COLLECTOR'S GUIDE TO CHILDREN'S BOOKS

1950–1975

VOLUME THREE

IDENTIFICATION
& VALUES

Diane McClure Jones • Rosemary Jones

cb

COLLECTOR BOOKS
A Division of Schroeder Publishing Co., Inc.

The current values in this book should be used only as a guide. They are not intended to set prices, which vary from one section of the country to another. Auction prices as well as dealer prices vary greatly and are affected by condition as well as demand. Neither the authors nor the publisher assumes responsibility for any losses that might be incurred as a result of consulting this guide.

Cover design: Beth Summers
Book design: Joyce Cherry
Book layout: Beth Ray

⤙⇒ *Searching For A Publisher?* ⇐⤙

We are always looking for knowledgeable people considered to be experts within their fields. If you feel that there is a real need for a book on your collectible subject and have a large comprehensive collection, contact Collector Books.

COLLECTOR BOOKS
P.O. Box 3009
Paducah, Kentucky 42002-3009
www.collectorbooks.com

Copyright © 2000 by Diane McClure Jones & Rosemary Jones

Contents

Acknowledgments

Special thanks to Suzanne and Truman Price of Monmouth, Oregon, who saved us both from brain meltdown with quick responses to our many questions. Eternal gratitude to Kris Walberg and Yvonne Walberg, who once again hauled out boxes of picturebooks from their private collection for us to use for the illustrations.

And special thanks to the many readers who have sent us encouraging notes, added information, or asked an inspired question. We appreciate all the input.

And hugs to Bob who puts up with us.

Introduction

Ever since the publication of the first volume of the *Collector's Guide to Children's Books*, people have asked us why we stopped at 1950. Now, in response to many requests from our readers, we're very pleased to present a whole new price guide that focuses on the years 1950 through 1975.

In the past few years, the favorite titles of the baby boom generation skyrocketed in popularity and collectibility as many parents sought to secure their childhood reading pleasures for their own children.

If you are a beginning collector, you will find that this period of children's books is a great place to start. Unlike earlier periods of children's publishing, a large supply of titles has become available through the secondary market of used bookstores, Internet auctions, and book sales. For a reasonable investment ($10 to $30 per title), you can start building a great collection for your children and grandchildren to enjoy.

Because of the greater number of books still available from this period, we've found that collectors place a strong emphasis on condition when purchasing a book. In general, they are looking for very good dust jackets on very good editions. There is also more interest in collecting first editions as opposed to finding any edition. In order to reflect the collectors' preferences, we've confined our price listings to hardcover books in very good condition and have given some extra information on identifying firsts in the back of this guide.

Book club editions are quite common for this period and usually command one-third to one-half of the listed price depending upon their rarity. For a few exceptional titles from this period, book club editions may be the only hardcover editions available, and in those instances command a higher price. Ex-library editions are not valued by all book dealers and most collectors, and therefore are generally sold as reading copies and priced in the $5 to $20 range with a good dust jacket.

Like our other price guides, we divided this guide into two main sections: books listed by author and books listed by series. We've also included a special section on the history of school readers for the fans of Dick and Jane and their many relatives.

As always, we found far more titles than we had room to list, so we gave priority to those books that we saw in other collections or in various shops and at antiquarian book shows. This let us confirm with our own eyes not only the details but also the quality and probable value. When this wasn't possible, we relied on recent auction house records, dealers' catalogs, and the many Internet databases linking bookstores across America.

We also did some checking against the Internet auction sites that have become a major resource for many of these books. You will find more information about Internet auctions at the end of this guide in the resources section.

Since so many of our readers enjoyed the illustrators' biographies, we added new biographies as well as expanded listings for illustrators working primarily during this period. You'll also find information there on the early works of many popular illustrators still working today.

As always, a number of research resources are listed at the end of this guide, including more Internet sites, identification of first editions, and a glossary.

Since the publication of Volume II, we've enjoyed receiving a number of letters and e-mail comments. We appreciate all the time and trouble taken by our readers to send us information on the books in their collections or to identify other authors and illustrators that would be of interest to collectors.

Reproduced here are some commonly asked questions and our answers. We welcome your suggestions for future price guides. Please address your comments to Rosemary Jones P.O. Box 9432, Seattle WA 98109, e-mail: lostlvs@aol.com. For those mailing their questions, please include a self-addressed stamped envelope for reply.

Question: *My book is signed by the author (or the illustrator). Does that make it more valuable?*

Answer: Certainly. Although it's fairly common to find signed books from this period (many authors listed are still alive today and willing to sign older copies during book tours), having a signature always adds to the value. How much it adds to the value depends on the popularity of the book and the author. For a very rare signature or extremely popular author, this can significantly increase the price. Prices in this guide are based upon unsigned books.

Question: *I think that I have a first edition but how do I tell? Is it worth more money?*

Answer: After 1950, the marking of first editions generally became more consistent. The first place to check is the copyright page (usually on the back of the title page). Most modern book collectors want first editions that are "first printings" of the book — often the first printing will be clearly stated on the copyright page. For books without this information clearly stated, like Grosset & Dunlap series books, the identifying of first editions becomes much harder. We've listed some basic clues in identifying firsts in the back of this guide. Experienced book dealers, collector's clubs or Internet newsgroups can be major sources of information when trying to identify firsts. Most people are very happy to share their knowledge with you.

The value of first editions varies based on the availability and collectibility of a title. If this is an exceptionally hard-to-find book, any edition may command a good price. For some books, only one or two editions were ever published, but if it is not a desired book by collectors, then the edition makes very little difference to the price. When the edition makes an exceptional difference to the value, we have tried to list that information.

Question: *I'm reading this dealer's catalog and don't understand the difference between good and very good. What do these things mean?*

Answer: Booksellers generally rank the condition of their stock by using terms such as good, very good, and fine. Good means that the book is clean and intact, with limited shelf wear and perhaps a few small marks such as the former owner's name neatly written on the endpaper. Very good means that the book looks almost new, with only very minor flaws on the jacket or text. Fine means that book or dust jacket looks new, as if nobody has ever touched it with human hands (fine is extremely rare in children's books that belonged to children). Individual booksellers have their own notions of good versus very good. If condition is a concern for you and you can't tell from the description what the book looks like, then ask for more information.

Question: *All I can remember about my favorite childhood book is that it was about a pony and there was a little boy in it. Any way that I might find the author or title? (This is still our most frequently asked question so we're repeating our answer from Volume II).*

Answer: If you have a book dealer specializing in children's books in your town, try asking that dealer. Children's librarians can also be a great help. On the Internet, the newsgroup called "rec.arts.books.children" does discussions like this every day, and the participants are truly wonderful at identifying books from bits and pieces of the plot.

Question: *I've been watching the e-Bay auctions and one title sold for $50 on one day and then another copy of the same title sold for $5 on the next day. What's going on and what is the book really worth?*

Answer: Auction prices are very volatile. Price often depends as much on who is bidding or how many bidders that auction attracted as on the actual item. Condition also makes an extreme difference in price. Perhaps one copy was in very good condition and the other copy was in poor condition.

When bidding on items, we check the availability of a title through other resources such as the Internet databases of used bookstores. This way, we can determine how rare a title is and how much we should reasonably expect to pay for a book in the same condition as the book being auctioned.

Question: *How do you set prices and for how long should I expect to find books at these prices?*

Answer: The prices in this guide are the average price seen. Most of the titles listed can be bought within a reasonable period of time at these prices.

Due to the increased availability of books in the secondary market spurred by the expansion of the Internet, we've found that the book prices in the low-to-medium range ($10 to $50) are fairly stable. We went back to our first book and ran a number of titles through the Internet (as well as actually looking in our local usedbook-stores). In most cases, we were able to find the same titles in good condition in the same price range as a few years ago, within a couple of weeks of searching.

Books marked as RARE in our earlier books or HARD-TO-FIND in this volume tend to be more volatile. These titles often increase substantially each year. That's why we've flagged such books for you.

Finally, certain circumstances, such as a publisher re-issuing a series like *Eloise* or a TV show based on a book like *Anne of Green Gables*, create new collector interest in an item and can dramatically affect prices.

We've always collected what we liked rather than worrying about future values. So, while not all of our books are monetary treasures, they are all treasured memories. Have fun collecting and don't forget to invest in some extra bookcases!

Explanation of Pricing

Prices of collectible books vary dramatically, due to changes in popularity of items. The revival of interest in an old novel for any reason, such as the production of a film based on the story, can create or increase demand.

We have based our prices on suggested prices received from a number of antiquarian book dealers.

All quoted prices are for hardcover books in good condition but WITHOUT dust jackets. When dust jacket pricing information is available, it is included and identified.

Book club editions are quite common for this period and usually command one-third to one-half of the listed price depending upon their rarity. For a few exceptional titles from this period, book club editions may be the only hardcover editions available, and in those instances command a higher price.

Ex-library editions are not valued by most collectors and all book dealers, and therefore are generally sold as reading copies and priced in the $5.00 to $20.00 range with a good dust jacket.

Good condition means clean, sound cover and spine without breaks or furred edges, clean undamaged pages, all pages and illustrations tightly attached. Price adjustments should be made for fingerprints, small tears, and loose pages. Large reductions are made for broken and seriously damaged covers, loose and missing pages, torn pages, water stains, and mold. In the case of children's books, other common damage found includes pencil and crayon marks.

First editions are noted. First state and other specific variations that dramatically alter the price of a particular volume have not been considered. This type of information is so specific and detailed that it needs to be obtained by the collector from a source specializing in a particular collection, such as a dealer or a club for collectors of a specific category.

Illustrations are a major factor in determining the price of a children's book. The illustrator is the major factor; the number and condition of the illustrations is the secondary factor.

Rare books are designated as such in the listings and not priced. A rare book is one that is extremely difficult to find, and the price is usually determined at the time of the sale. It will often depend solely on how much an individual collector wants the book. Auction prices can go into the thousands of dollars for a particular sale to a particular customer, but that price may never be paid again for an identical volume and is therefore not a reliable guide to pricing.

Investments: Because of the fragile nature of paper and the "well-handled" condition of most children's books, most collectors collect children's books for the joy of finding and owning them. Some of them may be excellent investments. Some may lose value. As we cannot guess which books will increase in value and which will decrease, we have in our own collections books that we acquired and love for their content rather than their potential monetary value.

Prices are for books in good condition but without dust jackets, except when noted.

A

AARDEMA, Verna
Why Mosquitoes Buzz in People's Ears, 1975 Dial (1976 Caldecott Award), oversize square hardcover, color illustrations by Leo and Diane Dillon. First edition with dust jacket: $100.00
First printing with 1976 Caldecott gold award sticker on dust jacket: $85.00
Later printings: ($20.00 with dust jacket) $10.00

ABRAHAMS, Anthony and Hilary
Polonius Penguin Learns to Swim, 1963 Franklin Watts, first edition, hardcover. ($15.00 with dust jacket) $10.00

ABRAHAMS, Roger D.
Jump-Rope Rhymes, 1969 U. of Texas Press, first edition, hardcover, 228 pages, color illustrations. ($30.00 with dust jacket) $15.00

ADAMS, Adrienne
Poetry of Earth, 1972 Charles Scribner, first edition, hardcover, illustrated by Adams. ($25.00 with dust jacket) $15.00
Woggle of Witches, 1971 Scribner, first edition, oversize hardcover. ($20.00 with dust jacket) $10.00

ADAMS, Richard
Tyger Voyage, 1976 Knopf, first American edition, oversize hardcover, color illustrations by Nicola Bayley, 30 pages. ($30.00 with dust jacket) $15.00
Watership Down, 1972 Collins, first UK edition, brown hardcover with gilt rabbit vignette. $1,000.00 or more with dust jacket.
Watership Down, 1972 Macmillan, first American edition, hardcover. ($35.00 with dust jacket) $15.00

ADAMSON, Gareth
Mr. Budge Builds His House, 1963 Chilton, first edition, hardcover, illustrations by author. ($15.00 with dust jacket) $10.00

ADDAMS, Charles
Charles Addams Mother Goose, 1967 Windmill Books, first edition, hardcover, illustrations by Addams. ($50.00 with dust jacket) $20.00
Homebodies, 1954 Simon and Schuster, first edition, hardcover, 90 pages, illustrations by author. ($25.00 with dust jacket) $15.00
Nightcrawlers, 1957 Simon and Schuster, first edi-

tion, hardcover, illustrations by author. ($60.00 with dust jacket) $20.00

ADKINS, Jan
Art and Industry of Sandcastles, 1971 Walker, first edition, hardcover. ($15.00 with dust jacket) $10.00

ADLER, Bill
Dear President Johnson, 1964 William Morrow, letters written to President L.B.J. by the children of America, illustrated by Charles M. Schulz. ($25.00 with dust jacket) $10.00

ADRIAN, Mary, see Series section, NATURE MYSTERIES
Rare Stamp Mystery, 1960 Hastings House, first edition, hardcover, 126 pages, illustrated by Lloyd Coe. ($25.00 with dust jacket) $10.00

AGLE, Nan Hayden, see Series section, THREE BOYS SERIES
Makon and the Dauphin, 1961 Scribner, small hardcover, b/w illustrations by Robert Frankenberg. ($25.00 with dust jacket) $15.00

AGREE, Rose H.
How To Eat A Poem & Other Morsels: Food Poems For Children, 1967 Pantheon, first edition, hardcover, illustrated by Peggy Wilson. ($20.00 with dust jacket) $10.00

AICHINGER, Helga
Elephant, the Mouse and the Flea, ca. 1966 Atheneum, first American edition, hardcover, illustrated endpapers, color illustrations by author. $25.00
Noah and the Rainbow, an Ancient Story, retold by Max Bolliger and translated by C. R. Bulla, 1972 Crowell, oversize hardcover, color illustrations. ($35.00 with dust jacket) $15.00
Rain Man, 1970 Watts, first American edition, hardcover, 27 pages, illustrations by author. ($25.00 with dust jacket) $15.00
Shepherd, 1966 Crowell, first American edition, oversize oblong picture book, color illustrations by author. $45.00

AIKEN, Conrad
Cats and Bats and Things With Wings, 1965 Atheneum, first edition, hardcover, illustrations by Milton Glaser. ($45.00 with dust jacket) $20.00

AIKEN, Joan, see Series section, WOLVES
All You've Ever Wanted, 1953 Jonathan Cape, first

edition, hardcover, illustrations by Pat Marriot. ($75.00 with dust jacket) $30.00

Arabel's Raven, (1972) 1974 printing Doubleday, hardcover, 118 pages, b/w illustrations by Quentin Blake. ($20.00 wth dust jacket) $10.00

Green Flash, 1971 Holt, first edition, hardcover. ($35.00 with dust jacket) $20.00

Kingdom and the Cave, 1960 Abelard-Schuman, first edition, hardcover, illustrations by Dick Hart. ($20.00 with dust jacket) $10.00

Mooncusser's Daughter, 1973 Viking Press, first American edition, hardcover. ($20.00 with dust jacket) $10.00

Whispering Mountain, 1968 Cape, first edition, small hardcover, 237 pages. ($50.00 with dust jacket) $20.00

ALAN, Sandy
Plaid Peacock, 1965 Pantheon, oblong picture book, color illustrations by Kelly Oechsli. $20.00

ALBEE, George Sumner
Three Young Kings, 1956 Watts, oversize hardcover picture book, brown/b/w illustrations by Ezra Jack Keats. ($15.00 with dust jacket) $10.00

ALBERTS, Frances Jacobs
Gift for Genghis Khan, 1961 Whittlesey House, first edition, hardcover, illustrations by Rafaello Busoni. ($20.00 with dust jacket) $10.00

ALDERSON, Brian
Cakes and Custard, 1974 Heinemann, first edition, oversize pictorial hardcover, color illustrated by Helen Oxenbury. ($40.00 with dust jacket) $15.00

ALDIS, Dorothy
We're Going to Town!, 1952 Bobbs-Merrill, first edition, 57 pages, illustrated end papers, Illustrated by Mary Gehr. ($15.00 with dust jacket) $10.00

ALDRICH, Bess Streeter
Journey Into Christmas and Other Stories, 1949 edition Appleton-Century, pictorial cover, 265 pages, illustrations by James Aldrich. $25.00

Journey Into Christmas and Other Stories, 1963 edition Appleton-Century, 239 pages, illustrations by Susanne Suba. $15.00

ALDRIDGE, Alan and **William PLOMER**
Butterfly Ball and Grasshopper Feast, 1975 Grossman/Viking, first American edition, pictorial hardcover, color illustrations by Aldridge. $30.00

ALEXANDER, Anne
Noise in the Night, 1960 Rand McNally, hardcover picture book, illustrated endpapers, color illustrations by Abner Grabeff. ($30.00 with dust jacket) $15.00

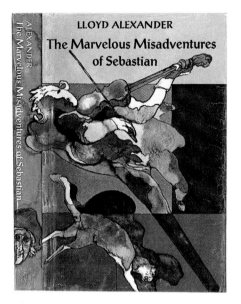

ALEXANDER, Lloyd, see Series section, PRYDAIN SERIES
Border Hawk, 1958 Farrar, hardcover. ($25.00 with dust jacket) $10.00

Cat Who Wished to Be a Man, 1973 Dutton, first edition, hardcover. ($30.00 with dust jacket) $15.00

Flagship Hope, 1960 Farrar, first edition, hardcover, 179 pages. ($35.00 with dust jacket) $15.00

Four Donkeys, 1972 Holt, first edition, hardcover, full page color illustrations by Lester Abrams. ($40.00 with dust jacket) $15.00

King's Fountain, 1971 E.P. Dutton, first edition, hardcover, illustrations by Ezra Jack Keats. ($40.00 with dust jacket) $15.00

Marvelous Misadventures of Sebastian, 1970 Dutton, first edition, hardcover, 204 pages, dust jacket illustration by Jacob Landau. ($60.00 with dust jacket) $15.00

My Five Tigers, 1956 Crowell, first edition, hardcover, b/w illustrations by Peggy Bacon. ($35.00 with dust jacket) $15.00

My Five Tigers, 1956 Cassell, London, first UK edition, hardcover, b/w illustrations by Peggy Bacon. ($50.00 with dust jacket) $15.00

Send for Ryan!, 1965 London, first edition, hardcover. ($25.00 with dust jacket) $10.00

Wizard in the Tree, 1975 Dutton, first edition, hardcover. ($25.00 with dust jacket) $15.00

ALEXANDER, Martha, b. Georgia
And My Mean Old Mother Will Be Sorry, Blackboard Bear, 1972 Dial, small oblong picture book, color illustrations by author. ($20.00 with dust jacket) $10.00

I'll Be the Horse If You'll Play with Me, 1975 Dial, small square picture book, color illustrations by author. ($25.00 with dust jacket) $10.00

I'll Protect You from the Jungle Beast, 1973 Dial, first edition, hardcover, illustrations by author. ($30.00 with dust jacket) $10.00

Maybe a Monster, 1968 Dial, small picture book, color illustrations by author. ($25.00 with dust jacket) $10.00

Nobody Asked Me if I Wanted a Baby Sister, 1977 Dial, first edition, small square picture book, color illustrations by author. ($25.00 with dust jacket) $10.00

No Ducks in Our Bathtub, 1973 Dial, small picture book, color illustrations by author. ($25.00 with dust jacket) $10.00

Sabrina, 1971 Dial, first edition, hardcover, illustrations by author. ($20.00 with dust jacket) $10.00

Story Grandmother Told, 1969 Dial, small picture book, color illustrations by author. ($25.00 with dust jacket) $10.00

We Never Get to Do Anything, 1970 Dial, small oblong picture book, color illustrations by author. ($25.00 with dust jacket) $10.00

ALEXANDER, Theroux
Great Wheadle Tragedy, 1975 David Godine, first edition, purple hardcover with pictorial paste-on, illustrated by Stan Washburn. ($65.00 with dust jacket) $30.00

ALLAN, Mabel Esther
Wood Street Secret, 1970 Abelard-Schuman, first edition, hardcover, illustrations by Shirley Hughes. ($25.00 with dust jacket) $15.00

ALLARD, Harry
Stupids Step Out, 1974 Houghton, oblong picture book hardcover, color illustrations by James Marshall. ($35.00 with dust jacket) $15.00

Tutti Frutti Case, ca. 1975 Prentice-Hall, first edition, hardcover, color illustrations by James Marshall. ($30.00 with dust jacket) $15.00

ALLEN, Elizabeth
Forest House, 1967 Dutton, first edition, hardcover, b/w illustrations by Paul Kennedy. ($20.00 with dust jacket) $10.00

ALLEN, Helen and others
WO-HE-LO, the Story of the Camp Fire Girls 1910-1960, 1961 Holt, Rinehart & Winston, first edition, hardcover. ($25.00 with dust jacket) $10.00

ALLEN, Jeffrey
Mary Alice, Operator Number 9, 1975 Little, Brown, hardcover picture book, color illustrations. ($25.00 with dust jacket) $15.00

ALLEN, Lorenzo
Fifer for the Union, 1970 Morrow, hardcover, 256 pages. $15.00

ALLEN, Thomas
Erie Canal, 1971 edition World Work, Tadworth Surrey, first edition UK, oblong pictorial hardcover, color illustrations by Peter Spier. ($20.00 with dust jacket) $10.00

ALLUM, Nancy
Monica Takes a Commission, 1965 Max Parrish, UK, first edition, green cloth with silver lettering on the spine. $10.00

ALMEDINGEN, E. M.
Stephen's Light, 1956 Holt, first edition, hardcover, 290 pages. ($25.00 with dust jacket) $10.00

ALTER, Robert Edmond
Dark Keep, 1962 Longmans, hardcover, b/w illustrations by Albert Orbaan. ($20.00 with dust jacket) $10.00

AMBRUS, Victor
Brave Soldier Janosh, 1967 Harcourt, first American edition, hardcover, color illustrations by author. ($35.00 with dust jacket) $20.00

Country Wedding, 1973 Collins, oversize illustrated hardcover, color illustrations by author. ($25.00 with dust jacket) $15.00

Mishka, 1975 Oxford, oversize picture book, color

illustrations by author. First edition with same-as-cover dust jacket: $85.00

Later printings: ($20.00 with dust jacket) $10.00

Seven Skinny Goats, 1970 Harcourt Brace Jovanovich, first edition, hardcover, illustrations by author. ($30.00 with dust jacket) $15.00

Sultan's Bath, 1971 Harcourt Brace Jovanovich, first edition, oversize hardcover, illustrations by author. ($30.00 with dust jacket) $15.00

AMERMAN, Lockhart

Cape Cod Casket, 1964 Harcourt, Brace & World, first edition, hardcover. ($45.00 with dust jacket) $20.00

Sly One, 1966 Harcourt, Brace & World, hardcover. ($25.00 with dust jacket) $15.00

AMON, Aline

Talking Hands, How to Use Indian Sign Language, 1968 Doubleday, first edition, hardcover, illustrated. ($35.00 with dust jacket) $20.00

ANCHARSVARD, Karin

Aunt Vinnie's Invasion, 1962 Harcourt, first US edition, hardcover, translated from Swedish by Anabelle Macmillan, illustrated by William M. Hutchinson. $15.00

Doctor's Boy, 1965 Harcourt, Brace, hardcover, 155 pages. ($20.00 with dust jacket) $10.00

ANDERSEN, Hans Christian

Little Mermaid, 1971 edition Harper, hardcover, illustrated by Edward Frascino. ($15.00 in dust jacket) $10.00

Nightingale, 1965 edition Harper, first edition, hardcover, illustrations by Nancy Ekholm Burkert. ($50.00 with dust jacket) $20.00

Seven Tales (copyright 1959), 1972 World's Work, London, first UK edition, color and b/w illustrations by Maurice Sendak. ($65.00 with dust jacket) $40.00

Snow Queen, 1974 Scribner, first edition, 95 pages, illustrated by Marcia Brown. ($60.00 with dust jacket) $25.00

Tinder Box, 1954 edition Polytint, London, oversize, retold by Joan Cherry, full color illustratons by Lucien Lowen. ($35.00 with dust jacket) $20.00

ANDERSON, Bertha

Eric Duffy, American, 1955 Little, Brown, first edition, hardcover, illustrations by Lloyd Coe. ($25.00 with dust jacket) $10.00

Tinker's Tim and the Witches, 1954 Little, Brown, Weekly Reader edition, hardcover, 147 pages, illustrations by Lloyd Coe. $15.00

THE BLIND CONNEMARA
C.W. Anderson

ANDERSON, C.W.

Blaze and the Gray Spotted Pony, 1968 Macmillan, first edition, hardcover, illustrations by author. ($60.00 with dust jacket) $20.00

Blind Connemara, 1971 Macmillan, first edition, hardcover, illustrations by author. ($25.00 with dust jacket) $10.00

C. W. Anderson's Complete Book of Horses and Horsemanship, 1963 Macmillan, hardcover, color illustrations by author. ($25.00 with dust jacket) $10.00

C.W. Anderson's Favorite Horse Stories, 1967 Dutton, first edition, hardcover, illustrations by author. ($20.00 with dust jacket) $10.00

Lonesome Little Colt, 1961 Macmillan, first edition, hardcover, illustrations by author. ($45.00 with dust jacket) $20.00

Outlaw, 1967 Macmillan, first edition, hardcover, illustrations by author. ($40.00 with dust jacket) $20.00

ANDERSON, Ella

Talking Mountain, 1962 Pickering & Inglis, first edition, hardcover, 96 pages. ($15.00 with dust jacket) $10.00

ANDERSON, Joy

Pai-Pai Pig, 1967 Harcourt Brace, first edition, hardcover, illustrations by Jay Yang. ($15.00 with dust jacket) $10.00

ANDERSON, Lonzo

Ponies of Mykillengi, 1966 Scribner, illustrated hardcover, color illustrations by Adrienne Adams. ($40.00 with dust jacket) $20.00

Two Hundred Rabbits, 1968 Viking, first edition, hardcover, 32 pages, picture book, color illustrations by Adrienne Adams. ($35.00 with dust jacket) $20.00

ANDREUS, Hans
Stilt Pedlar and Other Stories, 1970 Boyd and Oliver, first UK edition, pictorial green hardcover, b/w illustrations. $20.00

ANDREWS, Mary Evans
Hostage to Alexander, 1961 Longmans, first edition, hardcover. ($20.00 with dust jacket) $10.00
Lanterns Aloft, 1955 Longmans, first edition, hardcover, illustrations by Arthur Harper. ($15.00 with dust jacket) $10.00

ANGELO, Valenti
Merry Marcos, 1963 Viking, first edition, orange pictorial hardcover, b/w illustrations by Angelo. ($20.00 with dust jacket) $15.00
Tale of a Donkey, 1966 Viking, first edition, hardcover. ($45.00 with dust jacket) $20.00

ANGLUND, Joan Walsh
Childhood Is a Time of Innocence, 1964 Harcourt, first edition, small. ($25.00 in dust jacket) $10.00
Christmas Is a Time of Giving, 1961 Harcourt, first edition. ($15.00 in dust jacket) $10.00
Friend Is Someone Who Likes You, 1958 Harcourt, first edition. ($15.00 with dust jacket) $10.00
Look Out the Window, 1959 Harcourt, narrow, yellow cloth hardcover, short poems and two-color illustrations throughout by author. ($20.00 with dust jacket) $10.00
Pocketful of Proverbs, 1964 Harcourt, small. ($15.00 with slipcase) $5.00
Slice of Snow, 1970 Harcourt, first edition, small. ($25.00 in dust jacket) $10.00

ANNIXTER, Jane and **Paul**
Phantom Stallion, 1961 Golden Press, illustrated hardcover, illustrated by Robert Schultz. $15.00

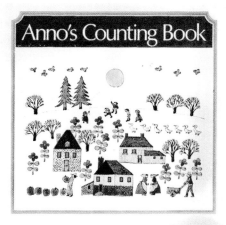

ANNO, Mitsumasa
Anno's Alphabet, 1975 Crowell, first American edition, square, color illustrated hardcover, color illustrations by author. SIGNED by author on title page, with dust jacket: $65.00
First edition with dust jacket: $35.00
Later editions: ($20.00 with dust jacket) $10.00
Anno's Counting Book, 1975 Harper Collins, oversize hardcover, color illustrations by author. First edition with dust jacket: $35.00
Later editions: ($20.00 with dust jacket) $10.00
Dr. Anno's Magical Midnight Circus, 1972 Weatherhill, oversize hardcover picture book, color illustrations by author. First edition with dust jacket: $45.00
Later editions: ($20.00 with dust jacket) $10.00
Topsy-Turvies, 1970 Walker/Weatherhill, oversize hardcover, 127 pages, full-page color illustrations by Anno. First edition with dust jacket: $35.00
Later editions: ($20.00 with dust jacket) $10.00
Upside-Downers, 1971 Weatherhill, oversize hardcover picture book, color illustrations by author. First edition with dust jacket: $35.00
Later editions: ($20.00 with dust jacket) $10.00

ANTHONY, Edward
Oddity Land, 1957 Doubleday, first edition, hardcover, illustrated by Erik Blegvad. ($25.00 with dust jacket) $15.00

APPEL, David
Comanche, the Story of America's Most Heroic Horse, 1951 World, first edition, hardcover, 224 pages, illustrations by James Daugherty. ($20.00 with dust jacket) $10.00

ARCHIBALD, Joe
Aviation Cadet, 1955 Longmans, first edition, hardcover. ($15.00 with dust jacket) $10.00
Long Pass, 1966 Macrae Smith Company, first edition, hardcover. ($15.00 with dust jacket) $10.00

13

ARDIZZONE, Aingelda
Night Ride, 1973 Longmans Young Books, first edition, oversize oblong yellow pictorial hardcover, color illustrations throughout by Edward Ardizzone. ($65.00 with dust jacket) $30.00

ARDIZZONE, Edward
Dick Whittington, edited by Kathleen Lines, 1970 Walck, first American edition, hardcover, color illustrations by Ardizzone. ($30.00 with dust jacket) $15.00

J. M. Barrie's Peter Pan, story of the play edited by Eleanor Graham, 1963 Scribner, first edition, hardcover, color and b/w illustrations by Ardizzone. ($50.00 with dust jacket) $20.00

Johnny the Clockmaker, 1960 Oxford Press, first edition, hardcover, illustrations by author. ($25.00 with dust jacket) $10.00

Lucy Brown and Mr. Grimes, (1937) 1971 edition Walck, first American printing of 1971 edition, oversize hardcover, color illustrations by author. ($100.00 with dust jacket) $40.00

Paul, the Hero of the Fire, 1963 Walck, first American edition, b/w and color illustrations by author. ($50.00 with dust jacket) $30.00

Peter the Wanderer, 1964 Walck, first American edition, hardcover, illustrations by author. ($40.00 with dust jacket) $20.00

Stories from the Bible, retold by Walter de la Mare, 1961 edition Faber, London, first edition, oversize hardcover, 420 pages, illustrations by Ardizzone. ($100.00 with dust jacket) $40.00

Tim and Charlotte, 1951 Oxford Press, first American edition, oversize hardcover, color illustrations by author. ($150.00 with dust jacket) $40.00

Tim All Alone, 1957 Oxford Press, first edition, oversize hardcover, color illustrations by author. ($125.00 with dust jacket) $40.00

Young Ardizzone, autobiographical, 1971 Macmillan, first American edition, oversize hardcover, color illustrations by author. ($60.00 with dust jacket) $25.00

ARKHURST, Joyce Cooper
Adventures Of Spider: West African Folk Tales, 1964 Little, Brown, first edition, hardcover, illustrations by Jerry Pinkney. ($30.00 with dust jacket) $15.00

ARMER, Alberta
Troublemaker, 1966 World, pictorial hardcover. $10.00

ARMOUR, Richard
Animals on the Ceiling, 1964 McGraw-Hill, first edition, hardcover, illustrated by Paul Galdone. ($65.00 with dust jacket) $25.00

Through Darkest Adolescence, with Tongue in Cheek and Pen in Checkbook, 1963 McGraw-Hill, hardcover, illustrated by Susan Perl. $15.00

Year Santa Went Modern, 1964 McGraw-Hill, first edition, hardcover, Illustrated by Paul Galdone. ($65.00 with dust jacket) $25.00

ARMSTRONG, Richard
Secret Sea, 1966 David McKay, hardcover, 150 pages. ($20.00 with dust jacket) $10.00

ARMSTRONG, William H.
Sounder, 1969 Harper, Newbery edition, hardcover. ($30.00 with dust jacket) $15.00

Sour Land, 1971 Harper, first edition, pictorial hardcover. ($45.00 with dust jacket) $15.00

Through Troubled Waters, 1973 Harper, hardcover. ($15.00 with dust jacket) $10.00

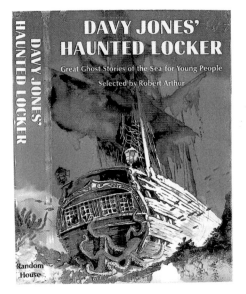

ARTHUR, Robert, see also Three Investigators
Davy Jones' Haunted Locker, 1965 Random House, oversize illustrated glossy hardcover, illustrations by Joseph Cellini. ($20.00 with dust jacket) $10.00
Ghosts and More Ghosts, 1963 Random House, first edition, hardcover. ($15.00 with dust jacket) $10.00

ARTHUR, Ruth
On The Wasteland, 1975 Gollancz, first edition, brown hardcover, 159 pages, drawings by Margery Gill. ($20.00 with dust jacket) $10.00

ARUNDEL, Jocelyn
Dugan and the Hobo, 1960 Whittlesey House, first edition, hardcover, b/w illustrations by Wesley Dennis. ($25.00 with dust jacket) $15.00
Jingo, Wild Horse of Abaco, 1959 McGraw Hill, first edition, hardcover, illustrated endpapers, 137 pages, b/w illustrations by Wesley Dennis. ($35.00 with dust jacket) $15.00
Simba of the White Mane, 1958 Whittlesey House, first edition, hardcover, illustrations by Wesley Dennis. ($30.00 with dust jacket) $15.00

ASCH, Frank
George's Store, 1969 McGraw Hill, oblong hardcover picture book, b/w illustrations by author. ($25.00 with dust jacket) $15.00
Rebecka, 1972 Harper, first edition. ($30.00 with dust jacket) $15.00
In the Eye of the Teddy, 1973 Harper, first edition, oblong hardcover. ($25.00 with dust jacket) $15.00

ASENDORF, James
Bear Seeds, 1969 Little, Brown, first edition, hardcover, illustrations by Ingrid Fetz. ($20.00 with dust jacket) $10.00

ASH, Frank
Blue Balloon, 1971 McGraw-Hill, first edition, hardcover. ($35.00 with dust jacket) $15.00

ASIMOV, Isaac, see also Lucky Starr
Best New Thing, 1971 World, first edition, oblong hardcover. ($30.00 with dust jacket) $15.00
Mars, 1967 Follet Beginning Science Book, first edition, hardcover, 32 pages, color illustrations by Herb Herrick. ($15.00 with dust jacket) $10.00
Stars, 1968 Follet Beginning Science Book, first edition, hardcover, 30 pages, color illustrations by Herb Herrick. ($15.00 with dust jacket) $10.00

ASTURIAS, Miguel Angel
Talking Machine, 1971 Doubleday, first edition, oblong hardcover, color illustrations by Jacqueline Duheme. ($100.00 with dust jacket) $30.00

ATTWELL, Lucie
Lucie Attwell's Annual, 1974 edition Dean & Son, London, 93 pages, illustrated hardcover, Attwell illustrations, stories by Penelope Douglas. $45.00

ATWOOD, Adeline
Treasure of the Sun, 1954 Houghton Mifflin, first edition, hardcover. $15.00

ATWOOD, Ann
Little Circle, 1967 Scribner, oversize hardcover picture book, photo-illustrated cover, color photograph illustrations by author. $15.00

AUGUSTA, Josef
Book of Mammoths, 1963 Hamlyn, London, oversize tan hardcover, 92 pages, 20 color plates by Zdenek Burian. ($110.00 with dust jacket) $65.00
Prehistoric Animals, undated ca. 1950s Hamlyn, London, oversize tan hardcover, 92 pages, 60 color plates by Zdenek Burian. ($110.00 with dust jacket) $65.00

AUSLANDER, Joseph
Riders at the Gate, 1958 Macmillan, first edition. hardcover, illustrations by Boris Artzybasheff. ($35.00 with dust jacket) $20.00

AUSTIN, Margot
Archie Angel, 1957 Dutton, first edition, oversize hardcover, illustrations by author. ($30.00 with dust jacket) $15.00
Churchmouse Stories, 1956 Dutton, hardcover, illustrated by author. ($30.00 in dust jacket) $15.00
Cousin's Treasure, 1960 Dutton, first edition, hardcover, 45 pages, b/w illustrations by author. ($20.00 with dust jacket) $10.00
Lutie, 1944 Dutton, oversize, hardcover, illustrated boards, illustrations by author. ($20.00 with dust jacket) $10.00
Poppet, 1949 Dutton, hardcover, illustrated by author. ($20.00 in dust jacket) $15.00
Three Silly Kittens, 1950 Dutton, illustrated by author. ($20.00 in dust jacket) $10.00

AVERY, Gillian
To Tame a Sister, 1961 Van Nostrand, first American edition, hardcover, illustrations by John Verney. ($15.00 with dust jacket) $10.00
Call of the Valley, 1968 Holt, hardcover. ($15.00 with dust jacket) $10.00
Elephant War, 1960 Holt, first edition, hardcover. ($20.00 with dust jacket) $10.00

AVERY, Ira
Five Fathers of Pepi, 1955 Bobbs-Merrill, first edition, hardcover. ($20.00 with dust jacket) $10.00

AVERILL, Esther
When Jenny Lost Her Scarf, 1951 Harper, small hardcover, color illustrations by author. ($25.00 with dust jacket) $10.00

AWDRY, Rev. Wilbert, see Series section, THOMAS THE TANK ENGINE

AYER, Jacqueline
Nu Dang and His Kite, 1959 Harcourt, oversize oblong picture book, illustrated endpapers, color illustrations by author. ($35.00 with dust jacket) $15.00
Paper-Flower Tree, 1962 Harcourt, oversize oblong picture book, illustrated endpapers, color illustrations by author. ($35.00 with dust jacket) $15.00

AYML, Marcel
Magic Pictures: More about the Wonderful Farm, 1954 Harper & Brothers, first edition, hardcover, photos of Ayml and Sendak. ($300.00 with dust jacket) $75.

B

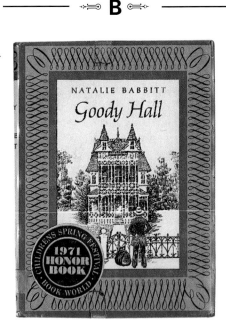

BABBITT, Natalie
Devil's Storybook, 1974 Farrar, first edition, hardcover, illustrations by author. ($25.00 with dust jacket) $10.00
Goody Hall, 1971 Farrar, Honor Book edition, hardcover, 176 pages, b/w illustrations by author. ($20.00 with dust jacket) $10.00
Phoebe's Revolt, 1968 Farrar, oblong hardcover, illustrated endpapers, brown/b/w illustrations by author. ($25.00 with dust jacket) $15.00
Search For Delicious, 1969 Farrar, first edition, hardcover. ($30.00 with dust jacket) $10.00
Something, 1970 Farrar, first edition, hardcover, illus-

trations by author. ($30.00 with dust jacket) $15.00
Tuck Everlasting, 1975 Farrar, hardcover. First edition with hardcover: $75.00 Later editions: ($20.00 with dust jacket) $10.00

BABBITT, Samuel
Forty-Ninth Magician ,1966 Pantheon Books, first edition, hardcover, illustrations by Natalie Babbitt. ($35.00 with dust jacket) $20.00

BABCOCK, J.C.
Waybent, 1954 Hutchinson, London, first edition, hardcover, b/w illustrations by Margaret Wetherbee. ($15.00 with dust jacket) $10.00

BACH, Alice
Day after Christmas, 1975 Harper, first edition, hardcover, color illustrations by Mary Chalmers. ($25.00 with dust jacket) $15.00
Smartest Bear and His Brother Oliver, 1975 Harper, first edition, hardcover, illustrations by Steven Kellogg. ($20.00 with dust jacket) $10.00

BACH, Richard
Stranger to the Ground, 1963 Harper, hardcover, illustrated. First edition with dust jacket $100.00 Later printings: ($25.00 with dust jacket) $15.00

BACON, Martha
In the Company of Clowns, 1973 edition Little, Brown, hardcover. $15.00

BACON, Peggy
Ghost of Opalina, or Nine Lives, 1967 Little, Brown, first edition, hardcover, 243 pages, illustrated by author. Hard to find. First edition with dust jacket: $100.00
Later printings: ($30.00 with dust jacket) $20.00
Magic Touch, 1968 Little, Brown, hardcover, 112 pages. ($25.00 with dust jacket) $15.00
Oddity, 1962 Pantheon, hardcover, 71 pages, b/w illustrations by author. ($25.00 with dust jacket) $15.00

BACON, Phillip, editor
Golden Book Picture Atlas of the World, 1960 Golden Books, 6 volume set, hardcover, maps, illustrations. Set of 6 volumes: $65.00

BAILEY, Bernadine
Picture Book of Oregon, 1954 Albert Whitman, first edition, oblong hardcover, 32 pages, color illustrations by Kurt Wiese. ($25.00 with dust jacket) $15.00

BAILEY, Carolyn Sherwin
Enchanted Village, 1950 Viking, first edition, hard-

cover, illustrated by Eileen Evans. ($25.00 with dust jacket) $10.00

Finnegan II: His Nine Lives, 1953 Viking, first edition, tall hardcover, illustrations by Kate Seredy. ($50.00 with dust jacket) $20.00

BAIN, Bernard E. with Dale KRAMER
My 100 Children, 1954 Simon & Schuster, first edition, hardcover. ($15.00 with dust jacket) $10.00

BAKER, Betty
Shaman's Last Raid, 1963 Harper, first edition, hardcover, illustrations by Leonard Shortall. ($15.00 with dust jacket) $10.00

Stranger and Afraid, 1972 Macmillan, first edition, hardcover, 161 pages. ($15.00 with dust jacket) $10.00

BAKER, Margaret J.
Away Went Galloper, (1962) 1964 Encyclopedia Britannica Press, tweed hardcover, b/w illustrations by Norman Thelwell. ($20.00 with dust jacket) $10.00

Bears Back in Business, 1967 Farrar, first American edition, hardcover, illustrated. $20.00

Castaway Christmas, 1963 Farrar, hardcover, 158 pages, b/w illustrations by Richard Kennedy. ($20.00 with dust jacket) $10.00

Four Farthings and a Thimble, 1950 Longmans, first edition, hardcover, b/w illustrations by Decie Merwin. $30.00

Hannibal and the Bears, 1966 Farrar, hardcover. ($20.00 with dust jacket) $10.00

Hijinks Joins the Bears, 1969 Farrar, first American edition, hardcover, illustrated by Leslie Wood. ($25.00 with dust jacket) $15.00

Homer Goes to Stratford, 1958 Prentice Hall, hardcover, illustrated by W. T. Mars. $15.00

Porterhouse Major, 1967 Prentice-Hall, hardcover with b/w illustrations. $15.00

BALCH, Glenn
Lost Horse, 1950 Grosset, hardcover. $10.00

Spotted Horse, 1961 Crowell, first edition, hardcover. ($20.00 with dust jacket) $10.00

BALDNER, Gaby
Joba and the Wild Boar, 1961 Hastings, oversize oblong hardcover picture book, color illustrations by Gerhard Oberlander, English/German text. ($25.00 with dust jacket) $15.00

BALDWIN, Anne Norris
Sometimes Island, 1969 Norton, first edition, hardcover, illustrations by Charles Robinson. ($25.00 with dust jacket) $15.00

BALDWIN, Clara
Little Tuck, 1959 Doubleday, first edition, hardcover, illustrations by Paul Galdone. ($35.00 with dust jacket) $15.00

BALDWIN, Ruth M.
100 Rhyming Alphabets in English, 1972 Southern Illinois U. Press, first edition, oversize hardcover, 296 pages. ($50.00 with dust jacket) $35.00

BALET, Jan
Joanjo, 1967 Delacorte, oversize oblong hardcover picture book, color illustrations by author. ($30.00 with dust jacket) $15.00

What Makes an Orchestra?, 1951 Oxford University Press, first edition, hardcover, illustrations by author. ($35.00 with dust jacket) $20.00

BALIAN, Lorna
Humbug Witch, 1965 Abingdon, first edition, hardcover. ($30.00 with dust jacket) $15.00

I Love You, Mary Jane, 1967 Abingdon, first edition, hardcover. ($20.00 with dust jacket) $10.00

Sometimes It's Turkey, Sometimes It's Feathers, 1973 Abingdon, first edition, hardcover. ($20.00 with dust jacket) $10.00

BALKOFF-DROWNE, Tatiana and Meredith
Helen Take Wing!, 1963 Viking, first edition, hardcover. ($15.00 with dust jacket) $10.00

BALL, Zachary
Tent Show, 1964 Holiday House, hardcover, illustrations by William Moyers. ($15.00 with dust jacket) $10.00

BANGERT, Ethel E.
Polly Perry, TV Cook, 1959 Putnam, first edition, green hardcover,185 pages. ($20.00 with dust jacket) $10.00

BANKS, Richard
Mysterious Leaf, 1954 Harcourt, Brace, first edition, hardcover, illustrated by Irene Haas. ($20.00 with dust jacket) $10.00

BANNON, Laura
Big Brother, 1950 Albert Whitman, pictorial hardcover, illustrated endpapers, color illustrations by author. ($30.00 with dust jacket) $15.00
Famous Baby-Sitter, 1960 Albert Whitman, first edition, hardcover with paste-on pictorial, color illustrations by author. ($45.00 with dust jacket) $20.00
Gift of Hawaii, 1961 Whitman, illustrated hardcover, oversize, illustrated endpapers, color illustrations by author. ($20.00 with dust jacket) $10.00
Hat for a Hero, 1954 Whitman, illustrated hardcover, oversize, illustrated endpapers, color illustrations by author. ($30.00 with dust jacket) $15.00
Horse On A Houseboat, 1951 Albert Whitman, first edition, hardcover, illustrations by author. ($40.00 with dust jacket) $20.00
Katy Comes Next, 1959 Albert Whitman, oversize hardcover, color and b/w illustrations by author. ($50.00 with dust jacket) $25.00
Mind Your Child's Art: A Guide for Parents and Teachers, 1952 Pellegrini & Cudahy Publishers, first edition, oversize, color and b/w illustrations by author. ($30.00 with dust jacket) $15.00
When the Moon is New, 1953 Whitman, illustrated hardcover, oversize, illustrated endpapers, color illustrations by author. ($25.00 with dust jacket) $15.00
Whistle For a Pilot: A Story of Nova Scotia and High Tides, 1959 Houghton Mifflin, first edition, hardcover, color and b/w illustrations by author. ($30.00 with dust jacket) $15.00

BARBER, Anne Viccars
Childhood in Egypt, 1968 Geoffrey Bles, London, first edition, hardcover. ($30.00 with dust jacket) $15.00
Days at Wickham, 1966 Geoffrey Bles, London, oblong picture book, color frontispiece, b/w illustrations by author. ($15.00 with dust jacket) $10.00

BARBER, Antonia
Affair of the Rockerbye Baby, 1966 Jonathan Cape, London, hardcover. ($40.00 with dust jacket) $15.00

BARBER, Noel
Adventures at Both Poles, 1963 Heinemann, first edition, hardcover, illustrations by photos. ($25.00 with dust jacket) $15.00

BARFIELD, Owen
Silver Trumpet, (1925) 1968 edition Eerdmann, purple hardcover with silver printing, oversize, b/w illustrations by Betty Beeby. ($25.00 with dust jacket) $15.00

BARLOW, Roger, see Series section, SANDY STEELE

BARNET, George
Mrs. Talky and Jim Spot, 1959 Macmillan, first edition, small hardcover, 32 pages, illustrations by Anne Fleur. ($40.00 with dust jacket) $15.00

BARR, Stringfellow
Copydog in India, 1955 Viking, hardcover, illustrations by Kurt Wiese. ($25.00 with dust jacket) $15.00

BARRETT, Judi
Peter's Pocket, 1974 Atheneum, small oblong hardcover picture book, red print and brown line drawings on yellow paper, illustrations by Julia Noonan. ($15.00 with dust jacket) $10.00

BARRY, Robert
Riddle of Castle Hill, 1968 McGraw Hill, pictorial hardcover. ($25.00 with dust jacket) $10.00
Mr. Willowby's Christmas Tree, 1965 McGraw-Hill, hardcover, illustrated by George Wilde. ($25.00 with dust jacket) $10.00

BARRY, Robert E.
Faint George, 1957 Houghton, oblong oversize picture book, red/b/w illustrations by author. ($85.00 with dust jacket) $25.00

BARTH, Edna
Day Luis Was Lost, 1971 Little, Brown, first edition, hardcover, illustrated by Lilian Obligado. ($20.00 with dust jacket) $10.00

BARTHELME, Donald
Slightly Irregular Fire Engine or the Hithering Thithering Djinn, 1971 Farrar, first edition, green hardcover, illustrated with 19th century engravings. ($100.00 with dust jacket) $40.00

BARTON, Byron
Applebet Story, 1973 Viking, first edition, oblong oversize hardcover, illustrations by author. ($35.00 with dust jacket) $15.00

Hester, 1975 Greenwillow, hardcover picture book, color illustrations by author. ($30.00 with dust jacket) $15.00

Where's Al?, 1972 Seabury, oblong picture book, color illustrations by author. ($40.00 with dust jacket) $15.00

BARUCH, Dorothy W.
I Would Like to Be a Pony and Other Wishes, 1959 Harper, first edition, hardcover, illustrations by Mary Chalmers. ($20.00 with dust jacket) $10.00

BASKIN, Esther
Creatures of Darkness, 1962 Little, Brown, oversize hardcover, illustrations by Leonard Baskin. First edition with dust jacket: $65.00 Later printings: ($35.00 with dust jacket) $20.00

BASKIN, Hosea and Leonard
Hosie's Alphabet, 1972 Viking, oversize hardcover picture book, color illustrations by Leonard Baskin. ($35.00 with dust jacket) $20.00

BASON, Lillian
Isabelle and the Library Cat, 1966 Lothrop, oversize hardcover picture book, color illustrations by Kurt Werth. ($20.00 with same-as-cover dust jacket) $10.00

BASSER, V.
Bright-Eyes, the Glider Possum, 1957 Sydney, first edition, hardcover, 72 pages, illustrations by R. Richardson. ($35.00 with dust jacket) $20.00

BATCHELOR, Julie Forsyth
Sea Lady, 1956 Harcourt, Brace, first edition, hardcover, illustrations by William Hutchinson. ($20.00 with dust jacket) $10.00

BATE, Norman
*When Cave Men Painted,*1963 Scribners, first edition, hardcover, two-color illustrations by author. ($15.00 with dust jacket) $10.00

BATES, H. E.
*Achilles the Donkey,*1963 Franklin-Watts, first edition, hardcover. ($30.00 with dust jacket) $15.00

Achilles and the Twins, 1964 Dennis Dobson, London, first edition, hardcover, illustrations by Carol Barker. ($45.00 with dust jacket) $15.00

BAWDEN, Nina
Peppermint Pig, 1975 Victor Gollancz, first edition, hardcover, 160 pages, illustrated by Alexy Pendle. ($35.00 with dust jacket) $20.00

Squib, 1971 Victor Gollancz, first edition UK, hardcover, illustrations by Shirley Hughes. ($15.00 with dust jacket) $10.00

Three on the Run, 1964 Lippincott, hardcover, b/w illustrations by Wendy Worth. ($30.00 with dust jacket) $15.00

Witch's Daughter, 1966 Victor Gollancz Ltd., first edition, hardcover, illustrated by Shirley Hughes. ($15.00 with dust jacket) $10.00

BAYLOR, Byrd
Before You Came This Way, 1969 Dutton, hardcover picture book, brown tone illustrations by Tom Bahti. ($25.00 with dust jacket) $10.00

Coyote Cry, 1972 Lothrop, Lee, Shepard, first edition, hardcover, illustrations by Symeoni Shimin. ($45.00 with dust jacket) $15.00

One Small Blue Bead, 1965 Macmillan, first edition, hardcover, full page illustrations by S. Shimin. ($50.00 with dust jacket) $15.00

Everybody Needs a Rock, 1974 Scribner, oblong hardcover picture book, 3-color illustrations by Peter Parnall. ($25.00 with dust jacket) $10.00

When Clay Sings, 1972 Charles Scribner, first edition, hardcover, illustrated by Tom Bahti. ($20.00 with dust jacket) $10.00

BAUMANN, Hans
Crotchety Crocodile, 1960 Oxford, first edition, hardcover, color illustrations by Ulrik Schramm. ($20.00 with dust jacket) $10.00

I Marched With Hannibal, 1962 Walck, hardcover, map and b/w illustrations by Ulrik Schramm. ($20.00 with dust jacket) $10.00

Son of Columbus, 1957 Oxford, hardcover, b/w illustrations by William Stobbs. ($20.00 with dust jacket) $10.00

BEALER, Alex W.
Picture-Skin Story, 1957 Holiday, oblong hardcover picture book, color illustrations by author. $30.00

BEATTY, Hetty
Blitz, 1961 Weekly Reader Children's Book Club, yellow hardcover, illustrations by Joshua Tolford. ($15.00 with dust jacket) $10.00
Bucking Horse, 1957 Houghton Mifflin, oversize square hardcover, scratchboard drawings. ($40.00 with dust jacket) $20.00
Rebel: The Reluctant Racehorse, 1968 Houghton Mifflin, hardcover. ($15.00 with dust jacket) $10.00

BEATTY, Jerome, Jr.
Clambake Mutiny, 1964 Young Scott, first edition, hardcover, 68 pages, illustrations by Tomi Ungerer. ($40.00 with dust jacket) $15.00

BEATTY, John and **Patricia**
Holdfast, 1972 Morrow, hardcover, 222 pages. Dust jacket art by Franz Altschuler. ($20.00 with dust jacket) $10.00

BEATTY, Patricia
Blue Stars Watching, 1969 William Morrow, first edition, small hardcover, 191 pages. ($20.00 with dust jacket) $10.00
Hail Columbia, 1970 Morrow, hardcover, illustrations by Liz Dauber. ($20.00 with dust jacket) $10.00
Rufus, Red Rufus, 1975 Morrow, first edition, hardcover, illustrations by Ted Lewin. ($20.00 with dust jacket) $10.00

BECHDOLT, Jack
Mystery at Hurricane Hill, 1951 Dutton, hardcover. ($15.00 with dust jacket) $10.00

BECKER, John
Near Tragedy at the Waterfall, 1964 Pantheon, first edition, hardcover, illustrations by Virginia Campbell. ($20.00 with dust jacket) $10.00

BEE, Clair, see Series section, CHIP HILTON

BEHN, Harry
House Beyond the Meadow: An Excursion into Fairyland, 1955 Pantheon, first edition, hardcover, 46 pages. ($35.00 with dust jacket) $15.00
Windy Morning, 1953 edition Harcourt, first edition thus, hardcover, illustrations by author. ($20.00 with dust jacket) $10.00

BEIER, Ulli
When the Moon Was Big and Other Legends from New Guinea, 1972 Sydney, first edition, oversize hardcover, drawings by Georgina Beier. ($30.00 with dust jacket) $15.00

BEIM, Jerrold
Country School, 1955 Morrow, first edition, hardcover, illustrated by Louis Darling. ($25.00 with dust jacket) $10.00

BELL, Norman
Weightless Mother, 1967 Follett, first edition, hardcover, illustrated by W.T. Mars. ($20.00 with dust jacket) $10.00

BELL, Thelma Harrington
Yaller-Eye, 1951 Viking, first edition, hardcover, illustrations by Corydon Bell. ($35.00 with dust jacket) $15.00

BELLAIRS, John
Face in The Frost, 1969 Macmillan, first edition, hardcover, illustrations by Marilyn Fitschen. ($45.00 with dust jacket) $15.00
Figure in the Shadows, 1975 Weekly Reader Books, illustrated hardcover, illustrations by Mercer Mayer. $15.00
House with a Clock in its Walls, 1973 Dial, hardcover, 179 pages, b/w illustrations by Edward Gorey. First edition with dust jacket: $70.00 Weekly Reader edition: $15.00
Pedant and the Shuffly, 1966 Macmillan, first edition, hardcover, 79 pages, illustrations by Marilyn Fitschen. ($65.00 with dust jacket) $20.00
St. Fidgeta and Other Parodies, 1966 Macmillan, first edition, hardcover, 123 pages, illustrated by Marilyn Fitschen. ($30.00 with dust jacket) $20.00

BELLOC, Hilaire
Bad Child's Book of Beasts and More Beasts for Worse Children, (ca. 1890s) 1966 edition Grosset, color illustrated hardcover, illustrated endpapers, 45 pages, color illustrations throughout by Harold Berson. ($35.00 same-as-cover dust jacket) $20.00

BELTING, Natalia
Summer's Coming In, 1970 Holt, first edition, hardcover, illustrated by Adrienne Adams. ($25.00 with dust jacket) $15.00
Whirlwind Is a Ghost Dancing, 1974 Dutton, oblong hardcover, color illustrations by Leo and Diane Dillon. ($25.00 with dust jacket) $15.00
Winter's Eve, 1969 Holt, first edition, hardcover, illustrations by Alan E. Cober. ($25.00 with dust jacket) $15.00

BEMELMANS, Ludwig, see Series section, MADELINE SERIES
Italian Holiday, 1961 Houghton Mifflin, first edition, oversize hardcover, illustrations by author. ($60.00 with dust jacket) $30.00
Sunshine: a Story about the City of New York., 1950 Simon Schuster, first edition, oversize, pictorial boards, illustrated endpapers, color and b/w illustrations throughout by author. ($125.00 in dust jacket) $55.00
World of Bemelmans, 1955 Viking, first edition, hardcover, illustrations by author. ($25.00 with dust jacket) $10.00

BENARY-ISBERT, Margot
Blue Mystery, 1957 Harcourt, Brace, first edition, pictorial hardcover. ($30.00 with dust jacket) $10.00

BENCHLEY, Nathaniel
Feldman Fieldmouse: A Fable, 1971 Harper, first edition, hardcover, illustrations by Hilary Knight. ($25.00 with dust jacket) $15.00
Ghost Named Fred, 1968 Harper, I Can Read, first edition, hardcover. ($30.00 with dust jacket) $15.00

BENEDICT, Dorothy P.
Bandoleer, 1963 Pantheon, first edition, hardcover, illustrations by Joseph Papin. ($40.00 with dust jacket) $20.00

BENEDICT, Lois Trimble
Canalboat Mystery, 1966 Atheneum, first edition, hardcover. ($20.00 with dust jacket) $10.00

BENNETT, Anna Elizabeth
Little Witch, 1953 Lippincott, first edition, hardcover, illustrations by Helen Stone. ($50.00 with dust jacket) $15.00

BENNETT, Susan
Underground Cats, 1974 Macmillan, first edition, hardcover, illustrated. ($15.00 with dust jacket) $10.00

BENTON, Robert
Little Brother, No More, 1960 Knopf, first edition, oversize hardcover picture book, color and b/w illustrations by author. $15.00

BERENSTAIN, see Series section, BERENSTAIN BEARS

BERESFORD, Elisabeth
Magic World, 1964 Bobbs-Merrill, hardcover, 153 pages, illustrations by Janina Domanska. ($25.00 with dust jacket) $10.00
Vanishing Garden, 1965 Funk & Wagnalls, first edition, 160 pages, illustrations by Judith Valpy. ($25.00 with dust jacket) $10.00

BERESFORD-HOWE, Constance
Book of Eve, 1973 Little, Brown, first edition, hardcover, 170 pages. ($20.00 with dust jacket) $10.00

BERG, Jean
Mr. Koonan's Bargain, 1971 Nautilus Books, first edition, hardcover, illustrations by Carolyn Bentley. ($20.00 with dust jacket) $10.00
Wee Little Man, 1963 Follett, first edition, hardcover, Beginning-To-Read Book. ($20.00 with dust jacket) $10.00

BERG, Karin and Hans
Greenland through the Year, 1973 Scoll Press, first American edition, oversize hardcover, 22 pages, illustrations by authors. ($20.00 with dust jacket) $10.00

BERKEY, Helen
Aunty Pinau's Banyan Tree, 1967 Charles E. Tuttle, first edition, hardcover, illustrated by Raymond Lanterman. ($20.00 with dust jacket) $10.00

BERNA, Paul
Horse Without a Head, 1958 Pantheon, hardcover, 182 pages, b/w illustrations by Richard Kennedy. ($15.00 with dust jacket) $10.00
Mule on the Expressway, 1967 Pantheon, first US edition, hardcover, 167 pages, illustrations by Gareth Floyd. ($20.00 with dust jacket) $10.00

BERNARD, Art
Dog Days, 1969 Caldwell Caxton, first edition, hardcover, 204 pages, b/w illustrations. ($25.00 with dust jacket) $15.00

BERNE, Eric
Happy Valley, 1968 Grove Press, hardcover, color illustrations by Sylvie Selig. ($20.00 with dust jacket) $10.00

BERRISFORD, Judith M.
Sue's Circus Horse, 1951 University of London Press, first edition, hardcover, 174 pages, illustrations by Leslie Atkinson. ($20.00 with dust jacket) $10.00

BERSON, Harold
Balarin's Goat, 1972 Crown Publishers, hardcover, color illustrations by Harold Berson. ($20.00 with dust jacket) $10.00
Bear Named George, 1969 Crown, hardcover, illustrations by author. ($20.00 with dust jacket) $10.00

Boy, the Baker, the Miller and More, 1974 Crown Publishers, green illustrated hardcover, illustrated by Harold Berson. ($20.00 with dust jacket) $10.00
Moose is Not a Mouse, 1975 Crown Publishers, first edition, oversize pictorial hardcover, 26 pages, color illustrations by author. ($20.00 with dust jacket) $10.00
Thief Who Hugged a Moonbeam, 1972 Seabury Press, hardcover, illustrations by author. ($20.00 with dust jacket) $10.00

BEST, Herbert, see Series section, DESMOND

BESTON, Henry
Chimney Farm Bedtime Stories, 1966 Holt Rinehart Winston, first edition, hardcover. ($20.00 with dust jacket) $10.00

BETTINA, see EHRLICH, Bettina

BIALK, Elisa
Colt of Cripple Creek, 1953 World, first edition, hardcover, illustrations by Edward Shenton. ($25.00 with dust jacket) $10.00

BIANCO, Pamela
Little Houses Far Away, 1951 Oxford first edition, hardcover, 87 pages, b/w illustrations by author. ($55.00 with dust jacket) $20.00
Look-Inside Easter Egg, 1953 Oxford, hardcover, square, 32 pages, color illustrations by author. ($65.00 with dust jacket) $40.00

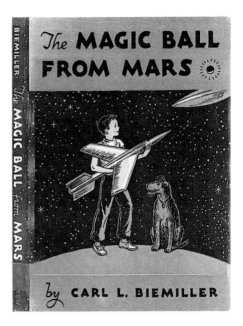

BIEMILLER, Carl, see Series section, HYDRONAUTS
Magic Ball from Mars, (1953) 1960 edition Mor-

row, hardcover, 127 pages, b/w illustrations by Kathleen Voute. ($20.00 with dust jacket) $10.00

BILLING, Graham
Forbush and the Penguins, 1966 Holt, first edition, hardcover, 192 pages. ($25.00 with dust jacket) $15.00

BILLOUT, Guy
Number 24, 1973 Harlin Quist, first edition, hardcover, 21 pages. ($30.00 with dust jacket) $15.00

BINZEN, Bill
Alfred, the Little Bear, 1970 Garden City, hardcover. ($20.00 with dust jacket) $10.00

BIRO, Val
Gumdrop and the Farmer's Friend, 1968 Follett, oversize hardcover, pictorial boards, illustrated. ($20.00 with dust jacket) $10.00
Gumdrop in Double Trouble, 1975 Brockhampton Press, first edition, illustrated by author. $15.00
Gumdrop on the Move, 1970 Follett, first edition, orange hardcover, author illustrated. ($20.00 with dust jacket) $10.00

BISHOP, Claire Huchet
All Alone, 1953 Viking, hardcover, illustrated endpapers, b/w illustrations by Feodor Rojankovsky. ($50.00 with dust jacket) $20.00
Big Loop, 1955 Viking, first edition, hardcover, illustrated by Carles Fontsere. ($35.00 with dust jacket) $15.00
Twenty and Ten, 1952 Viking, first edition, tall hardcover, illustrated endpapers, b/w illustrations by William Pene duBois. ($60.00 with dust jacket) $30.00

BISHOP, Curtis
Sideline Quarterback, 1960 Lippincott, first edition, hardcover. ($15.00 with dust jacket) $10.00

BISHOP, Elizabeth
Ballad of the Burglar of Babylon, 1968 Farrar, first edition, hardcover, woodcut color illustrations by Ann Grifalconi. Hard to find. ($100.00 with dust jacket) $40.00

BISHOP, Morris, editor
Renaissance Storybook, 1971 Cornell University, first edition, hardcover. ($20.00 with dust jacket) $10.00

BLACK, Mary Martin
Summerfield Farm, 1951 Viking, first edition, oversize hardcover, 143 pages, illustrations by Wesley Dennis. ($35.00 with dust jacket) $20.00

BLAINE, John, see Series section RICK BRANT

BLAINE, Marge
Terrible Thing Happened at Our House, 1972 Parents', oversize illustrated hardcover picture book, color illustrations throughout by John C. Wallner. ($20.00 with dust jacket) $15.00

BLAIR, Peter
Coming of Pout, 1969 Little, Brown, first edition, hardcover, illustrations by Trina Schart Hyman. ($20.00 with dust jacket) $10.00

BLAKE, Pamela
Peep-Show, a Little Book of Rhymes, 1973 Macmillan, first edition, square hardcover. ($20.00 with dust jacket) $10.00

BLAKESTON, Oswell
Working Cats, 1963 Elek Books, UK, first edition, oversize hardcover, illustrations by photographs. ($40.00 with dust jacket) $20.00

BLAKEY, Madge Beattie and **Carol COLLIVER**
Calypso Island, 1970 Westminster Press, first edition, hardcover, illustrations by Al Fiorentino. ($20.00 with dust jacket) $10.00

BLEGVAD, Lenore
Mr. Jensen & Cat, 1965 Harcourt, first edition, small hardcover picture book, b/w and color illustrations by Erik Blegvad. ($40.00 with dust jacket) $15.00

BLISHEN, Edward
Oxford Book of Poetry for Children, 1963 Franklin Watts, first edition, purple hardcover, 168 pages, illustrated by Brian Wildsmith. ($35.00 with dust jacket) $15.00

BLOCH, Bertram
Little Laundress and the Fearful Knight, 1954 Doubleday, first edition, hardcover. ($35.00 with dust jacket) $20.00

BLOUGH, Glenn
Bird Watchers and Bird Feeders, 1963 McGraw Hill/Whittlesey House, first edition, hardcover, illustrations by Jeanne Bendik. ($15.00 with dust jacket) $10.00
Tree on the Road to Turntown, 1953 Whittlesey, oversize hardcover picture book, color illustrations by Jeanne Bendik. ($20.00 with dust jacket) $10.00

BLUE, Rose
How Many Blocks Is the World?, 1970 Franklin

Watts, first edition, hardcover, 52 pages, illustrations by Harold James. ($25.00 with dust jacket) $15.00

BLUME, Judy

Blubber, 1974 Bradbury Press, hardcover. First edition with dust jacket: $90.00 Later printings: ($25.00 with dust jacket) $15.00

Iggie's House, 1970 Bradbury Press, probable first, hardcover. ($20.00 with dust jacket) $10.00

Otherwise Known as Sheila the Great, 1972 Dutton, hardcover, 118 pages, dust jacket illustration by Roy Doty. First edition with dust jacket: $75.00 Later printings: ($20.00 with dust jacket) $15.00

Then Again, Maybe I Won't, 1971 Bradbury Press, first edition, hardcover, 164 pages. ($40.00 with dust jacket) $15.00

BLYTON, Enid, see Series section, ADVENTURE; FAMOUS FIVE; FIVE FINDER-OUTERS; NODDY; SECRET SEVEN

English author Blyton wrote mystery/adventure novels for children, created numerous series, and is credited with 600 titles. Many of her books are still in print, especially in paperback editions.

Birds of the Wayside and Woodland, 1952 Warne, London, hardcover, 350 pages, color illustrations. ($20.00 with dust jacket) $10.00

Brer Rabbit's a Rascal, 1965 Dean, London, hardcover. ($20.00 with dust jacket) $10.00

Buttercup Farm Family, 1952 Lutterworth Press, London, hardcover, illustrated by Ruth Gervis. ($15.00 with dust jacket) $10.00

Enid Blyton's Circus Book, 1951 Latimer House, London, hardcover, 160 pages, b/w illustrations. $20.00

Enid Blyton's Storytime Book, 1964 Dean & Son Ltd., first edition, hardcover, green boards, black lettering,184 pages, 130 b/w illustrations. ($15.00 with dust jacket) $10.00

My Favourite Enid Blyton Story Book, 1964 Golden Pleasure Books Ltd., first edition, hardcover, blue pictorial boards. $20.00

Mystery That Never Was, 1961 Collins, first edition, hardcover. ($40.00 with dust jacket) $20.00

Pixie Land Storybook, 1966 Collins, first edition, hardcover, illustrations by Rene Cloke. $15.00

Pole Star Family, 1957 Lutterworth Press, London, hardcover. ($20.00 with dust jacket)

Rat-A-Tat Mystery, 1956 Collins, first edition, hardcover. ($30.00 with dust jacket) $10.00

Rubadub Mystery, 1954 Collins, first edition thus, hardcover, 256 pages, illustrations by Gilbert Dunlop. ($20.00 with dust jacket) $10.00

Six Bad Boys, 1955 British edition, hardcover, illustrated by Mary Gernat. $15.00

Tales After Tea, 1963 Collins, hardcover. $10.00

Tales of Brave Adventure, 1963 Dean, first edition. ($15.00 with dust jacket) $10.00

Wishing-Chair Again, 1950 George Newnes, London, first edition, red hardcover, illustrations by Hilda McGavin. ($15.00 with dust jacket) $10.00

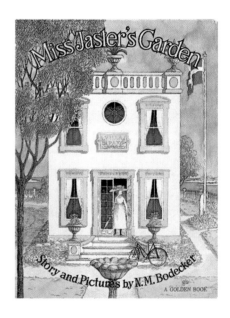

BODECKER, N. M.

It's Raining Said John Twaining, 1973 Atheneum, first edition, oblong oversize pictorial paper covered hardcover, illustrations by Bodecker. ($30.00 with dust jacket) $15.00

Miss Jaster's Garden, 1972 Western Publishing, oversize Golden Book, color illustrated paper-over-board cover, map endpapers, 29 pages, color illustrations throughout by author. $65.00

Mushroom Center Disaster, 1974 Atheneum, first edition, small hardcover, 48 pages, b/w illustrations by Eric Blegvad. ($60.00 with dust jacket) $30.00

BODEN, Hilda
Pony Girl, 1959 Lutterworth, London, first edition, hardcover, 124 pages. ($15.00 with dust jacket) $10.00
Storm Over Wales, 1969 David McKay, hardcover, 152 pages. ($15.00 with dust jacket) $10.00

BOEGEHOLD, Betty
Pawpaw's Run, 1968 Dutton, hardcover, illustrations by Christine Price. ($15.00 with dust jacket) $10.00
Pippa Mouse, 1973 Knopf, first US edition, hardcover, illustrated by Cyndy Szekeres. ($20.00 with dust jacket) $10.00

BOER, Friedrich, editor
Igloos, Yurts and Totem Poles, 1957 Pantheon, hardcover, 124 pages, illustrations. $10.00

BOLLIGER, Max
Fireflies, 1970 Atheneum, first American edition, oversize hardcover, 32 pages, illustrated by Jiri Trnka. ($30.00 with dust jacket) $15.00

BOLLIGER-SAVELLI, Antonella
Knitted Cat, 1971 Macmillan, square hardcover picture book, color illustrations by author. ($35.00 with dust jacket) $15.00

BOLTON, Mimi
Merry-Go-Round Family, 1954 Coward McCann, first edition, hardcover. ($25.00 with dust jacket) $10.00

BOND, Gladys Baker, b. 1912
Adventures with Hal, ca. 1965 Whitman, hardcover, 156 pages, illustrated by Polly Bolian. $15.00

BOND, Jean Carey
Brown Is a Beautiful Color, 1969 Franklin Watts, first edition, hardcover, illustrated by Barbara Zuber. ($15.00 with dust jacket) $10.00

BOND, Michael, see Series section, PADDINGTON, THURSDAY
Olga Meets Her Match, 1975 Hastings, first US edition, Olga da Polga book, small hardcover, b/w illustrations by Hans Helwig. ($35.00 with dust jacket) $15.00
Tales of Olga da Polga, 1971 Macmillan, b/w illustrations by Hans Helwig. ($35.00 with dust jacket) $15.00

BOND, Susan McDonald
Tale of a Red Tempered Viking, 1968 Grove Press, first edition, hardcover, illustrated endpapers, illustrations by Sally Trinkle. ($50.00 with dust jacket) $20.00

BONNER, M.G.
Real Book About Crime Detection, 1957 Garden City Books, 215 pages. $10.00

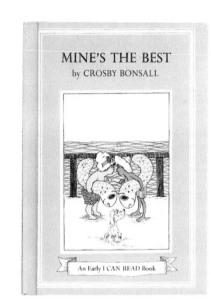

BONSALL, Crosby
And I Mean it, Stanley, 1974 Harper, first edition, easy reader, hardcover picture book, color illustrations by author. ($30.00 with dust jacket) $10.00
Case of the Dumb Bells, 1966 Harper, first edition, easy reader, hardcover picture book, color illustrations by author. ($20.00 with dust jacket) $10.00
Case of the Hungry Stranger, 1963 Harper, first edition, easy reader, hardcover picture book, color illustrations by author. ($30.00 with dust jacket) $10.00
Here's Jellybean Reilly, 1966 Harper, first edition, hardcover, photograph illustrations by Ylla Bonsall. ($25.00 with dust jacket) $10.00
Mine's the Best, 1973 Harper, first edition, hardcover, illustrations by author. ($40.00 with dust jacket) $20.00
Piggle, 1973 Harper, first edition, easy reader, hardcover picture book, color illustrations by author. ($30.00 with dust jacket) $15.00

BONTEMPS, Arna
Lonesome Boy, 1955 Houghton, first edition, hardcover, b/w illustrations by Feliks Topolski. ($80.00 with dust jacket) $20.00
Mr. Kelso's Lion, 1970 Lippincott, first edition, hardcover, 48 pages, illustrated by Len Ebert. ($25.00 with dust jacket) $15.00

Sam Patch, High, Wide and Handsome Jumper, 1951 Houghton, oblong hardcover picture book, b/w and color illustrations by Paul Brown. ($50.00 with dust jacket) $20.00

Story of George Washington Carver, 1954 Grosset & Dunlap, first edition, hardcover, 181 pages, illustrated. ($45.00 with dust jacket) $20.00

BOOZ, Elisabeth Benson
Treat in a Trout, 1955 Houghton, 63 pages. ($35.00 with dust jacket) $20.00

BORACK, Barbara
Grandpa, 1967 Harper, hardcover picture book, color illustrations by Ben Shecter. ($20.00 with same-as-cover dust jacket) $10.00

Someone Small, 1969 Harper, first edition, hardcover, illustrations by Anita Lobel. ($20.00 with dust jacket) $10.00

BORBIN, William
Horse in the House, 1964 Coward McCann, 288 pages, hardcover. $40.00.

BORLAND, Hal
Dog Who Came To Stay, 1961 Lippincott, first edition, hardcover. ($25.00 with dust jacket) $10.00

Penny, 1972 Lippincott, first edition, hardcover, illustrated by Taylor Oughton. $10.00

BORLAND, Kathryn and **Helen SPEICHER**
Good-Bye to Stony Crick, 1975 McGraw-Hill, Weekly Reader edition, hardcover, illustrated by Deanne Hollinger. $10.00

BORNEMARK, Gullan and **Pauline T. DYER**
Play-Game Song Book, 1964 Allyn and Bacon, first edition, hardcover, illustrations by Ylva Kallstrom-Eklund. Two 33⅓ vinyl records inside cover pockets. $35.00

BOSTON, L. M., see Series section, GREEN KNOWE
Memory in a House, 1973 Macmillan, first American edition, hardcover with gilt, 142 pages, illustrated from drawn plans and photographs. ($50.00 with dust jacket) $20.00

Nothing Said, 1971 Harcourt, first American edition, hardcover, 64 pages, illustrations by Peter Boston. ($25.00 with dust jacket) $15.00.

Sea Egg, 1967 Harcourt, first edition, hardcover, illustrated by Peter Boston. ($20.00 with dust jacket) $10.00

BOTHWELL, Jean
Missing Violin, 1959 Harcourt, first edition, hardcover, Artur Marokvia. ($15.00 with dust jacket) $10.00

BOTT, R.
Chess Apprentice, 1960 Collins, first edition, hardcover, illustrated endpapers. ($25.00 with dust jacket) $10.00

BOUTWELL, E.
Sailor Tom, 1960 World, first edition, hardcover, illustrations by Kurt Werth. ($15.00 with dust jacket) $10.00

BOWER, Barbra
Scarecrow of Scatterbrook Farm, 1947 Putnam, hardcover with illllustration of Worzel Gummidge, b/w Illustrations by Ursula Koering. ($20.00 with dust jacket) $10.00

BOWMAN, Jeanne
Neighborhood Nurse, 1968 Arcadia, hardcover, 188 pages. ($20.00 with dust jacket) $10.00

BOYLAN, Eleanor
How to Be a Puppeteer, 1970 McCall, first edition, hardcover, illustrated by Tomie de Paola. ($20.00 with dust jacket) $10.00

BOYLE, Joyce
Muskoka Holiday, 1953 Macmillan, hardcover, illustrated by Geoffrey Whittam. $10.00

BRADBURY, Bianca
Amos Learns to Talk, 1950 Rand McNally Elf book, hardcover. $10.00

Laughter in Our House, 1964 Washburn, 183 pages. ($25.00 in dust jacket) $10.00

Loner, 1970 Houghton Mifflin, first edition, hardcover, 140 pages, illustrations by John Gretzer. ($15.00 with dust jacket) $10.00

BRADBURY, Ray
Halloween Tree, 1972 Knopf, first edition, hard-

cover, b/w illustrations by Joseph Mugnaini. ($40.00 with dust jacket) $15.00

S is for Space, 1966 Doubleday, 234 pages, hardcover. $25.00

Switch on the Night, 1955 Pantheon, first edition, square hardcover, color illustrations by Madeleine Gekiere. Hard to find. ($250.00 with dust jacket) $75.00

BRADLEY, Duane
Cappy and the Jet Engine, 1957 Lippincott, first edition, hardcover, illustrations by Alice Cosgrove. ($30.00 with dust jacket) $15.00

Mystery at the Shoals, 1962 Lippincott, first edition, hardcover, 124 pages, illustrations by Velma Ilsley. ($20.00 with dust jacket) $10.00

BRADLEY, Helen
And Miss Carter Wore Pink, Scenes from an Edwardian Childhood, 1971 Cape, first edition UK, oversize square hardcover, color illustrations by author. ($30.00 with dust jacket) $15.00

And Miss Carter Wore Pink, Scenes from an Edwardian Childhood, 1971 Holt, first edition, hardcover, color illustrations. ($30.00 with dust jacket) $15.00

'In the Beginning,' Said Great-Aunt Jane, 1975 Jonathan Cape, first edition UK, oversize hardcover, 32 pages, color illustrations by author. ($30.00 with dust jacket) $15.00

Miss Carter Came With Us, 1974 Little, Brown, first American edition, hardcover, 31 pages, color illustrations by author. ($20.00 with dust jacket) $10.00

BRADLEY, Marion Zimmer
Colors of Space, 1963 Monarch Books. $15.00

BRADY, Eilis
All In! All In!, 1975 Dublin, 196 pages, photo illustrations. ($20.00 with dust jacket) $10.00

BRADY, Irene
Mouse Named Mus, 1972 Houghton Mifflin, first edition, hardcover, b/w illustrations. ($15.00 with dust jacket) $10.00

Owlet the Great Horned Owl, 1974 Houghton Mifflin, first edition, hardcover, 40 pages, illustrated by Irene Brady. ($15.00 with dust jacket) $10.00

BRAND, Christianna
Naughty Children, 1963 Dutton, first edition, hardcover, illustrations by Edward Ardizzone. ($40.00 with dust jacket) $20.00

Nurse Matilda, 1964 Dutton, first edition, hardcover, illustrations by Edward Ardizzone. ($40.00 with dust jacket) $20.00

BRANDENBERG, Franz
I Once Knew a Man, 1970 Macmillan, illustrated hardcover picture book, b/w/orange illustrations by Alika. ($25.00 with dust jacket) $15.00

Secret for Grandmother's Birthday, 1975 Greenwillow, oversize hardcover picture book, color illustrations by Alika. ($20.00 with dust jacket) $10.00

BRANLEY, Franklyn
Timmy and the Tin-Can Telephone, 1959 Crowell, hardcover picture book, color and b/w illustrations by Paul Galdone. ($15.00 with dust jacket) $10.00

BRANT, Irving
Friendly Cove, 1963 Bobbs-Merrill, first edition, hardcover. ($20.00 with dust jacket) $10.00

BRENNAN, Nicholas
Olaf's Incredible Machine, 1973 Windmill, oversize hardcover picture book, color illustrations by author. ($30.00 with dust jacket) $10.00

BRENNER, Anita
Timid Ghost, 1966 Young Scott, oversize hardcover picture book, color illustrations by Jean Charlot. $15.00

BRENNER, Barbara
Flying Patchwork Quilt, 1965 Young Scott, first edition, hardcover, illustrations by Fred Brenner. ($25.00 with dust jacket) $15.00

Summer of the Houseboat, 1968 Knopf, first edition, hardcover, illustrations by Fred Brenner. ($15.00 with dust jacket) $10.00

BRENNER, Leah
Artist Grows Up in Mexico, 1953 Beechhurst, first edition, hardcover, 16 line drawings by Diego Rivera. ($40.00 with dust jacket) $20.00

BRENT, Stuart
Mr. Toast and the Woolly Mammoth, 1966 Viking, first edition, hardcover. ($15.00 with dust jacket) $10.00

BRENTANO, Clemens
Tale of Gockel, Hinkel & Gackeliah, 1961 Random House, first edition, hardcover, illustrated endpapers, b/w illustrations by Maurice Sendak. ($150.00 with dust jacket) $50.00

BREWER, Jo
Mysterious Treasure of Cloud Rock, 1953 Dutton, first edition, hardcover. ($15.00 with dust jacket) $10.00

BREWSTER, Benjamin (Franklin Brewster Folsom), see Series section, WILDERNESS MYSTERY
Baby Elephant, 1950 Wonder Books, illustrations by Peter Duncan. $10.00
Big Book of the Real Circus, 1951 Grosset & Dunlap, illustrations by Gail Phillips. $15.00
First Book of Firemen, 1956 Watts, hardcover, illustrations by Jeanne Bendick. ($20.00 with dust jacket) $10.00

BREWTON, Sara and **John E.**
Christmas Bells are Ringing, 1951 Macmillan, first edition, red hardcover. $20.00

BRICE, Clare
Dog for Davie's Hill, 1957 Macmillan, Weekly Reader Book Club edition, hardcover, illustrated by author. $10.00

BRICK, John
Eagle of Niagara, the Story of David Harper and His Indian Captivity, 1955 Doubleday, first edition, hardcover. ($15.00 with dust jacket) $10.00

BRIDGMAN, Betty
Lullaby for Eggs, 1955 Macmillan, first edition, color illustrated hardcover, 28 pages, color illustrations by Elizabeth Orton Jones. ($30.00 with dust jacket) $20.00

BRIGGS, Raymond
Complete Father Christmas, 1973 Hamish Hamilton, London, first edition, pictorial glazed boards, color illustrations by author. $45.00
Fairy Tale Treasury, 1972 McCann, glossy pictorial oversize hardcover, illustrations by author. $30.00
Father Christmas, 1973 Hamish Hamilton, London, first edition, pictorial glazed boards, color illustrations by author. ($45.00 with dust jacket) $25.00
Father Christmas, 1973 Random House, first American edition, oversize hardcover, comic strip illustrations in color by author. ($25.00 with dust jacket) $10.00
Father Christmas Goes on Holiday, 1975 Coward-McCann, first American edition, oversize hardcover picture book, color cartoon illustrations by author. ($50.00 with same-as-cover dust jacket) $20.00 Later editions: ($15.00 with dust jacket) $10.00
Fee-Fi-Fo-Fum, 1964 Coward-McCann, first American edition, 40 pages, illustrations by author. ($45.00 with dust jacket) $25.00
Midnight Adventure, 1975 Hamish Hamilton, hardcover, illustrations by author. $25.00
Mother Goose Treasury, 1966 Yearling, oversize, color illustrations by Briggs. $40.00
Ring-a-Ring o' Roses, 1962 Coward-McCann, first US edition, oversize picture book, 48 pages, color illustrations by Briggs. ($80.00 with dust jacket) $50.00
Strange House, 1961 Hamish Hamilton, pictorial hardcover, illustrations by author. $25.00
White Land, a Picture Book of Traditional Rhymes and Verses, 1963 Coward-McCann, first edition, oversize hardcover, b/w and color illustrations by Briggs. ($25.00 with dust jacket) $15.00

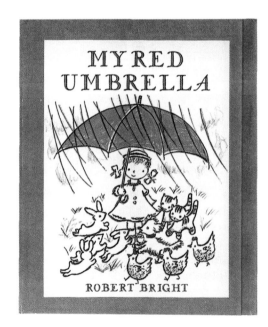

BRIGHT, Robert, see Series section, GEORGIE
Friendly Bear, 1957 Doubleday, first edition, oversize hardcover, illustrations by author. ($30.00 with dust jacket) $15.00

Gregory: the Noisiest and Strongest Boy In Grangers Grove, 1969 Doubleday, color illustrations by author. $15.00

Miss Pattie, 1954 Doubleday, hardcover, oversize pictorial hardcover, illustrated in color by the author. $30.00

My Red Umbrella, 1959 Morrow, small hardcover, red/white/black illustrations by author. ($20.00 with dust jacket) $10.00

Richard Brown and the Dragon, 1952 Doubleday, illustrated by author. ($25.00 with dust jacket) $10.00

Which Is Willy? 1962 Doubleday, illustrated by author. ($30.00 with dust jacket) $15.00

BRIMS, Bernagh
Runaway Riders, 1963 Bobbs-Merrill, hardcover. ($20.00 with dust jacket) $10.00

BRINDZE, Ruth, see Series section, ALL ABOUT SERIES
Story of Our Calendar, 1949 Vanguard, pictoral boards, cloth spine, illustrations by Helene Carter. $12.00

BRINK, Carol Ryrie
Highly Trained Dogs of Professor Petit, 1953 Macmillan, first edition, green hardcover. ($20.00 with dust jacket) $10.00

Louly, 1974 Macmillan, hardcover, b/w illustrations by Ingrid Fetz. ($20.00 with dust jacket) $10.00

Pink Motel, 1959 Macmillan, first edition, hardcover, illustrations by Sheila Greenwald. ($25.00 with dust jacket) $10.00

Winter Cottage, 1968 Macmillan, first edition, hardcover. ($25.00 with dust jacket) $10.00

BRINSMEAD, H. F.
Seasons of the Briar, 1965 Australia, first edition, 202 pages, illustrations by William Papas. ($45.00 with dust jacket) $25.00

BRISTOL, Jane Curtis
Little Prickly Weed, 1963 Allied, hardcover, illustrated by Mary Richards Gibson. ($25.00 with dust jacket) $15.00

BRITTEN, Benjamin and **Imogen HOLST**
Wonderful World of Music, 1958 Doubleday, oversize hardcover, 69 pages, illustrations by Ceri Richards. $20.00

BRO, Margueritte
Su-Mei's Golden Year, 1950 Doubleday, first edition, hardcover, illustrations by Kurt Wiese. ($20.00 with dust jacket) $10.00

BROCK, Betty
No Flying in the House, 1970 Harper, first edition, small pictorial hardcover, 139 pages, illustrated by Wallace Tripp. ($50.00 with dust jacket) $30.00

BROCK, Emma L.
Ballet For Mary, 1954 Knopf, first edition, 83 pages, hardcover, pictorial endpapers, illustrations in color and b/w. $15.00

Come On-Along, Fish!, 1956 Knopf, first edition, illustrated hardcover. $10.00

Plaid Cow, 1961 Knopf, first edition, hardcover, illustrations by author. ($25.00 with dust jacket) $15.00

Three Ring Circus, 1950 Knopf, first edition, hardcover. ($30.00 with dust jacket) $15.00

BROGER, Achim
Good Morning, Whale, 1974 Macmillan, first edition, hardcover, illustrated by Gisela Kalow. ($35.00 with dust jacket) $20.00

BROMHALL, Winifred
Middle Matilda, 1962 Knopf, oblong oversize hardcover picture book, color and b/w illustrations by author. ($35.00 with dust jacket) $15.00

BRONSON, Wilfrid S.
Cats, 1950 Harcourt, first edition, oversize hardcover, illustrations by author. ($75.00 with dust jacket) $40.00
Freedom and Plenty: Ours to Save, 1953 Harcourt, first edition, hardcover, b/w illustrations. ($30.00 with dust jacket) $15.00

BRONTE, Charlotte
Search for Happiness, (1829) 1969 edition Simon & Schuster, first American edition thus, hardcover, color illustrations by Carolyn Dinan. ($20.00 with dust jacket) $10.00

BROOKS, Mary
Adventures of Rufus, 1969 Locke, pictorial boards, oversize, 60 pages, illustrated by author. $15.00

BROOKS, Robert
Run, Jump, Bump Book, 1971 Little, Brown, first edition, hardcover, illustrations by David M. McPhail. ($20.00 with dust jacket) $10.00

BROOKS, Walter, see Series section, FREDDY
Henry's Dog, Henry, 1965 Knopf, illustrated by Aldren Watson. ($50.00 with dust jacket) $35.00
Jimmy Takes Vanishing Lessons, 1965 Knopf, illustrated by Donald Alan Bolognese. ($50.00 with dust jacket) $35.00

BROUGH, James
Dog Who Lives at the Waldorf, 1964 Little, Brown, hardcover, illustrated by Vasiliu. $20.00

BROWER, Brock
Inchworm War and the Butterfly Peace, 1970 Doubleday, first edition, hardcover, color illustrations by Arnold Roth. ($25.00 with dust jacket) $15.00

BROWN, Antony
Dangerfoot, 1966 Meredith, first US edition, hardcover, 187 pages. ($45.00 with dust jacket) $20.00

BROWN, Beth
All Horses Go to Heaven, 1963 Grosset, b/w illustrations by F. Vaugh. $15.00

Blinkie, 1956 Prentice-Hall, hardcover, b/w illustrations by Marin Barry. $15.00

BROWN, Bill and **Rosalie**
Big Rig, 1959 McCann, hardcover, illustrated by Peter Burchard. ($15.00 with dust jacket) $10.00

BROWN, Eleanor F.
Colt from Horse Heaven Hills, 1956 Julian Messner, first edition, hardcover. ($20.00 in dust jacket) $10.00
Horse For Peter, 1957 Julian Messner, first edition, hardcover, illustrated by Pers Crowell. ($20.00 in dust jacket) $10.00

BROWN, Gladys E.
Tico Bravo: Shark Hunter, 1954 Little, Brown, first edition, hardcover, b/w illustrations by Scott Maclain. ($15.00 with dust jacket) $10.00

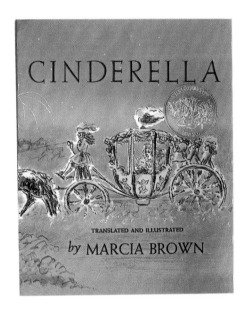

BROWN, Marcia
Backbone of the King, the Story of Paka'a and his Son Ku, 1966 Scribner, first edition, hardcover, 57 linoleum block illustrations by the author. ($50.00 with dust jacket) $20.00 Later editions: ($25.00 with dust jacket) $15.00
Cinderella, (Perrault), 1954 Atheneum, 1955 Caldecott Award edition, hardcover, color illustrations by author. ($30.00 with dust jacket) $15.00
Dick Whittington and His Cat, 1950 Scribner, oversize color illustrated hardcover, three-color illustrations by author. ($15.00 with dust jacket) $10.00
Felice, 1958 Scribner, oversize hardcover picture book, color illustrations by author. ($50.00 with dust jacket) $20.00

How, Hippo, 1969 Scribner, first edition, hardcover, illustrations by author. ($40.00 with dust jacket) $15.00

Neighbors, 1967 Charles Scribner, first edition, oversize hardcover picture book, color illustrations by author. ($30.00 with dust jacket) $15.00

Once a Mouse, 1961 Scribner, (1962 Caldecott Award), hardcover, color illustrations by author. First edition with dust jacket: $125.00
Later editions: ($25.00 with dust jacket) $15.00

Skipper John's Cook, 1951 Scribner, oversize hardcover picture book, red/b/w illustrations by author. ($35.00 with dust jacket) $15.00

Tamarindo!, 1960 Scribner's, oversize hardcover, color illustrations by author. ($30.00 with dust jacket) $10.00

BROWN, Margaret Wise

Duck, 1952 Harper, first edition, oversize hardcover, photograph illustrations by Ylla. ($75.00 with dust jacket) $30.00

Home for a Bunny, 1961 Golden Book, illustrated hardcover, illustrated by Garth Williams. $15.00

Quiet Noisy Book, 1950 Harper, first edition, oversize hardcover, 34 pages, color illustrations by Leonard Weisgard. ($50.00 with dust jacket) $15.00

Seven Stories about a Cat Named Sneaker, 1955 William Scott, first edition, hardcover, illustrated by Jean Charlot. ($90.00 with dust jacket) $30.00

Steamroller, 1974 Walker, oblong hardcover picture book, color illustrations by Evaline Ness. ($30.00 with dust jacket) $10.00

Three Little Animals, 1956 Harper, oversize illustrated hardcover picture book, 28 pages, color illustrations by Garth Williams. ($40.00 with dust jacket) $20.00

Young Kangaroo, 1955 Scott, hardcover, illustrated boards, illustrations by Symeon Shimin. $15.00

BROWN, Paul

Cats of Destiny, 1950 Scribner, first edition, hardcover, illustrations by author. ($35.00 with dust jacket) $15.00

BROWNER, Richard

Every One Has a Name, 1961 Walck, first edition, hardcover, illustrations by Emma Landau. ($15.00 with dust jacket) $10.00

BROWNJOHN, Alan

Brownjohn's Beasts, 1970 Scribner, first edition, hardcover, 48 pages, illustrations by Carol Lawson. ($20.00 with dust jacket) $10.00

BRUCE, Dana, editor
My Brimful Book, 1960 Platt & Munk, oversize illustrated hardcover, illustrations by Tasha Tudor, Margot Austin, and Wesley Dennis. $60.00

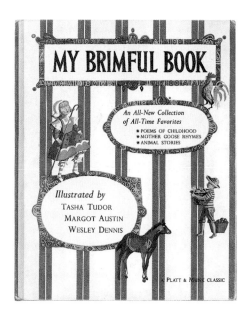

My Brimful Book, Dana Bruce, editor

BRYAN, Ashley

Ox of the Wonderful Horns and Other African Folktales, 1971 Atheneum, first edition, oversize hardcover, illustrated by color and b/w woodcuts. ($40.00 with dust jacket) $20.00

BRYAN, Dorothy and **Marguerite**

Four Puppies Who Wanted a Home, 1950 Wonder Books, color illustrations. $15.00

BRYSON, Bernarda

Gilgamesh, ca. 1967 Holt, first edition, oversize hardcover, color illustrations by author. ($25.00 with dust jacket) $10.00

BUCHANAN, William

Ghost of Dagger Bay, 1963 Abelard Schuman, hardcover, 189 pages. ($15.00 with dust jacket) $10.00

BUCHWALD, Art

Bollo Caper, a Fable for Children of All Ages, 1974 Garden City, first edition, hardcover. ($15.00 with dust jacket) $10.00

BUCK, Margaret Waring

Pets From the Pond, 1958 Abingdon, hardcover, illustrated by author. ($20.00 with dust jacket) $10.00

Where Do They Go In Winter, 1968 Abingdon Press, first edition, hardcover, illustrations by author. ($20.00 with dust jacket) $10.00

BUCK, Pearl, editor
Fairy Tales of the Orient, 1965 Simon & Schuster, first edition, hardcover. ($50.00 with dust jacket) $20.00

BUCKERIDGE, Anthony, see Series section, JENNINGS

BUCKLER, Helen
Wo-He-Lo, the Story of the Campfire Girls, 1960 Holt, first edition, hardcover, 308 pages. ($20.00 with dust jacket) $10.00

BUCKLEY, Helen
Grandfather and I, 1959 Lothrop, oversize hardcover picture book, color illustrations by Paul Galdone. ($20.00 with dust jacket) $10.00
Josie's Buttercup, 1967 Lothrop, pictorial hardcover, color illustrations by Evaline Ness. ($35.00 with dust jacket) $15.00
Some Cheese for Charles, 1963 Lothrop, small oblong hardcover, illustrations by Evaline Ness. ($40.00 with dust jacket) $15.00

BUCKLEY, Isabelle P.
Guide to a Child's World, 1951 Holt, first edition, small hardcover, 115 pages. ($20.00 with dust jacket) $10.00

BUCKLEY, Mary
Six Brothers and a Witch, 1969 Bobbs Merrill, first edition, hardcover, illustrations by Francoise Webb. ($15.00 with dust jacket) $10.00

BUEHR, Walter
Birth of a Liner, 1961 Little, Brown, hardcover, 119 pages, illustrated by author. $30.00

BUFF, Conrad and **Mary**
Apple and the Arrow, 1951 Houghton, illustrated hardcover, color and b/w illustrations by authors. $25.00
Elf Owl, 1958 Viking, first edition, hardcover, illustrations by authors. ($35.00 in dust jacket) $20.00
Forest Folk, 1962 Viking, illustrated hard cover, illustrated endpapers, brown ink illustrations by author. $15.00
Hah Nee of the Cliff Dwellers, 1956 Houghton, first edition, illustrated hardcover, color and b/w illustrations by authors. ($35.00 in dust jacket) $20.00
Kemi, an Indian Boy Before the White Man Came, 1966 Ward Ritchie Press, first edition, hardcover, illustrations by authors. ($55.00 in dust jacket) $20.00
Magic Maize, 1953 Houghton, illustrated hardcover, color and b/w illustrations by authors. ($35.00 in dust jacket) $20.00

BUFANO, Remo
Remo Bufano's Book of Puppetry, edited by Arthur Rich-mond, 1951 Macmillan, first edition, hardcover, illustrations by author. ($20.00 with dust jacket) $10.00

BULL, Angela
Wayland's Keep, 1966 Holt, first edition, hardcover, illustrations by Emily McCully. ($25.00 in dust jacket) $10.00

BULL, Peter
Teddy Bear Book, 1970 Random House, first American edition, oversize hardcover, illustrated. ($50.00 in dust jacket) $20.00

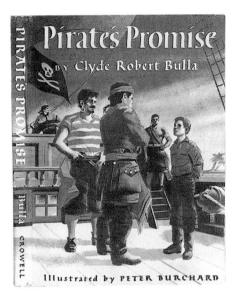

BULLA, Clyde Robert
Down the Mississippi, 1954 Crowell, first edition, hardcover. ($15.00 with dust jacket) $10.00
Eagle Feather, 1953 Crowell, first edition, hardcover, illustrations by Tom Two Arrows, includes three songs. ($20.00 with dust jacket) $10.00
Jonah and the Great Fish, 1970 Crowell, first edition, oversize hardcover, illustrations by Helga Aichinger. ($35.00 with dust jacket) $15.00
Moon Singer, 1969 Crowell, Weekly Reader Children's Book Club Edition, 38 pages, illustrations by Trina Schart Hyman. $15.00
Pirate's Promise, 1958 Crowell, hardcover, 87 pages, b/w illustrations by Peter Burchard. ($15.00 in dust jacket) $10.00
Poppy Seeds, 1955 Crowell, first edition, hardcover, illustrations by Jean Charlot. ($15.00 with dust jacket) $10.00
Robert John Billington: Friend of Squanto, 1956 Crowell, illustrated by Peter Burchard. ($15.00 in dust jacket) $10.00
Riding the Pony Express, 1948 Crowell, hardcover, illustrations by Grace Paull. ($20.00 in dust jacket) $10.00
Song of Saint Francis, 1952 Crowell, first edition, hardcover, illustrations by Valenti Angelo. ($50.00 with dust jacket) $20.00

BURCH, Robert
Jolly Witch, 1975 Dutton, first edition, yellow hardcover, 32 pages, illustrations by Leigh Grant. ($25.00 with dust jacket) $15.00

BURCHARD, Peter
Carol Moran, 1958 Macmillan, first edition, hardcover, illustrations by author. ($20.00 with dust jacket) $10.00
River Queen, 1957 Macmillan, first edition, oversize hardcover, 40 pages, color illustrations by author. ($45.00 with dust jacket) $20.00

BURGESS, Thornton W.
Aunt Sally's Friends in Fur, or the Woodhouse Night Club, 1955 Little, Brown, first edition, hardcover, photos by the author. ($40.00 with dust jacket) $15.00
Now I Remember, an Autobiography, 1960 Little, Brown, first edition, hardcover. ($45.00 with dust jacket) $20.00

BURGOYNE, Leon E.
State Champs, 1951 Winston, first edition, hardcover. Dust jacket illustrated by Joseph Bolden. ($15.00 with dust jacket) $10.00

BURGOYNE, Peter
Contraband Castle, 1960 Blackie, first edition UK, hardcover, 190 pages, illustrations by David Emerson. ($15.00 with dust jacket) $10.00

BURKETT, Molly and **John**
Foxes Three, 1975 Lippincott, first American edition, brown hardcover. ($15.00 with dust jacket) $10.00

BURMAN, Ben, see Series section, CATFISH BEND

BURMAN, Edor
Bears of Big Stream Valley, 1968 Delacorte Press, translated from Swedish, first American edition, hardcover, illustrations by Harald Wiberg. $15.00

BURN, Doris
Andrew Henry's Meadow, 1965 Coward McCann, oversize hardcover picture book, b/w illustrations by author. ($50.00 with dust jacket) $20.00
Summerfolk, 1968 Weekly Reader edition, illustrated hard cover, b/w illustrations by author. $15.00

BURNETT, Carol
What I Want to Be When I Grow Up, 1975 Simon & Schuster, first edition, hardcover, illustrated by Sheldon Secunda photos. ($15.00 with dust jacket) $10.00

BURNFORD, Sheila
Incredible Journey, 1961 Hodder & Stoughton, first edition UK, hardcover, full page illustrations by Carl Burger. ($20.00 with dust jacket) $10.00
Incredible Journey, 1961 Little Brown, first edition, hardcover. ($100.00 with dust jacket) Later editions: ($20.00 with dust jacket) $10.00

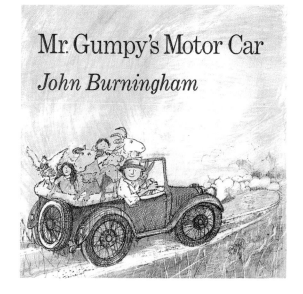

BURNINGHAM, John
Around the World in Eighty Days, 1972 Jonathan Cape, first edition, oversize hardcover, 95 pages, color illustrations by author. ($50.00 with dust jacket) $20.00
Borka, 1963 Random House, oversize hardcover picture book, color illustrations by author. $25.00
Mr. Firkin and the Lord Mayor of London, 1967 Bobbs Merrill, first edition, hardcover, illustrations by author. ($45.00 with dust jacket) $20.00
Mr. Gumpy's Outing, 1970 Holt, oversize hardcover picture book, color illustrations by author. ($35.00 with dust jacket) $15.00
Mr. Gumpy's Motor Car, (1973) 1976 HarperCollins, first American edition, oversize hardcover, color illustrations by author. ($45.00 with dust jacket) $20.00
Seasons, 1971 Bobbs Merrill, first American edition, oversize hardcover picture book, color illustrations by author. ($30.00 with dust jacket) $10.00

BURNS, Robert
Hand in Hand We'll Go, 1965 edition Crowell, poetry collection, 31 pages, illustrations by Nonny Hogrogian. ($30.00 with dust jacket) $15.00

BURROUGHS, Edgar Rice
I Am a Barbarian, 1967 Edgar Rice Burroughs, Inc., first edition, hardcover, gilt-lettered maroon cloth, illustrated by John Coleman Burroughs. ($200.00 with dust jacket) $40.00

BURROUGHS, Polly
Honey Boat, 1968 Little, Brown, hardcover, illustrations by Garrett Price. ($20.00 with dust jacket) $10.00

BURT, Olive W.
Wind Before the Dawn, 1964 John Day, hardcover, 188 pages. ($20.00 with dust jacket) $10.00
First Woman Editor, Biography of Sarah J. Hale, 1960 Messner, hardcover. ($20.00 with dust jacket) $10.00

BURTON, Hal
Real Book about Treasure Hunting, 1953 Garden City, hardcover. $10.00
Walton Boys and the Gold in the Snow, 1948 Whitman, illustrated by Robert Doremus. ($20.00 in dust jacket) $10.00

BURTON, Hester
Beyond the Weir Bridge, 1970 Thomas Crowell, first American edition, hardcover, 221 pages, illustrations by Victor G. Ambrus. ($25.00 with dust jacket) $10.00

BURTON, Katherine
Door of Hope, 1963 Hawthorn, first edition, hardcover, illustrated endpapers by Frank Nicholas. ($15.00 with dust jacket) $10.00

BURTON, Philip
Green Isle, 1974 Dial Press, first edition, hardcover, color illustrations by Robert Andrew Parker. ($25.00 with dust jacket) $10.00

BURTON, Richard
Christmas Story, 1964 Morrow, first edition, hardcover, illustrations by Lydia Fruhauf. ($15.00 with dust jacket) $10.00

BURTON, Virginia Lee
Calico the Wonder Horse or The Saga of Stewy Stinker, 1950 Houghton Mifflin, oblong yellow pictorial hardcover, 58 pages, illustrations by author. ($40.00 with dust jacket) $15.00
Maybelle, the Cable Car, 1952 Houghton, first edition, square hardcover picture book, color illustrations by author. ($125.00 with dust jacket) $75.00
Life Story, 1962 Houghton, first edition, oblong oversize hardcover, illustrated. ($50.00 with dust jacket) $20.00

BUTLER, Francelia, editor
*Skip Rope Book ,*1963 Dial, first edition, hardcover, illustrations by Gail E. Haley. ($15.00 with dust jacket) $10.00

BUTTERWORTH, Oliver
Enormous Egg, 1956 Little, Brown, hardcover, illustrations by Louis Darling. ($20.00 with dust jacket) $10.00

BUTTERWORTH, W. E.
Helicopter Pilot, 1967 Norton, first edition, hardcover. ($20.00 with dust jacket) $10.00
Return To Racing – A Flying Wheels Book, 1971 Grosset & Dunlap, hardcover, illustrated. $20.00

BUTTERS, Dorothy Gilman
Papa Dolphin's Table, 1955 Knopf, first edition, hardcover, illustrated by Kurt Werth. ($15.00 with dust jacket) $10.00

BUTTS, Marie
Misfortunes of Ogier the Dane, 1964 Blair, first edition, hardcover, illustrated by Mitzi Shewmake. $15.00

BYARS, Betsy
Winged Colt of Casa Mia, 1973 Viking Press, first edition, hardcover, illustrated by Richard Cuffari. ($20.00 with dust jacket) $10.00

BYFIELD, Barbara
Glass Harmonica, 1967 Macmillan, oversize hardcover, 160 pages, illustrations by author. ($40.00 with dust jacket) $25.00
(*Glass Harmonica* was later reprinted as *Book of Weird*)
Haunted Spy, 1969 Doubleday, hardcover, illustrated by author. ($20.00 with dust jacket) $10.00
Haunted Churchbell, 1971 Doubleday, hardcov-

er, illustrated by author. ($20.00 with dust jacket) $10.00
Haunted Ghost, 1973 Doubleday, hardcover, illustrated by author. ($20.00 with dust jacket) $10.00
Haunted Tower, 1976 Doubleday, hardcover, illustrated by author. ($20.00 with dust jacket) $10.00

⋙ **C** ⋘

CAFFREY, Nancy
Horse Haven, 1955 Dutton, first edition, hardcover, b/w illustrations by Paul Brown. Hard to find. ($100.00 with dust jacket) $30.00
Scene from the Saddle,, 1958 Dutton, first edition, oblong hardcover, 88 pages, full-page black and white photos by A. L. Waintrob. ($40.00 with dust jacket) $20.00

CAINES, Jeannette
Abby, 1973 Harper, first edition, oblong hardcover picture book, b/w illustrations by Steven Kellogg. ($20.00 same-as-cover dust jacket) $10.00

CALDWELL, John C.
Let's Visit Vietnam, 1966 John Day, hardcover, b/w photo illustrations. ($20.00 with dust jacket) $10.00

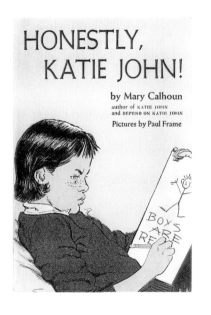

CALHOUN, Mary
Katie John, 1960 Harper, hardcover, illustrations by Paul Frame. ($25.00 with dust jacket) $10.00
Depend on Katie John, 1961 Harper, hardcover, illustrations by Paul Frame. ($25.00 with dust jacket) $10.00
Honestly, Katie John!, 1963 Harper, hardcover, b/w illustrations by Paul Frame. ($25.00 with dust jacket) $10.00

Mermaid of Storms, 1970 Morrow, first edition, hardcover, color illustrations by Janet McCaffery. ($20.00 with dust jacket) $10.00
Pixie and the Lazy Housewife, 1969 Morrow, first edition, oblong hardcover picture book, color illustrations by Janet McCaffrey. ($20.00 with dust jacket) $10.00
Sweet Patootie Doll, 1957 Morrow, oversize hardcover picture book, two-color illustrations by Roger Duvoisin. ($30.00 with dust jacket) $15.00
Thieving Dwarfs, 1967 William Morrow, first edition, hardcover, illustrated by Janet McCaffery. ($20.00 with dust jacket) $10.00
Wobble, the Witch Cat, 1958 Morrow, first edition, oversize hardcover picture book, 30 pages, color illustrations by Roger Duvoisin. ($30.00 with dust jacket) $20.00

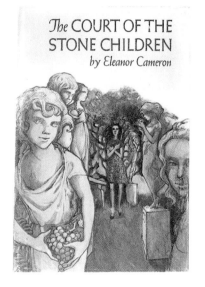

CAMERON, Eleanor, see Series section, MUSHROOM PLANET
Court of Stone Children, 1973 Dutton, first edition, hardcover, dust jacket illustrated by Trina Schart Hyman. ($50.00 same-as-cover dust jacket)
Later editions: ($25.00 with dust jacket) $10.00
Beast With the Magical Horn, 1963 Little Brown, first edition, hardcover, illustrations by Joe and Beth Krush. ($50.00 with dust jacket) $20.00
Mysterious Christmas Shell, 1961 Little Brown, first edition, hardcover, illustrations by Joe and Beth Krush. ($30.00 with dust jacket) $15.00
Room Made of Windows, 1971 Little Brown, hardcover, illustrations by Trina Schart Hyman. ($30.00 with dust jacket) $15.00
Spell Is Cast, 1964 Little Brown, hardcover, illustrations by Joe and Beth Krush. ($40.00 with dust jacket) $15.00
Terrible Churnadyne, 1959 Little Brown, hardcov-

er, illustrations by Joe and Beth Krush. ($60.00 with dust jacket) $20.00

CAMPBELL, Elizabeth A.
Nails to Nickels, the Story of American Coins Old and New, 1960 Little, Brown, first edition, hardcover, illustrations by Leonard Weisgard. ($20.00 with dust jacket) $10.00

CAMPBELL, Julie (Julie Campbell Tatham), see Series section GINNY GORDON; TRIXIE BELDEN
Rin Tin Tin's Rinty, 1954 Whitman, hardcover, pictorial endpapers. ($15.00 with dust jacket) $5.00

CAMPBELL, Mary Mason
New England Butt'ry Shelf Almanac, 1970 World Publishing, first edition, hardcover, color and b/w illustrations by Tasha Tudor. ($60.00 with dust jacket) $30.00

CAMPBELL, Roy
Mamba's Precipice, 1954 John Day, first edition, hardcover. ($15.00 with dust jacket) $10.00

CAMPBELL, Sam
Beloved Rascals, 1957 Bobbs-Merrill, first edition, hardcover, illustrated. ($30.00 with dust jacket) $20.00
Moose Country, 1950 Bobbs-Merrill, first edition, hardcover, illustrations by Bob Myers. ($25.00 with dust jacket) $10.00
Sweet Sue's Adventures, 1959 Bobbs-Merrill, first edition, hardcover, photo illustrations. ($15.00 with dust jacket) $10.00

CANNON, Bettie
Begin the World Again, 1961 Scribner, first edition, hardcover. ($15.00 with dust jacket) $10.00

CAPEK, Josef
Harum Scarum, 1963 edition W. W. Norton, first American edition, hardcover, illustrated boards, b/w illustrations. $15.00

CAPPE, Jeanne
Cinderella and Other Stories, 1957 Grosset & Dunlap, illustrated hardcover, color illustrations. $20.00

CARDEN, Priscilla
Vanilla Village, 1952 Ariel, oversize hardcover picture book, color and b/w illustrations by Jay Barnum. ($15.00 with dust jacket) $10.00
Aldo's Tower, 1954 Ariel, oversize hardcover picture book, color and b/w illustrations by Kurt Werth. ($15.00 with dust jacket) $10.00

CAREY, Mary
Gnome Mobile, 1967 Grosset, hardcover, from the Walt Disney Movie, illustrated by John Soli. $15.00
Story of Walt Disney's Motion Picture Mary Poppins, 1964 Whitman, pictorial boards, b/w and color illustrations. $20.00

CARIGIET, Alois
Anton and Anne, 1969 Walck, oblong oversize picture book, color illustrations by author. ($50.00 with dust jacket) $20.00
Anton the Goatherd, 1966 Walck, oblong oversize picture book, color illustrations by author. ($50.00 with dust jacket) $20.00

Do You Want to Be My Friend?, Eric Carle

CARLE, Eric
Do You Want to Be My Friend?, 1971 Crowell, picture hardcover, few words, color illustrations by author. ($30.00 with dust jacket) $15.00

CARLETON, Barbee Oliver
Witches' Bridge, 1967 Holt Rinehart Winston, first edition, hardcover. ($40.00 with dust jacket) $15.00

CARLSON, George
Funtime Crossword Puzzles for Juniors, 1955 Platt Munk, hardcover. ($15.00 with dust jacket) $10.00

CARLSON, Natalie
Chalou, 1967 Harper, pictorial cover. $10.00
Carnival in Paris, 1962 Harper, first edition, hardcover, illustrations by Fermin Rocker. ($20.00 with dust jacket) $10.00
Happy Orpheline, 1957 Harper, oversize illustrated hardcover, b/w illustrations by Garth Williams. ($25.00 with dust jacket) $15.00
Hortense the Cow for a Queen, 1957 Harcourt, first edition, hardcover. ($20.00 in dust jacket) $15.00

Jean-Claude's Island ,1963 Harper, first edition, hardcover. ($30.00 with dust jacket) $15.00

Letter on the Tree, 1964 Harper, illustrated hardcover. ($20.00 with dust jacket) $15.00

Luigi of the Streets, 1967 Harper, hardcover, b/w illustrations by Emily McCully. ($20.00 with dust jacket) $10.00

Marie Louise's Heyday, 1975 Scribners, first edition, hardcover. ($20.00 with dust jacket) $10.00

*Sailor's Choice,*1966 Harper, first edition, hardcover, illustrations by George Loh. ($30.00 with dust jacket) $10.00

Sashes Red and Blue, 1956 Harper, hardcover, illustrated by Rita Fava. ($15.00 with dust jacket) $10.00

Song of the Lop-Eared Mule, 1961 Harper, hardcover, illustrated by Janina Domanska. ($20.00 in dust jacket) $15.00

Talking Cat and Other Stories of French Canada, 1952 Harper, first edition, red hardcover, frontispiece and b/w illustrations by Roger Duvoisin. ($50.00 with dust jacket) $20.00

Tomahawk Family, 1960 Harper, illustrated hardcover. $15.00

CARMER, Carl

Pets at the White House, 1959 Dutton, first edition, illustrated by Sam Savitt. ($20.00 in dust jacket) $10.00

CARMICHAEL, John, editor

My Greatest Day in Baseball, 1951 Grosset, hardcover. $15.00

CARPENTER, Frances

Holiday in Washington, 1958 Alfred Knopf, first edition, hardcover, illustrations by George Fulton. ($15.00 with dust jacket) $10.00

Mouse Palace, 1964 McGraw Hill, hardcover, illustrated by Adrienne Adams. ($25.00 in dust jacket) $15.00

Rebel Schoolgirl, 1956 Blackie, hardcover. $10.00

CARR, Harriett

Young Viking of Brooklyn, 1961 Viking, illustrated by Dorothy Bayley Morse. ($15.00 in dust jacket) $10.00

CARR, Judith

Gipsy at Greywalls, 1955 Blackie, hardcover. ($20.00 with dust jacket) $10.00

CARRICK, Carol

Old Mother Witch, 1975 Seabury, hardcover picture book, color illustrations by Donald Carrick. ($20.00 with dust jacket) $10.00

The Tree
DONALD CARRICK

CARRICK, Donald

Tree, 1971 Macmillan, easy reader picture book, hardcover, color illustrations by author. ($20.00 with dust jacket) $10.00

CARRICK, Malcolm

Wise Men of Gotham, 1973 Collins, first edition, oversize, illustrated boards, color and b/w illustrations Malcolm Carrick. ($30.00 with dust jacket) $15.00

CARROLL, Jimmy

Singing Mother Goose Book, 1955 Winston, hardcover with 78 rpm record. $15.00

CARROLL, Lewis

Alice in Wonderland, 1955 edition Whitman, illustrated hardcover, illustrations by Roberta Paflin. $10.00

Alice in Wonderland, 1970 edition Whitman Classics, hardcover, promotional copy, "Free when you buy 2-lb. can of Folger's coffee" on cover, illustrated by Ted Schroeder. $10.00

CARROLL, Ruth and Latrobe

Beanie, 1953 Oxford, first edition, oversize hardcover, illustrations by authors. ($40.00 with dust jacket) $20.00

Bumble Pup, 1968 Walck, hardcover picture book, illustrations by author. $15.00

Old Mrs. Billups and the Black Cats, 1961 Walck, first edition, hardcover, illustrations by author. ($40.00 with dust jacket) $20.00

Picnic Bear, 1966 Walck, first edition, green hardcover, illustrations by author. ($15.00 with dust jacket) $10.00

Rolling Downhill, 1973 Walck, hardcover picture book, illustrations by author. $15.00

Runaway Pony, Runaway Dog, 1963 Walck, first edition, hardcover, illustrations by Ruth Carroll. ($30.00 with dust jacket) $15.00

Tough Enough and Sassy, 1958 Walck, red hardcover, illustrations by author. ($20.00 with dust jacket) $15.00

Tough Enough's Pony, 1957 Walck, hardcover, illustrations by author. ($25.00 with dust jacket) $15.00

CARRUTHERS, Janet
Forest Is My Kingdom, 1958 edition Oxford, hardcover. $10.00

CARSON, John F.
Hotshot, 1961 Farrar, hardcover, 192 pages. ($25.00 with dust jacket) $15.00

CARSON, Rachel
Sea Around Us, Special Edition for Young Readers, 1958 Golden Press, oversize hardcover, 165 pages, illustrated by Rene Martin. ($20.00 with dust jacket) $10.00

CARTER, ANGELA
Donkey Prince, 1970 Simon & Schuster, first edition, hardcover, illustrations by Eros Keith. ($60.00 with dust jacket) $20.00

Miss Z: The Dark Young Lady, 1970 Simon & Schuster, first edition, hardcover, illustrations by Eros Keith. ($80.00 with dust jacket) $20.00

CARTER, Page
Mystery in Little Breeze Street, 1967 Follett, first edition, hardcover. ($15.00 with dust jacket) $10.00

CASE, Victoria
Applesauce and Sugar, 1960 Doubleday, hardcover, b/w illustrations by Reisie Lonette. ($20.00 with dust jacket) $10.00

CASSEDY, Sylvia
Marzipan Day on Bridget Lane, 1967 Doubleday, first edition, hardcover, 64 pages, illustrated by Margot Tomes. ($20.00 with dust jacket) $10.00

CASTELLANOS, Jane
Tomasito and the Golden Llamas, 1968 Golden Gate, hardcover, b/w illustrations by Robert Corey. ($15.00 with dust jacket) $10.00

CASTLE, Frances
Sisters' Tale, 1968 Bodley Head, first edition, hardcover, 208 pages. ($15.00 in dust jacket) $10.00

CASWELL, Maryanne
Pioneer Girl, 1964 McGraw-Hill, Toronto, first edition, hardcover, illustrations by Douglas Johnson. ($15.00 with dust jacket) $10.00

CATALDO, John W.
Words and Calligraphy For Children, 1969 Reinhold, first edition, hardcover, color illustrations. ($15.00 with dust jacket) $10.00

CATHERALL, Arthur
Pirate Sealer, 1953 Children's Press, first edition, small hardcover with silver gilt, 188 pages. ($25.00 with dust jacket) $10.00

CATTON, Bruce
Banners at Shenandoah, 1955 Garden City, first edition, hardcover. ($15.00 with dust jacket) $10.00

CAUDILL, Rebecca, see Series section, BONNIE BOOKS
Did You Carry the Flag Today, Charlie?, 1966 Holt, first edition, hardcover. illustrations by Nancy Grossman, 94 pages. ($15.00 with dust jacket) $10.00

Certain Small Shepherd, 1965 Holt, hardcover, illustrated by William Pene Du Bois. ($25.00 with dust jacket) $15.00

Pocketful of Cricket, 1964 Holt, first edition, oversize hardcover, color illustrations by Evaline Ness. ($25.00 with dust jacket) $10.00

CAVANAH, Frances
Abe Lincoln Gets His Chance, 1959 Rand, McNally, hardcover. $10.00

Jenny Lind and Her Listening Cat, 1961 Vanguard, first edition, hardcover, illustrations by Paul Frame. ($25.00 with dust jacket) $15.00

CAVANNA, Betty
Angel on Skis, 1957 Morrow, first edition, hardcover, 255 pages. ($15.00 with dust jacket) $10.00

Boy Next Door, 1956 Morrow, first edition, hardcover, 253 pages. ($30.00 with dust jacket) $10.00

Fancy Free, 1961 Morrow, first edition, hardcover. ($15.00 with dust jacket) $10.00

Going on Sixteen, 1956 Westminster Press, hardcover. ($15.00 in dust jacket) $10.00

Lasso Your Heart, 1952 Westminster Press, hardcover, illustrated endpapers. ($15.00 in dust jacket) $10.00

Mystery at Love's Creek, 1965 Morrow, first edition, hardcover. ($15.00 in dust jacket) $10.00

Scarlet Sail, 1959 Morrow, hardcover. ($15.00 in dust jacket) $10.00

Spring Comes Riding, 1950 Westminster Press, hardcover, illustrations by Beth and Joe Krush. ($20.00 with dust jacket) $10.00

Stars in Her Eyes, 1958 Morrow, first edition, hardcover. ($25.00 with dust jacket) $10.00

CEDER, Georgiana
Joel, the Potter's Son, 1954 Abingdon, first edition, hardcover, illustrations by Helen Torrey. ($15.00 with dust jacket) $10.00

CHACONAS, Doris J.
Way the Tiger Walked, 1970 Simon & Schuster, oblong, illustrated paper-over-board cover, color illustrations throughout by Frank Bozzo. ($40.00 with same-as-cover dust jacket) $25.00

CHAFFIN, Lillie D.
Bear Weather, 1969 Macmillan, first edition, oversize hardcover, illustrations by Helga Aichinger. ($15.00 with dust jacket) $10.00

CHALMERS, Mary
Come for a Walk with Me, 1955 Harper, pictorial boards. ($20.00 with dust jacket) $15.00

CHALMERS, Audrey
Hector and Mr. Murfit, 1953 Viking, hardcover, illustrated by author. $15.00
High Smoke, 1950 Viking, first edition, hardcover, illustrations by author. ($25.00 with dust jacket) $15.00

CHAMBERLAIN, George
Lord Buff and Silver Star, 1955 Barnes, first edition, hardcover. ($20.00 with dust jacket) $10.00

CHAMBERS, Maria Christina
Boy Heroes of Chapultepec, a Story of the Mexican War, 1953 Winston, illustrations by Joseph Krush. ($20.00 with dust jacket) $10.00

CHANDLER, Edna Walker
Cowboy Andy, 1959 Random House, Beginner Books, hardcover, illustrated by E. Raymond Kintsler. $15.00
Cowboy Sam and the Fair, 1953 Beckley-Cardy, hardcover, illustrated by Jack Merryweather. $15.00
Cowboy Sam and the Rodeo, 1951 Beckley-Cardy, small hardcover. $15.00
Five Cent, Five Cent, 1967 Whitman, illustrated by Betty Stull. ($20.00 with dust jacket) $10.00
Crystal Pie, 1965 Duell, Sloan and Pearce, first edition, hardcover, illustrations by William Ferguson. ($15.00 with dust jacket) $10.00

CHAPMAN, Jean
Do You Remember What Happened, 1969 Angus and Robertson, first edition, hardcover, illustrations by Edward Ardizzone. ($25.00 with dust jacket) $15.00

CHARLIP, Remy
Harlequin, 1973 Parents', oversize hardcover, illustrated endpapers, color illustrations by author. ($20.00 with dust jacket) $10.00
Thirteen, 1975 Parents', oversize hardcover, color illustrations by author. ($20.00 with dust jacket) $10.00

CHARLOT, Martin
Sunnyside Up, 1972 Weatherhill, first edition, oversize hardcover, double plates and no dialogue, illustrations by author. $75.00 with dust jacket
Sunnyside Up, 1972 Island Heritage edition, oversize hardcover, 56 pages. ($20.00 with dust jacket) $10.00

CHASE, Mary (Pulitzer winning playwright of *Harvey*)
Wicked Pigeon Ladies in the Garden, 1968 Knopf, hardcover, 115 pages, b/w illustrations by Don Bolognese. ($25.00 with dust jacket) $15.00

CHASE, Mary Ellen
Edge of Darkness, 1957 Norton, hardcover. ($15.00 with dust jacket) $10.00
Sailing the Seven Seas, 1958 Houghton, first edition, illustrated by J. Cosgrave. ($15.00 with dust jacket) $10.00
Victoria: a Pig in a Pram, 1963 Norton, small, 58 pages, b/w illustrations by Paul Kennedy. ($25.00 with dust jacket) $10.00
White Gate, 1954 Norton, first edition, hardcover, illustrations by Nora Unwin. ($25.00 with dust jacket) $10.00

CHAUCER, Geoffrey
Chanticleer and the Fox, 1958 edition Crowell, first edition thus, hardcover, illustrated by Barbara Cooney. ($50.00 with dust jacket) $20.00

CHAUNCY, Nan
Half a World Away, 1962 Oxford, first edition, hardcover, illustrated by Annette Macarthur-Onslow. ($20.00 with dust jacket) $10.00
Lighthouse Keeper's Son, 1969 Oxford, first edition, hardcover, illustrations by V.G. Ambrus. ($30.00 with dust jacket) $15.00

CHEKHOV, Anton
Kashtanka, 1961 Walck, first American edition, tall hardcover, 49 pages, color illustrations by William Stobbs. ($20.00 with dust jacket) $10.00

CHENAULT, Nell
Parsifal Rides the Time Wave, 1962 Little Brown, illustrated hardcover, b/w illustrations by Vee Guthrie. ($25.00 with dust jacket) $10.00

CHENEY, Cora
Doll of Lilac Valley, 1959 Knopf, first edition, hardcover, b/w illustrations by Carol Beech. ($25.00 with dust jacket) $10.00
Girl at Jungle's Edge, 1962 Knopf, hardcover. ($25.00 with dust jacket) $15.00
Skeleton Cave, 1959 Holt, first edition, small hardcover, illustrations by Paul Galdone. ($20.00 with dust jacket) $10.00

CHERNEY, Janet
Pickles and Jane, 1975 Viking, hardcover, brown-tone illustrations by Lilian Obligado. ($15.00 in dust jacket) $5.00

CHESHIRE, Gifford P.
River of Gold ,1955 Aladdin, first edition, hardcover, illustrations by Fiore Mastri. ($15.00 with dust jacket) $10.00

CHIDSEY, Donald
Rod Rides High, 1960 Doubleday, first edition, hardcover. ($15.00 with dust jacket) $10.00

CHILDRESS, Alice
Hero Ain't Nothin' but a Sandwich, 1973 Coward McCann, small hardcover, 126 pages. ($30.00 with dust jacket) $10.00

CHILD STUDY ASSOCIATION OF AMERICA
Holiday Storybook, 1952 Crowell, first edition, hardcover, illustrations by Phoebe Erickson. ($25.00 with dust jacket) $10.00

CHILDS, Elizabeth
Fun of Being Good, 1954 Platt Munk, hardcover. $20.00

CHILDS, Fay
Wacheera, Child of Africa, 1965 Criterion Books, hardcover, 152 pages. ($15.00 with dust jacket) $5.00

CHITHAM, Edward
Ghost in the Water, 1973 Longmans, London, hardcover, first edition. ($60.00 with dust jacket) $20.00

CHONZ, Selina
Florina and the Wild Bird, 1953 Walck, first US edition, oversize hardcover, color illustrations by Alois Carigiet. ($75.00 in dust jacket) $35.00

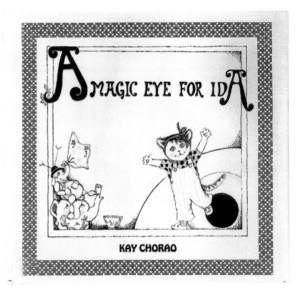

CHORAO, Kay
Ida Makes a Movie, 1974 Seabury, yellow hardcover, color illustrations by author. ($20.00 with dust jacket) $10.00
Magic Eye for Ida, 1973 Seabury, small oblong hardcover, color illustrations by author. ($20.00 with dust jacket) $10.00

CHRISTENSEN, Jack and Lee
Forgotten Rainbow, 1960 Morrow, first edition, hardcover, illustrations by author. ($25.00 with dust jacket) $10.00

CHRISTENSEN, Gardell Dano
Mrs. Mouse Needs a House, 1958 Henry Holt, hardcover, illustrated. ($20.00 with dust jacket) $10.00

CHRISTOPHER, John (b. 1922), See also TRIPODS and SWORD of SPIRITS
Wild Jack, 1974 Macmillan, hardcover. ($40.00 with dust jacket) $15.00
Beyond the Burning Lands, 1971 Macmillan edition, hardcover, 170 pages, dust jacket painting by Emanuel Schongut. ($20.00 with dust jacket) $10.00
White Mountains, 1967 Macmillan, first edition, hardcover. ($20.00 with dust jacket) $10.00
White Voyage, 1961 Simon & Schuster, first edition, hardcover. ($25.00 with dust jacket) $15.00

CHRISTOPHER, Matt
Desperate Search, 1973 Little, Brown, first edition, blue hardcover, 116 pages, illustrated by Leslie Morrill. ($15.00 with dust jacket) $10.00
Front Court Hex, 1974 Little, Brown, illustrated by Byron Goto. ($15.00 with dust jacket) $10.00
Look Who's Playing First Base, 1971 Little, Brown, first edition, hardcover, illustrated by Harvey Kidder. ($15.00 with dust jacket) $10.00
Miracle at the Plate, 1967 Little, Brown, hardcover, b/w illustrations by Foster Caddell. ($15.00 with dust jacket) $10.00
Mystery Coach, 1973 Little, Brown, hardcover, illustrations by Harvey Kidder. ($15.00 with dust jacket) $10.00
Team That Couldn't Lose, 1967 Little, Brown, hardcover, illustrated by Foster Caddell. ($15.00 with dust jacket) $10.00

CHUBB, Thomas Caldecot
Prince Henry the Navigator and the Highways of the Sea, 1970 Viking Press, first edition, hardcover. ($25.00 with dust jacket) $10.00

CHURCHILL, Sarah
Prince with Many Castles and Other Stories, 1967 Leslie Frewin, first edition, oversize hardcover, illustrated by Eric Critchley. ($25.00 with dust jacket) $10.00

CHUTE, B. J.
Moon and the Thorn, 1961 Dutton, first edition, hardcover. ($15.00 with dust jacket) $10.00

CHWAST, Jacqueline
How Mr. Berry Found a Home and Happiness Forever, 1968 Simon & Schuster, first edition, hardcover. ($20.00 with dust jacket) $10.00
When the Baby-Sitter Didn't Come, 1967 Harcourt, Brace & World, first edition, hardcover, illustrated by Jacqueline Chwast. ($50.00 with dust jacket) $15.00

CHWAST, Seymour and **Martin Stephen MOSKOF**
Still Another Children's Book, 1972 McGraw-Hill, first edition, hardcover, illustrated by authors. ($65.00 with dust jacket) $30.00

CIARDI, John
I Met a Man, 1961 Houghton Mifflin, hardcover, illustrated by Robert Osborn. ($40.00 in dust jacket) $20.00
John J. Plenty and Fiddler Dan, 1963 Lippincott, hardcover, illustrated by Madeleine Gekiere. ($40.00 in dust jacket) $20.00
Man Who Sang the Sillies, 1961 Lippincott, first edition, hardcover, illustrations by Edward Gorey. ($75.00 with dust jacket) $40.00
Monster Den, 1966 Lippincott, first edition, hardcover, drawings by Edward Gorey. ($70.00 with dust jacket) $20.00
You Know Who, 1964 Lippincott, first edition, hardcover, illustrations by Edward Gorey. ($55.00 with dust jacket) $20.00
You Read to Me, I'll Read to You, 1962 Lippincott, first edition, hardcover, drawings by Edward Gorey. ($35.00 with dust jacket) $20.00

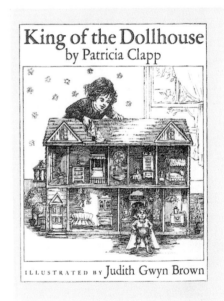

CLAPP, Patricia
King of the Doll House, 1974 Lothrop Lee, hardcover, 94 pages, b/w illustrations by Judith Gwyn Brown. ($35.00 with dust jacket) $20.00

CLARE, Helen, see Series section, FIVE DOLLS

CLARK, Ann Nolan

Bear Cub, 1965 Viking, first edition, hardcover, illustrations by Charles Frace. ($35.00 with dust jacket) $15.00

Blue Canyon Horse, 1954 Alan Houser, 1954, hardcover. ($20.00 in dust jacket) $10.00

Looking for Something, 1952 Viking, first edition, hardcover, Illustrated by Leo Politi. ($50.00 with dust jacket) $20.00

Medicine Man's Daughter, 1963 Bell Books, first edition, hardcover, illustrations by Donald Bolognese. ($40.00 with dust jacket) $20.00

Santiago, 1955 Viking, hardcover, color illustrated endpapers, b/w illustrations by Lynd Ward. ($30.00 with dust jacket) $10.00

Secret of the Andes, 1965 Viking, first edition, hardcover, illustrations by Jean Charlot. ($50.00 with dust jacket) $20.00

Third Monkey, 1956 Viking, first edition, hardcover, color illustrations. ($40.00 with dust jacket) $15.00

Tia Maria's Garden, 1963 Viking, first edition, hardcover, 47 pages, color illustrations by Ezra Jack Keats. ($40.00 with dust jacket) $20.00

World Song, 1960 Viking, first edition, hardcover, illustrations by Kurt Wiese. ($20.00 with dust jacket) $10.00

CLARK, Billy C.

Goodbye, Kate, 1964 Putnam, hardcover, 247 pages. ($20.00 with dust jacket) $10.00

CLARK, Denis

Boomer, 1966 Viking, hardcover, b/w illustrations by Gifford Ambler. ($15.00 with dust jacket) $10.00

CLARK, Electa

Tony For Keeps, A Story of a House On Wheels, 1955 Winston, first edition, hardcover, 186 pages, illustrations by Lisl Weil. ($15.00 with dust jacket) $10.00

CLARK, Joan

Thomasina and the Trout Tree, 1971 Tundra, square hardcover, color illustrations by Ingeborg Hiscox. ($20.00 with dust jacket) $10.00

CLARK, Leonard

All Along, Down Aong, 1971 Longman Young, first edition, hardcover, color and b/w illustrations by Pauline Baynes. ($30.00 with dust jacket) $15.00

CLARK, Margaret Goff

Mystery of the Missing Stamps, 1967 Funk & Wagnalls, hardcover, b/w illustrations by Vic Donohue. ($15.00 with dust jacket) $10.00

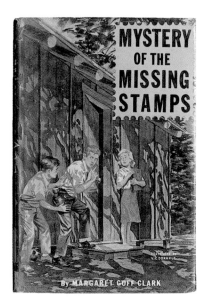

CLARK, Mavis Thorpe

Iron Mountain, 1971 Macmillan, hardcover, 204 pages. ($15.00 with dust jacket) $10.00

CLARK, Roger

Ride the White Tiger, 1959 Little Brown, hardcover, b/w illustrations by Kim. ($15.00 with dust jacket) $10.00

CLARKE, Arthur C.

Islands in the Sky, 1957 Winston, first edition, hardcover. ($50.00 with dust jacket) $15.00

CLARKE, Pauline

Return of the Twelves (British title: *Twelve & Gennii*), 1963 Coward, hardcover, illustrations by Bernarda Bryson, Carnegie Medal. ($20.00 with dust jacket) $10.00

CLARKSON, Ewan

Running of the Deer, 1972 Dutton, first edition, hardcover, illustrated by David Stone. ($30.00 with dust jacket) $15.00

CLEARY, Beverly, see Series section, HENRY HUGGINS, RAMONA

Ellen Tibbits, 1951 Morrow, first edition, hardcover, illustrations by Louis Darling. ($30.00 with dust jacket) $15.00

Emily's Runaway Imagination, 1961 Morrow, first edition, b/w illustrations by Beth and Joe Krush. ($35.00 with dust jacket) $20.00

Fifteen, 1956 Morrow, hardcover, illustrated by Joe and Beth Krush. ($30.00 with dust jacket) $10.00

Jean and Johnny, 1959 Morrow, b/w illustrations by Beth and Joe Krush. ($30.00 with dust jacket) $10.00

Luckiest Girl, 1958 Morrow, first edition, hardcover. ($50.00 with dust jacket) $15.00

Mitch and Amy, 1967 Morrow, hardcover, illustrations by George Porter. ($20.00 with dust jacket) $10.00

Mouse and the Motorcycle, (Ralph story), 1965 Morrow, first edition, hardcover, b/w illustrations by Louis Darling. ($30.00 with dust jacket) $10.00

Otis Spafford, 1953 Morrow, hardcover, b/w illustrations by Louis Darling. ($20.00 with dust jacket) $10.00

Runaway Ralph, 1970 Morrow, hardcover, b/w illustrations by Louis Darling. ($20.00 with dust jacket) $10.00

Sister of the Bride, 1963 Morrow, first edition, b/w illustrations by Beth and Joe Krush. ($35.00 with dust jacket) $20.00

Socks, 1973 Morrow, first edition, hardcover, 157 pages, b/w illustrations by Beatrice Darwin. ($30.00 with dust jacket) $15.00

Two Dog Biscuits, 1961 Morrow, oblong hardcover, illustrated endpapers, two-color illustrations by Mary Stevens. ($30.00 with dust jacket) $10.00

CLEWES, Dorothy

Mystery of the Scarlet Daffodil, 1953 Coward McCann, first edition. hardcover, illustrated by J. Marianne Moll. ($15.00 with dust jacket) $10.00

CLIFFORD, Eth

Bear Before Breakfast, 1962 Putnam, oversize hardcover, color illustrations by Kelly Oeschsli. ($25.00 with dust jacket) $10.00

King Who Was Different, 1969 Bobbs-Merrill, first edition, hardcover, Francoise Webb. ($15.00 with dust jacket) $10.00

Red is Never a Mouse, 1960 Bobbs-Merrill, first edition, oversize hardcover, illustrations by Bill Heckler. ($30.00 with dust jacket) $15.00

Why Is an Elephant Called an Elephant?, 1966 Bobbs-Merrill, first edition, hardcover, illustrated by Jackie Lacy. ($25.00 with dust jacket) $10.00

CLIFFORD, Peggy

Gnu and the Guru Go Behind the Beyond, 1970 Houghton Mifflin, first edition, pictorial hardcover. ($30.00 with dust jacket) $15.00

CLIFTON, Lucille

Boy Who Didn't Believe in Spring, 1973 Dutton, oblong hardcover, color illustrations by Brinton Turkle. ($30.00 with dust jacket) $10.00

Don't You Remember?, 1973 Dutton, square hardcover, color illustrations by Evaline Ness. ($40.00 with dust jacket) $15.00

Everett Anderson's Christmas Coming, 1971 Holt, Rinehart and Winston, first edition, oblong hardcover, illustrations by Evaline Ness. ($40.00 with dust jacket) $15.00

My Brother Fine With Me, 1975 Holt, oversize hardcover, illustrated endpapers. b/w illustrations by Moneta Barnett. ($40.00 with dust jacket) $15.00

Some of the Days of Everett Anderson, 1970 Holt, Rinehart and Winston, first edition, hardcover, illustrations by Evaline Ness. ($40.00 with dust jacket) $15.00

Times They Used to Be, 1974 Holt, first edition, small hardcover, b/w illustrations by Susan Jeschke. ($60.00 with dust jacket) $20.00

CLOSE, Jessie

Warping of Al, 1950 Harper, first edition, hardcover. ($15.00 with dust jacket) $10.00

CLUFF, Tom

Minutemen of the Sea, 1955 Follett, hardcover, 223 pages. $10.00

CLYMER, Eleanor

Big Pile of Dirt, 1968 Holt, oblong hardcover, brown/black illustrations by Robert Shore. ($25.00 with dust jacket) $10.00

Chipmunk in the Forest, 1965 Atheneum, hardcover, b/w illustrations. $20.00

Hamburgers – and Ice Cream for Dessert, 1975 Dutton, first edition, hardcover, illustrations by Roy Doty. ($20.00 with dust jacket) $10.00

How I Went Shopping and What I Got, 1972 Holt, small hardcover, b/w/gold illustrations by Trina Schart Hyman. ($30.00 with dust jacket) $10.00

Leave Horatio Alone, 1974 Atheneum, first edition, small hardcover, color illustrations by Robert Quackenbush. ($25.00 with dust jacket) $10.00

Luke Was There, 1973 Holt, first edition, hardcover, b/w illustrations by Diane deGroat. ($20.00 with dust jacket) $10.00

Me and the Eggman, 1972 Dutton, first edition, small hardcover, b/w illustrations by David Stone. ($30.00 with dust jacket) $10.00

Mr. Piper's Bus, 1961 Dodd Mead, b/w illustrations by Kurt Wiese. ($20.00 with dust jacket) $10.00

Take Tarts as Tarts Is Passing, 1974 Dutton, first edition, small hardcover, two-color illustrations by Roy Doty. ($20.00 with dust jacket) $10.00

COATSWORTH, Elizabeth

Bess and the Sphinx, 1967 Macmillan, first edition, pictorial boards, illustrated by Bernice Loewenstein. ($25.00 with dust jacket) $10.00

Captain's Daughter, 1950 Macmillan, first edition, hardcover, 198 pages. ($25.00 with dust jacket) $15.00

Indian Mound Farm, 1969 Macmillan, 62 pages, hardcover. ($25.00 with dust jacket) $10.00

Desert Dan, 1960 Viking, first edition, orange hardcover, illustrations by Harper Johnson. ($40.00 with dust jacket) $15.00

Enchanted London 1952 Dent and Sons, first edition UK, hardcover, 121 pages, illustrated by Joan Kiddell-Monroe. ($20.00 with dust jacket) $10.00

Indian Mound Farm, 1969 Macmillan, first edition, hardcover, illustrations by Fermin Rocker. ($25.00 with dust jacket) $15.00

Night and the Cat, 1950 Macmillan, first edition, hardcover, illustrated by Foujita. ($35.00 with dust jacket) $15.00

Secret, 1965 Macmillan, first edition, hardcover, illustrations by Don Bolognese. ($15.00 with dust jacket) $10.00

Silky, 1953 Pantheon, first edition, hardcover, illustrations by John Carroll. ($25.00 with dust jacket) $15.00

Sparrow Bush, 1966 Norton, hardcover, 63 pages, engraving illustrations by Stefan Martin. ($25.00 with dust jacket) $10.00

They Walk In the Night, 1969 Norton, hardcover, illustrated by Stefan Martin. ($25.00 with dust jacket) $10.00

Thief Island, 1962 Macmillan, hardcover. $10.00

Troll Weather, 1967 Macmillan, illustrated by Ursula Arndt. ($25.00 with dust jacket) $10.00

Wishing Pear, 1951 Macmillan, hardcover, 64 pages, illustrations by Ralph Roy. $10.00

You Say You Saw a Camel, 1958 Row, Peterson, first edition, hardcover, illustrations by Brinton Turkel. ($25.00 with dust jacket) $10.00

Wanderers, 1972 Four Winds Press, first edition, hardcover, illustrated by Trina Schart Hyman. ($40.00 with dust jacket) $15.00

COBB, Vicki

SuperSuits, 1975 Lippincott, first edition, hardcover. ($15.00 with dust jacket) $10.00

COBURN, John B.

Anne and the Sand Dobbies, 1964 edition Seabury, first edition, hardcover. ($25.00 with dust jacket) $10.00

COCKETT, Mary

Pelican Park, 1969 Warne, first edition, hardcover, color illustrations by Frank Francis. ($25.00 with dust jacket) $15.00

COFFIN, Lewis

Fog Boat, 1957 Lothrop, first edition, hardcover, 128 pages, illustrations by Gil Miret. ($20.00 with dust jacket) $10.00

COGGINS, Herbert

I Am A Mouse, 1959 Abelard-Schuman, first edition, hardcover, illustrations by Judith Brook. ($20.00 with dust jacket) $10.00

COGGINS, Jack

Boys in the Revolution, 1967 Stackpole, hardcover. $10.00

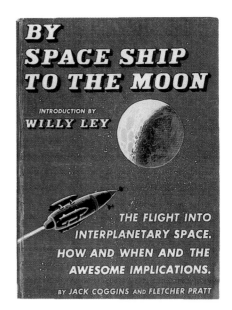

COGGINS, Jack and **Fletcher PRATT**

By Space Ship to the Moon, 1952 Random House, oversize illustrated glossy hardcover, illustrated endpapers, b/w and color illustrations by author. $15.00

Rockets, Jets, and Guided Missles for Space Ships, 1951 Random House, hardcover. ($20.00 in dust jacket) $15.00

COHN, Emil Bernhard

Stories and Fantasies from the Jewish Past, 1961 Jewish Pub. Soc. of America, first edition, hardcover, 262 pages. ($15.00 with dust jacket) $10.00

COLE, Natalie Robinson

Children's Arts from Deep Down Inside, 1966 John Day, first edition, hardcover, photos. ($20.00 with dust jacket) $10.00

COLE, William

Folk Songs of England, Ireland, Scotland and Wales, 1961 Doubleday, first American edition, hardcover, two-color illustrations by Edward Ardizzone. First edition with dust jacket: $95.00

I Went To the Animal Fair, 1958 World Publishing, hardcover, illustrations by Colette Rosselli. ($25.00 with dust jacket) $15.00

Oh What Nonsense, 1966 Viking, first edition, hardcover, illustrated by Tomi Ungerer. ($30.00 with dust jacket) $15.00

That Pest Jonathan, 1970 Harper, first edition, pictorial boards, illustrations by Tomi Ungerer. ($45.00 with same-as-cover dust jacket) $25.00

COLETTE

Boy and the Magic. (L'Enfant et les Sortileges), 1964 Putnam, first edition, oblong hardcover, color illustrations by Gerard Hoffnung. ($40.00 with dust jacket) $15.00

COLLIER, Ethel

Birthday Tree, 1961 William Scott, hardcover, illustrations by Honore Guilbeau. ($20.00 with dust jacket) $10.00

COLLIER, James Lincoln and **Christopher**

My Brother Sam Is Dead, 1974 Four Winds Press, hardcover, Newbery Award edition. ($20.00 with dust jacket) $10.00

COLLIN, Hedvig

Nils, Globetrotter, 1957 Viking first edition, small hardcover, 189 pages, b/w illustrations by author. ($15.00 with dust jacket) $10.00

COLLINS, Ruth P.

Runaway Camel, 1968 Crown, Weekly Reader edition, pictorial hardcover, 96 pages, b/w illustrations by Harold Berson. $10.00

COLMAN, Hila

Classmates by Request, 1968 William Morrow, hardcover, 187 pages. $10.00

Peter's Brownstone, 1963 Morrow, hardcover, illustrations by Leonard Weisgard. ($20.00 with dust jacket) $10.00

COLVER, Anne

Lucky Four, 1960 Duell Sloan and Pearce, hardcover, illustrations by Albert Orbaan. ($15.00 with dust jacket) $10.00

Nobody's Birthday, 1961 Knopf, small hardcover, color illustrations by Marvin Bileck. ($20.00 with dust jacket) $10.00

Old Bet, 1957 Knopf, oversize hardcover, illustrated endpapers, color illustrations by Tony Palazzo. ($20.00 with dust jacket) $10.00

Secret Castle, 1960 Knopf, first edition, small hardcover, b/w illustrations by Vaike Low. ($25.00 with dust jacket) $10.00

Yankee Doodle Painter, 1955 Knopf, first edition, hardcover, illustrations by Lee Ames. ($20.00 with dust jacket) $10.00

COMMAGER, Evan

Tenth Birthday, 1954 Bobbs-Merrill, first edition, hardcover. ($20.00 with dust jacket) $10.00

COMMINS, Dorothy

Lullabies of the World, 1967 Random House, first edition, illustrations by author. ($30.00 with dust jacket) $20.00

CONE, Molly, see Series section, MISHMASH

CONFORD, Ellen

Dear Lovey Heart, I Am Desperate, 1975 Little Brown, first edition, hardcover. ($25.00 with dust jacket) $10.00

Dreams of Victory, 1973 Little Brown, hardcover, illustrations by Gail Rockwell. ($20.00 with dust jacket) $10.00

Just the Thing for Geraldine, 1974 Little Brown Weekly Reader edition, hardcover, color illustrations by John Larrecq. ($20.00 with dust jacket) $10.00

Luck of Pokey Bloom, 1975 Little Brown, Weekly Reader edition, pictorial hardcover. $10.00

Me and the Terrible Two, 1974 Little Brown, hardcover. $15.00

Why Can't I Be William?, 1972 Little Brown, first edition, hardcover. ($15.00 with dust jacket) $10.00

CONKLIN, Gladys

Elephants of Africa, 1972 Holiday House, hardcover, illustrations by Joseph Cellini. ($20.00 with dust jacket) $10.00

CONKLING, Fleur

Bingity-Bangity School Bus, 1950 Wonder Books,

Grosset, first edition, small, illustrated hardcover, illustrated endpapers, color illustrations by Ruth Wood. $20.00 Later editions: $10.00

CONRAD, Barnaby
Zorro: a Fox in the City, 1971 Garden City, first edition, hardcover, illustrated. ($15.00 with dust jacket) $10.00

COOK, Bernadine
Little Fish that Got Away, 1956 Scott, square hardcover, two-color illustrations by Crockett Johnson. ($30.00 with dust jacket) $15.00
Curious Little Kitten, 1961 Hale, library binding, hardcover. ($15.00 with dust jacket) $10.00

COOK, George S.
Fish Heads and Fire Ants, 1973 Young Scott, wide hardcover, b/w illustrations by H. B. Vestal. ($60.00 with dust jacket) $20.00

COOK, Olive
Coon Holler, 1958 Longmans, hardcover, 179 pages. $15.00

COOKE, Alistair
Christmas Eve, 1952 Knopf, first edition, hardcover, color illustrations by Simont. ($30.00 with dust jacket) $15.00

COOKE, Donald
Powder Keg: Story of the Bermuda Gunpowder Mystery, 1953 Winston, hardcover. $10.00

COOLIDGE, Olivia
Come By Here, 1970 Houghton, first edition, hardcover, 239 pages, b/w illustrations by Milton Johnson. ($25.00 with dust jacket) $15.00
Marathon Looks at the Sea, 1967 Houghton, first edition, 246 pages, illustrations by Bea Holmes. ($25.00 with dust jacket) $15.00

COOMBS, Charles
Skyrocketing into the Unknown, 1954 Morrow, hardcover. $10.00

COOMBS, Patricia, see Series section, DORRIE
Lisa and the Grompet, 1970 Lothrop, Lee, hardcover, two-color illustrations by author. ($35.00 with dust jacket) $15.00
Lobo and Brewster, 1971 Lothrop, Lee, hardcover, color illustrations by author. ($35.00 with dust jacket) $15.00
Molly Mullet, 1975 Lothrop, Lee, hardcover, color illustrations by author. ($35.00 with dust jacket) $15.00
Mouse Cafe, 1970 Lothrop, Lee, square hardcover, two-color illustrations by author. ($35.00 with dust jacket) $15.00
Waddy and His Brother, 1963 Lothrop, Lee, hardcover, color illustrations by author. ($45.00 with dust jacket) $15.00. Ex-library: ($15.00 with dust jacket) $10.00

COONEY, Barbara
American Speller, an Adaptation of Noah Webster's Blue-Backed Speller, 1960 Crowell, first edition, hardcover, color illustrations by author. ($30.00 with dust jacket) $20.00
Chanticleer and the Fox, story from Chaucer, 1958 Crowell, oversize hardcover, color illustrations by Cooney. First edition with dust jacket: $75.00. 1959 Caldecott Award edition: ($35.00 with dust jacket) $15.00
Christmas, 1967 Crowell, hardcover, illustrations by author. ($20.00 with dust jacket) $10.00
Little Juggler, Adapted from an old French Legend, 1961 Hastings House, hardcover, illustrations by Cooney. ($25.00 with dust jacket) $15.00

COOPER, Elizabeth
Fish from Japan, 1969 Harcourt, oversize hardcover, color illustrations by Joe and Beth Krush. ($35.00 with dust jacket) $15.00

COOPER, Gordon
Hour in the Morning, 1974 edition Dutton, hardcover, 153 pages, illustrations by Philip Gough. ($20.00 with dust jacket) $10.00

COOPER, John R.
Mel Martin Baseball Stories: The College League Mystery, 1953 Books, Inc., hardcover. ($30.00 with dust jacket) $15.00

Mel Martin Baseball Stories: The Southpaw's Secret, 1947 Books, Inc., hardcover. ($30.00 with dust jacket) $15.00
Phantom Homer, 1952 Garden City, hardcover. $10.00

COOPER, Margaret
Ice Palace ,1966 Macmillan, first edition, hardcover, illustrated by Harold Goodwin. ($15.00 with dust jacket) $10.00

COOPER, Page
Pat's Harmony ,1954 edition World Junior Library, hardcover. ($20.00 with dust jacket) $10.00
Amigo Circus Horse, World, hardcover, illustrated by Henry Pitz. $10.00
Silver Spurs to Monterey, 1956 World, first edition, hardcover. ($25.00 with dust jacket) $10.00

COOPER, Susan, see Series section, DARK IS RISING
Dawn of Fear, 1970 Harcourt, first edition, hardcover. ($40.00 with dust jacket) $15.00

CORBETT, Scott
Baseball Trick, 1965 Little Brown, hardcover. ($15.00 with dust jacket) $10.00
Case of the Silver Skull, 1974 Little, Brown, hardcover. ($30.00 with dust jacket) $10.00
Case of the Ticklish Tooth, 1971 Atlantic Monthly Press, first edition, hardcover, illustrations by Paul Frame. ($15.00 with dust jacket) $10.00
Disappearing Dog Trick, 1965 Little Brown, hardcover. ($20.00 with dust jacket) $10.00
Great Custard Pie Panic, 1974 Little Brown, hardcover, color illustrations by Joe Mathieu. ($25.00 with dust jacket) $15.00

CORCORAN, Barbara
Row of Tigers, 1969 Atheneum, first edition, hardcover, illustrations by Allan Eitzen. ($15.00 with dust jacket) $10.00

CORCOS, Lucille
City Book, 1972 Golden Press, oversize hardcover, 93 pages, map endpapers, color illustrations throughout. $25.00

CORDDRY, Thomas
Kibby and the Red Elephant, 1973 J. Philip O'Hara, first edition, hardcover, illustrations by Carl Kock. ($20.00 with dust jacket) $10.00
Kibby's Big Feat, 1970 Follett, first edition, hardcover, illustrations by Quentin Blake. ($35.00 with dust jacket) $15.00

CORNISH, Sam
Your Hand in Mine, 1970 Harcourt, small hardcover, b/w illustrations by Carl Owens. ($15.00 with dust jacket) $10.00

COSGROVE, Stephen
Hucklebug, 1975 Grolier, tall narrow hardcover, pictorial boards, illustrations by Robin James. $10.00

COST, March
Bittter Green of the Willow, 1967 Chilton Books, 6 color plates by Anderson. ($25.00 in dust jacket) $10.00

COTHRAN, Jean
Magic Bells, 1949 Aladdin, first edition, 140 pages, hardcover, illustrations by Peter Burchard. ($25.00 with dust jacket) $10.00
Magic Calabash: More Folk Tales, 1956 David McKay, first edition, hardcover. ($35.00 with dust jacket) $15.00

COURLANDER, Harold
Kantchil's Lime Pit, 1950 Harcourt, first edition, hardcover, 150 pages, illustrations by Robert W. Kane. ($15.00 with dust jacket) $10.00

COUSINS, Margaret
Christmas Gifts, 1952 edition Doubleday, small hardback. $15.00

COVEN, Edwina
Cookery Tales of Oaktree Kitchen, 1959 Wingate, London, first edition, hardcover, illustrated by Edgar Spenceley. ($20.00 with dust jacket) $10.00

COWDEN, Jean Gibbons
Maribelle's Corner, 1960 Pageant Press, first edi-

tion, hardcover, illustrated. ($15.00 with dust jacket) $10.00

COX, Donald
Stations in Space: Our Stepping Stones to the Stars, 1960 Holt, first edition, hardcover, illustrations by Kocher. ($15.00 with dust jacket) $10.00

COX, Lee Sheridan
Andy & Willie Super Sleuths, 1967 Scribner, Weekly Reader edition, illustrated hardcover. $15.00

COY, Harold
Real Book about Gold, 1954 Garden City, hardcover. ($25.00 in dust jacket) $10.00

CRAIGIE, Dorothy
Little Train, 1950 Eyre, London, small oblong hardcover, map endpapers, color illustrations by author. ($20.00 with dust jacket) $10.00

CRAWFORD, Marion
Little Princesses, 1950 Harcourt, first edition, hardcover. ($20.00 with dust jacket) $10.00

CRAYDER, Dorothy
She, the Adventuress, 1973 Atheneum hardcover, 188 pages. ($20.00 with dust jacket) $10.00

CREDLE, Ellis
Big Doin's on Razorback Ridge, 1956 Thomas Nelson, hardcover, illustrated endpapers. ($20.00 with dust jacket) $10.00
Big Fraid, Little Fraid, 1968 Nelson, illustrated hardcover, orange illustrations. ($20.00 with dust jacket) $10.00
Monkey See, Monkey Do, 1968 Thomas Nelson, first edition, hardcover. ($25.00 with dust jacket) $10.00

CRIST, Eda and Richard
Good Ship Spider Queen, 1953 Bobbs-Merrill, first edition, hardcover, illustrations by author. ($15.00 with dust jacket) $10.00

CREWS, Donald
We Read: A to Z, 1967 Harper, square hardcover, 52 pages, color illustrations by author. ($65.00 with dust jacket) $35.00

CROCKER, Betty
Betty Crocker's New Boys and Girls Cook Book, 1965 Golden Press, first edition, oversize, spiral bound, picture boards. $15.00

CROMAN, Dorothy
Mystery of Steamboat Rock, 1956 Putnam, hardcover, illustrations by Charles Greer. ($20.00 with dust jacket) $10.00

CROMPTON, Richmal
Frost at Morning, 1950 Hutchinson, London, first edition, hardcover. ($35.00 with dust jacket) $20.00
Jimmy Again, 1951 London, first edition, hardcover. ($45.00 with dust jacket) $20.00
William and the Witch, 1964 George Newnes, UK, hardcover, illustrations by Thomas Henry and Henry Ford, gilt titles and gilt picture of William on spine. First edition with dust jacket: $95.00 Later editions: ($35.00 with dust jacket) $15.00
William and the Masked Ranger, 1966 Newnes, hardcover. First edition with dust jacket: $95.00 Later editions: ($35.00 with dust jacket) $15.00

CROSS, Genevieve
Trip to the Yard, 1952 Garden City, oversize picture book, illustrations by Hartwell and Dixon. $15.00

CROWELL, Ann
Hogan for the Bluebird, 1969 Scribner, hardcover, 127 pages. ($20.00 with dust jacket) $10.00

CRUMP, Irving
Boy's Life Book of Scout Stories, 1952 Doubleday, hardcover. ($15.00 with dust jacket) $10.00

CULFF, Robert
World of Toys, 1969 Paul Hamlyn, oversize first edition, hardcover, color and black and white photographs. ($40.00 with dust jacket) $20.00

CUMMING, Marian
Just Like Nancy, 1953 Harcourt, first edition, hardcover. ($25.00 with dust jacket) $10.00

CUMMINGS, E.E.
Fairy Tales, 1965 Harcourt, first edition, hardcover, illustrations by John Eaton. ($30.00 with dust jacket) $15.00

CUNLIFFE, John
Farmer Johns Buys a Pig, 1964 London: Andre Deutsch, first edition, hardcover, illustrations by Carol Barker. ($40.00 with dust jacket) $20.00

CUNNINGHAM, Julia
Drop Dead, 1965 Pantheon, hardcover, b/w illustrations by James Spanfeller. ($35.00 with dust jacket) $15.00
Macaroon, 1962 Pantheon, first edition, hardcover, 64 pages, illustrations by Evaline Ness. ($20.00 with dust jacket) $10.00
Onion Journey, 1967 Pantheon, small hardcover, color illustrations by Lydia Cooley. ($20.00 with dust jacket) $10.00
Treasure is the Rose, 1973 Pantheon, first edition, hardcover, 99 pages, illustrations by Judy Graese. ($25.00 with dust jacket) $15.00
Viollet, 1966 Pantheon, hardcover, b/w illustrations by Alan Cober. ($20.00 with dust jacket) $10.00

CUNNINGHAM, Mary
Paris Hat, 1958 Funk and Wagnalls, first edition, hardcover. ($15.00 with dust jacket) $10.00

CURREN, Polly
Family for Sarah Ann, 1962 Bobbs-Merrill, first edition, hardcover, illustrations by Kelly Oechsli. $20.00

CURRO, Evelyn Malone
Great Circus Parade, 1963 Holt, Little Owl Book, small, oblong illustrated hardcover, illustrated endpapers, color illustrations by author. $40.00

The Great Circus Parade by Evelyn Malone Curro

CURRY, Jane Louise
Ice Ghosts Mystery, 1972 Atheneum, first edition, hardcover.($20.00 with dust jacket) $10.00
Mindy's Mysterious Miniature, 1970 Harcourt, first edition, 157 pages, illustrations by Charles Robinson. ($25.00 with dust jacket) $10.00
Watchers, 1975 Atheneum, hardcover, 232 pages. ($30.00 with dust jacket) $10.00

CURTIS, Mattie Lamb
Blizzard, 1970 Dutton, Weekly Reader Book Club edition, hardcover, illustrated boards by Charles Robinson. $10.00

CUSHMAN, Jean
Golden Play Book of American History Stamps, 1953 Simon Schuster, stamps intact and not pasted in. $20.00

⇢ **D** ⇠

DAHL, Roald
Charlie and the Chocolate Factory, 1964 Knopf, hardcover, b/w illustrations by Joseph Schindelman. First edition with dust jacket: $95.00 Later printings: ($20.00 with dust jacket) $10.00
Charlie and the Great Glass Elevator, 1972 Knopf, first edition, hardcover, b/w illustrations by Joseph Schindelman. ($55.00 with dust jacket) $20.00 Later editions ($25.00 with dust jacket) $10.00
Danny, Champion of the World, 1975 Knopf, hardcover, illustrations by Jill Bennett. ($25.00 with dust jacket) $10.00
Fantastic Mr. Fox, 1970 Knopf, first edition, hard-

cover, illustrations by Donald Chaffin. ($30.00 with dust jacket) $20.00

James and the Giant Peach, 1961 Knopf, early edition, hardcover, 119 pages, color illustrations by Nancy Burkert. ($35.00 with dust jacket) $15.00

Magic Finger, 1966 Harper, illustrations by William Pene DuBois. ($35.00 with dust jacket) $15.00

DAIRS, Marilyn Kornreich

Music Dictionary, 1956 Doubleday, first edition, hardcover. ($25.00 with dust jacket) $15.00

DALGLIESH, Alice

America Travels, 1961 Macmillan, hardcover, 134 pages. ($20.00 with dust jacket) $10.00

Bears on Hemlock Mountain, 1952 Scribner, small hardcover, b/w/blue illustrations by Helen Sewell. ($50.00 with dust jacket) $20.00

Columbus Story, 1955 Scribner, first edition, hardcover, 28 pages, color plates by Leo Politi. ($100.00 with dust jacket) $30.00

Thanksgiving Story, 1954 Scribner, first edition, oversize hardcover, illustrations by Helen Sewell. ($50.00 with dust jacket) $20.00

DALTON, Alene

Caroline Kennedy First Lady Dress Up Book, 1963 Roylton House Publishers, first edition, hardcover, illustrations by photo of the young Caroline Kennedy on cover. Charlotte Jetter illustrations of Caroline in First Ladies' dresses from Martha Washington to Jacqueline Kennedy. $65.00

DALY, Kathleen

Ladybug, Ladybug, 1969 American Heritage Press, first edition, hardcover, illustrations by Susan Carlton Smith. ($40.00 with dust jacket) $20.00

Wild Animals Babies, 1958 Simon & Schuster, Little Golden Book #332, "A" edition, Illustrated by Feodor Rojankovsky. $15.00

DALY, Maureen

Ginger Horse, 1964 Dodd Mead, hardcover, double-page color illustrated title page, b/w illustrations by Wesley Dennis. ($25.00 with dust jacket) $15.00. Weekly Reader Book Club edition, $10.00

Patrick Visits the Farm, 1959 Dodd, Mead, first edition, hardcover, illustrations by Ellie Simmons. ($15.00 with dust jacket) $10.00

Rosie, the Dancing Elephant, 1967 Dodd, Mead, first edition, hardcover, illustrations by Lorence Bjorklund. ($25.00 with dust jacket) $15.00

Small War of Sergeant Donkey, 1966 Dodd, Mead, first edition, hardcover, illustrations by Wesley Dennis. ($30.00 with dust jacket) $15.00

DANA, Barbara

Spencer and His Friends, 1966 Atheneum, first edition, hardcover, illustrated by Jacqueline Chwast. ($15.00 with dust jacket) $10.00

DANA, Doris

Elephant and His Secret, 1974 Atheneum, oversize hardcover, text in English and Spanish, double page woodcut color illustrations by Antonio Frasconi. ($30.00 with dust jacket) $15.00

DANIELS, Guy (translator)

Falcon Under the Hat, Russian Merry Tales and Fairy Tales, 1969 Funk and Wagnalls, first edition, hardcover, illustrated by Feodor Rojankovsky. ($25.00 with dust jacket) $15.00

DANSKA, Herbert

Street Kids, 1970 Knopf, 160 pages, hardcover. ($20.00 with dust jacket) $10.00

DARBY, Gene, see Series section, TIME MACHINE

Pudgy, the Beaver, 1963 Benefic Press, tan hardcover, square, illustrated by Edward Miller. $20.00

DARINGER, Helen F.

Debbie of the Green Gate, 1950 Harcourt, first edition, hardcover. ($20.00 with dust jacket) $10.00

Flower of Araby, 1958 Harcourt, first edition, hardcover. ($25.00 with dust jacket) $10.00

Like A Lady, 1955 Harcourt, first edition, hardcover, illustrated by Susan Knight ($20.00 with dust jacket) $10.00

Yesterday's Daughter, 1964 Harcourt, Brace, first edition, hardcover. ($20.00 with dust jacket) $10.00

DAUGHERTY, Charles Michael
Where the Condor Nests, 1955 Viking, first edition, hardcover, illustrations by author. ($25.00 with dust jacket) $10.00

DAUGHERTY, James
Landing of the Pilgrims, 1950 Random House, hardcover, illustrated by author. $20.00
Of Courage Undaunted: Across the Continent with Lewis & Clark, 1964 Viking, oversize hardcover. $20.00
West of Boston, Yankee Rhymes and Doggerel, 1956 Viking Press, first edition, hardcover, 95 pages, drawings by author. ($35.00 with dust jacket) $15.00

DAUGHERTY, Sonia
Ten Brave Men, 1951 Lippincott, illustrated by James Daugherty. ($30.00 with dust jacket) $15.00

D'AULAIRE, Ingri and Edgar
Benjamin Franklin, 1950 Doubleday, first edition, hardcover hardcover, color illustrations by authors. First edition with dust jacket: $60.00. Later editions: ($25.00 with dust jacket) $15.00
Columbus, 1955 Doubleday, hardcover hardcover, color illustrations by authors. First edition with dust jacket: $75.00. Later editions: ($25.00 with dust jacket) $15.00
D'Aulaire's Book of Greek Myths, 1962 Doubleday, first edition, oversize hardcover, 192 pages, color illustrations by authors. First edition with dust jacket: $75.00. Later editions: ($25.00 with dust jacket) $15.00
Magic Meadow, 1958 Garden City, first edition, hardcover, illustrations by authors. ($50.00 with dust jacket) $20.00
Trolls, 1972 Garden City, first edition, oversize hardcover, color illustrations by authors. ($50.00 with dust jacket) $20.00

DAVID, Peter
How Jacky Bunny Came to Parson's Wood, 1950 John Martin's House, Friendly Book, hardcover, color illustrations throughout by Nino Carbe. $15.00

DAVIDSON, Louis B. and Eddie DOHERTY
Captain Marooner, 1952 Thomas Crowell, blue hardcover. $10.00

DAVIDSON, Sandra Calder
Sylvester and The Butterfly Bomb, 1972 Doubleday, first edition, oversize hardcover. ($20.00 with dust jacket) $15.00

DAVIES, Anthea
White Horse With Wings, 1968 Macmillan, first edition, hardcover, illustrated by Brigitte Bryan. ($25.00 with dust jacket) $15.00

DAVIES, Jack, Ken ANNAKIN, and Allen ANDREWS
Monte Carlo or Bust! Those Daring Young Men in their Jaunty Jalopies., 1969 Dennis Dobson, first edition, oversize hardcover, illustrations by Searle. ($50.00 with dust jacket) $20.00

DAVIS, Clive
Message from Space, 1961 Dodd, Mead, hardcover, 95 pages. $35.00

DAVIS, Lavinia R.
Danny's Luck, 1953 Doubleday, first edition, oblong hardcover, illustrated endpapers. color illustrations by Hildegard Woodward. ($60.00 with dust jacket) $25.00
Donkey Detectives, 1955 Doubleday, hardcover, illustrations by Jean Porter. ($20.00 with dust jacket) $10.00
Island City, 1961 Doubleday, hardcover. ($25.00 with dust jacket) $10.00
Janey's Fortune, 1957 Doubleday Book Club edition, hardcover. ($15.00 with dust jacket) $10.00
Sandy's Spurs, 1951 Doubleday, first edition, hardcover. ($30.00 with dust jacket) $10.00
Secret of Donkey Island, 1952 Doubleday, first edition, hardcover, 246 pages, illustrations by Jean Porter. ($20.00 with dust jacket) $10.00

DAVIS, Norman
Picken's Treasure Hunt, 1955 Oxford, first edition, hardcover, illustrations by Winslade.($50.00 with dust jacket) $20.00

DAVIS, Reda
Martin's Dinosaur, 1959 Crowell, first edition, oversize hardcover, red/b/w illustrations by Louis Slobidkin. ($30.00 with dust jacket) $15.00

DAVIS, Russell G.
Choctaw Code, 1961 McGraw Hill, hardcover. $15.00

DAWLISH, Peter, see Series section, DAUNTLESS

DAWSON, A.J.
Finn the Wolfhound, 1963 Harcourt, Brace & World, first American edition, hardcover. ($15.00 with dust jacket) $10.00

DAY, Veronique
Landslide, 1963 Coward, McCann, first American edition, hardcover, 158 pages, illustrations by Margaret Tomes. ($35.00 with dust jacket) $10.00

DAYTON, Mona
Earth and Sky, 1969 Harper, hardcover, illustrations by Roger Duvoisin. ($35.00 with dust jacket) $10.00

DeANGELI, Arthur Craig
Door In the Wall, 1968 Doubleday, adapted from *Hole In The Wall* by Marguerite De Angeli, first edition, hardcover, illustrated by Marguerite de Angeli. ($20.00 with dust jacket) $10.00

DeANGELI, Marguerite
Black Fox of Lorne, 1956 Doubleday, first edition, hardcover, illustrations by author. ($25.00 with dust jacket) $10.00

Book of Nursery and Mother Goose Rhymes, 1954 Doubleday, first edition, hardcover, illustrations by author. ($40.00 with dust jacket) $20.00

Fiddlestrings, 1974 Doubleday, first edition, hardcover, 143 pages, b/w illustrations by author. ($35.00 with dust jacket) $10.00

Just Like David, 1951 Garden City, first edition, pictorial green boards, b/w and two-color illustrations by author. ($40.00 with dust jacket) $20.00

Marguerite de Angeli's Book of Nursery and Mother Goose Rhymes, 1953 Doubleday, pictorial boards, illustrations by author. $25.00

Old Testament, 1960 edition Doubleday, oversize hardcover, illustrations by DeAngeli. First with dust jacket: $65.00 ($30.00 with dust jacket) $10.00

Pocket Full of Posies, a Merry Mother Goose, 1961 Garden City, oversize, hardcover, illustrated by author. $25.00

Ted and Nina Story Book, 1964 Doubleday, oblong, illustrations by author. ($30.00 in dust jacket) $20.00

DeBANKE, Cecile
More Tabby Magic, 1961 Hutchinson, first edition, hardcover, illustrations by Nora S. Unwin. ($35.00 with dust jacket) $15.00

DeBORHEGYI, Suzanne
Secret of Sacred Lake, 1967 Holt, first edition, hardcover, b/w illustrations by David Stone. ($15.00 with dust jacket) $10.00

DeBRUNHOFF, Laurent see Series section, BABAR; SERAFINA
Bonhomme, 1965 Pantheon, pictorial hardcover, illustrations by author. $15.00

Bonhomme and the Huge Beast, 1974 Pantheon, hardcover, illustrations by author. ($20.00 with dust jacket) $10.00

Gregory and Lady Turtle in the Valley of the Music Trees, translated by Richard Howard, 1971 Pantheon Books, hardcover with illustrated boards, orange endpages, black and white illustrations. $15.00

DECKER, Duane
Catcher from Double-A, 1950 Morrow, pictorial hardcover, 188 pages. $40.00

Fast Man on a Pivot, 1951 Morrow, hardcover. ($75.00 with dust jacket) $30.00

Hit and Run, 1950 Morrow, hardcover. ($75.00 with dust jacket) $30.00

Mister Shortstop, 1954 Morrow, hardcover. ($75.00 with dust jacket) $30.00

Rebel in Right Field, 1972 Morrow, hardcover. ($100.00 with dust jacket) $35.00

DEDMON, Richard K.
Frances the Pig, 1974 Barnyard Press, hardcover. $15.00

DEE, Ruby
Glowchild and Other Poems, 1972 Odarki Books/Third Press, first edition, hardcover, 111 pages. ($25.00 with dust jacket) $10.00

DEGH, Linda, editor
Folktales of Hungary, 1965 Routledge & Kegan, first edition, hardcover. ($20.00 with dust jacket) $10.00

DEHN, Paul
Cat's Whiskers, 1963 Longmans, Green, first edition, hardcover, black and white photos by Ronald Spillman. ($40.00 with dust jacket) $20.00

Quake, Quake, Quake: A Leaden Treasury of English Verse, 1961 Simon & Schuster, first edition, hardcover, 109 pages, illustrations by Edward Gorey. ($55.00 with dust jacket) $25.00

DeJONG, Dola
House on Charlton Street, 1962 Scribner, hardcover, 157 pages. ($20.00 with dust jacket) $10.00

One Summer's Secret, 1963 David McKay, first edition, hardcover. ($15.00 with dust jacket) $10.00

DeJONG, Meindert
Along Came A Dog, 1953 Harper, pictoral boards, illustrations by Maurice Sendak. ($50.00 with dust jacket) $25.00

Easter Cat, 1971 Macmillan, first edition, hardcover, illustrations by Lillian Hoban. ($20.00 with dust jacket) $10.00

Far Out the Long Canal, 1964 Harper, hardcover, 231 pages, illustrations by Nancy Grossman. ($20.00 with dust jacket) $10.00

Good Luck, Duck, 1950 Harper, first edition, oversize hardcover, 57 pages, color illustrations by Marc Simont. ($65.00 with dust jacket) $25.00

Horse Came Running, 1970 Luterworth, first edition, hardcover. ($35.00 with dust jacket) $15.00

Horse Came Running, 1970 Macmillan, pictorial hardcover, illustrated by Paul Sagsoorian. $15.00

Hurry Home, Candy, 1953 Harper, first edition, hardcover, illustrations by Maurice Sendak. ($40.00 with dust jacket) $20.00

Journey From Peppermint Street, 1968 Harper, National Book Award Winner, first edition, hardcover, illustrations by by Emily McCully. ($40.00 with dust jacket) $25.00

Little Cow and the Turtle, 1955 Harper, illustrated hardcover, 173 pages, b/w illustrations by Maurice Sendak. ($40.00 with dust jacket) $20.00

Wheel on the School, 1954 Harper, first edition, hardcover, illustrations by Maurice Sendak. ($45.00 with dust jacket) $20.00

DeLa IGLESIA, Maria Elena
Oak That Would Not Pay, 1968 Pantheon Books, first edition, green hardcover, 34 pages, illustrations by Jerome Snyder. ($50.00 with dust jacket) $25.00

DeLaROCHE, Mazo
Bill and Coo, 1958 Macmillan, first edition, illustrations by Eileen A. Soper. ($35.00 with dust jacket) $15.00

DeLAGE, Ida
Good Morning, Lady, 1974 Garrard, Illustrated boards, 32 pages, drawings by Tracy McVay. $10.00

Witchy Broom, 1969 Garrard, pictorial hardcover, illustrated by Walt Peaver. $15.00

DeLaMARE, Walter, editor
Tom Tiddler's Ground: A Book of Poetry for Children, 1961 Knopf, first American edition, hardcover, illustrations by Margery Gill. ($20.00 with dust jacket) $10.00

DeLEEUW, Adele
Donny, the Boy Who Made a Home for Animals, 1957 Little, Brown, first edition, hardcover. ($15.00 with dust jacket) $10.00

It's Fun to Cook, 1952 Macmillan, first edition, hardcover. ($15.00 with dust jacket) $10.00

DeLEEUW, Adele and **Cateau**
Strange Garden, 1958 Little, Brown, first edition, hardcover, illustrations by Meg Wohlberg. ($20.00 with dust jacket) $10.00

DeLEEUW, Cateau
Breakneck Betty, 1957 World, first edition, hardcover, 219 pages. ($25.00 with dust jacket) $15.00

Fear in the Forest, 1960 Nelson, Weekly Reader Book Club edition, 127 pages, hardcover. $10.00

Give Me Your Hand, 1960 Little, Brown, hardcover, 240 pages. ($25.00 with dust jacket) $10.00

DELETAILLE, Albertine
Home For My Kittens, 1966 Golden Press, first edition, hardcover. ($25.00 with dust jacket) $10.00

DelREY, Lester
Space Flight: The Coming Exploration of the Universe, 1959 Golden Library of Knowledge, illustrations. $10.00

Infinite Worlds of Maybe, 1968 Holt, hardcover, 192 pages. ($25.00 with dust jacket) $15.00

DEMING, Richard
Famous Investigators: Real Life Stories, 1963 Whitman, hardcover, illustrated by Arnie Kohn. $10.00

de PAOLA, Tomie
Cloud Book, 1975 Holiday House, first edition, blue oversize hardcover, 32 pages, color illustrations by author. ($20.00 with dust jacket) $10.00

Fight the Night, 1968 Lippincott, first edition, hardcover, illustrated by author. $30.00

Journey of the Kiss, 1970 Hawthorne Books, first edition, hardcover, illustrated by author. ($30.00 with dust jacket) $15.00

Michael Bird-Boy, 1975 Prentice-Hall, first edition, illustrated glossy hardcover, color illustrations by author. ($20.00 with dust jacket) $10.00

Nana Upstairs and Nana Downstairs, 1973 Putnam, hardcover, square, illustrated by author. ($25.00 with dust jacket) $10.00

Strega Nona, 1975 Prentice-Hall, Caldecott Honor Book, brown hardcover with gilt design on front and gilt titles on spine, color illustrations by author. ($35.00 with dust jacket) $15.00

Watch Out for the Chicken Feet in Your Soup, 1974 Prentice-Hall, hardcover, illustrations by author. ($30.00 with dust jacket) $15.00

DeREGNIERS, Beatrice Schenk
Boy, the Rat and the Butterfly, 1971 Atheneum, first edition, hardcover, illustrations by H. and R. Shekerjian. ($20.00 with dust jacket) $15.00

Cats Cats Cats Cats Cats, 1958 Pantheon, hardcover, illustrations by Bill Sokol. ($50.00 with dust jacket) $20.00

Circus, 1966 Viking, first edition, hardcover, photograph illustrations by Al Giese. ($20.00 with dust jacket) $10.00

David and Goliath, 1965 Viking, first edition, oversize hardcover, 28 pages, color illustrations by Richard M. Powers. ($25.00 with dust jacket) $15.00

Giant Story, 1953 Harper, probable first, oversize hardcover, blue/b/w illustrations by Maurice

Sendak. ($65.00 with dust jacket) $25.00

It Does Not Say Meow, 1972 Seabury, square hardcover, color illustrations by Paul Galdone. $15.00

Little Girl and Her Mother, 1963 Vanguard, first edition, oblong oversize hardcover, pink/b/w illustrations by Esther Gilman. ($30.00 with dust jacket) $15.00

Little House of Your Own, 1954 Harcourt, first edition, narrow hardcover, b/w illustrations by Irene Haas. ($50.00 with dust jacket) $20.00

May I Bring a Friend?, 1965 Atheneum, Caldecott Award, medal on dust jacket, hardcover, illustrations by Beni Montresor. ($20.00 with dust jacket) $10.00

Red Riding Hood, 1972 Atheneum, first edition, hardcover. 42 pages, two-color illustrations by Edward Gorey. ($75.00 with dust jacket) $30.00

Something Special, 1958 Harcourt, hardcover, window opening pages, illustrations by Irene Haas. ($25.00 with dust jacket) $15.00

What Can You Do with a Shoe?, 1955 Harper, oblong hardcover, pink/b/w illustrations by Maurice Sendak. First edition with dust jacket: $35.00. Later printings: ($15.00 with dust jacket) $10.00

What Happens Next?, 1959 Macmillan, hardcover, illustrated by Remo Farrugio. ($15.00 with dust jacket) $10.00

Willy O'Dwyer Jumped in the Fire, 1968 Atheneum, first edition, hardcover, illustrated by Beni Montresor. ($30.00 with dust jacket) $15.00

DERLETH, August, see Series section, MILL CREEK

Country of the Hawk, 1952 Aladdin Books, first edition, hardcover, b/w illustrations by Bjorklund. $15.00

DeROSSO, H. A.

Rebel, 1961 Whitman, first edition, book #1548, color illustrated boards, 212 pages. illustrated by Adam Szwejkowski. $10.00

DERWENT, Lavinia

Return to Sula, 1971 Gollancz, first edition, hardcover, illustrations by Louise Annand. ($30.00 with dust jacket) $15.00

DESMOND, Alice Curtis

Teddy Koala: Mascot of the Marines, 1962 Dodd, Mead, first edition, hardcover, illustrated by Sam Savitt, pictorial appendix by author. ($20.00 with dust jacket) $10.00

DEUTSCH, Babette

I Often Wish, 1966 Funk & Wagnalls, first edition, oversize blue hardcover, illustrations by Eva Cellini. ($20.00 with dust jacket) $10.00

DEVEAUX, Alexis

Na-Ni, 1973 Harper, first edition, square pictorial hardcover, b/w illustrations by author. ($35.00 with dust jacket) $15.00

DEVLIN, Wende and **Harry**

Cranberry Thanksgiving, 1971 Parents' Magazine Press, first edition, pictorial hardcover, color illustrations. $20.00

How Fletcher was Hatched, 1969 Parents' Magazine Press, illustrated boards and end papers. $12.00

DeVRIES, Leonard

Little Wide-Awake, 1967 World, first US edition, oversize, b/w and color illustrations. $45.00

DICK, Trella

Bridger's Boy, 1965 Follett, first edition, hardcover. ($25.00 with dust jacket) $15.00

Tornado Jones, 1953 Follett, first edition, 286 pages, illustrations by Mary Stevens. ($20.00 with dust jacket) $10.00

DICKENS, Charles

Captain Boldheart/Magic Fishbone, 1964 edition Macmillan, first thus, oversize hardcover, color illustrations by Hilary Knight. ($50.00 with dust jacket) $20.00

Christmas Carol, 1961 edition World, first edition thus, hardcover, 110 pages, color and b/w illustrations by Ronald Searle. ($40.00 with dust jacket) $20.00

Magic Fishbone, 1953 edition Vanguard, first edition, oversize pictorial boards with cloth spine, first thus, 36 pages, color and b/w illustrations by Louis Slobodkin. ($50.00 with dust jacket) $30.00

DICKENS, Monica
Cobbler's Dream, 1963 Coward-McCann, first edition, hardcover. ($25.00 with dust jacket) $15.00
House at World's End, 1970 Garden City, first American edition, hardcover. ($25.00 with dust jacket) $10.00
Summer at World's End, 1971 Heinemann, London, first edition, hardcover. ($15.00 with dust jacket) $10.00

DICKINSON, Alice
First Book of Prehistoric Animals, 1954 Franklin Watts, hardcover, illustrated by Helene Carter. ($15.00 with dust jacket) $10.00

DICKINSON, Peter, see Series section, CHANGES
Dancing Bear, 1973 Little, Brown, illustrated by John Smee, first American edition. ($30.00 with dust jacket) $15.00
Green Gene, 1973 Pantheon, first American edition, hardcover. ($20.00 with dust jacket) $10.00
Lizard in the Cup, 1972 Harper, first American edition, hardcover. ($25.00 with dust jacket) $10.00
Poison Oracle, 1974 Pantheon, first American edition, hardcover. ($25.00 with dust jacket) $10.00

DICKSON, Marguerite
Bennett High, 1953 Longmans, first edition, hardcover. ($80.00 with dust jacket) $20.00

DIETZ, Lew, see Series section, JEFF WHITE

DIETZEL, Paul
Go, Shorty, Go, 1965 Bobbs-Merrill, first edition, hardcover. ($15.00 with dust jacket) $10.00

DILLMAN, Mary Alma
Wee Folk; "About the Elves in Nova Scotia," 1953 University of New Brunswick Press, first edition, hardcover, 67 pages, illlustrated by Gordon MacLelland and Karl Cameron. ($20.00 with dust jacket) $10.00

DILLON, Eilis
Family of Foxes, 1964 Funk & Wagnalls, first edition, hardcover, 118 pages, b/w illustrations. ($20.00 with dust jacket) $10.00
Sea Wall, 1965 Farrar, first edition, hardcover, b/w illustrations by W. T. Mars. ($15.00 with dust jacket) $10.00

DINES, Glen
Bull Wagon: Strong Wheels for Rugged Men, 1963 Macmillan, hardcover, illustrations by author. ($30.00 with dust jacket) $15.00

Fabulous Flying Bicycle, 1960 Macmillan, illustrations by author. ($20.00 with dust jacket) $10.00
Gilly and the Whicharoo, 1968 Lothrop, hardcover, illustrations by author. ($25.00 with dust jacket) $15.00
Indian Pony, 1963 Macmillan, hardcover, illustrations by author. ($30.00 with dust jacket) $15.00
Mysterious Machine, 1957 Macmillan, hardcover, map endpapers, b/w illustrations by author. ($20.00 with dust jacket) $10.00
Overland Stage, 1961 Macmillan, hardcover, illustrations by author. ($30.00 with dust jacket) $15.00
Pitidoe, the Color Maker, 1959 Macmillan, oversize hardcover, color illustrations by author. ($20.00 with dust jacket) $10.00
Tiger in the Cherry Tree, 1958 Macmillan, first edition, hardcover, illustrations by author. ($50.00 with dust jacket) $20.00
Useful Dragon of Sam Ling Toy, 1958 Macmillan, oversize hardcover, color illustrations by author. ($40.00 with dust jacket) $20.00

DISKA, Pat
Andy Says Bonjour, 1954 Vanguard, oversize illustrated hardcover, red/b/w illustrations by Chris Jenkins. ($25.00 with dust jacket) $15.00

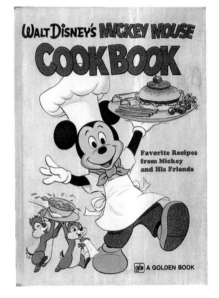

DISNEY, Walt, Studios
Walt Disney Thumper Annual, edited by R. H. Taylor, 1952 Odhams Press, oversize hardcover with gilt lettering, 93 pages, illustrated endpapers, color illustrations by studio throughout. ($75.00 with dust jacket) $30.00
Walt Disney's Mickey Mouse Cookbook, 1975 edition Golden Press, oversize hardcover, color endpapers, color illustrations throughout. $40.00

DIXON, Paige
Silver Wolf, 1973 Atheneum, first edition, hardcover, illustrated by Ann Brewster. ($15.00 with dust jacket) $10.00

DOANE, Pelagie
Book of Nature, 1952 Oxford University Press, first edition, oversize hardcover, color illustrations by author. ($35.00 with dust jacket) $20.00

DOBBS, Rose
Once-Upon-A-Time Story Book, 1958 Random House, first edition, hardcover, illustrated. $25.00

DOBLER, Lavina
Glass House at Jamestown, 1957 Dodd Mead, first edition, hardcover. ($15.00 with dust jacket) $10.00

DOBRIN, Arnold
Going To Moscow and Other Stories, 1973 Four Winds Press, first edition, hardcover, 47 pages, color illustrations by author. ($20.00 with dust jacket) $10.00
Taro and the Sea Turtles, 1966 Coward-McCann, first edition, oblong hardcover, illustrations by author. ($15.00 with dust jacket) $10.00

DOLBIER, Maurice
Lion in the Woods, 1955 Little, Brown, first edition, hardcover, illustrations by Robert Henneberger. ($40.00 with dust jacket) $20.00
Paul Bunyan, 1959 Random House, first edition, hardcover, illustrations by Leonard Fisher. ($25.00 with dust jacket) $15.00
Torten's Christmas Secret, 1951 Little, Brown, first edition, hardcover, color illustrations by Robert Henneberger. ($60.00 with dust jacket) $30.00

DOLCH, Edward W.
Old World Stories for Pleasure Reading, 1952 Garrard, first edition, hardcover, 166 pages, illustrations by Marguerite Dolch. ($20.00 with dust jacket) $10.00

DOMANSKA, Janina
Din Dan Don It's Christmas, 1975 Greenwillow, hardcover, illustrations by author. ($20.00 with dust jacket) $10.00
If All The Seas Were One Sea, 1971 Macmillan, hardcover, color illustrations by author. ($30.00 with dust jacket) $15.00
Marilka, 1970 Macmillan, first edition, hardcover, color illustrations by author. ($20.00 with dust jacket) $10.00
Palmiero and the Ogre, 1967 Macmillan, first edition, oblong hardcover, color illustrations by author. ($20.00 with dust jacket) $10.00
There Is a Turtle Flying, 1969 Macmillan, hardcover, illustrations by author. ($15.00 with dust jacket) $10.00
Tortoise and the Tree, 1978 Greenwillow, hardcover, illustrations by author. ($30.00 with dust jacket) $15.00
Turnip, 1969 Macmillan, first edition, oblong hardcover, color illustrations by author. ($20.00 with dust jacket) $10.00
What Do You See?, 1974 Macmillan, first edition, oversize hardcover, color illustrations by author. ($25.00 with dust jacket) $15.00

DONOVAN, John
Good Old James, 1975 Harper, first edition, small hardcover, b/w illustrations by James Stevenson. ($15.00 with dust jacket) $10.00
I'll Get There. It Better Be Worth the Trip, 1969 Harper, hardcover. ($15.00 with dust jacket) $10.00
Remove Protective Coating a Little at a Time, 1973 Harper, first edition, hardcover. ($25.00 with dust jacket) $15.00

DOUGLAS, William O.
Exploring the Himalaya, 1958 Random House, first edition, hardcover, illustrated with b/w photos and drawings. ($15.00 with dust jacket) $10.00

DOW, Edith
How to Make Doll Clothes: A Book for Daughters, Mothers, & Grandmothers, 1953 Coward-McCann, first edition, hardcover, illustrated by author. ($15.00 with dust jacket) $10.00

DOWNER, Marion
David and the Seagulls, 1956 Lothrop, Lee, first edition, hardcover, illustrations by photos. ($45.00 with dust jacket) $15.00

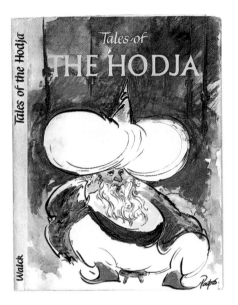

DOWNING, Charles
Tales of the Hodja, 1965 Walck, first American edition, hardcover, 98 pages, color illustrations throughout by William Papas. ($25.00 with dust jacket) $10.00

DRAGONWAGON, Crescent
Strawberry Dress Escape, 1975 Scribner, hardcover, illustrations by Lillian Hoban. ($15.00 with dust jacket) $10.00
When Light Turns into Night, 1975 Harper, first edition, oblong hardcover, color illustrations by Robert Andrew Parker. ($15.00 with dust jacket) $10.00

DRAGT, Tonke
Towers of February, (1973) 1975 Morrow, first American edition, hardcover, fantasy. ($15.00 with dust jacket) $10.00

DROWNE, Tatiana Balkoff
But Charlie Wasn't Listening, 1961 Heinemann, first edition, oblong pictorial hardcover, 30 pages, two-color illustrations by Helen Meredith. ($60.00 with dust jacket) $30.00

DuBOIS, Theodora
High King's Daughter, 1965 Ariel Books, first edition, hardcover. ($20.00 with dust jacket) $15.00

DuBOIS, William Pene, b. Nutley, N. J.
Alligator Case, 1965 Harper, oversize hardcover, 64 pages, color illustrations by author. ($20.00 with dust jacket) $10.00
Bears of Koala Park Present Bear Circus for Our Friends the Kangaroos, 1971 Viking, first edition, hardcover, illustrations by author. ($50.00 with dust jacket) $20.00

Call Me Bandicoot, 1970 Harper, hardcover, 64 pages, color illustrations by author. ($50.00 with dust jacket) $20.00
Forbidden Forest, 1968 Chatto & Windus, first edition, oversize hardcover, color illustrations by author. ($20.00 with dust jacket) $10.00
Giant, 1954 Viking, hardcover, 124 pages, b/w illustrations by author. First edition with dust jacket: $125.00. Later printings through 1966 ($50.00 with dust jacket) $20.00
Horse in the Camel Suit, 1967 Harper, first edition, square hardcover, 80 pages, color illustrations by author. ($50.00 with dust jacket) $20.00
Lion, 1956 Viking, first edition, oversize hardcover, illustrated endpapers, color illustrations by author. ($50.00 with dust jacket) $20.00
Mother Goose for Christmas, 1973 Viking, first edition, hardcover, 40 pages, illustrated endpapers, color illustrations by author. ($50.00 with dust jacket) $20.00
Peter Graves, 1950 Viking, first edition, oversize hardcover, illustrated endpapers, b/w illustrations by author. ($50.00 with dust jacket) $20.00
Porko von Popbutton, 1969 Harper, first edition, hardcover, 80 pages, illustrations by author. ($100.00 with dust jacket) $50.00
Squirrel Hotel, 1952 Viking, first edition, hardcover, illustrations by author. ($50.00 with dust jacket) $20.00

DUDDINGTON, Natalie, translator
Russian Folk Tales, 1969 Funk & Wagnalls, first edition, blue hardcover, 144 pages, illustrations by Dick Hart. ($25.00 with dust jacket) $15.00

DUDLEY, Nancy
Linda Goes to a TV Studio, 1957 Coward McCann, illustrated hardcover, b/w illustrations by Sofia. ($15.00 with dust jacket) $10.00
Linda Goes to the Hospital, 1953 Coward McCann, illustrated hardcover, b/w illustrations by Sofia. ($15.00 with dust jacket) $10.00

DUGGAN, Alfred
Leopards and Lilies, 1954 Waybright, first edition, 280 pages. ($20.00 with dust jacket) $10.00

DuJARDIN, Rosamund, see Series section, MARY RHODES; TOBY HEYDON; PAM AND PENNY

DUNCAN, Lois
Debutante Hill, 1958 Dodd, Mead, first edition, hardcover. ($20.00 with dust jacket) $10.00
I Know What You Did Last Summer, 1973 Little Brown, hardcover. ($25.00 with dust jacket) $10.00
Middle Sister, 1960 Dodd Mead, hardcover. ($25.00 with dust jacket) $10.00

Ransom, 1966 Doubleday, first edition, hardcover. ($20.00 with dust jacket) $10.00

DURRELL, Gerald
Donkey Rustlers, 1968 Collins, first edition, hardcover, 144 pages, b/w illustrations. ($25.00 with dust jacket) $15.00
Donkey Rustlers, 1968 Viking, first American edition, 158 pages, illustrations by Robin Jacques. ($25.00 with dust jacket) $10.00

DURYEA, Elizabeth
Long Christmas Eve, 1974 Houghton, small hardcover, color illustrations by Lisl Weil. ($20.00 with dust jacket) $10.00

DUVOISIN, Roger, see Series section, PETUNIA, VERONICA
A for the Ark, 1952 Lothrop, oversize hardcover, color illustrations by author. ($25.00 with dust jacket) $15.00
Crocodile in the Tree, 1972 Bodley Head, first edition, oversize hardcover, color illustrations by author. ($25.00 with dust jacket) $15.00
Donkey-Donkey, 1968 edition Parents, hardcover, illustrations by author. $15.00
Easter Treat, 1954 Knopf, oversize pictorial hardcover, yellow/b/w illustrations by author. $25.00
Happy Hunter, 1961 Lothrop, first edition, hardcover. ($25.00 with dust jacket) $15.00
House of Four Seasons, 1956 Lothrop, oversize pictorial hardcover, illustrated endpapers, color illustrations by author. ($30.00 with dust jacket) $15.00
Miller, His Son, and Their Donkey, Aesop, 1962 Whittlesey House, McGraw Hill, first edition, color illustrations by Duvoisin. ($25.00 with dust jacket) $15.00.
Missing Milkman, 1967 Knopf, pictorial hardcover, illustrations by author. $25.00
One Thousand Christmas Beards, 1955 Knopf, hardcover, illustrated endpapers, color illustrations by author. ($60.00 with dust jacket) $30.00
Two Lonely Ducks, 1955 Knopf, oblong hardcover, illustrated endpapers, two-color illustrations by author. $25.00

DYNES, Ivah Merwin
Merry Fiddle: Happy Memories of a Kansas Girlhood in the Nineties, 1959 Exposition Press, first edition, hardcover. ($15.00 with dust jacket) $10.00

E

EAGEN, William
Tall Boots and Yellow Legs, 1972 Carlton Press, limited edition, hardcover. ($30.00 with dust jacket) $15.00

EAGER, Edward, see Series section, HALF MAGIC
Magic or Not, 1959 Harcourt, first edition, hardcover, b/w illustrations by N. M. Bodecker. ($65.00 with dust jacket) $20.00
Mouse Manor, 1952 Ariel, first edition, hardcover, illustrated endpapers. b/w illustrations by Beryl Bailey-Jones. ($65.00 with dust jacket) $20.00
Well-Wishers (sequel to *Magic or Not*), 1960 Harcourt, hardcover, b/w illustrations by N. M. Bodecker. ($60.00 with dust jacket) $20.00

EARLE, Olive L.
Paws, Hoofs, and Flippers, 1954 Morrow, first edition, hardcover, illustrated by author. ($25.00 with dust jacket) $10.00

EARNSHAW, Brian
Dragonfall and the Space Cowboys, 1972 Methuen, first edition, small hardcover. ($20.00 with dust jacket) $10.00

EASTWICK, Ivy
O Deck the Stable, 1961 Mowbray & Co, first edition, hardcover, illustrated by Nora S. Unwin. ($45.00 with dust jacket) $20.00

EATON, Anne Thaxter
Welcome Christmas!, 1955 Viking Press, first edition, hardcover, illustrations by Valenti Angelo. ($35.00 with dust jacket) $15.00

EBERLE, Irmengarde
Evie and the Wonderful Kangaroo, 1955 Knopf, first edition, hardcover, illustrations by Louis Slobodkin. ($35.00 with dust jacket) $15.00

ECKERT, Allan W.
Crossbreed, 1968 Little, Brown, first edition, hardcover, illustrations by Karl E. Karalus. ($30.00 with dust jacket) $15.00
Incident at Hawk's Hill, 1971 Little, Brown, first edition, hardcover, 173 pages, illustrations by John Schoenherr. ($35.00 with dust jacket) $15.00

EDMONDS, Walter D.
Beaver Valley, 1971 Little, Brown, first edition, hardcover, illustrations by Lelsie Morrill. ($40.00 with dust jacket) $15.00
Story of Richard Storm, 1974 Little, Brown, oversize picture book hardcover, first edition, color illustrations by William Sauts Bock. ($20.00 with dust jacket) $10.00

EDMONDSON, Madeleine
Witch's Egg, 1974 Seabury, oversize hardcover, b/w illustrations by Kay Chorao. ($25.00 with dust jacket) $15.00

EDWARDS, Julie (Andrews)
Last of the Really Great Whangdoodles, 1974 Harper, first edition, hardcover. ($20.00 with dust jacket) $10.00
Mandy, 1971 Harper, first edition, square hardcover, b/w illustrations by Judith Gwyn Brown. ($30.00 with dust jacket) $15.00

EDWARDS, Monica
Cats of Punchbowl Farm, 1964 Garden City, first edition, hardcover, illustrations by photos. ($25.00 with dust jacket) $15.00

EGNER, Thorbjorn
Singing Town, 1959 Macmillan, first American edition, hardcover, 106 pages, illustrations by author. ($25.00 with dust jacket) $15.00

EHRLICH, Bettina
Cocolo's Home, 1950 Harper, oversize picture book hardcover, color and b/w illustrations by author. ($35.00 with dust jacket) $15.00
Dolls, 1963 Ariel Books, first edition, small, pictorial hardcover, illustrations by author. ($30.00 with dust jacket) $20.00
For the Leg of a Chicken, 1960 Watts, first American edition, oversize hardcover, color illustrations by author. ($50.00 with dust jacket) $20.00
Horse for the Island, 1952 Hamish Hamilton, London, first edition, hardcover, 213 pages, illustrations by author. ($20.00 with dust jacket) $10.00
Pantaloni, 1957 Harper, oversize picture book hardcover, color and b/w illustrations by author. ($40.00 with dust jacket) $15.00
Paolo and Panetto, 1960 Watts, first US edition, oversize hardcover, 32 pages, illustrations by author. ($75.00 with dust jacket) $30.00
Piccolo, 1954 Harper, miniature size book, color and b/w illustrations by author. $40.00
Trovato, 1959 Ariel, oversize picture book hardcover, color and b/w illustrations by author. $35.00

EICHENBERG, Fritz
Ape in a Cape, 1952 Harcourt, oversize alphabet hardcover, illustrated endpapers, color illustrations by author. ($25.00 with dust jacket) $15.00

ELDON, Magdalen
Bumble, 1950 Collins, first edition, hardcover, oversize, 46 pages, illustrations by author. ($50.00 with dust jacket) $20.00
Highland Bumble, 1952 Collins, first edition, oversize hardcover, color illustrations by author. ($45.00 with dust jacket) $20.00
Snow Bumble, 1952 Scribner, first American edition, illustrations by author. ($65.00 with dust jacket) $25.00

ELIOT, T.S.
Cultivation of Christmas Tree, 1956 edition Farrar, black hardcover, 5 double-page line drawings in gold and black, typography and decorations by Enrico Arno. $30.00

ELKIN, Benjamin
Gillespie and the Guards, 1956 Viking, first edition, two-color illustrations by James Daugherty. ($50.00 with dust jacket) $15.00
Loudest Noise in the World, 1954 Viking, two-color illustrations by James Daugherty. ($20.00 with dust jacket) $10.00
Six Foolish Fishermen, 1957 Watertower, first edition, laminated boards, oversize, illustrated by Katherine Evans. $15.00

ELLIOTT, Bruce
Magic as a Hobby, New Tricks for Amateur Performers, 1958 Gramercy Publishing, first edition, hardcover, illustrations by L. V. Lyons. ($25.00 with dust jacket) $15.00

ELLISON, Virginia
Pooh Get-Well Book – Recipes and Activities to Help You Recover from Wheezles and Sneezles, 1973 Dutton, first edition, hardcover, 82 pages, b/w illustrations. ($50.00 with dust jacket) $25.00
Pooh Cook Book, 1969 Dutton, first edition, oversize, yellow decorated hardcover, Shepard illustrations. ($35.00 with dust jacket) $15.00
Pooh Party Book, 1971 Dutton, first edition, hardcover. ($35.00 with dust jacket) $15.00

ELMS, F. Raymond
Let's Take a Trip, Stories and Pictures of the Marvels of Our Country, 1951 Whitman, first edition, hardcover. ($15.00 with dust jacket) $10.00

ELRICK, George S., see Series section, LASSIE
Major Matt Mason: Moon Mission, 1968 Whitman Big Little Book, book #22, full-color pictures. $12.00

ELTING, Mary
Answers and More Answers, 1961 Grosset, hardcover. $10.00
Hopi Way, 1969 M. Evans, first edition, hardcover, illustrations by Louise Mofsie. ($20.00 with dust jacket) $10.00
Machines at Work, 1953 Garden City, red and white hardcover, illustrated endpapers, illustrated by Laszlo Roth. $15.00
Lady the Little Blue Mare, 1950 Whitman Cozy Corner book, illustrated by Florence S. Winship. $10.00

Drummer Hoff, Barbara Emberley

EMBERLEY, Barbara
Drummer Hoff, 1968 Prentice-Hall, Caldecott Award, color illustrations by Ed Emberley. ($25.00 with dust jacket) $15.00

EMBERLEY, Ed
Klippity Klop, 1974 Little, Brown, first edition, hardcover, two-color illustrations by author. ($30.00 with dust jacket) $15.00
Punch & Judy, a Play for Puppets, 1965 Little Brown, first edition, hardcover, illustrations by author. ($20.00 with dust jacket) $10.00
Rosebud, 1966 Little Brown, first edition, oversize hardcover, 32 pages, illustrations by author. ($25.00 with dust jacket) $15.00

EMBLEM, Don and Betty
Palomino Boy, 1948 Viking, first edition, illustrations by Lynd Ward. ($20.00 with dust jacket) $10.00

EMERY, Anne
Sweet Sixteen, 1956 MacRae Smith, hardback. ($15.00 in dust jacket) $10.00

EMETT, Rowland
New World for Nellie, 1953 Harcourt, first edition, oversize hardcover, illustrated by author. ($35.00 with dust jacket) $15.00

EMMET, Betts
Adventures Here and There, 1950 American Book Company, green cloth hardcover. $10.00
Around Green Hills, 1958 American Book Company, hardcover with photo illustration, reader. $10.00

ENGDAHL, Sylvia
Journey Between Worlds, 1970 Atheneum, first edition, 236 pages, illustrations by James and Ruth McCrea. ($35.00 with dust jacket) $15.00

ENGEMAN, Jack
Airline Stewardess, a Picture Story, 1966 Lothrop, hardcover. $20.00

ENGLE, Paul
Golden Child, 1962 Dutton, first edition, hardcover, illustrations by Leonard Fisher. ($30.00 with dust jacket) $15.00

ENGVICK, Ed
Lullabies & Night Songs, 1969 Bodley Head, first edition, oversize hardcover, songs set to music by Alec Wilder and illustrated by Maurice Sendak. ($45.00 with dust jacket) $25.00

ENRIGHT, Elizabeth
Tatsinda, 1963 Harcourt, first edition, 80 pages, hardcover, illustrations by Irene Haas. ($35.00 with dust jacket) $20.00
Zeee, 1965 Harcourt, small hardcover, 46 pages, b/w and color illustrations by Irene Haas. ($25.00 with dust jacket) $15.00
Gone-Away Lake, 1957 Harcourt, first edition, hardcover, illustrations by Beth and Joe Krush. ($35.00 with dust jacket) $15.00
Return to Gone-Away, 1961 Harcourt, first edition, hardcover. ($25.00 with dust jacket) $10.00

ENRIGHT, W. J.
Sailor Jim's Cave, a Mystery of Buried Treasure in Florida, 1951 Dodd, Mead, first edition, hardcover, illustrations by author. ($20.00 with dust jacket) $10.00

EPP, Margaret
Prairie Princess, 1967 Moody Press, hardcover, illustrated by Robert Doares. $15.00
Princess and the Pelican, 1968 Moody Press, hardcover, illustrated by Robert Doares. $15.00

EPPENSTEIN, Louise
Sally Goes to the Circus Alone, 1953 Platt & Munk, square, illustrated red hardcover, 44 pages, pictorial endpapers, illustrations by Jean Staples. $20.00

ERWIN, Betty
Aggie, Maggie, and Tish, 1965 Little, Brown, first edition, hardcover. ($40.00 with dust jacket) $15.00
Behind the Magic Line, 1969 Little, Brown, first edition, hardcover, b/w illustrations. ($25.00 with dust jacket) $15.00
Go to the Room of the Eyes, 1969 Little, Brown, first edition, hardcover, b/w illustrations by Irene Burns. ($25.00 with dust jacket) $15.00
Summer Sleigh Ride, 1966 Little, Brown, first edition, hardcover. ($25.00 with dust jacket) $15.00
Where's Aggie?, 1967 Little, Brown, first edition, hardcover, b/w illustrations by Paul Kennedy. ($25.00 with dust jacket) $15.00
Who is Victoria?, 1973 Little, Brown, first edition, hardcover, b/w illustrations by Kathleen Anderson. ($20.00 with dust jacket) $10.00

ESCHMEYER, R. W.
Al Alligator, 1953 Fisherman Press, first edition, pictorial boards, 49 pages, illustrated endpapers, illustrated by Roy K. Wills. $10.00
Mac Mallard, 1953 Fisherman Press, first edition, pictorial boards, 49 pages, illustrated endpapers, illustrated by Francis W. Davis. $10.00
Tommy Trout, 1952 Fisherman Press, first edition, pictorial boards, 49 pages, illustrated endpapers, illustrated by Edwin Fulwider. $10.00
Willie Whitetail, 1953 Fisherman Press, first edition, pictorial boards, 49 pages, illustrated endpapers, illustrated by Roy K. Wills. $10.00

ESPY, Hilda Cole
Quiet, Yelled Mrs. Rabbit, 1958 J.B. Lippincott, hardback. $10.00

ESTES, Eleanor
Ginger Pye, 1951 Harcourt, first edition, 250 pages, b/w illustrations by author. ($20.00 with dust jacket) $10.00
Lollipop Princess, a Play for Paper Dolls in One Act, 1967 Harcourt, Brace & World, first edition, oblong pink hardcover, illustrations by author. ($100.00 with dust jacket) $50.00
Miranda the Great, 1967 Harcourt, first edition,

hardcover, b/w illustrations by Edward Ardizzone. ($30.00 with dust jacket) $15.00
Pinky Pye, 1958 Harcourt, first edition, hardcover, b/w illustrations by Edward Ardizzone. ($30.00 with dust jacket) $15.00
Witch Family, 1960 Harcourt, hardcover, b/w illustrations by Edward Ardizzone. ($30.00 with dust jacket) $15.00
Tunnel of Hugsy Goode, 1972 Harcourt, hardback, drawings by Edward Ardizzone. $25.00.

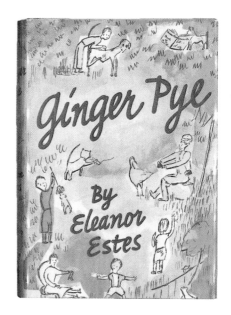

ESTRADA, Doris
Periwinkle Jones, 1965 Doubleday, first edition, hardcover, 94 pages, illustrations by JoAnn Stover. ($20.00 with dust jacket) $10.00

ETCHEMENDY, Teje
Tales of Old Russia, 1964 Rand McNally, first edition, hardcover, color and b/w illustrations. ($25.00 with dust jacket) $15.00

ETS, Marie Hall
Another Day, 1953 Viking, oblong hardcover, b/w illustrations by author. ($40.00 with dust jacket) $20.00
Beasts and Nonsense, 1952 Viking, first edition, illustrations by author. ($40.00 with dust jacket) $20.00
Cow's Party, 1958 Viking, first edition, oversize hardcover, 32 pages, illustrations by author. ($40.00 with dust jacket) $20.00
Elephant in a Well, 1972 Viking, oblong hardcover, b/w illustrations by author. ($40.00 with dust jacket) $20.00
Gilberto and the Wind, 1963 Viking, oversize hardcover, color illustrations by author. $20.00
Jay Bird, 1974 Viking, hardcover. ($25.00 in dust jacket) $15.00

Just Me, 1965 Viking, oblong hardcover, b/w illustrations by author. ($40.00 with dust jacket) $20.00

Mister Penny's Circus, 1961 Viking, first edition, hardcover, illustrations by author. ($40.00 with dust jacket) $20.00

Mister Penny's Race Horse, 1956 Viking, first edition, hardcover, illustrated endpapers, illustrations by author. ($35.00 with dust jacket) $15.00

Nine Days to Christmas, 1959 Viking, first edition, oversize hardcover, 1960 Caldecott Award book, color illustrations by Ets. ($100.00 with dust jacket) $40.00

Talking Without Words: (I Can, Can You?), 1968 Viking, oblong hardcover, b/w illustrations by author. ($45.00 with dust jacket) $15.00

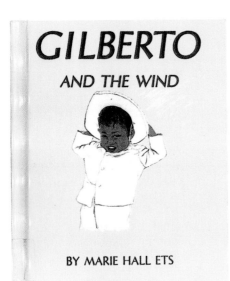

EVANS, Eva Knox
Snow Book, 1965 Little, Brown, first edition, hardcover, illustrations by Aldren Watson. ($20.00 with dust jacket) $15.00

EVANS, Katherine
Bundle of Sticks, 1967 Hale library edition, illustrations by author. ($15.00 with dust jacket) $10.00

Mice that Ate Iron, 1963 Albert Whitman, first edition, hardcover, color illustrations by author. ($30.00 with dust jacket) $15.00

Man, the Boy, and the Donkey, 1958 Albert Whitman, first edition, hardcover, color illustrations by author. ($30.00 with dust jacket) $15.00

One Good Deed Deserves Another, 1964 Doubleday, first edition, hardcover, illustrations by author. ($30.00 with dust jacket) $15.00

EVANS, Ruth
Jungle of Tonza Mara, 1963 Macmillan, first edition, oversize hardcover, 69 pages, color illustrations by Lawrence B. Smith. $25.00

EVARTS, Hal G.
Secret of the Himalayas, 1962 Scribner, illustrated hardcover. ($20.00 with same-as-cover dust jacket) $15.00

Smugglers' Road, 1968 Scribner, illustrated hardcover. ($20.00 with same-as-cover dust jacket) $15.00

Talking Mountain, 1966 Scribner, illustrated hardcover. ($20.00 with same-as-cover dust jacket) $15.00

Treasure River, 1964 Scribner, illustrated hardcover. ($20.00 with same-as-cover dust jacket) $15.00

EVATT, Harriet
Army in Pigtails, 1962 Bobbs-Merrill, first edition, hardcover, illustrations by author. ($30.00 with dust jacket) $15.00

Big Indian and Little Bear, 1955 Bobbs-Merrill, first edition, hardcover, illustrated endpapers, color and illustrations by author. ($40.00 with dust jacket) $20.00

Davy Crockett, Big Indian and Little Bear, 1955 Bobbs-Merrill, first edition, hardcover, illustrations by author. ($40.00 with dust jacket) $20.00

Mystery of the Alpine Castle, 1962 Bobbs-Merrill, first edition, hardcover, illustrations by author. ($30.00 with dust jacket) $15.00

Mystery of the Lonesome Manor, 1962 Bobbs-Merrill, first edition, hardcover, illustrations by David Stone. ($20.00 with dust jacket) $10.00

Papoose Who Wouldn't Keep Her Stockings On, 1954 Bobbs-Merrill, hardcover, color and b/w illustrations by author. ($40.00 with dust jacket) $20.00

Secret of the Old Coach Inn, 1959 Bobbs-Merrill, first edition, hardcover, illustrations by David Stone. ($15.00 with dust jacket) $10.00

Secret of the Singing Tower, 1953 Bobbs-Merrill, first edition hardcover. ($15.00 with dust jacket) $10.00

Secret of the Solitary Cove, 1964 Bobbs-Merrill, first edition, hardcover, illustrations by Paul Kennedy. ($25.00 with dust jacket) $15.00

Secret of the Whispering Willow, 1950 Bobbs-Merrill, hardcover. ($15.00 with dust jacket) $10.00

You Can't Keep a Squirrel on the Ground, 1961 Bobbs-Merrill, oversize hardcover, first edition, color and b/w illustrations by author. ($20.00 with dust jacket) $15.00

EVERNDEN, Margery
Knight of Florence, 1950 Random House, first edition, hardcover, illustrations by Rafaello Busoni. ($20.00 with dust jacket) $15.00

EVERS, Helen and Alf
Baby Bunny, 1951 Wonder Books, small hardcover, illustrations by author. $10.00

Bobby's Happy Days, 1953 Rand McNally, first edition, hardcover, illustrations by Marjorie Cooper. ($20.00 with dust jacket) $10.00

Chatterduck, 1956 Checkerboard Press, Elf Book, first edition, hardcover, color illustrations by authors. $20.00

Copy-Kitten, 1957 Rand McNally, illustrated hardcover, color illustrations by authors. $10.00

Crosspatch, 1954 Rand McNally, illustrated hardcover, color illustrations by authors. $10.00

Plump Pig, 1956 Rand McNally Elf Book, illustrated hardcover, color illustrations by authors. $15.00

EYRE, Katherine Wigmore

Children of the Light, 1967 Lippincott, first edition, hardcover, illustrated by Artur Marokvia. ($25.00 with dust jacket) $15.00

Chinese Box, 1959 Appleton, first edition, hardcover. ($25.00 with dust jacket) $15.00

Monks' Court, 1966 Appleton, first edition, hardcover. ($15.00 with dust jacket) $10.00

Sandlewood Fan, 1968 Meredith, first edition, hardcover. ($15.00 with dust jacket) $10.00

F

FAHY, Julian

Ants to Zebra, Animal Verses for Children, 1953 Exposition Press, first edition, small hardcover, oblong, 93 pages, brown/white illustrations by Eleanor Reindollar. ($20.00 with dust jacket) $15.00

FAIRMAN, Paul W.

Forgetful Robot, 1968 Holt, first edition, hardcover. ($20.00 with dust jacket) $10.00

FAIRWEATHER, Jessie Home

Happiest Christmas, 1955 edition Whitman Top Tales, pictorial cover, illustrated by Irma Wilde. $10.00

FALKNER, Frederick

Aqualung Twins and the 'Iron Crab,' 1959 Dent & Sons Ltd., first edition, hardcover, illustrated by Frank Grey. ($30.00 with dust jacket) $15.00

FALL, Thomas

Canalboat to Freedom. 1969 Dial, hardcover. ($30.00 with dust jacket) $15.00

Goat Boy of Brooklyn, 1968 Dial Press, first edition, hardcover, 192 pages, b/w illustrations by Fermin Rocker. ($25.00 with dust jacket) $10.00

FANNIN, Cole

Leave It to Beaver, 1962 Whitman, small, color illustrated boards. $20.00

Lucy and the Madcap Mystery, 1963 Whitman, hardcover, small, color illustrated boards. $30.00

Real McCoys and the Danger at the Ranch, 1961 Whitman, hardcover. $20.00

FARALLA, Dana

Swanhilda-of-the-Swans, 1964 Blackie, London, hardcover, illustrated by Edward Ardizzone. ($30.00 with dust jacket) $15.00

Swanhilda-of-the-Swans, 1964 Lippincott, hardcover, illustrated by Harold Berson. ($30.00 with dust jacket) $20.00

Wonderful Flying-Go-Round, 1965 World, first edition, hardcover, illustrated by Harold Berson. ($40.00 with dust jacket) $20.00

FARBER, Norma

As I Was Crossing Boston Common, 1975 Dutton, first edition, wide hardcover, illustrated by Arnold Lobel. ($25.00 with dust jacket) $15.00

I Found Them in the Yellow Pages, 1973 Atlantic Monthly/Little, Brown, first edition, yellow hardcover, illustrated endpapers, illustrated by Marc Brown. ($25.00 with dust jacket) $15.00

This is the Ambulance Leaving the Zoo, 1975 Dutton, oblong pictorial hardcover, yellow/b/w illustrations by Tomie dePaola. $20.00

FARJEON, Eleanor

Children's Bells, 1960 Walck, first American edition, green hardcover, 212 pages, illustrated by Peggy Fortman. ($25.00 with dust jacket) $10.00

Grannie Gray, 1956 edition Oxford, hardcover, illustrated by Peggy Fortnum. $10.00

Little Bookroom: Eleanor Farjeon's Short Stories for Children Chosen by Herself, 1956 Oxford, illustrated by Edward Ardizzone. ($60.00 with dust jacket) $25.00

Mrs. Malone, 1962 Walck, first edition, hardcover, illustrated by Edward Ardizzone. ($50.00 with dust jacket) $20.00

Nursery in the Nineties, 1960 Oxford, first edition, hardcover, illustrated by photographs. Autobiographical material. ($35.00 with dust jacket) $20.00

FARLEY, Walter, see Series section, BLACK STALLION

FARLIE, Barbara L. and **CLARKE, Charlotte**
All About Doll Houses, 1975 Bobbs-Merrill, first edition, hardcover, 240 pages, photographs by O. Maya, illustrated by J. Ibarren. ($20.00 with dust jacket) $10.00

FARMER, Penelope
Castle of Bone, 1972 Atheneum, first edition, hardcover, 152 pages. ($50.00 with dust jacket) $15.00

FARWELL, G.
Riders to an Unknown Sea, 1963 Melbourne, first edition, hardcover, end-paper maps, illustrated by Frank Beck. ($30.00 with dust jacket) $15.00

FATIO, Louise, see Series section, HAPPY LION
Christmas Forest, 1950 Aladdin Books, hardcover, 24 pages, illustrations by Roger Duvoisin. $25.00

FAULKNER, Nancy
Rebel Drums, 1952 Doubleday, hardcover, 218 pages. $15.00
Secret of the Simple Code, 1965 Doubleday, hardcover, 205 pages. ($20.00 with dust jacket) $10.00
Side Saddle For Dandy, 1954 Doubleday, first edition, hardcover, illustrated by Marguerite de Angeli. ($25.00 with dust jacket) $15.00
Traitor Queen, 1963 Doubleday, hardcover. ($20.00 with dust jacket) $10.00
West Is On Your Left Hand, 1953 Doubleday, first edition, green hardcover. ($15.00 with dust jacket) $10.00

FAULKNER, William
Wishing Tree, 1964 Random House, first edition, hardcover, illustrated by Don Bolognese. ($50.00 with dust jacket) $20.00
Wishing Tree, Random House, first edition, hardcover, limited edition of 500, in slipcase. $200.00

FAY, Leo C. and **CLIFFORD, E.**
Blue Dog and Other Stories, 1966 Lyons and Carnahan, first grade reader, hardcover with illustrated boards, illustrated by Carol Burger, ex-school copy. $15.00

FECHER, Constance
Link Boys, 1971 Farrar, Straus & Giroux, first edition, hardcover, drawings by Richard Cuffari. ($15.00 with dust jacket) $10.00

FEELINGS, Muriel and **Tom**
Jambo Means Hello, 1974 Dial, hardcover, color illustrations by Tom Feelings. ($30.00 with dust jacket) $20.00

FEIL, Hila
Ghost Garden, 1975 Atheneum, hardcover, b/w illustrations by Thomas Quirk. ($20.00 with dust jacket) $10.00

FELTON, Harold
Fire-Fightin' Mose, Being an Account of the Life and Times of the World's Greatest Fire Fighter, 1955 Knopf, first edition, hardcover, illustrated by Aldren A. Watson. ($30.00 with dust jacket) $15.00
John Henry and His Hammer, 1964 Knopf, hardcover, 82 pages, sheet music included. $20.00
Mike Fink, Best of the Keel-Boatmen, 1960 Dodd-Mead, first edition, hardcover. ($20.00 with dust jacket) $10.00

FENNER, Phyllis
Circus Parade: Stories of the Big Top, 1954 Knopf, first edition, hardcover, illustrated by Lee Ames. ($20.00 with dust jacket) $10.00
Fools and Funny Fellows, 1969 Knopf, hardcover, 192 pages. $15.00
Giggle Box, 1953 Knopf, hardcover. ($35.00 with dust jacket) $15.00

FENTON, Edward
Duffy's Rocks, 1974 Dutton, hardcover. ($20.00 with dust jacket) $15.00
Island for a Pelican, 1963 Doubleday, first edition, hardcover, 60 pages, sepia illustrated by Dimitris Davis. ($25.00 with dust jacket) $15.00
Matter of Miracles, 1967 Holt, hardcover, 239 pages. $15.00
Penny Candy, 1970 Holt, first edition, oblong hardcover, illustrated by Edward Gorey. ($60.00 with dust jacket) $20.00

Riddle of the Red Whale, 1966 Doubleday, first edition, hardcover. ($25.00 with dust jacket) $10.00

FERGUSON, Charles W.
Abecedarian Book, 1964 Little, Brown, first edition, hardcover, 131 pages, illustrated by John Alcorn. ($20.00 with dust jacket) $10.00

FIELD, Rachel
Rachel Field Story Book, 1958 Doubleday, first edition, collection of short stories. $25.00

FIFE, Dale
Boy Who Lived in the Railroad Depot, 1968 Coward-McCann, first edition, hardcover, illustrated by Ingrid Fetz. ($15.00 with dust jacket) $10.00

FINCH, Christopher
Art of Walt Disney: From Mickey Mouse to the Magic Kingdoms, 1973 Harry B. Abrams, first edition, oversize hardcover, color throughout. In original mailing box, with dust jacket, $200.00

FINE, Warren
Mousechildren and the Famous Collector, 1970 Harper and Row, first edition, oversize hardcover, 57 pages, illustrated by Mercer Mayer. ($25.00 with dust jacket) $15.00

FINNEGAN, Elizabeth
Secret of the Stone Griffins, 1962 Bobbs Merrill, first edition, hardcover, 188 pages, illustrated by Reisie Lonette. ($15.00 with dust jacket) $10.00

FINNEY, Gertrude E.
Sleeping Mines, 1951 Longmans, first edition, hardcover. ($20.00 with dust jacket) $10.00

FISCHER, Hans
Birthday, 1954 Harcourt, Brace, oversize oblong pictorial boards, illustrations in color by Hans Fischer. ($30.00 with dust jacket) $15.00
Pitschi, 1953 Harcourt Brace, illustrated oblong hardcover, illustrated by author. ($150.00 with dust jacket) $30.00
Rum-Pum-Pum, 1951 Zurich, oversize pictorial boards, 14 pages, illustrated by author. $45.00

FISHBACK, Margaret
Child's Book of Natural History, 1969 Platt & Munk, first edition, hardcover, illustrated by Hilary Knight. ($40.00 with dust jacket) $20.00

FISHER, Aileen
Cricket In A Thicket, 1963 Scribner, hardcover, illustrations by Feodor Rojankovsky. ($30.00 with dust jacket) $15.00
Feathered Ones and Furry, 1961 Crowell, first edition, square hardcover, 39 pages, illustrated by

Eric Carle. ($20.00 with dust jacket) $10.00
Listen, Rabbit, 1964 Crowell, hardcover, illustrations by Symeon Shimin. $15.00
We Went Looking, 1968 Crowell, first edition, hardcover, illustrated by Marie Angel. ($35.00 with dust jacket) $15.00

FISHER, Dorothy Canfield
Fair World for All, 1952 Whittlesey House, United Nations book for children, hardcover, illustrated by Jeanne Bendick. ($20.00 with dust jacket) $10.00

FISHER, John
John Fisher's Magic Book, 1971 Prentice-Hall, first edition, hardcover, illustrated by T. dePaola. ($15.00 with dust jacket) $10.00

FISHER, Laura
Never Try Nathaniel, 1968 Holt, first edition, pictorial boards. $10.00

FISHER, Leonard
Across the Sea from Galway, 1975 Four Winds Press, first edition, hardcover, 103 pages, b/w illustrations by author. ($25.00 with dust jacket) $15.00

FISHER, Leonard Everett
Death of Evening Star, 1972 Doubleday, hardcover with silver lettering on spine, illustrated by author. ($20.00 with dust jacket) $10.00

FISHER, Margery
Open the Doors, 1967 World, first American edition, hardcover, illustrated by Edward Ardizzone. ($25.00 with dust jacket) $15.00
Who's Who in Children's Books: A Treasury of the Familiar Characters of Childhood, 1975 Holt Rinehart & Winston, first edition, hardcover, 399 pages, b/w and color illustrations. ($50.00 with dust jacket) $20.00

FITZGERALD, John, see Series section, GREAT BRAIN

FITZHUGH, Louise
Harriet the Spy, 1964 Harper, illustrated hardcover, 298 pages, b/w illustrations by author. ($20.00 with dust jacket) $10.00
Long Secret, 1965 Harper, first edition, hardcover. ($20.00 with dust jacket) $10.00
Nobody's Family is Going to Change, 1974 Farrar, Straus and Giroux, hardcover. ($20.00 with dust jacket) $10.00

FIX, Betty
Adventures of Idabell and Wakefield, 1946 Crosby House, Vol. 4 of Dolls Around the World, oversize, hardcover, illustrated endpapers, 50 pages, 16 full-page color illustrations. ($45.00 with dust jacket) $20.00

FLACK, Marjorie
Walter the Lazy Mouse, 1963 Doubleday, first edition, oversize hardcover, illustrated by Cyndy Szekeres. ($65.00 with dust jacket) $30.00

FLANNERY, Elizabeth
Foaling Barn, 1951 Barnes, first edition, oblong oversize hardcover. ($20.00 with dust jacket) $10.00

FLEISCHMAN, Sid, see Series sections, McBROOM
By the Great Horn Spoon!, 1963 Little, Brown, hardcover, illustrated by Eric von Schmidt. ($20.00 with dust jacket) $10.00
Chancy and the Grand Rascal, 1966 Little, Brown, first edition, hardcover, b/w illustrations by Eric von Schmidt. ($15.00 with dust jacket) $10.00
Ghost in the Noonday Sun, 1965 Little, Brown, hardcover, illustrated by Warren Chappell. ($20.00 with dust jacket) $10.00
Mr. Mysterious and Company, 1962 Little, Brown, hardcover, illustrated by Eric von Schmidt. ($20.00 with dust jacket) $10.00

FLEISHMAN, Seymour
Four Cheers for Camping, 1963 Albert Whitman, square oversize hardcover, color and b/w illustrations by author. ($30.00 with dust jacket) $15.00

FLEMING, Ian
Chitty Chitty Bang Bang the Magical Car, 1964 edition Jonathan Cape, London, first edition thus, hardcover, 46 pages, illustrated by John Burningham. ($60.00 with dust jacket) $30.00

FLETCHER, Helen Jill
Crayon, Chalk, Charcoal,, 1959 Stuttman, first edition, hardcover, illustrated by author. ($15.00 with dust jacket) $10.00
See and Do Book of Dolls and Doll Houses, 1959 Stuttman, first edition, hardcover, illustrated. ($20.00 with dust jacket) $10.00

FLETCHER, Sydney
Big Book of Indians, 1950 Grosset, first edition, oversize hardcover, color illustrations. $20.00

FLOETHE, Richard and **Louise**
Houses around the World, 1973 Scribners, first edition, hardcover, illustrated by authors. ($15.00 with dust jacket) $10.00

FLORA, James
Day the Cow Sneezed, 1957 Harcourt, hardcover, oversize, illustrations by author. $15.00
Fabulous Firework Family, 1955 Harcourt, first edition, hardcover, illustrated by author. ($25.00 with dust jacket) $15.00
Fishing With Dad, 1967 Harcourt, Brace, first edition, hardcover, illustrated by author. ($20.00 with dust jacket) $10.00
Leopold: the See-Through Crumbpicker, 1961 Harcourt, first edition, hardcover, illustrated by author. ($25.00 with dust jacket) $15.00

FLORY, Jane
Mr. Snitzel's Cookies, 1950 Rand McNally, small, pictorial boards, Junior Elf Book. $12.00

FOLSOM, Franklin (also wrote as Troy Nesbit or Benjamin Brewster)
Mystery at Rustlers' Fort, 1960 Harvey House, hardcover. $10.00

FONTANE, Theodore
Sir Ribbeck, 1969 Macmillan, first edition, hardcover, 32 pages, woodcut color illustrations by Nonny Hogrogian. ($40.00 with dust jacket) $20.00

FORD, Lauren
Lauren Ford's Christmas Book, 1963 Dodd, Mead, first edition, hardcover, illustrated by author. ($25.00 with dust jacket) $15.00

FOREMAN, Michael
War and Peas, 1974 Crowell, first edition, oversize hardcover, illustrated by author. ($25.00 with dust jacket) $15.00
Moose, 1972 Pantheon, first edition, yellow oversize hardcover. ($30.00 with dust jacket) $15.00

FOREST, Antonia, see Series section MARLOWS
Players' Boy, 1970 Faber, first edition, hardcover. ($50.00 with dust jacket) $25.00
Players and Rebels, 1971 Faber, first edition, hardcover. First edition with dust jacket: $50.00. Later editions: ($20.00 with dust jacket) $15.00

FORMAN, James
Cow Neck Rebels, 1969 Farrar, first edition, hardcover. $15.00

FORST, S. (Charlotte Peek).
Pipkin, 1970 Delacorte, first edition, hardcover, purple boards, gilt print spine, illlustrated by Robin Jacques. ($20.00 in dust jacket) $10.00

FOSTER, J.
Pete's Puddle, 1950 Houghton, first edition, hardcover, color illustrations by author. ($30.00 with dust jacket) $15.00

FOSTER, John T., see Series section MARCO
Gallant Gray Trotter, 1974 Dodd Mead, first edition, hardcover, 248 pages, illustrated by Sam Savitt. ($20.00 with dust jacket) $10.00

FOWLES, John
Cinderella, 1974 Little, Brown, first American edition, hardcover, illustrated by Sheilah Beckett. ($25.00 with dust jacket) $15.00

FOX, Mary Virginia
Ambush at Fort Dearborn, 1962 St. Martin's Press, first edition, small orange hardcover, illustrated by Lorence Bjorklund. ($20.00 with dust jacket) $10.00

FOX, Paula
Good Ethan, 1973 Bradbury Press, first edition, hardcover, illustrated by Arnold Lobel. ($50.00 with dust jacket) $20.00
Likely Place, 1967 Macmillan, first edition, hardcover, small, illustrated by Edward Ardizzone. ($40.00 with dust jacket) $15.00
Stone-Faced Boy, 1968 Bradbury Press, first edition, hardcover, illustrated by Donald Mackay. ($45.00 with dust jacket) $20.00

FRAME, Janet
Mona Minim and the Smell of the Sun, 1969 George Braziller, first edition, oversize hardcover, 94 pages, illustrated by Robin Jacques. ($25.00 with dust jacket) $15.00

FRANCES, Miss, see Series section DING DONG

FRANCHERE, Ruth
Willa, the Story of Willa Cather's Growing Up, 1958 Crowell, hardcover, illustrations by Leonard Weisgard. ($25.00 with dust jacket) $10.00

FRANCIS, Connie
For Every Young Heart, 1962 Prentice Hall, hardcover. ($25.00 in dust jacket) $10.00

FRANCIS, Sally
Goat that Went to School 1952 Rand McNally, hardcover. $10.00

FRANK, Janet
Daddies, 1953 Simon & Schuster, pictorial hardcover, illustrations by Tibor Gergely. $15.00

FRANKENBERG, Lloyd
*Poems of William Shakespeare,*1966 Crowell, first edition, hardcover, illustrated by Nonny Hogrogian. ($25.00 with dust jacket) $10.00

FRANKLIN, George Cory
Shorty's Mule, 1952 Houghton, Mifflin, first edition, pictorial hardcover, 47 pages, illustrations by William Moyers. ($15.00 with dust jacket) $10.00
Wild Animals of the Southwest, 1950 Houghton Mifflin, illustrated by L. D. Cram. ($15.00 with dust jacket) $10.00

FRANZEN, Nils-Olof
Agaton Sax and the Scotland Yard Mystery, 1969 Andre Deutsch, London, first edition, hardcover, 128 pages, illustrated by Quentin Blake. ($20.00 with dust jacket) $10.00
Agaton Sax and the Diamond Thieves, 1967 Delacorte, first edition, hardcover. ($15.00 with dust jacket) $10.00

FRASCONI, Antoni
House That Jack Built, 1958 Harcourt, Brace, first edition, oversize hardcover, text in French and English, illustrated by author. ($40.00 with dust jacket) $20.00
See and Say/ Guada e Parla/ Regarde et Parle/ Mira y Habla. A Picture Book in Four Languages, 1955 Harcourt Brace, hardcover, woodcuts by Antoni Frasconi. ($45.00 with dust jacket) $20.00

FRASER, Antonia
*History of Toys,*1966 Weidenfeld & Nicholson, oversize first edition, hardcover, illustrated. ($60.00 with dust jacket) $30.00

FRASER, Beatrice and **Ferrin**
Arturo and Mr. Bang, 1963 Bobbs-Merrill, first edition, hardcover, illustrated. ($45.00 with dust jacket) $20.00.

FRAZEE, Steve
Bonanza: Killer Lion, 1966 Whitman, illustrated hardcover, 212 pages. $10.00
Lassie, Trouble at Panter's Lake, 1972 Whitman, hardcover, full-color cover by Al Andersen, b/w illustrations by Adam Szwejkowski. $10.00
Lassie Lost in the Snow, 1969 Whitman, illustrated hardcover, illustrations by Larry Harris. $10.00

FREEDLEY, George
Mr. Cat, 1960 Howard Frisch, hardcover, illustrated by

Victor J. Dowling. ($25.00 with dust jacket) $15.00

More Mr. Cat and a Bit of Amber Too, 1962 Howard Frisch, first edition, hardcover, illustrated by Victor J. Dowling. ($35.00 with dust jacket) $20.00

FREELING, Anne
Ranjit of the Circus Ring, 1959 Roy Publishers, first edition, hardcover, 208 pages, illustrated by Paul Marriott. ($15.00 with dust jacket) $10.00

FREEMAN, Barbara
Broom-Adelaide, 1965 Little Brown, hardcover. $15.00

Forgotten Theatre, 1967 Faber and Faber, London, first edition, hardcover. ($40.00 with dust jacket) $20.00

Name on the Glass, 1964 Faber and Faber, first edition, hardcover, illustrated by Barbara Freeman. ($45.00 with dust jacket) $20.00

FREEMAN, Don
Corduroy, 1968 Viking, first edition, hardcover, color illustrations by author. ($30.00 with dust jacket) $15.00. Later illustrated hardcover editions: $15.00

Dandelion, 1964 Viking, first edition, hardcover, two-color illustrations by author. ($30.00 with dust jacket) $15.00

Guard Mouse, 1967 Viking, first edition, oversize hardcover, pictorial paper covered boards, illustrated by author. ($50.00 with dust jacket) $30.00

Hattie the Backstage Bat, 1970 Viking, first edition, hardcover, illustrated by Don Freeman. ($50.00 with dust jacket) $20.00

Norman the Doorman, 1959 Viking, oversize hardcover, 64 pages, color endpapers, full-page or double-page color illustrations on every page. ($50.00 with dust jacket) $20.00

Turtle and the Dove, 1964 Viking Press, first edition, hardcover. ($20.00 with dust jacket) $10.00

Will's Quill, 1975 Viking, first edition, oversize hardcover, illustrated by author. ($30.00 with dust jacket) $20.00

FRENCH, Fiona
King Tree, 1973 Oxford University Press, first edition, pictorial oversize hardcover, illustrated by author. ($35.00 with dust jacket) $15.00

FRESCHET, Berniece
Kazue Jumping Mouse, 1970 Crowell Publishing, first edition, hardcover, b/w illustrations by K. Mizumura. ($15.00 with dust jacket) $10.00

Year on Muskrat Marsh, 1974 Charles Scribner, first edition, oblong tan decorated hardcover, 56 pages, b/w drawings by Peter Parnell. ($15.00 with dust jacket) $10.00

FRIEDMAN, Frieda
Carol From the Country, 1971 William Morrow, hardcover, 191 pages. ($15.00 with dust jacket) $10.00

Ellen and the Gang, 1963 Morrow, first edition, hardcover, illustrated by Jacqueline Tomes. ($20.00 with dust jacket) $10.00

FRIEDRICH, Otto and Priscilla
Easter Bunny that Overslept, 1957 Lothrop, Lee, first edition, hardcover, illustrated by Adrienne Adams. ($50.00 with dust jacket) $20.00

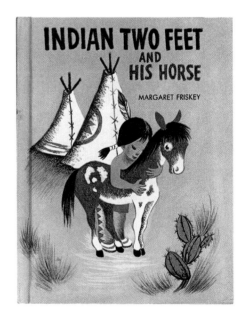

FRISKEY, Margaret
Indian Two Feet and His Horse, (1959) 1970 edition Childrens Press, illustrated hardcover, color illustrations by Katherine Evans. $20.00

True Book of Birds We Know, 1954 Childrens Press, first edition, hardcover, color illustrations by Anna Pistorius. ($15.00 with dust jacket) $10.00

FRITZ, Jean
Then What Happened, Paul Revere?, 1973 Coward

McCann, red hardcover, 45 pages, illustrations by Margot Tomes. ($20.00 with dust jacket) $10.00

FROST, Frances
Rocket Away, 1953 McGraw-Hill, first edition, hardcover, illustrated by Paul Galdone. ($45.00 with dust jacket) $20.00

FROST, Lesley
Really Not Really, Devon Adair, first edition, hardcover illustrated by Barbara Remington. ($25.00 with dust jacket) $10.00

FRY, Christopher
Boat that Mooed, 1965 Macmillan, first edition, oversize hardcover, 27 pages, illustrated by Leonard Weisgard. ($20.00 with dust jacket) $15.00

FRY, Rosalie
Castle Family, 1966 Dutton, first edition, hardcover, illustrated by Margery Gill. ($25.00 with dust jacket) $15.00
Snowed Up, 1970 Farrar, Straus, & Giroux, first edition, hardcover, illustrated by Robin Jacques. ($20.00 with dust jacket) $10.00

FUJIKAWA, Gyo
Mother Goose Nursery Rhymes, 1969 Collins, first edition UK, illustrated by author. ($15.00 with dust jacket) $10.00

G

GAG, Flavia
Four Legs and a Tail, 1952 Henry Holt, first edition, hardcover, illustrations by the author. $15.00

GAGE, Joseph H.
Beckoning Hills; a Story of the Italians of California, 1951 Winston, first edition, hardcover. ($20.00 with dust jacket) $10.00

GAGE, Wilson
Bib Blue Island, 1964 World, first edition, hardcover, illustrated by Glen Rounds. ($15.00 with dust jacket) $10.00
Dan and the Miranda, 1962 World Publishing, hardcover, illustrations by Glen Rounds. $15.00
Ghost of Five Owl Farm, 1966 Collins, hardback. $10.00
Secret of Crossbone Hill, 1959 World, first edition, hardcover. ($20.00 with dust jacket) $10.00
Wild Goose Tale, 1961 World, first edition, blue hardcover,112 pages, illustrated by Glen Rounds. ($20.00 with dust jacket) $10.00

GALDONE, Paul
Frog Prince, 1975 McGraw Hill, pictorial hardcover, illustrated by Galdone. $10.00
History of Mother Twaddle and the Marvelous Achievements of Her Son Jack, 1974 Seabury Press, first edition, hardcover, illustrated by Paul Galdone. ($35.00 with dust jacket) $20.00
House that Jack Built, 1961 McGraw Hill, hardcover, illustrated by Galdone. ($15.00 with dust jacket) $10.00
Little Red Hen, 1973 Houghton Mifflin, green hardcover, 37 pages, illustrated in color. $15.00
Little Red Riding Hood, 1974 McGraw Hill, hardcover, illustrated by Galdone. ($15.00 with dust jacket) $10.00
Monkey and the Crocodile, 1969 Seabury, oversize hardcover, illustrated by Galdone. $15.00

GALLANT, Roy A.
Exploring Mars, 1956 Garden City, first edition, oversize hardcover, 62 pages, color illustrations and diagrams. ($25.00 with dust jacket) $10.00

GALLICO, Paul
Boy Who Invented the Bubble Gun, 1974 Delacorte Press, hardcover. ($15.00 with dust jacket) $10.00
Day Jean-Pierre Joined the Circus, 1970 Franklin Watts, hardcover, color and b/w illustrations by Gioia Fiammenghi. ($20.00 with dust jacket) $15.00
Day Jean-Pierre was Pignapped, 1964 Heinemann, first edition, hardcover, illustrated by Edmund Dulac. ($50.00 with dust jacket) $20.00
Day The Guinea-Pig Talked, 1963 Heinemann, London, first edition, hardcover. ($25.00 with dust jacket) $15.00
Ludmilla. A Legend of Liechtenstein, 1959 Doubleday, first edition, small hardcover, color illustrations by Reisie Lonette. ($20.00 with dust jacket) $10.00
Manxmouse, The Mouse Who Knew No Fear, 1968 Coward-McCann, first edition, hardcover, b/w illustrations by Grahame-Johnstones. ($30.00 with dust jacket) $15.00
Snowflake, 1953 Doubleday, first edition, hardcover. ($20.00 with dust jacket) $10.00
Thomasina, The Cat Who Thought She Was God, 1957 Doubleday, first edition, hardcover. ($25.00 with dust jacket) $10.00

GALLIENNE, Eva
Seven Tales by H. C. Andersen, 1959 Harper & Row, first American edition, blue boards, gold edge design and title letters, illustrations by Maurice Sendak. ($100.00 with dust jacket) $30.00. Later editions: ($20.00 with dust jacket) $15.00

GANNETT, Ruth, see Series section DRAGON
Katie and the Sad Noise, 1961 Random House, first edition, hardcover, illustrated by Ellie Simmons. ($65.00 with dust jacket) $20.00

GARBER, Nancy
Amy's Long Night, 1970 Whitman Tell-A-Tale, hardcover, illustrated by Lynn Wheeling. $10.00

GARBER, Nellia Burman
Sparky, a True Monkey Tale, 1954 Review and Herald, hardcover with pictorial cover, illustrated by Arlo Greer. $25.00

GARBUTT, Bernard
Up Goes the Big Top, 1966 Golden Gate Jr. Books, hardcover picture book. ($20.00 with dust jacket) $10.00

GARD, Joyce
Talargain, 1964 Holt, hardcover. ($25.00 with dust jacket) $10.00

GARD, Robert E.
Devil Red, 1963 Duell, Sloan and Pearce, first edition, hardcover. ($15.00 with dust jacket) $10.00

GARDNER, John
Dragon, Dragon and Other Tales, 1975 Knopf, first edition, hardcover, 73 pages. ($40.00 with dust jacket) $20.00
Gudgekin the Thistle Girl & Other Tales, 1976 Alfred Knopf, b/w illustrations by Michael Sporn. ($25.00 with dust jacket) $10.00
In the Suicide Mountains, 1973 Knopf, first edition, hardcover. ($60.00 with dust jacket) $20.00

GARDNER, Martin
Annotated Alice, 1960 Clarkson N. Potter, includes *Alice's Adventures in Wonderland & Through the Looking Glass* by Lewis Carroll, with the Tenniel illustrations, introduction and margin notes by Martin Gardner, oversize, beige hardcover with silver lettering, 352 pages. ($50.00 with dust jacket) $25.00

GARELICK, May
What Makes a Bird a Bird?, 1969 Follett, first edition, hardcover, illustrated by Leonard Weisgard. ($20.00 with dust jacket) $10.00

GARFIELD, James B.
Follow My Leader, 1957 Viking, first edition, hardcover, illustrated by Robert Greiner. ($25.00 with dust jacket) $10.00

GARFIELD, Leon
Black Jack, 1968 Longmans Young, hardcover. $10.00
Captain's Watch, 1972 Heinemann, hardcover, illustrated by Trevor Ridley. ($15.00 with dust jacket) $10.00
Child O'War, 1972 Collins, first edition, 127 pages, hardcover, illustrated with paintings and diagrams. ($30.00 with dust jacket) $15.00
Drummer Boy, 1970 Longmans, first edition, hardcover, b/w illustrations by Antony Maitland. ($35.00 with dust jacket) $15.00
God Beneath the Sea, 1970 Longmans, first edi-

tion, hardcover, illustrations by Charles Keeping. ($75.00 with dust jacket) $30.00
Sound of Coaches, 1974 Viking, first American edition, hardcover. ($25.00 with dust jacket) $10.00

GARFIELD, Nancy
Tuesday Elephant, 1968 Crowell, first edition, hardcover, b/w illustrations by Tom Feelings. ($15.00 with dust jacket) $10.00

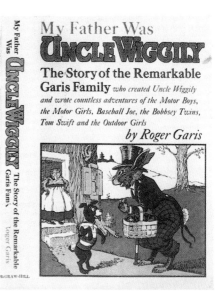

GARIS, Roger
My Father Was Uncle Wiggily, 1966 McGraw-Hill, first edition, hardcover, 217 pages, photos. ($40.00 with dust jacket) $20.00

GARLAND, Rosemary, editor
My Bedtime Book of Two-Minute Stories, 1969 Grosset & Dunlap, illlustrated boards, 123 pages, illustrated by Tony Escott and Sally Wellman. $15.00

GARNER, Alan
Hamish Hamilton Book of Goblins, edited by Garner, 1969 Hamish Hamilton, first edition, hardcover, illustrated by Krystyna Turska. ($15.00 with dust jacket) $10.00
Moon of Gomrath, 1963 Collins, first edition, hardcover. ($40.00 with dust jacket) $20.00
Owl Service, 1968 Walck, first American edition, hardcover, 202 pages. ($30.00 with dust jacket) $15.00
Weirdstone of Brisingamen, 1960 Philomel, first edition, hardcover, Garner's first book. ($50.00 with dust jacket) $20.00

GARNETT, Eve
Holiday at the Dew Drop Inn, 1962 Vanguard, hardcover. ($15.00 with dust jacket) $10.00
Book of the Seasons, 1952 Oxford, first edition, over-

size hardcover, 80 pages, color and b/w illustrations by Garnett. ($35.00 with dust jacket) $20.00

GARNETT, Richard
Jack of Dover, 1966 Vanguard Press, first edition, green hardcover, illustrated by Graham Oakley. ($15.00 with dust jacket) $10.00

GARRISON, Christian
Little Pieces of the West Wind, 1975 Bradbury Press, first edition, oblong blue hardcover, double-page color illustrations by Diane Goode. ($25.00 with dust jacket) $15.00

GARSON, Eugenia
Laura Ingalls Wilder Songbook, 1968 Harper & Row, oversize, pictorial boards, illustrated by Garth Williams. Arranged for piano and guitar by Herbert Haufrecht. $25.00

GARST, Shannon
Jim Bridger: The Greatest of Mountain Men, 1952 Houghton Mifflin, hardcover, illustrations by Wm. Moyers. $25.00
Wild Bill Hickok, 1952 Julian Messner, first edition, hardcover, 183 pages, illustrations. ($25.00 with dust jacket) $10.00

GARTHWAITE, Marion
Thomas and the Red Headed Angel, 1959 Messner, hardcover, illustrated by Lorence Bjorklund. $20.00

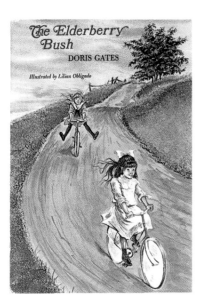

GATES, Doris
Becky and the Bandit, 1955 Ginn, school reader, gold cloth hardcover, ex-school copy, illustrations by Paul Lantz. $15.00
Cat and Mrs. Cary, 1965 Viking, first edition, hard-

cover, b/w illustrations by Peggy Bacon. ($35.00 with dust jacket) $20.00
Elderberry Bush, 1967 Viking, hardcover, 160 pages, b/w illustrations by Lilian Obligado. ($30.00 with dust jacket) $10.00
Golden God: Apollo, 1973 Viking, hardcover, illustrations by Constantinos Coconis. ($30.00 with dust jacket) $10.00
Little Vic, 1951 Viking, first edition, hardcover, illustrated by Kate Seredy. ($35.00 with dust jacket) $20.00
Lord of the Sky: Zeus, 1972 Viking, hardcover, illustrations by Robert Handville. ($35.00 with dust jacket) $15.00
Two Queens of Heaven, 1974 Viking, first edition, oversize, 94 pages, b/w illustrations by Trina Schart Hyman. ($35.00 with dust jacket) $15.00
Warrior Goddess: Athena, 1972 Viking, hardcover, illustrations by Don Bolognese. ($30.00 with dust jacket) $15.00

GAULT, William Campbell
Stubborn Sam, 1969 Dutton, first edition, hardcover. ($15.00 with dust jacket) $10.00
Thunder Road, 1962 Dutton, hardcover. $10.00

GAY, Zhenya
Bits and Pieces, 1958 Viking, first edition, hardcover. ($35.00 with dust jacket) $15.00
I'm Tired of Lions, 1961 New York. Viking, first edition, oversize hardcover, ($35.00 with dust jacket) $15.00
Jingle Jangle, 1955 edition Viking, hardcover, pictures by the author. ($25.00 with dust jacket) $10.00
Nicest Time of Year, 1960 Viking, first edition, green pictorial hardcover. ($20.00 with dust jacket) $10.00
Small One, 1958 Viking, first edition, oversize hardcover, illustrated by author. ($50.00 with dust jacket) $20.00
Who's Afraid?, 1965 Viking, first edition, hardcover illustrations by the author. ($25.00 with dust jacket) $10.00
Wonderful Things!, 1954 Viking, first edition, hardcover. ($25.00 with dust jacket) $15.00

GAY-KELLY, Doreen
Bea's Best Friend, 1975 Prentice-Hall, first edition, hardcover, 27 pages, b/w photographs of clay models. ($25.00 with dust jacket) $15.00

GEE, Maurine H.
Jeff and the River, 1961 Morrow, first edition, hardcover, illustrated by Charles Geer. ($15.00 with dust jacket) $10.00

GEIS, Darlene
Rattle-Rattle Dump Truck, 1958 Wonder Books, illustrated boards, illustrations by Carl Bobertz. $10.00

GENDEL, Evelyn
Tortoise and Turtle, 1960 Simon & Schuster, first edition, yellow boards with lime green cloth spine, illustrated endpapers, illustrations by Hilary Knight. ($45.00 with dust jacket) $20.00
Tortoise and Turtle Abroad, 1963 Simon & Schuster, first edition, hardcover, illustrated by Hilary Knight. ($50.00 with dust jacket) $30.00

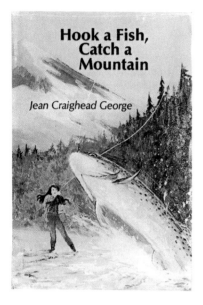

GEORGE, Jean Craighead
Hook a Fish, Catch a Mountain, 1975 Dutton, hardcover. ($20.00 with dust jacket) $10.00
Julie of the Wolves, 1972 Harper, first edition, hardcover, illustrated by John Schoenherr. ($20.00 with dust jacket) $10.00
Spring Comes to the Ocean, 1965 Crowell, first edition, hardcover, illustrated by John Wilson. ($20.00 with dust jacket) $10.00
Thirteen Moons/ Moon of the Mountain Lion, 1968 Crowell, first edition, hardcover, illustrated by Winifred Lubell. ($20.00 with dust jacket) $10.00

GEORGIADY, Nicholas P. and ROMANO, Louis G.
Gertie the Duck, 1959 Follett, hardcover, first grade reader, illustrated by Dagmar Wilson. ($35.00 with dust jacket) $15.00

GERVAISE, Mary
Belinda Rides to School, 1960 Lutterworth, first edition, hardcover. ($20.00 with dust jacket) $10.00
Farthingale Fete, 1955 Nelson, first edition, hardcover, illustrated. ($15.00 with dust jacket) $10.00
Mandy, Dandy and Co., 1962 Nelson, first edition, hardcover, illustrated. ($15.00 with dust jacket) $10.00
Secret of Pony Pass, 1965 Lutterworth, first edition, hardcover. ($20.00 with dust jacket) $10.00

GIBBS, Alonzo
Least Likely One, 1964 Lothrop, Lee, first edition, hardcover. ($35.00 with dust jacket) $15.00
Son of a Mile-Long Mother, 1970 Bobbs-Merrill, first edition, hardcover, 78 pages, line drawings by Mary Frank. ($15.00 with dust jacket) $10.00

GIDAL, Sonia
Children's Village in Israel, 1950 Meier Shfeya Behrman House, hardcover, 48 pages, photo illustrations by Tim Gidal. $35.00

GILBERT and SULLIVAN
HMS Pinafore, 1966 edition Watts, hardcover, with drawings by Anne and Janet Grahame. $20.00
Duke of the Plaza Toro, 1969 Macmillan, hardcover, illustrated boards, pictures by Rosemary Wells. $15.00.

GILBERT, John
Golden Book of Buccaneers, 1975 edition Golden Press, first edition, hardcover, illustrated by Edward Mortelmans. ($20.00 with dust jacket) $10.00

GILBERT, Kenneth
Cruise of the Dipsy-Do, 1954 Henry Holt, first edition, hardcover. ($15.00 with dust jacket) $10.00
Triple-Threat Patrol, 1953 Holt, first edition, hardcover. ($20.00 with dust jacket) $10.00

GILBERT, Miriam
Karen Gets a Fever, 1961 Lerner, hardcover. $15.00.

GILBERT, Nan
365 Bedtime Stories, 1955 Whitman, hardcover, illustrations by Jill Elgin. $15.00
Unchosen, 1963 Harper, hardcover. $10.00
Dog for Joey, 1967 Harper & Row, first edition, hardcover. ($40.00 with dust jacket) $20.00

GILES, Janice Holt
Johnny Osage, 1960 Houghton Mifflin, hardcover, illustrated endpapers. ($15.00 with dust jacket) $10.00
Miss Willie, 1951 Houghton Mifflin, hardcover. ($15.00 with dust jacket) $10.00
Tara's Healing, 1951 Houghton Mifflin, hardcover. ($15.00 with dust jacket) $10.00

GILLESPIE, T.H.
Zoo-Man Stories, 1960 Taplinger, pictorial hardcover, b/w illustrations by Len Fullerton. ($20.00 with dust jacket) $10.00

GILLETT, Mary
Bugles at the Border, 1968 Winston-Salem, first edition, hardcover, illustrated by Bruce Tucker. ($15.00 with dust jacket) $10.00

GILLHAM, Charles E.
Eskimo Folk-Tales from Alaska, 1955 Batchworth Press, first edition, hardcover, illustrated by Chanimun. ($30.00 with dust jacket) $15.00

GILMORE, D. H.
Christopher Cricket's Favourite Tales, 1950 Angus & Robertson, Sydney, first edition, hardcover, color and b/w illustrations. $35.00

GIOVANNETTI
Nothing But Max, 1959 Macmillan, first edition, oversize hardcover, 85 pages, b/w illustrations by author. ($30.00 with dust jacket) $15.00

GIOVANNI, Nikki
Spin a Soft Black Song, 1971 Hill & Wang, first edition, oversize square hardcover, illustrated by Charles Bible. ($50.00 with dust jacket) $20.00

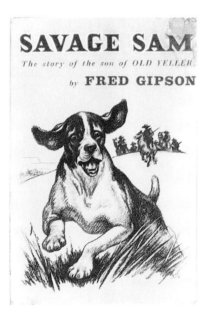

GIPSON, Fred
Cowhand, 1953 Harper, first edition, hardcover. ($25.00 with dust jacket) $15.00
Old Yeller, 1957 Hodder & Stoughton, first edition UK, hardcover. ($20.00 with dust jacket) $10.00
Savage Sam, 1962 Harper, hardcover, 214 pages, b/w illustrations by Carl Burger. ($25.00 with dust jacket) $10.00
Trail-Driving Rooster, 1955 Harper & Row, hardcover, illustrated by Marc Simont. ($25.00 with dust jacket) $10.00

GIPSON, Morrell
Mr. Bear Squash-You-All-Flat, 1950 Wonder Book, small hardcover, color illustrations. Hard-to-find. $250.00

GIRVAN, Helen
Down Bayberry Lane, 1955 Westminster, first edition, hardcover. ($25.00 with dust jacket) $10.00
Hidden Pond, 1951 Dutton, first edition, hardcover, illustrated by Albert Orbaan. ($20.00 with dust jacket) $10.00

GLEMSER, Bernard
Radar Commandos, A Story of World War II, 1953 Winston. first edition, hardcover, illustrated by Avison. ($15.00 with dust jacket) $10.00

GLUBOK, Shirley
Fall of the Incas, 1967 Macmillan, hardcover, oversize, illustrations based on Huaman Poma's drawings. $20.00

GNOLI, D.
Orestes or The Art of Smiling, 1961 Simon & Schuster, first edition, oversize hardcover, color illustrations by author. ($30.00 with dust jacket) $15.00

GOBLE, Paul and **Dorothy**
Lone Bulll's Horse Raid, 1973 Bradbury, oversize hardcover, color illustrations by Paul Goble. ($30.00 with dust jacket) $15.00

GODDEN, Rumer
Candy Floss, 1960 edition Viking, hardcover, 65 pages, color and b/w illustrations by Adrienne Adams. ($25.00 with dust jacket) $10.00
Dolls' House, 1962 edition Viking, first thus, gray hardcover, 136 pages, color and b/w illustrations by Tasha Tudor. First edition with dust jacket: $200.00. Later editions: ($25.00 with dust jacket) $15.00
Greengage Summer, 1958 Viking, first edition, hardcover, 218 pages. ($25.00 with dust jacket) $10.00

Home is the Sailor, 1964 Macmillan, first edition, hardcover, color and b/w illustrations by Jean Primrose. ($40.00 with dust jacket) $20.00

Impunity Jane, 1954 Viking, first edition, hardcover, illustrated by Adrienne Adams. ($50.00 with dust jacket) $20.00

Little Plum, 1963 Viking, first edition, hardcover, illustrated by Jean Primrose. ($20.00 with dust jacket) $10.00

Miss Happiness and Miss Flower, 1961 London Macmillan, London, first edition, hardcover, illustrated by Jean Primrose. ($75.00 with dust jacket) $30.00

Miss Happiness and Miss Flower, Viking, hardcover, 82 pages, illustrated end papers, drawings by Jean Primrose. ($50.00 with dust jacket) $15.00

Mouse House, 1957 Viking, hardcover, illustrated by Adrienne Adams. ($35.00 with dust jacket) $15.00

Mousewife, 1951 Viking, first edition, hardcover, b/w illustrations by William Pene du Bois. ($125.00 with dust jacket) $40.00

Mr. McFadden's Hallowe'en, 1975 Viking, first edition, hardcover, 127 pages. ($35.00 with dust jacket) $15.00

Operation Sippacik, 1969 Viking, first edition, hardcover, illustrated by Capt. James Bryan. ($35.00 with dust jacket) $15.00

Tale of the Tales, the Beatrix Potter Ballet, 1971 Warne, first edition, oversize hardcover, illustrated. ($40.00 with dust jacket) $20.00

GOETZ, Delia

Mountains, 1962 Morrow Junior Books, first edition, hardcover, illustrated by Louis Darling. ($20.00 with dust jacket) $10.00

Tropical Rain Forests, 1957 Morrow Junior Books, first edition, hardcover, illustrated by Louis Darling. ($20.00 with dust jacket) $10.00

GOFFSTEIN, M. B.

Brookie and Her Lamb, 1967 Farrar, hardcover, b/w illustrations by author. ($45.00 with dust jacket) $20.00

Goldie and the Dollmaker, 1969 Farrar, hardcover, illustrated by author. ($45.00 with dust jacket) $20.00

Little Schubert, 1972 Harper, first edition, hardcover, illustrations by author. Includes record by Peter Schaaf. With dust jacket and record: $45.00

Me and My Captain, 1974 Farrar, hardcover. ($30.00 with dust jacket) $15.00

Two Piano Tuners, 1970 Farrar, hardcover, 65 pages, b/w illustrations by author. ($30.00 with dust jacket) $15.00

GOLD, Sharlya

Potter's Four Sons, 1970 Doubleday, hardcover. $10.00

GOLDIN, Augusta

Spider Silk, 1964 Crowell, hardcover, pictorial cover, Let's-Read-And-Find-Out series edition, illustrated by Joseph Low. $10.00

GOLDING, Amy Thomas

Miniature Travelers, 1956 Marshall Jones, first edition, hardcover, illustrated. ($25.00 with dust jacket) $15.00

GOLDMARK, Josephine

Impatient Crusader, Florence Kelly's Life Story, 1953 University of Illinois, first edition, hardcover. ($35.00 with dust jacket) $20.00

GOOD, Loren D.

Panchito, 1955 Coward-McCann, first edition, hardcover, illustrated by Nicholas. ($20.00 with dust jacket) $10.00

GOOD, Mabel Tinkiss

At the Dark of the Moon, 1956 Macmillan, first edition, hardcover, illustrated by Clare Bice. ($30.00 with dust jacket) $15.00

GOODALL, John S.

Adventure of Paddy Pork, 1968 Harcourt, Brace & World, first edition, hardcover. ($45.00 with dust jacket) $20.00

GORDON, Alvin

Inherit the Earth, Stories from Mexican Ranch Life, 1963 U of Arizona Press, first edition, hardcover, illustrated by Ted De Grazia. ($50.00 with dust jacket) $20.00

GORDON, Ethel Edison

Where Does the Summer Go?, 1967 Crowell, first edition. ($35.00 with dust jacket) $15.00

GORDON, Patricia

Taming of Giants, 1950 Viking, Junior Literary Guild

selection, first edition, hardcover, illustrated by Garry MacKenzie. ($15.00 with dust jacket) $10.00

GOREY, Edward
Amphigorey, 1972 Putnam, first edition, hardcover, illustrated by author. ($85.00 with dust jacket) $30.00
Amphigorey Too, 1975 Putnam, first edition, oversize hardcover, illustrated by author. ($60.00 with dust jacket) $25.00
Blue Aspic, 1968 Meredith Press, first edition, hardcover, illustrated by author. ($60.00 with dust jacket) $25.00
Doubtful Guest, 1957 Doubleday, first edition, hardcover, illustrated by author. ($200.00 with dust jacket) $50.00
Fletcher and Zenobia, with Victoria Chess, 1967 Meredith Press, first edition, small square hardcover. ($35.00 with dust jacket) $15.00
Gilded Bat, 1966 Simon & Schuster, first edition, pictorial hardcover, illustrated by author. ($60.00 with dust jacket) $25.00
Hapless Child, 1961 Dodd Mead,, first edition, hardcover, illustrated by Edward Gorey. ($50.00 with dust jacket) $20.00
Haunted Looking Glass, 1959 Random House, first edition, hardcover, 311 pages, stories chosen and illustrated by Gorey. ($30.00 with dust jacket) $15.00
Listing Attic, 1954 Duell, Sloan and Pearce, first edition, small hardcover, illustrated by author. ($100.00 with dust jacket) $50.00
Remembered Visit, A Story Taken From Life, 1965 Simon & Schuster, first edition, hardcover, illustrated by Gorey. ($100.00 with dust jacket) $40.00
Unstrung Harp, 1953 Duell, Sloan and Pearce, first edition, hardcover, illustrated by author. Gorey's first book. ($300.00 with dust jacket) $75.00
Utter Zoo, 1967 Meredith Press, first edition, hardcover, 56 pages, illustrations by author. ($80.00 with dust jacket) $30.00

GORFINKLE, Lilliam K.
Bianca, 1959 Rand McNally, first edition, hardcover, illustrated by Silvia Rosenberg. ($25.00 with dust jacket) $15.00

GORHAM, Maurice
Showmen and Suckers, An Excursion on the Crazy Fringe of the Entertainment World, 1951 Marshall, London, green boards, b/w illustrations by Edward Ardizzone. ($45.00 with dust jacket) $20.00

GORHAM, Michael
Real Book About Cowboys, 1952 Garden City, hardcover, illustrations by C. L. Hartman. $10.00

GORSE, Golden
Mary in the Country, 1955 Country Life, London, first edition, hardcover, 162 pages, illustrated by E. H. Shepard. ($25.00 with dust jacket) $15.00

GOTTLIEB, Robin
Mystery of the Jittery Dog, 1966 Walker, first edition, hardcover, illustrated by Mimi Korach. ($15.00 with dust jacket) $10.00

GOUDGE, Elizabeth
Linnets and Valerians, 1964 Brockhampton Press, first edition, hardcover. ($70.00 with dust jacket) $30.00. Later editions: $20.00

GOUGH, Catherine
Young Readers Guide to Music, Boyhoods of Great Composers, 1960 Oxford U Press, first edition, pictorial laminated hardcover, illustrated endpapers, b/w illustrations by Edward Ardizzone. $25.00

GOVAN, Christine, see Series section MYSTERY
Year the River Froze, 1959 World, first edition, hardcover. ($20.00 with dust jacket) $10.00

GOVAN, Margaret
Trail of the Red Canoe, 1954 Dent, first edition, hardcover, illustrated by Margot Lovejoy. ($20.00 with dust jacket) $10.00

GRAHAM, Janette Sargeant
Venture at Lake Tahogan, 1956 Longmans, Green, first edition, hardcover. ($15.00 with dust jacket) $10.00

GRAHAM, John
Crowd of Cows, 1968 Harcourt, Brace, hardcover, illustrated by Feodor Rojankovsky. $15.00

GRAHAM, Lorenz
David He No Fear, 1971 Crowell, first edition, hardcover, illustrated by Ann Grifalconi woodcuts. ($25.00 with dust jacket) $15.00
I, Momolu, 1966 Crowell, first edition, hardcover, 226 pages. ($25.00 with dust jacket) $10.00

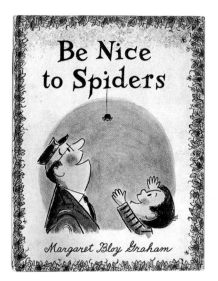

GRAHAM, Margaret Bloy, see Series section HARRY THE DOG

Be Nice to Spiders, 1967 Harper, Weekly Reader edition, illustrated hardcover, color illustrations by author. $15.00

Benjy and the Barking Bird, 1971 Harper & Row, first edition, oversize hardcover, illustrated by author. ($35.00 with dust jacket) $15.00

Benjy's Dog House, 1973 Harcourt, Brace, first edition, oversize hardcover, illustrated by author. ($60.00 with dust jacket) $25.00

GRAHAM, Rosemary

Furry Forest Bears, 1956 McClelland and Stewart, Toronto, first edition, small hardcover, illustrated endpapers, 143 pages, illustrated by author. ($30.00 with dust jacket) $15.00

GRAHAME, Kenneth

Wind in the Willows, 1959 Methuen, London, first edition thus UK, hardcover, new color plates by Shepherd. ($100.00 with dust jacket) $40.00

GRAMATKY, Hardie

Happy's Christmas, 1970 Putnam, first edition, hardcover, illustrated by author. ($40.00 with dust jacket) $20.00

Little Toot on the Mississippi, 1974 World's Work, first edition UK, pictorial hardcover, illustrated endpapers, color and b/w illustrations by author. ($30.00 with dust jacket) $20.00

Nikos and the Sea God, 1963 Putnam, first edition, hardcover, illustrated by author. ($30.00 with dust jacket) $20.00

GRANNAN, Mary, see Series section MAGGIE MUGGINS

Just Mary's Brown Book, 1957 Thomas Allan Ltd. Toronto, first edition, small hardcover, 150 pages, based on CBC radio series, illustrated by Pat Patience. ($25.00 with dust jacket) $10.00

GRANT, Bruce

Boy Scout Encyclopedia, 1952 Rand McNally, first edition, oversize hardcover, illustrated by Fiore and Jackie Mastri. ($60.00 with dust jacket) $20.00

Pancho, a Dog of the Plains, 1958 World, first edition, hardcover. ($15.00 with dust jacket) $10.00

Star-Spangled Rooster, 1961 World, first edition, hardcover, illustrated by W.T. Mars. ($20.00 with dust jacket) $10.00

GRATTAN, Madeleine

Jexium Island, 1957 Viking, first edition, hardcover, 184 pages, illustrated by William Pene du Bois. ($45.00 with dust jacket) $20.00

GRAVES, Robert

Ann at Highwood Hall, Poems for Children, 1964 Cassell, London, first edition, hardcover, illustrated by Edward Ardizzone. ($35.00 with dust jacket) $20.00

Big Green Book, 1962 Crowell-Collier, first edition, green hardcover, oversize, illustrations by Maurice Sendak. ($50.00 with dust jacket) $20.00

Greek Gods and Heroes, 1960 Doubleday, hardcover, illustrated by Dimitris Davis. ($20.00 with dust jacket) $10.00

Penny Fiddle, 1960 Doubleday, first American edition of collection of Graves' poems, hardcover, illustrated by Edward Ardizzone. ($35.00 with dust jacket) $20.00

Poor Boy who Followed his Star, 1968 Garden City, first edition, hardcover, illustrated by Alice Meyer-Wallace. ($15.00 with dust jacket) $10.00

Siege and Fall of Troy, 1962 Doubleday, first edition, hardcover, illustrations by Walter Hodges. $15.00

Two Wise Children, 1966 Harlin Quist, first edition, hardcover, illustrated by Ralph Pinto. ($25.00 with dust jacket) $10.00

GRAY, Elizabeth Janet

I Will Adventure, 1962 Viking, hardcover, 208 pages, illustrated endpapers, full page b/w illustrations by by Corydon Bell. ($25.00 with dust jacket) $10.00

GRAY, Genevieve

Ghost Story, 1975 Lothrop, hardcover. $15.00

GRAY, Nicholas Stuart

Apple-Stone, 1965 Dennis Dobson, hardcover, b/w illustrations by Charles Keeping. ($60.00 with dust jacket) $20.00

Grimbold's Other World, 1963 Meredith, first American edition, hardcover, 184 pages, b/w illustrations by Charles Keeping. ($50.00 with dust jacket) $20.00

Boys: Cats with Everything, 1968 Meredith, first edition, hardcover, photos by Robin Adler. ($20.00 with dust jacket) $10.00

Mainly in Moonlight, 1967 Meredith, first edition, hardcover, b/w illustrations by Charles Keeping. ($50.00 with dust jacket) $20.00

Over the Hills to Fabylon, (1954) 1970 edition Hawthorn, first American edition, hardcover, b/w illustrations by Charles Keeping. ($100.00 with dust jacket) $30.00. Ex-library: $15.00 with dust jacket

Stone Cage, 1963 Dobson, first edition, hardcover. ($65.00 with dust jacket) $25.00

Tinder-Box, a Play for Children, 1951 Oxford, illustrated by Joan Jefferson. ($15.00 with dust jacket) $10.00

GREEN, Alexander
Scarlet Sails, 1967 Scribners, first edition, hardcover, illustrated by Esta Nesbitt. ($20.00 with dust jacket) $10.00

GREEN, Ivan
Animals Under Your Feet, 1953 Grosset & Dunlap, oversize hardcover, 129 pages. $15.00

Splash and Trickle: A Conservation Story, 1970 Oddo Publishing, pictorial hardcover, illustrated by Bil Conner. $10.00

GREEN, Kathleen
Philip and the Pooka and Other Irish Fairy Tales, 1966 Lippincott, first edition, hardcover, 93 pages, illustrated by Vitoria de Larrea. ($20.00 with dust jacket) $10.00

GREEN, Nancy
Abu Kassim's Slippers, 1963, pictorial boards, illustrations by W.T. Mars. $10.00

GREEN, Phyllis
Nantucket Summer, 1974 Thomas Nelson, first edition, hardcover. ($30.00 with dust jacket) $20.00

GREEN, R. L.
Theft of the Golden Cat, 1955 Methuen, first edition, hardcover, illustrated by E. F. McGrath . $20.00

GREEN, Robert James
Hawk of the Nile, 1962 St. Martin's, first edition, green pictorial boards, 212 pages, illustrations by Shane Miller. $15.00

GREENE, Carla
I Want to be an Airplane Hostess, 1960 Grosset & Dunlap, first edition, oversize hardcover, illustrated by Frances Eckart. ($15.00 with dust jacket) $10.00

I Want to be a Bus Driver, 1957 Children's Press, first edition, hardcover, illustrated by Katherine Evans. ($15.00 with dust jacket) $10.00

GREENE, Graham
Little Fire Engine, 1973 Bodley Head, first edition

thus, oblong hardcover, 48 pages, illustrated by Edward Ardizzone. ($50.00 with dust jacket) $25.00

Little Horse Bus, 1974 Bodley Head, London, first edition, oblong oversize pictorial hardcover, color illustrations by Edward Ardizzone. ($150.00 with dust jacket) $40.00

Little Horse Bus, 1974 Doubleday, first American edition, hardcover, color illustrations by Edward Ardizzone. ($50.00 with dust jacket) $30.00

Little Steamroller, 1955 Lothrop, Lee, first American edition, square hardcover, 36 pages, color illustrations by Dorothy Craigie. ($300.00 with dust jacket) $60.00

Little Steamroller, 1974 Doubleday, first American edition thus, oversize hardcover, 46 pages, illustrated by Edward Ardizzone. ($50.00 with dust jacket) $20.00

GREENER, Leslie
Moon Ahead, 1951 Viking/Junior Literary Guild, hardcover, illustrated by William Pene DuBois. $15.00

GREENWOOD, Ted
Obstreperous, 1970 Atheneum, first edition, hardcover, 46 pages, color illustrations. ($15.00 with dust jacket) $10.00

GREGOR, Arthur
Little Elephant, 1956 Harper & Brothers, first edition, pictorial paper covered oversize hardcover, b/w photos by Ylla on every page. ($40.00 with dust jacket) $20.00

GRIEDER, Walter
Pierrot and His Friends in the Circus, 1967 Delacorte, first American edition, oversize hardcover, illustrated by author. ($40.00 with dust jacket) $20.00

GRIFALCONI, Ann
City Rhythms, 1965 Bobbs Merrill, first edition, decorated boards. $15.00

GRIFFITHS, Helen
Wild Heart, 1963 Doubleday, first edition, hardcover, illustrated by Victor Ambrus. ($20.00 with dust jacket) $10.00

GRILLEY, Virginia
Shilling for Samuel, 1957 Little, Brown, first edition, hardcover, illustrated by author. ($20.00 with dust jacket) $10.00

GRINGHUIS, Dirk
Here Comes the Bookmobile, 1952 Albert Whitman, first edition, hardcover, color illustrated cover. ($30.00 with dust jacket) $20.00

GRIPE, Maria
Elvis and His Friends, 1973 Delacorte, hardcover, illustrated by Harald Gripe. ($25.00 with dust jacket) $15.00

Hugo and Josephine, (1962) 1969 Delacorte, first American edition, hardcover, 168 pages, illustrated by Harald Gripe. ($40.00 with dust jacket) $15.00

Land Beyond, 1974 Delacorte, hardcover, illustrated by Harald Gripe. ($15.00 with dust jacket) $10.00

Night Daddy, 1972 Chatto, first edition, hardcover, illustrated by Harald Gripe. ($15.00 with dust jacket) $10.00

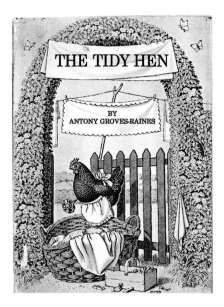

GROVES-RAINES, Antony

Tidy Hen, 1961 Harcourt Brace, first edition, small blue hardcover, full-page color illustrations by author. ($35.00 with dust jacket) $20.00

GRUENBERG, Sidonie Matsner, editor

Let's Hear a Story, 1961 Doubleday, first edition, hardcover, collection of stories and poems, illustrated by Dapner Wilson. ($45.00 with dust jacket) $20.00

Let's Read a Story, Modern, Gay Stories for Boys and Girls, 1957 Garden City, first edition, hardcover, illustrated by Virginia Parsons. ($30.00 with dust jacket) $15.00

Let's Read More Stories, 1960 Garden City, first edition, hardcover, illustrated. $30.00

GRUN, Bernard

Golden Quill, 1956 Putnam, first edition, hardcover. ($20.00 with dust jacket) $10.00

GUILLOT, Rene

Fodai and the Leopard-men, 1970 Funk & Wagnalls, first edition, hardcover, illustrated by Michel Jouin. ($25.00 with dust jacket) $15.00

GUIRMA, Frederic

Princess of the Full Moon, 1970 Macmillan, first edition, hardcover, illustrated by Frederic Guirma. ($40.00 with dust jacket) $20.00

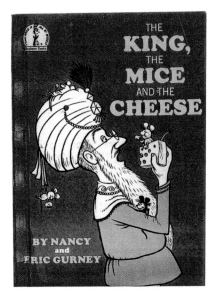

GURNEY, Eric

Gilbert, 1963 Prentice-Hall, first edition, hardcover, illustrated by author. ($15.00 with dust jacket) $10.00

Gurney's Guide to Feathered Friends, 1968 Morrow, first edition, text by Nancy Gurney, illustrated by Eric Gurney. ($20.00 with dust jacket) $10.00

How to Live with a Calculating Cat, 1965 Prentice Hall, hardcover, b/w illustrations by author. ($20.00 with dust jacket) $10.00

King, the Mice and the Cheese, with Nancy Gurney, 1965 Random House, first edition, hardcover, illustrated by authors. ($30.00 with dust jacket) $15.00

GURY, Jeremy

Wonderful World of Aunt Tuddy, 1958 Random House, first edition, oversize hardcover, color illustrations by Hilary Knight. ($100.00 with dust jacket) $30.00

GWYNNE, Fred

God's First World, 1970 Harper and Row, first edition, hardcover, illustrated by Fred Gwynne. ($20.00 with dust jacket) $10.00

King Who Rained, 1970 Prentice-Hall Books for Young Readers, first edition, hardcover, full-page color illustrations. ($30.00 with dust jacket) $15.00

Story of Ick, 1971 Windmill, first edition, hardcover, illustrated by author. ($20.00 with dust jacket) $10.00

⤞⇒ **H** ⇐⤝

HAAS, Irene

Maggie B., 1975 Atheneum, first edition, oversize hardcover. ($30.00 with dust jacket) $15.00

HACKETT, Walter

Swans of Ballycastle, 1954 Ariel Books, Weekly

Reader book club edition, blue boards, color illustrations by Bettina. ($20.00 with dust jacket) $10.00

HADER, Berta and **Elmer**
Ding Dong Bell: Pussy's in the Well, 1957 Macmillan, first edition, oversize hardcover, illustrated by authors. ($45.00 with dust jacket) $20.00
Friendly Phoebe, 1953 Macmillan, first edition, hardcover, illustrated by authors. ($45.00 with dust jacket) $25.00
Little Chip of Willow Hill, 1958 Macmillan, first edition, oversize hardcover, illustrated by authors. ($50.00 with dust jacket) $20.00
Mister Billy's Gun, 1960 Macmillan, first edition, oversize hardcover, illustrated by authors. ($40.00 with dust jacket) $20.00
Quack Quack, 1961 Macmillan, first edition, hardcover, illustrated by authors. ($25.00 with dust jacket) $15.00
Runaways, 1956 Macmillan, first edition, oversize hardcover, pictorial paper-covered hardcover, 38 pages, illustrated by authors. ($50.00 with dust jacket) $20.00
Spunky, the Story of a Shetland Pony, 1951 Macmillan, square first edition, 90 pages, color illustrations by authors. ($60.00 with dust jacket) $30.00
Squirrely of Willow Hill, 1950 Macmillan, first edition, hardcover, illustrated by authors. ($65.00 with dust jacket) $30.00
Wish on the Moon, 1954 Macmillan, first edition, oversize hardcover, color illustrations by authors. ($50.00 with dust jacket) $20.00

HAGER, Alice Rogers
Wonderful Ice Cream Cart, 1955 Macmillan, first edition, hardcover. ($20.00 with dust jacket) $10.00

HALE, Helen
Dale Evans and Danger in Crooked Canyon, 1958 Whitman, hardcover, illustrated by Henry Luhrs. ($20.00 with dust jacket) $10.00

HALE, Jeanne, Editor
Through Golden Windows: Adventures Here and There, 1958 Grolier, pictorial boards, 333 pages, color and b/w illustrations. $15.00

HALEY, Gail
Abominable Swamp Man, 1975 Viking, hardcover, b/w illustrations by author. ($20.00 with dust jacket) $10.00
Jack Jouet's Ride, 1973 Bodley Head, first edition, oversize hardcover. ($15.00 with dust jacket) $10.00
Story, A Story, an African Tale Retold, (1970) Atheneum, 1971 Caldecott Award edition, oblong oversize hardcover, color illustrations by author. ($40.00 with dust jacket) $20.00

HALL, Anna Gertrude
Cyrus Holt and the Civil War, 1965 Viking Press, hardcover. $15.00

HALL, Marjory
Valentine for Vinnie, 1965 Funk & Wagnells, hardcover. $10.00

HALL, Rosalyn
Tailor's Trick, 1955 Lippincott, first edition, hardcover, illustrated by Kurt Werth. ($15.00 with dust jacket) $10.00

HALL, William
Walking Hat, 1950 Knopf, illustrated boards, illustrated by Kurt Wiese. ($25.00 with dust jacket) $15.00
Winkies World, 1958 Doubleday, hardcover, illustrations by Roger Duvoisin. $15.00

HALLARD, Peter
Puppy Lost in Lapland, 1971 Weekly Reader, pictorial hardcover. $10.00

HALLSTEAD, William F.
Sky Carnival, 1969 David McKay, illustrated hardcover, 149 pages, dust jacket by Russ Anderson. ($20.00 with dust jacket) $10.00

HAMBERGER, John
Hazel Was An Only Pet, 1968 Norton, first edition, hardcover. ($20.00 with dust jacket) $10.00

HAMILTON, Esme
Children at Moyinish, 1957 Bodley Hall, first edition, hardcover, 159 pages, illustrated by Margery Gill. ($25.00 with dust jacket) $10.00

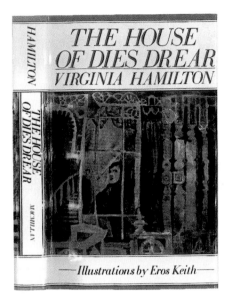

HAMILTON, Virginia
House of Dies Drear, 1968 Macmillan, first edition, hardcover, illustrated by Eros Keith. First edition with dust jacket: $60.00. Later editions: ($20.00 with dust jacket) $10.00
M. C. Higgins the Great, (1974) Macmillan, 1975 Newbery Medal edition, hardcover. ($20.00 with dust jacket) $10.00
Time-Ago Lost: More Tales of Jahdu, 1973 Macmillan, first edition, hardcover, illustrated. ($35.00 with dust jacket) $15.00
Zeely, 1967 Macmillan, first edition, hardcover, b/w illustrations by Symeon. Author's first book. Scarce. ($100.00 with dust jacket) $30.00. Ex-library copies: ($15.00 with dust jacket) $10.00

HAMMOND, Penny
Child's View of New York City, 1963 Doubleday, first edition, oversize, pictorial boards, photo illustrations by Katrina Thomas. ($25.00 with same-as-cover dust jacket) $15.00

HANSON, Joseph E.
Grandfather Todd of Old Cape Cod, 1959 David McKay, first edition, square hardcover, 64 pages, illustrated by Jean Porter. ($15.00 with dust jacket) $10.00

HARDENDORFF, Jeanne B., editor
Frog's Saddle Horse and Other Tales, 1968 Lippincott, first edition, hardcover, illustrated by Helen Webber. ($40.00 with dust jacket) $20.00

HARMER, Mabel
True Book of the Circus, 1955 Children's Press, hardcover, color and b/w illustrations by Loran Wilford. $15.00

HARNDEN, Ruth
Runaway Raft, 1968 Houghton, 155 pages. $20.00

HARNETT, Cynthia
Caxton's Challenge, 1960 World, first American edition, hardcover. ($15.00 with dust jacket) $10.00
Writing on the Hearth, 1973 Viking, first American edition, hardcover, color illustrations by Gareth Floyd. ($20.00 with Trina Schart Hyman illustrated dust jacket) $10.00

HARRIS, Christie
West with the White Chiefs, 1965 Atheneum, first edition, hardcover, 214 pages. ($20.00 with dust jacket) $10.00
You Have to Draw the Line Somewhere, 1968 Atheneum, hardcover. ($25.00 with dust jacket) $15.00

HARRIS, Cyril
Northern Exposure, 1963 Norton, first edition, hardcover, illustrated by Leonard Vosburgh. ($15.00 with dust jacket) $10.00

HARRIS, Joel Chandler
Brer Rabbit and Brer Fox, retold by Jane Shaw, 1969 Collins, U. K., oversize picture book, illustrated hardcover, color illustrations throughout by William Backhouse. $30.00
Animal Stories, 1954 copyright Junior Deluxe Editions, hardcover, illustrations by Jack Ezra Keats. $15.00

HARRIS, Leon A.
Great Picture Robbery, 1963 Atheneum, first edition, hardcover, illustrated by Joseph Schindelman. ($15.00 with dust jacket) $10.00

HARRIS, Ray
Adventures of Turkey, 1959 Collins, London, hardcover, illustrated by Geoffrey Whittam. ($20.00 with dust jacket) $15.00
Cruise of the Nifty Duck, 1955 Collins, London, first edition, hardcover. ($20.00 with dust jacket) $10.00
Turkey and Partners, 1954 Collins, London, first edition, hardcover, illustrated by Geoffrey Whittam. ($20.00 with dust jacket) $15.00

HARRIS, Rosemary
Moon in the Cloud, 1968 Macmillan, first US edition, 182 pages, hardcover. ($30.00 with dust jacket) $15.00

HARTER, Walter
Dog That Smiled, 1965 Macmillan, first edition, 102 pages, b/w illustrations by Charles W. Walker. $15.00

HARWOOD, David
Scouts Indeed!, 1967 Bell & Sons, London, first edition, hardcover. ($30.00 with dust jacket) $15.00

HASTINGS, Mary
Oliver, 1968 Random House, hardcover, adapted from the screenplay of the Columbia Pictures movie based on the book by Charles Dickens. $20.00

HATCH, Eric
Two and Two Is Six, 1969 Crown, first edition, hardcover, illustrated by Roseanne Burke. ($20.00 with dust jacket) $10.00

HATFIELD, John
Quintilian & the Curious Weather Shop, 1969 Jonathan Cape, London, first edition, hardcover, 110 pages, illustrated endpapers, illustrated. ($15.00 with dust jacket) $10.00

HAUFF, Wilhelm
Fairy Tales of Wilhelm Hauff, 1969 Abelard Schuman, first UK edition, hardcover, 222 pages, illustrated by Ulrik Schramm. $15.00
Monkey's Uncle, 1969 Farrar, Straus, first edition, hardcover, illustrated by Mitchell Miller. ($20.00 with dust jacket) $10.00

HAUTZIG, Esther
In the Park, an Excursion in Four Languages, 1968 Macmillan, first edition, 36 pages, illustrated by Ezra Jack Keats. ($40.00 with dust jacket) $15.00

HAVERS, Elinore
Pony to Catch, 1964 Lutterworth Press, first edition, hardcover. ($15.00 with dust jacket) $10.00
Pony Sleuths, 1966 Lutterworth, London, first edition, hardcover. ($15.00 with dust jacket) $10.00

HAVILAND, Virginia
Fairy Tale Treasury, 1972 Coward, McCann & Geoghegan, first American edition, hardcover, illustrated by Raymond Briggs ($50.00 with dust jacket) $30.00
Favorite Fairy Tales Told In Denmark, 1971 Little Brown, first edition, hardcover. ($25.00 with dust jacket) $10.00
Favorite Fairy Tales Told in England, 1959 Little Brown, first edition, hardcover, illustrated. ($20.00 with dust jacket) $10.00
Favorite Fairy Tales Told in Greece, 1970 Little Brown, first edition, hardcover, 90 pages, color and b/w illustrations by Nonny Hogrogian. ($50.00 with dust jacket) $20.00
Yankee Doodle's Literary Sampler of Prose, Poetry, & Pictures, 1974 Thomas Crowell, first edition, hardcover, 466 pages, illustrated. ($20.00 with dust jacket) $10.00

HAWKINS, Quail
Best Birthday, 1954 Junior Books, Doubleday, first edition, hardcover, illustrated by Antonio Sotomayor. ($15.00 with dust jacket) $10.00

HAY, Doddy
Hit the Silk, 1968 S. G. Phillips, first edition, hardcover. ($20.00 with dust jacket) $10.00

HAYES, Anna H.
Adventures of Hedvig & Lollie, 1961 Caxton, first edition, hardcover, illustrated by Carl A. Orrin. ($30.00 with dust jacket) $15.00

HAYES, Florence
Alaskan Hunter, 1959 Houghton, embossed design on hardcover, 248 pages, illustrated by Kurt Wiese. $15.00
Good Luck Feather, 1958 Houghton Mifflin, first edition, hardcover. ($25.00 with dust jacket) $10.00

HAYES, Marjorie
Robin on the River, 1950 Little Brown, first edition, hardcover. ($20.00 with dust jacket) $10.00

HAYNES, Nelma
Panther Lick Creek, 1970 Abingdon Press, first edition, hardcover, illustrated by William Moyers. ($15.00 with dust jacket) $10.00

HAYS, Wilma Pitchford
Cape Cod Adventure, 1964 Coward-McCann, hardcover, illustrated by Elinor Jaeger. ($15.00 with dust jacket) $10.00
Christmas on the Mayflower, 1956 Coward-McCann, first edition, hardcover, illustrated by Roger Duvoisin. ($35.00 with dust jacket) $15.00

Fourth of July Raid, 1959 Weekly Reader, pictorial hardcover, illustrated by Peter Burchard. $10.00

Horse that Raced a Train, 1959 Little, Brown, first edition, hardcover, illustrated by Wesley Dennis. ($25.00 with dust jacket) $15.00

Meriwether Lewis Mystery, 1971 Westminster Press, first edition, hardcover, b/w map, photos, drawings. ($15.00 with dust jacket) $10.00

HAYWOOD, Carolyn, see Series section EDDIE

Christmas Fantasy, 1972 Morrow, first edition, hardcover, illustrated by Glenys and Victor Ambrus. ($15.00 with dust jacket) $10.00

Robert Rows the River, 1965 William Morrow, first edition, hardcover, b/w illustrations by author. ($20.00 with dust jacket) $10.00

Taffy and Melissa Molasses, 1969 Morrow, first edition, hardcover, illustrated by author. ($25.00 with dust jacket) $10.00

HAZELTON, Elizabeth Baldwin

Day the Fish Went Wild, 1969 Scribners, first edition, hardcover, illustrated by Joe Servello. ($20.00 with dust jacket) $10.00

HAZELWOOD, Rex

Scout Annual, 1961 Pearson, hardcover, 224 pages, photos and drawings. ($15.00 with dust jacket) $10.00

HEARN, Lafcadio

Boy Who Drew Cats, 1963 Macmillan, first edition, hardcover. ($20.00 with dust jacket) $10.00

HEARN, Michael Patrick

Annotated World of Oz, (L. Frank Baum) 1973 edition Clarkson Potter, oversize hardcover, b/w

and color Denslow illustrations from original edition. ($30.00 with dust jacket) $20.00

HEATNERS, Anne

Thread Soldier, 1960 Harcourt, first edition, hardcover. ($15.00 with dust jacket) $10.00

HEFFERNAN, Helen, Mariam CRENSHAW, and Aline MERRITT

Mysterious Swamp Rider and Life in the Young Republic, 1955 Harr-Wagner, hardcover, illustrated by Warren Chase Merritt. $10.00

HEFTER, Richard

Noses and Toes, ca. 1974 Weekly Reader Book Club, oversize hardcover. $10.00

HEIDE, Florence Parry

Alphabet Zoop, 1970 McCall Publishing, first edition, hardcover, illustrated by Sally Mathews. ($25.00 with dust jacket) $15.00

Maximilian Becomes Famous, 1969 Funk & Wagnalls, first edition, hardcover, illustrated by Ed Renfro. ($25.00 with dust jacket) $15.00

Sebastian, 1968 Funk & Wagnalls, first edition, hardcover, "A Fun & Frolic Book", illustrated by Betty Fraser, music by Sylvia Worth Van Clief. ($15.00 with dust jacket) $10.00

HEIDERSTADT, Dorothy

Lois Says Aloha, 1963 Thomas Nelson, first edition, hardcover, illustrated by Charles Geer. ($15.00 with dust jacket) $10.00

HEILBRONER, Joan

This is the House Where Jack Lives, 1962 Harper, Weekly Reader edition, illustrated hardcover, illustrated by Aliki. $10.00

Happy Birthday Present, 1962 Harper, hardcover, illustrated by Mary Chalmers. $15.00

HEINLEIN, Robert

Citizen of the Galaxy, 1957 Scribner, hardcover. ($60.00 with dust jacket) $20.00

Have Space Suit, Will Travel, 1958 Scribner, hardcover. ($60.00 with dust jacket) $25.00

Orphans of the Sky, 1964 Putnam, first US edition, blue hardcover with yellow space capsule on cover. $75.00

HELLER, Suzanne

Misery, 1964 Paul Eriksson, small oblong hardcover, blue/white print and illustrations, illustrations by author. ($25.00 with dust jacket) $10.00

Misery Loves Company, 1962 Eriksson, small oblong hardcover, illustrated by author. ($20.00 with dust jacket) $10.00

More Misery, 1965 Eriksson, hardcover, illustrated by author. ($20.00 with dust jacket) $10.00

Story of a Fat Little Girl, 1966 Eriksson, first edition, small oblong hardcover, illustrated by author. ($25.00 with dust jacket) $10.00

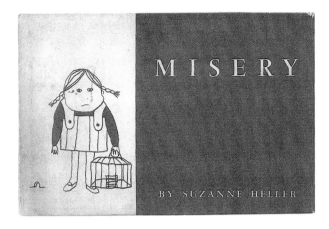

HELME, Eleanor and Nance PAUL

Joker and Jerry, 1955 edition Eyre & Spottiswood, hardcover, full page b/w illustrations by Cecil Aldin. ($20.00 with dust jacket) $10.00

HELMERICKS, Bud

Arctic Hunter, 1955 Little, Brown, first edition, hardcover, illustrated by Henry Bugbee Kane. ($15.00 with dust jacket) $10.00

Oolak's Brother, 1953 Little, Brown, first edition, hardcover, illustrated by Henry Bugbee Kane. ($25.00 with dust jacket) $10.00

HELPS, Racey

Barnaby and the Scarecrow, 1955 Collins, illustrated by author. ($30.00 with dust jacket) $15.00

Blow-Away Balloon, 1967 World, hardcover. ($20.00 with dust jacket) $10.00

Clean Sweep, 1967 Chilton, first edition, hardcover. ($20.00 with dust jacket) $10.00

Tale of Hunky Dory, 1958 Collins, first edition, hardcover, 46 pages, color illustrations by author. ($25.00 with dust jacket) $15.00

*Two from a Teapot,*1966 Chilton Books, first edition, hardcover, color and b/w illustrations by author. ($25.00 with dust jacket) $15.00

HENRY, Marguerite

Album of Horses, 1951 Rand McNally, first edition, hardcover, color and b/w illustrations by Wesley Dennis. ($35.00 with dust jacket) $20.00

Black Gold, 1957 Rand McNally, first edition, hardcover, black boards with gold text, illustrated endpapers, illustrated by Wesley Dennis. ($35.00 with dust jacket) $20.00

Born to Trot, 1950 Rand McNally, first edition, oversize hardcover, illustrated by Wesley Dennis. ($50.00 with dust jacket) $20.00

Brighty of the Grand Canyon, 1953 Rand McNally, oversize hardcover, illustrated by Dennis. ($45.00 with dust jacket) $20.00

Cinnabar, the One O'Clock, 1956 Rand McNally, first edition, oversize hardcover, illustrated by Wesley Dennis. ($50.00 with dust jacket) $20.00

Five O'Clock Charlie, 1962 Rand McNally, oversize hardcover, illustrated by Wesley Dennis. ($40.00 with dust jacket) $15.00

Gaudenzia, Pride of the Palio, 1960 Rand McNally, red hardcover with gilt lettering, oversize, 237 pages, illustrated endpapers, b/w and color illustrations by Lynd Ward. ($30.00 with dust jacket) $15.00

Wagging Tails, An Album of Dogs, 1955 Rand McNally, first edition, oversize hardcover, 64 pages, illustrated by Wesley Dennis. ($20.00 with dust jacket) $15.00

HENRY, Vera

*Ong, the Wild Gander,*1966 Lippincott, first edition, hardcover, illustrated by Fermin Rocker. ($20.00 with dust jacket) $10.00

HERBERT, Crystal, editor

Royal Children Today, 1954 Putnam, first edition, hardcover. ($15.00 with dust jacket) $10.00

HERBERT, Don

Mr. Wizard's Science Secrets, 1952 Popular Mechanics, hardcover, illustrated. $10.00

HERNDON, Betty Boulton

Adventures in Cactus Land, 1953 Caxton, hardcover with gilt lettering, color frontispiece, illustrated endpapers, b/w illustrations by author. ($35.00) $10.00

HERRMANN, Frank

Giant Alexander and the Circus, 1966 McGraw-Hill, first American edition, hardcover, illustrated by George Him. ($30.00 with dust jacket) $15.00

HERRMANNS, Ralph

Children of the North Pole, 1964 Harcourt, first edition, hardcover, illustrated by author with photographs. ($20.00 with dust jacket) $10.00

HESSELBERG, Erik

Kon-Tiki and I, 1950 Rand McNally, oversize hardcover, 74 pages, illustrated by author. ($25.00 with dust jacket) $10.00

HEWETT, Anita

Little Yellow Jungle Frogs, 1960 Barnes, first edition, hardcover, illustrated by Charlotte Hough. ($15.00 with dust jacket) $10.00

Mrs. Mopple's Washing Line, 1966 McGraw Hill, first edition, hardcover, color illustrations by Robert Broomfield. ($25.00 with dust jacket) $10.00

HICKOK, Lorena
Story of Eleanor Roosevelt, 1959 Grosset, hardcover. ($15.00 with dust jacket) $10.00

HIEATT, Constance
Castle of Ladies, 1973 Crowell, first edition, hardcover, illustrated by Norman Laliberte. ($50.00 with dust jacket) $20.00

Joy of the Court, 1973 Thomas Y. Crowell, first edition, hardcover, illustrated by Pauline Baynes. ($50.00 with dust jacket) $20.00

HILDICK, E., see Series section McGURK

HILL, Denise
Coco the Gift Horse, 1966 Collins, London, first edition, blue hardcover. ($15.00 with dust jacket) $10.00

HILL, Eileen Sheila
Five Little Princesses from Tuppieland, 1953 Story Book Press, Dallas, first edition, small hardcover, 66 pages. ($35.00 with dust jacket) $15.00

HILL, Lorna, see Series section DANCING PEELS; MARJORIE; SADLER WELLS; VICARAGE CHILDREN

HILL, Margaret
Extra-Special Room, 1962 Little, Brown, first edition, hardcover. ($30.00 with dust jacket) $10.00

Hostess in the Sky, 1955 Little, Brown, first edition, hardcover. ($25.00 with dust jacket) $15.00

HILLARY, Sir Edmund, editor
Boys' Book of Exploration, 1957 Cassell, first edition, hardcover, halftone illustrations. ($35.00 with dust jacket) $20.00

HILLIER, Caroline
Winter's Tales for Children, 1965 MacMillan, first edition, hardcover, illustrated by Hugh Marshall. ($15.00 with dust jacket) $10.00.

HINTON, S.E.
Outsiders, 1967 Viking, first edition, hardcover, $100.00 with dust jacket. Later printings: ($20.00 with dust jacket) $10.00

That Was Then, This Is Now, 1971 Viking, hardcover. ($20.00 with dust jacket) $10.00

HIRSH, Marilyn
How the World Got Its Color, 1972 Crown, first

edition, oversize blue hardcover, illustrated. ($35.00 with dust jacket) $20.00

HITCHCOCK, Alfred, see Series section ALFRED HITCHCOCK AND THE THREE INVESTIGATORS; ALFRED HITCHCOCK ANTHOLOGIES
Alfred Hitchcock's Solve Them Yourself Mysteries, 1963 Random House, hardcover. $10.00

HOAG, Florence
I Love My Grandma, 1960 Whitman, pictorial hardcover, illustrations by Dagmar Wilson. $10.00

HOBAN, Lillian
Sugar Snow Spring, 1973 Harper, first edition, illustrated hardcover, 39 pages, illustrated by author. ($20.00 with dust jacket) $10.00

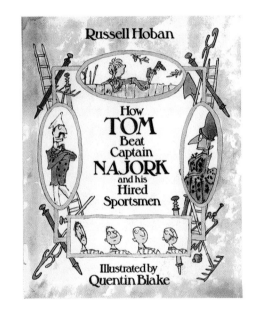

HOBAN, Russell
Baby Sister for Frances, 1964 Harper, first edition, cloth spine, pictorial boards, oversize, 32 pages. $75.00

Bargain for Frances, 1970 Harper, oversize hardcover, illustrated by Lillian Hoban. ($25.00 with dust jacket) $15.00

Bedtime for Frances, 1960 Harper, oversize, illustrated hardcover, b/w/green illustrations by Garth Williams. $25.00

Dinner at Alberta's, 1975 Crowell, first edition, hardcover, illustrated by James Marshall. ($30.00 with dust jacket) $15.00

Egg Thoughts and Other Frances Songs, 1972 Harper, first edition, hardcover, illustrations by Lillian Hoban. ($40.00 with dust jacket) $15.00

Herman the Loser, 1961 Harper, first edition, 32 pages, illustrated by Lillian Hoban. ($40.00 with dust jacket) $20.00

How Tom Beat Captain Nojork and His Hired Sportsmen, 1974 Atheneum, first edition, oversize hardcover, color illustrations by Quentin Blake. ($125.00 with dust jacket) $30.00

Emmett Otter's Jug-Band Christmas, 1971 Parents' Magazine Press, hardcover, color illustrations by Lillian Hoban. $20.00

Letitia Rabbit's String Song, 1973 Coward McCann, small hardcover, water color illustrations by Mary Chalmers. $20.00

Pedalling Man and Other Poems, 1969 World's Work, hardcover, 33 pages, illustrated by Lillian Hoban. ($50.00 with dust jacket) $20.00

Save My Place, 1967 Norton, library edition, hardcover, color illustrations by Lillian Hoban. ($25.00 with dust jacket) $15.00

Some Snow Said Hello, 1963 Harper, first edition, hardcover, illustrated by Lillian Hoban. ($35.00 with dust jacket) $20.00

Story of Hester Mouse, 1969 World's Work Ltd., first edition, hardcover, illustrated by Lillian Hoban. ($20.00 with dust jacket) $10.00

Tom and the Two Handles, 1965 Harper, illustrated boards, illustrated by Lillian Hoban. $10.00

London Men and English Men, 1962 Harper, oblong hardcover, illustrations by Lillian Hoban. $15.00

HOBART, Lois
Elaine Forrest, Visiting Nurse, 1959 Messner, hardcover. $15.00

Strangers Among Us, 1957 Funk & Wagnalls, first edition, hardcover. ($20.00 with dust jacket) $10.00

HOBERG, Marielis
One Summer in Majorca, 1961 Abelard-Schuman, first American edition, hardcover, illustrated by Hans Georg Lenzen. ($20.00 with dust jacket) $10.00

HODEIR, Andre
Warwick's 3 Bottles, 1966 Grove Press, first edition, hardcover, color illustrations throughout by Tomi Ungerer. ($25.00 with dust jacket) $15.00

HODGES, C. Walter
Overland Launch, 1970 Coward-McCann, first US edition, hardcover. ($25.00 with dust jacket) $10.00

HODGES, Elizabeth Jamison
Free As A Frog, 1969 Addison-Wesley, first edition, hardcover, illustrated by Paul Diovanopoulos. ($20.00 with dust jacket) $10.00

Serendipity Tales, 1966 Atheneum, first edition, hardcover, illustrated by June Atkin Corwin. ($15.00 with dust jacket) $10.00

HODGES, Margaret
Baldur and the Mistletoe: A Myth of the Vikings, 1974 Little, Brown, first edition, hardcover, illustrated by Gerry Hoover. ($25.00 with dust jacket) $10.00

Fire Bringer: A Paiute Indian Legend, 1972 Little, Brown, first edition, hardcover, illustrated by Peter Parnall. ($20.00 with dust jacket) $10.00

Gorgon's Head, A Myth from the Isles of Greece, 1972 Little, Brown, oversize square hardcover, illustrated by Charles Mikolaycak. $25.00

Making of Joshua Cobb, 1971 Farrar, Straus, Giroux, first edition, hardcover, illustrated by Richard Cuffari. ($25.00 with dust jacket) $10.00

Sing Out Charlie!, 1968 Farrar, first edition, hardcover, illustrated by Velma Isley. $10.00

Wave, 1964 Houghton Mifflin, pictorial hardcover, oversize, color illustrations by Blair Lent. $20.00

HODGSON, Ila
Bernadette's Busy Morning, 1968 Parents' Magazine Press, first edition, oversize oblong hardcover, illustrated by John E. Johnson. $25.00

HOFF, Syd
Sammy the Seal, 1959 Harper, I Can Read book, hardcover, illustrated by author. ($15.00 with dust jacket) $10.00

HOFFMANN, Heinrich
Mountain-Bounder, 1967 Macmillan, first edition, hardcover, illustrated by Heinrich Hoffmann. ($20.00 with dust jacket) $10.00

HOFFMANN, Hilde
City & Country Mother Goose, 1969 American Heritage Press, hardcover, illustrations by author. ($25.00 with dust jacket) $15.00

HOFSINDE, Robert (Gray-Wolf)
Indian's Secret World, 1955 Morrow, first edition, hardcover, illustrated by author. ($25.00 with dust jacket) $15.00

HOGAN, Inez
Cubby Bear and the Book, 1961 Dutton, first edition, hardcover. ($50.00 with dust jacket) $25.00
Eager Beaver, 1963 Dutton, first edition, hardcover, illustrated by author. ($50.00 with dust jacket) $20.00
Koala Bear Twins, 1955 Dutton, first edition, hardcover. ($50.00 with dust jacket) $20.00
Littlest Satellite, 1958 Dutton, first edition, hardcover. ($50.00 with dust jacket) $20.00
Twin Otters and the Indians, 1962 Dutton, first edition, hardcover. ($50.00 with dust jacket) $20.00
Twin Puppies, 1959 Dutton, first edition, hardcover. ($40.00 with dust jacket) $15.00

HOGBEN, Lawrence
Wonderful World of Mathematics, 1955 Garden City, glossy pictorial oversize hardcover, illustrated. $25.00

HOGG, Beth and **Garry**
Young Traveler in Norway, 1955 Dutton, first edition, hardcover, illustrated by photos and maps. ($20.00 with dust jacket) $10.00

HOGNER, Dorothy Childs
Dusty's Return, 1950 Oxford, first edition, hardcover, illustrated by Nils Hogner. ($15.00 with dust jacket) $10.00

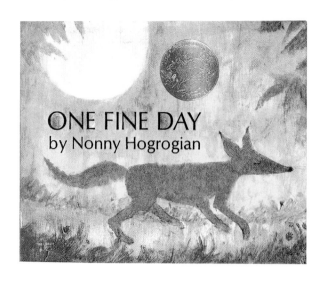

HOGROGIAN, Nonny
Billy Goat and His Well-Fed Friends, 1972 Harper, first edition, hardcover, illustrated by author. ($20.00 with dust jacket) $10.00
Handmade Secret Hiding Places, 1975 Overlook Press, first edition, hardcover, illustrated by author. ($20.00 with dust jacket) $15.00

Hermit and Harry and Me, 1972 Little Brown, first edition, hardcover, illustrated by author. ($25.00 with dust jacket) $15.00
One Fine Day, 1971 Macmillan, hardcover, 1972 Caldecott Award, illustrated by author. ($20.00 with dust jacket) $10.00
One I Love, Two I Love, and Other Loving Mother Goose Rhymes, 1972 Dutton, first edition, hardcover, illustrated by author. ($30.00 with dust jacket) $15.00
Renowned History of Little Red Riding Hood, 1967 Crowell, first edition, small hardcover, 32 pages, color illustrations by author. ($45.00 with dust jacket) $20.00
Rooster Brother, 1974 Macmillan, first edition, oblong hardcover, illustrated by author. ($30.00 with dust jacket) $15.00
Vasilisa the Beautiful, translated by Whitney, 1971 Macmillan, first edition, hardcover, illustrated by Hogrogian. ($20.00 with dust jacket) $10.00

HOLBERG, Ruth Langland
Three Birthday Wishes, 1953 Crowell, square, 122 pages, hardcover, illustrated endpapers, b/w illustrations by Lisl Weil. $10.00

HOLBROOK, Stewart H.
Mr. Otis, 1958 Macmillan, first edition, oversize hardcover, 71 pages, color plates. ($20.00 with dust jacket) $10.00

HOLL, Adelaide
Lisette, 1962 Lothrop, first edition, hardcover, 26 pages, illustrated by Roger Duvoisin. ($45.00 with dust jacket) $20.00

HOLLADAY, Virginia
Bantu Tales, 1970 Viking, first edition, illustrated hardcover, 95 pages, illustrated by Rocco Negri. ($20.00 with dust jacket) $10.00

HOLLAND, Marion
Big Ball of String, 1958 Collins, first edition UK, pictorial hardcover, illustrated by author. ($100.00 with dust jacket) $30.00
Billy Had a System, 1958 Knopf, hardcover, 184 pages, illustrated by author. ($30.00 with dust jacket) $15.00
Billy's Clubhouse, 1955 Knopf, first edition, hardcover. ($30.00 with dust jacket) $15.00
Every Girl's Horse Stories, 1956 Grosset, hardcover, b/w illustrations. ($15.00 with dust jacket) $10.00
No Children, No Pets, 1956 Knopf, hardcover, 181 pages, b/w illustrations by author. ($30.00 with dust jacket) $15.00
No Room for a Dog, 1959 Random House, hardcover, illustrated by Albert Orbaan. ($30.00 with dust jacket) $15.00

Teddy's Camp-Out, 1963 Knopf, hardcover, illustrated by author. ($30.00 with dust jacket) $15.00
Tree for Teddy, 1957 Knopf, hardcover, 59 pages. ($30.00 with dust jacket) $15.00

HOLLAND, Vyvyan
Explosion of Limericks, 1967 Funk & Wagnalls, oversize hardcover, b/w illustrations by Sprod. ($30.00 with dust jacket) $15.00

HOLLANDER, John
Book of Various Owls, 1963 Norton, first edition, oversize hardcover, illustrated by Tomi Ungerer. ($30.00 with dust jacket) $15.00

HOLLING, Holling Clancy
Minn of the Mississippi, 1951 Houghton, first edition, 86 pages, Newbery Honor book, illustrated by author. ($65.00 with dust jacket) $20.00
Pagoo, 1957 Houghton, oversize hardcover, 87 pages, color illustrations by author. ($65.00 with dust jacket) $20.00

HOLM, Anne
North to Freedom, 1963 Harcourt, Brace & World, first American edition, hardcover. ($20.00 with dust jacket) $10.00

HOLMAN, Felice
At the Top of My Voice, 1970 Norton, first edition, hardcover, illustrated by Edward Gorey. ($65.00 with dust jacket) $25.00
Blackmail Machine, 1968 Macmillan, first edition, hardcover. ($20.00 with dust jacket) $10.00
Cricket Winter, 1967 Norton, first edition, hardcover, illustrated by Ralph Pinto. ($15.00 with dust jacket) $10.00
Escape of the Giant Hogstalk, 1974 Scribners, first edition, hardcover, illustrated by Ben Shecter. ($20.00 with dust jacket) $10.00
Silently, the Cat and Miss Theodosia, 1965 Macmillan, first edition, hardcover, illustrated by H. Dinnerstein. ($25.00 with dust jacket) $15.00

HOLMELUND, Else, see MINARIK, Else Holmelund

HONOUR, Alan
Cave of Riches, 1956 McGraw-Hill, hardcover. $10.00

HOOPER, Muriel
Amelia and the Robber Rats, 1962 Bockhampton Press, first edition, hardcover. ($25.00 with dust jacket) $15.00

HOOVER, Helen
Animals at My Doorstep, 1966 Parents' Magazine Press, hardcover, with illustrated boards. $15.00
Gift of the Deer, 1967 Knopf, hardcover. $15.00

HOPKINS, Marjorie
And the Jackal Played the Masinko, 1969 Parents' Magazine Press, first edition, embossed design on oblong brown cloth, illustrated endpapers, illustrated by Olivia Cole. ($25.00 with dust jacket) $15.00

HORGAN, Paul
Saintmaker's Christmas Eve, 1955 Farrar, first edition. $20.00

HORWICH, Dr. Frances (TV's Miss Frances), see Series section DING DONG SCHOOL

HOUGHTON, Leighton
Phantom Rider, 1958 Lutterworth, London, first edition, hardcover, 158 pages, color illustrations. ($15.00 with dust jacket) $10.00

HOUSE, Charles
Lonesome Egg, 1968 Norton, first edition, hardcover. ($15.00 with dust jacket) $10.00

HOUSMAN, Laurence
Cotton-Wooleena, 1967 Doubleday, first edition, hardcover, 58 pages. ($25.00 with dust jacket) $15.00

HOUSTON, James
Wolf Run: A Caribou Eskimo Tale, 1971 Harcourt, Brace, first edition, hardcover, b/w illustrations by author. ($25.00 with dust jacket) $15.00

HOWARD, Max
People Papers, 1974 Harlin Quist, first edition, hardcover, illustrated. ($20.00 with dust jacket) $10.00

HOWARD, Vernon
California Ho!, 1950 Pickering and Inglis, London, first edition, hardcover, color frontispiece, 128 pages. ($15.00 with dust jacket) $10.00
Complete Book of Children's Theater, 1969 Doubleday, first edition, hardcover. ($20.00 with dust jacket) $15.00

HOYT, Edwin P.
Horatio's Boys, The Life and Works of Horatio Alger, Jr., 1974 Radnor Chilton, hardcover, illustrated. ($40.00 with dust jacket) $20.00

HUBBARD, Douglas
In Old Virginia City, 1966 Ginn, hardcover, illustrated by Ed Vella. $10.00

HUGHES, Ted
Season Songs, 1975 Viking, first edition, oversize

hardcover, full-page color illustrations by Leonard Baskin. ($40.00 with dust jacket) $15.00

Tiger's Bones and Other Plays for Children, 1974 Viking Press, first edition, hardcover, 141 pages, b/w illustrations by Alan E. Cober. ($30.00 with dust jacket) $20.00

HUGHES, Virginia, see Series section PEGGY LANE

HUME, Lotta Carswell
Favorite Children's Stories from China and Tibet, 1962 Tuttle, first edition, gilt dragon and lettering on red square hardcover, 119 pages, 12 full-page color illustrations plus b/w, illustrated by Lo Koon-chiu. ($45.00 with dust jacket) $25.00

HUME, Ruth and Paul
Lion of Poland: the Story of Paderewski, 1962 Hawthorn, hardcover, illustrated by Lili Rethi. ($30.00 with dust jacket) $15.00

HUNGERFORD, Edward Buell
Fighting Frigate, 1947 Follett, hardcover. ($60.00 for author-signed copy in dust jacket) $20.00

HUNT, Blanche Seale
Little Brown Koko Has Fun, 1952 American Colortype, oversize hardcover with paste-on-pictorial, 96 pages, illustrated by Dorothy Wagstaff. $45.00

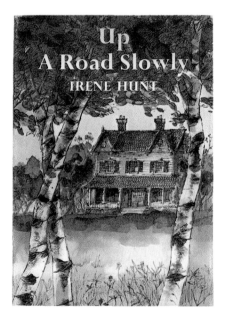

HUNT, Irene
Across Five Aprils, 1964 Follett, first edition, hardcover. ($20.00 with dust jacket) $10.00
No Promises in the Wind, 1970 Follett, first edition, hardcover. ($20.00 with dust jacket) $10.00
Trail of Apple Blossoms, 1968 Follett, first edition,

hardcover, illustrated by Don Bolognese. ($40.00 with dust jacket) $15.00

Up a Road Slowly, 1966 Follett, hardcover. Jacket illustration by Don Bolognese. First edition with dust jacket: $60.00. Later editions: ($20.00 with dust jacket) $15.00

HUNT, Mabel Leigh
Cupola House, 1961 Lippincott, first edition, hardcover, illustrated by Nora S. Unwin. ($20.00 with dust jacket) $10.00
Johnny-Up and Johnny-Down, 1962 Lippincott book club edition, pictorial cover, illustrated by Harold Berson. $10.00
Ladycake Farm 1952 Lippincott, first edition, hardcover, illustrated by Clotilde Funk. ($20.00 with dust jacket) $10.00
Miss Jellytot's Visit, 1955 Lippincott, first edition, hardcover, b/w illustrations by Velma Ilsley. ($30.00 with dust jacket) $15.00
Singing Among Strangers, 1954 Lippincott, first edition, hardcover, illustrated by Irene Gibian. ($35.00 with dust jacket) $15.00

HUNT, Maxine
General's Daughter, 1960 Julian Messiner, hardcover. ($20.00 with dust jacket) $10.00

HUNTER, Mollie
Sound of Chariots, 1972 Harper, hardcover. ($15.00 with dust jacket) $10.00
Stranger Came Ashore, 1975 Harper, hardcover. ($25.00 with dust jacket) $10.00
Stronghold, 1973 Hamish Hamilton, Carnegie Medal book, hardcover. ($35.00 with Charles Keeping with dust jacket) $15.00

HURD, Edith Thatcher
Caboose, 1951 Lothrop, first edition, hardcover. ($50.00 with dust jacket) $20.00

Catfish, 1970 Viking, first edition, hardcover, illustrated by Clement Hurd. ($50.00 with dust jacket) $20.00

Day the Sun Danced, 1965 Harper, first edition, hardcover. ($30.00 with dust jacket) $15.00

Johnny Littlejohn, 1957 Lothrop, first edition, hardcover, illustrated. ($30.00 with dust jacket) $15.00

Somebody's House, 1953 Lothrop, first edition, hardcover, 43 pages, two-color illustrations by Clement Hurd. ($50.00 with dust jacket) $20.00

Wilson's World, 1971 Harper, oversize hardcover. ($15.00 with dust jacket) $10.00

HURLIMANN, Bettina

Seven Houses, My Life with Books, 1968 World, first edition, hardcover, illustrated. ($25.00 with dust jacket) $15.00

Three Centuries of Children's Books in Europe, 1968 World, first American edition, hardcover, plate illustrations. ($50.00 with dust jacket) $20.00

HURLIMANN, Ruth

Mouse with the Daisy Hat, 1971 David White, oversize hardcover. ($35.00 with dust jacket) $15.00.

HURLONG, Lena F.

Adventures of Jaboti on the Amazon, 1968 Abelard, illustrated by John Vernon Lord. ($25.00 with dust jacket) $10.00

HUTCHINS, Pat

Silver Christmas Tree, 1972 Macmillan, hardcover, illustrated. $15.00

Wind Blew, 1974 Macmillan, first edition, oblong pictorial hardcover, color illustrations by author. ($20.00 with dust jacket) $10.00

HUTCHINS, Ross

Travels of Monarch X, 1966 Rand McNally, first edition, hardcover, illustrated by Jerome P. Connolly. $15.00

HUTCHISON, C.

Toward Daybreak, 1950 Harper, first edition, hardcover, three illustrations by Marc Chagall. ($25.00 with dust jacket) $15.00

HUXLEY, Aldous

Crows of Pearblossom, 1967 edition Chatto and Windus, first edition, hardcover, green, illustrated by Barbara Cooney. ($20.00 with dust jacket) $10.00

Crows of Pearblossom, 1967 edition Random House, Weekly Reader edition, pictorial boards, illustrated by Barbara Cooney. $10.00

Hyde, Dayton O.

Cranes In My Corral, 1971 Dial Press, first edition, hardcover, illustrations by Lorence Bjorklund. ($15.00 with dust jacket) $10.00

HYMAN, Trina Schart

How Six Found Christmas, 1969 Little Brown, first edition, hardcover, illustrated by author. ($35.00 with dust jacket) $20.00

IBBOTSON, EVA

Great Ghost Rescue, 1975 Walck, hardcover, illustrations Giulio Maestro. ($25.00 with dust jacket) $15.00

IBBOTSON, M. C.

Robertson, Ugly & Nohow, 1968 Pantheon, hardcover, b/w illustrations by Edward McLachlan. ($20.00 with dust jacket) $10.00

IDELL, ALBERT

Corner Store, 1953 Doubleday, Book Club edition, hardcover. ($20.00 with dust jacket) $10.00

ILSEY, Velma

Long Stocking, 1959 Lippincott, first edition, hardcover. ($30.00 with dust jacket) $15.00

INGER, Nan

Katie and Nan Go to Sea, 1964 Harcourt, 160 pages, hardcover, illustrations by Eva Zetterland. ($25.00 with dust jacket) $15.00

IPCAR, Dahlov

Black and White, 1963 Alfred A. Knopf, first edition, hardcover, verse, illustrations by author. ($20.00 with dust jacket) $15.00

Bright Barnyard, 1966 Knopf, 34 pages, illustrations by author. ($30.00 with dust jacket) $15.00

Brown Cow Farm, 1959 Doubleday, first edition, oblong oversize hardcover, illustrations by author. ($40.00 with dust jacket) $20.00

Cat at Night, 1969 Doubleday, hardcover, illustrations by author. ($40.00 with dust jacket) $20.00

Cat Came Back, 1971 Knopf, first edition, purple oversize hardcover with gilt, color illustrations by author. ($50.00 with dust jacket) $25.00

Horses of Long Ago, 1965 Doubleday, oversize hardcover picture book, 61 pages. ($25.00 with dust jacket) $15.00

One Horse Farm, 1950 Doubleday, first edition, oblong oversize hardcover, illustrations by author. ($40.00 with dust jacket) $15.00

Queen of Spells, 1973 Viking, first edition, hardcover. ($30.00 with dust jacket) $10.00

Sir Addlepate and the Unicorn, 1971 Garden City, first edition, hardcover, color illustrations by author. ($20.00 with dust jacket) $10.00

Whispering and Other Things, poetry, 1967 Knopf, oversize hardcover, illustrations by author. ($30.00 with dust jacket) $15.00

Wonderful Egg, 1958 Doubleday, first edition, hardcover, illustrations by author. ($45.00 with dust jacket) $25.00

IRESON, Barbara

Faber Book of Nursery Stories, 1966 Faber & Faber, London, hardcover, illustrations by Shirley Hughes. ($30.00 in with dust jacket) $15.00

IVENS, Dorothy

Long Hike, 1956 Viking Press, first edition, hardcover, illustrated. ($25.00 with dust jacket) $10.00

IVES, Burl

Sailing on a Very Fine Day, 1954 Rand McNally, first edition, Elf Book, small hardcover, silver spine, illustrations by Bernice and Lou Myers. $15.00

J

JABLONSKI, Edward

Great War Stories of World War I, 1965 Whitman, hardcover, green pictorial boards, illustrations by Arnie Kohn. $10.00

JACKSON, Edgar N.

Green Mountain Hero, 1961 Lantern, first edition, hardcover. ($15.00 with dust jacket) $10.00

JACKSON, Gary

Shorty Carries the Ball, 1952 Follett, first edition, hardcover. ($15.00 with dust jacket) $10.00

JACKSON, Jacqueline and William PERLMUTTER

Endless Pavement, 1973 Seabury, hardcover, illustrations by Richard Cuffari. $10.00

JACKSON, Jesse

Tessie, 1968 Harper, first edition, hardcover 243 pages, pictures by Harold James. ($35.00 with dust jacket) $15.00

JACKSON, Kathryn

Cowboys and Indians, (1948) 1968 edition Golden, oversize hardcover pictorial boards, 76 pages, illustrations by Gustaf Tenggren. $40.00

Animals Merry Christmas, 1975 edition Golden, glossy hardcover, 68 pages, illustrations by Richard Scarry. $30.00

Farm Stamps, 1957 Simon and Schuster, hardcover. $15.00

Pirates, Ships and Sailors, 1950 Simon and Schuster, first edition, glossy illustrated hardcover, color illustrations by Gustaf Tenggren. $20.00

Winter Tales, 1967 edition Golden Press, small, hardcover, color and b/w illustrations. $15.00

JACKSON, Paul

Rookie Catcher, 1966 Hasting House, hardcover. ($20.00 with dust jacket) $10.00

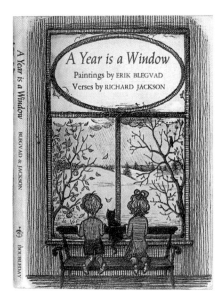

JACKSON, Richard

Year is a Window, 1963 Doubleday, pictorial hardcover, color illustrations by Erik Blegvad. ($25.00 with dust jacket) $10.00

JACKSON, Shirley

Famous Sally, 1966 Harlin Quist, first edition, hardcover with gilt, color illustrations by Charles B. Slackman. ($50.00 with dust jacket) $20.00

Life Among the Savages, 1953 Farrar, Straus, hardcover. ($15.00 with dust jacket) $10.00

JACOBS, Flora Gill
Doll House Mystery, 1958 Coward-McCann, first edition, hardcover, illustrated. ($25.00 with dust jacket) $15.00

JACOBS, Frank
Alvin Steadfast on Vernacular Island, 1965 Dial, yellow cloth hardcover, 64 pages, b/w illustrations by Edward Gorey. ($60.00 with dust jacket) $30.00

JACOBS, Joseph
Buried Moon, 1969 Bradbury, first edition, square hardcover, illustrations by Susan Jeffers. ($20.00 with dust jacket) $15.00

JACOBS, Leland B.
Belling the Cat and Other Stories, 1960 Golden Press, hardcover, 28 pages, illustrations by Berson. $15.00
Just Around The Corner, 1964 Holt, Rinehart and Winston, Weekly Reader edition, hardcover. $10.00

JACOBSON, Ethel and **Florence HARRISON**
Curious Cats, 1969 Funk & Wagnalls, first edition, oversize hardcover, photographs. ($25.00 with dust jacket) $15.00

JAEGER, Karel
Bull That Was Terrifico, 1956 John Day, first American edition, hardcover, illustrated by Cam. ($20.00 with dust jacket) $10.00

JAFFE, Rona
Last of the Wizards, 1961 Simon & Schuster, first

edition, hardcover, color and b/w illustrations by E. Blegvad. ($15.00 with dust jacket) $10.00

JAGENDORF, M. A.
Ghost of Peg Leg Peter and Other Stories of Old New York, 1965 Vanguard, hardcover, illustrations by Lino Lipinsky. ($30.00 with dust jacket) $15.00

JAMES, Kathleen
Basement Clown, 1972 Victor Gollancz, London, first edition, red hardcover, gilt spine letters, 126 pages, pictures by Richard Kennedy. ($15.00 with dust jacket) $10.00

JANSSON, Tove, see Series section MOOMIN
Summer Book, 1974 Pantheon Books, first American edition, hardcover. ($30.00 with dust jacket) $20.00

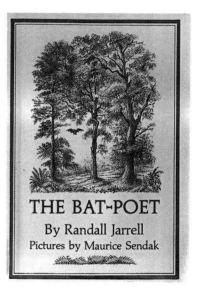

JARRELL, Randall
Animal Family, 1965 Pantheon, first edition, hardcover, illustrations by Maurice Sendak. ($65.00 with dust jacket) $20.00
Bat-Poet, 1965 Macmillan, hardcover, 43 pages, illustrations by Maurice Sendak. ($45.00 with dust jacket) $20.00
Gingerbread Rabbit, 1964 Macmillan, first edition, hardcover, illustrations by Garth Williams. First edition $150.00 with dust jacket. Later editions: ($20.00 with dust jacket) $10.00
Snow-White and the Seven Dwarfs: Tale from Brothers Grimm, 1972 Farrar, first edition, hardcover, full page color plates by Nancy Ekholm Burkert. ($25.00 with dust jacket) $15.00

JENKINS, Alan
Kingdom of the Elephants, 1963 Follett, first edition, hardcover. ($25.00 with dust jacket) $15.00

JENKINS, Louise
Bayou Hunter, 1958 Bobbs Merrill, first edition, hardcover. ($15.00 with dust jacket) $8.00

JENNINGS, Michael
Mattie Fritts and the Flying Mushroom, 1973 Windmill, first edition, white hardcover, 93 pages, b/w illustrations by N. M. Bodeker. ($20.00 with dust jacket) $10.00

JENNINGS, Paul
Great Jelly of London, 1967 Faber & Faber, London, first edition, hardcover, 32 pages, colored text and full page illustrations by Gerald Rose. ($35.00 with dust jacket) $20.00

JENNY, Anne
Fantastic Story of King Brioche, 1973 Lothrop Lee, hardcover, illustrations by Jocelyne Pache. ($15.00 with dust jacket) $10.00

JENSEN, Lee
Pony Express, 1955 Grosset, first edition, hardcover. ($25.00 with dust jacket) $10.00

JESSUP, Ronald
Wonderful World of Archaeology, 1956 Garden City, first edition, oversize hardcover, 69 pages, illustrated. ($20.00 with dust jacket) $10.00

JETER, Jacky
Cat and the Fiddler, 1968 Parents' Magazine Press, illustrated hardcover, illustrations by Lionel Kalish. $15.00

JEWELL, Nancy
Cheer Up, Pig!, 1975 Harper and Row, first edition, small hardcover, 32 pages, color illustrated drawings by Ben Shecter . ($20.00 with dust jacket) $10.00
Try and Catch Me, 1972 Harper, first edition, oversize hardcover, 32 pages, illustrations by Leonard Weisgard. ($25.00 with dust jacket) $10.00

JEWETT, Eleanore
Cobblers' Knob, 1967 Viking, hardcover, illustrated. ($25.00) $15.00
Big John's Secret, 1962 Viking, hardcover. ($25.00) $15.00
Mystery at Boulder Point, 1949 Viking, hardcover. ($35.00) $15.00

JEWETT, Sarah Orne
White Heron, a Story of Maine, 1963 Crowell, first edition, hardcover, color illustrations by Barbara Cooney. ($30.00 with dust jacket) $15.00

JOHNS, Captain W.E., see Series section BIGGLES
Worlds Of Wonder, 1962 Hodder & Stoughton, first edition, hardcover. ($40.00 with dust jacket) $15.00

JOHNSON, Annabel and **Edgar**
Golden Touch, 1963 Harper & Row, pictorial hardcover. $15.00

JOHNSON, Barbara Greenough
Big Fish, 1959 Little Brown, first edition, hardcover, illustrations by Mary Greenough. ($15.00 with dust jacket) $10.00

JOHNSON, Crockett
Ellen's Lion, 1959 Harper, first edition, illustrated hardcover, 62 pages, illustrations by author. ($65.00 with dust jacket) $20.00
Emperor's Gifts, 1965 Holt Rinehart Winston, first edition, hardcover, illustrations by Johnson. ($25.00 with dust jacket) $10.00
Gordy and the Pirate, 1965 Putnam, blue hardcover, 46 pages. ($20.00 with dust jacket) $10.00
Harold and the Purple Crayon, 1955 Harper, first edition, hardcover, illustrations by author. ($50.00 with dust jacket) $20.00
Harold and the Purple Crayon, later book club editions, illustrated hardcover. $15.00
*Lion's Own Story,*1963 Harper and Row, first edition, hardcover, 63 pages, illustrations by author. ($75.00 with dust jacket) $30.00
Picture for Harold's Room, 1960 Harper I Can Read Book, illustrated hardcover, illustrations by author. $15.00

JOHNSON, Eleanor
Magic Carpet, 1954 Charles E. Merrill, Treasury of Literature Readtext Series, hardcover. $30.00

JOHNSON, Elisabeth
Three-In-One Prince, 1961 Little Brown, first edition, hardcover, illustrations by Ronnie Solbert. ($15.00 with dust jacket) $10.00

JOHNSON, Enid
Right Job For Judith, 1962 Messner, hardcover. $10.00
Bill Williams: Mountain Man, 1952 Julian Messner, first edition, hardcover, illustrations by Richard Bennett. ($15.00 with dust jacket) $10.00

JOHNSON, Gerald W.
Pattern For Liberty, 1952 McGraw Hill, first edition, oversize obling hardcover with gilt lettering, 146 pages, 32 full-page color plates by artists: Frank Reilly, Simon Greco, James Bingham. ($45.00 with dust jacket) $30.00

JOHNSON, James Ralph
Lost on Hawk Mountain, 1954 Follett Publishing, first edition, hardcover, illustrations by author. ($25.00 with dust jacket) $10.00

JOHNSON, Lois
Happy Birthdays Round the World, 1967 Rand McNally, small hardcover, 128 pages. ($15.00 with dust jacket) $10.00

JOHNSON, Ryerson
Upstairs and Downstairs, 1962 Crowell, first edition, hardcover, illustrations by Lisl Weil. ($50.00 with dust jacket) $30.00

JOHNSON, Winifred
Stained Glass House, 1965 Macrae Smith, hardcover. $10.00

JOHNSTON, Johanna
Great Gravity the Cat, 1958 Alfred A. Knopf, first edition, hardcover, illustrations by Kurt Wiese. ($20.00 with dust jacket) $10.00
Penguin's Way, 1962 Doubleday, first edition, hardcover, b/w/blue/yellow illustrations by Leonard Weisgard. ($25.00 with dust jacket) $15.00

JOHNSTON, Minton
How the Littlest Cherub Was Late for Christmas, 1967 Abington Press, first edition, hardcover, illustrations by Ralph McDonald. ($20.00 with dust jacket) $10.00

JOHNSTON, William
Dr. Kildare and the Magic Key, 1964 Whitman, pictorial hardcover, illustrations by Al Andersen and Jason Art Studio. $15.00
F Troop, the Great Indian Uprising, 1967 Whitman, hardcover, illustrations by Larry Pelini. $25.00
Gilligan's Island, 1966 Whitman. illustrated hardcover, illustrated endpapers, 212 pages. $10.00
Munsters and the Great Camera Caper, 1965 Whitman, illustrated hardcover, authorized edition based on the tv series, illustrated by Arnie Kohn. $25.00
Munsters and the Last Resort, 1966 Whitman, illustrated hardcover. $25.00

JONES, Diana Wynne
Cart and Cwidder, 1975 Macmillan, first UK edition, hardcover. ($30.00 with dust jacket) $15.00
Eight Days of Luke, 1975 Macmillan, hardcover. ($25.00 with dust jacket) $15.00
Ogre Downstairs, (1974) 1975 Dutton, first American edition, hardcover. ($30.00 with dust jacket) $15.00

JONES, Dorothy Holder
Those Gresham Girls, 1965 Funk & Wagnalls, illustrated hardcover. $ 20.00

JONES, DuPre
Adventures of Gremlin, 1966 Lippincott, first edition, hardcover, illustrated by Edward Gorey. ($150.00 with dust jacket) $50.00

JONES, Elizabeth Orton
Song of the Sun, St. Francis of Assisi, 1952 Macmillan, first edition, oversize hardcover, illustrations by Jones. ($50.00 with dust jacket) $20.00

JONES, Hettie
Longhouse Winter, 1972 Holt, Rinehart & Winston, first edition, hardcover. ($20.00 with dust jacket) $10.00

JONES, Mary Alice
Tell Me About Christmas, 1958 Rand, first edition, hardcover, color illustrations by Marjorie Cooper. ($30.00 with dust jacket) $10.00
Tell Me About Heaven, 1956 Rand McNally, first edition, oversize hardcover, 70 pages, illustrations by Marjorie Cooper. ($30.00 with dust jacket) $10.00

JONES, Raymond F.
Stories of Great Physicians, 1963 Whitman, hardcover. ($15.00 with dust jacket) $8.00
Voyage to the Bottom of the Sea, 1965 Whitman, glossy illustrated hardcover, illustrations by Leon Jason Studios. $10.00

JOSLIN, Sesyle
Baby Elephant's Baby Book, 1964 Harcourt Brace, first edition, small hardcover, two-color illustrations by Leonard Weisgard. ($35.00 with dust jacket) $15.00
Baby Elephant's Trunk, 1961 Harcourt Brace, first edition, hardcover, illustrations by Leonard

Weisgard. ($30.00 with dust jacket) $15.00

Doctor George Owl, 1970 Houghton Mifflin, first edition, illustrated hardcover, illustrated by Lisl Weil. ($25.00 with dust jacket) $15.00

Pinkety Pinkety, 1966 Harcourt Brace & World, first edition, pink oblong hardcover, illustrations by Luciana Roselli. ($25.00 with dust jacket) $15.00

Please Share that Peanut!, 1965 Harcourt, first edition, hardcover, 60 pages, illustrations by Simms Taback. ($25.00 with dust jacket) $15.00

Qu'Est-Ce Qu'On Dit, Mon Petit?, 1966 Young Scott, first edition thus, oblong hardcover. French translation of "What Do You Say, Dear?" ($50.00 with dust jacket) $25.00

Senor Baby Elephant the Pirate, 1962 Harcourt, Brace, first edition, hardcover, 96 pages, illustrations by Leonard Weisgard. ($20.00 with dust jacket) $15.00

What Do You Say, Dear? a Book of Manners for All Occasions, 1958 Scott Young, first edition, small hardcover, illustrations by Maurice Sendak. ($100.00 with dust jacket) $40.00

JUDSON, Clara Ingram

Andrew Jackson, 1954 Follett, first edition, hardcover. ($25.00 with dust jacket) $10.00

JUPO, Frank

Up the Trail and Down the Street, 1956 Macmillan, first edition, oversize hardcover, 38 pages, color illustrations by author. ($20.00 with dust jacket) $10.00

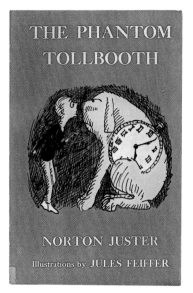

JUSTER, Norton

Alberic the Wise and Other Journeys, 1965 Pantheon, first edition, hardcover, illustrations by Pomenico Gnoli. ($40.00 with dust jacket) $15.00

Phantom Toll Booth, 1961 Random House, hardcover, map endpapers, illustrations by Jules Feiffer. ($20.00 with dust jacket) $10.00

K

KAHL, Ann

Francis Discovers the World, 1962 Luce, hardcover, color illustrations by author. $25.00

KAHL, Virginia

Giants, Indeed!, 1974 Scribner, Weekly Reader Book Club edition, hardcover, color illustrations by author. $20.00

Habits of Rabbits, 1957 Scribner, first edition, hardcover, illustrated. ($45.00 with dust jacket) $20.00

KAHN, Joan

Some Things Dark and Dangerous, 1971 Bodley Head or Harper Row, hardcover. ($25.00 with dust jacket) $10.00

Some Things Fierce and Fatal: 14 Suspense Stories, Some Fact, Some Fiction, 1971 Harper and Row, hardcover. ($20.00 with dust jacket) $10.00

Some Things Strange and Sinister, 1973 Bodley Head or Harper Row, hardcover. ($25.00 with dust jacket) $10.00

Some Things Weird and Wicked, 1976 Pantheon, hardcover. ($20.00 with dust jacket) $10.00

KALB, Jonah

How to Play Baseball Better than You Did Last Year, 1974 Macmillan, oversize hardcover, 148 pages, illustrated. ($15.00 with dust jacket) $10.00

Kids' Candidate, 1975 Houghton Mifflin, first edition, hardcover, illustrated by Sandy Kossin. ($20.00 with dust jacket) $10.00 Weekly Reader edition: $10.00

KALNAY, Francis

Richest Boy in the World, 1959 Harcourt, Brace,

first edition, hardcover, illustrated by W. T. Mars. ($20.00 with dust jacket) $10.00

KALUSKY, Rebecca
Is It Blue as a Butterfly?, 1965 Prentice-Hall, first edition, hardcover, color illustrations by Aliki. ($20.00 with dust jacket) $10.00

KAMPMANN, Ulla
Eva and Her Grandmother's Cat, 1968 Follett, hardcover, color illustrations by author. ($25.00 with dust jacket) $15.00

KANE, Sharon
Little Mommy, 1967 Golden Press, hardcover, color illustrations by author. $20.00

KANTOR, MacKinlay
Lobo, 1957 World, hardcover, b/w illustrations by Irene Layne. ($25.00 with dust jacket) $15.00

KANTROWITZ, Mildred
Good-bye Kitchen, 1972 Parents, hardcover, illustrated endpapers, color illustrations by Mercer Mayer. $25.00
I Wonder if Herbie's Home Yet, 1971 Parents, pictorial hardcover, color illustrations by Tony DeLuna. $20.00
Maxie, 1970 Parents, pictorial hardcover, color illustrations by Emily McCully. $20.00

KAPP, Paul
Cat Came Fiddling, and other Rhymes of Childhood, 1956 Harcourt, Brace, first edition, oversize hardcover, 80 pages, illustrated by Irene Haas. ($20.00 with dust jacket) $10.00

KASSIRER, Norma
Doll Snatchers, 1969 Viking, hardcover, b/w illustrations by Donald Mackay. ($25.00 with dust jacket) $10.00

KASTNER, Erich
Baron Munchhausen: His Wonderful Travels & Adventures, 1957 edition Messner, hardcover, color illustrations by Walter Trier. ($25.00 with dust jacket) $15.00
Little Man, 1966 Knopf (translation by James Kirkup), first American edition, illustrations by Rick Schrieter. ($20.00 with dust jacket) $10.00
Little Man and the Big Thief, 1969 Knopf, first American edition, hardcover, b/w illustrations by Stan Mack. ($25.00 with dust jacket) $10.00
Puss in Boot, 1957 Messner, hardcover, color illustrations by Walter Trier. $20.00

KAUFMAN, Joseph
Snowman Book, ca. 1965 Golden Press Shape Book, pictorial softcover, color illustrations by author. $15.00

KAUFMANN, Alicia
No Room for Nicky, 1969 Hawthorne, hardcover, red/brown illustrations by Vicki De Larrea. ($25.00 with dust jacket) $15.00

KAULA, Edna
One Two Buckle My Shoe, 1951 Whitman, book 2466, color illustrated hardcover, color illustrations by author. $25.00

KAWAGUCHI, Sanae
Taro's Festival Day, 1957 Little, Brown, first edition, oblong hardcover, 41 pages, illustrated. ($20.00 with dust jacket) $10.00

KAY, Helen
Henri's Hands for Pablo Picasso, ca. 1965 Abelard-Schuman, hardcover, b/w and color illustrations by Victor Ambrus. ($25.00 with dust jacket) $15.00
House of Many Colors, ca. 1963 Abelard-Schuman, hardcover, b/w and color illustrations by Lilian Obligado. ($25.00 with dust jacket) $15.00

KEATS, Ezra Jack
Apt. 3, 1972 Macmillan, hardcover, color illustrations by author. ($35.00 with dust jacket) $15.00
Dreams, 1974 Macmillan, first edition, oversize hardcover, color illustrations by author. ($35.00 with dust jacket) $15.00
God is in the Mountain, 1966 Holt, first edition, oversize hardcover. ($35.00 with dust jacket) $15.00
Goggles!, 1969 Macmillan, first edition, hardcover, color illustrations by author. ($45.00 with dust jacket) $25.00
Jennie's Hat, 1966 Harper, hardcover, color illustrations by author. $20.00

John Henry, 1965, first edition, oversize hardcover, color illustrations by author. ($45.00 with dust jacket) $15.00

Letter to Amy, 1968 Harper, first edition, hardcover, 32 pages, color illustrations by author. ($25.00 with dust jacket) $15.00

Little Drummer Boy, 1968 Macmillan, first edition, oblong hardcover, words and music by Davis, Onorati and Simeone, color illustrations by author. ($45.00 with dust jacket) $15.00

Louie, 1975 Greenwillow Books, first edition, hardcover, illustrated by author. ($15.00 with dust jacket) $10.00

My Dog Is Lost!, 1960 Thomas Crowell, first edition, hardcover, illustrations by Pat Cherr. ($20.00 with dust jacket) $15.00

Night, 1969 Atheneum, first edition, hardcover, photographs by Beverly Hall. ($25.00 with dust jacket) $15.00

Peter's Chair, 1967 Harper, first edition, hardcover, illustrations by author. ($25.00 with dust jacket) $15.00

Pet Show, 1972 Macmillan, book club edition, hardcover, color illustrations by author. $15.00

Slates!, 1973 Franklin Watts, first edition, hardcover, illustrations by author. ($35.00 with dust jacket) $15.00

Snowy Day, 1962 Viking, 1963 Caldecott Award, first edition, hardcover, color illustrations by author. $65.00 with dust jacket. Later editions: ($20.00 with dust jacket) $10.00

Whistle for Willie, 1964 Viking, hardcover, color illustrations by author. $20.00

KEATS, John
Naughty Boy, 1965 Viking, hardcover, b/w/red illustrations by Ezra Jack Keats. ($35.00 with dust jacket) $15.00

KEEPING, Charles
Black Dolly, the Story of a Junk Cart Pony, 1966 Brockhampton Press, Leicester, picture book, 33 pages, pictorial paper covered boards, illustrated endpapers, double-page color illustrations. ($35.00 with dust jacket) $15.00

Richard, 1973 Oxford University Press, first edition, hardcover, illustrations by author. ($30.00 with dust jacket) $15.00

Wasteground Circus, 1975 Oxford University Press, first edition, hardcover. ($40.00 with dust jacket) $15.00

KEITH, Harold
Bluejay Boarders, 1972 Crowell, hardcover, color illustrations by Harold Berson. $20.00

KELLER, Frances
Contented Little Pussy Cat, ca. 1949 Platt Munk, hardcover, color illustrations by Adele Werber and Doris Laslo. ($25.00 with dust jacket) $15.00

Curious Little Owl, ca. 1957 Platt Munk, hardcover, color illustrations by Adele Werber and Doris Laslo. ($25.00 with dust jacket) $15.00

KELLOGG, Steven
Island of Skog, 1971 Dial Press, first edition, pink oblong hardcover, illustrations by author. ($20.00 with dust jacket) $10.00

KELLY, Eric
In Clean Hay, 1953 Macmillan, hardcover, color illustrations by Maud and Miska Petersham. ($45.00 with dust jacket) $20.00

KELLY, Rosalie
Great Toozy Takeover, 1975 Putnam, first edition, hardcover. ($20.00 with dust jacket) $10.00

KELLY, Walt
Songs of the Pogo, 1956 Simon & Schuster, first edition, hardcover, 152 pages, illustrations by author. ($60.00 with dust jacket) $30.00

Ten Ever-Lovin' Blue-Eyed Years with Pogo, 1959 Simon & Schuster, first edition, oversize hardcover, 288 pages, illustrations by author. ($45.00 with dust jacket) $20.00

Uncle Pogo So So Stories, ca. 1953 Simon & Schuster, first edition, oversize softcover cartoon book. $50.00

KENDALL, Lace
Mud Ponies, 1963 Coward McCann, hardcover, color illustrations by Eugene Fern. $25.00

Kennedy, Jean
Nunga Punga & The Booch, 1975 Charles Scribner, first edition, hardcover, 91 pages, illustrated endpapers, b/w drawings by Anne Burgess. ($15.00 with dust jacket) $10.00

KENNEDY, Mary
Come and See Me, 1966 Harper, hardcover, b/w/blue illustrations by Martha Alexander. ($25.00 with dust jacket) $10.00

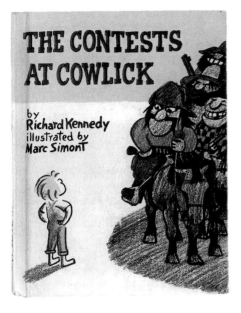

KENNEDY, Richard
Contests at Cowlick, ca. 1975 Little Brown, Weekly Reader edition, illustrated hardcover, color illustrations by Marc Simont. $15.00

KENNEDY., X. J.
One Winter Night in August, 1975 Atheneum, hardcover, b/w illustrations by David McPhail. $15.00

KENT, Jack
Grown-Up Day, 1969 Parents' Magazine Press, first edition, color illustrated paper over hardcover, color illustrations. $15.00
Mrs. Mooley, 1973 Golden Books, Artists and Writers Guild Book, first edition, hardcover, color illustrations. ($25.00 with dust jacket) $15.00
Wizard of Wallaby Wallow, 1971 Parents', Weekly Reader edition, illustrated hardcover, color illustrations by Jack Kent. $15.00

KENT, Margaret
Lucky Thirteen, 1960 Pantheon, hardcover, b/w illustrations by Imre Hofbauer. ($20.00 with dust jacket) $10.00

KERR, Judith
When Willy Went to the Wedding, 1973 Parents', hardcover, color illustrations by author. $30.00

KERR, M. E.
Son of Someone Famous, 1974 Harper and Row, first edition, hardcover, 226 pages. ($35.00 with dust jacket) $15.00

KESSELL, Joseph
Lion, 1962 Knopf, first edition, hardcover. illustrations by Harper Johnson. ($40.00 with dust jacket) $20.00

KESSELMAN, Wendy
Time for Jody, 1975 Harper, small oblong hardcover, b/w illustrations by Gerald Dumas. ($20.00 with dust jacket) $10.00

KESSLER, Ethel and Leonard
All Aboard the Train, 1964 Doubleday, first edition, hardcover, color illustrations by Leonard Kessler. ($25.00 with dust jacket) $15.00
All for Fall, 1974 Parents, hardcover, illustrated endpapers, color illustrations by Leonard Kessler. ($20.00 with dust jacket) $10.00
Kick, Pass and Run, 1966 Harper, pictorial hardcover, b/w/brown/green illustrations by author. $15.00
Last One in is a Rotten Egg, 1969 Harper, hardcover, color illustrations by author. $15.00
Splish Splash!, 1973 Parents', color illustrated hardcover, illustrated endpapers, color illustrations by authors. $15.00
Tale of Two Bicycles, 1971 Lothrop, Lee, hardcover, color illustrations by author. $15.00

KEY, Alexander
Escape to Witch Mountain, 1963 Westminster, first edition, hardcover. ($50.00 with dust jacket) $20.00
Forgotten Door, 1965 Westminster, first edition, hardcover. ($50.00 with dust jacket) $20.00
Mystery of the Sassafras Chair, 1967 Westminster, illustrated library binding hardcover. $20.00

KEY, Ted
Biggest Dog in the World, 1960 Dutton, first edition, oversize hardcover, 72 pages, illustrations by author. ($25.00 with dust jacket) $10.00

KIDWELL, Carl
Arrow in the Sun, 1961 Viking, first edition, hardcover. ($15.00 with dust jacket) $10.00

KIMMEL, Margaret Mary
Magic in the Mist, 1975 Atheneum, hardcover, first edition, illustrated by Trina Schart Hyman. ($25.00 with dust jacket) $15.00

KING, Alexander
Memoirs of a Certain Mouse, 1965 McGraw-Hill, green hardcover, 93 pages. ($25.00 with dust jacket) $10.00
Great Ker-Plunk, 1962 Simon & Schuster, first edition, hardcover, illustrated by Robin Alexander. ($35.00 with dust jacket) $15.00

KING, Clive
Hamid of Aleppo, 1958 Macmillan, first edition, oversize hardcover, 47 pages, illustrations by Giovanetti. $15.00
Town That Went South, 1959 Macmillan, first edition, hardcover, illustrations by Maurice Bartlett. ($15.00 with dust jacket) $10.00

KING, Helen
Willy, 1971 Doubleday, first edition, hardcover, illustrations by Carole Byard. ($20.00 with dust jacket) $10.00

KING, Robin
Pioneers: A Badger Book, 1959 Whitman, glossy color pictorial hardcover, 92 pages, illustrated endpapers, illustrations in color by Charles Beck. $15.00

KINGMAN, Lee
Flivver the Heroic Horse, 1958 Garden City, first edition, hardcover, illustrations by Eric Blegvad. ($35.00 with dust jacket) $15.00
House of the Blue Horse, 1960 Doubleday, first edition, hardcover. ($20.00 with dust jacket) $10.00
Magic Christmas Tree, 1956 Ariel Books, Farrar, first edition, hardcover, illustrated endpapers, watercolor illustrations by Bettina. ($40.00 with dust jacket) $20.00
Mikko's Fortune, 1963 Cadmus Library Edition, hardcover, color illustrations by Arnold Edwin Bare. $10.00
Peter's Pony, 1963 Doubleday, first edition, hardcover, illustrations by F. Lasell. ($25.00 with dust jacket) $15.00

KIPLING, Rudyard
Elephant's Child, 1969 edition Follett, first edition, hardcover, 48 pages, color illustrations by Ulla Kampmann. ($30.00 with dust jacket) $20.00

KIRKUP, James
Insect Summer, 1971 Knopf, first edition, hardcover, b/w woodcuts by Naoko Matsubara. ($20.00 with dust jacket) $10.00

KIRTLAND, Elizabeth
Buttons in the Back, A Cameo of Yesterday that Makes a Better Today, 1958 Vangard, first edition, hardcover, illustrated by David Levine. ($25.00 with dust jacket) $15.00

KJELGAARD, Jim, see Series section BIG RED
Black Fawn, 1958 Dodd Mead, hardcover. ($25.00 with dust jacket) $10.00
Fawn in the Forest and Other Wild Animal Stories, 1963 Dodd Mead, first edition, hardcover. ($15.00 with dust jacket) $10.00
Two Dogs and a Horse, 1964 Dodd, Mead, Weekly Reader edition, pictorial hardcover. $10.00

KLEIN, Leonore
Can You Guess, 1953 Wonder Books, laminated hardcover. $10.00
Happy Surprise, 1952 Wonder Books, laminated hardcover, illustrations by Ruth Wood. $10.00

KLEINHANS, T.J.
Printer's Devil From Wittenberg, 1962 Augsburg, hardcover. $15.00

KLOSE, Ellen Sue
Tick-a Tock-a Clock, 1957 Review and Herald, pictorial hardcover, decorated endpapers, 158 pages, illustrations by Stanley Dunlap, Jr. $20.00

KNAPP, Sally
Sink the Basket, 1953 Crowell, hardcover, 186 pages. $10.00

KNIGHT, Clayton
Big Book of Real Helicopters, 1955 Grosset & Dunlap, oversize hardcover, 28 pages, color illustrations by author. $20.00
Real Book about our Armed Forces, 1959 Garden City, hardcover, illustrations by author. $10.00

KNIGHT, Hilary, see Series section NUTSHELL LIBRARY
Animal Garden, a story by Ogden Nash, 1965 M. Evans, first edition, square hardcover, double-page color illustrations by Hilary Knight. ($65.00 with dust jacket) $30.00
Sylvia the Sloth, 1969 Harper & Row, first edition, hardcover, a roundabout story, illustrations by author. $50.00
Where's Wallace?, 1964 Harper book club edition, hardcover. ($35.00 with dust jacket) $15.00

KNOPF, Mildred O.
Around the World Cookbook for Young People, 1966 Knopf, first edition, hardcover. ($15.00 with dust jacket) $10.00

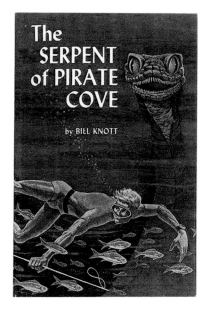

KNOTT, Bill
Dwarf on Black Mountain, 1967 Steck-Vaughn, hardcover, illustrations by Ben Smith. ($20.00 with dust jacket) $10.00
Junk Pitcher, 1963 Follett, hardcover. ($20.00 with dust jacket) $10.00
Secret of the Old Brownstone, 1963 Steck-Vaughn, hardcover, 131 pages. ($15.00 with dust jacket) $10.00
Serpent of Pirate Cove, 1971 Steck-Vaughn, hardcover, 151 pages. Wrap-around illustration dust jacket by Frank O'Leary. ($20.00 with dust jacket) $10.00
Taylor Street Irregulars, 1970 Steck-Vaughn, hardcover. ($25.00 with dust jacket) $10.00

KNOTT, Leonard
Children's Book of the Great Lakes, 1946, oversize hardcover, pictorial boards, 32 pages, duotone illustrations throughout. $15.00
Children's Guide to Canada's Capital, 1952 Brunswick Press, oversize hardcover, illustrations by Jacques Gagnier $20.00

KNUDSEN, Lynne
Follett Book of Cradle Songs. Lullabies from Around the World, 1967 Follett, first edition, hardcover, illustrated by Jacqueline Tomes. ($25.00 with dust jacket) $15.00

KOCH, Dorothy
I Play at the Beach., 1955 Holiday House, oversize hardcover, illustrated endpapers, color illustrations by Feodor Rojankovsky. $25.00

KOERING, Ursula
Adventures of Winnie and Bly, 1947 Little Brown, hardcover, illustrated endpapers, illustrations by author. $10.00

KOHLER, Julilly H.
Razzberry Jamboree, Crowell, first edition, hardcover, illustrations by Henry Pitz. ($15.00 with dust jacket) $10.00

KOHN, Bernice
Beachcomber's Book, 1970 Viking, first edition, pictorial hardcover, oblong, 96 pages, illustrations by Arabelle Wheatley and Laurel Brown. ($30.00 with dust jacket) $20.00

KOMAIKO, Jean and **Kate ROSENTHAL**
Your Family Tree, 1963 Parents, illustrated hardcover, illustrated by Denman Hampson. $15.00

KONIGSBURG, E. L.
About the B'nai Bagels, 1969 Atheneum, oversize hardcover, illustrations by author. ($20.00 with dust jacket) $10.00
Altogether, One at a Time, 1971 Atheneum, hardcover, illustrated. ($20.00 with dust jacket) $10.00
Dragon in the Ghetto Caper, 1974 Atheneum, first edition, hardcover, illustrations by author. ($20.00 with dust jacket) $10.00
From the Mixed-Up Files of Mrs. Basil E. Frankweiler, 1967 Atheneum, first edition, 162 pages, illustrations by author. ($200.00 with dust jacket) $30.00
From the Mixed-Up Files of Mrs. Basil E. Frankweiler, 1968 Atheneum, first printing of Newbery Medal edition, 162 pages, illustrations by author. ($60.00 with dust jacket) $20.00
Later editions: ($20.00 with dust jacket) $10.00
jennifer, hecate, macbeth, william mckinley and me, elizabeth, 1967 Atheneum, hardcover, Newbery Honor award on dust jacket. ($20.00 with dust jacket) $10.00
Proud Taste For Scarlet and Minniver, 1973 Atheneum, first edition, hardcover, illustrated by author. ($25.00 with dust jacket) $10.00

KORINETZ, Juri
There Far Beyond the River, (1968 Russia) 1973 Brockhampton Press, first edition UK, 189 pages. $30.00

KORSCHUNOW, Irina
Piebald Pup, 1958 McDowell, first edition, hardcover. ($40.00 with dust jacket) $20.00

KOSOVA, Maria and **Vladislav STANOVSKY**
African Tales of Magic and Mystery, 1970 Hamlyn,

London, first edition, hardcover, illustrated by Karel Teissig. ($15.00 with dust jacket) $10.00

KOTZWINKLE, William

Elephant Boy, 1970 Farrar, Straus, & Giroux, first edition, hardcover, illustrations by Joe Servello. ($65.00 with dust jacket) $20.00

Return of Crazy Horse, 1971 Farrar, first edition, oversize hardcover, illustrations by Joe Servello. ($75.00 with dust jacket) $30.00

Ship that Came Down the Gutter, 1970 Pantheon, first edition, hardcover, illustrations by Joe Servello. ($60.00 with dust jacket) $20.00

Supreme, Superb, Exalted and Delightful, One and Only Magic Building, 1973 Farrar, Straus & Giroux, first edition, hardcover, 4-color woodcuts. ($30.00 with dust jacket) $15.00

KRAHN, Fernando

April Fools, 1974 Dutton book club, first edition, small hardcover, illustrations by author. ($30.00 with dust jacket) $15.00

Gustavus and Stop, 1969 Dutton, first edition, hardcover, illustrations by author. ($30.00 with dust jacket) $15.00

Journeys of Sebastian, 1968 Delacorte, first edition, hardcover, illustrations by author. ($30.00 with dust jacket) $15.00

How Santa Claus Had a Long and Difficult Journey Delivering his Presents, 1970 Delacorte Press, first edtion, a Seymour Lawrence Book, wordless book with two color illustrations. ($45.00 with dust jacket) $20.00

KRAMER, Robert

Big Train Book, 1958 McGraw-Hill, first edition, ring-bound cut-out cover in shape of train engine, wheels turn, ten double-sided boards, illustrations by Cober. $30.00

KRAMER, Walter Smith

Treasure at Bar X, 1955 Dodd Mead, hardcover, 149 pages, b/w illustrations by Gerald McCann. $15.00

KRAMON, Florence

Wallpaper for Eugene's Room, 1967 Follet, first edition, hardcover. ($15.00 with dust jacket) $10.00

KRANTZ, Hazel

100 Pounds of Popcorn, 1961 Vanguard, hardcover, illustrations by Charles Geer. ($30.00 with dust jacket) $15.00

Freestyle for Michael, 1964 Vanguard, hardcover, illustrations by Charles Geer. ($20.00 with dust jacket) $10.00

Secret Raft, 1965 Vanguard, Weekly Reader edition, pictorial hardcover, 190 pages, illustrations by Charles Geer. $15.00

KRASILOVSKY, Phyllis

Girl Who Was a Cowboy, 1965 Garden City, first edition, blue pictorial hardcover w/red spine, 31 pages, red/b/w illustrations by Cyndy Szekeres. ($15.00 with dust jacket) $10.00

Man Who Didn't Wash His Dishes, 1950 Parents', illustrated hardcover, illustrations by Barbara Cooney. $15.00

Scaredy Cat, 1959 Macmillan, first edition, hardcover. ($25.00 with dust jacket) $15.00

Very Little Boy, 1962 Doubleday, first edition, hardcover, four-color illustrations. ($25.00 with dust jacket) $15.00

KRAUS, Robert

Amanda Remembers, 1965 Harper, first edition, hardcover, illustrations. ($45.00 with dust jacket) $20.00

Christmas Cookie Sprinkle Snitcher, 1969 Simon &

Schuster, hardcover, 32 pages, color illustrations by Virgil Franklin Partch, hard to find. $150.00

First Robin, 1965 Windmill Books, illustrated, glossy pictorial boards, color illustrations by Virgil Franklin Partch. $15.00

Hello Hippopotamus, 1969 Windmill Books, first printing, hardcover, color illustrations. ($30.00 with dust jacket) $20.00

Littlest Rabbit, 1961 Harper and Row, pictorial hardcover, illustrated. $15.00

Milton the Early Riser, 1972 Windmill Books, oversize hardcover, illustrations by Jose Aruego. ($30.00 with dust jacket) $15.00

My Son the Mouse, 1966 Harper, hardcover. ($40.00 with dust jacket) $15.00

Mouse at Sea, 1959 Harper, first edition, hardcover, 32 pages, illustrations. ($30.00 in dust jacket) $20.00

Owliver, 1974 Prentice Hall, first edition, small hardcover, illustrations by Jose Aruego and Ariane Dewey. ($20.00 with dust jacket) $10.00

Trouble with Spider, 1962 Harper, first edition. ($55.00 with dust jacket) $25.00

Tree That Stayed Up Until Next Christmas, 1972 Windmill Books, hardcover, 32 pages, illustrated by Edna Eicke. $25.00

Whitney Darrow, Jr.'s Unidentified Flying Elephant, 1968 Windmill Books, hardcover. $35.00

Whose Mouse are You?, 1970 Macmillan, oversize hardcover, illustrations by Jose Aruego. ($25.00 with dust jacket) $15.00

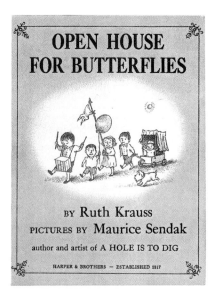

KRAUSS, Ruth

Bouquet of Littles, 1963 Harper and Row, small hardcover, illustrations by Jane Flora. $20.00

Hole is to Dig, 1952 Harper, small hardcover, illustrated by Maurice Sendak. First edition: $250.00 with dust jacket. Later editions: ($30.00 with dust jacket) $15.00

I'll Be You and You Be Me, 1954 Harper and Row, first edition, hardcover, illustrated by Maurice Sendak. ($200.00 with dust jacket) $50.00

Open House for Butterflies, 1960 Harper, first edition, small illustrated yellow hardcover with black spine, brown print, b/w illustrations by Maurice Sendak. ($150.00 with dust jacket) $40.00. Later editions: ($30.00 with dust jacket) $15.00

KRAVETZ, Nathan

Way of the Condor, 1970 Crown, first edition, hardcover, illustrated by W. T. Mars. ($35.00 with dust jacket) $15.00

KREMENTZ, Jill

Sweet Pea, a Black Girl Growing Up in the Rural South, 1969 Harcourt, Brace and World, first edition, oversize hardcover, 94 pages, photos. ($40.00 with dust jacket) $20.00

KRISKOVIC, Josip

Milan and His Runaway Uncle, 1970 Stackpole, first edition, 128 pages, hardcover. ($20.00 with dust jacket) $10.00

KRUEGER, Louise

Scarecrow, 1962 Ivan Obolensky, first edition, hardcover, illustrated by author. ($20.00 with dust jacket) $10.00

KRUMGOLD, Joseph

And Now Miguel, 1953 Crowell, hardcover, color illustrated endpapers, illustrations by Jean Charlot. ($30.00 with Newbery Medal dust jacket) $10.00

Henry 3, 1967 Atheneum, first edition, hardcover, illustrations by Alvin Smith. ($20.00 with dust jacket) $10.00

Most Terrible Turk, 1969 Crowell, first edition, hardcover, 42 pages, b/w illustrations by Michael Hampshire. ($20.00 with dust jacket) $10.00

Onion John, 1959 Crowell, Newbery Award edition, hardcover, b/w illustrations by Symeon Shimin. ($20.00 with dust jacket) $10.00

KRUSS, James

My Great-Grandfather, the Heroes and I, (1967) 1973 Atheneum, first US edition, hardcover, 244 pages. ($30.00 with dust jacket) $15.00

KRUTCH, Joseph

Most Wonderful Animals that Never Were, 1969 Houghton Mifflin, hardcover. ($25.00 with dust jacket) $15.00

KUBIE, Nora Benjamin

King Solomon's Navy, 1954 Harper, first edition, hardcover. ($15.00 with dust jacket) $10.00

KUBINYI, Laszlo
Zeki and the Talking Cat Shukru, 1970 Simon & Schuster, first edition, hardcover. ($20.00 with dust jacket) $10.00

KUBLER, Arthur
Tomaya, 1971 Longman Young, first edition, oversize hardcover, color illustrations by author. ($15.00 with dust jacket) $10.00

KUMIN, Maxine W.
Beach Before Breakfast, 1964 Putnam, first edition, hardcover, illustrations by Leonard Weisgard. ($25.00 with dust jacket) $15.00

KUNHARDT, Dorothy
Once There Was A Little Boy, 1956 Viking, first edition, oversize hardcover, illustrations by Helen Sewell. ($50.00 with dust jacket) $20.00

KUNHARDT, Philip B. Jr.
Hats Make You Happy, 1957 Sterling, first edition, hardcover, b/w photos. ($25.00 with dust jacket) $10.00

A PRAIRIE BOY'S WINTER
Paintings and Story by William Kurelek

KURELEK, William
Lumberjack, 1974 Houghton Mifflin, first American edition, oblong hardcover, 25 pages, illustrated. ($20.00 with dust jacket) $10.00
Prairie Boy's Winter, 1973 Houghton Mifflin, first edition, blue hardcover, illustrations by author. ($15.00 with dust jacket) $10.00

KUSKIN, Karla
Any Me I Want to Be: Poems, 1972 Harper and Row, first edition, hardcover. ($30.00 with dust jacket) $15.00
Walk the Mouse Girls Took, 1967 Harper and Row,

first edition, hardcover, 32 pages. ($60.00 with dust jacket) $20.00
Which Horse Is William?, 1959 Harper and Row, first edition, hardcover. ($45.00 with dust jacket) $20.00

KUWABARA, Minoru
Cut and Paste, 1958 Astor, first edition, oversize hardcover. ($35.00 with dust jacket) $20.00

——————— ⇒ **L** ⇐ ———————

LACH, Alma
Child's First Cook Book, 1950 Hart, first edition, hardcover, illustrated by Doris Stolberg. ($20.00 with dust jacket) $15.00

LADD, Elizabeth
Indians on the Bonnet, 1971 Morrow, illustrated hardcover, illustrations by Richard Cuffari. $10.00
Meg and Melissa, 1964 Morrow, hardcover. ($20.00 with dust jacket) $10.00
Year of the Pheasants, 1957 Morrow, first edition, hardcover. ($20.00 with dust jacket) $10.00

LaFARGE, Phyllis
Christmas Adventure, 1974 Holt, Rinehart & Winston, first edition, hardcover, illustrated by Ray Cruz. ($15.00 with dust jacket) $10.00

LAIRD, Jenny
James and MacArthur: A Novel about Two Cats. 1951 Longmans, Green, first edition, hardcover, b/w illustrations by Peggy Bacon. ($25.00 with dust jacket) $15.00

LAMBERT, Janet
Boy Wanted, 1959 Dutton, hardcover. First with

dust jacket: $100.00. Later printings: ($25.00 with dust jacket) $15.00

Dream for Susan, 1954 Grosset, hardcover. ($45.00 with dust jacket) $15.00

First of All, 1966 Dutton, first edition, hardcover. ($100.00 with dust jacket) $35.00

Hi, Neighbor, 1968 Dutton, hardcover. First edition with dust jacket: $150.00

Sweet as Sugar, 1967 Dutton, first edition, green hardcover. Lambert's fifitieth book. First edition with dust jacket: $150.00

We're Going Steady, 1958 Dutton, hardcover. First with dust jacket: $100.00. Later printings: ($25.00 with dust jacket) $15.00

LAMORISSE, Albert

Red Balloon, 1956 Doubleday, first American edition, oversize hardcover, b/w and color photos from film. ($35.00 with dust jacket) $20.00

Red Balloon, 1956 Children's Choice Book Club, hardcover. $20.00

White Mane, 1954 Dutton, first edition, oversize hardcover, 44 pages, photo illustrations from film. ($30.00 with dust jacket) $20.00

LAMPMAN, Evelyn.

Go Up the Road, 1972 Atheneum, first edition, hardcover. $10.00

Mrs. Updaisy, 1963 Doubleday, first edition, hardcover, illustrations by Cyndy Szekers. ($15.00 with dust jacket) $10.00

Rock Hounds, 1958 Doubleday, first edition, hardcover, illustrated by author. ($25.00 with dust jacket) $10.00

Shy Stegosaurus of Cricket Creek, 1955 Doubleday, 220 pages, illustrations by Hubert Buel. ($45.00 with dust jacket) $20.00

Special Year, 1959 Doubleday, first edition, hardcover. $10.00

Witch Doctor's Son, 1954 Doubleday, first edition, hardcover, illustrations by Richard Bennet. ($35.00 with dust jacket) $15.00

LAMPORT, Felicia

Scrap Irony, 1961 Houghton Mifflin, first edition, hardcover, illustrations by Edward Gorey. ($25.00 with dust jacket) $15.00

LANCER, Jack, see Series section CHRISTOPHER COOL

LANCASTER, Osbert

Facades and Faces, 1950 John Murray, London, first edition, yellow hardcover, 64 pages, b/w illustrations by author. ($20.00 with dust jacket) $10.00

LANDECK, Beatrice

Echoes of Africa in Folk Songs of the Americas, 1961

David McKay, blue hardcover, illustrations by Alexander Dobkin. ($45.00 with dust jacket) $25.00

Wake Up and Sing! Folk Songs From America's Grassroots, 1969 Morrow, hardcover, illustrations by Bob Blansky. ($35.00 with dust jacket) $20.00

LANE, Fred

Patrol to the Kimberleys, 1955 Prentice-Hall, first edition, hardcover, illustrated by photos. ($15.00 with dust jacket) $10.00

LANE, Neola Tracy

Grasshopper Year, 1960 Lippincott, first edition, hardcover. ($20.00 with dust jacket) $10.00

LANES, Selma G.

Down the Rabbit Hole: Adventures and Misadventures in the Realm of Children's Literature, 1971 Atheneum, first edition, hardcover, 239 pages, with illustrations from other children's books including works by Maurice Sendak, Denslow, Garth Williams. $15.00

LANGEHOUGH, Mabel

Lost Letter and Other Stories, 1958 Augsburg, first edition, tan hardcover, 111 pages. $20.00

LANGSTAFF, John

Frog Went A Courtin', 1955 Harcourt, (1956 Caldecott Award), oversize hardcover, color illustrations by Feodor Rojankovsky. ($30.00 with dust jacket) $15.00

Golden Vanity, 1972 Harcourt Brace Jovanovich, first edition, hardcover, illustrated by David Gentleman. ($15.00 with dust jacket) $10.00

On Christmas Day in the Morning!, 1959 Harcourt Brace, first edition, hardcover, illustrations by Antony Groves-Raines. ($20.00 with dust jacket) $10.00

Over in the Meadow, 1957 Scott, Foresman, special First Talking Storybook edition, oversize pictorial hardcover, with music record, illustrations by Feodor Rojankovsky, $40.00 with record, $15.00 without record.

LANGTON, Jane

Diamond in the Window, 1962 Harper, early printing, hardcover, 242 pages, illustrations by Erik Blegvad. ($50.00 with dust jacket) $20.00

Swing in the Summerhouse, 1967 Harper, first edition, hardcover, illustrations Erik Blegvad. ($80.00 with dust jacket) $30.00

Astonishing Stereoscope, 1971 Harper, first edition, hardcover, illustrations Erik Blegvad. ($80.00 with dust jacket) $30.00

LANIER, Sterling

War for the Lot, A Tale of Fantasy and Terror,

1969 Follett, first edition, hardcover, illustrations by Robert Baumgartner. ($35.00 with dust jacket) $15.00

LANSING, E.H.
Sure Thing For Shep, 1956 Crowell, first edition, hardcover, 179 pages, b/w illustrations by Ezra Jack Keats. ($40.00 with dust jacket) $20.00

LARSON, Henry V.
Ride Like an Indian, 1958 Whittlesey House, hardcover, 140 pages, color frontispiece, illustrated by Wesley Dennis. ($25.00 with dust jacket) $10.00

LATHAM, Jean
Man Who Never Snoozed, 1961 Macmillan, first edition, hardcover, illustrations by Sheila Greenwald. ($30.00 with dust jacket) $15.00
When Homer Honked, 1961 Macmillan, first edition, hardcover, illustrations by Cynbdy Szekeres. ($15.00 with dust jacket) $10.00

LATHAM, John
Meskin Hound, 1958 Putnam, hardcover, illustrations by Nick Eggenhofer ($15.00 with dust jacket) $10.00

LATHROP, Dorothy
Dog in the Tapestry Garden, 1962 Macmillan, first edition, hardcover, 42 pages, illustrations by author. ($50.00 with dust jacket) $20.00

LATHROP, West
Unwilling Pirate, 1951 Random House, first edition, hardcover, 277 pages. $15.00

LATTIMORE, Eleanor
Cousin Melinda, 1961 Morrow, first edition, hardcover, illustrated endpapers, illustrations by author. $15.00
Indigo Hill, 1950 Morrow, first edition, hardcover, illustrations by author. ($25.00 with dust jacket) $15.00
Janetta's Magnet, 1963 Morrow, first edition, hardcover, 126 pages, illustrations by author. ($25.00 with dust jacket) $15.00
Laurie and Company, 1962 Morrow, first edition, hardcover, 128 pages, illustrated endpapers, illustrations by author. ($20.00 with dust jacket) $10.00
Mexican Bird, 1955 Morrow, first edition, hardcover. ($20.00 with dust jacket) $10.00
Molly in the Middle, 1956 Morrow, hardcover, 127 pages, illustrated endpapers. $12.00
Search for Christina, 1967 Morrow, hardcover, 128 pages, illustrated endpapers, illustrations by author. ($20.00 with dust jacket) $10.00

LAUBER, Patricia
Adventure At Black Rock Cave, 1959 Random House, hardcover, illustrations by Leonard Shortall. ($20.00 with dust jacket) $10.00
Found: One Orange-Brown Horse, 1957 Random House, hardcover, illustrated endpapers. $20.00
Look It Up Book of 50 States, 1957 Random House, first edition, oversize hardcover, color illustrations by Robert Borst. $15.00
Runaway Flea Circus, 1958 Random House, first edition, hardcover, illustrated by Catherine Barnes. First edition with dust jacket: $35.00. Later printings: ($20.00 with dust jacket) $10.00

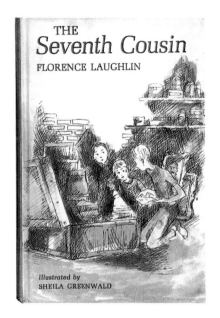

LAUGHLIN, Florence
Seventh Cousin, 1966 Macmillan, illustrated hardcover. $10.00

LAURENCE, Margaret
Jason's Quest, 1970 McClelland & Stewart, first edition, hardcover, 211 pages, illustrations by Staffan Torell. ($125.00 with dust jacket) $40.00

LAURITZEN, Jonreed
Glitter-Eyed Wouser, 1960 Little Brown, first edition, hardcover. ($20.00 with dust jacket) $10.00
Ordeal of the Young Hunter, 1954 Little Brown, first edition, hardcover, illustrations by Hoke Denetsosie. ($30.00 with dust jacket) $15.00

LAWRENCE, Cynthia
Barbie's New York Summer, 1962 Random House, first edition, small hardcover. ($35.00 with dust jacket) $15.00
Barbie Solves a Mystery, 1963 Random House, hardcover, illustrations by Clyde Smith. $12.00

LAWRENCE, John
Rabbit and Pork Rhyming Talk, 1975 Crowell, first

edition, small oblong hardcover, color woodcut illustrations. ($35.00 with dust jacket) $20.00

LAWSON, Robert

Capt. Kidd's Cat, 1956 Little Brown, hardcover, illustrated by author. ($30.00 with dust jacket) $15.00

Great Wheel, 1957 Viking Press, hardcover, illustrations by author. First edition with dust jacket: $85.00. Later editions: ($20.00 with dust jacket) $15.00

Mr. Revere and I, 1953 Little Brown, first edition, oversize hardcover, illustrations by author. First edition with dust jacket: $100.00. Later editions: ($30.00 with dust jacket) $15.00

Smeller Mart, 1950 Viking, first edition, hardcover, illustrations by author. First edition with dust jacket: $85.00 Later editions: ($20.00 with dust jacket) $15.00

Tough Winter, 1954 Viking, first edition, hardcover, 128 pages, illustrated endpapers, illustrations by author. First edition with dust jacket: $65.00. Later editions: ($20.00 with dust jacket) $15.00

LAZARUS, Keo Felker

Gismo, 1970 Follett, hardcover, b/w illustrations by Leonard Shortall. ($25.00 with dust jacket) $10.00

LEACH, Maria

Luck Book, 1964 World, first edition, hardcover, illustrations by Kurt Werth. ($30.00 with dust jacket) $15.00

Rainbow Book of American Folk Tales and Legends, 1958 World, first edition, oversize hardcover, 318 pages, color and b/w illustrations by Marc Simont. ($65.00 with dust jacket) $30.00

LEAF, Anne Sellers

Gingerbread Man, 1965 Rand McNally Elf Book, small, color illustrated boards. $10.00

LEAF, Munro

Being an American Can Be Fun, 1964 Lippincott, first edition, hardcover, illustrations by author. ($15.00 with dust jacket) $10.00

Geography Can Be Fun, 1951 Lippincott, first edition, oversize hardcover, 63 pages, b/w illustrations by author. $30.00

History Can Be Fun, 1950 Lippincott, first edition, oversize hardcover, b/w illustrations by author. ($50.00 with dust jacket) $30.00

Reading Can Be Fun, 1953 Lippincott, first edition, hardcover, illustrations by author. ($30.00 with dust jacket) $10.00

Lucky You, 1955 Lippincott, first edition, oversize hardcover, b/w illustrations by author. ($35.00 with dust jacket) $15.00

Three Promises to You, 1957 Lippincott, oblong hardcover, line drawings. $15.00

Turnabout, 1967 Lippincott, first edition, hardcover, illustrated by author. ($20.00 with dust jacket) $15.00

LEAR, Edward

Dong with a Luminous Nose, 1969 Young Scott, first edition thus, hardcover, illustrations by Edward Gorey. ($50.00 with dust jacket) $20.00

Four Little Children Who Went Around the World, 1968 edition Macmillan, first thus, blue hardcover, 44 pages, b/w illustrations by Arnold Lobel. ($50.00 with dust jacket) $20.00

Jumblies, 1968 edition Young Scott, first edition thus, hardcover, illustrations by Edward Gorey. ($50.00 with dust jacket) $25.00

Lear's Nonsense Verses, 1967 edition Grosset & Dunlap, first American edition, hardcover, illustrated by Tomi Ungerer. ($40.00 with dust jacket) $20.00

New Vestments, 1970 edition Bradbury Press, first edition, hardcover, illustrations by Arnold Lobel. ($35.00 with dust jacket) $15.00

Nonsense Book, 1956 edition Garden City, first edition thus, oversize hardcover, 188 pages, illustrations by Tony Palazzo. $40.00

Owl and the Pussycat, 1961 edition Doubleday, first edition thus, hardcover, illustrations by William Pene Du Bois. ($25.00 with dust jacket) $15.00

LEDERER, William J.

Timothy's Song, 1965 Norton, first edition, hardcover, 41 pages, illustrations by Edward Ardizzone. $15.00

LEE, Dave

Tailor and his Two Button Day, 1971 Carolrhoda Books, oblong oversize hardcover, illustrations by Sally King Brewer. $15.00

LEE, Elizabeth

Quorum of Cats, 1963 Elek Books, UK, first edition, hardcover, illustrations by Peter Kneebone. ($25.00 with dust jacket) $15.00

LEE, Tanith
Animal Castle, 1972 Farrar, first American edition. ($25.00 with dust jacket) $15.00
Dragon Hoard, 1971 Farrar, first American edition, hardcover, b/w illustrations by Graham Oakley. ($35.00 with dust jacket) $15.00
East of Midnight, 1977 Macmillan, London, first edition, hardcover. ($35.00 with dust jacket) $15.00

LEE, Wayne
Bat Masterson, 1960 Whitman, pictorial hardcover. $15.00

LEEK, Sybil
Jackdaw and the Witch, 1966 Prentice Hall, first American edition, hardcover, illustrations by Barbara Efting. $10.00

LeGALLIENNE, Eva, translator
Seven Tales by H. C. Andersen, 1959 Harper & Brothers, first edition, oversize hardcover, illustrations by Maurice Sendak. ($100.00 with dust jacket) $40.00. Later editions: ($20.00 with dust jacket) $10.00

LeGUIN, Ursula, see Series section EARTHSEA TRILOGY

LEICHMAN, Seymour
Boy Who Could Sing Pictures, 1968 Doubleday, first edition, oversize hardcover, 59 pages, picture book, color and b/w illustrations. ($20.00 with dust jacket) $10.00

LEIGH, Roberta
Tomahawk and the River of Gold, 1960 Pelham, London, first edition, ochre boards stamped with a gilt pictorial, 96 pages. $10.00

LEIGHTON, Clare
Where Land Meets Sea – The Tide Line of Cape Cod, 1954 Rinehart, first edition, oversize hardcover, 202 pages, wood engraving illustrations. ($50.00 with dust jacket) $20.00

LEIGHTON, Margaret
Story of Florence Nightingale, 1952 Grosset, hardcover, Signature Books edition. ($20.00 with dust jacket) $10.00
Story of General Custer, 1954 Grosset, hardcover, illustrations by Nicholas Eggenhofer. $10.00

LEISER, Harry W.
Lost Canyon of the Navajos, 1960 Criterion, first edition, hardcover. ($15.00 with dust jacket) $10.00

LEITCH, Pat
To Save a Pony, 1960 Hutchinson, London, first edition, brown decorated hardcover. ($35.00 with dust jacket) $10.00

L'ENGLE, Madeleine
Camilla, 1965 Delacorte, first edition, hardcover, 278 pages. First edition with dust jacket: $35.00. Later editions: ($20.00 with dust jacket) $15.00
Circle Of Quiet, 1972 Farrar, first edition, hardcover, 246 pages. First edition with dust jacket: $50.00. Later editions: ($20.00 with dust jacket) $15.00
Dance in the Desert, 1969 Farrar, first edition, hardcover, illustrations by Symeon Shimin. First edition with dust jacket: $35.00. Later editions: ($20.00 with dust jacket) $15.00
Moon by Night, 1963 Ariel Books, first edition, hardcover, 218 pages. First edition with dust jacket: $75.00. Later editions: ($20.00 with dust jacket) $15.00.
Wind in the Door, 1973 Farrar, Straus & Giroux, first edition, hardcover. First edition with dust jacket: $35.00. Later editions: ($20.00 with dust jacket) $15.00.
Wrinkle in Time, 1962 Farrar, hardcover, 211 pages. First edition with dust jacket: $150.00. Later editions: ($20.00 with dust jacket) $15.00
Young Unicorns, 1969 Farrar, hardcover. ($20.00 with dust jacket) $15.00

LENSKI, Lois, see Series section AMERICAN REGIONAL; ROUNDABOUT AMERICA
Flood Friday, 1956 Lippincott, hardcover. ($150.00 with dust jacket) $50.00
I Like Winter, ca. 1950 Walck, small, red hardcover, 48 pages, illustrated endpapers, page of music, red/green/black illustrations by Lenski. ($40.00 with dust jacket) $20.00

I Went for a Walk, 1958 Walck, tan hardcover, music by Clyde Robert Bulla, illustrations by Lenski. First edition with dust jacket: $100.00. Ex-library: ($15.00 with dust jacket) $10.00

Little Sioux Girl, 1958 Scott Foresman school edition, white pictorial hardcover, 128 pages, illustrations by author. $25.00

Papa Small, 1951 Walck, first edition, hardcover, illustrations by author. ($65.00 with dust jacket) $25.00

San Francisco Boy, 1955 Lippincott, first edition, hardcover, 176 pages, illustrations by author. ($100.00 with dust jacket) $40.00

Songs of Mr. Small, 1954 Oxford, first edition, 40 pages, music by C. R. Bulla, color illustrations by author. ($100.00 with dust jacket) $40.00

We Are Thy Children, with Clyde Bulla, 1952 Crowell, first edition, oblong hardcover, illustrations by Lenski. ($50.00 with dust jacket) $25.00

LEODHAS, Sorche Nic

All in the Morning Early, 1963 Holt, Rinehart & Winston, first edition, hardcover, illustrations by Evaline Ness. ($30.00 with dust jacket) $15.00

Ghosts Go Haunting, 1965 Holt, first edition, blue hardcover, 128 pages, b/w illustrations by Nonny Hogrogian. ($50.00 with dust jacket) $20.00

Kellyburn Braes, 1968 Holt, first edition, hardcover, illustrations by Evaline Ness. ($35.00 with dust jacket) $15.00

Laird of Cockpen, 1969 Holt, Rinehart & Winston, first edition, hardcover, illustrations by Adrienne Adams. ($25.00 with dust jacket) $15.00

LEONARD, Burgess

One-Man Backfield, 1953 Lippincott, hardcover. ($20.00 with dust jacket) $10.00

Rookie Southpaw, 1951 Lippincott, first edition, hardcover. ($45.00 with dust jacket) $15.00

LEONARD, Nellie M.

Grandfather Whiskers, M. D., 1953 Crowell, first edition, hardcover. $20.00

LERNER, Marguerite Rush

Dear Little Mumps Child, ca. 1959 Lerner Publications, illustrated hardcover. $20.00

LeSIEG, Theo (Dr. Seuss), see Series section BEGINNER BOOKS

Eye Book, 1968 Random House, illustrated hardcover, illustrations by Roy McKie. $10.00

Ten Apples Up on Top!, 1961 Random House, illustrated hardcover, illustrations by Roy McKie. $10.00

Would You Rather Be a Bullfrog?, 1975 Random House, hardcover. $10.00

LESSER, Milton

Star Seekers, 1953 Winston, first edition, hardcover. ($70.00 with dust jacket) $20.00

LEVENSON, Dorothy

Magic Carousel, 1967 Parents', pictorial hardcover, illustrations by Ati Forberg. $10.00

LEVINE, Lois and Rosalie SCHMIDT

Kids in the Kitchen Cookbook, 1968 Macmillan Book Club, hardcover, 182 pages. ($15.00 with dust jacket) $10.00

LEVINE, Rhoda

Quiet Story, 1965 Atheneum, first edition, hardcover, illustrations by Rosalie Richards. ($35.00 with dust jacket) $15.00

LEVOY, Myron

Penny Tunes and Princesses, 1972 Harper, first edition, oversize hardcover, color illustrations by Ezra Jack Keats. ($35.00 with dust jacket) $15.00

Witch of Fourth Street and Other Stories, 1972 Harper & Row, first edition, pictorial hardcover. $20.00

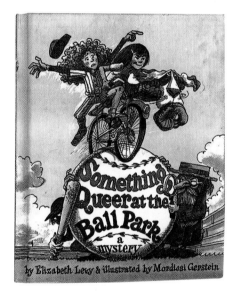

LEVY, Elizabeth

Something Queer at the Ball Park, 1975 Delacorte, Weekly Reader, oversize pictoral hardcover, color illustrations by Mordicai Gerstein. $20.00

LEVY, Mimi Cooper

Caravan from Timbuktu, 1961 Viking, first edition, hardcover. ($15.00 with dust jacket) $10.00

LEWELLEN, J.

Tee Vee Humphrey, 1957 Knopf, first edition, hardcover. ($15.00 with dust jacket) $10.00

LEWIS, C. S., see Series section CHRONICLES OF NARNIA

LEWIS, Frank
Johnny's Secret, 1975 Rand McNally Storytime Book, color illustrated hardcover, color illustrations by Marjorie Cooper. $15.00

LEWIS, Hilda (Evelyn Gibbs)
Gentle Falcon, 1952 London, first edition, hardcover, b/w illustrations by Evelyn Gibbs. ($15.00 with dust jacket) $10.00

LEWIS, Janet
Keiko's Bubble, 1961 Doubleday, first edition, hardcover, illustrations by Kazue Mizumura. ($60.00 with dust jacket) $15.00

LEWIS, Jean
Hong Kong Phooey and the Fortune Cookie Caper, 1975 Rand McNally, hardcover. $10.00

LEWIS, Oscar
Sacramento River, 1970 Holt, Rinehart, Winston, first edition, blue hardcover, 89 pages, illlustrated by Michael Hampshire. ($25.00 with dust jacket) $15.00

LEWIS, Roger
Puppets and Marionettes, 1952 Knopf, first edition, red hardcover, 44 pages, illustrations by author. ($20.00 with dust jacket) $10.00

LEWIS, Shari
Dear Shari, 1963 Stein & Day, first edition, hardcover, illustrations by Susan Perl. ($15.00 with dust jacket) $10.00

LEWIS, Thomas P.
Dragon Kite, 1974 Holt, Rinehart and Winston, first edition, oversize hardcover, two-color illustrations throughout by Errol Le Cain. ($30.00 with dust jacket) $15.00

LEWTHWAITE, Margaret
Changing the Guard at Buckingham Palace, 1953 Arthur Barker, London, first edition, hardcover, illustrated endpapers, illustrated. ($20.00 with dust jacket) $10.00

LEXAU, Joan M.
Emily and the Klunky Baby and the Next-Door Dog, 1972 Dial, pictorial hardcover, color illustrations by Martha Alexander. ($50.00 with dust jacket) $20.00
Finders Keepers, Losers Weepers, 1967 Lippincott, hardcover, 34 pages, illustrated by Tomie de Paola. ($25.00 with dust jacket) $15.00

L'HOMMEDIEU, Dorothy K.
Pompon, 1955 Ariel Books, first edition, hardcover, illustrations by Marie C. Nichols. ($30.00 with dust jacket) $15.00

LIFFRING, Joan
Jim and Alan on a Cotton Farm, 1959 Follett, first edition, hardcover, illustrated by photos by author. ($25.00 with dust jacket) $15.00

LIFTON, Betty Jean
Silver Crane, 1971 Seabury, first edition, hardcover. ($20.00 with dust jacket) $10.00

LINDE, Gunnel
Chimney-Top Lane, 1965 Harcourt, first American edition, hardcover, 160 pages, illustrations by Ilon Wikland. ($15.00 with dust jacket) $10.00
Invisible League and the Royal Ghost, 1970 Harcourt, first US edition, 188 pages, illustrations by Eric Palmquist. ($20.00 with dust jacket) $10.00

LINDGREN, Astrid, see Series section PIPPI
Cherry Time at Bullerby, (Swedish 1961) 1964 Methuen, first edition UK, small hardcover, 93 pages, illustrations by Ilon Wikland. ($30.00 with dust jacket) $15.00
Children of Noisy Village, 1962 Viking, first edition, hardcover. ($25.00 with dust jacket) $10.00
Christmas in the Stable, 1963 Coward-McCann, pictorial boards, illustrations by Harald Wiberg. $15.00
Emil's Pranks, 1971 Follett, first edition, hardcover, illustrations by Bjorn Berg. ($15.00 with dust jacket) $10.00
Emil and His Clever Pig, 1974 Brockhampton Press, first edition, hardcover, illustrated ($75.00 with dust jacket) $30.00
Karlsson-on-the-Roof, (1955) 1971 Viking, first American edition, 128 pages, illustrations by Marianne Turner. ($45.00 with dust jacket) $20.00
Skrallan and the Pirates, 1967 Doubleday, first edition, hardcover, 48 pages, illustrated with photos by Sven-Eric Deler and Stig Hallgren. ($70.00 with dust jacket) $30.00

LINDMAN, Maj
Sailboat Time, 1951 Albert Whitman, pictorial hardcover, color illustrations by author. $55.00
Snipp, Snapp, Snurr Learn to Swim, 1954 Whitman, first printing, continuation of series, oversize blue hardcover with paste-on pictorial, color illustrations by author. ($90.00 with same-as-cover dust jacket) $50.00

LINDOP, Audrey Erskine
Adventures of the Wuffle, 1966 McGraw-Hill, hard-

cover, first American edition, illustrations by William Stobbs. ($15.00 with dust jacket) $10.00

LINDOP, Edmund
Hubert, the Traveling Hippopotamus, 1961 Little Brown, first edition, oversize hardcover. $15.00

LINDSAY, Barbara
Captain Kangaroo's Surprise Party, 1958 Simon & Schuster, first edition, hardcover, illustrations by Edwin Schmidt. ($15.00 with dust jacket) $10.00

LINES, Kathleen
Ring of Tales, 1959 Franklin Watts, first American edition, hardcover. ($40.00 with dust jacket) $15.00

LINGSTROM, Freda, editor
BBC Children's Annual, 1958 Burke, London, first edition, hardcover, anthology of verse, b/w illustrations and six color plates. ($20.00 with dust jacket) $10.00

LINN, J.R. and **DONALDSON, Dorothy**
Laughing Letters, 1967 Holt Rinehart, illustrated hardcover. $20.00
Wings of Wonder, 1969 Holt Rinehart, hardcover. $20.00

LIONNI, Leo
Alexander and the Windup Mouse, 1969 Random House, first edition, oversize hardcover, color illustrations by author. ($40.00 with dust jacket) $15.00
Color of His Own, 1975 Pantheon, first edition, hardcover, illustrations by author. ($30.00 with dust jacket) $15.00
Greentail Mouse, 1973 Pantheon Books, first edition, oversize blue hardcover, illustrations by author. ($20.00 with dust jacket) $15.00
Swimmy, 1963 Pantheon, first edition, oversize hardcover, Caldecott Honor book, color illustrations by author. ($55.00 with dust jacket) $20.00

LIPKIND, William
Boy with a Harpoon, 1952 Harcourt Brace, first edition, green hardcover, illustrations by Nicholas Mordvinoff. $15.00
Chaga, 1955 Harcourt, oversize green hardcover. ($40.00 with dust jacket) $20.00
Finders Keepers, 1951 Harcourt, (1952 Caldecott Award), illustrated hardcover, illustrations by Nicholas Mordvinoff. ($30.00 with dust jacket) $15.00
Nubber Bear, 1966 Harcourt, first edition, hardcover, illustrations by Roger Duvoisin. $25.00
Professor Bull's Umbrella, 1954 Viking, first edition, oversize hardcover, illustrations by Georges Schreiber. ($40.00 with dust jacket) $15.00
Sleepyhead, 1957 Harcourt, Brace, first edition, hardcover, illustrations by Nicholas Mordvinoff. ($25.00 with dust jacket) $15.00

LIPPMAN, Peter J.
New at the Zoo, 1969 Harper and Row, first edition, hardcover, 32 pages. ($30.00 with dust jacket) $15.00
Plunkety Plunk, 1963 Ariel, first edition, hardcover, color illustrations. ($25.00 with dust jacket) $15.00

LITCHFIELD, Sarah
Hello Alaska, 1951 Whitman, oversize hardcover, 32 pages, map endpapers, color and b/w illustrations by Kurt Wiese. $25.00

LITTLE, Jean
From Anna, 1972 Harper & Row, first edition, pictorial hardcover. $15.00
Look Through My Window, 1970 Harper & Row, first edition, hardcover, illustrations by Joan Sandin. ($45.00 with dust jacket) $20.00
Mine for Keeps, 1962 Little Brown, illustrated hardcover. ($25.00 with dust jacket) $10.00
When the Pie Was Opened, Poems, 1968 Little, Brown, first edition, hardcover. ($25.00 with dust jacket) $10.00

LITTLE, Mary E.
ABC for the Library, 1975 Atheneum, hardcover. ($20.00 with dust jacket) $10.00

LITTLEDALE, Harold
Alexander, 1964 Parents Magazine Press, first edition, red hardcover, color illustrations by Tom Vroman. ($25.00 with dust jacket) $15.00

LIVELY, Penelope
Driftway, 1972 Dutton, first edition, hardcover. ($20.00 with dust jacket) $10.00
Ghost of Thomas Kempe, 1973 Dutton, first Ameri-

can edition, hardcover, b/w illustrations by Antony Maitland. ($40.00 with dust jacket) $15.00

Whispering Knights, 1971 Dutton, first edition, hardcover. ($20.00 with dust jacket) $10.00

LIVINGSTON, Myra Cohn
I'm Waiting, 1966 Harcourt, Brace, first edition, brown hardcover, b/w illustrations by Erik Blegvad. ($20.00 with dust jacket) $10.00

LIVINGSTON, Richard R.
Hunkendunkens, 1968 Harcourt, Brace & World, first edition, hardcover picture book, illustrated by Harriet Pincus. ($20.00 with dust jacket) $15.00

LLOYD, Norris
Billy Hunts the Unicorn, 1964 Hastings House, first edition, tall hardcover, illustrations by Robin Lloyd Papish. $15.00

LOBEL, Anita
Troll Music, 1966 Harper, Weekly Reader edition, illustrated hardcover, illustrations by author. ($20.00 with dust jacket) $10.00

LOBEL, Arnold
Bears of the Air, 1965 Harper, pictorial hardcover, illustrations by author. $15.00

Comic Adventures of Old Mother Hubbard and her Dog, 1968 Bradbury Press, small hardcover, color illustrations by author. ($20.00 with dust jacket) $10.00

Frog and Toad are Friends, 1970 Harper, first edition, hardcover, 64 pages, illustrations by author. ($25.00 with dust jacket) $10.00

Frog and Toad are Friends, 1970 Harper I Can Read Book edition, small glossy hardcover, 64 pages, illustrations by author. $10.00

Giant John, 1964 Harper, first edition, oversize hardcover, illustrations by author. ($45.00 with dust jacket) $15.00

Holiday for Mister Muster, 1963 Harper and Row, first edition, oblong hardcover, illustrations by author. ($60.00 with dust jacket) $20.00

Man Who Took the Indoors Out, 1974 Harper, first edition, hardcover, illustrations by author. ($15.00 with dust jacket) $10.00

Mouse Tales, 1972 Harper, I Can Read Book, first edition, hardcover, 64 pages, color illustrations by author. ($45.00 with dust jacket) $15.00

On the Day Peter Stuyvesant Sailed into Town, 1971 Harper, first edition, oblong hardcover, illustrations by author. ($25.00 with dust jacket) $15.00

Owl at Home, 1975 Harper, Weekly Reader edition, pictorial hardcover. ($20.00 with dust jacket) $10.00

Zoo for Mister Muster, 1962 Harper, oblong hardcover, two-color illustrations by author. ($20.00 with dust jacket) $10.00

LOCKE, Elsie
End of the Harbour, 1968 Jonathan Cape, London, first edition, blue hardcover with gilt spine, 207 pages, illustrated by Katarina Mataira. ($20.00 with dust jacket) $10.00

LONDON, Carolyn
Zarga's Shadow, 1966 Duell, Sloan and Pearce, first edition, hardcover. ($30.00 with dust jacket) $15.00

LONG, Eula
Pirate's Doll, 1956 Knopf, orange hardcover, 71 pages, four-color illustrations by author. ($15.00 with dust jacket) $10.00

LONGFELLOW
Story of Hiawatha, adapted by Allen Chaffee, 1951 Random House edition, glossy pictorial hardcover, illustrations by Armstrong Sperry. $15.00

LONGSTRETH, T. Morris
Scarlet Force, the Making of the Mounted Police, 1966 Macmillan, Toronto, hardcover. $10.00

LOPSHIRE, Robert
How to Make Filbbets, Etc., ca. 1964 Random House, hardcover. $10.00

LORCA, Federico Garcia
Lieutenant Colonel and the Gypsy, 1971 Doubleday, first edition, hardcover. ($20.00 with dust jacket) $10.00

LORD, Beman
Quarterback's Aim, ca. 1950 Henry Z. Walck, hardcover. ($20.00 with dust jacket) $10.00

LORD, John Vernon and Janet BURROWAY
Giant Jam Sandwich, Verses by Janet Burroway,

1972 Houghton-Mifflin, hardcover, full color illustrations by John Vernon Lord. $10.00

LOUDEN, Claire and **George**
Rain in the Winds, a Story of India, 1953 Scribner, first edition, hardcover, illustrations by authors. ($50.00 with dust jacket) $20.00

LOUGHLIN, Kataryn
Miss Abby Fitch-Martin, 1952 Coward-McCann, hardcover. ($20.00 with dust jacket) $10.00

LOURIE, Richard
Soldier and Tsar in the Forest, 1972 Farrar, Straus and Giroux, first edition, oversize hardcover, illustrations by Uri Shulevitz. ($20.00 with dust jacket) $10.00

LOUVAIN, Robert
Walt Disney's White Wilderness: Animals of the Arctic, 1957 Giant Little Golden Book, hardcover, color illustrations. $15.00
Walt Disney's Wildlife of the West: Animals of the Plains, Mountains and Desert, 1958 Golden Press, pictorial hardcover with photo of bison, 56 pages, from Golden Library of Knowledge, with full-color photos. $10.00

LOVE, Margaret
Explorer for an Aunt, 1967 Follett, hardcover. ($15.00 with dust jacket) $8.00

LOVELACE, Maude Hart
Betsy and the Great World, 1952 Crowell, hardcover, b/w illustrations by Vera Neville. ($250.00 with dust jacket) $80.00
Trees Kneel at Christmas, 1951 Crowell, first edi-

tion, hardcover, illustrations by Gertrude Herrick Howe. ($150.00 with dust jacket) $50.00

LOW, Elizabeth
Mouse, Mouse, Go Out of My House, 1958 Little Brown, first edition, hardcover, illustrated by Ronni Solbert. ($20.00 with dust jacket) $10.00
Snug in the Snow, 1963 Little Brown, hardcover, three-color illustrations by Ronni Solbert. ($15.00 with dust jacket) $10.00

LOWE, Edith
Fluffy is Lost, 1960 John Martin, pictorial hardcover, illustrated by Katharine Howe. $15.00

LUBELL, Winifred and **Cecil**
Rosalie, the Bird Market Turtle, 1966 Dobson, London, first edition UK, pictorial hardcover. $15.00
Rosalie, the Bird Market Turtle, 1962 Rand McNally, hardcover, Weekly Reader edition. $10.00

LUND, Doris Herold
I Wonder What's Under, 1970 Parents', illustrated hardcover and endpapers, illustrations by Janet McCaffery. $10.00

LUND, Gilda
Red Riding Hood and Goldilocks and the Three Bears, 1958 Wills & Hepworth, Ladybird Book Series 413, hardcover, illustrations. $15.00

LYNCH, Patricia, see Series section BROGEEN
.
LYON, Eleanor
Secret of Hermit's Bay, 1962 Follett, first edition, hardcover. ($20.00 with dust jacket) $10.00
Cathie Runs Wild, 1960 Follett, hardcover, illustrated by Greta Elgaard. $15.00

LYON, Elinor
House in Hiding, 1950 Coward McCann, hardcover, 229 pages, illustrations by R. M. Powers. ($35.00 with dust jacket) $20.00

LYONS, Dorothy
Bluegrass Champion (Harlequin Hullabaloo), 1949 Grosset, blue tweed cover, illustrated by Wesley Dennis. ($20.00 with dust jacket) $10.00
Dark Sunshine, 1951 Harcourt Brace, pictorial hardcover. $15.00

LYSTAD, Mary
James and the Jaguar, 1972 Putnam, Weekly Reader edition, Illustrated hardcover, oblong, illustrated by Cyndy Szekeres. $15.00

LYTTLETON, Kay, see Series section JEAN CRAIG

M

MAAS, Dorothy
Sugar-Candy Heart , 1968 Harcourt, Brace & World, first edition, pink hardcover, 61 pages, b/w illustrations by author. ($25.00 with dust jacket) $10.00

MacALPINE, Margaret
Black Gull of Corrie Lochan, 1965 Prentice Hall, first American edition, hardcover, 105 pages. ($25.00 with dust jacket) $10.00

MacARTHUR-ONSLOW, Annette
Minnie, 1971 Sydney, Ure Smith, first edition, oversize green hardcover with gilt lettering, 64 pages, line drawings. ($20.00 with dust jacket) $10.00
Uhu, 1969 Knopf, first edition, hardcover, illustrations by author. ($25.00 with dust jacket) $15.00

MACAULAY, David
Cathedral: The Story of Its Construction, 1973 Houghton Mifflin, oversize hardcover, 79 pages, illustrations by author. First edition with dust jacket: $35.00. Later editions: ($20.00 with dust jacket) $10.00

MacDONALD, Betty, see Series section MRS. PIGGLE-WIGGLE
Nancy and Plum, 1952 Lippincott, first edition, hardcover. Hard-to-find. ($250.00 with dust jacket) $100.00

MacDONALD, George
Light Princess, 1962 edition Crowell, first thus, oversize hardcover, illustrations by William Pene du Bois. ($50.00 with dust jacket) $20.00
Light Princess, 1969 edition Farrar, Straus and Giroux, first edition thus, hardcover, illustrations by Maurice Sendak. ($50.00 with dust jacket) $20.00

MacDOUGAL, Mary Katherine
Black Jupiter, 1960 Broadman Press, first edition, hardcover, illustrated by William Moyers. ($20.00 with dust jacket) $10.00

MacGREGOR, A.J.
Bunnikin's Picnic Party, undated Wills & Hepworth, England, ca. 1960s, Ladybird Book, hardcover, color illustrations. ($15.00 with dust jacket) $10.00
Piggly Plays Truant, undated Wills & Hepworth, England, ca. 1960s, Ladybird Book, hardcover, color illustrations. ($15.00 with dust jacket) $10.00
Pippety's Unlucky Day, undated Wills & Hepworth, England, ca. 1960s, Ladybird Book, hardcover, color illustrations. ($15.00 with dust jacket) $10.00

MacGREGOR, Ellen, see Series section MISS PICKERELL

Mr. Pingle and Mr. Buttonhouse, 1957 Whittlesey House, first edition, hardcover, illustrations by Paul Galdone. ($40.00 with dust jacket) $20.00

MacINTYRE, E.
Jane Likes Pictures, 1959 Collins, first edition, hardcover, illustrated reader. ($15.00 with dust jacket) $10.00

MACK, Angela
Fortress of the Eagles, 1968 Brockhampton Press, first edition, hardcover, 151 pages. ($15.00 with dust jacket) $10.00

MacKELLAR, William
Two for the Fair, 1958 McGraw-Hill, first edition, hardcover. ($25.00 with dust jacket) $10.00

MacKENZIE, Compton
Theseus, 1972 Aldus Books, first edition, hardcover, map on back endpaper, color illustrations by William Stobbs. ($25.00 with dust jacket) $15.00

MacKENZIE, Kathleen
Three Of A Kind, 1956 Evans, London, first edition, hardcover, 190 pages. ($15.00 with dust jacket) $10.00

MacLELLAN, Esther and Catherine SCHROLL
Suzy and the Dog School, 1953 Ariel, first edition, small square hardcover, illustrated endpapers, 46 pages, b/w illustrations by Margaret Bradfield. ($40.00 with dust jacket) $15.00

MacLEOD, Ruth
Cheryl Downing, School Nurse, 1964 Messner, white pictorial hardcover. $10.00

MacMILLAN, Miriam
Etuk, the Eskimo Hunter, 1950 Dodd Mead, first edition, hardcover, illustrations by Kurt Wiese. ($15.00 with dust jacket) $10.00

MADDEN, Warren
Enormous Turtle, 1954 Bobbs-Merrill, first edition, small hardcover. ($15.00 with dust jacket) $10.00

MADISON, Winifred
Max's Wonderful Delicatessen, 1972 Little, Brown, first edition, hardcover, b/w illustrations by James Armstrong. ($20.00 with dust jacket) $10.00

MAGGS, William
Head-Hunter's Moon, 1958 Kingfisher, London, hardcover, 183 pages. ($20.00 with dust jacket) $10.00

MAGOON, Marian W.
Ojibway Drums, 1955 Longmans, first edition, hard

cover, 146 pages, illustrations by Larry Toschik. ($15.00 with dust jacket) $10.00

MAHOOD, Kenneth
Laughing Dragon, 1970 Scribner, first edition, oversize hardcover, illustrations by author. ($15.00 with dust jacket) $10.00

MAHY, Margaret
Princess and the Clown, 1971 Franklin Watts, oversize hardcover, color illustrations by Carol Barker. $15.00
Ultra-Violet Catastrophe! or the Unexpected Walk with Great Uncle Magnus Pringle, 1975 Parents' Press, first edition, hardcover, illustrations by Brian Froud. ($45.00 with dust jacket) $20.00

MAIDEN, Cecil
Song For Young King Wenceslas, 1969 Addison-Wesley, first edition, hardcover, illustrations by Cary. ($25.00 with dust jacket) $15.00
Speaking of Mrs. McCluskie, 1962 Vanguard Press, first edition, hardcover, 43 pages, illustrations by Hilary Knight. ($60.00 with dust jacket) $30.00

MAITLAND, Antony
Ben Goes to the City, 1967 Delacorte, oversize hardcover, two-color illustrations by author. ($15.00 with dust jacket) $10.00

MAITLAND, Hugh, see Series section BRAD FORREST

MALCOLM, Anthony, see Series section JENNINGS

MALKUS, Alida
Colt of Destiny, 1950 Winston, hardcover, illustrated. ($20.00 with dust jacket) $10.00
Story of Good Queen Bess, 1953 Grosset, hardcover, illustrated by Douglas Gorsline. ($15.00 with dust jacket) $10.00

MALVERN, Gladys
Great Garcias, 1958 Longmans, tan illustrated hardcover. $15.00
Meg's Fortune, 1950 Messner, tan hardcover, 182 pages, decorations by Corinne Malvern. ($20.00 with dust jacket) $10.00

MANN, Arthur
Jackie Robinson Story, 1950 Grosset, hardcover. $30.00

MANNING, Rosemary
Dragon in Danger, 1959 Constable, hardcover, illustrations by Constance Marshall. ($25.00 with dust jacket) $10.00
Dragon in Danger, 1960 Doubleday, hardcover,

illustrations by Constance Marshall. ($25.00 with dust jacket) $10.00
Green Smoke, 1957 Doubleday, hardcover, illustrations by Constance Marshall. ($30.00 with dust jacket) $10.00

MANNING-SANDERS, Ruth
Book of Magic Animals, 1975 Dutton, first US edition, oversize hardcover, 127 pages, illustrations by Robin Jacques. ($25.00 with dust jacket) $10.00
Book of Monsters, 1975 Methuen, first edition, hardcover. ($60.00 with dust jacket) $30.00
Jonnikin and the Flying Basket, 1969 Oxford University Press, first edition, hardcover, illustrations by Victor. G. Ambrus. ($15.00 with dust jacket) $10.00
Tortoise Tales, 1972 Thomas Nelson, first American edition, hardcover. ($25.00 with dust jacket) $10.00

MANSO, Leo
Wild West, 1950 World, Rainbow Playbook, first edition, spiral bound pictorial hardcover, forms three scenes, includes unpunched pages of punchouts. $75.00

MANTLE, Winifred
Penderel Puzzle, 1966 Holt, Rinehart & Winston, first edition, hardcover. ($15.00 with dust jacket) $10.00
Question of the Painted Cave, 1965 Holt, Rinehart & Winston, first edition, hardcover. ($25.00 with dust jacket) $10.00

MARGOLIS, Richard
Upside-Down King, 1971 Windmill Books, first edition, oversize hardcover. ($25.00 with dust jacket) $15.00

MARK, David
Sheep of the Lal Bagh, 1967 Parents, pictorial boards, illustrations by Lionel Kalish. $10.00

MARRIOTT, Alice
Indian Annie: Kiowa Captive 1965 David McKay, first edition, hardcover, illustrations by Allan Thomas. ($25.00 with dust jacket) $15.00

MARSDEN, Monica
Matter of Clues, 1962 Children's Press, green hardcover. ($15.00 with dust jacket) $10.00

MARSH, Gwen
Land of No Strangers, 1951 Oxford University, first edition, hardcover, 80 pages, color illustrations by Jean Garside. ($20.00 with dust jacket) $15.00

MARSHALL, Archibald
Edward the Dragon, 1967 Dutton, first American edition, oblong hardcover, illustrations by Edward Ardizzone. ($25.00 with dust jacket) $10.00

MARSHALL, Helen Lowrie
Starlight and Candleglow, 1971 Doubleday, first edition, hardcover, 64 pages, illustrations by Paul Bacon. ($20.00 with dust jacket) $10.00

MARSHALL, James
Guest, 1975 Houghton Mifflin, first edition, hardcover, 39 pages, illustrated by James Marshall. ($15.00 with dust jacket) $10.00
My Boy John that Went to Sea, 1966 Hodder and Stoughton, first edition, hardcover. 128 pages, full-page map. ($25.00 with dust jacket) $15.00
Yummers, 1973 Houghton Mifflin, first edition, hardcover, illustrations by author. ($30.00 with dust jacket) $15.00

MARTIGNONI, Margaret
Every Child's Story Book, A Horn of Plenty of Good Reading for Boys and Girls, 1959 Franklin Watts, oversize red hardcover, illustrations by Gioia Flammenghi. ($30.00 with dust jacket) $15.00

MARTIN, Bill and **Bernard**
Silver Stallion, 1949 Tell Well Press, picture cover binding with illustrated color endpapers and color illustrations. ($25.00 with dust jacket) $10.00
Wild Horse Roundup, 1950 Tell Well Press, first edition, oversize hardcover, 33 pages, color illustrations by author. ($45.00 with dust jacket) $20.00

MARTIN, Bill Jr.
Wizard, 1970 Holt Rinehart, hardcover, illustrations by Sal Murdocca. $10.00

MARTIN, Charles
Cowboy Charley, 4-H Champ, 1953 Viking, first edition, hardcover, illustrated by Taylor Oughton. ($20.00 with dust jacket) $10.00

MARTIN, David
Spiegel the Cat, 1971 Clarkson Potter, first American edition, oversize hardcover, 113 pages, illustrations by Roy McKie. ($15.00 with dust jacket) $10.00

MARTIN, George with **Fred GWYNNE**
Battle of the Frogs and the Mice, an Homeric Fable, 1962 Dodd, Mead, hardcover, b/w illustrations by Fred Gwynne. $40.00

MARTIN, Gregory
Boy and His Friend the Blizzard, 1962 Harper, first edition, hardcover, illustrations by Brian Wildsmith. ($25.00 with dust jacket) $15.00

MARTIN, Magdalene
Happy Ever After, 1969 Young World Productions, first edition, oversize hardcover, color illustrations by Janet and Anne Grahame Johnstone. ($30.00 with dust jacket) $20.00

MARTIN, Marcia, see Series section DONNA PARKER

MARTIN, Patricia Miles
Dog and the Boat Boy, 1969 Putnam, first edition, hardcover, illustrations by Earl Thollander. ($20.00 with dust jacket) $10.00
Grandma's Gun, 1968 Golden Gate Jr. Books, first edition, hardcover, illustrations by Robert Corey. ($35.00 with dust jacket) $15.00

MARQUAND, Josephine
Chi Ming and the Writing Lesson, 1970 Franklin

Watts, first edition, hardcover, color illustrations by Pearl Binder. ($15.00 with dust jacket) $10.00

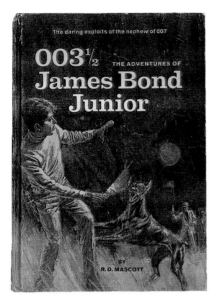

003½, Adventures of James Bond Junior, R. D. Mascott

MASCOTT, R. D.
003½, Adventures of James Bond Junior, 1968 Random House, pictorial hardcover, illustrations by Michael Jackson. $40.00

MASHA
Masha's Cats and Kittens, 1970 American Heritage Press, first edition, oversize hardcover, color illustrations by Masha. ($35.00 with dust jacket) $15.00

MASON, Arthur
Major and His Camels, 1953 Macmillan, first edition, hardcover, illustrations by Zhenya Gay. ($40.00 with dust jacket) $20.00
Wee Men of Bally Wooden, 1952 Viking, first edition, hardcover, illustrations by Robert Lawson. ($50.00 with dust jacket) $20.00

MASON, Miriam
Benjamin Lucky, 1956 Macmillan, first edition, hardcover, illustrations by Vee Guthrie. ($25.00 with dust jacket) $15.00
Gray-Nosed Kitten, 1950 Houghton, 118 pages, b/w illustrations, dust jacket by Marie Nichols. ($20.00 with dust jacket) $15.00
Hominy and This Blunt-Nosed Arrow, 1950 Macmillan, first edition, hardcover, illustrations by George and Doris Hauman. ($30.00 with dust jacket) $15.00
Stevie and His Seven Orphans, 1964 Houghton Mifflin, Weekly Reader edition, pictorial hardcover. $10.00
Young Mr. Meeker and His Exciting Journey to

Oregon, 1952 Bobbs Merrill, first edition, hardcover, illustrations by Sandra James. ($15.00 with dust jacket) $10.00

MASSIE, Diane Redfield
Baby Beebee Bird, 1963 Harper, first edition, hardcover, color illustrations by author. ($25.00 with dust jacket) $15.00
MacGregor Was a Dog, 1965 Parents' Magazine Press, first edition, hardcover, illustrations by author. ($20.00 with dust jacket) $10.00
Turtle and a Loon and Other Fables, 1965 Atheneum, first edition, hardcover, illustrations by author. ($25.00 with dust jacket) $15.00

MASTERS, Elaine
Ali and the Ghost Tiger, 1970 Westminster Press, first edition, green hardcover, 154 pages, illustrated by ink and brush drawings by author. ($25.00 with dust jacket) $15.00

MATSUTANI, Miyoko
Crane Maiden, 1968 Parents' Magazine Press, first edition, oversize pictorial hardcover, unpaginated, illustrated by Chihiro Iwasaki. $15.00
Fisherman Under the Sea, 1969 Parents' Magazine, pictoral hardcover, watercolor illustrations by Chihiro Iwasaki. $15.00

MATTHIESSEN, Peter
Seal Pool, 1972 Doubleday, first edition, pictorial hardcover, illustrations by William Pene du Bois. Hard to find. First edition with dust jacket: $350.00

MATTIESSEN, Wilhelm
Potato King and Other Folk Tales, 1969 Burke, London, first edition, hardcover, 207 pages, illustrations by Ruth Bartlett. ($30.00 with dust jacket) $15.00

MAUERSBERGER, Helga
Sun: Cockadoodledo Tells the Story of the Sun and the Seasons of the Year, 1961 Franklin Watts, oversize red hardcover, illustrations by Bischoff and Winter. $20.00

MAUGHAM, W. Somerset
Princess September, (1930) 1969 edition Harcourt, Brace, first edition, oversize red hardcover, color illustrations by Jacqueline Ayer. ($35.00 with dust jacket) $20.00
Princess September, 1970 edition Collins, London, illustrated endpapers, color illustrations by Jacqueline Ayer. ($20.00 with dust jacket) $15.00

MAURIAC, Francois
Holy Terror, 1967 Funk & Wagnalls, orange hardcover, first American edition, 63 pages, translated by Anne Carter, illustrated by Ingrid Fetz. ($25.00 with dust jacket) $10.00

MAUZEY, Merritt
Cotton Farm Boy, 1953 Henry Schuman, oversize hardcover, lithograph illustrations by Merritt Mauzey. ($50.00 with dust jacket) $25.00

MAXWELL, Gavin
Otters' Tale, Longmans, first edition, hardcover. ($25.00 with dust jacket) $15.00

MAY, Charles Paul
Michael Faraday and the Electric Dynamo, 1961 Watts, first edition, hardcover, 144 pages. ($25.00 with dust jacket) $15.00

MAY, Julian
Show Me the World of Modern Airplanes, 1959 Pennington, first edition, hardcover, illustrations. ($15.00 with dust jacket) $10.00

MAYALL and WYCKOFF
Sky Observer's Guide, 1959 Golden Press, first edition, illustrated hardcover, paintings and diagrams by John Polgreen. $65.00.

MAYBERRY, Genevieve
Eskimo of Little Diomede, 1961 Follett, first edition, hardcover, illustrations by W. T. Mars. ($30.00 with dust jacket) $15.00

MAYER, Herbert
Story of Little Ajax, 1949 Television Station WXEL, Cleveland, Channel 9, pictorial boards with black spine, drawings by Frances Mayer. TV station giveaway. Copyright 1949 by Empire Coil Co. $25.00

MAYER, Marianna and **Mercer**
Me and My Flying Machine, 1971 Parents, hardcover, color illustrations by Mercer Mayer. $15.00

MAYER, Mercer, see Series section FROG
Boy, a Dog and a Frog, 1974 Collins, London, first edition, pictorial hardcover, 32 pages, illustrations by author. ($15.00 with dust jacket) $10.00
Frog On His Own, 1973 Dial, first edition, small hardcover, illustrations by author. $20.00
Liza Lou and the Yeller Belly Swamp, 1976 Four Winds Press, glossy oversize pictorial hardcover, illustrated endpapers, color illustrations by author. $50.00
Great Cat Chase, 1974 Four Winds, small oblong hardcover, wordless book, illustrations by author. ($30.00 with dust jacket) $15.00
Silly Story, 1972 Parents, hardcover, illustrations by author. $10.00
There's a Nightmare in my Closet, 1968 Dial, first edition, oversize hardcover, color illustrations by Mayer. ($85.00 with dust jacket) $30.00. Later editions: ($25.00 with dust jacket) $15.00
What Do You Do with a Kangaroo?, 1973 Four Winds Press, illustrations by author. ($40.00 with dust jacket) $15.00

MAYNE, William
Chorister's Cake, (1956) undated Bobbs Merrill, 160 pages, hardcover, illustrations by C. W. Hodges. ($45.00 with dust jacket) $20.00
Earthfasts, 1966 Dutton, hardcover, 154 pages. ($25.00 with dust jacket) $15.00

MAZER, Harry
Snow Bound, 1973 Delacorte, first edition, hardcover. ($20.00 with dust jacket) $10.00

MAZER, Norma
Figure of Speech, 1973 Delacourt, first edition, hardcover. ($20.00 with dust jacket) $10.00

I, Trissy, 1971 Delacorte, first edition, hardcover. ($20.00 with dust jacket) $10.00

Saturday, the Twelfth of October, 1975 Delacorte, first edition, hardcover. ($20.00 with dust jacket) $10.00

McAULEY, Frank

George and Herbert, 1959 Macmillan, hardcover, illustrations by George Wilde. $15.00

McCALLUM, John and Dave STIDOLPH

Coit Fishing Pole Club Beginner's Book of Fishing, 1958 Prentice-Hall, green hardcover, 176 pages, 42 drawings by Carl Bobertz, 29 copper engravings by Jon Gnagy. ($20.00 with dust jacket) $10.00

McCLELLAND, Hugh

Magic Lasso, 1963 St. Martin's Press, first edition, hardcover, illustrations by McClelland. ($40.00 with dust jacket) $20.00

McCLINTOCK, Theodore

Animal Close-Ups, 1958 Aberlard-Schuman, hardcover, 160 pages, photo illustrations. $15.00

McCLOSKEY, Robert

Burt Dow, Deep-Water Man, 1963 Viking, oversize pictorial hardcover, 63 pages, illustrations by author. ($30.00 with dust jacket) $15.00

Homer Price, 1971 Viking, color pictorial hardcover, illustrations by author. ($20.00 with dust jacket) $10.00

One Morning in Maine, 1952 Viking, first edition, oversize hardcover, 64 pages, illustrations by author. $50.00

Time of Wonder, 1957 Viking, 1958 Caldecott Award edition, oversize hardcover, 63 pages, illustrations by author. ($35.00 with dust jacket) $20.00

McCRACKEN, Harold

Winning of the West, 1955 Garden City Books, first edition, hardcover, illustrated by Lee Ames. ($35.00 with dust jacket) $20.00

McCREADY, T. L.

Biggity Bantam, 1960 revised edition Warne, first edition UK, beige hardcover, color and b/w illustrations by Tasha Tudor. First edition with dust jacket: $150.00. Later editions: ($25.00 with dust jacket) $15.00

McCULLERS, Carson

Sweet as a Pickle and Clean as a Pig, 1964 Houghton Mifflin, first edition, hardcover, illustrations by Rolf Gerard. ($100.00 with dust jacket) $30.00

McCULLOCH, Margaret

Second Year Nurse, 1957 Westminster Press, first edition, hardcover, illustrations by Georgi Helms. ($15.00 with dust jacket) $10.00

McDERMOTT, Gerald

Arrow to the Sun, 1974 Viking, (1975 Caldecott Award), first edition, hardcover. ($20.00 with dust jacket) $10.00

Stonecutter, 1975 Viking, first edition, hardcover, 31 pages, color illustrations by author. ($50.00 with dust jacket) $20.00

McDEVITT, Jean

Twins and Trusty, 1958 Row, Peterson, first edition, hardcover, b/w illustrations. ($15.00 with dust jacket) $10.00

McDONALD, Lucile

For Glory and the King, 1969 Meredith, first edition, hardcover. ($25.00 with dust jacket) $10.00

Mystery of Catesby Island, 1950 Junior Literary Guild, hardcover. $15.00

McFARLANE, Leslie

Last of the Great Picnics, 1965 McClelland & Stewart, first edition, orange hardcover, illustrations by Lewis Parker. ($20.00 with dust jacket) $10.00

McGINLEY, Phyllis

Lucy McLocket, 1959 Lippincott, first edition, oversize hardcover, 48 pages, illustrations by Roberta McDonald. ($40.00 with dust jacket) $15.00

Make Believe Twins, 1951 Lippincott, first edition, oversize hardcover, 48 pages, illustrations by Roberta McDonald. ($35.00 with dust jacket) $15.00

Merry Christmas, Happy New Year, 1958 Viking, first edition, hardcover, illustrations by Ilonka Karasz. ($35.00 with dust jacket) $20.00

Most Wonderful Doll in the World, 1950 J.B. Lippincott, 64 pages, hardcover, color illustrations and drawings by Helen Stone. ($20.00 with dust jacket) $10.00

McGOVERN, Ann

If You Lived with the Circus, 1971 Scholastic, glossy hardcover, illustrations by Ati Forberg. $15.00

Squeals and Squiggles and Ghostly Giggles, 1973 Four Winds Press, first edition, hardcover, illustrations by Jeffrey Higginbottom. ($25.00 with dust jacket) $15.00

Too Much Noise, 1967 Houghton Mifflin, brown hardcover with embossed design. ($15.00 with dust jacket) $10.00

Treasury of Christmas Stories, 1960 Four Winds Press, hardcover, 152 pages, includes authors Anne Wood, Nolan, Chute, Howells, Gillespie, Andersen, Steffens, Poe, Crandall, Mead, Fisher, and hymn verses. $15.00

Zoo, Where Are You?, 1964 Harper, oversize hardcover, illustrations by Ezra Jack Keats. ($25.00 with dust jacket) $15.00

McGOWEN, Tom
Apple Strudel Soldier, 1968 Follett, first edition, hardcover, illustrations by John E. Johnson. ($25.00 with dust jacket) $15.00
Only Glupmaker in the U.S. Navy, 1966 Whitman, pictorial hardcover, color drawings. $15.00
Sir Machinery, 1970 Follett, hardcover. ($25.00 with dust jacket) $15.00

McGRAW, Eloise Jarvis
Crown Fire, 1951 Coward-McCann, hardcover, 254 pages. ($30.00 with dust jacket) $15.00
Golden Goblet, 1961 Coward-McCann, hardcover, dust jacket by R. M. Powers. ($25.00 with dust jacket) $10.00
Mara, Daughter of the Nile, 1953 Coward McCann, first edition, hardcover. Hard to find. ($100.00 with dust jacket) $40.00
Master Cornhill, 1973 Atheneum, hardcover. ($35.00 with dust jacket) $15.00
Sawdust in His Shoes, 1950 Coward-McCann, hardcover, 246 pages. ($25.00 with dust jacket) $10.00

McGREGOR, Ellen
Theodore Turtle, 1955 Whitlesey House, first edition, hardcover, color and b/w illustrations by Paul Galdone. ($15.00 with dust jacket) $10.00

McHARGUE, Georgess
Mermaid and the Whale, 1973 Holt, first edition, oversize hardcover, picture book, color illustrations by Robert Andrew Parker. ($30.00 with dust jacket) $15.00

McILVANE, Jane
Cammie's Challenge, 1962 Bobbs Merrill, first edition, hardcover, illustrations by Wesley Dennis. ($25.00 with dust jacket) $15.00

McINNES, John A.
Toy-Box, 1970 Nelson, Toronto, hardcover. $20.00

McKENZIE, Ellen
Drujienna's Harp, 1971 Dutton, first edition, hardcover. ($25.00 with dust jacket) $15.00

McKENZIE, John
Rebels in Buckskin, 1966 Exposition Press, hardcover. ($20.00 with dust jacket) $10.00

McKEOWN, Martha Ferguson
Come to Our Salmon Feast, 1959 Binfords & Mort, first edition, hardcover, b/w photos by Archie W. McKeown. ($15.00 with dust jacket) $10.00

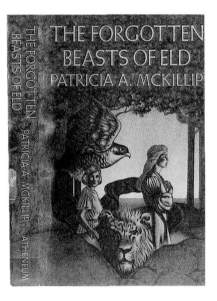

McKILLIP, Patricia
House on Parchment Street, 1973 Atheneum, hardcover. ($40.00 with dust jacket) $20.00
Forgotten Beasts of Eld, 1974 Atheneum, first edition, hardcover. ($90.00 with dust jacket) $30.00. Later editions: ($20.00 with dust jacket) $10.00
Throne of the Errill of Sherrill, 1973 Atheneum, first edition, hardcover. ($40.00 with dust jacket) $20.00

McKIM, Audrey
Andy and the Gopher, 1959 Little, Brown, first edition, hardcover, 119 pages, b/w illustrations by Ronni Solbert. $25.00

McKOWN, Robin
Boy Who Woke Up in Madagascar, 1967 Putnam, first edition, hardcover, illustrations by Robert Quakenbush. ($30.00 with dust jacket) $15.00
Foreign Service Girl, 1959 Putnam, hardcover. ($15.00 with dust jacket) $10.00

Rakoto and the Drongo Bird, 1966 Lothrop, Lee and Shepard, oversize blue hardcover, 52 pages, color illustrations by Robert Quackenbush. $15.00

McLACHLAN, Edward
Simon in the Land of Chalk Drawings, 1969 Follett, first edition, blue hardcover, illustrated endpapers, 29 pages, illustrations by author. ($20.00 with dust jacket) $10.00

McLELLAND, Isabel
Hi! Teacher, 1952 Holt, first edition, hardcover, illustrated by Mary Stevens. ($15.00 with dust jacket) $10.00

McLEOD, Emilie
Bear's Bicycle, 1975 Little, Brown, first edition, hardcover, illustrations by David McPhail. ($25.00 with dust jacket) $15.00

McMEEKIN, Isabel
Ban-Joe & Grey Eagle, 1951 Franklin Watts, hardcover. $10.00
Kentucky Derby Winner, Grosset, Famous Horse Stories, hardcover. $10.00

McNEER, May
American Story, 1963 Ariel Books, first edition, oversize hardcover, illustrations by Lynd Ward. ($35.00 with dust jacket) $20.00
*Armed With Courage,*1957 Abingdon, first edition, hardcover, illustrated by Lynd Ward. ($25.00 with dust jacket) $15.00
Canadian Story, 1963 Ariel Books, first edition, oversize hardcover, illustrations by Lynd Ward. ($35.00 with dust jacket) $20.00
Give Me Freedom, 1964 Abingdon, first edition, hardcover, illustrations by Lynd Ward. ($50.00 with dust jacket) $20.00
My Friend Mac, 1960 Houghton Mifflin, first edition, hardcover, illustrations by Lynd Ward. ($35.00 with dust jacket) $15.00
Stranger in the Pines, 1971 Houghton Mifflin, first edition, hardcover, illustrations by Lynd Ward. ($40.00 with dust jacket) $20.00
Up a Crooked River, 1952 Viking, first edition, hardcover, illustrated endpapers, illustrated by Lynn Ward. ($20.00 with dust jacket) $15.00
Wolf of Lambs Lane, 1967 Houghton Mifflin Company, first edition, hardcover, illustrations by Lynd Ward. ($35.00 with dust jacket) $20.00

McNEILL, Janet
Prisoner in the Park, 1971 Faber & Faber, hardcover. ($40.00 with dust jacket) $15.00

McSWIGAN, Marie
Snow Treasure, 1960 Dutton, first edition, hardcover, b/w illustrations by Mary Reardon. ($20.00 with dust jacket) $10.00

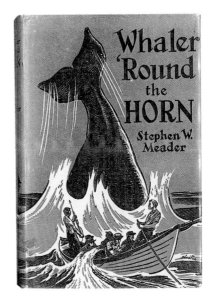

MEADER, Stephen W.
Cedar's Boy, 1960 edition Harcourt, Brace, beige hardcover, illustrated by Lee Townsend. Sequel to *Red Horse Hill*. ($30.00 with dust jacket) $15.00
Whaler 'Round the Horn, 1950 Harcourt, hardcover, map illustrated endpapers, b/w illustrations by Edward Shenton. ($30.00 with dust jacket) $15.00
Who Rides In The Dark?, 1965 Harcourt, first edition, hardcover, illustrations by James MacDonald. ($30.00 with dust jacket) $15.00

MEADOWCRAFT, Enid LaMonte
Story of Crazy Horse, 1954 Grosset & Dunlap, first edition, hardcover. ($15.00 with dust jacket) $10.00
Story of Davy Crockett, 1952 Grosset, brown hardcover, illustrated by Charles B. Falls. ($15.00 with dust jacket) $8.00

MEANS, Florence Crannell
It Takes All Kinds, 1964 Houghton Mifflin, orange hardcover. ($20.00 with dust jacket) $10.00

MEANY, Tom
Magnificent Yankees, 1963 Grosset & Dunlap, hardcover, Big League Baseball Library edition. $10.00

MEEK, Colonel S.P.
Hans, a Dog of the Border Patrol, 1951 Knopf, first edition, hardcover. ($30.00 with dust jacket) $15.00

MEIER, Mariann
Young Traveler in Switzerland, 1954 Dutton, first edition, hardcover, illustrated by photos and maps. ($15.00 with dust jacket) $10.00

MEIGS, Cornelia
Wild Geese Flying, 1957 Macmillan, Weekly Reader edition, hardcover, illustrations by Charles Geer. ($15.00 with dust jacket) $10.00

MELIN, Grace Hathaway
Maria Mitchell. Girl Astronomer, 1960 Bobbs-Merrill, first edition, hardcover. ($25.00 with dust jacket) $10.00

MELLIN, Jeanne
Horses Across America, 1953 Dutton, first edition, hardcover. ($15.00 with dust jacket) $10.00

MEMMEN, Carol
Woodland Queen, 1963 Vantage Press, first edition, oversize hardcover, 30 pages. ($20.00 with dust jacket) $10.00

MENDEL, Jo, see Series section TUCKER

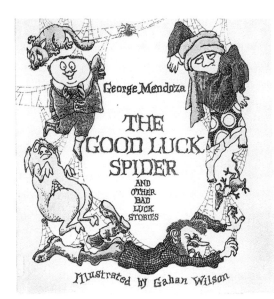

MENDOZA, George
Crack in the Wall, and Other Terribly Weird Tales, 1968 Dial, hardcover, b/w Mercer Mayer. ($40.00 with dust jacket) $20.00
Fearsome Brat, 1971 Lothrop Lee, hardcover, illustrated by Frank Bozzo. $15.00
Good Luck Spider, 1970 Doubleday, square hardcover, b/w George Mendoza. ($30.00 with dust jacket) $15.00
Herman's Hat, 1969 Doubleday, first edition, oblong hardcover, illustrations by Frank Bozzo. ($30.00 with dust jacket) $15.00
Inspector, 1970 Garden City, first edition, decorated oblong small hardcover, illustrated by Peter Parnall. ($30.00 with just jacket) $20.00
Marcel Marceau Alphabet Book, 1970 Doubleday,

first edition, hardcover, color photographs by Milton H. Greene. ($25.00 with dust jacket) $10.00
Practical Man , 1968 Lothrop, Lee & Shepard, first edition, hardcover, illustrated by Imero Gobbato. ($35.00 with dust jacket) $15.00

MENOTTI, Gian-Carlo
Amahl and the Night Visitors, narrative adaptation by Frances Frost, 1952 edition Whittlesey House, red hardcover, 89 pages, illustrated endpapers, illustrated in color and black and white by Roger Duvoisin. $15.00
Help, Help, The Globolinks!, 1970 edition McGraw-Hill, first edition thus, hardcover, color illustrations by Milton Glaser. ($30.00 with dust jacket) $15.00

MEREDITH, Nicolete
Milestone Summer, 1962 Whitman, hardcover, decorations by Arnie Kohn. $10.00

MERRIAM, Eve
Gaggle of Geese, 1960 Knopf, oversize hardcover, illustrations by Paul Galdone. ($25.00 with dust jacket) $10.00
There Is No Rhyme for Silver, 1962 Atheneum, first edition, hardcover, b/w illustrations by Joseph Schindelman. ($15.00 with dust jacket) $10.00

MERRILL, Jean
Boxes, 1953 Coward McCann, hardcover, illustrated in color by Ronni Solbert. ($35.00 with dust jacket) $20.00
Elephant Who Liked to Smash Small Cars, 1967 Pantheon, first edition, oversize hardcover, illustrations by Ronni Solbert. ($30.00 with dust jacket) $20.00
Pushcart War, 1964 William Scott, illustrated hardcov-

er, 223 pages, b/w illustrations by Ronni Solbert. ($25.00 with same-as-cover dust jacket) $15.00

MERWIN, Decie
Robin and Mr. Jones, 1953 Oxford, yellow hardcover, 112 pages, illustrations by author. ($20.00 with dust jacket) $10.00
Scottish Treasure Mystery, 1960 Lippincott, hardcover. ($15.00 with dust jacket) $10.00
Somerhaze Farm, 1958 Lippincott, hardcover. ($15.00 with dust jacket) $10.00

MEYER, Louis
Gypsy Bears, 1971 Little Brown, first edition, yellow oversize hardcover, 53 pages, b/w illustrations by author. ($25.00 with dust jacket) $10.00

MEYER, Margaret
Mei Ling's Mountain, 1968 Chilton, hardcover. ($20.00 with dust jacket) $10.00

MEYER, Renate
Hide-and-Seek, 1969 Bodley Head, London, first edition, oblong oversize hardcover, 24 pages, color illustrations. ($30.00 with dust jacket) $15.00

MEYERHOFF, Nancy
Let's Go Shopping, 1958 Wonder Books, hardcover, illustrations by Guyon Brooke. $15.00

MEYERS, Barlow
Champions All the Way, 1960 Whitman, hardcover. $10.00
Janet Lennon at Camp Calamity, 1962 Whitman, glossy color pictorial hardcover, small. $15.00
Janet Lennon: Adventure at Two Rivers, 1961 Whitman, glossy color pictorial hardcover, illus-

trated by Ken Sawyer. $10.00
Janet Lennon and the Angels, 1963 Whitman, orange pictorial hardcover, illustrated by Adam Szwjkowski. $20.00
Restless Gun, 1959 Whitman, hardcover. $25.00
Walt Disney's Annette, Mystery at Medicine Wheel, 1964 Whitman, glossy pictorial hardcover, illustrated endpapers, illustrations by Robert L. Jenney and Maxine McCaffrey. $10.00

MEYERS, Susan
*Melissa Finds a Mystery,*1966 Dodd, Mead, first edition, hardcover. Winner of Calling All Girls Prize Competition. ($15.00 with dust jacket) $10.00

MICHAEL, Maurice and **Pamela**
Fairy Tales from Bohemia, 1968 Follett, first edition, hardcover, 182 pages, b/w illustrations by John Lathey. ($30.00 with dust jacket) $15.00

MICHELSON, Florence
Lassie and the Cub Scout, 1966 Whitman, blue hardcover, illustrated by Al Anderson. $10.00

MIEGS, Cornelia
Fair Wind to Virginia, 1955 Macmillan, first edition, hardcover, illustrations by John C. Wonstler. ($20.00 with dust jacket) $10.00

MIERS, Earl Schenck
Kid Who Beat the Dodgers and Other Sports Stories, 1954 World, first edition, hardcover, illustrations by Paul Galdone. ($15.00 with dust jacket) $10.00
Pirate Chase, 1965 Holt, Rinehart, hardcover. $15.00
Rebel's Roost: The Story of Old Williamsburg, 1956 Colonial Williamsburg, Inc., red and black and gilt decorative hardcover, illustrated by Fritz Kredel. $15.00

MIKHALKOV, Sergei
Jolly Hares, 1969 Progress Publishers, Moscow, first English edition, hardcover, illustrations by Y. Rachev. ($30.00 with dust jacket) $15.00

MIKLOWITZ, Gloria D.
Zoo That Moved, 1968 Follett, hardcover, color and b/w illustrations by Don Madden. ($25.00 with dust jacket) $10.00

MILES, Miska
Kickapoo, 1961 Little Brown, first edition, hardcover, illustrations by Wesley Dennis. ($15.00 with dust jacket) $10.00

MILHOUS, Katherine
Appolonia's Valentine, 1954 Charles Scribner, first

edition, oversize hardcover, color illustrations by author. ($60.00 with dust jacket) $15.00

Egg Tree, 1950 Scribner, 1951 Caldecott Award, hardcover, color illustrations by author. ($35.00 with dust jacket) $20.00

Patrick and the Golden Slippers, 1951 Scribner, red oversize hardcover, color illustrations by author. ($35.00 with dust jacket) $15.00

Through These Arches, 1964 Lippincott, oblong hardcover, 96 pages, color illustrations by author. ($35.00 with dust jacket) $15.00

With Bells On, 1955 Scribners, first edition, oversize hardcover, illustrations by author. ($35.00 with dust jacket) $20.00

MILLER, Albert G., see Series section FURY
Bambi Gets Lost, 1972 Random House book club, hardcover, illustrated by Disney Animation. $10.00

MILLER, Basil, see Series section KOKO; SILVER STAR
Ken and the Navajo Treasure Map, 1955 Zondervan, hardcover. $10.00

Ken Follows the Chuck Wagon, 1950 Zondervan, hardcover. ($25.00 with dust jacket) $10.00

Range Hero, 1954 Zondervan, hardcover. $10.00

MILLER, Edna
Mousekin Finds a Friend, 1967 Macdonald, London, first edition, green hardcover, watercolor illustrations by author. ($35.00 with dust jacket) $20.00

MILLER, Eugenia
Sign of the Salamander, 1967 Holt, hardcover. ($30.00 with dust jacket) $10.00

Golden Spur, 1964 Holt, hardcover. $10.00

MILLER, Helen Topping
Christmas with Robert E. Lee, 1958 Longmans, Green, first edition, hardcover, 79 pages. ($15.00 with dust jacket) $10.00

MILLER, Katherine
Apollo, 1970 Houghton Mifflin, first edition, oversize hardcover, 80 pages, woodcuts by Vivian Berger. ($30.00 with dust jacket) $15.00

MILLER, Warren
Goings-on at Little Wishful, 1959 Harcourt, first edition, oblong hardcover, illustrations by Edward Sorel. ($35.00 with dust jacket) $15.00

King Carlo of Capri, 1958 Harcourt Brace, first edition, hardcover, illustrations by Edward Sorel. ($20.00 with dust jacket) $10.00

MILLIGAN, Spike
Badjelly the Witch, 1973 Michael Joseph, first edi-

tion, hardcover, illustrations by author. ($20.00 with dust jacket) $15.00

MILLS, Annette
Colonel Crock, 1953 Harrap, London, first edition, hardcover, 96 pages, 4 color plates and b/w illustrations by Edward Andrews. $10.00

MILNE, A. A.
Once on a Time. . ., (1917)1962 edition New York Graphic Society, first edition thus, illustrated by Susan Perl. ($45.00 with dust jacket) $25.00

Pooh's Birthday Book, 1963 Dutton, small, color illustrated hardcover, illustrated endpapers, Shepard illustrations. $12.00

Prince Rabbit and the Princess Who Could Not Laugh, 1966 edition Dutton, hardcover, numerous color and b/w illustrations by Mary Shepard. $15.00

Winnie Ille Pu, in Latin, translation by Alexander Lenard, 1962 Dutton, illustrations by Ernest Shepard. ($25.00 with dust jacket) $15.00

MINARIK, Else Holmelund, see Series section LITTLE BEAR
Cat and Dog, 1960 Harper, first edition, hardcover. ($25.00 with dust jacket) $10.00

Little Giant Girl and Elf Boy, 1963 Harper & Row, first edition, hardcover, illustrations by Garth Williams. $100.00 with dust jacket. Later editions: ($20.00 with dust jacket) $10.00

No Fighting, No Biting!, 1958 Harper, 62 pages, illustrations by Maurice Sendak. First edition with dust jacket: $300.00. Later printings: ($25.00 with dust jacket) $10.00

Winds that Come from Far Away, 1964 Harper Row, 32 pages, hardcover, illustrations by Joan Phyllis Berg. ($25.00 with dust jacket) $15.00

MINSHALL, Vera
Call of the High Road, 1967 Zondervan, hardcover. $10.00

MIRSKY, Reba Paeff
Nomusa and the New Magic, 1962 Follett, first edition, hardcover, 189 pages, illustrations by W. T. Mars. ($20.00 with dust jacket) $10.00
Thirty-One Brothers and Sisters, 1952 Wilcox and Follett, hardcover, illustrated. ($20.00 with dust jacket) $10.00

MITCHELL, Ehrman
Ponies for Young People, 1960 Van Nostrand, first edition, hardcover, illustrated with photographs. ($20.00 with dust jacket) $10.00

MITCHELL, Elyne
Kingfisher Feather, 1962 Hutchinson, hardcover, illustrations by Grace Huxtable. $30.00

MITZUMURA, Kazue
If I Built a Village, 1971 Thomas Crowell, first edition, hardcover. ($50.00 with dust jacket) $20.00
If I Were A Cricket..., 1973 Thomas Crowell, first edition, hardcover, illustrated. ($30.00 with dust jacket) $15.00

MOFFET, Enid
Mervyn's Secret, 1969 Pickering & Inglis Snowdrop series, illustrated hardcover. $10.00

MOHAN, Beverly
Punia and the King of the Sharks, 1964 Follett, first edition, hardcover, illustrations by Don Bolognese. ($40.00 with dust jacket) $20.00

MOLLOY, Anne
Mystery of the Pilgrim Trading Post, 1964 Hastings House, Weekly Reader edition, illustrated hardcover, 160 pages, b/w illustrations by Floyd James Torbert. $10.00
Secret of the Old Salem Desk, 1955 Ariel, first edition, hardcover. ($15.00 with dust jacket) $10.00
Where Away, 1952 Houghton Mifflin, hardcover. ($20.00 with dust jacket) $10.00

MONCURE, Jane
On Christmas Morning, 1963 Dandelion House, hardcover, illustrations by Kathryn Hutton. $15.00

MONJO, F. N.
Me and Willie and Pa, 1973 Simon & Schuster, first edition, oversize hardcover, illustrations by David Gorsline. ($30.00 with dust jacket) $15.00
One Bad Thing About Father, 1970 Harper, first edition, hardcover, illustrations by Rocco Negri. ($20.00 with dust jacket) $10.00
Rudi and the Distelfink, 1972 Dutton, first edition, hardcover, illustrations by George Kraus. ($15.00 with dust jacket) $10.00
Secret of the Sachem's Tree, 1972 Coward McCann, first edition, hardcover, illustrations by Margot Tomes. ($20.00 with dust jacket) $10.00
Vicksburg Veteran, 1971 Simon and Schuster, first edition, hardcover, 62 pages, b/w illustrations. ($30.00 with dust jacket) $15.00

MONSELL, Helen A.
Her Own Way, the Story of Lottie Moon, ca. 1958 Broadman Press, hardcover, illustrations by Henry C. Pitz. $10.00
Susan Anthony, Girl Who Dared, 1954 Bobbs-Merrill, first edition, hardcover, b/w 1954 illustrations. ($25.00 with dust jacket) $15.00

MONTGOMERY, Herb and Mary
Mongoose Magoo, 1968 Oddo Publishing, illustrated hardcover. $15.00

MONTGOMERY, Jean
Wrath of Coyote, 1968 Morrow, hardcover. ($30.00 with dust jacket) $10.00

MONTGOMERY, Rutherford G., see Series section GOLDEN STALLION; KENT BARSTOW
Claim Jumpers of Marble Canyon, 1956 Knopf, first edition, hardcover, illustrated. ($20.00 with dust jacket) $10.00
In Happy Hollow, 1958 Garden City, first edition, hardcover, illustrated by Harold Berson. ($20.00 with dust jacket) $10.00
Kildee House, 1949 Doubleday, hardcover, 209 pages, illustrations by Barbara Cooney. 1950 Newbery honor book. ($20.00 with dust jacket) $10.00
Klepty, 1961 Duell Sloan Pearce, first edition, hardcover, 83 pages. ($15.00 with dust jacket) $10.00
McGonnigle's Lake, 1953 Doubleday, first edition, hardcover, 219 pages, illustrations by Garry MacKenzie. ($20.00 with dust jacket) $10.00
Pekan the Shadow, 1970 Caxton, first edition, hardcover, b/w illustrations. ($25.00 with dust jacket) $10.00
Walt Disney's Cougar, 1961 Golden Press, first edition, pictorial hardcover, illustrations by Robert Magnusen. $20.00

MOODY, Ralph
Fields of Home, 1953 W.W. Norton, first edition, brown hardcover, illustrations by Edward Shenton. $40.00
Horse of a Different Color, Reminiscences of a Kansas Drover, 1968 W.W. Norton, first edition, hardcover. ($20.00 with dust jacket) $10.00

MOON, Sheila
Hunt Down the Prize, 1971 Atheneum, first edition, hardcover. ($25.00 with dust jacket) $15.00
Knee-Deep in Thunder, 1967 Atheneum, first edition, hardcover. ($30.00 with dust jacket) $15.00

MOORE, Clement C.
Night Before Christmas, 1961 edition Grosset & Dunlap, first edition thus, hardcover, illustrated by Gyo Fujikawa. ($75.00 with dust jacket) $20.00
Night Before Christmas, 1962 Worcester, first edition, miniature red leather hardcover with gilt edges, illustrations by Tasha Tudor. First edition with dust jacket: $200.00. Later editions: ($25.00 with dust jacket) $15.00

MOORE, Doris Langley
E. Nesbit, a Biography, 1966 Chilton, first edition, hardcover. Photographs. ($25.00 with dust jacket) $15.00

MOORE, Elizabeth
Something to Jump For, 1960 Country Life, London, first edition, hardcover, 100 pages, b/w plate illustrations by John Lobban. ($35.00 with dust jacket) $20.00

MOORE, Jane Shearer
Story of Toby, 1957 Rand McNally, illustrated hardcover, oversize. $15.00

MOORE, Lilian
Little Raccoon and No Trouble at All, 1972 McGraw Hill Weekly Reader Book Club, hardcover, illustrated by Giolia Fiammenghi. $10.00
Magic Spectacles and Other Easy-to-Read Stories, 1965 Parents, illustrated hardcover, 70 pages, illustrations by Arnold Lobel. $15.00
Snake That Went to School, 1957 Easy To Read Book, Random House, pictorial boards, illustrations by Mary Stevens. $10.00

MOORE, Margaret
Willie Without, 1951 Coward McCann, red pictorial hardcover, 86 pages, illustrated by Nora S. Unwin. ($20.00 with dust jacket) $10.00

MOORE, Marianne
Puss in Boots, the Sleeping Beauty and Cinderella, 1963 Macmillan, first edition, hardcover, pastel illustrations by Eugene Carlin. ($40.00 with dust jacket) $20.00

MOORE, Nancy
Unhappy Hippopotamus, 1957 Vanguard, first edition, pictorial hardcover, illustrations by Edward Leight. ($50.00 with dust jacket) $20.00

MOORE, Ruth Nulton
Hiding the Bell, 1968 Westminster Press, first edition, hardcover, illustrated by Andrew A. Snyder. ($20.00 with dust jacket) $10.00

MOREL, Eve
Fairy Tales and Fables, 1970 Grosset & Dunlap, glossy oversize hardcover, 77 pages, color illustrations by Gyo Fujikawa. $15.00

MOREY, Walt
Angry Waters, 1969 Dutton, hardcover, first edition, illustrations by Richard Cuffari. ($20.00 with dust jacket) $10.00
Canyon Winter, 1972 Dutton, first edition, hardcover. Dust jacket by Michael Hampshire. ($35.00 with dust jacket) $15.00
Deep Trouble, 1971 Dutton, first edition, hardcover. ($20.00 with dust jacket) $10.00
Gentle Ben, 1965 Dutton, first edition, hardcover,

191 pages, illustrations by John Schoenherr. ($25.00 with dust jacket) $10.00
Gloomy Gus, 1973 Dutton, hardcover. ($15.00 with dust jacket) $10.00
Kavik the Wolf Dog, 1968 Dutton, first edition, 192 pages, illustrations by Peter Parnell. ($35.00 with dust jacket) $20.00

MORGAN, Henry
O-Sono and the Magician's Nephew and the Elephant, 1964 Vanguard, first edition, hardcover. ($20.00 with dust jacket) $10.00

MORGENSTERN, Christian
Great Lalula and Other Nonsense Rhymes, 1969 Putnam, first American edition, hardcover, color illustrations by Ladislav Svatos. ($15.00 with dust jacket) $10.00

MORRIS, Marcus, editor
Eighth Eagle Annual, 1956 Hulton, 173 pages, illustrations include color and comics. $25.00

MORROW, Betty
See Up the Mountain, 1958 Harper & Row, hardcover, illustrated by Winifred Lubell. $10.00

MORROW, Suzanne Stark
Inatuk's Friend, 1968 Little, Brown, first edition, hardcover, illustrated by Ellen Raskin. ($20.00 with dust jacket) $10.00

MORTON, Miriam
Harvest of Russian Children's Literature, 1967 University of California Press, first edition, oversize hardcover, anthology. ($45.00 with dust jacket) $25.00

MOSEL, Arlene
Funny Little Woman, (1972) Dutton, 1973 Caldecott Award edition, oblong oversize green hardcover, color illustrations by Blair Lent. ($50.00 with dust jacket) $20.00
Tikki Tikki Tembo, 1968 Rinehart, hardcover picture book, color illustrations. ($20.00 with dust jacket) $15.00

MOSKIN, Marietta
Lysbet and the Fire Kittens, 1973 Coward McCann, first edition, hardcover, 48 pages, color and b/w drawings by Margot Tomes. ($25.00 with dust jacket) $10.00

MOSS, Elaine
Polar, 1975 A. Deutsch, London, first edition, oversize hardcover picture book, color illustrations by Jeanne Baker. $20.00

MOWAT, Farley
Black Joke, 1962 McClelland, first edition, 177 pages, illustrations by D. Johnson. ($60.00 with dust jacket) $20.00
Boat Who Wouldn't Float, 1969 Atlantic Monthly, first American edition, 241 pages. $15.00
Curse of the Viking Grave, 1966 McClelland, first edition, 243 pages, illustrations by Charles Greer. ($50.00 with dust jacket) $30.00
Dog Who Wouldn't Be, 1957 Little Brown, first edition, hardcover, 238 pages, illustrations by Paul Galdone. ($50.00 with dust jacket) $15.00
Never Cry Wolf, 1963 McClelland, first edition, 243 pages. ($50.00 with dust jacket) $20.00
Owls in the Family, 1973 McClelland, hardcover, illustrated by Robert Frankenberg. ($30.00 with dust jacket) $15.00

MOZLEY, Charles
Sleeping Beauty, 1972 Mulberry, first American edition, purple glossy hardcover with 3-D picture, illustrations by Charles Mozley. $15.00

MUHLENWEG, Fritz
Big Tiger and Christian, Their Adventures in Mongolia, 1954 Jonathan Cape, London, first edition in English, UK, hardcover, 558 pages, two-page map, color endpapers, illustrated by Rafaello Busoni. ($110.00 with dust jacket) $25.00

MUIR, Marcie, editor
Strike-A-Light Bushranger and Other Australian Tales, 1972 Hamish Hamilton, first edition, hardcover. ($20.00 with dust jacket) $10.00

MULLING, Vera Cooper
Kala and the Sea Bird, 1966 Golden Gate Junior Books, blue illustrated boards, illustrated by Earl Thollander. ($15.00 with dust jacket) $8.00

MURPHY, Robert
Certain Island, 1967 M. Evans, first edition, hardcover. ($20.00 with dust jacket) $10.00

MURPHY, Shirley Rousseau
Elmo Doolan and the Search for the Golden Mouse, 1970 Viking, first edition, hardcover, illustrations by Fritz Kredl. ($20.00 with dust jacket) $10.00

MURRAY, Jane W.
Walk the High Horizon, 1974 Westminster, hardcover. ($25.00 with dust jacket) $15.00

MUSGRAVE, Florence
Trailer Tribe, 1955 Ariel Books, first edition, hardcover. ($25.00 with dust jacket) $15.00

MYERBERG, Michael
Hansel and Gretel, 1955 Fernand & Spertus, hardcover, illustrated with scenes from the Michael Myerberg motion picture with puppet-like characters. $15.00

MYERS, Byrona
Turn Here for Strawberry Roan, 1950 Bobbs-Merrill, first edition, hardcover, 134 pages, illustrations by Anne Marie Jauss. $15.00

MYERS, Walter Dean
Fast Sam, Cool Clyde, and Stuff, 1975 Viking, first edition, hardcover 190 pages. ($30.00 with dust jacket) $10.00

N

NAGEL, Stina
Little Boys, 1965 Gibson, Norwalk, hardcover, color and b/w illustrations. ($20.00 with dust jacket) $10.00

NAGY, Gil
No More Dragons, 1969 Lothrop Lee, hardcover, illustrations by William Wiesner. $10.00

NASH, Ogden
Animal Garden, 1965 M. Evans, hardcover, illustrations by Hilary Knight. ($50.00 with dust jacket) $20.00
Boy Is A Boy: The Fun of Being a Boy, 1960 Watts, first edition, oversize hardcover. ($20.00 with dust jacket) $10.00
Christmas that Almost Wasn't, 1957 Little, Brown, first edition, hardcover, color illustrations by Linell Nash. ($20.00 with dust jacket) $10.00
Cruise of the Aardvark, 1967 M. Evans, first edition, red hardcover, illustrations by Wendy Watson. ($40.00 with dust jacket) $20.00
Girls are Silly, 1962 Franklin Watts, orange hardcover, illustrations by Lawrence Beall Smith. ($50.00 with dust jacket) $20.00
New Nutcracker Suite and Other Innocent Verses, 1962 Little, Brown and Company, first edition, hardcover, illustrations by Ivan Chermayeff. ($20.00 with dust jacket) $10.00
Santa Go Home, 1966 Little Brown, first edition, green hardcover, 56 pages, illustrated with 40 drawings by Robert Osborn. ($35.00 with dust jacket) $20.00
Untold Adventures of Santa Claus, 1964 Little Brown, first edition, hardcover, illustrations by Walter Lorraine. ($25.00 with dust jacket) $15.00

NAVARRA, John Gabriel
Turtle in the House, 1968 Doubleday, first edition, hardcover, illustrations by Kiyoaki Komoda. ($20.00 with dust jacket) $15.00

NAYLOR, Phyllis Reynolds
To Make a Wee Moon, 1969 Follett, first edition, hardcover, 190 pages, illustrations by Beth and Joe Krush. ($25.00 with dust jacket) $10.00

NEFF, Priscilla Holton
Little Miss Callie, 1955 Longmans, Green, first edition, hardcover. ($15.00 with dust jacket) $10.00

NELSEN, Alix
Raggedy Ann & Andy's Green Thumb Book, 1975 Bobbs Merrill, first edition, dark green hardcover, illustrated. ($45.00 with dust jacket) $20.00

NELSEN, Donald
Sam and Emma, 1971 Parents' Magazine Press, first edition, oblong illustrated hardcover, 38 pages, color illustrations by Edward Gorey. ($50.00 with dust jacket) $20.00

NELSON, Marg
Mystery on a Full Moon, 1970 Farrar, hardcover. $10.00

NESBIT, E.
Long Ago When I Was Young, 1966 Whiting & Wheaton, London, first edition, hardcover, illustrated by Edward Ardizzone. ($45.00 with dust jacket) $20.00

NESBIT, Troy (Franklin Brewster Folsom), see Series section WILDERNESS MYSTERY
Diamond Cave Mystery, (1954) 1964 edition Whitman, green pictorial hardcover. $10.00
Jinx of Payrock Canyon, 1954 Whitman, blue pictorial hardcover, b/w illustrations by Ursula Koering. $15.00
Sand Dune Pony, 1954, glossy pictorial hardcover, illustrated endpapers, illustrated. $15.00
Forest Fire Mystery, 1962 Whitman, red hardcover, illustrations by Shannon Stirnweis. $10.00
Indian Mummy Mystery, 1953 Whitman, orange pictorial hardcover, illustrations by Paul Busch. $15.00
Mystery at Rustler's Fort, 1954 Whitman, pictorial hardcover. $15.00
Wagon Train, 1959 Whitman, blue pictorial hardcover. $15.00

NESS, Evaline
Amelia Mixed the Mustard and Other Poems, 1975 Scribner, first edition, brown oversize hardcover, selected poems, color illustrations by Ness. ($35.00 with dust jacket) $20.00
Do You Have the Time, Lydia?, 1971 Dutton, first edition, hardcover. ($25.00 with dust jacket) $10.00

Double Discovery, 1965 Scribner, first edition, oversize hardcover, 32 pages, color illustrations by author. ($35.00 with dust jacket) $15.00

Gift for Sula Sula, 1963 Scribner, first edition, oversize hardcover, color illustrations by author. ($25.00 with dust jacket) $10.00

Girl and the Goatherd or This and That and Thus and So, 1970 Dutton, first edition, oversize blue hardcover, color illustrations by author. ($25.00 with dust jacket) $10.00

Joey and the Birthday Present, 1971 McGraw Hill, first edition, hardcover, illustrations by author. ($35.00 with dust jacket) $20.00

Josefina February, 1963 Scribner, orange hardcover, illustrations by author. ($30.00 with dust jacket) $15.00

Long, Broad and Quickeye, 1969 Scribner, first edition, oversize hardcover, illustrations by author. ($35.00 with dust jacket) $15.00

Mr. Miacca, 19967 Holt Rinehart, first edition, hardcover, illustrated. ($45.00 with dust jacket) $20.00

Old Mother Hubbard and Her Dog, 1972 Holt, first edition, illustrations by author. ($30.00 with dust jacket) $15.00

Pavo and the Princess, 1964 Scribners, first edition, hardcover, illustrations by author. ($55.00 with dust jacket) $20.00

Sam, Bangs & Moonshine, 1966 Holt, 1967 Caldecott Medal edition, oversize, hardcover, illustrated endpapers, b/w/brown/green illustrations throughout by author. ($35.00 with dust jacket) $20.00

Sam, Bangs & Moonshine, Weekly Reader edition, hardcover. $10.00

Story of Ophelia, edited by Mary Gibbons, 1954 Doubleday, first edition, hardcover, 32 pages, illustrations by Ness. ($65.00 with dust jacket) $30.00

Tom Tit Tot, 1965 Scribner, first edition, oversize hardcover, illustrations by author. ($35.00 with dust jacket) $15.00

Veck Eck, 1974 Dutton, first edition, oblong hardcover, 36 pages, color illustrations by author. ($25.00 with dust jacket) $15.00

NETHERCLIFT, Beryl
Snowstorm, 1967 Knopf, first edition, hardcover. ($40.00 with dust jacket) $15.00

NETT, Roger
Thorntree Meadows, 1957, Houghton Mifflin, first edition, hardcover. ($20.00 with dust jacket) $10.00

NEUMEYER, Peter
Why We Have Day and Night, 1970 Young Scott, first edition, pictorial hardcover, color and b/w illustrations by Edward Gorey. ($40.00 with dust jacket) $20.00

NEURATH, Marie
Exploring Under the Sea, 1959 Lothrop, first American edition, hardcover, 36 pages, illustrations by author. $15.00

Jungle, 1963 Lothrop, first American edition, hardcover, 36 pages, illustrations by author. $15.00

NEWELL, Audrey
Seashells in Action, 1973 Walker, first edition, hardcover, illustrated by author. ($20.00 with dust jacket) $10.00

NEWELL, Crosby
Make Believe Book, 1959 Wonder Books, laminated illustrated hardcover. $10.00

NEWELL, Hope
Mary Ellis, Student Nurse, 1958 Harper and Row, illustrated hardcover. ($20.00 with dust jacket) $10.00.

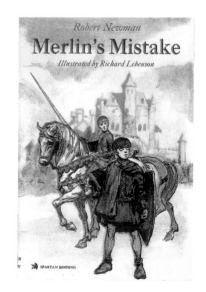

NEWMAN, Robert
Merlin's Mistake, 1970 Atheneum, first edition, hardcover, b/w illustrations by Richard Lebenson. ($25.00 with dust jacket) $10.00

NICHOLS, Beverley

Beverley Nichols' Cats' A. B. C., 1960 Jonathan Cape, first edition, hardcover, illustrated by Derrick Sayer. ($30.00 with dust jacket) $15.00

Stream That Stood Still, 1948 Jonathan Cape, London, first edition, hardcover, illustrated endpapers, b/w line drawings throughout by Richard Kennedy. $60.00

NICHOLS, Marie C.

Ten Portraits of Real Dogs, Selection of Favoritie Dog Stories, compiled by W. Harper, 1950 Houghton Mifflin, first edition, hardcover, illustrations by Nichols. ($50.00 with dust jacket) $20.00

NICHOLS, Ruth

Ceremony of Innocence, 1969 Faber and Faber, London, first edition, hardcover. ($30.00 with dust jacket) $15.00

Marrow of the World, 1972 Atheneum, illustrations Trina Schart Hyman. ($30.00 with dust jacket) $15.00

Walk Out of the World, 1969 Harcourt, illustrations Trina Schart Hyman. ($30.00 with dust jacket) $15.00

Walk Out of the World, 1969 Longmans, Toronto, hardcover. ($50.00 with dust jacket) $20.00

NICHOLSON, John D.

White Buffalo, 1965 Platt & Munk, red illustrated hardcover, brown/white illustrations by Roger Vernam. $15.00

NICLAS, Yolla

Island Shepherd, 1959 Viking, first edition, hardcover, photos by author. ($60.00 with dust jacket) $25.00

NIKLEWICZOWA, Maria

Sparrow's Magic, 1970 Parents' Press Magazine,

first edition, hardcover, color illustrations by Fuyuji Yamanaka. ($40.00 with dust jacket) $20.00

NOBLE, Trinks Hakes

Jimmy's Boa Ate the Wash, 1960 Dial, Weekly Reader edition, glossy hardcover, illustrations by Steven Kellogg. $15.00

NOEL, Bernard

Sinbad the Sailor, 1972 Doubleday, first edition, hardcover, full page b/w drawings by Alain LeFoll. ($15.00 with dust jacket) $10.00

NORDSTROM, Ursula

Secret Language, 1960 Harper, hardcover, illustrations by Mary Chambers. $20.00

NORELIUS, Einar

Jim, Jock and Jumbo, 1946 Dutton, first edition, oversize hardcover, full-page color illustrations. $35.00

NORMAN, Charles

Mr. Upstairs and Mr. Downstairs: Introducing Jane Johnquil and her Father, 1950 Harper, first edition, hardcover, illustrations by Margaret Graham. ($20.00 with dust jacket) $15.00

Orimha of the Mohawks, 1961 Macmillan, first edition, hardcover, 94 pages, illustrations by Johannes Troyer. ($20.00 with dust jacket) $10.00

NORMAN, Lilith

Flame Takers, 1973 Collins, first edition, hardcover. 126 pages. ($35.00 with dust jacket) $20.00

NORTH, Sterling

Hurry, Spring!, 1966 Dutton first edition, hardcover, 58 pages, illustrations. ($15.00 with dust jacket) $10.00

Little Rascal, 1965 Dutton, first edition, hardcover, illustrations by Carl Burger. ($25.00 with dust jacket) $15.00

Raccoons are the Brightest People, 1966 Dutton, hardcover, photo illustrations. $15.00

Rascal: A Memoir of a Better Era, 1963 Dutton, hardcover, illustrations by John Schoenherr. ($20.00 with dust jacket) $10.00

Wolfling, 1969 Dutton, first edition, hardcover, illustrated by John Schoenherr. ($15.00 with dust jacket) $10.00

NORTON, Andre

Crystal Gryphon, 1972 Atheneum, hardcover. First edition stated on copyright page, with dust jacket: $150.00. Later editions: ($25.00 with dust jacket) $10.00

Crystal Gryphon, 1973 Gollancz, first UK edition, hardcover. ($95.00 with dust jacket) $25.00

Dark Piper, 1969 Gollancz Ltd., hardcover. ($25.00 with dust jacket) $10.00

Forerunner Foray, 1974 Longman Young Books, 1974, first edition, hardcover, 286 pages. ($25.00 with dust jacket) $10.00

Fur Magic, 1968 World, hardcover. ($20.00 with dust jacket) $10.00

Here Abide Monsters, 1974 Atheneum, hardcover. First edition with dust jacket: $50.00. Later editions: ($20.00 with dust jacket) $10.00

Huon of the Horn, 1951 Harcourt, illustrations by Joe Krush. First edition stated on copyright page, with dust jacket: $125.00. Later editions: ($25.00 with dust jacket) $15.00

Ice Crown, 1970 Viking, first edition, hardcover, 256 pages. With Laszlo Gal illustrated dust jacket. ($30.00 with dust jacket) $15.00

Jargoon Pard (sequel to *Crystal Gryphon*), 1974 Atheneum, hardcover. First edition with dust jacket: $50.00. Later editions: ($20.00 with dust jacket) $10.00

Knave of Dreams, 1975 Viking, hardcover. First edition with dust jacket: $35.00

Lavender-Green Magic, 1974 Crowell, first edition, hardcover, 241 pages, illustrations by Judith Gwyn Brown. ($50.00 with dust jacket) $20.00

Octagon Magic, 1967 World, first edition, hardcover. ($50.00 with dust jacket) $20.00

Steel Magic, 1965 World, hardcover, illustrations by Robin Jacques. First edition with dust jacket: $95.00. Later editions: ($20.00 with dust jacket) $15.00

Storm Over Warlock, 1960 World, hardcover. ($20.00 with dust jacket) $10.00

Quest Crosstime, 1965 Viking, hardcover. ($30.00 with dust jacket) $15.00

NORTON, Bertha and **Andre NORTON**

Bertie and May, 1971 Hamish Hamilton, first edition UK, hardcover, illustrations by Fermin Rocker. ($15.00 with dust jacket) $10.00

NORTON, Mary, see Series section BORROWERS

Are All the Giants Dead?, 1975 Harcourt Brace, first American edition, hardcover, b/w illustrations by Brian Froud. ($35.00 with dust jacket) $15.00

Bed-Knob and Broomstick, 1968 edition Dent, UK, hardcover, illustrations by Erik Blegvad. ($15.00 with dust jacket) $10.00

Bed-Knob and Broomstick, 1971 edition Harcourt Brace, hardcover, illustrations by Erik Blegvad. ($30.00 with dust jacket) $15.00

Poor Stainless: A New Story About the Borrowers, 1971 Harcourt, hardcover, illustrations Joe and Beth Krush. ($25.00 with dust jacket) $10.00

NYE, Nelson C.

Caliban's Colt, 1950 Dodd, Mead, first edition, hardcover, 278 pages. ($20.00 with dust jacket) $10.00

NYE, Robert

Cricket, 1975 Bobbs-Merrill, first edition, hardcover, illustrations by Shelley Freshman. ($25.00 with dust jacket) $15.00

NYGAARD, Jacob Bech

Tobias, the Magic Mouse, 1968 Harcourt, Brace & World, first American edition, blue hardcover, illustrated by Ib Spang Olsen. ($25.00 with dust jacket) $15.00

O

OAKES, Vanya

Willy Wong, American, 1952 Messner, hardcover, 174 pages, graphic on front cover, pictorial endpapers, illustrated by Weda Yap. $15.00

OAKLEY, Graham

Church Mice at Bay, 1978 Macmillan, London, first edition, hardcover. ($25.00 with dust jacket) $10.00

Church Mouse, 1972 Macmillan, London, first edition, hardcover, illustrated by author. ($25.00 with dust jacket) $10.00

OAKLEY, Helen

Horse on the Hill, 1957 Alfred A. Knopf, first edition, hardcover. ($20.00 with dust jacket) $10.00

O'BRIEN, Margaret

My Diary, 1947 Lippincott, first edition, illustrated by author. ($30.00 with dust jacket) $20.00

O'BRIEN, Robert C.

Mrs. Frisby and the Rats of NIMH, 1971 Atheneum, illustrated by Zena Bernstein. First edition with dust jacket: $150.00. Later printings: ($20.00 with dust jacket) $15.00

O'CONNELL, Jean S.
Doll House Caper, 1975 Crowell, first edition, hardcover, b/w illustrations by Erik Blegvad. ($20.00 with dust jacket) $10.00

O'CONNOR, Betty
Better Homes and Gardens Story Book, 1950 Meredith, first edition, oversize hardcover. ($35.00 with dust jacket) $15.00

O'CONNOR, Edwin
Benjy, a Ferocious Fairy Tale, 1957 Little Brown, first edition, decorated hardcover, 143 pages, illustrated by Ati Forberg. ($30.00 with dust jacket) $10.00

O'CONNOR, Patrick
Beyond Hawaii, 1969 Washburn, hardcover. $10.00
Watermelon Mystery, 1955 Washburn, first edition, hardcover. ($15.00 with dust jacket) $10.00

O'CONNOR, Richard
Young Bat Masterson, 1967 McGraw-Hill, 128 pages, illustrated. ($15.00 with dust jacket) $10.00

O'DELL, Scott
Black Pearl, 1967 Houghton Mifflin, first edition, black hardcover with gilt, illustrated by Milton Johnson. ($30.00 with dust jacket) $15.00
Dark Canoe , 1968 Houghton Mifflin, first edition, hardcover, illustrated by Milton Johnson. ($15.00 with dust jacket) $10.00
Hawk That Dare Not Hunt By Day, 1975 Houghton Mifflin, first edition, hardcover, Family Bookshelf edition. ($20.00 with dust jacket) $10.00
Island of the Blue Dolphins, 1960 Houghton Mifflin, hardcover, 184 pages. Newbery Medal Award Winner. ($20.00 with dust jacket) $15.00

Journey to Jericho, 1969 Houghton Mifflin, first edition, hardcover, 41 pages, illustrated by Leonard Weisgard. ($30.00 with dust jacket) $15.00
King's Fifth, 1966 Houghton Mifflin, hardcover, 264 pages, illustrated by Samuel Bryant. ($20.00 with dust jacket) $10.00
Sing Down the Moon, 1970 Houghton Mifflin, first edition, hardcover. ($30.00 with dust jacket) $15.00

OESCHLI, Helen
Peter Bull, 1971 Viking, first edition, oversize hardcover, color illustrations by Kelly Oechsli. ($25.00 with dust jacket) $15.00

O'FAOLAIN, Eileen
Shadowy Man, 1949 Longmans Green, London, first edition, square hardcover, 120 pages, illustrated by Phoebe Llewellyn Smith. $20.00
White Rabbit's Road, 1950 Longmans, first edition, hardcover, 138 pages, illustrated by Phoebe Llewllyn. ($30.00 with dust jacket) $15.00

OFFIT, Sidney
Boy Who Made a Million, 1968 St. Martin's Press, first edition, hardcover, illustrated by Mercer Mayer. ($40.00 with dust jacket) $20.00

OGILVIE, Elisabeth
Fabulous Year, 1958 McGraw Hill, hardcover. ($20.00 with dust jacket) $10.00

O'GRADY, Rohon
Pippin's Journal or Rosemary Is for Remembrance, 1962 Macmillan, first American edition, hardcover, 230 pages b/w illustrations by Edward Gorey. ($30.00 with dust jacket) $15.00
Pippin's Journal or Rosemary Is for Remembrance, 1962 Gollancz, London, first edition UK, blue hardcover, 230 pages b/w illustrations by Edward Gorey. ($60.00 with dust jacket) $20.00

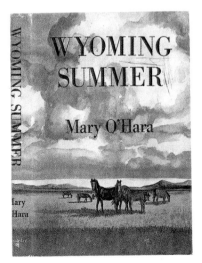

O'HARA, Mary
Green Grass of Wyoming, 1946 Lippincott, first edition, hardcover, 319 pages. ($25.00 with dust jacket) $10.00
Musical in the Making, 1966 Markane Publishing, first edition, hardcover. ($25.00 with dust jacket) $15.00
Wyoming Summer, 1963 Doubleday, hardcover, 286 pages. ($20.00 with dust jacket) $10.00

OKSNER, Robert M.
Incompetent Wizard, 1965 William Morrow, first edition, tall hardcover, 30 pages, illustrated by Janet McCaffery. ($25.00 with dust jacket) $15.00

OLDRIN, John
Eight Rings on His Tail, 1956 Viking, first edition, hardcover, illustrated by Kurt Wiese. ($20.00 with dust jacket) $10.00
Round Meadow, 1951 Viking, first edition, oversize hardcover, 80 pages, illustrated by Kurt Wiese. ($20.00 with dust jacket) $10.00

OLDS, Elizabeth
Deep Treasure, 1958 Houghton Mifflin, first edition, red hardcover, 38 pages, illustrated by author. $15.00
Riding the Rails, 1948 Houghton Mifflin, first edition, red hardcover, 47 pages, illustrated by author. $20.00

O'LEARY, Michael
Great Automobile Club, 1968 Constable Young, first edition, hardcover, illustrated by John Haslam. ($25.00 with dust jacket) $10.00

OLIVER, Marjorie Mary
A-Riding We Will Go, 1951 Lutterworth, London, first edition, green hardcover, 125 pages, b/w illustrations by Stanley Lloyd. ($30.00 with dust jacket) $15.00

OLSEN, Aileen
Big Fish, 1970 Lothrop, Lee & Shepard, orange hardcover, illustrated by Imero Gobbato. ($20.00 with dust jacket) $10.00

OLSON, Gene
Ballhawks, 1950 Westminster Press, first edition, hardcover. ($20.00 with dust jacket) $10.00
Roaring Road, 1962 Dodd Mead, hardcover. ($30.00 with dust jacket) $15.00

O'NEILL, Elizabeth and **Mary**
Nursery History of England, undated ca. 1950s Nelson, hardcover with gilt motif and lettering, 168 pages, illustrated by George Morrow and Marjory Whittington, color plates throughout. $35.00

O'NEILL, Mary
Hailstones and Halibut Bones, 1961 Doubleday, first

edition, oversize hardcover, illustrated by Leonard Weisgard. ($15.00 with dust jacket) $10.00
White Palace, 1966 Crowell, first edition, blue oversize hardcover, color and b/w illustrations by Nonny Hogrogian. ($50.00 with dust jacket) $20.00

OPIE, Iona and **Peter**
Children's Games in Street and Playground, 1969 Oxford University Press, first edition, hardcover. $35.00
Classic Fairy Tales, 1974 London, Oxford, first edition, hardcover, illustrated. ($50.00 with dust jacket) $20.00
Oxford University Nursery Rhyme Book, 1955 Oxford University Press, hardcover, first edition, 223 pages, 400+ woodcuts from 18th and 19th century children's books, plus 150 illustrations by Joan Hassall. ($70.00 with dust jacket) $30.00

OPPENHEIM, Shulamith
Selchie's Seed, 1975 Bradbury Press, hardcover, 83 pages. ($20.00 with dust jacket) $10.00

O'REILLY, John
Glob, 1952 Viking, hardcover, 63 pages, b/w illustrations by Walt Kelly. ($30.00 with dust jacket) $15.00

ORGEL, Doris
Bartholomew, We Love You, 1972 Knopf, first edition, hardcover, 54 pages, b/w illustrations by Pat G. Porter. ($35.00 with dust jacket) $20.00
Heart of Stone: A Fairy Tale, 1964 Macmillan, first edition, hardcover, illustrated by David Levine. ($25.00 with dust jacket) $15.00
Story of Lohengrin: The Knight of the Swan, 1966 Putnam, first edition, hardcover, based on the opera by Richard Wagner, illustrated by Herbert Danska. ($20.00 with dust jacket) $10.00

ORMSBY, Virginia H.
Cunning is Better than Strong, 1960 Lippincott, hardcover, 112 pages. ($15.00 with dust jacket) $8.00

ORRMONT, Arthur
Master Detective Allan Pinkerton, 1965 Messner, hardcover. ($20.00 with dust jacket) $10.00

ORSKA, Krystyna and **Miriam PETERSON**
Special Collection: Illustrated Poems for Children, 1973 Hubbard Press, first edition, oversize hardcover, half-bound in navy leatherette, white cloth boards, gilt lettering, color illustrations by Orska. ($50.00 with dust jacket) $35.00

ORTON, Helen Fuller
Mystery in the Apple Orchard, 1954 Lippincott, first edition, hardcover, illustrated by Robert Doremus. ($30.00 with dust jacket) $10.00

OSBORNE, Chester G.
First Puppy, 1953 Wilcox & Follett, first edition, hardcover, illustrated by Richard Osborne. ($30.00 with dust jacket) $15.00
Wind and the Fire, 1959 Prentice Hall, hardcover, illustrated by Rafaello Busoni. ($20.00 with dust jacket) $10.00

OSBORNE, Rosalie
Let's Be Somebody, 1956 Banks Upshaw, Dallas, hardcover. $15.00

OSTRANDER, Sheila
Gadgets and Gifts for Girls to Make, 1962 Gramercy, hardcover, contains material from "Calling All Girls" and "Teen-Age Ingenue" magazines, illustrated by author. $15.00

OTERDAHL, Jeanna
Island Summer, 1964 Harcourt, Brace, first American edition, small hardcover, illustrated by Birgitta Nordenskjold. ($20.00 with dust jacket) $10.00

OTTO, Margaret G.
Man in the Moon, 1957 Henry Holt, first edition, illustrated by Paul Galdone. $20.00
Pumpkin, Ginger and Spice, 1954 Henry Holt, first edition, hardcover, illustrated by Barbara Cooney. ($25.00 with dust jacket) $10.00

OUSLEY, Odille and **David H. RUSSELL**
Around the Corner, 1949 Ginn, reader, pictorial hardcover, 240 pages, color illustrations. $18.00
Little White House, revised edition 1957 Ginn and Company, school reader, 191 pages. $15.00
On Cherry Street, 1948 Ginn Basic Reader, hardcover, color illustrations. $15.00
Under the Apple Tree, 1953 Ginn Basic Readers-Enrichment Series, hardcover, illustrated. $10.00

OVERTON, Jenny
Thirteen Days of Christmas, 1972 Greenwillow Books, hardcover, 118 pages. ($20.00 with dust jacket) $10.00

OXENBURY, Helen
Helen Oxenbury's A B C of Things, 1971 Franklin Watts, first edition, hardcover. ($35.00 with dust jacket) $15.00
Hunting of the Snark, Lewis Carroll poem (1970 Heinemann), 1970 Franklin Watts, first edition thus, pictorial oversize hardcover, illustrated by Oxenbury. ($35.00 with dust jacket) $20.00
Number of Things, 1967 William Heineman Ltd., first edition UK, hardcover, color illustrations, counting book. ($25.00 with dust jacket) $10.00

Number of Things, 1967 Delacorte, oblong oversize hardcover, color illustrations, counting book. ($40.00 with dust jacket) $20.00
Pig Tale, 1973 Heinemann, first edition UK, hardcover, 32 pages, illustrated by author. ($60.00 with dust jacket) $30.00

———— ◦⇒ **P** ⇐◦ ————

PACE, Mildred Mastin
Old Bones, the Wonder Horse, 1955 McGraw-Hill, first edition, hardcover, illustrated by Wesley Dennis. ($20.00 with dust jacket) $10.00

PALAZZO, Tony
Giant Playtime Nursery Book, 1959 Garden City Books, first edition, hardcover, illustrated by author. ($40.00 with dust jacket) $20.00
Mister Whistle's Secret, 1953 Viking, first edition, oversize hardcover. ($25.00 with dust jacket) $15.00
Passel of Possums and other Animal Families, 1968 Lion Press, first edition, hardcover. $20.00
Pig for Tom, 1963 Garrard, first edition, hardcover, illustrated by author. ($15.00 with dust jacket) $10.00
Tales of Don Quixote, 1958 Garden City, first edition, glossy hardcover, illustrated by author. ($25.00 with dust jacket) $10.00

PALEY, Claudia
Benjamin the True, 1969 Little Brown, first edition, pictorial hardcover, 192 pages, illustrated by Trina Schart Hyman. ($35.00 with dust jacket) $15.00

PALMER, Candida
Kim Ann and the Yellow Machine, 1972 Ginn,

magic circle book, illustrated hardcover, illustrated by Mercer Mayer. $15.00

Ride on High, 1960 Scott, Foresman, Second Talking Storybook Box, orange hardcover, illustrated by H. Tom Hall. ($35.00 with record) $10.00.

PALMER, C. Everard
Cloud with the Silver Lining, 1966 Pantheon Books, first edition, hardcover, 164 pages, illustrated. ($30.00 with dust jacket) $15.00

PALMER, Mary B.
Dolmop of Dorkling, 1967 Houghton Mifflin, first edition, hardcover, illustrated by Fen Lasell. ($25.00 with dust jacket) $10.00

No-Sort-of-Animal, 1964 Houghton Mifflin, first edition, hardcover, illustrated by Abner Graboff. ($20.00 with dust jacket) $10.00

PALMER, Robin
Dragons, Unicorns And Other Magical Beasts, 1966 Walck, oversize hardcover, illustrated by Don Bolognese. ($30.00 with dust jacket) $20.00

PANETTA, George
Kitchen Is Not a Tree, 1970 Norton, first edition, hardcover, illustrated by Joe Servello. ($15.00 with dust jacket) $10.00

PANTER, Carol
Beany and his New Recorder, 1972 Four Winds Press, first edition, hardcover, illustrated by Imero Gobbato. ($30.00 with dust jacket) $20.00

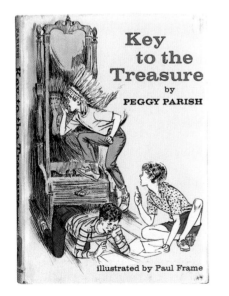

PARISH, Peggy, see Series section AMELIA BEDELIA
Clues in the Woods, 1968 Macmillan, Weekly Reader edition, pictorial hardcover, illustrations by Paul Frame. $10.00

Dinosaur Time, 1974 Harper & Row, first edition, hardcover, I Can Read Book, 3-color illustrations by Arnold Lobel. ($25.00 with dust jacket) $15.00

Good Hunting, Little Indian, 1962 Young Scott, hardcover. ($25.00 with dust jacket) $15.00

Key to the Treasure, 1966 Macmillan, pictorial hardcover, illustrations by Paul Frame. $15.00

Let's Be Indians, 1962 Harper, first edition, hardcover, illustrated by Arnold Lobel. ($25.00 with dust jacket) $15.00

My Book of Manners, 1963 Golden Press, hardcover, illustrated by Richard Scarry. $15.00

PARKER, Bertha Morris
My Big Book of the Seasons, 1966 edition Golden Press, illustrated oversize hardcover, illustrated by Eloise Wilkin. $25.00

PARKINSON, Ethelyn
Elf King Joe, 1968 Abindgon Press, first edition, hardcover, illustrated by Cornellia Brown. ($25.00 with dust jacket) $10.00

Good Old Archibald, 1960 Weekly Reader Book Club, Abingdon Press, illustrated hardcover, 160 pages, illustrated by Mary Stevens. $10.00

PARSONS, Arthur H. Jr.
Horn that Stopped the Band, 1954 Franklin Watts, first edition, oversize hardcover, illustrated by Lynd Ward. ($35.00 with dust jacket) $15.00

PASCHALL, Janie Lowe
Present for the Princess, 1959 Rand McNally, first edition, laminated illustrated hardcover, illustrated endpapers, Illustrations by Elizabeth Webbe. $20.00

PATERSON, James Hamilton
House in the Waves, 1970 Phillips, hardcover. $20.00

PATERSON, Katherine
Of Nightingales that Weep, 1974 Thomas Crowell, hardcover, 170 pages, yellow linen, hardcover with red lettering, illustrated by Haru Wells. ($30.00 with dust jacket) $20.00

PATON, Frances Gray
Good Morning, Miss Dove, 1954 Dodd, Mead, hardcover, b/w illustrations. $10.00

PAUL, Aileen
Kids Cooking Complete Meals, 1975 Doubleday, first edition, hardcover, illustrated by John Delulio. ($20.00 with dust jacket) $10.00

PAULI, Bertha
Little Town of Bethlehem, 1963 Sloan and Pearce,

first edition, blue hardcover with gilt design, color illustrated end papers, illustrated by Fritz Kredel. ($25.00 with dust jacket) $15.00

PAULL, Grace
Come to the City, 1959 Abelard, oversize hardcover, 40 pages, illustrations by author. $20.00
Freddy the Curious Cat, 1958 Doubleday, illustrated hardcover, picture book, illustrations by author. $20.00

PAYNE, Joan Balfour
General Billycock's Pigs, 1961 Hastings House, blue hardcover, 64 pages, illustrated by author. ($30.00 with dust jacket) $15.00
General Billycock's Pigs, 1961 Hastings House, Weekly Reader edition, illustrated hardcover. $10.00

PEARCE, Philippa
Dog So Small, 1962 Constable, first edition, hardcover, illustrated by Antony Maitland. ($30.00 with dust jacket) $15.00
Squirrel Wife, 1972 Crowell, first American edition, hardcover, illustrated by Derek Collard. ($30.00 with dust jacket) $15.00
Tom's Midnight Garden, 1959 Lippincott, (Carnegie medal winner), first American edition, hardcover, b/w illustrations Susan Einzig. ($50.00 with dust jacket) $20.00
What the Neighbors Did and Other Stories, 1972 Longmans Young Books, first edition, green hardcover with gilt lettering on spine, 120 pages, b/w text illustrations by Faith Jaques.($30.00 with dust jacket) $15.00

PEARL, Jack
Invaders Dam of Death, 1967 Whitman, hardcover, illustrated by Robert Jenney. $20.00

Space Eagle – Operation Doomsday, 1967 Whitman, hardcover, illustrated by Arnie Kohn. $10.00

PEASE, Howard
Dark Adventure, 1950 Doubleday, probable first edition, hardcover. ($75.00 with dust jacket) $30.00
Shipwreck, 1957 Doubleday, first edition, hardcover. ($100.00 with dust jacket) $30.00

PECK, Richard
Don't Look and It Won't Hurt, 1972 Holt Rinehart, first edition, hardcover. ($25.00 with dust jacket) $10.00
Ghost Belonged to Me, 1975 Viking, hardcover. ($20.00 with dust jacket) $10.00
Representing Super Doll, 1974 Viking, first edition, hardcover. ($25.00 with dust jacket) $10.00

PECK, Robert Newton
Day No Pigs Would Die, 1972 Knopf, first edition, hardcover. ($20.00 with dust jacket) $10.00

PEDERSEN, Elsa
House Upon A Rock, 1968 Atheneum, book club edition, hardcover, 218 pages, illustrated by Charles Shaw. $10.00
Mystery on Malina Straits, A Story of Alaska, 1963 Ives Washburn, illustrated by Bernard Case. ($20.00 with dust jacket) $10.00

PEET, Bill
Ant and the Elephant, 1972 Houghton Mifflin, oversize hardcover, color illustrations by author. ($25.00 with dust jacket) $10.00
Caboose Who Got Loose, 1971 Houghton Mifflin, oversize hardcover, color illustrations by author. ($25.00 with dust jacket) $10.00
Capyboppy, 1966 Houghton Mifflin, oversize hard-

cover, color illustrations by author. ($25.00 with dust jacket) $10.00

Cyrus the Unsinkable Sea Serpent, Houghton Mifflin, hardcover, color illustrations by author. ($20.00 with dust jacket) $10.00

Fly Homer Fly, 1969 Houghton Mifflin, hardcover, color illustrations by author. ($20.00 with dust jacket) $10.00

Merle, the High Flying Squirrel, 1974 Houghton Mifflin, hardcover, color illustrations by author. ($20.00 with dust jacket) $10.00

Jennifer and Josephine, 1967 Houghton Mifflin, hardcover, color illustrations by author. ($20.00 with dust jacket) $10.00

Randy's Dandy Lions, 1964 Houghton Mifflin, hardcover. ($25.00 with dust jacket) $10.00

Whingdingdilly, 1970 Houghton Mifflin, oversize hardcover, color illustrations by author. ($20.00 with dust jacket) $10.00

Worldly Pig, 1965 Houghton Mifflin, hardcover, color illustrations by author. ($20.00 with dust jacket) $10.00

WumpWorld, 1970 Houghton Mifflin, hardcover, color illustrations by author. ($20.00 with dust jacket) $10.00

PENNEY, R. L.
Penguins Are Coming!, 1969 Harper Row, Science I Can Read, illustrated hardcover. $15.00

PEPPE, Rodney
Simple Simon, 1972 Holt, Rinehart and Winston, first American edition, hardcover, illustrated by Peppe. ($30.00 with dust jacket) $20.00

PERKINS, Al
Ear Book, Bright and Early Book, 1968 Random House, illustrated hardcover picture book, illustrated by William O'Brian. $10.00

Nose Book, Bright and Early Book, 1970 Random House, illustrated hardcover picture book, illustrated by Roy McKie. $10.00

PERKINS, Marlin
Zooparade, 1954 Rand-McNally, first edition, hardcover, 96 pages, b/w illustrations by Seymour Fleishman, color illustrations by Paul Bransom. ($25.00 with dust jacket) $15.00

PERKINS, Wilma Lord
Fannie Farmer Junior Cook Book New and Revised Edition, (1942) 1957 Little Brown, green hardcover, illustrated by Martha Powell Setchell. ($30.00 with dust jacket) $20.00

PERRAULT, Charles
Cinderella, or The Little Glass Slipper, 1954 edition Scribners, hardcover, illustrated by Marcia Brown. $15.00

Cinderella, or The Little Glass Slipper, 1954 edition Troll, illustrated hardcover, illustrated by Marcia Brown. $15.00

PERRET, Denise and **Mary ECKLEY**
Young French Chef, 1969 Platt & Munk, hardcover. ($25.00 with dust jacket) $15.00

PERRIN, Noel
Amateur Sugar Maker, 1972 Hanover: University Press of New England/"Vermont Life Magazine," first edition, small hardcover, b/w illustrations by Robert MacLean. ($20.00 with dust jacket) $10.00

PERRINE, Mary
Nannabah's Friend, 1970 Houghton Mifflin, first edition, illustrated hardcover, illustrated by Leonard Weisgard. $10.00

PESSIN, Deborah
Michael Turns the Globe, 1950 Union of American Hebrew Congregations, small hardcover, b/w illustrations. $15.00

PETER, John
McCall's Giant Golden Make It Book, 1953 Simon Schuster, oversize hardcover, illustrations. $15.00

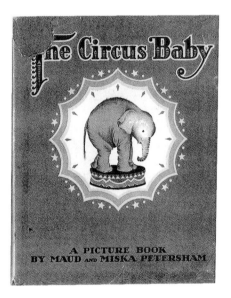

PETERSHAM, Maud and **Miska**
Circus Baby, 1950 Macmillan, oversize picture book, orange hardcover, full-page color pictures throughout. ($40.00 with dust jacket) $20.00

Joseph and His Brothers, 1958 Macmillan, hardcover, illustrated by authors. ($30.00 with dust jacket) $20.00

Peppernuts, 1958 Macmillan, first edition, small hardcover, illustrated by authors. ($35.00 with dust jacket) $20.00

Shepherd Psalm, 1962 Macmillan, first edition, oversize hardcover, illustrated by author. ($40.00 with dust jacket) $20.00

Silver Mace, A Story of Williamsburg. 1956 Macmillan, first edition, pictorial hardcover, illustrated by authors. ($30.00 with dust jacket) $20.00

Story of the Presidents, 1953 Macmillan Company, first edition, oversize hardcover, illustrated by authors. ($50.00 with dust jacket) $20.00

PETERSON, Hans, see Series section MAGNUS
Big Snowstorm, 1975 Coward, McCann, & Geoghegan, first edition, hardcover, illustrated by Harald Wiberg. ($15.00 with dust jacket) $10.00

PETERSON, Harold
History of Body Armor, 1968 Scribner, oversize hardcover, illustrated by Daniel D. Feaser. $20.00

PETRY, Ann
Tituba of Salem Village, 1964 Crowell, first edition, hardcover. Hard to find. ($75.00 with dust jacket) $20.00

PEYTON, K.M.
Sea Fever, 1963 World, first edition, hardcover. ($15.00 with dust jacket) $10.00

PFLUG, Betsy
Funny Bags, 1968 Van Nostram, first edition. ($25.00 with dust jacket) $15.00

PHELAN, Joseph
Whale Hunters, 1969 Time Life, first edition, hardcover, color and b/w illustrated by Phelan. ($15.00 with dust jacket) $10.00

PHILBROOK, Clem
Live Wire, 1966 Hastings House, first edition, hardcover, 126 pages. ($15.00 with dust jacket) $10.00

PHILBROOK, Elizabeth
Hobo Hill, 1954 Viking, first edition, hardcover, illustrated by Don Freeman. ($20.00 with dust jacket) $10.00

PHILBROOK, Rose
Wings of Dr. Smidge, 1954 Caxton, first edition, hardcover, illustrated by Jim Bolin. ($35.00 with dust jacket) $15.00

PHIPSON, Joan
Birkin, 1966 Harcourt, first American edition, hardcover, 224 pages, illustrated by Margaret Horder. ($25.00 with dust jacket) $15.00

Cross Currents, 1967 Harcourt, first American edition, hardcover, 190 pages, illustrated by Margaret Horder. ($25.00 with dust jacket) $15.00

Haunted Night, 1970 Harcourt, hardcover. ($25.00 with dust jacket) $15.00

Threat to the Barkers, 1965 Harcourt, first American edition, hardcover, 224 pages, illustrated by Margaret Horder. ($25.00 with dust jacket) $15.00

PHLEGER, Fred
Ann Can Fly, 1959 Random House, Beginner Books, oversize, pictorial hardcover, illustrated by Robert Lopshire. ($30.00 with dust jacket) $15.00

Red Tag Comes Back, 1961 Harper, first edition, hardcover, illustrated by Arnold Lobel. ($20.00 with dust jacket) $10.00

PIATTI, Celestino
Happy Owls, 1964 Atheneum, first American edition, oblong oversize hardcover, color illustrations by author. ($40.00 with dust jacket) $15.00

Nock Family Circus, 1968 Atheneum, first American edition, oblong oversize hardcover, color illustrations by author. ($55.00 with dust jacket) $35.00

PICARD, Barbara Leone
Story of Rama and Sita, 1960 Harrap, London, first edition, small hardcover, illustrated by Charles Stewart. ($35.00 with dust jacket) $15.00

PICCARD, Joan Russell
Adventure on the Wind, 1971 Nash Publishing, hardcover, 174 pages, illustrated by Hollis Willford. ($15.00 with dust jacket) $8.00

PIERCE, Robert
Grin and Giggle Book, 1972 Golden Press, first edition, oversize, pictorial hardcover. $35.00

PIERS, Helen
Grasshopper and Butterfly, 1975 McGraw-Hill, first

edition, hardcover, color illustrations by Pauline Baynes. ($20.00 with dust jacket) $10.00

PILGRIM, Anne
Clare Goes to Holland, 1962 Abelard-Schuman, illustrated hardcover. $10.00

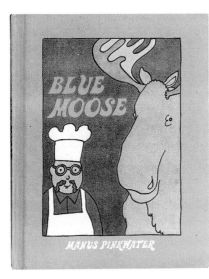

PINKWATER, Daniel Manus
Blue Moose, 1975 Dodd Mead, Weekly Reader edition, illustrated hardcover, b/w illustrations by author. $10.00

PINTO, Oreste, Lt. Col.
Boys' Book of Secret Agents, 1955 Cassell & Company Ltd., first edition, red hardcover with gilt lettering, 170 pages. ($25.00 with dust jacket) $15.00

PIPER, Roberta
Little Red, 1963 Methuen, London, first edition, hardcover, 137 pages, illustrated by Elisabeth Grant. ($15.00 with dust jacket) $10.00

PLACE, Marian
Resident Witch, 1970 Washburn, pictorial hardcover. $15.00

PLASMATI, Valdine
Algernon and the Pigeons, 1963 Viking, first edition, hardcover, illustrated by Kazue Mizumura.($30.00 with dust jacket) $15.00

PLATT, Kin
Big Max, 1965 Harper and Row, I Can Read Mystery, first edition, hardcover, 64 pages. ($35.00 with dust jacket) $15.00

PLATT, Rutherford
Worlds of Nature, 1965 Golden Press, hardcover, illustrated with photos, based on the Walt Disney Motion Picture Series. $10.00

PLIMPTON, George
Rabbit's Umbrella, 1955 Viking, first edition, hardcover, illustrated by William Pene du Bois. ($40.00 with dust jacket) $20.00
Rabbit's Umbrella, 1955 Viking, first edition, hardcover, illustrated by William Pene du Bois. Author-signed copy, with dust jacket: $200.00

PLISS, Louise
Strange Journey of Kippy Brooks, 1965 Reilly & Lee, first edition, hardcover. ($25.00 with dust jacket) $10.00

PLOTZ, Helen, editor
Imagination's Other Place: Poems of Science and Mathematics, 1955 Crowell, hardcover, 197 pages, wood engravings by Clare Leighton. $15.00

POHLMANN, Lillian
Myrtle Albertina's Song, 1958 Coward-McCann, hardcover, b/w illustrations by Erik Blegvad. ($35.00 with dust jacket) $20.00

POLITI, Leo
Boat for Peppe, 1950 Scribner, first edition, hardcover, illustrated by Politi. ($75.00 with dust jacket) $30.00
Bunker Hill, Los Angeles. Reminiscences of Bygone Days, 1964 Dester-Southwest, first edition, hardcover, color illustrations by Politi. ($100.00 with dust jacket) $60.00
Butterflies Come, 1957 Scribners, first edition, oversize hardcover, 28 pages, illustrated by author. ($50.00 with dust jacket) $20.00
Lito and the Clown, 1964 Scribner, pictorial hardcover, color illustrations by author. ($100.00 with dust jacket) $60.00
Little Leo, 1951 Scribner, first edition, hardcover, illustrated by author. ($50.00 with dust jacket) $20.00
Mieko, 1969 Scott Foresman edition, oversize hardcover, illustrated by author. ($50.00 with dust jacket) $20.00
Mission Bell, 1953 Scribner, first edition, oversize hardcover, illustrated by author. ($50.00 with dust jacket) $20.00
Moy Moy, 1960 Scribner, first edition, hardcover, color and b/w illustrations by author. ($50.00 with dust jacket) $20.00
Nicest Gift, 1973 Scriber, first edition, hardcover, illustrated by author. ($80.00 with dust jacket) $45.00
Poinsetta, 1967 Palm Desert, Best-West Publications, first edition, hardcover, color illustrations. ($100.00 with dust jacket) $50.00

POLITZER, Anie
My Journals and Sketchbooks by Robinson Crusoe, 1974 Harcourt Brace Jovanovich, first edi-

tion, oversize hardcover, b/w sketches by Michel Politzer. ($20.00 with dust jacket) $15.00

POLLAND, Madeleine
Town Across the Water, 1973 Holt, first edition, hardcover, 175 pages, illustrated by Esta Nesbett. ($25.00 with dust jacket) $10.00

POLLARD, Nan
Circus, 1952 Samuel Lowe, Bonnie Book, hardcover. $15.00
Tubby's Birthday Party, 1960 Samuel Lowe, Bonnie Book, hardcover. $10.00

POLLOCK, Dean
Joseph, Chief of the Nez Perce, 1950 Binfords & Mort, Portland, 1950, illustrated oversize orange hardcover, 63 pages, illustrated by author. ($15.00 with dust jacket) $10.00

POOLE, Josephine
Moon Eyes, 1967 Atlantic Monthly, first American edition, hardcover, 151 pages. ($20.00 with dust jacket) $10.00

POPE, Elizabeth M.
Perilous Gard, 1974 Houghton Mifflin, first edition, hardcover. ($65.00 with dust jacket) $25.00
Sherwood Ring, 1958 Houghton Mifflin, first edition, hardcover. ($50.00 with dust jacket) $20.00

PORTER, Ella Williams
Wind's in the West, 1950 Macmillan, first edition, hardcover. ($15.00 with dust jacket) $10.00

PORTER, Mark
Duel on the Cinders, 1960 Simon & Schuster, first edition, hardcover.($25.00 with dust jacket) $10.00
Overtime Upset, 1960 Simon & Schuster, first edition, hardcover. ($25.00 with dust jacket) $10.00

POSTGATE, Oliver and **Peter FIRMIN**
Noggin and the Moon Mouse, 1967 David White, orange hardcover, illustrated endpapers, 48 pages, illustrated by author. ($30.00 with dust jacket) $20.00

POSTON, Elizabeth
Baby's Song Book, 1971 Crowell, first edition, oversize hardcover. ($40.00 with dust jacket) $30.00

POTHAST-GIMBERG, C.E.
Corso the Donkey, 1962 Constable, first American edition, translated by Hilda van Stockum, hardcover, illustrated by Elly van Beek. $30.00

POTTER, Jeffrey
Robin Is a Bear, 1958 Viking, first edition, hardcov-

er, illustrated by Johannes Troyer. ($25.00 with dust jacket) $15.00

POTTER, Miriam Clark
Copperfield Summer, 1967 Follett, first edition, hardcover. First edition with dust jacket: $50.00. Later editions: ($20.00 with dust jacket) $15.00
Nine Rabbits and Another, 1957 Wonder Books, small hardcover, color illustrations. $10.00

POWELL, Jessie
Country Cock and City Dragon, 1966 Whiting and Wheaton, London, first edition, hardcover, illustrated by Bernadette Watts. ($15.00 with dust jacket) $10.00

PRATCHETT, Terry
Carpet People, 1971 Colin Smythe, first edition, dark green hardcover, gilt title on spine, 195 pages, b/w illustrations by author. First edition: $500.00 with dust jacket.

PRELUTSKY, Jack
Lazy Blackbird and Other Verses, 1969 Macmillan Canada, first American edition, hardcover, 22 pages, full-color drawings by Janosch. ($25.00 with dust jacket) $15.00
Terrible Tiger, 1970 Macmillan, London, first edition, oversize illustrated hardcover, color illustrations by Arnold Lobel. ($50.00 with dust jacket) $20.00
Three Saxon Nobles and Other Verses, 1969 Macmillan, first edition, oversize illustrated hardcover, color illustrations by Eva Johanna Rubin. ($25.00 with dust jacket) $15.00

PRESTON, Edna Mitchell
Toolittle, 1969 Viking, first edition, hardcover, illustrated. ($25.00 with dust jacket) $15.00

PREUSSLER, Otfried
Further Adventures of the Robber Hotzenplotz, 1970 Abelard-Schuman, London, hardcover, illustrated by F.J. Tripp. ($40.00 with dust jacket) $20.00
Robber Hotzenplotz, 1965 Abelard-Schuman, London, hardcover, illustrated by F.J. Tripp. ($40.00 with dust jacket) $20.00

PRICE, Al
Haunted by a Paintbrush, 1968 Children's Press, illustrated hardcover, 31 pages. $15.00

PRICE, Christine
Happy Days A UNICEF Book of Birthdays, Name Days and Growing Days, 1969 UNICEF, first edition, hardcover, illustrated by author. ($12.00 with dust jacket) $6.00
Three Golden Nobles, 1951 Longmans, first edition, hardcover, illustrated endpapers, illustrated by author. ($15.00 with dust jacket) $10.00

PRIESTLEY, J. B.
Snoggle, 1972 Harcourt, Brace, first American edition, hardcover, illustrated by Barbara Flynn. ($75.00 with dust jacket) $30.00
Wonderful World of Theatre, 1959 Garden City, glossy pictorial boards, color photo illustrations by Evans Kempster. $20.00

PRIESTLEY, Lee
Teacher for Tibby, 1960 Morrow, first edition, hardcover, 96 pages, illustrated by Theresa Sherman. ($15.00 with dust jacket) $10.00

PRISHVIN, M.
Treasure Trove of the Sun, 1952 Viking, first edition, oversize hardcover, illustrated by Feodor Rojankovsky. ($50.00 with dust jacket) $20.00

PROKOFIEFF, Serge
Peter and the Wolf, 1970 edition Bancroft, London, oblong hardcover, illustrated endpapers, full-page illustrations by Franz Haacken. $30.00

PROTHEROE, Ruth Hepburn
Little Chief of the Gaspe, 1955 Abelard-Schuman, first edition, hardcover, illustrated by Nils Hogner. ($25.00 with dust jacket) $10.00

PROTTER, Eric
Monster Festival: Classic Tales of the Macabre, 1965 Vanguard, first edition, half-bound gilt-stamped hardcover, color and b/w illustrations by Edward Gorey. ($60.00 with dust jacket) $30.00

PROVENSEN, Alice and **Martin**
Aesop's Fables, adapted by Louis Untermeyer, 1965 Golden Press, oversize hardcover, 92 pages, color illustrations by authors. ($35.00 with dust jacket) $20.00
First Noel, 1959 Golden Press, "A" printing, illustrated glossy hardcover, color illustrations by authors. $25.00
Golden Treasury of Myths and Legends, edited by Anne Terry White, 1959 Golden Press, oversize pictorial hardcover, color illustrations by authors. $45.00
My Little Hen, 1973 Random House, first edition, square hardcover, illustrated endpapers, 32 pages, color illustrations by authors. ($30.00 with dust jacket) $15.00
Play on Words, 1972 Random House, oversize glossy illustrated hardcover, illustrated by authors. $25.00
Provensen Book of Fairy Tales, 1971 Random House, first edition, hardcover, color illustrations by authors. ($35.00 with dust jacket) $20.00
What Is a Color?, 1967 Golden Press, oversize pictorial hardcover, color illustrations by authors. $35.00
Who's in the Egg?, 1970 Western, first edition, hardcover, color illustrations by authors. ($35.00 in dust jacket) $20.00

PROYSEN, Alf, see Series section MRS. PEPPERPOT
Goat That Learned to Count, 1961 Webster, hardcover, illustrations by Bjorn Berg. $20.00
Town That Forgot It Was Christmas, 1961 Gelles-Widmer, glossy pictorial hardcover, illustrations by Nils Stodberg. $25.00

PURCELL, John Wallace
True Book of African Animals, 1954 Children's Press, green hardcover, illustrated by Katherine Evans. $10.00

139

PUTTCAMP, Rita
Borrowed Boots, 1956 Viking Press, first edition, hardcover, illustrated by Clifford Geary. ($15.00 with dust jacket) $10.00

PUZO, Mario
Runaway Summer of Davie Shaw, 1966 Platt & Munk, first edition, hardcover, illustrated by Stewart Sherwood. ($50.00 with dust jacket) $20.00

PYLE, Howard
King Stork, 1973 edition Little Brown, first edition thus, illustrated oversize hardcover, 48 pages, color illustrations by Trina Schart Hyman. ($50.00 with dust jacket) $30.00

PYNE, Mabel
Story of Religion, 1954 Houghton Mifflin, first edition, hardcover, illustrated by author. ($15.00 with dust jacket) $10.00

──── *⇒ Q ⇐* ────

QUAYLE, Eric
Ballantyne the Brave, 1967 Rupert Hart-Davis, London, first edition, hardcover, 316 pages, 8 plates. ($50.00 with dust jacket) $20.00

QUIGG, Jane
Jiggy Likes Nantucket, 1953 Oxford, first edition, hardcover, illustrated by Zhenya Gay. ($25.00 with dust jacket) $15.00
Judy and Her Turtle Osmond, 1960 Macmillan, first edition, blue hardcover, illustrated by Peggy Bacon. ($20.00 with dust jacket) $10.00
Trolling with Susie Bennett, 1961 Macmillan, first edition, hardcover, illustrated by Peggy Bacon. ($15.00 with dust jacket) $10.00

──── *⇒ R ⇐* ────

RABOFF, Ernest
Art For Children, 1968 Garden City, first edition, oversize hardcover, illustrated by Marc Chagall, 15 full-color plates. ($15.00 with dust jacket) $10.00

RACHLIS, Eugene, and **John C. EWERS**
Indians of the Plains, 1960 American Heritage Junior Library, Harper, pictorial oversize hardcover, illustrated with painting, prints, photographs. $15.00

RAILLON, Madeleine
Secret of Gold, 1965 Harcourt, Brace, first American edition, hardcover. ($15.00 with dust jacket) $10.00

RAISZ, Erwin
Mapping the World, 1956 Abelard-Schuman, hardcover, 114 pages, illustrated. $20.00

RALLS, Alice M and **Ruth E. GORDON**
Daughter of Yesterday, A Pioneer Child Looks Back at Early Johannesburg, 1975 Howard Timmins, first edition, hardcover. ($25.00 with dust jacket) $15.00

RAMBEAU, John and **Nancy**
Jim Forest and the Bandits, 1959 Harr Wagner, pictorial hardcover, color illustrations. $15.00
Jim Forest and the Flood, 1967 Harr Wagner, hardcover. $10.00
Mystery of the Midnight Visitor, 1962 Field Educational Publications, hardcover. $10.00

RAND, Ann
Umbrella, Hats and Wheels, 1961 Harcourt, Brace, first edition, hardcover, illustrated by Jerome Snyder. ($30.00 with dust jacket) $15.00

RANDALL, Janet
Miracle of Sage Valley, 1958 Longmans, Green, first edition, hardcover. $20.00

RANKIN, Louise
Daughter of the Mountains, 1965 Viking, hardcover. ($20.00 with dust jacket) $10.00
Gentling of Jonathan, 1950 Viking, first edition, hardcover, illustrated by Lee Townsend. ($15.00 with dust jacket) $10.00

RANSOME, Arthur
Fool of the World and the Flying Ship, 1968 Farrar,

color illustrations by Uri Shuleritz, 1969 Caldecott Award. ($30.00 with dust jacket) $15.00

RAPAPORT, Stella F.
Horse Chestnut Hideway, 1959 Putnam, first edition, hardcover, illustrated by author. ($25.00 with dust jacket) $10.00

RAPOSO, Joe and **Jeffrey MOSS**
Sesame Street Song, 1971 Simon Schuster, first edition, oversize yellow/tan hardcover, 127 pages, drawings by Loretta Trezzo. ($30.00 with dust jacket) $15.00

RASKIN, Ellen
Figgs & Phantoms, 1974 Dutton, first edition, yellow hardcover, 154 pages, b/w illustrations by author. ($30.00 with dust jacket) $15.00
Moe Q. McGlutch, He Smoked Too Much, 1973 Parents', oversize pictorial hardcover, illustrated by author. $15.00
Moose Goose and Little Nobody, 1974 Weekly Reader Book, illustrated hardcover. $15.00
Mysterious Disappearance of Leon (I Mean Noel), 1971 Dutton, ($25.00 with dust jacket) $10.00
Nothing Ever Happens on My Block, 1966 Atheneum, small oblong hardcover, color illustrations by author. ($20.00 with dust jacket) $10.00
Silly Songs and Sad, 1967 Thomas Y. Crowell, first edition, oblong yellow pictorial hardcover, illustrated by Ellen Raskin. ($30.00 with dust jacket) $15.00
Who, Said Sue, Said Whoo?, 1973 Atheneum, first edition, hardcover. ($30.00 with dust jacket) $15.00

RASPE, R. E.
Life and Adventures of Baron Munchausen, 1969 edition Pantheon, oversize hardcover,

Ronald Searle illustrations. ($30.00 with dust jacket) $20.00

RATHJEN, Carl Henry
Hot Rod Road, 1968 Whitman, color pictorial hardcover, 210 pages, illustrated. $15.00

RATZEBERGER, Anna
Pets, 1954 Rand McNally, illustrated hardcover, illustrated by Elizabeth Webbe. $15.00
Animal Mothers and Babies, 1961 Rand McNally Junior Elf Book, small, hardcover, picture book. $10.00

RAU, Margaret
Yellow River, 1969 Julian Messner, first edition, hardcover, 95 pages, illustrated by Haris Petie. ($15.00 with dust jacket) $10.00

RAUCH, Mabel Thompson
Little Hellion, 1960 Duell, Sloan and Pearce, first edition, hardcover. ($20.00 with dust jacket) $10.00

RAYMOND, John
Marvelous March of Jean Francois, 1965 Doubleday, first edition, hardcover, illustrated by Joseph Schindelman. ($15.00 with dust jacket) $10.00

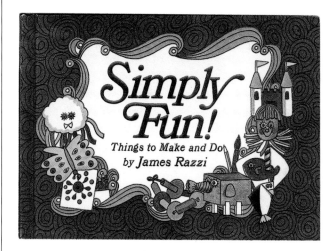

RAZZI, James
Don't Open This Box!, 1973 Parents', hardcover, illustrations by James Razzi. $20.00
Simply Fun! Things to Make and Do, 1968 Parents', illustrated oblong hardcover, 61 pages, illustrated by author. $20.00

READ, Elfreida
Spell of Chuchuchan; 1967 World, first American edition, hardcover, illustrated by Betty Fraser. ($20.00 with dust jacket) $10.00

READ, Miss

Christmas Mouse, 1973 Houghton Mifflin, first edition, hardcover, illustrated by J.S. Goodall. ($20.00 with dust jacket) $15.00

Fairacre Festival , 1968 Houghton Mifflin, first edition, hardcover, illustrated by Goodall. ($20.00 with dust jacket) $10.00

Farther Afield, 1975 Houghton Mifflin, first edition, hardcover. ($25.00 with dust jacket) $15.00

Miss Clare Remembers, 1963 Houghton Mifflin, first American edition, hardcover. ($25.00 with dust jacket) $10.00

Over the Gate, 1965 Houghton Mifflin, first American edition, hardcover, 236 pages, illustrated endpapers. ($25.00 with dust jacket) $10.00

Village School, 1959 Michael Joseph, London, hardcover, illustrated endpapers. ($20.00 with dust jacket) $15.00

REAVIN, Sam

Hurray For Captain Jane!, 1971 Parents' Magazine Press, first edition, pictorial hardcover. $15.00

REDFORD, Polly

Christmas Bower, 1967 Dutton, first edition, hardcover, 192 pages, illustrations by Edward Gorey. ($35.00 with dust jacket) $15.00

REED, Gwendolyn

Sand Lady, 1968 Lothrop, Lee & Shepard, pictorial hardcover, illustrated in color. ($15.00 with dust jacket) $10.00

REED, Harrison

Inky Puss, 1962 Winston-Salem, first edition, hardcover, illustrated. ($20.00 with dust jacket) $10.00

REED, Philip

Mother Goose and Nursery Rhymes, (1963) 1966 edition Atheneum, orange hardcover, 57 pages, color wood engravings by Reed. ($20.00 with dust jacket) $10.00

REES, Ennis

Brer Rabbit and His Tricks, 1967 Young Scott Books, first edition, hardcover, color illustrations by Edward Gorey. ($60.00 with dust jacket) $30.00

Fables from Aesop, 1966 Oxford, first edition, hardcover, illustrated by J.J. Grandville, (wood engravings Grandville made for an 1838 edition of *La Fontaine's Fables*). ($40.00 with dust jacket) $20.00

Lions and Lobsters and Foxes and Frogs, 1971 Young Scott Books, first edition, oblong hardcover, illustrated by Edward Gorey. ($40.00 with dust jacket) $20.00

Little Greek Alphabet, 1968 Prentice Hall, first edition, hardcover, illustrated by George Salter. ($30.00 with dust jacket) $20.00

More of Brer Rabbit's Tricks, 1968 Young Scott, oblong hardcover, color illustrations by Edward Gorey. ($60.00 with dust jacket) $30.00

REES, Leslie

Two-Thumbs: The Story of a Koala, 1950 John Sands, Sydney, first edition, hardcover, 44 pages, color illustrations by Margaret Senior. ($80.00 with dust jacket) $40.00

REESINK, Maryke

Fisherman's Family, 1968 Harcourt, Brace, first American edition, illustrated hardcover, cloth spine, illustrated by Georgette Apol. $15.00

Peter and the Twelve-Headed Dragon, 1970 Harcourt, Brace & World, first American edition, hardcover, illustrated by Adrie Hospes. ($25.00 with dust jacket) $15.00

Wishing Balloons, Holt, Rinehart, Winston, first edition, oversize hardcover, illustrated by Adrie Hospes. ($25.00 with dust jacket) $15.00

REEVES, James

Angel and the Donkey, 1970 McGraw-Hill, first American edition, oblong hardcover, 32 pages, illustrated by Edward Ardizzone. ($40.00 with dust jacket) $20.00

How the Moon Began, 1971 Abelard-Schuman, first American edition, oversize hardcover, illustrated by Edward Ardizzone. ($40.00 with dust jacket) $20.00

Lion that Flew, 1974 Chatto & Windus, first edition, hardcover, illustrated by Edward Ardizzone. ($40.00 with dust jacket) $20.00

More Prefabulous Animals, 1975 Heinemann, first edition, green hardcover with gilt, illustrated by Edward Ardizzone. ($30.00 with dust jacket) $15.00

One's None, Old Rhymes for New Tongues, 1969 Franklin Watts, illustrated hardcover, 125 pages, pictures by Bernadette Watts. ($15.00 with dust jacket) $10.00

Ragged Robin, 1961 Dutton, first edition, hardcover, illustrated by Jane Paton. ($15.00 with dust jacket) $10.00

Rhyming Will, 1968 McGraw Hill, blue hardcover, color and b/w illustrations by Edward Ardizzone. ($20.00 with dust jacket) $10.00

Story of Jackie Thimble, 1964 Dutton, first edition, small hardcover, 31 pages, b/w illustrations by Edward Ardizzone. ($40.00 with dust jacket) $20.00

Titus in Trouble, 1959 Bodley Head, London, first edition, tall hardcover, illustrated by Edward Ardizzone. ($50.00 with dust jacket) $20.00

REEVES, Katherine

Farmer's Cat Nap, 1956 Sterling, first edition, hardcover. ($25.00 with dust jacket) $10.00

Feather Bed for Toby Tod, 1959 Crowell, first edition, hardcover, illustrated by Grace Paull. ($20.00 with dust jacket) $10.00

REGLI, Adolph
Cowboy Stories, 1951 edition, Grosset & Dunlap, hardcover, illustrated by Charles Geer. ($15.00 with dust jacket) $8.00

REID, Alastair
I Will Tell You of a Town, 1956 Houghton, Mifflin, first edition, hardcover, color accented b/w illustrations by W. Lorraine. ($20.00 with dust jacket) $10.00
Ounce Dice Trice, 1958 Little Brown, first edition, hardcover, 57 pages, illustrations by Ben Shahn. ($35.00 with dust jacket) $15.00

REID, Hale C., Helen W. CRANE & Betty Ellen JENKINS
My Second Picture Dictionary, 1971 Ginn and Co., school reader, hardcover. $10.00

REID, Meta Mayne
Dawks and the Duchess, 1958 Macmillan, first edition, yellow hardcover. $15.00
With Angus in the Forest, 1963 Faber & Faber, first edition, hardcover, illustrated by Zelma Blakely. ($15.00 with dust jacket) $10.00

REINECKE, Esther E.
Tim and the Lucky Straw, 1969 Denison, illustrated green boards, illustrated by Dorothy Schaphorst. $10.00

REISNER, Robert
Graffitti: Two Thousand Years of Wall Writing, 1971 Cowles Book Company, first edition, hardcover, 204 pages, photos. ($15.00 with dust jacket) $10.00

RENICK, Marion
Bats and Gloves of Glory, 1956 Scribner, first edition, hardcover, illustrated by Pru Herrick. ($15.00 with dust jacket) $10.00
Buckskin Scout and Other Ohio Stories, 1953 World, first edition, hardcover, 192 pages, illustrated by Paul Galdone. ($15.00 with dust jacket) $10.00
Nicky's Football Team, 1951 Charles Scribner, pictorial hardcover, illustrated by Marian Honigman. $10.00
Pete's Home Run, 1952 Charles Scribner, hardcover, illustrated by Pru Herric. $10.00
Watch Those Red Wheels Roll, 1965 Charles Scribner, hardcover, illustrated by Leonard Shortall. ($15.00 with dust jacket) $10.00

RESSNER, Phil
August Explains, 1963 Harper & Row, oversize hardcover, illustrated by Crosby Bonsall. ($35.00 with dust jacket) $20.00

Dudley Pippin, 1965 Harper & Row, first edition, hardcover, illustrated by Arnold Lobel. ($35.00 with dust jacket) $20.00

REUSSWIG, William
Story of Crazy Horse, 1954 Grosset, hardcover. $10.00

REY, H.A. and Margaret, see Series section CURIOUS GEORGE
Find the Constellations, 1966 Houghton Mifflin, oversize hardcover, color illustrations by author. ($30.00 with dust jacket) $15.00
Stars, 1954 Houghton Mifflin, hardcover, illustrated by author. Dust jacket unfolds to map of constellations. ($40.00 with dust jacket) $20.00

REYNOLDS, Alfred
Adventures of Rattlesnake Ralph, 1973 Charles Scribner, blue hardcover. ($15.00 with dust jacket) $10.00

REYNOLDS, Barbara
Leonard Pepper, 1952 edition E M Hale. $20.00

REYNOLDS, Dickson
Perilous Prairie, 1956 Ryerson Press, Toronto, first edition, hardcover. ($15.00 with dust jacket) $10.00

REYNOLDS, Marjorie
Ride the Wild Storm, 1969 Macmillan, first edition, hardcover, b/w illustrations by Lorence F. Bjorklund. ($15.00 with dust jacket) $10.00

REYNOLDS, Pamela
Earth Times Two, 1970 Lothrop, Weekly Reader edition, pictorial cover. $10.00

RICCIUTI, Edward R.
Catch a Whale by the Tail, 1969 Harper and Row, first edition, hardcover, 61 pages, illustrated by Geoffrey Moss. ($15.00 with dust jacket) $10.00
Donald and the Fish that Walked, 1974 Harper and Row, "A Science I Can Read Book", hardcover, pictures by Syd Hoff. $15.00

RICH, Louise Dickinson
First Book of the China Clippers, 1962 Franklin Watts, first edition, hardcover, illustrated by Henry S. Gillette. $10.00.
Star Island Boy, 1968 Franklin Watts, first edition, hardcover. ($15.00 with dust jacket) $10.00

RICHLER, Mordecai
Jacob Two-Two Meets The Hooded Fang, 1975 Alfred A. Knopf, first edition, hardcover. ($15.00 with dust jacket) $10.00

RIDLE, Julia Brown
Hog Wild!, 1961 Harper and Row, hardcover. $10.00

RIEDMAN, Sarah
Clang! Clang! The Story of Trolleys, 1964 Rand McNally, orange hardcover, 112 pages. ($20.00 with dust jacket) $15.00

RIESENBERG, Felix
Story of the Naval Academy, 1958 Random House, first edition, hardcover, illustrations. $10.00

RIETVELD, Jane
ABC Molly, 1966 Norton, first edition, hardcover. ($20.00 with dust jacket) $10.00
Monkey Island, 1963 Viking, first edition, yellow hardcover, illustrated by Rietveld. $20.00
Wild Dog, 1953 Wilcox and Follett, first edition, hardcover, illustrated by author. ($20.00 with dust jacket) $10.00

RINEHART, Susan
Something Old, Something New, 1961 Harper, first edition, hardcover, 32 pages, illustrated by Arnold Lobel. ($50.00 with dust jacket) $20.00

RINKOFF, Barbara
Pretzel Hero, 1970 Parents' Magazine Press, first edition, hardcover, illustrated by Charles Mikolaycaak. $15.00

RITCHIE, Jean
Apple Seeds and Soda Straws: Some Love Charms and Legends, 1965 Walck, first edition, hardcover, 48 pages, illustrated by Don Bolognese. ($15.00 with dust jacket) $10.00

RITCHIE, Rita
Bicycles North! A Mystery on Wheels, 1973 Western Publishing, hardcover, illustrated by Ben Otero. $10.00
Silver Seven, 1972 Whitman, pictorial hardcover. $10.00

RIVKIN, Ann
Mystery of Disaster Island, 1975 Scholastic, illustrated hardcover, illustrated by Affie Mohammed. $10.00

ROACH, Marilynne
Mouse and the Song, 1974 Parents' Magazine Press, illustrated hardcover, illustrated by Joseph Low. ($20.00 with dust jacket) $10.00

ROBB, Esther Chapman
There's Something About a River, 1961 Duell, Sloan and Pearce, first edition, hardcover. ($45.00 with dust jacket) $20.00

ROBBIN, Irving
Explorations and Discoveries, 1961 Wonder Book, hardcover. $10.00

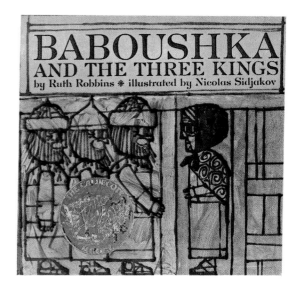

ROBBINS, Ruth
Baboushka and the Three Kings, 1960 Parnassus, 1961 Caldecott Award, hardcover, illustrated by Nicolas Sidjakov. ($30.00 with dust jacket) $15.00
Emperor and the Drummer Boy, 1962 Parnassus, hardcover. ($25.00 with dust jacket) $15.00

ROBERTS, Catherine
First Book of Sewing, 1956 Watts, color illustrated hardcover, illustrated endpapers, 67 pages, two-color illustrations by author. $15.00

ROBERTS, Suzanne
Spirit Town, 1972 Western Publishing, glossy hardcover illustrated by Charles Platt. $10.00

ROBERTSON, Keith, see Series section HENRY REED
If Wishes were Horses, 1967 Harper & Row, hardcover. $20.00
Missing Brother, 1950 Viking, first edition, red illustrated hardcover, illustrated by Rafaello Busoni. ($65.00 with dust jacket) $30.00
Money Machine, 1969 Viking, first edition, hardcover, 220 pages, illustrated by George Porter. $20.00

ROBINSON, Helen; Marion MONROE, and others
New Guess Who, 1965 Scott, Foresman, school reader, illustrated, pictorial hardcover of Dick, Jane, Sally, Pam, Penny and Mike. $50.00

ROBINSON, Jan M.
Christmas Dog, 1969 Lippincott, Weekly Reader edition, pictorial hardcover, illustrated by Joan Sandin. $10.00
December Dog, 1969 Lippincott, Weekly Reader edition, pictorial hardcover, illustrated by Joan Sandin. $10.00

ROBINSON, Jean O.
Francie, 1970 Follett, first edition, hardcover, illustrated by Joann Daley. ($15.00 with dust jacket) $10.00

ROBINSON, Joan
Charley, 1970 Coward McCann, first American edition, hardcover. ($15.00 with dust jacket) $10.00

ROBINSON, Kathleen
Designed by Suzanne, 1968 Lothrop, Lee, pink hardcover. ($15.00 with dust jacket) $10.00
When Debbie Dared, 1963 Whitman, hardcover, illustrated by Jim Tadych. $10.00
When Sara Smiled, 1962 Whitman, hardcover, cover and decorations by Mimi Korach. $10.00

ROBINSON, Tom
Lost Dog Jerry, 1952 Viking, first edition, hardcover, illustrated by Morgan Dennis. ($25.00 with dust jacket) $15.00

ROBINSON, Tom D.
An Eskimo Birthday, 1975 Dodd Mead, pictorial hardcover, illustrated by Glo Coalson. $15.00

ROBISON, Eleanor G.
Fun and Fancy, 1959 Ginn and Co., third grade reader, illustrated orange hardcover, some illustrations by Corrine Malvern. $15.00

ROCHE, Aloysius
Animals under the Rainbow, 1952 Broadwater, London, hardcover, 174 pages, wood engravings by Agnes Miller Parker. ($20.00 with dust jacket) $15.00

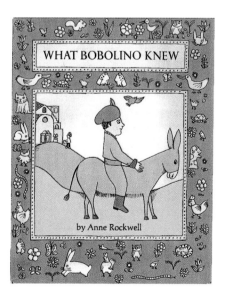

ROCKWELL, Anne
Glass, Stones and Crown, 1968 Atheneum, hardcover. $10.00

Gypsy Girl's Best Shoes, 1966 Parents' Magazine Press, hardcover. $10.00
Monkey's Whiskers, 1971 Parents' Magazine Press, pictorial hardcover. $10.00
Poor Goose, 1976 Crowell, first edition, hardcover. ($15.00 with dust jacket) $10.00
What Bobolino Knew, 1973 McCall, hardcover, 29 pages, color illustrations by author. ($15.00 with dust jacket) $10.00

ROCKWELL, Carey, see Series section TOM CORBETT

ROCKWELL, Molly and **Norman**
Willie Was Different, The Tale of an Ugly Thrushling, 1969 Funk & Wagnalls, hardcover, 42 pages, b/w and color illustrations by Norman Rockwell. Signed first edition with dust jacket: $100.00

ROCKWELL, Norman
My Adventures as an Illustrator, 1960 Doubleday, first edition, hardcover, b/w photos. $20.00

RODGERS and **HAMMERSTEIN**
Rodgers and Hammerstein's Saturday Matinee, 1956 Little Golden Books, A Golden Record Chest, 8 records in box. $70.00.

RODGERS, Mary
Billion For Boris, 1974 Harper & Row, first edition, hardcover, sequel to *Freaky Friday,* ($25.00 in pictorial Edward Gorey dust jacket) $20.00
Freaky Friday, 1972 Harper & Row, first edition, hardcover. ($20.00 with dust jacket) $10.00
Rotten Book, 1969 Harper and Row, first edition, hardcover, illustrated by Steven Kellogg ($60.00 with dust jacket) $30.00
Songs We Sing from Rodgers and Hammerstein, 1971 Golden Press, hardcover, 77 pages, illustrated by William Dugan. $25.00

ROGERS, Fred
Mister Rogers' Song Book, 1970 Random House, photo pictorial hardcover, oversize, 59 pages, illustrated by Steven Kellogg. ($20.00 with dust jacket) $15.00

ROJANKOVSKY, Feodor
Animals in the Zoo, 1962 Knopf, first edition, hardcover, illustrated by author. ($20.00 with dust jacket) $10.00
Rojankovsky's Wonderful Picture Book: An Anthology Illustrated by Feodor Rojankovsky, 1972 Golden Press, illustrated hardcover, 117 pages, illustrated endpapers, illustrated by F. Rojankovsky. $25.00

ROLAND, Betty
Jamie's Summer Visitor, 1964 Bodley Head, first edition, hardcover, illustrated by Prudence Seward. ($30.00 with dust jacket) $15.00

ROLERSON, Darrell
In Sheep's Clothing, 1972 Dodd, Mead, first edition, hardcover, illustrated by Ted Lewin. ($15.00 with dust jacket) $10.00

ROMANO, Louis G. and **Nicholas P. GEORGIADY**
This is a Department Store, 1962 Follett, hardcover, illustrated by Jim Collins. $10.00

ROOD, Ronald
Animals Nobody Loves, the Fascinating Story of Varmints, 1971 Stephen Greene Press, hardcover, 215 pages, b/w illustrations. ($15.00 with dust jacket) $10.00
How and Why Wonder Book of Insects, 1960 Grosset & Dunlap, Deluxe Edition, glossy pictorial cover, 48 pages. $15.00

ROOSE-EVANS, James
Odd and Great Bear, 1973 Andre Deutsch, first edition, blue hardcover, b/w illustrations by Brian Robb. ($20.00 with dust jacket) $10.00

ROOSEVELT, Eleanor and **Regina TOR**
Growing Toward Peace, 1960 Random House, first edition, oversize green hardcover, illustrated endpapers, b/w illustrations from photographs. ($50.00 with dust jacket) $20.00

ROSE, Ada Campbell, editor
Jack and Jill Round the Year Book, 1958 Little, Brown, first edition, hardcover, 339 pages. $25.00

ROSELLI, Auro
Cats of the Eiffel Tower, 1967 Delacorte Press, first edition, hardcover, illustrated by Laurent DeBrunhoff. ($65.00 with dust jacket) $40.00

ROSEN, Sidney
Galileo and the Magic Numbers, 1958 Little, Brown, first edition, hardcover. ($25.00 with dust jacket) $15.00

ROSS, Diana
Old Perisher, 1965 Faber & Faber, London, first edition, oversize hardcover, color and b/w illustrations by Edward Ardizzone. ($100.00 with dust jacket) $40.00

Bran Tub, 1954 Lutterworth, first edition, hardcover. ($20.00 with dust jacket) $10.00

ROTH, Mary Jane
Pretender Princess, 1967 Morrow, first edition, hardcover, illustrated by Sheila Greenwald. ($30.00 with dust jacket) $15.00

ROTHMAN, Joel
Antcyclopedia, 1974 Phinmarc Books, first edition, oversize hardcover, 30 pages, brown/white illustrated by Shelley Freshman. ($15.00 with dust jacket) $10.00

ROUNDS, Glen
Casey Jones: The Story of a Brave Engineer, 1968 Golden Gate Junior Books, first edition, hardcover, illustrated by author. $15.00
Hunted Horses, 1951 Holiday House, first edition, small, full-page illustrations by author. ($35.00 with dust jacket) $15.00
In the Woods and Other Small Matters, 1964 World, first edition, hardcover, illustrated by author. ($20.00 with dust jacket) $10.00
Wild Orphan, 1961 Holiday House, first edition, hardcover. ($15.00 with dust jacket) $10.00

ROWE, Viola
Practically Twins, 1963 Western Publishing, first edition, hardcover, 216 pages, cover illustration by Olinda Giacomini. $10.00
Way with Boys, 1957 Longmans, Green, hardcover, illustrated by Millard McGee. ($25.00 with dust jacket) $15.00

ROWLAND, Florence Wightman
Jade Dragons, 1954 Henry Z. Walck, hardcover. ($15.00 with dust jacket) $10.00

ROWLAND, Phyllis
George Goes to Town, 1958 Little, Brown, first edition, hardcover, 41 pages, illustrated. $15.00

ROWNTREE, Lester
Ronnie, 1952 Viking, blue hardcover, illustrated by Don Perceval. ($15.00 with dust jacket) $10.00

RUDSTROM, Lennart
Home, 1974 Putnam, first American edition, hardcover, watercolor illustrations by Carl Larsson. ($35.00 with dust jacket) $15.00

RUGGLES, Alice McGuffey
Story of the McGuffeys, 1950 American Book Company, small, hardcover, 133 pages, history of the McGuffey family, and the McGuffey school readers. ($20.00 with dust jacket) $10.00

RUGH, Belle Dorman
Path above the Pines, 1962 Houghton Mifflin, hardcover. ($20.00 with dust jacket) $10.00
Crystal Mountain, 1955 Houghton Mifflin, first edi-

tion, hardcover, illustrated by E. H. Shepard. ($45.00 with dust jacket) $25.00

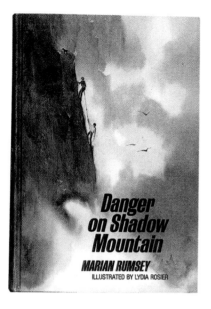

RUMSEY, Marian
Danger on Shadow Mountain, 1970 Morrow, Weekly Reader edition, illustrated hardcover, illustrated by Lydia Rosier. $10.00
Devil's Doorstep, 1966 Morrow Junior Books, first edition, hardcover, illustrated by W. T. Mars. ($15.00 with dust jacket) $10.00
Lost in the Desert, 1971 Morrow, Weekly Reader edition, illustrated hardcover. $10.00

RUNBECK, Margaret Lee
Miss Boo Is 16, 1956 Houghton Mifflin, first edition, hardcover, 263 pages. ($15.00 with dust jacket) $10.00

RUSH, Caroline
Tales of Mr. Pengachoosa, 1973 Crown, first edition, hardcover, 56 pages, illustrated by Dominique M. Strandquest. ($15.00 with dust jacket) $10.00

RUSHMORE, Helen
Bigfoot Wallace and the Hickory Nut Battle, 1970 Garrard, hardcover, 48 pages, illustrated by George Wilde. $20.00
Shadow of Robbers' Roost, 1960 World, Young American Book Club edition, color illustrated hardcover, 186 pages. $10.00

RUSS, Lavinia
Over the Hills and Far Away, 1968 Harcourt, Brace, Weekly Reader edition, pictorial hardcover, 160 pages. $10.00

RUSSELL, David H.
Roads to Everywhere, 1961 Ginn, orange pictorial hardcover. $20.00

RUSSELL, Franklin
Frightened Hare, 1965 Holt, Rinehart & Winston, first edition, hardcover. ($15.00 with dust jacket) $10.00

RUSSELL, Helen Ross
Clarion the Kildeer, 1970 Hawthorn, first edition, hardcover, illustrated by John Hamberger. ($15.00 with dust jacket) $10.00

RUSSELL, Solveig Paulson
Motherly Smith & Brother Bimbo, 1971 Abingdon, first edition, hardcover, illustrated by Susan Perl. ($15.00 with dust jacket) $10.00
White Sweater Must Be White, 1967 Grosset & Dunlap, hardcover, illustrated by Art Seiden. $10.00

RUST, Doris
Animals at Number Eleven, 1961 Faber & Faber, UK, first edition, hardcover, illustrated by Shirley Hughes. ($15.00 with dust jacket) $10.00

RYAN, Cheli Duran
Hildilid's Night, 1971 Macmillan, first edition, oblong hardcover, illustrated by Arnold Lobel. ($45.00 with dust jacket) $25.00
Paz, 1971 Macmillan, first edition, square blue hardcover, 39 pages, color illustrations by Nonny Hogrogian. ($40.00 with dust jacket) $20.00

———— ✦➤ **S** ◄✦ ————

SABOLY, Nicholas
Bring A Torch, Jeannette, Isabella, 1963 Scribner, first edition, hardcover, illustrated by Adrienne Adams. ($60.00 with dust jacket) $30.00

SACHS, Marilyn
Amy and Laura, 1966 Doubleday, hardcover. $10.00

SAINT-MARCOUX
Andalusian Guitar, 1961 Bodley Head, London, first edition, 176 pages, adapted from French by June Howe. ($15.00 with dust jacket) $10.00
Green Slippers, 1959 Bodley Head, London, first edition, 176 pages, adapted from French by Judy Taylor. ($15.00 with dust jacket) $10.00
Green Slippers, 1961 Reilly & Lee, first American edition, small green hardcover, adapted from French by Judy Taylor. ($20.00 with dust jacket) $10.00

SAINTSBURY, Dana
Squirrel that Remembered, 1951 Viking, tan hardcover. ($15.00 with dust jacket) $10.00

SAKADE, Florence
Japanese Children's Favorite Stories, 1962 Tuttle, oblong hardcover, color and black and white illustrations by Yoshisuke Kurosaki. $20.00

SALAS, Frieda
Tadao and the Magic Plant, 1966 Exposition Press, first edition, hardcover. ($15.00 with dust jacket) $10.00

SALISBURY, Kent
Ookpik Visits the USA, 1963 Golden Press, orange pictorial hardcover, includes magnetic Ookpik in his auto, illustrated by Beverly Edwards. $75.00

SAMSON, Anne S.
Lines, Spines and Porcupines, 1969 Doubleday, first edition, hardcover, illustrated by author. ($35.00 with dust jacket) $20.00

SAMSTAG, Nicholas
Kay-Kay Comes Home, 1962 Obolensky, Inc, first edition, pictorial hardcover, b/w illustrations by Ben Shahn. $30.00

SANDBURG, Carl
Wedding Procession of the Rag Doll and the Broom Handle and Who Was in It , 1968 edition Collins, first edition UK, hardcover, illustrated by Harriet Pincus. ($45.00 with dust jacket) $20.00

SANDBURG, Helga
Bo and the Old Donkey, 1965 Dial Press, first edition, hardcover, illustrated by Marian Morton. ($15.00 with dust jacket) $10.00
Joel and the Wild Goose, 1963 Dial Press, first edition, oblong pictorial hardcover, color illustrations by Thomas Daly. $20.00

SANDERLIN, George
First Around the World: A Journal of Magellan's Voyage, 1964 Harper & Row, pictorial hardcover. $15.00

SANDERS, Ann
Library Mice, Ariel Books, first edition, hardcover, illustrated by Eugene Fern. ($15.00 with dust jacket) $10.00

SANDERS, Martha
Alexander and the Magic Mouse, 1969 American Heritage Press, illustrated hardcover, 44 pages, illustrated by Philippe Fix. ($35.00 with dust jacket) $20.00

SANDERSON, Ivan
John and Juan in the Jungle, ca. 1950s edition Dodd, Mead, pictorial boards, illustrations by Miguel Covarrubias. $25.00

SANKEY, Marjorie
Holiday in Hiding, 1960 Harrap, London, hardcover, 160 pages, line drawings by W. F. Philips. ($15.00 with dust jacket) $10.00

SARGENT, Shirley
Pat Hawly, Pre-School Teacher, 1958 Dodd, Mead, hardcover. ($20.00 with dust jacket) $10.00

SARNOFF, Jean
Light the Candles! Beat the Drums! A Book of Holidays, 1979 Scribner, first edition, pictorial hardcover, illustrated by author. $15.00

SAROYAN, William
Color Me, 1963 Crowell-Collier Press, first edition, hardcover, illustrated by Murray Tinkelman. ($30.00 with dust jacket) $15.00
Tooth and My Father, 1974 Garden City, first edition, hardcover, illustrated by Suzanne Verrier. ($25.00 with dust jacket) $10.00

SARVER, Hannah
Square Peg, 1962 Funk & Wagnalls, hardcover. $15.00

SASEK, Miroslav, see Series section SASEK

SAUNDERS, F. Wenderoth
Building Brooklyn Bridge, 1965 Little Brown, first edition, illustrated. ($40.00 with dust jacket) $20.00

SAUNDERS, Rubie
Calling All Girls Party Book, 1966 Parents' Magazine Press, first edition, hardcover. ($25.00 with dust jacket) $15.00

SAVAGE, Blake (pseudonym of Harold Goodwin, see Series section RICK BRANT)
Assignment in Space, 1950 Whitman, hardcover ($20.00 with dust jacket) $10.00

Rip Foster Rides the Gray Planet, 1952 (Reprint of *Assignment*), hardcover.($20.00 with dust jacket) $10.00

SAVILLE, Malcolm
Buckinghams at Ravenswyke, 1972 Collins, London, hardcover. ($15.00 with dust jacket) $10.00

SAVITT, Sam
Wild Horse Running, 1973 Dodd, Mead, first edition, hardcover illustrated by author. ($20.00 with dust jacket) $10.00

SAVORY, Phyllis
Song of the Golden Birds, 1970 Timmins, Cape Town, oversize hardcover, 78 pages, illustrated by Jillian Hulme. ($50.00 with dust jacket) $25.00

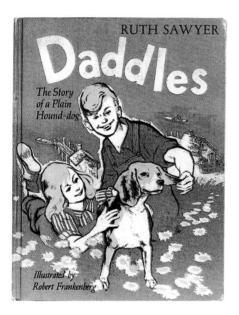

SAWYER, Ruth
Daddles, 1964 Little Brown, first edition, b/w illustrations by Robert Frankenberg. ($20.00 with dust jacket) $10.00

Enchanted Schoolhouse, 1956 edition Viking, hardcover, illustrated by Hugh Troy. ($20.00 with dust jacket) $10.00

Journey Cake, Ho!, 1953 Viking, oversize hardcover, illustrated endpapers, two-color illustrations throughout by Robert McCloskey. ($25.00 with dust jacket) $15.00

Little Red Horse, 1950 Viking, first edition, hardcover, illustrated by Jay Barnum. ($60.00 with dust jacket) $30.00

Maggie Rose – Her Birthday Christmas, 1952 Harper, hardcover, illustrated by Maurice Sendak. ($40.00 with dust jacket) $20.00

Year of the Christmas Dragon, 1960 Viking, first edition, hardcover, illustrated by Hugh Troy. ($40.00 with dust jacket) $20.00

SAY, Allen
Dr. Smith's Safari, 1972 Harper and Row, first edition, hardcover, 32 pages. ($45.00 with dust jacket) $20.00

SCARRY, Patricia M.
Jeremy Mouse Book, 1969 American Heritage Press, illustrated hardcover, illustrated by Hilary Knight. ($35.00 with dust jacket) $20.00

SCARRY, Richard, see Series section TINKER
Fables of La Fontaine, 1963 Doubleday, first edition, hardcover, color illustrations by author. ($40.00 with dust jacket) $20.00

I Am a Bunny, 1963 Golden Sturdy Book, narrow glossy hardcover, stiff pages, color illustrations by author. $25.00

Richard Scarry's ABC Word Book, 1971 Random House, illustrated hardcover, 61 pages, color illustrations by author. $25.00

Richard Scarry's Best Mother Goose Ever, 1970 Golden Book/Western, pictorial oversize hardcover, color illustrations by author. $15.00

Richard Scarry's Best Story Book Ever, 1967 Golden Book/Western, pictorial oversize hardcover, color illustrations by author. $20.00

Richard Scarry's Please and Thank You Book, 1973 Norcross, square hardcover, illustrated by author. ($20.00 with dust jacket) $10.00

What Do People Do All Day?, 1968 Random House, oversize hardcover, illustrated by author. ($40.00 with dust jacket) $20.00

SCHACKBURG, Dr. Richard
Yankee Doodle, 1965 Prentice Hall, oblong decorated hardcover, color woodcuts by Ed Emberley. $30.00

SCHAEFFER, Susan
Rhymes and Runes of the Toad, 1975 Macmillan, first edition, hardcover. ($15.00 with dust jacket) $10.00

SCHAEFFLER, Ursula
Thief and the Blue Rose, (1963) 1967 Harcourt, first American edition, oversize hardcover, color illustrations by author. ($35.00 with dust jacket) $20.00

SCHAFER, Jack
Stubby Pringle's Christmas, 1964 Houghton Mifflin, first edition, hardcover, illustrated by Lorence Bjorkland. ($100.00 with dust jacket) $40.00

SCHEER, Julian
Rain Makes Applesauce, 1964 Holiday House, oversize hardcover, illustrated by Marvin Bileck. 1965 Caldecott Honor winner. ($30.00 with dust jacket) $20.00

SCHERF, Margaret
Mystery of the Velvet Box, 1963 Franklin Watts, hardcover. ($15.00 with dust jacket) $10.00

SCHERMELE, Willy
Winkie and his Magic Flute, ca. 1950 Mulder & Zoon, Amsterdam, first edition, pictorial hardcover, 26 pages, color and b/w illustrations by author. $15.00

SCHICKEL, Richard.
Gentle Knight, 1964 Abelard-Schuman, first American edition, hardcover, illustrated by Quentin Blake. ($35.00 with dust jacket) $20.00

SCHIFFER, Herbert F. and **Peter B.**
Miniature Antique Furniture, 1972 Wynnewood Livingston, first edition, hardcover, photographic illustrations. ($35.00 with dust jacket) $20.00

SCHILLER, Barbara
Kitchen Knight, 1965 Holt, Rinehart and Winston, first edition, hardcover, illustrated by Nonny Hogrogian. ($20.00 with dust jacket) $10.00
White Rat's Tale, 1969 Holt, Rinehart & Winston, first edition, hardcover, illustrated by Adrienne Adams. ($40.00 with dust jacket) $20.00

SCHLEIN, Miriam
City Boy Country Boy, 1955 Children's Press, first edition, hardcover, illustrated by Katherine Evans. ($30.00 with dust jacket) $10.00
Oomi: The New Hunter, 1955 Abelard-Schuman, pictorial hardcover. $20.00

SCHLOAT, G. Warren, Jr.
Milk for You, 1951 Scribners, red hardcover. $20.00
Playtime For You, 1950 Scribner, first edition, oversize hardcover, photo illustrations. ($35.00 with dust jacket) $20.00

SCHMID, Eleonore
Horns Everywhere, 1968 Harlin Quist, first edition, hardcover, color illustrations by author. $45.00

SCHOLEFIELD, Edmund
L'il Wildcat, 1967 World, hardcover, illustrated by Paul France. ($15.00 with dust jacket) $10.00

SCHOOLLAND, Marian M.
Forest Folk at Work, 1960 Eerdmans, pictorial hardcover, illustrated by Reynold Weidenaar. $15.00

SCHREITER, Rick
Delicious Plums of King Oscar the Bad, 1967 Harlin Quist Books, oversize hardcover, color illustrations by author. ($20.00 with dust jacket) $15.00

SCHROEDER, Doris
Annie Oakley in Danger at Diablo, 1955 Whitman, pictorial hardcover. $20.00
Beverly Hillbillies, 1963 Whitman, glossy pictorial hardcover, illustrated. $10.00
Walt Disney's Annette and the Mystery at Moonstone Bay, 1962 Whitman, pictorial hardcover with illustrated by Adam Szwejkowski. $10.00
Walt Disney's Annette and the Desert Inn Mystery, 1962 Whitman, pictorial hardcover. $10.00
Lassie and the Forbidden Valley, 1959 Whitman, pictorial hardcover. $10.00
Patty Duke and the Mystery Mansion, 1964 Whitman, pictorial hardcover. $20.00
Rin Tin Tin and Call to Danger, 1957 Whitman, Screen Gems Authorized TV edition, pictorial hardcover. $10.00

SCHULZ, Charles M.
Charlie Brown's All-Stars, 1966 World, hardcover, illustrated by author. ($30.00 with dust jacket) $15.00
Charlie Brown's Christmas, 1965 World, first edition, square hardcover, illustrated by author. ($25.00 with dust jacket) $15.00
Happiness Is a Warm Puppy, 1962 Determined Productions, first edition, small square hardcover, brown & black pictorial paper over boards, 62 pages on heavy stock in a variety of colors, illustrated by author. ($20.00 with dust jacket) $10.00
Love is Walking Hand in Hand, 1965 San Francisco Determined Productions, first edition, hardcover, illustrated by author. ($25.00 with dust jacket) $15.00
It's The Great Pumpkin, Charlie Brown, 1967 World, first edition, oblong pictorial hardcover, illustrated in color. $25.00
Peanuts Lunch Bag Cook Book, 1974 Scholastic, first edition, hardcover. ($15.00 with dust jacket) $10.00
Snoopy and His Sopwith Camel, 1969 Holt, Rinehart, small illustrated hardcover, b/w drawing on alternate red and green pages. $20.00
Snoopy and the Red Baron, 1966 Holt, Rinehart, first edition, hardcover. ($40.00 with dust jacket) $20.00
Snoopy and the Red Baron, 1966 Holt, Weekly Reader edition, pictorial hardcover. $15.00
Young Pillars, 1958 Warner Press, hardcover. ($20.00 with dust jacket) $10.00
You're in Love, Charlie Brown, 1968 World, first edition, illustrated hardcover, illustrated by author. $15.00
Wit and Wisdom of Snoopy, 1967 Hallmark, pictorial hardcover. $10.00

SCHWALJE, Earl and Marjory
Cezar and the Music Maker, 1951 Knopf, first edition, hardcover, 77 pages, illustrated. ($15.00 with dust jacket) $10.00

SCHWARTZ, Julius
I Know a Magic House, 1956 Whittlesey, first edition, oversize hardcover, 32 pages, b/w and color illustrations by Marc Simont. ($30.00 with dust jacket) $15.00
Now I Know, 1955 Whittlesey House, first edition, oversize hardcover, 32 pages. ($20.00 with dust jacket) $15.00
Through the Magnifying Glass, 1954 McGraw-Hill, Whittlesey House, first edition, hardcover, 111 pages, illustrated by Jeanne Bendick. $12.00.

SCOTT, A.F.
Savage King of the Seven Seas, 1968 Geoffrey Chapman, London, illustrated hardcover, illustrated by Jacques Le Scanff. $20.00

SCOTT, Sally
Chica, 1954 Harcourt, Brace, first edition, hardcover, 114 pages, illustrated by Joe Krush. ($20.00 with dust jacket) $10.00
Judy's Surprising Day, 1957 Harcourt, Brace, first edition, hardcover, illustrated by Beth Krush. ($15.00 with dust jacket) $10.00

SCOTT, Thurman Thomas
Mark of a Champion, 1960 Longmans, first American edition, hardcover, illustrated by Edward Shenton. ($25.00 with dust jacket) $15.00

SEAGER, Joan
Mystery at Lynx Lodge, 1965 McGraw-Hill, hardcover. ($15.00 with dust jacket) $10.00

SEAMAN, David M.
Story of Rocks & Minerals, 1956 Seaman (A Guidebook for Young Collectors), hardcover. $15.00

SEARLE, Ronald
Back to the Slaughterhouse, 1951 MacDonald, UK, first edition, oversize hardcover, 96 pages, b/w illustrations by author. ($30.00 with dust jacket) $20.00
Dick Deadeye, 1975 Harcourt Brace Jovanovich, first American edition, oblong oversize hardcover, Searle interpretation of Gilbert and Sullivan opera, illustrated by author. ($45.00 with dust jacket) $20.00
Merry England, etc., 1957 Knopf, oversize hardcover, first edition, illustrated by author. ($40.00 with dust jacket) $20.00
More Cats, 1975 Stephen Greene edition, oversize hardcover, illustrated by author. ($25.00 with dust jacket) $15.00
Searle's Cats , 1967 Stephen Greene Press, first edition, hardcover, illustrated by author. ($25.00 with dust jacket) $15.00
Terror of St. Trinian's or Angela's Prince Charming, with Timothy Shy, 1952 Max Parrish, 128 pages, illustrated by author. ($30.00 with dust jacket) $15.00
Those Magnificent Men In Their Flying Machines, with Bill Richardson and Allen Andrews, 1965 Norton, first edition, hardcover, illustrated by author. ($20.00 with dust jacket) $10.00

SECHRIST, Elizabeth Hough, editor
13 Ghostly Yarns, 1963 Macrae Smith, pictorial hardcover, b/w illustrations by Albert Michini. ($30.00 with dust jacket) $15.00

SEED, Jenny
Voice of the Great Elephant, ca. 1968 Pantheon Books, first edition, tan hardcover, 178 pages. ($20.00 with dust jacket) $10.00

SEEMAN, Elizabeth
Talking Dog & the Barking Man, 1960 Franklin Watts, first edition, pictorial hardcover. ($20.00 with dust jacket) $10.00

SEIDLER, Rosalie
Grumpus and the Venetian Cat, 1964 Atheneum, first edition, hardcover, illustrated by Rosalie Seidler. ($20.00 with dust jacket) $10.00

SEIDMAN, M. S.
Who Woke the Sun?, 1960 Macmillan, first edition, hardcover, illustrated by Karla Kuskin. ($40.00 with dust jacket) $20.00

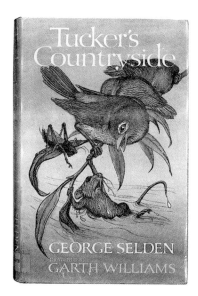

SELDEN, George
Cricket in Times Square, 1960 Farrar, hardcover, first edition, b/w illustrations by Garth Williams. ($50.00 with dust jacket) $20.00. Later editions: ($20.00 with dust jacket) $10.00
Dunkard, 1968 Harper, first edition, hardcover, illustrated by Peter Lippman. ($20.00 with dust jacket) $10.00
Garden Under the Sea, 1957 Viking, first edition, hardcover, illustrations by Garry MacKenzie. ($50.00 with dust jacket) $20.00
Genie of Sutton Place, 1973 Farrar Straus, first edition, hardcover, dust jacket by Leo and Diane Dillon. ($35.00 with dust jacket) $15.00
Harry Cat's Pet Puppy, 1973 Farrar, first edition, hardcover, illustrations by Garth Williams. ($50.00 with dust jacket) $20.00
I See What I See!, 1962 Ambassador Books, Toronto, hardcover, illustrated by Robert Galster. ($15.00 with dust jacket) $10.00
Tucker's Countryside, 1969 Farrar, first edition, hardcover, 165 pages, b/w illustrations by Garth Williams. ($40.00 with dust jacket) $20.00

SELF, Margaret Cabell
Shaggy Little Burro of San Miguel, 1965 Duell, Sloan and Pearce, New York, first edition, hardcover, illustrated by Betty Fraser. ($15.00 with dust jacket) $10.00

SELSAM, Millicent E.
Bug that Laid the Golden Eggs, 1967 Harper & Row, I Can Read science series, pictorial hardcover, photos by Harold Krieger. $10.00
Let's Get Turtles, 1965 Harper & Row, I Can Read science series, pictorial hardcover, illustrated by Arnold Lobel. $15.00
Play With Seeds, 1957 Morrow, first edition, hardcover, 93 pages. ($20.00 with dust jacket) $10.00
Play with Trees, 1950 Morrow, first edition, hardcover, illustrated by Scherer. ($20.00 with dust jacket) $10.00
Seeds and More Seeds, 1959 Harpers, first edition, hardcover, 60 pages, illustrated by Tomi Ungerer. ($100.00 with dust jacket) $30.00

SEMPE, Jean-Jacques
Young Nicolas, 1962 Bobbs-Merrill, square hardcover, decorative green boards, 121 pages. ($20.00 with dust jacket) $10.00

SENDAK, Jack
King of the Hermits, 1966 Farrar, Straus, first edition, illustrated by Margot Zemach. ($35.00 with dust jacket) $20.00
Magic Tears, 1971 Harper, first edition, hardcover, 58 pages, illustrated by Mitchell Miller. ($15.00 with dust jacket) $10.00

SENDAK, Maurice
First editions and first printings of early Sendak

books command high prices. However, his books are so popular, later books were given extremely large printings and are therefore available at lower costs. Most of his books have been re-printed in large quantities. The prices on these later printings are usually in the $20.00 to $30.00 range with dust jacket, and in the $15.00 range without dust jacket.

Dwarf Long-Nose, 1960 Random House, first edition, oversize hardcover, b/w illustrations by Sendak. First edition: $80.00 in dust jacket. Later editions: ($20.00 with dust jacket) $15.00

Hector Protector and As I Went Over the Water, 1965 Harper, oblong hardcover, illustrated and written by Sendak. First edition with dust jacket: $110.00. Later editions: ($20.00 with dust jacket) $15.00

Higglety Pigglety Pop! Or There Must Be More to Life, 1967 Harper, hardcover, 69 pages, dust jacket price $4.95. First edition with dust jacket: $50.00. Later editions: ($20.00 with dust jacket) $15.00

In the Night Kitchen, 1970 Harper illustrated white oversize hardcover, color illustrations by Sendak. (Some dust jacket indications of first: $4.95 price, "1070" on bottom inside flap, title list ending with *Higglety Pigglety Pop*), no Caldecott sticker. First edition with dust jacket: $150.00. Later editions: ($20.00 with dust jacket) $15.00

In the Night Kitchen, 1970 Bodley Head, first edition UK, illustrated white oversize hardcover, color illustrations by Sendak. First edition with dust jacket: $50.00

Juniper Tree, and Other Tales from Grimm, 1973 Farrar, hardcover, b/w illustrations by Maurice Sendak. Two volume set. First edition set: $100.00 with dust jackets and box. Later printings, 2-volume set: $35.00 with jackets and box.

Kenny's Window, 1956 Harper & Row, Sendak's first book, hardcover, illustrated by author. $75.00 Later editions: ($20.00 with dust jacket) $15.00

King Grisly-Beard, Grimm fairy tale, 1973 Farrar, hardcover, illustrated by Sendak. First edition with dust jacket: $80.00. Later editions: ($20.00 with dust jacket) $15.00

Lullabies and Night Songs. 1965 Harper, oversize hardcover, music by Alec Wilder, illustrated by Maurice Sendak. First edition with dust jacket: $80.00. Later editions: ($20.00 with dust jacket) $15.00

Seven Little Monsters, 1975 Harper & Row, oblong pictorial hardcover. First edition with dust jacket: $75.00. Later editions: ($20.00 with dust jacket) $15.00

Sign on Rosie's Door, 1969 Bodley Head, first edition UK, hardcover, illustrated by author. ($50.00 with dust jacket) $20.00

Sign on Rosie's Door, 1960 Harper, early edition, hardcover, illustrated by author. ($50.00 with dust jacket) $20.00

Very Far Away, 1957 Harper, small hardcover, 53 pages, pink/b/w illustrations by author. ($95.00 with dust jacket) $45.00

Where the Wild Things Are, 1963 Harper, unstated early edition, signed and dated by Sendak, June 1964, impressed gold Caldecott Medal on cover. Signed edition with dust jacket: $300.00. Later editions: ($20.00 with dust jacket) $15.00

SEREDY, Kate

Gypsy, 1951 Viking, first edition, oversize hardcover, 62 pages, illustrated by author. ($50.00 with dust jacket) $20.00

Gypsy, 1952 Harrap Ltd., first edition, small hardcover, illustrated by author. ($50.00 with dust jacket) $20.00

Lazy Tinka, 1962 Viking Press, first edition, hardcover, 56 pages, illustrated by author. ($20.00 with dust jacket) $10.00

Philomena, 1955 Viking, first edition, illustrated by author. ($50.00 with dust jacket) $25.00

Tenement Tree, 1959 Viking, first edition, hardcover, illustrated by author. ($50.00 with dust jacket) $25.00

SERLING, Rod

Twilight Zone, 1963 Grosset & Dunlap, pictorial hardcover. $10.00

Rod Serling's Twilight Zone Revisited, 1964 Grosset, illustrated by Earl Mayan. ($30.00 with dust jacket) $15.00

SERRAILLIER, Ian

Bishop and the Devil, 1971 edition Kaye and Ward London, first edition thus, oversize hardcover, illustrated by Simon Stern. ($25.00 with dust jacket) $15.00

Challenge of the Green Knight, 1967 Walck, first American edition, hardcover. ($30.00 with dust jacket) $15.00

Enchanted Island Stories from Shakespeare, 1964 Walck, first American edition, hardcover, color and b/w illustrations by Peter Farmer. ($30.00 with dust jacket) $20.00

Gorgon's Head, 1962 Walck, first American edition, hardcover. ($40.00 with dust jacket) $20.00

Silver Sword (later issued as *Escape from Warsaw*), 1968 Phillips, hardcover, 187 pages. ($30.00 with dust jacket) $15.00

Suppose You Met a Witch, 1973 edition Little Brown, first edition thus, hardcover, 34 pages, illustrated by Ed Emberley. ($40.00 with dust jacket) $20.00

Tale of Three Landlubbers, 1970 Coward-McCann, first American edition, hardcover, illustrated by Raymond Briggs. ($30.00 with dust jacket) $15.00

SERWER, Blanch Luria
Let's Steal the Moon, Jewish Tales, Ancient and Recent, 1970 Little, Brown, first edition, hardcover, illustrated by Trina Schart Hyman. ($30.00 with dust jacket) $15.00

SESKIN, Stephen
Stone in the Road, 1968 Van Nostrand, first edition, hardcover, illustrated by Ursula Arndt. $25.00

SETON, Anya
Mistletoe and Sword, 1955 Doubleday, first edition, hardcover. ($15.00 with dust jacket) $10.00

SEUSS, Dr. (Ted Geisel)
All books using the Dr. Seuss pseudonym were written and illustrated by Geisel. See Series section, BEGINNER BOOKS, for other books by Geisel. The Dr. Seuss books were so popular, the early printings were large, later printings were usually of equal quality, and first editions are often hard to identify. However, when they can be identified, they command high prices. At a recent Sotheby's auction, a first edition of *Cat in the Hat* sold for $3,500.00
Cat in the Hat, 1955 Houghton Mifflin, school edition. RARE
Cat in the Hat, 1955 Random House, trade edition, hardcover, oversize hardcover, color illustrations by author. First edition with dust jacket: $1,500.00. Later editions: ($20.00 with dust jacket) $10.00
Cat in the Hat Comes Back, 1958 Random House, Beginner Books, hardcover, glossy pictorial boards, color illustrations by author. First edition with dust jacket: $500.00. Later editions: ($20.00 with dust jacket) $10.00
Cat in the Hat Songbook, 1968 Collins, London, hardcover. ($40.00 with dust jacket) $20.00

Dr. Seuss's Sleep Book, 1962 Random House, glossy oversize hardcover, 54 pages, color illustrations by author. First edition with dust jacket: $500.00. Later editions: ($20.00 with dust jacket) $10.00
Happy Birthday to You!, 1959 Random House, hardcover, illustrated endpapers, full-color illustrations. First edition with dust jacket: $350.00. Later editions: ($20.00 with dust jacket) $10.00
Hop on Pop, 1964 Collins, UK, hardcover, illustrated by author. $15.00
Horton Hatches the Egg, 1962 Collins, UK, hardcover. First UK edition with dust jacket: $100.00. Later editions: ($20.00 with dust jacket) $10.00
Horton Hears a Who!, 1954 Random House, oversize hardcover, illustrated endpapers, color illustrations by author. First edition with dust jacket: $300.00. Later editions: ($20.00 with dust jacket) $10.00
How the Grinch Stole Christmas!, 1957 Random House, hardcover, illustrated by author. First edition with dust jacket: $700.00. Later editions: ($20.00 with dust jacket) $10.00
I Had Trouble in Getting to Solla Sollew, 1965 Random House, oversize hardcover, illustrated endpapers, color illustrations by author. First edition with dust jacket: $500.00 Later editions: ($20.00 with dust jacket) $10.00
If I Ran The Circus, 1956 Random House, hardcover. First edition with dust jacket: $700.00 Later editions: ($20.00 with dust jacket) $10.00
If I Ran The Zoo, 1950 Random House, oversize hardcover, color illustrations by author. First edition with dust jacket: $300.00. Later editions: ($20.00 with dust jacket) $10.00
On Beyond Zebra, 1955 Random House, oversize hardcover, illustrated by author. First edition with dust jacket: $600.00. Later editions: ($30.00 with dust jacket) $20.00
Sneetches and Other Stories, 1961 Random House, hardcover. First edition with dust jacket: $400.00. Later editions: ($20.00 with dust jacket) $10.00
Yertle the Turtle, 1958 Random House, trade edition, oversize hardcover, green glossy pictorial boards, color illustrations by author. First edition with dust jacket: $300.00. Later editions: ($20.00 with dust jacket) $10.00

SEVERN, David
Burglars and Bandicoots, 1952 Macmillan, first edition, small hardcover, 192 pages, illustrated by Kiddell-Monroe. ($25.00 with dust jacket) $15.00
Three at the Sea, 1959 Bodley Head, first edition, hardcover, illustrated by Margery Gill. ($15.00 with dust jacket) $10.00

SEYMOUR, Alta Halverson
Christmas Donkey, 1954 Follett, oversize red hardcover, 128 pages, illustrated by W. T. Mars. $12.00

SHACKCLOTH, Irene
Muddles of Mugwumpia, 1951 Hallcraft Publishing, first edition, hardcover. ($40.00 with dust jacket) $20.00

SHAHN, Ben
Maximus of Tyre, 1964 Pantheon, first edition, oblong hardcover. ($25.00 with dust jacket) $15.00

SHANE, Harold G. and **Kathleen B. HESTER**
Doorways to Adventure, 1966 Third Grade Reader, Laidlaw, hardcover, 191 pages, illustrations by Mary Miller Salem. $10.00
Stories to Remember, 1960 First Grade Reader, Laidlaw, hardcover, illustrations by Mary Miller Salem. $10.00

SHANNON, Terry
Trip to Quebec, 1963 Children's Press, first edition, hardcover, 32 pages, color illustrations by Charles Payzant. ($15.00 with dust jacket) $10.00

SHAPIRO, Irwin
Golden Book of America. Stories from our Country's Past, 1957 Simon & Schuster, first edition, hardcover, color and b/w photos. $15.00
Tall Tales of America, 1958 Guild Press, hardcover. $10.00
Twice Upon a Time, 1973 Weekly Reader edition, pictorial hardcover. $10.00

SHAPP, Martha and Charles
Let's Find Out What Electricity Does, 1975 Franklin Watts, revised edition, color illustrations by Leonard Shortall. $25.00

SHAROFF, Victor
Garbage Can Cat, 1969 Westminster Press, illustrated hardcover, illustrated by Howard N. Watson. ($15.00 with dust jacket) $10.00

SHARP, Margery, see Series section RESCUERS
Lost at the Fair, 1965 Little Brown, first edition, hardcover, illustrated by Rosalind Fry. ($35.00 with dust jacket) $15.00
Lost Chapel Picnic and Other Stories, 1973 Heinemann, first edition, hardcover. ($20.00 with dust jacket) $10.00
Magical Cockatoo, 1974 Heinemann, first edition, slim hardcover, line drawings by Faith Jaques. ($25.00 with dust jacket) $15.00
Martha, Eric and George, 1964 Little Brown, first edition, hardcover. ($20.00 with dust jacket) $10.00
Melisande, 1960 Little, Brown, first edition, hardcover, illustrated by Roy McKie. ($30.00 with dust jacket) $15.00
Rosa, 1970 Little Brown, first edition, hardcover. ($20.00 with dust jacket) $10.00

SHAW, Dick
Liberated Latin, 1951 Doubleday, first edition, hardcover, cartoon illustrations by O. Soglow. ($35.00 with dust jacket) $20.00

SHAW, Evelyn
Fish Out of School, 1970 Harper, first edition, glossy pictorial hardcover. ($20.00 with dust jacket) $10.00

SHAW, Richard
Owl Book, 1970 Warne, first edition, hardcover, 48 pages, illustrated by numerous artists. ($15.00 with dust jacket) $10.00

SHECTER, Ben
Across the Meadow, 1973 Doubleday, first edition, oversize hardcover, 30 pages, color illustrations. ($20.00 with dust jacket) $10.00

SHEEHY, Emma Dickson
Molly and the Golden Wedding, 1956 Henry Holt, first edition, hardcover, illustrated by Robert Henneberger. ($20.00 with dust jacket) $10.00

SHELDON, Ann, see Series section LINDA CRAIG

SHELDON, William D. and **Mary C. AUSTIN**
Fields and Fences, 1963 Allyn and Bacon, reader, hardcover, illustrated. $20.00
Magic Windows, 1963 Allyn and Bacon, hardcover, third grade reader, 272 pages. $10.00
Story Caravan, 1957 Allyn and Bacon, hardcover, illustrated. $15.00

SHEPARD, Ernest
Betsy and Joe, 1967 Metheun, first edition UK, grey hardcover with gilt, 78 pages, illustrated by author. ($40.00 with dust jacket) $20.00
Betsy and Joe, 1967 Dutton, first American edition, hardcover, illustrated by author. ($20.00 with dust jacket) $10.00

SHEPARD, Fern
Ozark Nurse, 1965 Arcadia House, hardcover. $15.00

SHERBURNE, Zoa
Almost April, 1965 Morrow, hardcover. ($15.00 with dust jacket) $10.00
Jennifer, 1959 Morrow, hardcover. ($15.00 with dust jacket) $10.00

SHERET, Rene
Dutch and the Jewel Robbers, 1973 Bobbs-Merrill, first edition, hardcover. ($30.00 with dust jacket) $10.00

SHERLOCK, Philip
West Indian Folk-Tales, 1966 Walck, first American edition, hardcover, illustrated by Joan Kiddell-Monro. ($20.00 with dust jacket) $10.00

SHERLOCK, Philip and Hilary
Ears and Tails and Common Sense, 1974 Crowell, first edition, hardcover, 124 pages, illustrated by Alika. ($25.00 with dust jacket) $15.00

SHERMAN, Alan
I Can't Dance, 1964 Harper and Row, first edition, hardcover, illustrated by Syd Hoff. ($20.00 with dust jacket) $15.00

SHERRILL, Dorothy
Santa Claus Bears, 1952 Crowell, first edition, small, illustrated. ($30.00 with dust jacket)

SHERWAN, Earl
Mask: The Door County Coon, 1963 Norton, first edition, oversize hardcover, 122 pages, illustrated by author. ($15.00 with dust jacket) $10.00

SHIPPEN, Katherine
Bridle for Pegasus, 1951 Viking, first edition, hardcover, illustrated by C. B. Falls, ($25.00 with dust jacket) $15.00

SHIRLEY TEMPLE BOOKS, see TEMPLE, Shirley

SHOTWELL, Louisa
Roosevelt Grady, 1963 World, first edition, hardcover. ($25.00 with dust jacket) $10.00

SHOWALTER, Jean B.
Around the Corner, 1966 Doubleday, first edition, oversize hardcover picture book, color and b/w illustrations by Roger Duvoisin. ($30.00 with dust jacket) $15.00

SHOWERS, Paul
In The Night, 1961 Crowell, "Let's Read and Find Out Book", hardcover, illustrated by Ezra Jack Keats. ($30.00 with dust jacket) $15.00

SHULEVITZ, Uri
Dawn, 1974 Farrar, Straus, first edition, hardcover, illustrated by author. ($30.00 with dust jacket) $15.00
Magician, 1973 Macmillan, first edition, hardcover, b/w illustrations by Shulevitz. ($35.00 with dust jacket) $15.00
Oh What A Noise!, 1971 Macmillan, first edition, hardcover, color illustrations by Shulevitz. ($45.00 with dust jacket) $20.00

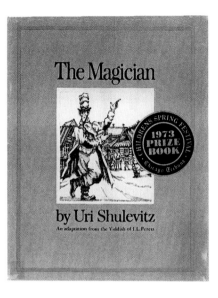

SHURA, Mary
Nearsighted Knight, 1964 Alfred A. Knopf, first edition, hardcover, illustrated by Adrienne Adams. ($20.00 with dust jacket) $10.00
Shoefull of Shamrock, 1965 Atheneum, hardcover, illustrated by Shura. ($20.00 with dust jacket) $10.00
Riddle of Raven's Gulch, 1975 Dodd, Mead, Weekly Reader series, hardcover, illustrated by Salem Tamer. $10.00
Valley of the Frost Giants, 1971 Lothrop, Lee & Shepard, first edition, hardcover, illustrated by Charles Keeping. ($25.00 with dust jacket) $15.00

SHURTLEFF, Bertrand
Colt of the Alican Road, 1951 Bobbs-Merrill, first edition, hardcover, 266 pages. ($30.00 with dust jacket) $15.00
Flying Footballs, 1951 Bobbs-Merrill, first edition, hardcover. ($20.00 with dust jacket) $10.00

SHUTTLESWORTH, Dorothy
Ecology Story, 1973 Doubleday, hardcover, illustrated by author. ($15.00 with dust jacket) $10.00

SICELOFF, David
Boy Settler in the Cherokee Strip, 1964 Caxton Printers, Ltd.; blue hardcover, map end papers, 249 pages, color frontispiece and 38 b/w illustrations by Alfred C. Dunn. ($20.00 with dust jacket) $10.00

SILLIMAN, Leland
Golden Cloud: Palomino of Sunset Hill, 1950 Winston, Toronto, first edition, hardcover. ($40.00 with dust jacket) $20.00

SILVERSTEIN, Shel
Giving Tree, 1964 Harper, hardcover, illustrated by

author. First edition with dust jacket: $50.00. Later editions: ($20.00 with dust jacket) $15.00

Lafcadio: The Lion Who Shot Back, 1963 Harper, hardcover, illustrated by author. First edition with dust jacket: $40.00. Later editions: ($20.00 with dust jacket) $15.00

L'Arbre Au Grand Coeur, (Giving Tree)1973 Harper, first French edition, hardcover, translated by Hila Feil. $40.00

Where the Sidewalk Ends, 1974 Harper, hardcover, b/w illustrations by author. First edition with dust jacket: $40.00. Later editions: ($20.00 with dust jacket) $15.00

SIMISTER, Florence Parker
Daniel and Drum Rock, 1963 Hastings House, hardcover, 128 pages. ($15.00 with dust jacket) $10.00

SIMMONS, Ellie
Wheels, 1968 McKay, first edition, small yellow hardcover, 26 pages, brown/white illustrations, picture book, no text. ($20.00 with dust jacket) $10.00

SIMON, Hilda
Young Pathfinder's Book of Snakes, 1963 Hart Publishing, first edition, hardcover, illustrated. ($30.00 with dust jacket) $15.00

SIMON, Leonard
Counting Lightly, 1964 Holt, pictorial hardcover, illustrated by Ted Schroeder. ($20.00 with dust jacket) $10.00

SIMON, Norma
Up and Over the Hill, 1957 Lippincott, first edition, hardcover, illustrated by Garry MacKenzie. ($15.00 with dust jacket) $10.00

SIMONT, Marc
Afternoon in Spain, 1965 Morrow, hardcover, color illustrations by author. ($20.00 with dust jacket) $10.00

Child's Eye View of the World, 1972 Delacorte, first edition, hardcover, 2-color illustrations by author. ($20.00 with dust jacket) $10.00

Contest at Paca, 1959 Harpers, first edition, hardcover, 60 pages. ($20.00 with dust jacket) $10.00

Opera Souffle, 1950 Henry Schuman, first edition, hardcover, decorated endpapers, illustrated by author. ($50.00 with dust jacket) $30.00

Polly's Oats, 1951 Harper, first edition, hardcover, illustrated by author. ($30.00 with dust jacket) $15.00

SIMPSON, Dorothy
Lesson for Janie, 1958 Lippincott, first edition, blue hardcover, illustrated endpapers, frontispiece. $15.00

SINCLAIR, Kenneth L.
Mystery Mine, 1951 Winston, first edition, hardcover, b/w illustrations by Sidney A. Quinn. ($25.00 with dust jacket) $10.00

SINGER, Isaac Bashevis
Alone in the Wild Forest, 1971 Farrar, first edition, hardcover, 80 pages, illustrations Margot Zemech. ($40.00 with dust jacket) $20.00

Elijah the Slave, 1970 Farrar, Straus and Giroux, first edition, oversize hardcover, illustrated by Antonio Frasconi. ($60.00 with dust jacket) $30.00

Fools of Chelm and Their History, 1973 Farrar, first edition, red hardcover, illustrated by Uri Shulevitz. ($30.00 with dust jacket) $15.00

Joseph and Koza, 1970 Farrar, first edition, hardcover, illustrated by Symeon Shimin. ($50.00 with dust jacket) $20.00

Mazel and Shllimazel, 1967 Farrar, first edition, hardcover, illustrated by Margot Zemach. ($30.00 with dust jacket) $15.00

Topsy-Turvy Emperor of China, 1971 Harper, first edition, hardcover, illustrated by William Pene DuBois. ($40.00 with dust jacket) $20.00

When Schemiel Went to Warsaw and Other Stories, 1968 Farrar, first edition, hardcover, illustrated by Margot Zemach. ($20.00 with dust jacket) $10.00

Zlateh the Goat and Other Stories, ca. 1966 Harper, first edition, hardcover, 90 pages, illustrated by Maurice Sendak. ($40.00 with dust jacket) $20.00

SINNICKSON, Tom
Child's Book of Planes, ca. 1950s Caxton Publishers, laminated illustrated hardcover, illustrated endpapers, illustrations. $15.00

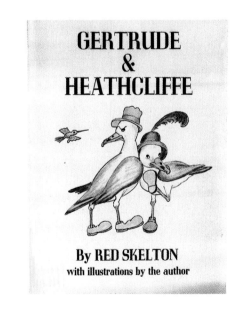

SKELTON, Red
Gertrude & Heathcliffe, 1974 Charles Scribner,

first edition, hardcover, 60 pages, b/w and color illustrations by author. $100.00 with dust jacket.

SLAUGHTER, Jean,
Horsemanship for Beginners: Riding, Jumping, and Schooling, 1952 Knopf, first edition, hardcover, illustrated. ($15.00 with dust jacket) $10.00

SLEATOR, William
Among the Dolls, 1975 Dutton, hardcover, illustrations Trina Schart Hyman. ($30.00 with dust jacket) $15.00
Blackbriar, 1972 Dutton, first edition, hardcover, 212 pages. ($20.00 with dust jacket) $10.00

SLEIGH, Barbara
Carbonel: King of Cats, (1955 Parrish), ca. 1957 Bobbs Merrill, illustrated by V. H. Drummond, hard-to-find. First American edition: ($175.00 with dust jacket) $135.00
Kingdom of Carbonel, 1960 edition Clarke Irwin, Canada, (also Bobbs-Merrill, first American edition,) illustrations by D.M. Leonard & Stephen P. Haas. ($150.00 with dust jacket) $75.00
No One Must Know, 1962 Bobbs-Merrill, first American edition, hardcover, illustrations by Jillian Willett. ($40.00 with dust jacket) $20.00
North of Nowhere, 1966 Coward-McCann, first American edition, hardcover, b/w illustrations. First edition with dust jacket: $90.00. Later editions: ($20.00 with dust jacket) $10.00
Stirabout Stories, 1972 Bobbs-Merrill, first American edition, hardcover. ($30.00 with dust jacket) $15.00

SLEPIANI, Jan.
Lester and the Sea Monster, 1964 Follett, hardcover, 32 pages, color illustrations by Richard E. Martin. $25.00

SLOANE, Eric
Cracker Barrel, 1967 Funk, first edition, oversize hardcover, 109 pages, illustrated by author. ($40.00 with dust jacket) $20.00
Our Vanishing Landscape, 1955 Funk, first edition, oversize hardcover, 107 pages, illustrated by author. $40.00

SLOANE, William
Space Space Space, 1953 Grosset, hardcover. ($20.00 with dust jacket) $10.00

SLOBODKIN, Florence
Sarah Somebody, 1969 Vanguard Press, first edition, hardcover, illustrated by Louis Slobodkin. ($20.00 with dust jacket) $10.00

SLOBODKIN, Louis
Colette and the Princess, 1965 Dutton, first edi-

tion, hardcover, illustrated by author. ($25.00 with dust jacket) $10.00
Excuse Me! Certainly, 1959 Vanguard, oblong hardcover, illustrated by author. ($30.00 with dust jacket) $10.00
Gogo, the French Sea Gull, 1960 Macmillan, first edition, oversize hardcover, illustrated by author. ($30.00 with dust jacket) $15.00
Late Cuckoo, 1962 Vanguard, first edition, oversize hardcover, color illustrations by author. ($35.00 with dust jacket) $15.00
Luigi and the Long-Nosed Soldier, 1963 Macmillan, first edition, hardcover, illustrated by author. ($30.00 with dust jacket) $15.00
Melvin the Moose Child, 1957 Macmillan, first edition, hardcover, color illustrations by author. ($40.00 with dust jacket) $20.00
Moon Blossom and the Golden Penny, 1963 Vanguard, hardcover, illustrated by author. ($30.00 with dust jacket) $15.00
One Is Good But Two Are Better, 1956 Vanguard, oversize hardcover, illustrated by author. ($35.00 with dust jacket) $15.00
Polka-Dot Goat, 1964 Macmillan, first edition, hardcover, color illustrations by author. ($20.00 with dust jacket) $10.00
Space Ship in the Park, 1972 Macmillan, first edition, hardcover, 168 pages, illustrated by author. ($30.00 with dust jacket) $10.00
Thank You, You're Welcome, 1957 Vanguard, oblong hardcover, color illustrations by author. ($30.00 with dust jacket) $15.00
Up High and Down Low, 1960 Macmillan, first edition, hardcover, illustrated by author. ($30.00 with dust jacket) $15.00
Wilbur and the Warrior, 1972 Vanguard, first edition, hardcover, 40 pages, illustrated by author. ($30.00 with dust jacket) $15.00
Yasu and the Strangers, 1965 Macmillan, first edition, oversize hardcover, color illustrations by author. ($35.00 with dust jacket) $15.00

SLOBODKINA, Esphyr
Flame, the Breeze, and the Shadow, 1969 Rand McNally, first edition, oversize orange decorated hardcover. ($30.00 with dust jacket) $15.00
Pezzo the Peddler and the Circus Elephant, 1967 edition Abelard, oversize hardcover picture book, illustrated by author. $20.00

SMILEY, Lavinia
Mr. Snodgrass's Holiday, 1958 Faber, first edition, oversize oblong hardcover, illustrated by author. ($20.00 with dust jacket) $10.00

SMILEY, Minerva
Billy's Search for Florida Undersea Treasure, 1954 Mercury Publications, Miami, first edition, oversize pictorial hardcover, 42 pages, illustrated by Russ Smiley. $15.00

SMITH, Agnes
Edge of the Forest, 1962 Viking Press, hardcover. $10.00

SMITH, Charles
Animal Fare, 1962 Garrett & Massie, first edition, hardcover picture book, wood block paintings, black and gray tones on yellow background, illustrated by author. ($40.00 with dust jacket) $20.00

SMITH, Dodie
Hundred and One Dalmatians, 1957 Viking, first American edition, green hardcover, illustrations by Janet and Anne Grahame-Johnstone. First edition with dust jacket: $300.00. Later editions: ($20.00 with dust jacket) $10.00
Starlight Barking, 1967 Heinemann, London, hardcover, 145 pages, illustrated by Janet and Anne Grahame-Johnstone. First UK edition with dust jacket: $65.00. Later editions: ($20.00 with dust jacket) $10.00
Starlight Barking, 1967 Simon and Schuster, first American edition, hardcover, illustrated by Janet and Anne Grahame-Johnstone First edition with dust jacket: $100.00. Later editions: ($20.00 with dust jacket) $10.00

SMITH, Doris Buchanan
Taste of Blackberries, 1973 Crowell, first edition, hardcover, illustrated by Charles Robinson. ($20.00 with dust jacket) $10.00

SMITH, Dorothy Hall
Tall Book of Christmas, 1954 Harper, first edition, tall hardcover, color illustrations by Gertrude Elliott Espenscheid. ($75.00 with dust jacket) $30.00

SMITH, E. Brooks and **MEREDITH, Robert**
Coming of the Pilgrims Told from Governor Bradford's

Firsthand Account, 1964 Little Brown, first edition, oversize oblong hardcover, illustrated by Leonard Everett Fisher. ($25.00 with dust jacket) $15.00

SMITH, Edesse Perry
Pokes of Gold, 1958 Dodd, Mead, first edition, 210 pages, hardcover, illustrated by Gerald McCann. ($20.00 with dust jacket) $10.00

SMITH, Emma
Emily's Voyage, 1966 Harcourt Brace, small hardcover, illustrated by Irene Haas, further adventures of Miss Emily Guinea-Pig. ($20.00 with dust jacket) $10.00
Emily, 1959 Thomas Nelson Ltd., first edition, red hardcover, illustrated endpapers, 8 color plates plus b/w illustrations by Katherine Wigglesworth. ($50.00 with dust jacket) $20.00

SMITH, Eunice Young
Jennifer Prize, 1951 Bobbs-Merrill, first edition, blue hardcover with gilt letters, 263 pages, b/w illustrations by author. ($20.00 with dust jacket) $10.00

SMITH, Kate
Kate Smith Stories of Annabelle, 1951 Tell Well Press, hardcover, illustrations by Bill and Bernard Martin, based on the original Annabelle stories by Jane Gale. ($40.00 with dust jacket) $20.00

SMITH, Mary Rowell
Of Course You Can, A Book of Rhymes for the Young, 1953 Exposition Press, first edition, blue hardcover, illustrated by George Hitt. ($25.00 with dust jacket) $15.00

SMITH, Robert Paul
Another Thing and Another Thing, 1959 Norton, first edition, hardcover, illustrated. ($15.00 with dust jacket) $10.00
How To Do Nothing With Nobody All Alone By Yourself, 1958 Norton, first edition, hardcover, 125 pages, illustrated by Elinor Goulding Smith. ($15.00 with dust jacket) $10.00

SMITH, Vian
Lord Mayor's Show, 1969 Doubleday, hardcover, 231 pages. ($20.00 with Sam Savitt dust jacket) $10.00

SMITH, William Jay
Laughing Time, 1955 Little, Brown, first edition, hardcover, color illustrations by Juliet Kepes. ($40.00 with dust jacket) $20.00
Puptents and Pebbles, a Nonsense ABC, 1959 Atlantic Monthly, first edition, oversize hardcover, 32 pages, color illustrations by Juliet Kepes. ($25.00 with dust jacket) $15.00

Typewriter Town, 1960 Dutton, first edition, over-size hardcover, 32 pages, b/w and color illustrations. ($45.00 with dust jacket) $25.00

SMUCKER, Barbara
Wigwam in the City, 1966 Dutton, first edition, hardcover, woodcut illustrations. ($20.00 with dust jacket) $10.00

SMYTHE, Pat, see Series section THREE JAYS
Jacqueline Rides for a Fall, 1957 Cassell, first edition, hardcover. ($15.00 with dust jacket) $8.00

SNEDEKER, Carolyn Dale
Theras and His Town, 1961 Doubleday 1961, hardcover, 238 pages. ($40.00 with dust jacket) $20.00

SNELLING, Lois
Secret of the Red Gourd, 1961 Funk & Wagnalls, first edition, hardcover. ($25.00 with dust jacket) $10.00
Treasure in the Valley, 1958 Funk & Wagnalls, first edition, hardcover. ($25.00 with dust jacket) $10.00
Yellow Cup Mystery, 1963 Funk & Wagnalls, first edition, hardcover. ($25.00 with dust jacket) $10.00

SNOW, Dorothea
Charmed Circle, 1964 Whitman, pictorial hardcover. $10.00
Circus Boy, War on Wheels, 1964 Whitman, pictorial hardcover. $20.00
Come, Chucky, Come, 1952 Houghton Mifflin, first edition, hardcover, illustrated by Joshua Tolford. ($30.00 with dust jacket) $15.00
Secret of the Stone Frog, 1959 Bobbs-Merrill, first edition, hardcover. ($15.00 with dust jacket) $10.00
That Certain Girl, 1964 Whitman, pictorial hardcover. $10.00

SNYDER, Agnes
Old Man on Our Block, 1964 Holt, small oblong hardcover, picture book, illustrations by Donald Lynch. $15.00
First Step, 1975 Holt, first edition, hardcover. ($15.00 with dust jacket) $8.00

SNYDER, Louis L.
First Book of World War 2, 1958 Franklin Watts, hardcover. ($20.00 with dust jacket) $10.00

SNYDER, Zilpha Keatley
Below the Root, 1975 Atheneum, first edition, hardcover, b/w illustrations by Alton Raible. ($40.00 with dust jacket) $20.00
Black and Blue Magic, 1966 Atheneum, first edition, hardcover, illustrated by Gene Holtan. ($30.00 with dust jacket) $15.00

Egypt Game, 1967 Atheneum, illustrated hardcover, b/w illustrations by Alton Raible. ($30.00 with dust jacket) $10.00
Truth about Stone Hollow, 1974 Atheneum, first edition, hardcover. ($30.00 with dust jacket) $15.00
Velvet Room, 1965 Atheneum, first edition, hardcover, 183 pages, illustrated by Alton Raible. ($50.00 with dust jacket) $20.00
Witches of Worm, 1972 Atheneum, first edition, hardcover, 183 pages, illustrated by Alton Raible. ($40.00 with dust jacket) $20.00

SOBOL, Donald, see Series section ENCYCLOPEDIA BROWN

SOEMER, Cecelia
Story of Maximilian the Mouse Who Went to School, 1956 David McKay, first American edition, hardcover. ($15.00 with dust jacket) $10.00

SOFTLY, Barbara
Magic People, 1966 Oliver & Boyd, London, first edition, green hardcover, 48 pages, two-tone text illustrations throughout by Gunvor Edwards. ($15.00 with dust jacket) $10.00

SOLBERT, Ronni
Song That Sings Itself, 1972 Bobbs-Merrill, first edition, hardcover, brown/orange illustrations by author. ($15.00 with dust jacket) $10.00

SOLLERS, Allan
Fox Story, 1963 Holt, first edition, illustrated hardcover, illustrated by William Reusswig. $15.00

SOMMERFELT, Aimee
My Name Is Pablo, 1966 Criterion Books, Young Amer-

ica Book Club edition, pictorial hardcover. $10.00
Road to Agra, 1962 Criterion Books, Weekly Reader edition, illustrated hardcover. $10.00

SONNEBORN, RUTH
Question and Answer Book of Space, 1965 Random House, hardcover. $10.00

SOPER, Eileen
Song of Lambert Mazo de la Roche, 1955 Macmillan, first edition, hardcover, illustrated by author. ($25.00 with dust jacket) $15.00
Wild Encounters, 1959 Routledge, first edition, hardcover, illustrated by Eileen Soper. $25.00
Wild Favours, 1963 Hutchinson, London, first edition, hardcover, b/w illustrations by author. ($30.00 with dust jacket) $15.00

SOREL, Edward
Making the World Safe for Hypocrisy, Swallow Press, first edition, oversize hardcover, color and black and white illustrations. ($30.00 with dust jacket) $20.00

SORENSEN, Virginia
Miracles on Maple Hill, 1956 Harcourt, Brace, hardcover, illustrated by Beth and Joe Krush. (1957 Newbery Award winner) ($25.00 with dust jacket) $15.00

SOTOMAYOR, Antonio
Kasha Goes to the Fiesta, 1967 Doubleday, first edition, orange hardcover. ($30.00 with dust jacket) $20.00

SOULE, Jean and **Nancy SCUTTLE**
Stowaway Mouse, 1969 Parents' Magazine, first edition, oblong hardcover, illustrated by Barbara Remington. ($35.00 with dust jacket) $15.00

SOUTHALL, Ivan, see Series section SIMON BLACK
Head in the Clouds, 1972 A&R, London, square oversize hardcover, illustrated by Richard Kennedy. $15.00
Let the Balloon Go, 1968 St. Martin's Press, red hardcover, illustrated by Ian Ribbons. ($15.00 with dust jacket) $10.00

SPARK, Muriel
Very Fine Clock, 1968 Alfred Knopf, first edition, hardcover, illustrated by Edward Gorey. ($80.00 with dust jacket) $25.00

SPARKS, Enid
Dana's Date with Trouble and Other True Stories, 1960 Southern Publishing, hardcover, illustrated by Vance Locke. $10.00

SPARROW, Gerald
No Other Elephant, 1962 Adventurers Club, London, hardcover, 192 pages. ($15.00 with dust jacket) $10.00

SPEARE, Elizabeth George
Bronze Bow, 1961 Houghton Mifflin, first edition, hardcover, 254 pages. ($20.00 with dust jacket) $10.00

SPEEVACK, Yetta
Spider Plant, 1965 Antheneum, first edition, hardcover. ($15.00 with dust jacket) $10.00

SPELLMAN, John W.
Beautiful Blue Jay and Other Tales of India, 1967 Little, Brown, first edition, hardcover, Jerry Pinkney. ($25.00 with dust jacket) $10.00

SPENCER, Ann
Cat Who Tasted Cinnamon Toast, 1968 Alfred A. Knopf, first edition, oversize hardcover, 70 pages. ($25.00 with dust jacket) $15.00

SPERRY, Armstrong
Great River, Wide Land, 1967 Macmillan, first edition, hardcover, color illustrations by author. ($20.00 with dust jacket) $10.00
South of Cape Horn: A Saga of Nat Palmer and Early Antarctic Exploration, 1958 Winston, first edition, hardcover, 180 pages, b/w illustrations by author. ($15.00 with dust jacket) $10.00

SPICER, Dorothy Gladys
Kneeling Tree, 1971 Coward-McCann, first edition, hardcover, illustrated by Barbara Morrow. ($25.00 with dust jacket) $10.00
Thirteen Devils, 1967 Coward-McCann, first edition, hardcover, illustrated by Sofia. ($15.00 with dust jacket) $10.00
Thirteen Ghosts, 1965 Coward-McCann, first edition, hardcover, illustrated by Sofia. ($20.00 with dust jacket) $10.00

161

SPIER, Peter
Hurrah, We're Outward Bound!, 1968 Garden City, first edition, small oblong hardcover, 41 pages, illustrated by Peter Spier. ($30.00 with dust jacket) $20.00
London Bridge Is Falling Down, 1967 Doubleday, oblong pictorial hardcover, illustrated by author. ($25.00 with dust jacket) $15.00
Star Spangled Banner, 1973 Garden City, first edition, oversize hardcover, illustrated by Spier, includes a poster. ($55.00 with poster and dust jacket) Book only: $15.00

SPILKA, Arnold
And the Frog Went Blah, 1972 Charles Scribner, first edition, hardcover, illustrated by Arnold Spilka ($30.00 with dust jacket) $15.00
Rumbudgin of Nonsense, 1970 Charles Scribner, first edition, hardcover. ($20.00 with dust jacket) $10.00

SPILLMAN, Ron and **RAMSAY, Jack**
Kittens on the Keys, 1961 Longmans, first edition, hardcover, photo illustrations. ($40.00 with dust jacket) $20.00

SPINK, Reginald
Hans Christian Andersen and His World, 1972 Thames & Hudson, London, first edition, square hardcover, 128 pages, photos, drawings, facsimiles throughout. ($30.00 with dust jacket) $15.00

SPOONER, Glenda
Silk Purse, 1953 Cassell, first edition, hardcover. ($25.00 with dust jacket) $15.00

SPRINKLE, Rebecca K.
Parakeet Peter, 1958 Rand McNally, hardcover, illustrated by Dorothy Grider. $10.00

SPYKMAN, E. C.
Edie on the Warpath, 1966 Harcourt, Brace, first edition, hardcover. ($30.00 with dust jacket) $15.00

STACK, Nicolete Meredith
Corky's Hiccups, 1968 Golden Press, hardcover, illustrated by Tom Sullivan. $15.00
King and Kerry Fair, 1960 Crowell, hardcover, illustrated by Nanny Hogrogrian. ($20.00 with dust jacket) $10.00
Milestone Summer, 1962 Whitman, hardcover, illustrated by Arnold Kohn. $15.00
Pierre of the Island, 1954 Bruce, hardcover, illustrated by Gertrude Williamson. $15.00
Rainbow Tomorrow, 1956 Bruce, hardcover, illustrated by George Pllard. $15.00
Two to Get Ready, 1953 Caxton, hardcover, illustrated by Gertrude Williamson. ($25.00 with dust jacket) $10.00

STAFFORD, Jean
Elphi, the Cat with the High IQ, 1962 Farrar, first edition, hardcover, illustrated by Eric Blegvad. ($75.00 with dust jacket) $30.00

STAFFORD, Kay
Ling Tang and the Lucky Cricket, 1964 Whittlesey House, hardcover, illustrated by Louise Zibold.($20.00 with dust jacket) $10.00

STAGG, James
Castle for the Kopcheks, 1964 Macmillan, first edition, hardcover. ($15.00 with dust jacket) $10.00

STAHL, Ben
Blackbeard's Ghost, 1965 Houghton, first edition, hardcover, illustrations by author. ($50.00 with dust jacket) $20.00
Secret of Red Skull (sequel to *Blackbeard's Ghost*), 1971 Houghton. first edition, hardcover. ($40.00 with dust jacket) $20.00

STAHL, P.J
Poor Minette, The Letters of Two French Cats, 1954 Rodale, first American edition, small hardcover, 41 pages, color illustrations by Grandville. $20.00

STANDER, Siegfried
Horse, 1969 edition World Publishing, gold hardcover, illustrated by Victor Ambrus. ($15.00 with dust jacket) $10.00

STANDON, Anna and **Edward**
Three Little Cats, Trois Petits Chats, 1967 Delacorte, first American edition, square oversize hardcover, illustrated. ($20.00 with dust jacket) $15.00

STANLEY-WRENCH, Margaret
Silver King, 1966 Hawthorn Books, first edition, hardcover. ($15.00 with dust jacket) $10.00

STANOVSKY, Vladislav
Fairy Tale Tree, 1961 Putnam, oversize hardcover, 452 pages, color illustrations by by Stanislav Kolibal. $50.00

STEELE, Mary Q.
Journey Outside, 1969 Viking, first edition, 144 pages, woodcut illustrations by Rocco Negri. ($35.00 with dust jacket) $15.00

STEELE, William O.
Davy Crockett's Earthquake, 1956 Harcourt Brace, first

edition, hardcover. ($20.00 with dust jacket) $10.00

Far Frontier, 1961 Harcourt Brace, Weekly Reader hardcover, illustrated by Paul Galdone. ($15.00 with dust jacket) $10.00

Flaming Arrows, 1957 Harcourt Brace, first edition, hardcover, illustrations. ($15.00 with dust jacket) $10.00

Trail Through Danger, 1965 Harcourt Brace, Young America Book Club edition, red hardcover, illustrated by Charles Beck. $10.00

Wilderness Journey, 1953 Harcourt Brace, hardcover, illustrated by Paul Galdone. $10.00

STEEN, Marguerite

Little White King, 1956 World Publishing, first edition, hardcover. ($25.00 with dust jacket) $10.00

STEIG, William

Abel's Island, 1976 Farrar, first edition, hardcover, illustrated by author, Newbery Medal winner. ($50.00 with dust jacket) $25.00

Agony in the Kindergarten, 1950 Duell, Sloan & Pearce, first edition, oversize hardcover, illustrated by author. ($50.00 with dust jacket) $20.00

Amos and Boris, 1971 Farrar, Straus & Giroux, first edition, hardcover, illustrated by author. ($20.00 with dust jacket) $10.00

Bad Speller, 1970 Simon & Schuster, first edition, hardcover, illustrated by author. ($30.00 with dust jacket) $15.00

C D B!, 1968 Simon & Schuster, yellow hardcover, small, puzzle book. ($20.00 with dust jacket) $10.00

Dominic, 1972 Farrar, first edition, hardcover, illustrated by author. ($40.00 with dust jacket) $20.00

Farmer Palmer's Wagon Ride, 1974 Farrar, first edition, oversize hardcover, illustrated by author. ($50.00 with dust jacket) $20.00

Real Thief, 1973 Farrar, first edition, red hardcover, 58 pages, b/w illustrations by author. ($60.00 with dust jacket) $25.00

STEINER, Alexis

Wild Duck, 1960 Franklin Watts, hardcover, full- and double-page color illustrations by Wilhelm Jaruska. ($20.00 with dust jacket) $15.00

STEINER, Charlotte

Bobby Follows the Butterfly, 1959 Macmillan, first edition, hardcover, illustrated endpapers, illustrated by author. ($20.00 with dust jacket) $10.00

I'd Rather Stay with You, 1965 Seabury Press, hardcover, color illustrations. $15.00

Red Riding Hood Goes Sledding, 1962 Macmillan, first edition, oversize hardcover, 27 pages. ($35.00 with dust jacket) $20.00

Red Riding Hood's Little Lamb, 1964 Knopf, color illustrations by the author. $15.00

Timmy Needs a Thinking Cap, 1961 Macmillan, first edition, hardcover. ($15.00 with dust jacket) $10.00

Tomboy's Doll, 1969 Lothrop Lee, oversize hardcover, illustrated by author. ($20.00 with dust jacket) $15.00

STEINMETZ-ROSS, Eulalie, editor

Blue Rose, 1966 Harcourt, collection of short stories, blue hardcover, 186 pages, b/w illustrations by Enrico Arno. ($20.00 with dust jacket) $10.00

STEPHENS, Mary Jo

Witch of the Cumberlands. 1974 Houghton Mifflin, first edition, hardcover, 243 pages, illustrated by Arvis Stewart. ($25.00 with dust jacket) $15.00

Zoe's Zodiac, 1971 Houghton Mifflin, first edition, hardcover, illustrated by Leonard Shortall. ($35.00 with dust jacket) $20.00

STEPTOE, John
Birthday, 1972 Holt, first edition, hardcover, illustrated by author. ($50.00 with dust jacket) $20.00
Stevie, 1969 Harper, pictorial hardcover, first edition, color illustrations by author. ($45.00 with dust jacket) $$20.00
Uptown, 1970 Harper, first edition, pictorial paper-covered hardcover. ($85.00 with dust jacket) $30.00

STERLING, Dorothy
Captain of the Planter: The Story of Robert Smalls, 1958 Doubleday, first edition, hardcover, illustrated by Ernest Crichlow. ($25.00 with dust jacket) $15.00
Fall Is here!, 1966 American Museum of Natural History, first edition, oversize hardcover, 96 pages, illustrated in color by Winifred Lubell. $20.00
Exploration of Africa, 1963 American Heritage, first edition, pictorial boards. $15.00

STERLING, Stewart
Kick of the Wheel, 1957 Prentice Hall, first edition, hardcover. ($20.00 with dust jacket) $10.00

STERNE, Emma Gelders
King Arthur and the Knights of the Round Table, 1966 Golden Press, first edition, decorated hardcover, 140 pages, illustrated by Gustaf Tenggren. $35.00
Long Black Schooner: The Voyage of the Amistad, 1968 Follett, first edition, hardcover, 192 pages. ($20.00 with dust jacket) $10.00

STEVENSON, James
Bear Who Had No Place to Go, 1972 Harper & Row, first edition, hardcover. ($25.00 with dust jacket) $10.00
Here Comes Herb's Hurricane!, 1973 Harper, first edition, small hardcover, b/w illustrations by author. ($30.00 with dust jacket) $15.00
If I Owned a Candy Factory, 1968 Greenwillow, first edition, illustrated by author. $20.00

STEVENSON, William
Bushbabies, 1965 Houghton Mifflin, hardcover. ($25.00 with dust jacket) $10.00

STEWART, Fiona
My Best Wild Animal Book, 1975 Dean & Son, illustrated hardcover. $25.00

STEWART, Mary
Crystal Cave, 1970 Morrow, first American edition, hardcover, illustrated by Gino d'Achille. ($20.00 with dust jacket) $10.00
Little Broomstick, 1972 Morrow, hardcover, 192 pages, b/w illustrations by Shirley Hughes. Wrap-around illustration on dust jacket. ($35.00 with dust jacket) $15.00
Ludo and the Star Horse, 1975 Morrow, first American edition, hardcover, illustrated by Gino d'Achille. ($20.00 with dust jacket) $10.00

STIRLING, Betty
Julie Otis, Student Nurse, 1956 Pacific Press, first edition, pictorial hardcover. $20.00
Ned of the Navajos, 1962 Pacific Press, first edition, pictorial hardcover, 136 pages, illustrated by James Converse. $20.00
This Is Where They Went, 1959 Pacific Press, pictorial hardcover, illustrated by Joseph Maniscalco. $20.00

STIRLING, Monica
Little Ballet Dancer, 1952 Lothrop, first edition, hardcover, illustrated by Helen Stone. ($25.00 with dust jacket) $15.00

St. JOHN, Wylly
Mystery of the Other Girl, 1971 Viking Press, first edition, hardcover. ($15.00 with dust jacket) $10.00

STOCKTON, Frank
Bee-Man of Orn, 1964 Holt, Rinehart and Winston, first edition thus, hardcover, color illustrations by Maurice Sendak. First edition with dust jacket: $70.00. Later editions: ($20.00 with dust jacket) $15.00
Griffin and the Minor Canon, 1963 Holt, first edition thus, hardcover, illustrated by Maurice Sendak. First edition with dust jacket: $100.00. Later editions: ($20.00 with dust jacket) $15.00
Ting A Ling Tales, 1955 Scribner, first edition thus,

164

hardcover, illustrated by Richard Floethe. ($20.00 with dust jacket) $10.00

STODDARD, Edward
First Book of Magic, 1953 Watts, first edition, hardcover, color illustrations by Robin King. $15.00

STOLZ, M. S.
Dog on Barkham Street, 1961 Harper, hardcover, Weekly Reader Children's Book Club Edition, illustrated by Leonard Shortall. ($20.00 with dust jacket) $10.00

STOLZ, Mary
Beautiful Friend and Other Stories, 1966 Harper, hardcover. ($20.00 with dust jacket) $15.00
Dragons of the Queen, 1969 Harper, illustrated hardcover, illustrated by Edward Frascino. ($20.00 with dust jacket) $10.00
Emmett's Pig, 1959 Harper & Bros., first edition, hardcover, 63 pages, illustrated by Garth Williams. ($40.00 with dust jacket) $20.00
By the Highway Home, 1971 Harper, hardcover, illustrated by Peggy Bacon. ($20.00 with dust jacket) $15.00
In a Mirror, 1953 Harper, first edition, hardcover. ($20.00 with dust jacket) $10.00
Ready or Not, 1953 Harper, first edition, hardcover, 243 pages. ($35.00 with dust jacket) $15.00
Second Nature, 1958 Harper, first edition, hardcover. ($25.00 with dust jacket) $15.00

STONE, Ethel B.
Wild Bill Hickok and the Indians, 1956 Rand McNally, Elfbook, small, hardcover, color illustrations. $10.00

STONE, Eugenia
Magpie Hill, 1958 Watts, first edition, hardcover, 150 pages, illustrated by Alan Moyler. ($25.00 with dust jacket) $15.00

STONE, Patti
Sandra, Surgical Nurse, 1961 Messner, blue pictorial hardcover. $15.00

STONG, Phil
Hirum, the Hillbilly, 1951 Dodd, Mead, hardcover, illustrated by Kurt Wiese. $10.00
Mississippi Pilot: With Mark Twain on the Great River, 1954 Garden City, first edition, hardcover, illustrated endpapers, 253 pages. ($20.00 with dust jacket) $10.00
Prince and the Porker, 1950 Dodd Mead, hardcover, illustrated by Kurt Wiese. First edition with dust jacket: $70.00

STOREY, David
Flight into Camden, 1960 Macmillan, first edition, hardcover. $10.00

STOUTENBURG, Adrien
Crocodile's Mouth, 1966 Viking, first edition, hardcover, b/w drawings by Glen Rounds. ($20.00 with dust jacket) $10.00

STOVER, Jo Ann
Binnies, and the Dogs and Cats from Everywhere, 197 Knopf, first edition, hardcover, 100 pages. ($25.00 with dust jacket) $15.00
Why . . . ? Because, 1961 McKay, hardcover. ($25.00 with dust jacket) $15.00

STOVER, Marjorie
Chad and the Elephant Engine, 1975 Atheneum, Weekly Reader edition, pictorial hardcover. $10.00.
Trail Boss in Pigtails, 1972 Atheneum, first edition, hardcover, 220 pages, illustrated by Lydia Dabcovich. ($20.00 with dust jacket) $10.00

STRANGER, Joyce
Casey, 1968 Harvill Press, London, first edition, hardcover, 190 pages. ($15.00 with dust jacket) $10.00
Paddy Joe, 1971 Collins, London, first edition, hardcover, 158 pages. Dustjacket illustration by Hans Helweg. ($15.00 with dust jacket) $10.00
Running Foxes, 1965 Hammond, London, first edition, hardcover, 127 pages. ($15.00 with dust jacket) $10.00

STREATFEILD, Noel (author of Shoes books)
Ballet Annual, 1959 Collins, first edition, oversize blue hardcover, 128 pages, illustrated, contributors include numerous writers and illustrators. $20.00
By Special Request, 1953 Collins, blue hardcover with gilt, 255 pages, b/w illustrations, short stories. $15.00
Children on the Top Floor, 1965 Random House, first American edition, hardcover. ($25.00 with dust jacket) $15.00
Family at Caldicott Place, 1967 Random, first American edition, pictorial hardcover, illustrated by Betty Maxey. $20.00
First Book of Ballet, 1953 Watts, first edition, hardcover, illustrated by Moses Soyer. ($25.00 with dust jacket) $15.00
Growing Summer, 1966 Collins, first edition, hardcover, illustrated by Edward Ardizzone. ($35.00 with dust jacket) $15.00
Noel Streatfeild Easter Holiday Book, 1974 Dent, green hardcover with gilt, b/w illustrations,($20.00 with dust jacket) $15.00
Years of Grace, a Book for Girls, 1950 Evans, London, hardcover. ($40.00 with dust jacket) $20.00

STREET, James
Pride of Possession, 1960 Lippincott, first edition, hardcover. ($25.00 with dust jacket) $15.00

STREET, Julia Montgomery
Fiddler's Fancy, 1955 Follett, first edition, pictorial hardcover, illustrated by Don Sibley. ($35.00 with dust jacket) $15.00

STRIKER, Fran, see Series section LONE RANGER; TOM QUEST

STRONG, Charles
Ranger's Arctic Patrol, 1952 Winston, 214 pages, illustrated by Kurt Weise. ($20.00 with dust jacket) $10.00
Seal Hunters, 1958 Dodd Mead, first edition, hardcover. $10.00
Real Book About the Antarctic, 1959 Garden City, hardcover, book club edition, illustrated by Albert Orbaan. ($15.00 with dust jacket) $10.00

STRUBLE, Virginia
Cactus, 1958 Bethany Press, green hardcover, 48 pages, two-color drawings by Lillian Thoele. $10.00

STURNER, Fred and **Adolph SELTZER**
What Did You Do When You Were a Kid?, 1973 Weathervane, hardcover. ($15.00 with dust jacket) $10.00

SUDDON, Alan
Cinderella, 1969 Oberon Press, London, silver lettering on blue hardcover, 29 full-color collage illustrations. $25.00

SUHL, Yuri
Simon Boom Gives a Wedding, 1973 Four Winds Press, hardcover, illustrated by Margot Zemach. ($15.00 with dust jacket) $10.00

SUIB, L. and **M. BROADMAN**
Marionettes On Stage!, 1975 Harper, first edition, hardcover, illustrated by drawings, photos. ($25.00 with dust jacket) $10.00

SULLIVAN, Pat
Felix the Cat, 1974 edition Wonder Books, small illustrated glossy hardcover. $10.00
Surprise for Felix, 1959 edition Wonder Books, small illustrated glossy hardcover. $15.00

SUMMERS, Dr. Edward G., editor
Mystery in the Sky, 1968 McGraw-Hill, hardcover. $10.00

SUMMERS, James
Heartbreak Hot Rod, 1958 Garden City, first edition, tan hardcover, 208 pages. ($20.00 with dust jacket) $10.00

SURANY, Anico
Golden Frog, 1973 G. P. Putnam, first edition, hardcover, color illustrations by Leonard Fisher. ($25.00 with dust jacket) $15.00

SUTCLIFF, Rosemary
Brother Dusty Feet, 1952 Oxford, first edition, hardcover, b/w illustrations by Walter Hodges. ($30.00 with dust jacket) $15.00
Dawn Wind, 1961 Oxford, first edition, hardcover, b/w illustrations by Charles Keeping. ($35.00 with dust jacket) $20.00
Eagle of the Ninth, 1959 Oxford, hardcover, illustrated by C. Walter Hodges. ($20.00 with dust jacket) $10.00
Knight's Fee, 1960 Oxford, first edition, hardcover, illustrated by Charles Keeping. ($60.00 with dust jacket) $20.00
Mark of the Horse Lord, 1965 Oxford, first edition, hardcover. ($40.00 with dust jacket) $20.00
Mark of the Horse Lord, 1965 Walck, first American edition, hardcover, 305 pages, illustrated by Charles Keeping. ($15.00 with dust jacket) $10.00
Sword at Sunset, 1963 Hodder & Stoughton, London, first edition, hardcover, 480 pages, map endpapers. ($30.00 with dust jacket) $15.00
Witch's Brat, 1970 Oxford, first edition, hardcover. ($30.00 with dust jacket) $15.00

SUTTON, Felix
Book of Clowns, 1953 Grosset, hardcover, illustrated by James Schucker. $20.00

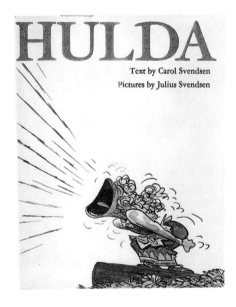

SVENDSEN, Carol
Hulda, 1974 Houghton, oversize hardcover picture book, color illustrations by Julius Svendsen. ($35.00 with dust jacket) $15.00

SWADOS, Harvey
Mystery of the Spanish Silver Mine, 1971 Doubleday, first edition, hardcover, color illustrations by Barbara Ninde Byfield. ($25.00 with dust jacket) $10.00

SWEAT, Lynn
Wonderful Hunting Dog, 1973 Macmillan, first edition, hardcover. ($15.00 with dust jacket) $10.00

SWENSON, Juliet Morgan
Book to Begin on Hawaii, 1963 Holt, Rinehart and Winston, first edition, hardcover, illustrated by Ezra Jack Keats. ($25.00 with dust jacket) $15.00

SWIFT, Helen Miller
Head Over Heels , 1968 Delacorte, first edition, hardcover. ($15.00 with dust jacket) $10.00

SWINFORD, Betty
White Panther, 1964 Zondervan, hardcover. ($20.00 with dust jacket) $10.00

SYMONDS, John
Elfrida and the Pig, 1959 Franklin Watts, oversize hardcover, illustrated by Edward Ardizzone. ($30.00 with dust jacket) $15.00
Tom and Tabby, 1964 Universe Books, glossy illustrated hardcover, color illustrations by Andre Francois. $20.00

T

TABER, Gladys
Conversations with Amber, 1973 Lippincott, hardcover. ($20.00 with dust jacket) $10.00
My Own Cape Cod, 1971 Lippincott, hardcover. ($20.00 with dust jacket) $10.00
Stillmeadow Road, 1962 Lippincott, first edition, hardcover, illustrated by Edward Shenton. ($25.00 with dust jacket) $10.00

TAGUE, Lola
Wonderful Merry Go Round, 1961 Lothrop, Lee & Shepard, pictorial hardcover, illustrated by Kurt Werth. ($20.00 with dust jacket) $10.00

TAKEICHI, Yasoo
Mighty Prince, 1971 edition Crown, first American edition, oblong oversize hardcover, illustrated by Sejima Yoshimasa. ($35.00 with dust jacket) $20.00

TALLON, Robert
Conversations: Cries, Croaks and Calls, 1963 Holt, first edition, hardcover, illustrated by Tallon. ($25.00 with dust jacket) $15.00.

TAMBURINE, Jean
How Now Brown Cow, 1967 Abingdon Press, first edition, hardcover, author illustrated. ($35.00 with dust jacket) $20.00

TASHJIAN, Virginia
Three Apples Fell from Heaven, Armenian Tales Retold, 1971 Little, Brown, first edition, hardcover, illustrated by Nonny Hogrogian. ($35.00 with dust jacket) $15.00

TATE, Joan
Wild Boy, 1972 Chatto, Boyd & Oliver, first edition, hardcover, 104 pages. ($15.00 with dust jacket) $10.00

TATHAM, Julie (see Julie Campbell), see Series section CHERRY AMES

TAYLOR, Arthur
Mr. Fizbee and the Little Troop, 1962 Random House, first edition, hardcover. ($25.00 with dust jacket) $10.00

TAYLOR, Sydney Bremer (1904 – 1978), see Series section ALL-OF-A-KIND FAMILY
Dog Who Came to Dinner, 1966 Follett, pictorial hardcover, illustrations by John Emil Johnson. $10.00
Mr. Barney's Beard, 1961 Follett Beginning-to-Read Book, hardcover, illustrations by Charles Gear. $10.00
Papa Like Everyone Else!, 1966 Follett, hardcover, illustrations by George Porter. $10.00

TAYLOR, Theodore
Teetoncey and Ben O'Neal, 1975 Doubleday, first edition, hardcover, 185 pages, illustrated by Richard Cuffari. ($25.00 with dust jacket) $15.00

TAZEWELL, Charles
Small One: Story for Those Who Like Christmas and Small Donkeys, 1958 Franklin Limited Edition, gilt decorated paper-over-board hardcover, 26 pages, designed by Donald E. Cooke, illustrated by Marian Ebert. $65.00

TEMPLE, Nigel
Seen and Not Heard: A Garland of Fancies for Victorian Children, 1970 Dial, first edition, hardcover, color illustrations. ($30.00 with dust jacket) $15.00

TEMPLE, Shirley
Shirley Temple's Fairyland, 1958 Random House, oversize laminated illustrated hardcover, color illustrations. $15.00
Shirley Temple's Favorite Tales of Long Ago, 1958

Random House, first edition, oversize laminated illustrated hardcover, color illustrations. $20.00

Shirley Temple's Stories that Never Grow Old, 1958 Random House, first edition, oversize hardcover, collection, color illustrations. ($20.00 with dust jacket) $10.00

Shirley Temple Treasury, 1959 Random House, first edition, oversize hardcover, illustrated by Robert Patterson drawings and photographs from films featuring Shirley Temple, including Heidi, Little Colonel, Rebecca of Sunnybrook Farm, Captain January. ($50.00 with dust jacket) $20.00

TEMPLE, Vere
How to Draw Pond Life, 1956 Studio Publications, London, first edition, small hardcover, b/w illustrations by author. ($15.00 with dust jacket) $10.00

TERRIS, Susan
Backwards Boots, 1971 Doubleday, first edition, oversize hardcover, 62 pages, illustrations by Rino Casalini. ($30.00 with dust jacket) $15.00

Upstairs Witch and Downstairs Witch, 1970 Doubleday, first edition, hardcover, illustrated by Olivia H. Cole. ($25.00 with dust jacket) $15.00

THALER, Mike
How Far Will a Rubber Band Stretch?, 1974 Parents', pictorial hardcover, illustrated endpapers, illustrations. $10.00

Prince and the Seven Moons, 1966 Macmillan, Master Library Edition, color pictorial hardcover, illustrated. ($15.00 with dust jacket) $10.00

Staff, 1971 Alfred A. Knopf, first edition, hardcover, 30 pages, illustrated in sepia /black by Joseph Schindelman. ($20.00 with dust jacket) $10.00

THANE, Elswyth
Mount Vernon Family, 1968 Crowell-Collier, hardcover, 152 pages, b/w illustrations. ($20.00 with dust jacket) $10.00

THARP, Edgar
Giants of Space, 1968 Grosset and Dunlap, translated by Charles Gottlieb, pictorial hardcover, charcoal sketches of astronauts. $15.00

THAYER, Ernest Lawrence
Casey at the Bat, 1954 edition Prentice-Hall, first edition thus, hardcover, illustrated by Paul Frame. ($15.00 with dust jacket) $10.00

THAYER, Jane
Cat That Joined The Club, 1967 Morrow, oversize hardcover. ($20.00 with dust jacket) $10.00

Gus and the Baby Ghost, 1972 William Morrow, Weekly Reader edition, illustrated by Seymour Fleishman. $10.00

Gus Was a Mexican Ghost, 1974 William Morrow, Weekly Reader edition, illustrated by Seymour Fleishman. $10.00

I Don't Believe in Elves, 1975 Morrow, first edition, hardcover. ($15.00 with dust jacket) $10.00

Popcorn Dragon, 1953 Morrow, hardcover picture book, illustrated by Jay Hyde Barnum. ($35.00 with dust jacket) $15.00

What's a Ghost Going to Do?, 1974 William Morrow, Weekly Reader edition, hardcover. $10.00

THELWELL, Norman
Belt-Up Motoring Manual, 1974 Methuen, first edition UK, hardcover, 128 pages, cartoon illustrations by author. ($20.00 with dust jacket) $10.00

Thelwell Country, 1959 Methuen, first edition, oversize hardcover picture book, b/w illustrations by author. ($35.00 with dust jacket) $20.00

Top Dog, Thelwell's Complete Canine Compendium, 1964 Methuen, first edition, hardcover. ($25.00 with dust jacket) $15.00

THIELE, Colin
Fire in the Stone, 1974 Harper, first American edition, hardcover. ($20.00 with dust jacket) $10.00

THOMAS, Dylan
Child's Christmas in Wales, 1954 James Laughlin, first edition, hardcover. ($120.00 with dust jacket) $40.00

Me and My Bike, 1965 McGraw-Hill, red oversize hardcover, 53 pages, illustrated. $20.00

THOMAS, Eleanor with Ernest TIEGS and Fay ADAMS
Your Town and Mine, 1954 Ginn, yellow and orange hardcover, school reader, color illustrations thoughout. $15.00

THOMAS, H. C.
Lee Baird, Son of Danger, 1957 Whitman, hardcover. $15.00

Red Ryder and the Adventure at Chimney Rock, 1957 Whitman, pictorial hardcover. $20.00

THOMAS, Maude Morgan
Sing in the Dark: A Story of the Welsh in Pennsylvania, 1954 Winston, first edition, hardcover, llustrated by Clifford H. Schule. ($25.00 with dust jacket) $15.00

THOMAS, Patricia
Stand Back Said the Elephant, I'm Going to Sneeze, 1971 Weekly Reader Book Club, hardcover, illustrations by Wallace Tripp. $10.00

THOMPSON, Kay, see Series section ELOISE
Miss Pooky Peckinpaugh, 1970 Harper, first edition, hardcover. First edition in dust jacket: $100.00. Later editions: ($30.00 with dust jacket) $15.00

THOMPSON, Mary Wolfe
Steadfast Heart, 1951 David McKay, hardcover. ($20.00 with dust jacket) $10.00

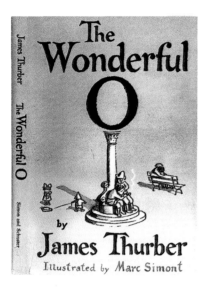

THURBER, James
Thirteen Clocks, 1957 Simon & Schuster, hardcover, blue/b/w illustrations by Marc Simont. First edition with dust jacket: $100.00. Later editions: ($25.00 with dust jacket) $10.00
Wonderful O, 1957 Simon & Schuster, hardcover, blue/b/w illustrations by Marc Simont. First edition with dust jacket: $65.00. Later editions: ($25.00 with dust jacket) $10.00

THURMAN, John
Patrol Leader's Handbook, Boy Scouts, London, first edition, hardcover, illustrated by Ken Sprague. ($35.00 with dust jacket) $20.00

THWAITE, Ann
House in Turner Square, 1960 Harcourt Brace, first edition, hardcover, illustrated by Robin Jacques. ($20.00 with dust jacket) $10.00
Waiting for the Party, 1974 Charles Scribner, first American edition, hardcover, b/w photos. ($25.00 with dust jacket) $15.00

TIBBER, Robert
Aristide, 1966 Dial Press, first edition, hardcover, illustrated by Quentin Blake. ($25.00 with dust jacket) $10.00

TICHENOR, Tom
Sir Patches and the Dragon, 1972 Aurora, Nashville, first edition, hardcover, 95 pages, color illustrations by Mary Helen Wallace. ($20.00 with dust jacket) $10.00

TITCOMB, Margaret
Voyage of the Flying Bird, 1963 Dodd, Mead, first edition, blue hardcover, illustrated by Joseph Feher. ($20.00 with dust jacket) $10.00

TITUS, Eve, see Series section ANATOLE; BASIL

TODD, Mary Fidelis
ABC & 1 2 3, 1955 Whittlesey House, red hardcover. ($15.00 with dust jacket) $10.00

TODD, Ruthven, see Series section SPACE CAT
Tan's Fish, 1958 Little, Brown, first edition, hardcover, illustrated by Theresa Sherman. ($35.00 with dust jacket) $20.00

TOEPPERWEIN, Emilie and **Fritz**
Charcoal and Charcoal Burners, 1950 Highland, Boerne, Texas, first edition, signed limited edition, hardcover, fold-out plate, map endpapers. ($45.00 with dust jacket) $20.00
Donkey Day, 1950 Highland, Boerne, Texas, first edition, hardcover, drawings in text. ($20.00 with dust jacket) $10.00

TOLBOOM, Wanda Neil
Tosie of the Far North, 1954 Aladdin Books, first edition, oversize hardcover, yellow cloth with blue spine, 64 pages, illustrated by Robert Bruce. ($45.00 with dust jacket) $$20.00

TOLES, Elsie and **Myriam**
Secret of Lonesome Valley and Life in the Range Country, 1955 Harr Wagner, hardcover. $15.00

TOLKIEN, J.R.R. (author of *Hobbit*) see series section Lord
Farmer Giles of Ham, 1950 edition Houghton Mifflin, first American edition thus, hardcover, 80 pages, color frontispiece, illustrated by Pauline Baynes. First edition with dust jacket: $100.00. Later editions: ($20.00 with dust jacket) $15.00
Road Goes Ever On, 1968 George Allen & Unwin Ltd., first edition, oversize white hardcover, 67 pages. Songs. ($50.00 with dust jacket) $25.00
Tree and Leaf, 1965 Houghton Mifflin, first edition, hardcover. ($75.00 with dust jacket) $30.00

TOLSTOI, Lev
Stories for Children, 1962 Progress Publishers, Moscow, oversize hardcover, b/w illustrations by Pakhomov, translated from Russian by Jacob Guralsky. $25.00

TOLSTOY, Nikolai
Founding of Evil Hold School, 1968 Allen, London, first edition, hardcover, 149 pages, illustrated by full page drawings by Robin Jacques. ($20.00 with dust jacket) $15.00

TOMERLIN, John
Sky Clowns, 1973 Dutton, first edition, orange hardcover, 184 pages. ($25.00 with dust jacket) $15.00

TOMPKINS, Walker A.
Roy Rogers and the Ghost of Mystery Rancho, 1950 Whitman, hardcover. $15.00

TOOLE-PAPLOW
Dennis the Menace, 1956 edition Rand McNally Elf Book, illustrated hardcover, small, color illustrations. $15.00

TORJESEN, Elizabeth
Captain Ramsay's Daughter, 1953 Lothrop, first edition, hardcover, illustrated by Adrienne Adams. ($20.00 with dust jacket) $10.00

TOUSEY, Sanford
Bill Clark, American Explorer, 1951 Whitman, hardcover, illustrated by author. ($25.00 with dust jacket) $10.00
Wild Bill Hickok, 1952 Whitman, hardcover. $15.00

TOVEY, Doreen
Donkey Work, 1963 Doubleday, first edition, blue hardcover, 138 pages, b/w illustrations by Maurice Wilson. ($30.00 with dust jacket) $15.00

TOWLE, Faith
Magic Cooking Pot, 1975 Houghton, oblong hardcover, batik illustrations by author. First edition with dust jacket: $85.00. Ex-library: $20.00

TOWNSEND, Doris
Dinny and Dreamdust, 1962 Doubleday Signal Book, first edition, pictorial hardcover, illustrated by Sam Savitt. $15.00

TOWNSEND, J. David
Five Trials of the Pansy Bed, 1967 Houghton Mifflin, first edition, hardcover, small, 59 pages, illustrated by Trina Schart Hyman. ($20.00 with dust jacket) $10.00

TOWNSEND, John Rowe
Pirate's Island, 1968 Oxford, first edition, hardcover, illustrated by Douglas Hall. ($20.00 with dust jacket) $10.00

TOWNSEND, Kenneth
Felix and the Bald-Headed Lion, 1967 Delacorte, hardcover, 31 pages, color illustrations by author. $15.00

TRACY, Don
Duck That Flew Backwards, 1950 Dial, hardcover, 49 pages. ($20.00 with dust jacket) $10.00

TRACY, T. H.
Book of the Poodle, 1950 Viking, first edition, oversize hardcover, photos plus illustrations by Flavia Gag. ($35.00 with dust jacket) $20.00

TRANTER, Nigel
Give a Dog a Bad Name, 1963 Collins, London, first edition, hardcover, 190 pages, b/w illustrations by Prudence Seward. ($15.00 with dust jacket) $10.00
Smoke Across the Highlands, 1964 Platt Munk, hardcover. ($15.00 with dust jacket) $10.00

TRAVEN, B. and BELTRAN, Alberto
Creation of the Sun and the Moon, 1968 Hill & Wang, first edition, hardcover, illustrated by Beltran. ($40.00 with dust jacket) $20.00

TRAVERS, P. L. (author of *Mary Poppins*)
About the Sleeping Beauty, 1975 McGraw-Hill, first edition, hardcover, 111 pages. ($25.00 with dust jacket) $10.00
Fox at the Manger, 1962 W.W. Norton, small hardcover, 75 pages, browntone engravings by Thomas Bewick. ($25.00 with dust jacket) $15.00
Friend Monkey, 1971 Harcourt, first American edition, hardcover, 284 pages, illustrated by Charles Keeping. ($30.00 with dust jacket) $15.00

TREADGOLD, Mary
Heron Ride, 1962 Jonathan Cape, London, first UK edition, hardcover. ($25.00 with dust jacket) $15.00
Winter Princess, (1962) 1964 Van Nostrand, first American edition, hardcover, 112 pages, illustrated by Pearl Falconer. ($35.00 with dust jacket) $20.00

TREECE, Henry
Ask for King Billy, 1955 Faber and Faber, first edition, hardcover, illustrated by Richard Kennedy. ($35.00 with dust jacket) $15.00
Men of the Hills, 1957 John Lane, hardcover. ($25.00 with dust jacket) $10.00
Queen's Brooch , 1967 Putnam, first edition, hardcover, 159 pages, illustrated by Brian Wildsmith. ($15.00 with dust jacket) $10.00

TREMBLAY, Jack
Ten Canadian Legends: A Story from Each Province in Canada, 1955 Brunswick Press, first edition, pictorial hardcover. $45.00

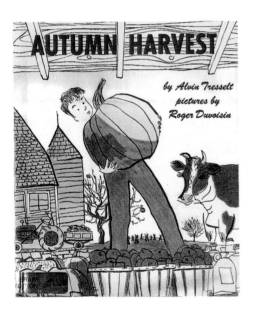

TRESSELT, Alvin
Autumn Harvest, 1951 Lothrop, first edition, oversize hardcover, illustrated by Roger Duvoisin. ($45.00 with dust jacket) $20.00
How Far Is Far? 1964 Parents' Magazine Press, pictorial hardcover, illustrated endpapers. ($20.00 with dust jacket) $10.00
Hide and Seek Fog, 1965 Lothrop, Lee, Reading Program edition, hardcover, illustrated by Roger Duvoisin. $10.00

TRESSELT, Alvin and Wilbur WHEATON
Elephant is Not a Cat, 1962 Parents' Magazine Press, illustrated hardcover, illustrated by Tom Vroman. ($15.00 with dust jacket) $10.00

TREZ, Denise and Alain
Rabbit Country, 1966 Viking, first edition, hardcover, illustrated by the authors. ($20.00 with dust jacket) $10.00

TRIPP, Edward
New Tuba, 1955 Oxford, first edition, hardcover, 103 pages. ($20.00 with dust jacket) $10.00

TROBISCH, David
Adventures of Pumpelhoober, 1971 Concordia, first edition, glossy hardcover, illustrated by Eva Bruchmann. $20.00

TRUCHOT, Theresa
Charcoal Wagon Boy, 1952 Binfords & Mort, first edition, red hardcover, 133 pages, full-page plates by M. Vols Winkler. ($15.00 with dust jacket) $10.00

TUDOR, Tasha
A is for Anna Belle, 1954 Oxford, oblong hardcover, illustrated by author. First edition with dust jacket: $200.00. Later editions: ($25.00 with dust jacket) $15.00
Around the Year, 1957 Oxford, yellow hardcover, illustrated by author. First edition with dust jacket: $100.00. Later editions: ($25.00 with dust jacket) $15.00
Becky's Christmas, 1961 Viking, hardcover, color illustrations. First edition with dust jacket: $150.00. Later editions: ($25.00 with dust jacket) $15.00
Corgiville Fair, 1971 Crowell, probable first edition, oblong hardcover with gilt animal illustration and lettering, color illustrations by author. First edition with dust jacket: $200.00. Later editions: ($30.00 with dust jacket) $15.00
Country Fair, (1940) 1968 Walck, enlarged first edition thus, hardcover, color illustrations by author. First edition with dust jacket: $100.00. Later editions: ($25.00 with dust jacket) $15.00
Doll's Christmas, 1950 Oxford, square red hardcover with paste-on-pictorial, illustrated by author. First edition with dust jacket: $200.00. Later editions: ($25.00 with dust jacket) $15.00
First Delights, 1966 Platt & Monk, hardcover, color illustrations by author. First edition with dust jacket: $75.00. Later editions: ($25.00 with dust jacket) $15.00
First Graces, 1955 Oxford, small hardcover, color illustrations by author. First edition with dust jacket: $100.00. Later editions: ($25.00 with dust jacket) $15.00
First Poems of Childhood., 1967 Platt & Munk, hardcover, illustrations by author. First edition with dust jacket: $170.00. Later editions: ($25.00 with dust jacket) $15.00
First Prayers, 1952 Oxford, small blue-gray hard-

cover, illustrated endpapers, 48 pages, color illustrations by author. First edition with dust jacket: $125.00. Later editions: ($25.00 with dust jacket) $15.00

1 is One, 1956 Oxford, pink oblong oversize hardcover, illustrated by author. First edition with dust jacket: $200.00. Later editions: ($25.00 with dust jacket) $15.00

Take Joy!, 1966 World, oblong oversize hardcover, color illustrations by author. First edition with dust jacket: $100.00. Later editions: ($20.00 with dust jacket) $15.00

Tasha Tudor's Favorite Stories, 1965 Lippincott, oversize hardcover, green cloth spine, pictorial boards. First edition with dust jacket: $125.00. Later editions: ($30.00 with dust jacket) $15.00

Tasha Tudor Book of Fairy Tales, 1961 Platt & Munk, oversize, pictorial cover. First edition with dust jacket: $150.00. Later editions: ($25.00 with dust jacket) $15.00

Twenty-Third Psalm, 1965 Worcester, Achille J. St. Onge, miniature green leather hardcover with gilt, color illustrations by author. First edition with dust jacket: $125.00

Wings from the Wind, 1964 Lippincott, hardcover, illustrated by author. First edition with dust jacket: $100.00. Later editions: ($20.00 with dust jacket) $15.00

TUNIS, Edwin
Chipmunk on the Doorstep, 1971 Crowell, first edition, hardcover, illustrated by author. ($30.00 with dust jacket) $15.00

TUNIS, John R.
Buddy and the Old Pro, 1955 Morrow, first edition, hardcover, illustrated by Jay Hyde. ($20.00 with dust jacket) $10.00

Go, Team Go!, 1954 William Morrow, first edition, hardcover. ($20.00 with dust jacket) $10.00

Grand National, 1973 Morrow, first edition, hardcover. ($20.00 with dust jacket) $10.00

Iron Duke, 1966 Harcourt, Brace, hardcover. ($15.00 with dust jacket) $10.00

TURKLE, Brinton
Adventures of Obadiah, 1972 Viking Press, first edition, hardcover, illustrated by author. ($20.00 with dust jacket) $15.00

Magic of Millicent Musgrave, 1967 Viking, first edition, hardcover. ($35.00 with dust jacket) $15.00

TURNBULL, Agnes Sligh
Jed, the Shepherd's Dog, 1957 Houghton Mifflin, oversize, 80 pages, hardcover, b/w illustrations by Sari. ($20.00 with dust jacket) $10.00

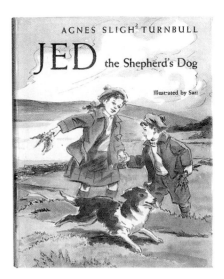

TURNER, Audrey
Betty Starling, Private Secretary, 1955 Lantern Press, pictorial hardcover. $20.00

TURNER, Mina
Town Meeting Means Me, 1951 Houghton Mifflin, hardcover, illustrated by Lloyd Coe. ($15.00 with dust jacket) $10.00

TURNER, Philip
Grange at High Force, 1965 Oxford, first edition, hardcover. ($15.00 with dust jacket) $10.00

Steam on the Line, 1968 Oxford, hardcover. ($15.00 with dust jacket) $10.00

TURNER, Robert
Gunsmoke, 1958 Whitman, illustrated hardcover. $15.00

TURNER, William O.
War Country, 1957 Houghton Mifflin, first edition, green hardcover. ($25.00 with dust jacket) $10.00

TURSKA, Krystyna
Magician of Cracow, 1975 Greenwillow Books, first edition, hardcover. ($20.00 with dust jacket) $10.00

Woodcutter's Duck, 1972 Macmillan, first edition, hardcover, illustrated by Krystyna Turska.($20.00 with dust jacket) $10.00

TUTE, Warren and Felix Fonteyn
Cockney Cats, 1953 Museum Press Limited, London, first edition, hardcover, 32 pages of photos. ($25.00 with dust jacket) $15.00

U

UCHIDA, Yoshiko
In-Between Miya, 1967 Scribner, hardcover, 128

pages, illustrated by Susan Bennett. ($20.00 with dust jacket) $10.00

Sea of Gold and Other Tales from Japan, 1965 Scribner, first edition, hardcover, illustrated by Marianne Yamaguchi. ($25.00 with dust jacket) $15.00

UDRY, Janice May

Let's Be Enemies, 1968 Harper, hardcover, illustrated by Maurice Sendak. First edition with dust jacket: $75.00. Later editions: ($20.00 with dust jacket) $15.00

Mean Mouse and Other Mean Stories, 1962 Harper, pictorial hardcover, color illustrations by Ed Young. ($50.00 with dust jacket) $25.00

Sunflower Garden, 1969 Harvey House, pictorial hardcover, illustrated by Beatrice Darwin. $10.00

Tree is Nice, 1956 Harper, (1957 Caldecott Award), hardcover, illustrated by Marc Simont. ($20.00 with dust jacket) $10.00

ULRICI, Rolf

Kai Conquers Brixholm, 1963 Bobbs-Merrill, first edition, hardcover, 163 pages, illustrated by Ulrik Schramm. ($15.00 with dust jacket) $10.00

UNDERWOOD, Betty

Tamarack Tree, 1971 Houghton Mifflin, first edition, hardcover, 230 pages, b/w illustrations by Bea Holmes. ($30.00 with dust jacket) $15.00

UNGERER, Tomi

Adelaide, 1959 Harper & Row, first edition, hardcover, 40 pages, illustrated by author. ($90.00 with dust jacket) $30.00

Ask Me a Question, 1968 Harper & Row, first edition, hardcover, 32 pages, illustrated by author. ($50.00 with dust jacket) $20.00

Astorybook (A Story Book), 1974 Franklin Watts, first edition, hardcover, illustrated by author. ($30.00 with dust jacket) $15.00

Beast of Monsieur Racine, 1971 Farrar, first edition, hardcover, illustrated by author. ($40.00 with dust jacket) $20.00

Hat, 1970 Parents' Magazine Press, oversize, illustrated hardcover, color illustrations throughout by author. $15.00

I Am Papa Snap and These Are My Favorite No Such Stories, 1971 Harper & Row, first edition, illustrated oversize hardcover, illustrated by author. ($35.00 with dust jacket) $20.00

No Kiss for Mother, 1973 Harper & Row, first edition, hardcover, 40 pages, color illustrations by author. ($35.00 with dust jacket) $20.00

Rufus, 1961 Harper & Row, first edition, hardcover, color illustrations by author. ($50.00 with dust jacket) $20.00

UNNERSTAD, Edith

Peep-Larssons Go Sailing, 1963 Macmillan, first edition, hardcover. ($20.00 with dust jacket) $10.00

Saucepan Journey, 1951 Macmillan, first edition, hardcover, illustrated by Louis Slobodkin. ($25.00 with dust jacket) $15.00

UNTERMEYER, Louis, editor

Aesop's Fables, 1965 Golden Press, first edition, oversize hardcover, 92 pages, illustrated by Alice and Martin Provensen. ($35.00 with dust jacket) $20.00

For You With Love, 1961 edition Golden Press, first edition, hardcover, illustrated by Joan Walsh Anglund, ($20.00 with dust jacket) $15.00

Pour Toi (For You), 1966 edition Golden Press, first edition, glossy hardcover, illustrated by Joan Walsh Anglund. $15.00

UNWIN, Nora S.

Joyful the Morning, 1963 David McKay, first edition, hardcover, illustrated by author. ($15.00 with dust jacket) $10.00

UPHAM, Elizabeth

Little Brown Bear, 1952 Platt & Munk, first edition thus, oversize hardcover, illustrated by Marjorie Hartwell. ($50.00 with dust jacket) $25.00

URMSTON, Mary

New Boy, 1950 Junior Literary Guild & Doubleday, hardcover. ($15.00 with dust jacket) $10.00

USHINSKY, K.

How a Shirt Grew in the Field, 1967 McGraw, first edition, oversize hardcover picture book, 30 pages, blue/red/white illustrated by Yaroslava. ($20.00 with dust jacket) $15.00

UTTLEY, Alison, (author of Little Grey Rabbit books), see Series section SNUG
Brown Mouse Book 1971 Heinemann, first edition, hardcover, 92 pages, four color plates, illustrated by Katherine Wigglesworth. ($50.00 with dust jacket) $30.00
Fuzzypeg's Brother, 1971 London Collins, first edition, small hardcover. $25.00
Hare and the Easter Eggs, 1952 Collins, first edition, small hardcover, 80 pages, color illustrations by Margaret Tempest. ($50.00 with dust jacket) $20.00
Lavendar Shoes, Eight Tales of Enchantment, 1970 Faber and Faber, hardcover. ($30.00 with dust jacket) $15.00
Litle Grey Rabbit and the Snow-Baby, 1973 Collins, first edition thus, hardcover, illustrated by Katherine Wigglesworth. ($40.00 with dust jacket) $20.00
Little Grey Rabbit's Third Painting Book, 1953 Collins, oversize hardcover, 6 color plates by Margaret Tempest, 8 illustrations to color. $45.00
Little Red Fox and the Wicked Uncle, 1954 Heinemann, first edition, hardcover, color illustrations by Katherine Wigglesworth. First edition with dust jacket: $85.00
Toad's Castle, 1951 Heinemann, first edition, hardcover, illustrated by Katherine Wigglesworth. $45.00

——— ⇒ **V** ⇐ ———

VALENTI, Angelo, illustrator
America, Ruth Tooze, 1956 Viking, first edition, oversize hardcover, illustrated by Valenti. ($40.00 with dust jacket) $20.00

VanBREDA, A.
Pleasure with Paper, 1956 Faber and Faber, 157 pages, hardcover, b/w illustrations. ($20.00 with dust jacket) $10.00

VANCE, Eleanor Graham
Everything Book, 1974 Golden Book, oversize, color illustrated paper-over-board cover, 140+ pages, color and b/w illustrations throughout by Trina Schart Hyman. $40.00

VANCE, Marguerite
Jeptha and the New People, 1960 Dutton, first edition, hardcover, illustrated by Robert MacLean. ($20.00 with dust jacket) $10.00

VanDerVEER, Judy
Wallace the Wandering Pig, 1967 Harcourt, Brace & World, first edition, hardcover, illustrated by Paul Galdone. ($25.00 with dust jacket) $15.00

VanHEUKELOM, A. S.
Arabella, the Heavenly Cat, 1966 Platt & Munk, hardcover. $15.00

VanLAMSWEERDE, Frans
Ziggy, What Animals Say, 1968 Ideals Publishing, oversize glossy illustrated hardcover, color illustrations by Frans VanLamsweerde. $20.00

VanLAMSWEERDE, Joyce
Ziggy and his Music, 1968 Ideals Publishing, oversize glossy illustrated hardcover, color illustrations by Frans VanLamsweerde. $15.00

VanLOON, Dirk
Papeek, 1970 Lippincott, first edition, hardcover, illustrated by Louis Glanzman. ($20.00 with dust jacket) $10.00

VanRHIJN, Aleid
Tide in the Attic, 1961 Criterion, pictorial hardcover. $10.00

VanSOMEREN, Liesje
Young Traveler in Holland, 1953 Dutton, first edition, hardcover, illustrated by photos and maps. ($20.00 with dust jacket) $10.00

VanSTOCKUM, Hilda
King Oberon's Forest, 1957 Viking, first edition, hardcover, illustrated by Brigid Marlin. ($35.00 with dust jacket) $15.00
Winged Man, 1962 edition Weekly Reader Book Club, illustrated hardcover. 10.00

VARNEY, Joyce
Half-Time Gypsy, 1966 Bobbs-Merrill, first edition, hardcover, illustrated by Trina Schart Hyman. ($25.00 with dust jacket) $10.00

VASILIU
Year Goes Round, 1964 John Day, oversize hardcover, illustrated by author. ($25.00 with dust jacket) $10.00

VAVRA, Robert
Felipe the Bullfighter, 1967 Harcourt Brace Jovanovich, first edition, hardcover illustrated by Robert Vavra photos. ($25.00 with dust jacket) $10.00
Tiger Flower, 1968 Reynal, first edition, hardcover, illustrated by Fleur Cowles. ($20.00 with dust jacket) $10.00

VEGLAHN, Nancy
Vandals of Treason House, 1974 Houghton Mifflin, first edition, hardcover.($20.00 with dust jacket) $10.00

VELTHUIJS, Max
Poor Woodcutter and the Dove, 1970 Delacorte Press, first American edition, hardcover, color illustrations. ($20.00 with dust jacket) $10.00

VENABLE, Max
Hurry the Crossing, 1974 Lippincott, first edition, hardcover. ($25.00 with dust jacket) $15.00

VENTURA, Piero
Book of Cities, 1975 Random House, first edition, oversize hardcover picture book, illustrated by author. ($30.00 with dust jacket) $15.00

VERMEER, Jackie and **Marian LARIVIERE**
Little Kid's Craft Book, 1973 Taplinger Publishing, first edition, hardcover, Illustrated by Paul McMaster and Lou Vermeer, b/w photos. ($15.00 with dust jacket) $10.00

VERRAL, Charles, see Series section BRAINS BENTON

VETTER, Marjorie, editor
Stories to Live By, 1960 Platt Munk, treasury of fiction from *American Girl* magazine, hardcover. $20.00

VICTOR, Joan Berg
Sh-h! Listen Again, Sounds of the Season, 1969 World, hardcover, author illustrated. ($15.00 with dust jacket) $10.00

VINTON, Iris
Folkways Omnibus of Children's Games, 1970 Stackpole Books, first edition, hardcover, 320 pages, illustrated by Alex D'Amato. ($15.00 with dust jacket) $10.00

VIORST, Judith
Alexander and the Terrible, Horrible, No Good, Very Bad Day, 1972 Atheneum, oversize hardcover, drawings by Ray Cruz. First edition with dust jacket: $50.00. Later editions: ($20.00 with dust jacket) $10.00
I'll Fix Anthony, 1969 Harper, hardcover, illustrations by Arnold Lobel. $15.00
My Mama Says There Ain't Any Zombies, Ghosts, Vampires, Creatures, Demons, Monsters, Fiends, Goblins, or Things, 1973 Atheneum, oversize hardcover, illustrated by Kay Chorao. ($20.00 with dust jacket) $15.00
Sunday Morning, 1968 Harper, hardcover, illustrations by Hilary Knight. $15.00

VIP [Virgil Partch]
VIP's Mistake Book, 1970 Windmill, first edition, pictorial orange hardcover, illustrated by author's cartoons. ($25.00 with dust jacket) $10.00

VOIGHT, Virginia Frances
Red Blade and the Black Bear, 1973 Dodd, Mead, first edition, red-stamped yellow hardcover, 157 pages. ($20.00 with dust jacket) $10.00

VonHIPPEL, Ursula
Story of the Nails Who Traded Houses, 1961 Coward-McCann, first edition, hardcover. ($25.00 with dust jacket) $10.00

VonSCHMIDT, Eric
Ballad of Bad Ben Bilge, 1965 Houghton Mifflin, first edition, oversize hardcover, 48 pages, illustrated by author. ($25.00 with dust jacket) $15.00
Mr. Chris and the Instant Animals, 1967 Houghton Mifflin, illustrated by author. ($20.00 with dust jacket) $15.00

──────── ⊷⇒ **W** ⇐⊶ ────────

WABER, Bernard, see Series section LYLE
Anteater Named Arthur, 1967 Houghton, first edition, oversize hardcover, two-color illustrations by author. ($30.00 with dust jacket) $15.00

WADSWORTH, Wallace
Choo-Choo the Little Switch Engine, 1954 Rand McNally Giant Book, pictorial oversize hardcover, color illustrations by Mary Jane Chase. $20.00
Modern Story Book, 1950 Rand McNally, oversize hardcover, 72 pages, revised and redesigned version of the 1941 title. ($50.00 with dust jacket) $25.00

WAGENVOORD, James
Hangin' Out – City Kids, City Games, 1974 Lippincott, first edition, hardcover. ($20.00 with dust jacket) $10.00

WAHL, Jan, see Series section PLEASANT FIELD-MOUSE
Cobweb Castle, 1968 Holt, first edition, hardcover, small, 32 pages, color illustrations by Edward Gorey. ($50.00 with dust jacket) $20.00
Doctor Rabbit, 1970 Delacorte, first edition, hardcover, illustrations by Peter Parnall. ($60.00 with dust jacket) $25.00
Furious Flycycle, 1968 Delacorte Press, first edition, blue hardcover, b/w illustrations by Fernando Krahn. ($15.00 with dust jacket) $10.00
Jeremiah Knucklebones, 1974 Holt, oblong hardcover. ($25.00 with dust jacket) $15.00
May Horses, 1969 Delacorte, first edition, hardcover, illustrated endpapers, illustrated by Blair Kent. ($30.00 with dust jacket) $15.00
Muffletump Storybook, 1975 Follett, first edition, hardcover, illustrated by Cyndy Szekeres. ($35.00 with dust jacket) $20.00
Mulberry Tree, 1970 Grosset & Dunlap, first edition, hardcover, illustrated by Feodor Rojankovsky. ($30.00 with dust jacket) $15.00
Wonderful Kite, 1970 Delacorte Press, first edition, hardcover, color illustrations by Uri Shulevitz. ($30.00 with dust jacket) $15.00

WALDEN, Amelia Elizabeth
Girl Called Hank, 1951 Morrow, first edition, hardcover. ($25.00 with dust jacket) $10.00
I Found my Love, 1956 Westminster, hardcover, 186 pages. ($20.00 with dust jacket) $10.00

WALKER, Barbara K.
How the Hare Told the Truth about His Horse, 1972 Parents' Magazine Press, illustrated hardcover, color illustrations by Charles Mikolaycak. $15.00
Korolu, the Singing Bandit, 1970 Crowell, first edition, hardcover. ($15.00 with dust jacket) $10.00
Stargazer to the Sultan, 1967 Parents' Magazine Press, first edition, hardcover.($20.00 with dust jacket) $10.00

WALKER, David
Sandy Was a Soldier's Boy, 1957 Houghton Mifflin, first edition, hardcover, illustrated by Dobson Broadhead. ($35.00 with dust jacket) $20.00

WALKER, Diana
Year of the Horse, 1975 Abelard-Schulman, first edition, hardcover. ($15.00 with dust jacket) $10.00

WALLACE, Ivy
Pookie Believes in Santa Claus, 1953 Collins, London, first edition, pictorial oversize hardcover, color and b/w illustrations. ($25.00 with dust jacket) $15.00
Pookie at the Seaside, 1956 Collins, pictorial hardcover. ($25.00 with dust jacket) $15.00
Snake Ring Mystery, 1966 Collins, first edition, hardcover. $15.00

WALLACE, May Nickerson
Race for Bill, 1951 Jr. Literary Guild and Thomas Nelson, hardcover, illustrated by Jean MacDonald Porter. ($15.00 with dust jacket) $10.00

WALLEY, Dean
Puck's Peculiar Petshop, 1970 Hallmark, hardcover, color illustrations by Roz Schanzer. ($15.00 with dust jacket) $10.00

WALSH, Jill Paton
Huffler, 1975 Farrar, first edition, hardcover, 84 pages, b/w illustrations by Juliette Palmer. ($20.00 with dust jacket) $10.00

WALSH, John
Truants, 1968 Rand McNally, first American edition, hardcover, illustrated by Edward Ardizzone. ($50.00 with dust jacket) $20.00

WALTERS, Marguerite
Up and Down and All Around, 1960 Franklin Watts, first edition, hardcover, illustrated by Susanne Suba. ($15.00 with dust jacket) $10.00

WALTON, Elizabeth Cheatham
Treasure in the Sand, 1960 Lothrop, first edition, hardcover, illustrated by Jo Polseno. ($20.00 with dust jacket) $10.00

WALTRIP, Lela and **Rufus**
Quiet Boy, 1961 Longmans Green, first edition, hardcover, illustrated by Theresa Kalab Smith. ($20.00 with dust jacket) $10.00
Quiet Boy, 1962 David McKay, Weekly Reader Book Club edition, hardcover, illustrated by Theresa Kalab Smith $10.00

WARD, Lynd
Biggest Bear, 1952 Houghton Mifflin, (1953 Caldecott Award) Weekly Reader edition, 84 pages, illustrated by author. ($30.00 with dust jacket) $15.00
Martin Luther, with May McNeer, 1955 Abingdon-Cokesbury, first edition, oversize hardcover. ($35.00 with dust jacket) $20.00
Nic of the Woods, 1965 Houghton Mifflin, first edition, hardcover. ($25.00 with dust jacket) $15.00
Silver Pony, 1973 Houghton Mifflin, first edition, hardcover, illustrated endpapers, b/w illustrations. First edition with dust jacket: $60.00. Later editions: ($25.00 with dust jacket) $15.00

WARD, Nanda
High Flying Hat, 1956 Ariel Books, first edition, hardcover, illustrated by Lynd Ward. ($35.00 with dust jacket) $15.00
Wellington and the Witch, 1959 Hastings House, first edition, hardcover. ($25.00 with dust jacket) $10.00

WARING, Gilchrist
City of Once Upon a Time, "A Children's True Story of Williamsburg in Virginia," 1965 Dietz Press, Richmond, oversize hardcover. $15.00

WARNER, Edythe
Siamese Summer, 1964 Viking, first edition, oversize hardcover, sepia illustrations. ($35.00 with dust jacket) $20.00

WARNER, Gertrude
Mike's Mystery, 1960 Albert Whitman, hardcover, pictorial hardcover. $10.00

WARNLOF, Anna Lisa
Boy Upstairs, 1963 Harcourt Brace & World, first American edition, hardcover. ($15.00 with dust jacket) $10.00

WARREN, Billy
Headquarters Ranch, 1954 David McKay, hardcover. ($15.00 with dust jacket) $10.00
Ride West Into Danger, Junior Literary Guild & David McKay, hardcover, 218 pages, illustrations. ($15.00 with dust jacket) $10.00
Golden Palomino, 1951 David McKay, first edition, hardcover, 199 pages, illustrated by author. ($15.00 with dust jacket) $10.00

WASHBURNE, Heluiz
Tomas Goes Trading, 1959 John Day, first edition, hardcover, 127 pages, illustrated by Jean MacDonald Porter. ($15.00 with dust jacket) $10.00

WASSERMAN, Selma and **Jack,** see Series section SAILOR JACK

WATSON, Helen Orr
Beano, Circus Dog, 1953 Ariel Books, hardcover, illustrated. ($15.00 with dust jacket) $10.00

WATSON, Jane Werner, see Series section FIRST GOLDEN and LITTLE GOLDEN
How to Tell Time, 1957 Little Golden Books, first edition, small hardcover, clock face: Gruen Precision, metal clock hands. $25.00
Dinosaurs and Other Prehistoric Reptiles, 1960 Giant Golden Book, Western Publishing, pictorial oversize hardcover, color illustrations by Rudolph F. Zallinger. $15.00
True Story of Smokey the Bear, 1955 Big Golden Book, hardcover, color illustrations by Feodor Rojankovsky. $35.00

WATSON, Nancy Dingman
Arabian Nights Picture Book, 1959 Garden City, oversize hardcover, 88 pages, color illustrations by Aldren A. Watson. $15.00

Pony Tales from Old English Nursery Rhymes, (selected by the author), 1961 Doubleday, illustrated by Aldren A. Watson. $15.00

WATSON, Wendy and Clyde
Father Fox's Pennyrhymes, 1971 Crowell, author illustrated. ($50.00 with dust jacket) $15.00
Tom Fox and the Apple Pie, 1972 Crowell, author illustrated. ($30.00 with dust jacket) $15.00
Quips and Quirks, 1975 Crowell, author illustrated. ($30.00 with dust jacket) $15.00

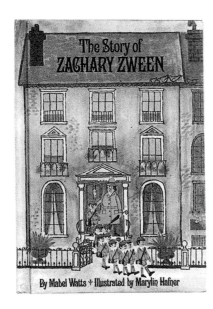

WATTS, Mabel
Boy Who Listened to Everyone, 1963 Parents' Magazine Press, hardcover, illustrated by Ervine Metzl. $10.00
Dozens of Cousins, 1950 McGraw-Hill, hardcover, illustrated by Roger Duvoisin. $10.00
King and the Whirlybird, 1969 Parents' Magazine Press, first edition, hardcover, illustrated by Harold Berson. ($15.00 with dust jacket) $10.00
Story of Zachary Zween, 1967 Parents' Magazine Press edition, color illustrated oversize hardcover, color illustrations by Marylin Hafner. $15.00
Yin Sun and the Lucky Dragon, 1969 Westminster Press, first edition, hardcover, illustrated by Tom H. Hall. ($25.00 with dust jacket) $10.00

WAYNE, Jenifer
Sprout, 1970 McGraw-Hill, Weekly Reader edition, illustrated hardcover, illustrated by Gail Owens. $10.00

WEBB, Addison
Song of the Seasons, 1950 Morrow, first edition, hardcover, illustrated by Charles J. Ripper. ($20.00 with dust jacket) $10.00

WEBB, Robert N.
Challenge of Ice, 1963 Whitman, pictorial hardcover. $10.00

WEBB, Wheaton P.
Twelve Labors of Wimpole Stout, 1970 Abingdon, first edition, hardcover, illustrated by Steele Savage. ($25.00 with dust jacket) $15.00

WEBER, Lenora Mattingly, see Series section BEANY MALONE
How Long Is Always?, 1970 Crowell, first edition, hardcover. First edition with dust jacket: $60.00. Later editions: ($20.00 with dust jacket) $15.00
Make a Wish for Me, 1956 Crowell, first edition, hardcover. Hard to find. First edition with dust jacket: $150.00
New and Different Summer, 1966 Crowell, first edition, hardcover, illustrated by Jo Polseno. First edition with dust jacket: $150.00

WEEKS, Sara
Tales of a Common Pigeon, 1960 Houghton Mifflin, first edition, hardcover, illustrated by Eric Von Schmidt. ($25.00 with dust jacket) $15.00

WEIL, Lisl
Golden Spinning Wheel, 1969 Macmillan, first edition, yellow illustrated hardcover, music by Antonin Dvorak. ($15.00 with dust jacket) $10.00
I Wish, I Wish, 1957 Houghton Mifflin, first edition, oversize hardcover, illustrated by author. ($25.00 with dust jacket) $15.00

WEIR, Rosemary, see Series section ALBERT THE DRAGON
Mike's Gang, 1966 Abelard-Schuman, Weekly Reader edition, pictorial hardcover. $10.00

WEISGARD, Leonard
Mr. Peaceable Paints, 1956 Scribner, first edition, oblong oversize pictorial hardcover, illustrated by author. ($45.00 with dust jacket) $20.00
Plymouth Thanksgiving, 1967 Doubleday, first edition, hardcover, illustrated by author. ($15.00 with dust jacket) $10.00
Under the Greenwood Tree, Shakespeare, 1950 edition Oxford, first edition thus, hardcover, illustrated by Weisgard. ($25.00 with dust jacket) $15.00

WEISS, Harvey
Big Cleanup, 1967 Abelard-Schuman, Weekly Reader edition, hardcover. $10.00

WEISS, Renee Karol
Bird from the Sea, 1970 Crowell, first edition,

oblong hardcover, illustrations by Ed Young. ($45.00 with dust jacket) $$20.00

WELCH, Ronald
Knight Crusader, 1960 edition Oxford, Toronto, hardcover, illustrated by William Stobbs. $25.00

WELLMAN, Alice
Tammy, Adventure in Hollywood, 1964 Whitman, pictorial hardcover, photo illustrations of Tammy and friends. $10.00

WELLMAN, Manly Wade
Master of Scare Hollow, 1964 Washburn, first edition, hardcover. ($35.00 with dust jacket) $15.00

WELLS, Helen, see Series section CHERRY AMES

WELLS, Luana M.
Children's Garden, 1960 Nelson, first edition, hardcover. ($25.00 with dust jacket) $15.00

WELLS, Rosemary
Noisy Nora, 1974 Dial Press, illustrated hardcover. ($35.00 with dust jacket) $20.00

WELTY, Eudora
Shoe Bird, 1964 Harcourt, Brace, first edition, illustrated by Beth Krush. ($85.00 with dust jacket) $30.00

WENNING, Elizabeth
Christmas Mouse, 1959 Henry Holt, first edition, hardcover, illustrated by Barbara Remington. ($30.00 with dust jacket) $15.00

Tall Book of Make-Believe, Jane Werner

WERNER, Jane
Giant Golden Book of Elves and Fairies with Assorted Pixies, Mermaids, Brownies, Witches, and Leprechauns, 1951 Simon & Schuster, first American edition, oversize pictorial hardcover, 76 pages, illustrated by Garth Williams. $200.00
Tall Book of Make-Believe, 1950 Harper, first edition, oversize illustrated hardcover, illustrated by Garth Williams. ($150.00 with dust jacket) $35.00
This World of Ours, 1959 Golden Press, first edition, hardcover, color illustrations by Eloise Wilkin. $20.00
Walt Disney's Vanishing Prairie, A True-Life Adventure, 1955 Simon & Schuster, first edition, hardcover, illustrated by color photographs. ($20.00 with dust jacket) $10.00

WERSBA, Barbara
Brave Balloon of Benjamin Buckley, 1963 Atheneum, first edition, oversize hardcover, b/w illustrations by Tomes. ($30.00 with dust jacket) $15.00
Do Tigers Ever Bite Kings?, 1966 Atheneum, first edition, hardcover, colored wood engravings, rhyming text. ($40.00 with dust jacket) $20.00
Dream Watchers, 1968 Atheneum, first edition, hardcover, 171 pages.($20.00 with dust jacket) $10.00
Land of Forgotten Beasts, 1964 Atheneum, first edition, hardcover. ($25.00 with dust jacket) $15.00
Let Me Fall Before I Fly, 1971 Atheneum, hardcover, illustrated by Mercer Mayer. ($25.00 with dust jacket) $15.00

WEST, Jerry, see Series section HAPPY HOLLISTERS

WEST, Tom
Story of the Pony Express/Heroes on Horseback, 1969 Four Winds Press, first edition, hardcover, photos, maps, illustrations. ($20.00 with dust jacket) $15.00

WESTLAKE, Veronica
Unwilling Adventurers, 1955 Blackie, first edition, hardcover, 205 pages. $10.00

WEXLER, Susan Stanhope
Story of Sandy, 1955 Bobbs-Merrill, first edition, hardcover. ($15.00 with dust jacket) $10.00

WHEELER, Benson
I, Becky Barrymore, 1959 Robert Speller, first edition, illustrated by actor Lionel Barrymore. ($35.00 with dust jacket) $20.00

WHEELER, Ruth
Bright Sunset: The Story of an Indian Girl, 1974 Lothrop, Lee & Shepard, first edition, hardcover,

b/w illustrations by Dorothy Matteson. ($35.00 with dust jacket) $20.00

WHITAKER, Helen Hart
Sing and Celebrate, 1961 Silver Burdett, hardcover, 60 pages, illustrations. $15.00

WHITCOMB, Jon
Coco, the Far-Out Poodle, 1963 Random House, first edition, hardcover, illustrated. ($20.00 with dust jacket) $10.00

WHITE, Anne H.
Junket, 1955 Junior Literary Guild and Viking Press, first edition, hardcover, 184 pages, illustrated endpapers, illustrated by Robert McCloskey. ($40.00 with dust jacket) $20.00
Story of Serapina, 1951 Junior Literary Guild and Viking Press, hardcover, illustrated by Tony Palazzo. ($25.00 with dust jacket) $15.00
Uninvited Donkey, 1957 Viking Press, Book Club edition. $10.00

WHITE, Besie
On Your Own Two Feet, 1955 Ariel Books, first edition, hardcover, illustrated by Joshua Tolford. ($20.00 with dust jacket) $10.00

WHITE, Constance M.
Ballet School Mystery, 1959 Hutchinson, hardcover. ($15.00 with dust jacket) $10.00
Young Artists, 1970 Hutchinson, first edition, hardcover. ($20.00 with dust jacket) $10.00

WHITE, Dale
Wild-Horse Trap, 1955 Viking, first edition, hardcover, illustrated by Richard Bennett. ($25.00 with dust jacket) $10.00

WHITE, Dori
Sarah and Katie, 1972 Harper & Row, hardcover. ($20.00 with dust jacket) $10.00

WHITE, E. B.
Charlotte's Web, 1952 Harper, hardcover, b/w illustrations by Garth Williams. First American edition with dust jacket: $450.00 Later editions: ($20.00 with dust jacket) $10.00
Trumpet of the Swan, 1970 Harpers, hardcover, 210 pages, b/w illustrations by Edward Frascino. ($20.00 with dust jacket) $10.00

WHITE, Edward and Muriel
Famous Subways and Tunnels of the World, 1953 Random House, first edition, green pictorial hardcover, 96 pages, indexed, pictorial endpapers, illus-

trated by Robin King. ($25.00 with dust jacket) $10.00

WHITE, Robb
Up Periscope, 1956 Doubleday, first edition, hardcover. ($25.00 with dust jacket) $15.00

WHITE, Stewart Edward
Magic Forest, 1952 Macmillan, first edition, hardcover, illustrated. ($15.00 with dust jacket) $10.00

WHITMAN, Doris
Hand of Apollo, 1969 Follett, first edition, hardcover, illustrated by Paul Hogarth. ($20.00 with dust jacket) $10.00

WHITMAN, Walt
Lines from Walt Whitman: Overhead the Sun, 1969 edition Farrar, Straus and Giroux, first edition thus, oversize hardcover, woodcut illustrations by Antonio Frasconi. ($60.00 with dust jacket) $25.00

WHITNEY, Phyllis
Linda's Homecoming, 1950 Grosset & Dunlap, hardcover. ($20.00 with dust jacket) $10.00

WHITNEY, Thomas P., translator
Story of Prince Ivan, the Firebird, and the Gray Wolf, 1968 Scribner, first edition, oblong hardcover, illustrated by Nonny Hogrogian. ($35.00 with dust jacket) $20.00

WHYTE, Jenny Bell
Adelaide Stories, 1972 Simon & Schuster, first edition, hardcover, 76 pages, illustrated by Annabelle Prager. ($20.00 with dust jacket) $10.00

WIBBERLEY, Leonard
Ballad of the Pilgrim Cat, 1962 Washburn, first edition, hardcover, illustrated by Erik Blegvad. ($30.00 with dust jacket) $15.00
Epics of Everest, 1954 Junior Literary Guild and Ariel, book club edition, illustrated by Genevieve Vaughan-Jackson, map endpapers. ($15.00 with dust jacket) $10.00
Hands of Cormac Joyce, 1960 Putnam, first edition, hardcover, illustrated by Richard Bennett. ($20.00 with dust jacket) $10.00

WIEMER, Rudolf Otto
Good Robber Willibald, 1968 Atheneum, first American edition, hardcover. ($35.00 with dust jacket) $15.00

WIESE, Kurt
Groundhog and His Shadow, 1959 Viking Press,

first edition, hardcover, illustrated by author. ($25.00 with dust jacket) $15.00

Thief in the Attic, 1965 Viking, illustrated hardcover, color illustrations by author. $15.00

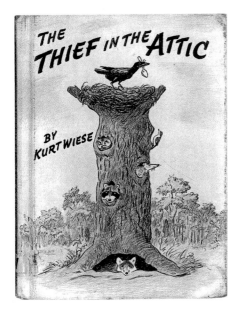

WILD, Robin and Jocelyn
Mouse Who Stole a Zoo, 1972 Coward, McCann, & Geoghegan, first American edition, hardcover. ($20.00 with dust jacket) $10.00

WILDE, Irma
Christmas Puppy, 1953 Wonder Books, small pictorial hardcover, color illustrations. $15.00
Puppy Who Found a Boy, with George Wilde, 1951 Wonder Books, small pictorial hardcover, color illustrations. $20.00
Farm Animals, 1960 McLoughlin, narrow glossy illustrated hardcover, stiff glossy pages, color illustrations by Wilde. $15.00

WILDER, Laura Ingalls, see Series section LITTLE HOUSE
West from Home: Letters of Laura Ingalls Wilder, 1974 Harper and Row, first edition, hardcover, edited by Roger Lea MacBride. ($15.00 with dust jacket) $10.00

WILDSMITH, Brian, author-illustrator
Brian Wildsmith's ABC, 1962 Franklin Watts, first American edition, oversize hardcover, 52 pages, full-page color illustration throughout. $15.00
Brian Wildsmith's Birds, 1967 Franklin Watts, first American edition, hardcover, 34 pages, color illustrations by author. $25.00
Brian Wildsmith's Wild Animals, 1967 Watts, first edition, oblong oversize pictorial hardcover, illustrated by author. ($25.00 with dust jacket) $15.00

Lion and the Rat, a Fontaine fable, 1963 Oxford, London, first edition, oversize hardcover, illustrated by author. ($30.00 with dust jacket) $15.00
Little Wood Duck, 1973 Jonathan Cape, London, pictorial oversize hardcover, illustrated by author. ($35.00 with dust jacket) $20.00
Miller, the Boy and the Donkey, (based on a fable by La Fontaine), 1969 Oxford University Press, first edition, hardcover, color illustrated by author. ($20.00 with dust jacket) $15.00
Nursery Rhymes, Mother Goose, 1964 Oxford University Press, first edition, hardcover, illustrated by author. $30.00
Owl and the Woodpecker, 1971, London, oversize hardcover, illustrated by author. ($35.00 with dust jacket) $20.00
Python's Party, 1974 Franklin Watts, oversize hardcover, 32 pages, color illustrations by author. ($30.00 with dust jacket) $15.00

WILKIN, Eloise, illustrator
Baby's Mother Goose, 1958 Golden Press, oversize glossy hardcover, color illustrations by Wilkin. $50.00

WILLARD, Barbara
Charity at Home, 1965 Harcourt, Brace, hardcover. ($15.00 with dust jacket) $10.00
Sprig of Broom, 1971 Dutton, first edition, hardcover. ($35.00 with dust jacket) $15.00

WILLARD, Nancy
Sailing to Cythera and Other Anatole Stories, 1974 Harcourt Brace Jovanovich, first edition, hardcover, 72 pages, illustrations by David McPhail. ($15.00 with dust jacket) $10.00

WILLCOX, K. M.
Candlelight Angel, 1960 Mowbray & Co. Ltd., first edition, hardcover, 188 pages, illustrated by Jennifer Miles. ($15.00 with dust jacket) $10.00

WILLIAMS, Anne Sinclair
Secret of the Round Tower, 1968 Random House, hardcover, 87 pages, full-page illustrations by J.C. Kocsis. ($25.00 with dust jacket) $15.00

WILLIAMS, Barbara
Kevin's Grandma, 1975 Dutton, first edition, hardcover, illustrated by Kay Chorao. ($25.00 with dust jacket) $15.00

WILLIAMS, Eric
Wooden Horse, 1959 Collins, London, red hardcover. ($15.00 with dust jacket) $10.00

WILLIAMS, Garth
Adventures of Benjamin Pink, 1951 Harper, first edition, hardcover, b/w illustrations by author. Hard to find. ($75.00 with dust jacket) $40.00
Baby Animals, copyright 1952 Simon & Schuster Golden Book, small, illustrated slick paper-over-board cover, stiff pages, color illustrations throughout by Williams. $20.00
Rabbits' Wedding, 1958 Harper and Row, oversize hardcover, color illustrations by author. First edition with dust jacket: $150.00

WILLIAMS, Gladys
Semolina Silkpaws Comes to Catstown, 1967 Hart, first American edition, hardcover. ($25.00 with dust jacket) $15.00

WILLIAMS, J. R.
Oh, Susanna!, 1963 Putnam, first edition, hardcover, illustrated by Albert Orbaan. ($25.00 with dust jacket) $15.00

WILLIAMS, Jay, see Series section DANNY DUNN
Cookie Tree, 1967 Parents' Magazine, pictorial oversize hardcover, color illustrations by Blake Hampton. $20.00
King With Six Friends, 1968 Parents' Magazine, first edition, oversize hardcover, orange endpapers, illustrated by Imero Gobbato. $15.00
Practical Princess, 1969 Parents' Magazine, pictorial hardcover. $15.00
Seven at One Blow, 1972 Parents' Magazine Press, first edition, hardcover, illustrated by Friso Henstra. ($20.00 with dust jacket) $10.00
Tournament of the Lions, 1960 Walck, first edition, hardcover, illustrated by Ezra Jack Keats. ($25.00 with dust jacket) $15.00
What Can You Do With a Word?, 1966 Collier, first edition, Beginning Reader, hardcover. $10.00

WILLIAMS, M. P.
Nigerian Holiday, 1959 Pickering & Inglis, yellow hardcover, color frontispiece. ($15.00 with dust jacket) $10.00

WILLIAMS, Ursula Moray
Earl's Falconer, 1961 William Morrow, hardcover. ($15.00 with dust jacket) $10.00
Malkin's Mountain, 1971 Thomas Nelson, first American edition, hardcover, illustrated by Shirley Hughes. ($20.00 with dust jacket) $10.00
Nine Lives of Island Mackenzie, 1959 Chatto & Windus, London, first edition, oversize hardcover, 128 pages, color illustrated endpapers, b/w illustrations by Edward Ardizzone. ($100.00 with dust jacket) $40.00
Picnic with the Aunts, 1972 Chatto & Windus, first edition, green oversize hardcover, color illustrations by Faith Jacques. ($25.00 with dust jacket) $15.00
Secrets of the Wood, 1955 Harrap, first edition, hardcover, 127 pages, illustrated by author. ($40.00 with dust jacket) $20.00

WILLOUGHBY, Louisa
Fairyland Tales, 1970 Collins, London, laminated pictorial hardcover, illustrated endpapers, 28 pages, color illustrations by Rene Cloke. $15.00

WILLS, Jonathan
Travels of Magnus Pole, 1975 Houghton, first edition, oversize hardcover, color illustrations by author. $15.00

WILSON, Catherine
Fantasy In Orbit, 1975 Carlton, first edition, hardcover. ($15.00 with dust jacket) $10.00

WILSON, Erle
Minado the Devil Dog, a Novel of the Quebec Woods,

1955 Andre Deutsch, London, first edition, hardcover, 191 pages. ($25.00 with dust jacket) $15.00

WILSON, Gahan
Bang Bang Family, 1974 Charles Scribner, first edition, hardcover, illustrated by author. ($50.00 with dust jacket) $20.00

WINDSOR, Mary
Mr. Gallagher's Donkey, 1950 Garden City, first edition, pictorial hardcover, illustrated by Elsie Dariern. ($40.00 with dust jacket) $20.00

WINDSOR, Patricia
Summer Before, 1973 Harper, pictorial hardcover. $20.00

WINN, Marie
Fireside Book of Fun & Game Songs, 1974 Simon & Schuster, first edition, hardcover, illustrated by Whitney Darrow Jr. ($25.00 with dust jacket) $10.00
What Shall We Do and Allee Galloo!, 1970 Harper & Row, first edition, hardcover, illustrated by Karla Kuskin. ($30.00 with dust jacket) $15.00

WINSLOW, Marjorie
Mud Pies and Other Recipes, 1961 Macmillan, small, green hardcover, b/w illustrations by Erik Blegvad. ($35.00 with dust jacket) $15.00

WINSOR, Frederick
Space Child's Mother Goose, 1958 Simon & Schuster, first edition, hardcover, b/w illustrations by Marian Parry. ($45.00 with dust jacket) $20.00

WINTER, Howard
Wonders of the Animal Kingdom, 1959 Golden Glow

Sales, first edition, pictorial hardcover, sealed and including 20 packets of stamps. $75.00

WINTER, Klaus and **Helmut BISCHOFF**
Forester Pfeffer, 1960 Franklin Watts, first American edition, oversize hardcover. ($30.00 with dust jacket) $15.00

WINTERFIELD, Henry
Castaways in Lilliput, 1960 Harcourt, hardcover. ($25.00 with dust jacket) $10.00
Star Girl, 1957 Harcourt, hardcover. ($20.00 with dust jacket) $10.00

WISBESKI, Dorothy
Picaro, a Pet Otter, 1971 Hawthorn Books, first edition, oblong hardcover, illustrated by Edna Miller. ($20.00 with dust jacket) $10.00

WISE, William
Lazy Young Duke of Dundee, 1970 Rand McNally, first edition, oversize hardcover, 47 pages. ($35.00 with dust jacket) $20.00

WISE, Winifred E.
Revolt of the Darumas, 1970 Parents' Magazine, first edition, illustrated oblong hardcover, illustrated by Beverly Komoda. $25.00

WISEMAN, B.
Morris is a Cowboy, a Policeman and a Baby Sitter, 1960 Harper, I Can Read book, pictorial hardcover. $10.00
Morris Goes to School, 1970 Harper, I Can Read book, pictorial hardcover. $10.00

WITHERIDGE, Elizabeth P.
Mara Journeys Home, 1957 Abingdon, first edition, hardcover, 128 pages, illustrated by Lucille Wallower. ($15.00 with dust jacket) $10.00
Never Younger, Jeannie, 1957 Atheneum, illustrated hardcover. $10.00

WITHERS, Carl
Grindstone of God: A Fable Retold, 1970 Holt, Rinehart and Winston, first edition, hardcover, illustrated by Bernarda Bryson. ($25.00 with dust jacket) $10.00

WITTY, Paul and **Florence BRUMBAUGH**
Fun and Frolic, 1955 D.C. Heath, school reader, hardcover, illustrated by Emma Bock. $15.00

WOJCIECHOWSKA, Maia
Don't Play Dead Before You Have To, 1970 Harper & Row, hardcover. ($15.00 with dust jacket) $10.00

Life and Death of a Brave Bull, 1972 Harcourt, first edition, hardcover, illustrated by John Groth. ($25.00 with dust jacket) $10.00

Shadow of a Bull, 1965 Atheneum, hardcover, 165 pages. ($15.00 with dust jacket) $10.00

WOLF, Bernard

Jamaica Boy, 1971 Cowles, first edition, hardcover, photographs by author. ($20.00 with dust jacket) $10.00

WOLFF, Janet

Let's Imagine Thinking Things Up, 1961 Dutton, glossy illustrated hardcover, 30 pages, illustrated by Bernard Owett. $20.00

WOLHEIM, Donald, see Series section MIKE MARS

WONDRISKA, William

All By Myself, 1963 Holt, Rinehart and Winston, first edition, hardcover. ($25.00 with dust jacket) $15.00

Puff, 1960 Pantheon, pictorial hardcover. $20.00

WOOD, Frances E.

Tommy of Bar A Ranch, 1951 Whitman Cozy Corner Book, hardcover, illustrated by E. Dart. $15.00

WOOD, James Playsted

Admirable Cotton Mather, 1971 Seabury Press, hardcover. ($15.00 with dust jacket) $10.00

Hound, a Bay Horse, and a Turtle Dove, 1963 Pantheon, hardcover. ($15.00 with dust jacket) $10.00

WOOD, Kerry

Great Chief Maskepetoon, Warrior of the Crees, 1957 Macmillan, Toronto, hardcover. ($15.00 with dust jacket) $10.00

Wild Winter, 1954 Houghton Mifflin, first edition, hardcover, illustrated by Victor Mays. ($25.00 with dust jacket) $10.00

WOOD, Nancy

Little Wrangler, 1966 Doubleday, first edition, hardcover, illustrated by Myron Wood, photos. ($40.00 with dust jacket) $20.00

WOODBERRY, Joan

Cider Duck, 1969 Macmillan of Australia, first edition, hardcover, illustrated by Molly Stephens. ($25.00 with dust jacket) $15.00

Come Back Peter, 1968 Adelaide Rigby, hardcover, 103 pages, illustrated by George Tetlow. ($15.00 with dust jacket) $10.00

WOODS, Hubert C.

Child of the Arctic, 1962 Follett, first edition, hardcover, 173 pages, illustrated. ($15.00 with dust jacket) $10.00

WOODS, Joan

Maudie's Mush Pots, 1963 Abingdon, red hardcover, 32 pages, illustrations in color by William Thackeray. $25.00

WOODY, Regina

Almena's Dogs, 1965 Ariel Books, hardcover. $20.00

WOOLLEY, Catherine, see Series section GINNIE

Libby Looks for a Spy, 1970 Morrow, pictorial hardcover. $10.00

Railroad Cowboy, 1951 William Morrow, first edition, hardcover, illustrated by Iris Beatty Johnson. ($30.00 with dust jacket) $10.00

WORCESTER, Donald, see Series section LONE HUNTER

WORCESTER, Gurdon S.

Singing Flute, 1963 Ivan Obolensky, first edition, hardcover, illustrated by Irene Burns. ($25.00 with dust jacket) $15.00

WORMSER, Richard

Kidnapped Circus, 1968 Morrow, Weekly Reader edition, hardcover, illustrated by Don Bolognese. $10.00

WORSTELL, Emma Vietor

Jump the Rope Jingles, 1961 Macmillan, oblong pictorial hardcover, illustrated by Sheila Greenwald. ($20.00 with dust jacket) $10.00

WRIGHT, Anna Rose

Offshore Summer, 1957 Houghton Mifflin, first edition, hardcover, 183 pages, b/w illustrations by Ursula Koering. $10.00

WRIGHT, Dare, see Series section EDITH

WRIGHT, Frances Fitzpatrick

Daybreak at Sampey Place, 1954 Abingdon Press, hardcover, illustrated endpapers, illustrated by Margaret Ayer. $10.00

Surprise at Sampey Place, 1950 Abingdon Press, hardcover, illustrated endpapers, illustrated by Margaret Ayer. ($20.00 with dust jacket) $10.00

WRIGHTSON, Patricia

Feather Star, 1963 Harcourt, first American edition, hardcover, 160 pages, illustrated by Noela Young. $15.00

Racecourse for Andy, 1968 Harcourt, first edition, hardcover, 156 pages, illustrated by Margaret Horder. $15.00

WRISTON, Hildreth
Show Lamb, 1953 Abingdon, first edition, hardcover, 191 pages, illustrated by Peter Burchard. ($15.00 with dust jacket) $10.00

WUORIO, Eva-Lis
Canadian Twins, 1956 Jonathan Cape, first edition, hardcover. ($15.00 with dust jacket) $10.00
Happiness Flower, 1969 World, first edition, hardcover, 78 pages, illustrated by Don Bolognese. ($25.00 with dust jacket) $15.00
Land of Right Up and Down, 1964 World, first edition, hardcover, color and b/w illustrations by Edward Ardizzone. ($30.00 with dust jacket) $15.00
October Treasure, 1967 Holt, Rinehart, hardcover, 191 pages. ($25.00 with dust jacket) $10.00
Return of the Viking, 1955 Clarke, Irwin & Company Limited, Toronto, blue hardcover. $10.00
Venture at Midsummer, 1967 Holt, first edition, hardcover. ($30.00 with dust jacket) $15.00

WYATT, George, see Series section BRAINS BENTON

WYLER, Rose
Child's First Book Of Everyday Adventure, 1953 Grosset & Dunlap, hardcover. ($15.00 with dust jacket) $10.00
Exploring Space, 1958 Simon & Schuster, first edition, hardcover, illustrated by Tibor Gergely. $10.00
Story of the Ice Age, (with Gerald Ames), 1956 Harper, hardcover, illustrated by Thomas Voter. $15.00

WYNDHAM, Lee
How and Why Wonder Book of Ballet, 1961 Grosset & Dunlap, illustrated hardcover, illustrations. $10.00

WYNDHAM, Robert, editor
Chinese Mother Goose Rhymes, 1968 World, first edition, hardcover, illustrated by Ed Young. ($20.00 with dust jacket) $10.00

WYNNE, Pamela
Tide Has Turned, 1957 Collins, hardcover. ($15.00 with dust jacket) $10.00

WYSE, Lois
Grandfathers Are to Love, 1967 Parents', first edition, small hardcover, illustrated. ($25.00 with dust jacket) $15.00
I Wish Every Day Were My Birthday, 1967 World, first edition, hardcover, illustrated by Donald Leake. ($15.00 with dust jacket) $10.00

YASHIMA, Taro
Crow Boy, 1955 Viking Press, hardcover. ($25.00 with dust jacket) $15.00

YATES, Elizabeth
On That Night, 1969 Dutton, first edition, hardcover, 92 pages, illustrated by James Barkley. ($20.00 with dust jacket) $10.00
Rainbow Round the World: A Story of UNICEF, 1954 Bobbs-Merrill, first edition, green hardcover. ($15.00 with dust jacket) $10.00

YEOMAN, John
Mouse Trouble, 1972 Macmillan, Weekly Reader edition, illustrated hardcover, illustrated by Quentin Blake. $15.00

YEP, Laurence
Sweetwater, 1973 Harper, first edition, hardcover, illustrated by Julia Noonan. $15.00

YLLA
Little Bears, 1954 Harper, oversize hardcover, 30 pages, illustrated by Ylla. ($45.00 with dust jacket) $30.00

YOLEN, Jane
Bird of Time, 1971 Crowell, first edition, hardcover, illustrated by Mercer Mayer. ($30.00 with dust jacket) $15.00
Boy Who Had Wings, 1974 Crowell, first edition, oversize hardcover, illustrated by Helga Aichinger. ($50.00 with dust jacket) $20.00
Emperor and the Kite, 1967 World, Caldecott Honor book, oblong hardcover, illustrated by Ed Young. ($30.00 with dust jacket) $20.00
Girl Who Cried Flowers, 1974 Crowell, color illustrations by David Palladini. First edition with dust jacket: $50.00. Later editions: ($20.00 with dust jacket) $15.00
Inway Investigators or Mystery at McCracken's Place, 1969 Seabury Press, first edition, hardcover, illustrated by Allan Eitzen. ($15.00 with dust jacket) $10.00
Minstel and the Mountain, 1967 World Publishing, small hardcover, illustrated in full-color on every other page by Anne Rockwell. ($25.00 with dust jacket) $15.00
Rainbow Rider, 1974 Crowell, blue hardcover with gilt, illustrated by Michael Foreman. ($35.00 with dust jacket) $15.00
Ring Out! A Book of Bells, 1974 Clarion, hardcover, b/w illustrations by Richard Cuffari. ($25.00 with dust jacket) $15.00

See This Little Line?, 1963 David McKay, first edition, hardcover, illustrated by Kathleen Elgin. ($15.00 with dust jacket) $10.00

Seventh Mandarin, 1970 Seabury Press, first edition, hardcover, color illustrations by Ed Young. ($15.00 with dust jacket) $10.00

YORK, Carol Beach
Mystery of the Spider Doll, 1973 Watts, hardcover. $10.00

Ten O'Clock Club, 1970 Franklin Watts, first edition, hardcover. ($20.00 with dust jacket) $10.00

Tree House Mystery, 1973 Weekly Reader edition, hardcover, illustrated by Reisie Lonette. $10.00

YORK, Suzannah
In Search of Unicorns, 1973 Hodder and Stoughton, first edition, oversize brown buckram hardcover with gilt, pictorial endpapers, color and b/w illustrations by Wendy Hall. ($65.00 with dust jacket) $25.00

YORTY, Jean
Far Wilderness, 1966 William B. Eerdmans, first edition, hardcover, b/w drawings. ($15.00 with dust jacket) $10.00

YOUNG, Bob and Jan
Across the Tracks, 1958 Julian Messner, hardcover. $10.00

YOUNG, Doris, editor
Kim's Cookbook, 1971 Red Farm Studio, first edition, hardcover, spiral bound, b/w illustrations by Ellen Nelson. $25.00

YOUNG, Miriam
Miss Suzy, 1964 Parents', illustrated hardcover, illustrated endpapers, color illustrations by Arnold Lobel. $20.00

YOUNG, Percy
Ding Dong Bell, "A First Book of Nursery Rhymes," co-authored with Edward Ardizzone, 1957 Dennis Dobson, London, first edition, decorated hardcover, 143 pages, illustrated. ($40.00 with dust jacket) $20.00

YOUNG, Scott
Clue of the Dead Duck, 1962 Little, Brown, hardcover. ($15.00 with dust jacket) $10.00

YOUNGBERG, Norma R.
Nyla and the White Crocodile, 1963 Review and Herald, pictorial hardcover, decorated endpapers, illustrated by Thomas Dunbebin. ($20.00 with dust jacket) $10.00

──── ◦⇒ **Z** ⇐◦ ────

ZAFFO, George J.
Big Book of Real Fire Engines, 1950 Grosset & Dunlap, first edition, oversize pictorial hardcover, illustrated by Zaffo. $20.00

ZAHN, Muriel
Grimsel, Story of a Valiant Saint Bernard and Three Boys in the Swiss Alps, 1953 Bobbs-Merrill, first edition, gold-stamped blue hardcover, 178 pages, illustrated by William Walsh. ($15.00 with dust jacket) $10.00

ZALBEN, Jane Breskin
Basil and Hillary, 1975 Macmillan, first edition, hardcover. ($45.00 with dust jacket) $20.00

ZANINI, G.
Dinosaur Book, 1973 Greenwich House, pictorial hardcover, illustrated by G. B. Bertelli. $25.00
Later editions: $10.00

ZAPF, Marjorie A.
Mystery of the Great Swamp, 1967 Atheneum, Weekly Reader edition. $10.00

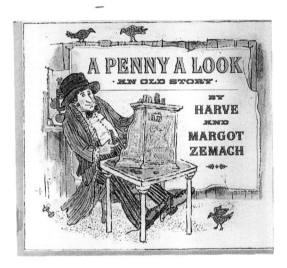

ZEMACH, Harve
Awake and Dreaming, 1970 Farrar, Straus & Giroux, oversize blue hardcover, illustrated by Margot Zemach. ($35.00 with dust jacket) $15.00

Duffy and the Devil, 1973 Farrar, 1974 Caldecott Award, hardcover, illustrated by Margot Zemach. ($30.00 with dust jacket) $15.00

Judge, An Untrue Tale, 1969 Bodley Head, first edition UK, oblong oversize hardcover. ($30.00 with dust jacket) $15.00

Mommy, Buy Me a China Doll, 1966 Follett, hardcover, adaptation of old Ozarks song, color illustrations by Margot Zemach. ($20.00 with dust jacket) $10.00

Penny a Look, An Old Story, 1973 Farrar, first edition, hardcover, color illustrations by Margot Zemach. ($40.00 with dust jacket) $20.00

Princess and Froggie, with Kaethe Zemach, 1975 Farrar, first edition, blue hardcover, illustrated by Margot Zemach. ($20.00 with dust jacket) $10.00

Salt, 1965 Follett, hardcover picture book, illustrated by Margot Zemach. ($20.00 with dust jacket) $10.00

Small Boy Is Listening, 1959 Houghton Mifflin, first edition, small hardcover, 30 pages, b/w illustrations by Margot Zemach, first book by Zemachs. ($60.00 with dust jacket) $30.00

Speckled Hen: A Russian Nursey Rhyme, 1966 Holt, hardcover, illustrated by Margot Zemach. ($30.00 with dust jacket) $15.00

Too Much Nose: An Italian Tale, 1967 Holt, first edition, hardcover. ($20.00 with dust jacket) $10.00

ZHELEZNOVA, Irina, editor

Vasilisa the Beautiful, Russian Fairy Tales, 1966 Progress Publishers, Moscow, first edition, green hardcover with gilt, 213 pages, color illustrations throughout. ($30.00 with dust jacket) $15.00

ZIEGLER, Ursina

Peppino, 1971 Atheneum, hardcover, illustrated by Sita Jucker. ($25.00 with dust jacket) $15.00

Squaps the Moonling, 1969 Atheneum, first American edition, pictorial hardcover, color illustrations by Sita Jucker. ($40.00 with dust jacket) $25.00

ZIJLSTRA, Tjerk

Benny and His Geese, 1975 McGraw-Hill, first edition, hardcover, illustrated by Ivo de Weerd. ($20.00 with dust jacket) $15.00

ZIMELMAN, Nathan

Look Hiroshi!, 1972 Aurora Publishers, first edition, hardcover, woodcut illustrated by Dan Quest. ($20.00 with dust jacket) $10.00

Tales of Butcher Bobcat and Chipper Chipmunk, 1972 Christopher Publications, first edition, small hardcover, 163 pages, illustrated. ($15.00 with dust jacket) $10.00

To Sing a Song as Big as Ireland, 1967 Follett, first edition, oversize hardcover, 32 pages, pastel illustrations by Terence O'Flaherty O'Flynn. ($20.00 with dust jacket) $10.00

ZIMMERMAN, Naomi

Baby Animals, 1955 Rand McNally Storytime Book, color illustrated paper-over-board hardcover, oversize, color illustrations throughout by Marge Opitz. $15.00

ZINDEL, Paul

Pardon Me, You're Stepping on My Eyeball, 1976 Harper, first edition, illustrated hardcover. ($40.00 with same-as-cover dust jacket) $20.00

Pigman, 1968 Harper Row, first edition, hardcover. ($35.00 with dust jacket) $20.00

ZINER, Feenie

Hiding, 1963 Golden Gate Junior Books, first edition, hardcover, illustrations by Zeke Ziner. ($45.00 with dust jacket) $20.00

ZION, Gene, see Series section HARRY THE DOG

All Falling Down, 1951 Harper, pictorial hardcover, illustrated by Margaret Bloy Graham. ($15.00 with dust jacket) $10.00

ZOLOTOW, Charlotte

Big Brother, 1960 Harper, small pictorial hardcover, illustrated by Mary Chalmers. ($25.00 with dust jacket) $15.00

Bunny Who Found Easter, 1959 Parnassus Press, green hardcover with embossed outline of bunnies, illustrated by Betty Peterson. ($25.00 with dust jacket) $15.00

I Have a Horse of My Own, 1964 Crowell, first edition, hardcover, 28 pages, illustrated by Yoko Mitsuhashi. ($25.00 with dust jacket) $15.00

Mr. Rabbit and the Lovely Present, 1962 Harper, oblong pictorial boards, pictures by Maurice Sendak. First edition: $100.00. Later editions: $10.00

Quarreling Book, 1963 Harper, first edition, hardcover, illustrated by Arnold Lobel. ($25.00 with dust jacket) $15.00

Rose, A Bridge, and A Wild Black Horse, 1964 Harper and Row, first edition, hardcover, illustrated by Uri Shulevitz. ($35.00 with dust jacket) $15.00

Sky Was Blue, 1963 Harper and Row, first edition, hardcover, illustrations by Garth Williams. ($35.00 with dust jacket) $15.00

Storm Book, 1952 Harper, oversize pictorial hardcover, color illustrations by Margaret Bloy Graham. ($25.00 with dust jacket) $15.00

Summer Night, 1974 Harper, hardcover, color illustrations by Ben Shecter. ($15.00 with dust jacket) $10.00

Unfriendly Book, 1975 Harper & Row, first edition, small with pictorial hardcover, b/w illustrations by William Pene DuBois. ($25.00 with dust jacket) $15.00

Prices are for each hardcover book in good condition but without dust jacket, except when noted.

A

ADVENTURE SERIES, Enid Blyton, ca. 1944 – 1955, Macmillan, UK, hardcover, illustrated by Stuart Tresilian. Early British editions featured light hardcover with contrasting picture stamped on cover. First editions: ($100.00 with dust jacket) $30.00
Later editions: ($35.00 with dust jacket) $15.00
Island of Adventure
Castle of Adventure
Valley of Adventure
Sea of Adventure
Mountain of Adventure
Ship of Adventure
Circus of Adventure
River of Adventure

ADVENTURE IN SPACE SERIES, Willy Ley, 1957-1958 Guild Press, glossy illustrated hardcover, 44 pages, illustrated by John Polgreen. $20.00
Golden Press editions: $15.00
Space Pilots
Space Stations
Man Made Satellites

ALBERT THE DRAGON SERIES, Rosemary Weir, 1960s Abelard-Schuman, hardcover, illustrated by Quentin Blake. $20.00
Albert the Dragon, 1961
Further Adventures of Albert the Dragon, 1964
Albert the Dragon and the Centaur, 1968

ALFRED HITCHCOCK AND THE THREE INVESTIGATORS SERIES, Random House, color illustrated paper-over-board covers, graveyard illustration endpapers, b/w full page illustrations, about 150 pages, series titles listed on back cover. First editions generally list to self.
Three teens investigate crimes at the instigation of movie director Alfred Hitchcock (1899 – 1980), who appears briefly in the introduction or closing chapters. Robert Arthur (1909 – 1969), an editor at the Alfred Hitchcock Mystery Magazine, wrote 10 of the early titles in the 43-book series. Following Hitchcock's death, books #31 through #43 used a fictional film director named Hector Sebastian. Later titles are the most difficult to find, due to the limited number of printings. After 1979 the series name changed to *Three Investigators* and reprints of earlier stories had the titles revised, dropping the Hitchcock reference. These later reprints and are usually priced at about $10.00.
Probable firsts: $40.00
Early printings, hardcovers: $20.00
1970s Scholastic paperbacks: $5.00
Secret of Terror Castle, 1964, Robert Arthur
Mystery of the Stuttering Parrot, 1964, Robert Arthur
Mystery of the Whispering Mummy, Robert Arthur
Mystery of the Green Ghost, 1965, Robert Arthur
Mystery of the Vanishing Treasure, 1966, Robert Arthur
Secret of Skeleton Island, 1966, Robert Arthur
Mystery of the Fiery Eye, 1967, Robert Arthur
Mystery of the Silver Spider, 1967, Robert Arthur
Mystery of the Screaming Clock, 1968, Robert Arthur
Mystery of the Moaning Cave, 1968, William Arden
Mystery of the Talking Skull, 1969, Robert Arthur
Mystery of the Laughing Shadow, 1969, William Arden
Secret of the Crooked Cat, 1970, William Arden
Mystery of the Coughing Dragon, 1970, Nick West
Mystery of the Flaming Footprints, 1971, Alfred Carey
Mystery of the Singing Serpent, 1972, Alfred Carey
Mystery of the Shrinking House, 1972
Mystery of Monster Mountain, 1973
Secret of Phantom Lake, 1973
Secret of the Haunted Mirror, 1974
Mystery of the Dead Man's Riddle, 1974

ALFRED HITCHCOCK ANTHOLOGIES, 1960s Random House, oversize illustrated hardcover, illustrated endpapers, 200+ pages, two-color illustrations, collections of short stories by noted mystery writers matching the title theme. ($20.00 with dust jacket) $10.00

Alfred Hitchcock and The Three Investigators, cover and graveyard endpapers.

Alfred Hitchcock's Haunted Houseful, 1961
Alfred Hitchcock's Ghostly Gallery, 1962
Alfred Hitchcock's Daring Detectives, 1969
Alfred Hitchcock's Sinister Spies, 1966
Alfred Hitchcock's Monster Museum
Alfred Hitchcock's Spellbinders in Suspense

ALL ABOUT SERIES, Random House, hardcover, pictorial boards, illustrations. ($15.00 with dust jacket) $10.00
All About Dinosaurs, R. C. Andrews, 1953
All About the Sea, F. Lane, 1953
All About Whales, R. C. Chapman, 1954
All About the Insect World, Lane, 1954
All About Famous Inventors and Their Inventions, Pratt, 1955
All About our Changing Rocks, White, 1955
All About the Flowering World, Lane, 1956
All About Moths and Butterflies, Lemmon, 1953
All About Famous Inventors and their Inventions, Fletcher, 1955
All About Strange Beasts of the Present, Lemmon, 1957
All About Animals and Their Young, McClung, 1958
All About Monkeys, Lemmon, 1958
All About Rockets and Jets, Pratt, 1958
All About the Ice Age, Patricia Lauber, 1959
All About Fish, Carl Burger, 1960
All About Undersea Exploration, Ruth Brindze, 1960
All About Aviation, Loomis, 1964

ALL-OF-A-KIND FAMILY SERIES, Sidney Taylor, various publishers and illustrators. Early printings: ($75.00 with dust jacket) $20.00
All-of-a-Kind Family, 1951 Wilcox and Follett, illus-

trated by Helen John
More All-of-a-Kind Family, 1954 Wilcox, illustrated by Mary E. Stevens
All-of-a-Kind Family Uptown, 1958 Wilcox, illustrated by Mary E. Stevens
All-of-a-Kind Family Downtown, 1972, b/w illustrations by Beth and Joe Krush, oversize, 187 pages, wrap-around illustration dust jacket
Ella of All-of-a-Kind Family, 1978 Dutton, illustrated by Gail Owens

ALVIN FERNALD SERIES, Clifford B. Hicks, 1970s Holt, Weekly Reader edition, illustrated hardcover, illustrated by Bill Sokol. $15.00
Alvin Fernald, Superweasel, 1974
Alvin Fernald, Mayor for a Day
Alvin Fernald, Foreign Trader
Alvin's Secret Code
Marvelous Inventions of Alvin Fernald

AMELIA BEDELIA SERIES, Peggy Parish, Harper & Row, Weekly Reader Book Club, "An I Can Read Book", 64 pages, pictorial hardcover, illustrated by Fritz Siebel or Wallace Tripp. ($20.00 with dust jacket) $10.00
Amelia Bedelia, 1963
Thank You, Amelia Bedelia, 1964
Amelia Bedelia and the Surprise Shower, 1969
Come Back, Amelia Bedelia, 1971
Play Ball, Amelia Bedelia, 1972

AMERICAN HERITAGE BOOK OF THE PRESIDENTS SERIES, ca. 1976 Dell, 12 volume series, illustrated hardcover, color illustrated endpapers, color and b/w illustrations throughout. Each: $20.00

AMERICAN HERITAGE LANDMARK BOOKS, see
LANDMARK BOOKS

AMERICAN HERITAGE SERIES, Aladdin Books,
hardcover. ($20.00 with dust jacket) $10.00
Back of Beyond, George Franklin, 1952
Wildcat, the Seminole, Electa Clark, 1956
King of the Clippers, Edmund Collier, 1955
Pirates of the Spanish Main, Hamilton Cockran, 1961

AMERICAN REGIONAL STORIES SERIES, Lois
Lenski, 1950s Lippincott, hardcover, illustrated
endpapers, b/w illustrations by author.
First edition: ($150.00 with dust jacket) $25.00
Later printings: ($40.00 with dust jacket) $15.00
Houseboat Girl
San Francisco Boy
Corn-Farm Boy
Texas Tomboy
Cotton in My Sack
Boom Town Boy
Coal Camp Girl
Mama Hattie's Girl
Prairie School
Blue Ridge Billy
Strawberry Girl
Bayou Suzette
Judy's Journey

Shoo-Fly Girl
Deer Valley Girl

ANATOLE SERIES, Eve Titus, Whittlesey House
(McGraw Hill), small, hardcover, 32 pages, b/w illus-
trations by Paul Galdone. The first title is a Calde-
cott Honor book. ($35.00 in dust jacket) $15.00
Oversize editions with color illustrations, 32
pages. ($60.00 with dust jacket) $30.00
Weekly Reader editions: $10.00
Anatole, 1956
Anatole and the Cat, 1957
Anatole and the Robot, 1960
Anatole Over Paris, 1961
Anatole and the Poodle, 1965
Anatole and the Piano, 1966
Anatole and the Thirty Thieves
Anatole in Italy
Anatole and the Toyshop, 1970

ARTHUR SERIES, Lillian Hoban, Harper, I Can
Read books, small, illustrated hardcovers, color
illustrations by author. $10.00
Arthur's Halloween Costume
Arthur's Christmas Cookies
Arthur's Honey Bear, 1973 Harper, hardcover. First
edition with dust jacket: $40.00. Later editions:
($20.00 with dust jacket) $10.00

American Regional Stories Series, Lois Lenski

⇒ B ⇐

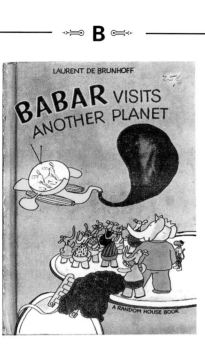

BABAR SERIES, created by Jean de Brunhoff (1899 – 1937) continued and revised by Laurent de Brunhoff, color illustrations by authors. Random House editions usually issued in illustrated oversize hardcover, with matching dust jacket. ($20.00 with same-as-cover dust jacket) $15.00 Some price exceptions on first editions and editions by other publishers are noted below.

Le Roi Babar, 1953 edition France, first edition of revision, laminated ilustrated hardcover. $50.00

Babar's Picnic

Babar's Fair

Babar and the Professor, 1957

Babar and Zephyr, 1957

Babar's Castle

Babar's French Lessons, 1965 Cape, London, first edition UK. ($75.00 in dust jacket) $30.00

Babar Comes to America, 1965 Random House, first edition. ($50.00 in dust jacket) $20.00

Babar's Spanish Lessons, 1965

Babar Loses his Crown, 1967

Babar's Trunk

Babar's Birthday Surprise

Adventures of Babar on Television, 1969 Metheun Ltd., first edition thus, UK, white glazed oversize pictorial boards. $20.00

Babar Visits Another Planet, 1972 Random House Beginner Book

Meet Babar and his Family

Babar and the Wully-Wully

Babar Saves the Day

Babar's Bookmobile, 1974 Random House, four books, each approximately 4 x 4-1/2 inches, oblong, paper-over-board illustrated hardcover, 16 pages, color illustrations, packaged together in a color illustrated cardboard slipcase. Complete package: $35.00. Individual books: $5.00 The titles include:

Babar's Concert

Babar to the Rescue

Babar Bakes a Cake

Babar's Christmas Tree

Babar, Related Pop-Up Books: pop-up book prices require pop-up and mechanicals all to be in very good working condition.

Pop-Up Babar's Games, 1968 Random House, pictorial hardcover, color illustrations, pop-ups and pull tab animations. $35.00

Babar's Moon Trip, 1969 Random House, pictorial hardcover, color illustrations, pop-ups and pull tab animations. $35.00

BASIL OF BAKER STREET SERIES, Eve Titus, Whittlesey House (McGraw Hill), hardcover, about 96 pages, b/w illustrations by Paul Galdone. ($25.00 with dust jacket) $10.00

Basil of Baker Street, 1958

Basil and the Lost Colony, 1964

Basil and the Pigmy Cats, 1971

Basil in Mexico, 1975

BEANY MALONE BOOKS, Lenora Mattingly Weber, Crowell, hardcover. Hard-to-find books. First edition with dust jacket: $225.00. Later printings: ($50.00 with dust jacket) $25.00

Leave it to Beany!, 1950

Beany Has a Secret Life, 1955

Come Back, Wherever You Are, 1969

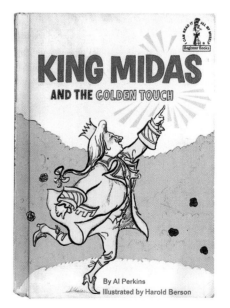

Beginner Books, Random House

BEGINNER BOOKS, Random House, also see

BERENSTAIN BEARS.
Color illustrated oversize hardcover, color illustrations throughout, limited vocabulary. Following is a small sample of the many titles. (First editions of favorites can command much higher prices, but most were issued in extremely large printings, are easily available and priced accordingly.) ($20.00 with dust jacket) $15.00

Cerf, Bennett (Random House publisher)
Bennett Cerf's Book of Riddles, 1960, color illustrations by Roy McKie, first edition. $25.00

Eastman, P. D.
Are You My Mother?, 1960 color illustrations by author
Best Nest, 1968, color illustrations by author
Go, Dog, Go!, 1961 color illustrations by author
Sam and the Firefly, 1958, color illustrations by author

LeSeig, Theo. (pseudonym used by Ted Geisel for books that he wrote but did not illustrate)
Ten Apples Up on Top, 1961 color illustrations by Roy McKie
I Wish I Had Duck Feet, 1965
I Can Write!: A Book by Me, Myself, 1971
In a People House, 1972
Wacky Wednesday, 1974
Would You Rather Be a Bullfrog?, 1975

Palmer, Helen (Helen Geisel):
Fish Out of Water, 1961, color illustrations by P. D. Eastman.
Do You Know What I'm Going to Do Next Saturday?, 1963 photgraph illustrations by Lynn Fayman.

Perkins, Al
Travels of Doctor Doolittle, adaptation, Lofting, 1967, color illustrations by Philip Wende.
Meet Chitty Chitty Bang Bang, adaptation, Fleming, 1968, color illustrations by B. Tobey.
King Midas and the Golden Touch, 1969, color illustrations by Harold Berson.

Seuss, Dr. (pseudonym used by Ted Geisel for books that he wrote and illustrated) See Author section, SEUSS, Dr., for first edition prices.
Cat In the Hat, 1955
One Fish Two Fish Red Fish Blue Fish, 1959
Green Eggs and Ham, 1960
Hop on Pop, 1963
Dr. Seuss's ABC Book, 1963
Fox in Socks, 1965
Cat in the Hat Dictionary, ca. 1966, published in English, British spellings, French, and Spanish versions
My Book About Me, 1969
There's A Wocket in My Pocket!, 1973
Oh the Thinks You Can Think!, 1975

Stone, Rosetta (pseudonym of Mike Frith and Ted Geisel)
Because a Little Bug Went Ka-Choo

BEGINNER BOOKS, Bright & Early Readers: $15.00
Dr. Seuss (Ted Geisel)
Foot Book, 1968
Shape of Me, 1973
Marvin K. Mooney, Will You Please Go Now!, 1974
LeSieg, Theo
Eye Book, 1968, color illustrations by McKie
Perkins, Al
Ear Book, 1968
Hand, Hand, Fingers, Thumb, 1969, color illustrations by Eric Gurney

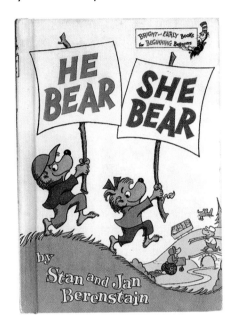

BERENSTAIN BEARS BOOKS, Stan and Jan Berenstain, author-illustrators, 1970s Random House. (Series continues today, with 100+ titles.)
Beginner Books, oversize color illustrated hardcover, color illustrations by authors: $15.00
Bears' Almanac
Big Honey Hunt
Bike Lesson
Bears' Picnic
Bear Scouts
Bears' Vacation
Bears' Christmas
Bear Detectives
Bright and Early Books, color illustrated hardcover picture books, color illustrations throughout by authors. $15.00
Inside, Outside, Upside Down
Bears on Wheels
Old Hat, New Hat
Bears in the Night
B Book
C is for Clown
He Bear She Bear

Big Red, LeMoult dust jacket

BIFF BREWSTER SERIES, Andy Adams (Walter B. Gibson/Maxwell Grant), ca. 1960 Grosset, blue-gray hardcover. First editions are not clearly marked, but are usually judged by title being last on title list.

Brazilian Gold Mine Mystery, 1960. ($25.00 with dust jacket) $10.00

Mystery of the Chinese Ring, 1960. ($25.00 with dust jacket) $10.00

Hawaiian Sea Hunt Mystery, 1960. ($25.00 with dust jacket) $10.00

African Ivory Mystery, 1961. First edition: $50.00 with dust jacket. Later editions: ($25.00 with dust jacket) $10.00

Mystery of the Ambush in India, 1962. First edition: $75.00 with dust jacket. Later editions: ($25.00 with dust jacket) $10.00

Mystery of the Tibetan Caravan, 1963. First edition: $65.00 with dust jacket. Later editions: ($25.00 with dust jacket) $10.00

Egyptian Scarab Mystery, 1963. First edition: $65.00 with dust jacket. Later editions: ($25.00 with dust jacket) $10.00

BIG RED SERIES, Jim Kjelgaard, Holiday House book club editions: ($15.00 with dust jacket) $10.00. Grosset, pictorial hardcover editions: $15.00

Big Red, (1945) 1964 Holiday House, book club edition, hardcover, color frontispiece and b/w illustrations by Shannon Stirnweis. Dust jacket illustration by Adolph LeMoult

Irish Red, Son of Big Red, 1951 Grosset, pictorial hardcover

Outlaw Red, 1953 Holiday House, book club edition, hardcover, endpapers and b/w illustrations signed Ames

BIGGLES BOOKS, Captain W.E. Johns (1893 – 1968), new titles, continuation of series started in 1932, various publishers, including Hodder & Stoughton, Oxford, Brockhampton, Dean, Thames, or Marks and Spencer. Johns continued to write new books until his death in 1968, while working on the uncompleted *Biggles Does Some Homework,* the book in which Biggles was supposed to retire. Hardcovers, probable first editions: ($40.00 with dust jacket) $10.00. Later editions: ($25.00 with dust jacket) $10.00. Dean laminated pictorial hardcovers, probable first editions of later 1960s titles: $35.00. Dean pictorial hardcovers, other editions: $10.00

Biggles Gets His Men, 1950
Another Job for Biggles, 1951
Biggles Goes to School, 1951
Biggles Works It Out, 1952
Biggles Takes the Case, 1952
Biggles Follows On, 1952
Biggles, Air Detective, 1952
Biggles and the Black Raider, 1953
Biggles in the Blue, 1953
Biggles in the Gobi, 1953
Biggles of the Special Air Police, 1953

Biggles Cuts It Fine, 1954
Biggles and the Pirate Treasure, 1954
Biggles Foreign Legionnaire, 1954
Biggles Pioneer Airfighter, 1954
Biggles in Australia, 1955
Biggles' Chinese Puzzle, 1955
Biggles of 266, 1956
No Rest For Biggles, 1956
Biggles Takes Charge, 1956
Biggles Makes Ends Meet, 1957
Biggles of the Interpol, 1957
Biggles on the Home Front, 1957
Biggles Presses On, 1958
Biggles on Mystery Island, 1958
Biggles Buries a Hatchet, 1958
Biggles in Mexico, 1959
Biggles' Combined Operation, 1959
Biggles at the World's End, 1959
Biggles and the Leopards of Zinn, 1960
Biggles Goes Home, 1960
Biggles and the Poor Rich Boy, 1960
Biggles Forms a Syndicate, 1961
Biggles and the Missing Millionaire, 1961
Biggles Goes Alone, 1962
Orchids for Biggles, 1962
Biggles Sets a Trap, 1962
Biggles Takes It Rough, 1963
Biggles Takes a Hand, 1963
Biggles' Special Case, 1963
Biggles and the Plane That Disappeared, 1963
Biggles Flies to Work, 1963
Biggles and the Lost Sovereigns, 1964
Biggles and the Black Mask, 1964
Biggles Investigates, 1964
Biggles Looks Back, 1965
Biggles and the Plot That Failed, 1965
Biggles and the Blue Moon, 1965
Biggles Scores a Bull, 1965
Biggles in the Terai, 1966
Biggles and the Gun Runners, 1966
Biggles Sorts It Out, 1967
Biggles and the Dark Intruder, 1967
Biggles and the Penitent Thief, 1967
Biggles and the Deep Blue Sea, 1967
Boy Biggles, 1968
Biggles in the Underworld, 1968
Biggles and the Little Green God, 1969
Biggles and the Noble Lord, 1969
Biggles Sees Too Much, 1970

Biggles related titles:

Biggles Breaks the Silence, Brockhampton Press, ca. 1960, W.E. Johns. Small (48 pages). Illustrated by "Kay." Hardcover, $12.00 (with dust jacket $25.00).

Biggles Air Detective Omnibus, W.E. Johns, Hodder & Stoughton, ca. 1956. Collection of Biggles stories (at least three omnibus editions issued by Hodder).

Hardcover, $15.00 (with dust jacket $30.00).

Daily Mail Boy's Annual, John Bellamy (editor), ca. 1950s, hardcover collections of stories printed in the boy's magazine. Editions with "Biggles" stories, $12.00 (with dust jacket, $30.00).

BILLY BUNTER BOOKS, Frank Richards (pseudonym of Charles Harold St. John Hamilton, 1876 – 1961), 1947 – 1965 Skilton or Cassells, 38 titles. Bunter stories began as magazine pieces for "The Magnet" (1908 to 1940). English publisher Skilton printed the books through 1952, after which Cassells took over the series. Another English publisher, Hawk, began printing facsimile hardcovers of early titles in the 1990s. Early editions were issued with color frontispiece and black-and-white illustrations. Illustrators included R. J. MacDonald and C.H. Chapman. Some books issued after Hamilton's death were finished by other authors. Prices in England tend to be much higher than US prices.

Billy Bunter, Charles Skilton editions, 1947 – 1952: ($35.00 with dust jacket) $15.00

Billy Bunter, Cassell hardcover reprints of Skilton, ca. 1950 – 1960s of same titles: ($20.00 with dust jacket) $10.00

Billy Bunter of Greyfriars School, 1947
Billy Bunter's Banknote, 1948
Billy Bunter's Barring Out, 1948
Billy Bunter in Brazil, 1949
Billy Bunter's Christmas Party, 1949
Bessie Bunter of Cliff House School, 1949
Billy Bunter's Benefit, 1950
Billy Bunter Among the Cannibals, 1950
Billy Bunter's Postal Order, 1951
Billy Bunter Butts In, 1951
Billy Bunter and the Blue Mauritius, 1952, harder-to-find than other Skilton titles because it is the last, hardcover $20.00 (with dust jacket $60.00).

Billy Bunter, titles first published by Cassell, hardcover: Firsts with dust jacket, $30.00. Later editions: ($20.00 with dust jacket) $10.00

Billy Bunter's Beanfeast, 1952
Billy Bunter's Brainwave, 1953
Billy Bunter's First Case, 1953
Billy Bunter the Bold, 1954
Bunter Does His Best, 1954
Billy Bunter's Double, 1955
Backing Up Billy Bunter, 1955
Lord Billy Bunter, 1956
Banishing of Billy Bunter, 1956
Billy Bunter's Bolt, 1957
Billy Bunter Afloat, 1957
Billy Bunter's Bargain, 1958
Billy Bunter the Hiker, 1958
Bunter Out of Bounds, 1959
Bunter Comes for Christmas, 1959

Bunter the Bad Lad, 1960
Bunter Keeps it Dark, 1960
Billy Bunter's Treasure Hunt, 1961
Billy Bunter at Butlins, 1961
Bunter the Ventriloquist, 1961
Bunter the Caravanner, 1962
Billy Bunter's Bodyguard, 1962
Big Chief Bunter, 1963
Just Like Bunter, 1963
Bunter the Stowaway, 1964
Thanks to Bunter, 1964
Bunter the Sportsman, 1965
Bunter's Last Fling, 1965

BLACK STALLION SERIES and **ISLAND STALLION SERIES**, Walter Farley, ca. 1941 – 1971 Random House, hardcover, 18 books. By the 1950s, Random House generally identified books in both of Farley's horse series as belonging to the Black Stallion series, with some novels featuring characters from both series. First editions (first printing) are clearly marked on the copyright page.
1950s first edition hardcover: ($25.00 with dust jacket) $10.00
1960s first edition hardcover: ($20.00 with dust jacket) $15.00
Later hardcover editions: ($15.00 with dust jacket) $10.00
Black Stallion titles published after 1950:
Blood Bay Colt, 1950
Island Stallion's Fury, 1951
Black Stallion's Filly, 1952
Black Stallion Revolts, 1953
Black Stallion's Sulky Colt, 1954
Island Stallion Races, 1955
Black Stallion's Courage, 1956
Black Stallion Mystery, 1957
Horse Tamer, 1958

Black Stallion and Flame, 1960
Black Stallion Challenged, 1964
Black Stallion's Ghost, 1969
Black Stallion and the Girl, 1971
Black Stallion, Related books, Farley, Random House (I Can Read Beginner Books), color endpapers and full color illustrations by James Schucker. Hard-to-find with dust jacket. (List from $50.00 to $95.00 with dust jacket) $15.00
Little Black, a Pony, 1961
Little Black Goes to the Circus, 1963

BONNIE AND DEBBIE BOOK SERIES, Rebecca Caudill, 1950 – 1960 Winston, small hardcover, b/w illustrations by Decie Merwin. ($35.00 with dust jacket) $15.00
Schoolhouse in the Woods
Up and Down the River
Happy Little Family
Schoolhouse in the Parlor

BORROWERS SERIES, Mary Norton, Harcourt, hardcover, b/w illustrations by Beth and Joe Krush. First editions: $75.00 with dust jacket. Later editions: ($20.00 with dust jacket) $10.00
Borrowers, 1953
Borrowers Afield, 1955
Borrowers Aloft
Borrowers Afloat, 1959
Adventures of the Borrowers, 1967 Harcourt, Brace & World, first edition, hardcover, includes the four books of the Borrowers in one volume: *Borrowers, Borrowers Afloat, Borrowers Afield,* and *Borrowers Aloft*. ($60.00 with dust jacket) $20.00

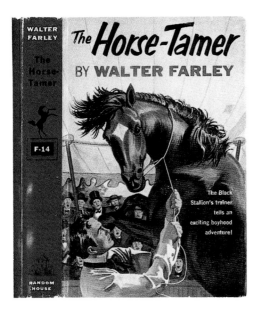

Black Stallion Series, 1958 dust jacket

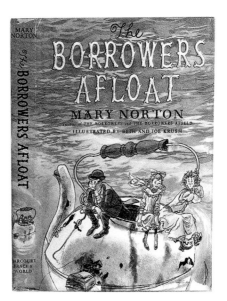

BOY SCOUTS OF AMERICA PUBLICATIONS, mid-1950s through 1975, hardcover. $15.00
Boy Scouts of America Cub Scout Song Book, 1955
Boy Scouts of America Handbook for Boys, 1958
Boy Scouts of America Boy Scout Handbook, 1965
Boy Scouts of America Den Chief's Denbook, 1968

BRAD FORREST ADVENTURE SERIES, Hugh Maitland, Longmans, Canada, hardcover, 8 titles, a young Canadian's adventures in other parts of the world. ($15.00 with dust jacket) $10.00
Brad Forrest's Calgary Adventure, 1964
Brad Forrest's Hong Kong Adventure, 1964
Brad Forrest's Los Angeles Adventure, 1964
Brad Forrest's Madagascar Adventure, 1964
Brad Forrest's New York Adventure, 1965
Brad Forrest's Yucatan Adventure, 1965
Brad Forrest's Halifax Adventure, 1965
Brad Forrest's London Adventure, 1965

BRAINS BENTON, Charles Spain Verral and George Wyatt, 1959 – 1960 Whitman, hardcover, pictorial hardcovers. $20.00
ca. 1960s Golden Press, yellow spine, illustrated hardcover. $15.00
Case of the Missing Message
Case of the Counterfeit Coin
Case of the Stolen Dummy
Case of the Roving Rolls
Case of the Waltzing Mouse
Case of the Painted Dragon

BROGEEN THE LEPRECHAUN SERIES, Patricia Lynch, Macmillan, hardcover, illustrated by Ralph Pinto or H. B. Vestal. ($45.00 with dust jacket) $20.00
Brogeen Follows the Magic Tune, 1952
Brogeen and the Lost Castle, 1956
Brogeen and the Black Enchanter, 1958
Brogeen and the Little Wind, 1971
Brogeen and the Bronze Lizard, 1975

BRONC BURNETT SERIES, Wilfred McCormick, late 1940s – 1960s Grosset, hardcover, a dozen plus titles, and some by Putnam. ($20.00 with dust jacket) $10.00
Legion Tourney
Eagle Scout
Grand Slam Home
Rambling Halfback
Stranger in the Backfield
Go-Ahead Runner

BUCKSKIN BOOKS SERIES, ca. 1960s Macmillan, hardcover. ($15.00 with dust jacket) $10.00
Danger In the Cove, Thompson
Heroine of Long Point, Benham

Boy and the Buffalo, Wood
Scout Who Led an Army, Ballantyne
Adventure at the Mill, Barbara and Heather Bramwell
Man with the Yellow Eyes, Catherine Clark
Escape From Grand Pre, Thompson

BUTTONS SERIES, Edith McCall, 1950s Beckley-Cardy, also Benefic Press, church school books, hardcover, illustrated. $10.00
Buttons at the Farm, 1955
Buttons Go Camping
Buttons and the Little League, 1961
Buttons and the Pet Parade, 1961

C

CATFISH BEND BOOKS, Ben Lucien Burman, 1960s George Harrap, hardcover, illustrated by Alice Cady. ($15.00 with dust jacket) $10.00
High Water at Catfish Bend
Seven Stars for Catfish Bend
Owl Hoots Twice at Catfish Bend

CAVALCADE BOOKS SERIES, Doubleday, hardcover, historical fiction by a variety of authors. ($20.00 with dust jacket) $10.00
Eagle of Niagara, John Brick, 1955
Witch of Merthyn, Llewellyn, 1954
Bride of Liberty, Frank Yerby
Flame of Hercules, Richard Llewellyn, 1955
Mississippi Pilot: With Mark Twain on the Great River, Phil Stong, 1954

CHANGES TRILOGY, Peter Dickenson, Little Brown (American editions), English science fiction trilogy, hardcover. ($20.00 with dust jacket) $10.00
Weathermonger, 1969
Heartsease, 1969
Devil's Children, 1970

CHERRY AMES SERIES, Helen Wells or Julie Tatham, Grosset. There were 27 books written between 1943 and 1968. A planned 28th book was not published. A few of the later books had small printings and therefore command a higher price, which is listed after the title.
Most plain hardcovers: ($30.00 with dust jacket) $15.00.
Illustrated hardcover: $20.00
Student Nurse, 1943
Senior Nurse, 1944
Army Nurse, 1944
*Chief Nurse,*1944
*Flight Nurse,*1945
Veterans' Nurse, 1946

Private Duty Nurse, 1946
Visiting Nurse, 1947
Cruise Nurse, 1948
At Spencer, 1949
Night Supervisor, 1950
Mountaineer Nurse, 1951
Clinic Nurse, 1952
Dude Ranch Nurse, 1953
Rest Home Nurse, 1954
Country Doctor's Nurse, 1955
Boarding School Nurse, 1955
Department Store Nurse, 1956
Camp Nurse, 1957
At Hilton Hospital, 1959
Island Nurse, 1960
Rural Nurse, 1961
Staff Nurse, 1962
Companion Nurse, 1964
Jungle Nurse, 1965
Mystery in the Doctor's Office, 1966, illustrated
    hardcover, hard-to-find. $50.00
Ski Nurse Mystery, 1968, illustrated hardcover,
    hard-to-find. $50.00

CHIP HILTON SPORTS SERIES, Clair Bee, Grosset &
    Dunlap, red tweed hardcover, sport design endpa-
    pers, b/w illustrations. ($30.00 with dust jacket) $15.00
Touchdown Pass, 1948
Championship Ball, 1948
Strike Three, 1949
Clutch Hitter, 1949
Hoop Crazy, 1950

Pitchers' Duel, 1950
Pass and a Prayer, 1951 65/
Dugout Jinx, 1952
Freshman Quarterback, 1952
Backboard Fever, 1953
Fence Busters, 1953
Ten Seconds to Play, 1955
Fourth Down Showdown, 1956
Tournament Crisis, 1957
Hardcourt Upset, 1957
Hardcourt Upset, 1957, first edition, signed by
    Clair Bee. Hard to find. $400.00
Pay-Off Pitch, 1958
No-Hitter, 1959
Triple-Threat Trouble, 1960
Backboard Ace, 1961
Buzzer Basket, 1962
Comeback Cagers, 1963
Home Run Feud, 1964
Hungry Hurler, 1966

CHRISTOPHER COOL, TEEN AGENT SERIES, Jack
    Lancer, Grosset, illustrated hardcover. $15.00
X Marks the Spy, 1967
Mission: Moonfire, 1967
Department of Danger, 1967
Ace of Shadows, 1968
Heads You Lose, 1968
Trial by Fury, 1969

CHRONICLES OF NARNIA SERIES, C. S. Lewis, ca.
    1950s Macmillan editions, hardcover, b/w illus-

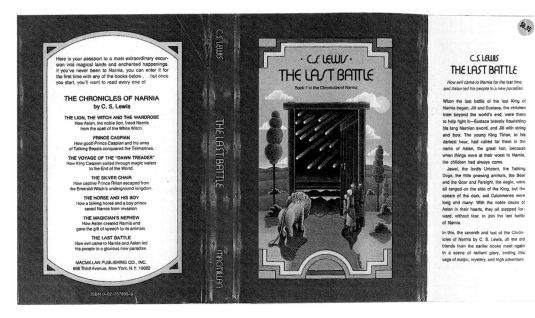

Chronicles of Narnia Series, dust jacket by Roger Hane

trations by Pauline Baynes, dust jacket illustration by Roger Hane. Reprints are plentiful. Later reprints: ($20.00 with dust jacket) $10.00

Lion, the Witch and the Wardrobe, 1950, first edition with dust jacket: RARE

Prince Caspian, 1951, first edition, ($300.00 with dust jacket) $50.00

Voyage of the Dawn Treader, 1952, first edition, oversize hardcover ($500.00 with dust jacket) $50.00

Silver Chair, 1953, first edition, ($250.00 with dust jacket) $50.00

Horse and his Boy, 1954, first edition, ($250.00 with dust jacket) $50.00

Magician's Nephew, 1954, first edition, ($200.00 with dust jacket) $40.00

Magician's Nephew, 1955, Bodley Head, London, oversize green hardcover with silver lettering, first English edition listed at $1000 with dust jacket.

Last Battle, 1956, first edition, ($200.00 with dust jacket) $40.00

Last Battle, 1956 Geoffrey Bles, London, first UK edition, light blue hardcover with silver gilt lettering, listed at $700.00 with dust jacket

CLARENCE THE DOG SERIES, Patricia Lauber, Coward-McCann, illustrated hardcover. $20.00

Clarence, the TV Dog, 1955, illustrated by Leonard Shortall

Clarence Turns Sea Dog, 1959, illustrated by Leonard Shortall.

Clarence and the Burglar, adapted by Monjo, 1973, illustrated by Paul Galdone

Clarence and the Cat, adapted from a chapter in first book, 1977, illustrated by Paul Galdone

COLOSSAL CORCORAN SERIES, W. Ingram Morgan (pseudonym of R.G. Campbell), 1952 Cole Publishing, Australia, hardcover, illustrated by Wally Driscoll. ($20.00 with dust jacket) $10.00

Colossal Corcoran in Mystery Valley
Colossal Corcoran on Skull Atoll
Colossal Corcoran in the Caribbean
Colossal Corcoran on Smoke Island
Colossal Corcoran in the Hindu Kush Mountains

CORNERSTONES OF FREEDOM SERIES, 1960s Children's Press, hardcover, numerous titles, illustrated, by various authors. ($15.00 with dust jacket) $10.00

Story of the Statue of Liberty
Story of the Lewis & Clark Expedition
Story of the USS Arizona
Story of the Constitution
Story of the Declaration of Independence
Story of the Supreme Court
Story of the Alamo
Story of the Gettysburg Address
Story of the Conestoga Wagon
Story of the Mayflower
Story of Monticello
Story of the Bonhomme Richard

CURIOUS GEORGE SERIES, H.A. Rey (1898 – 1977) and Margaret Rey (b. 1906), Houghton Mifflin, oversize hardcover, illustrated by authors. Margaret Rey continued to do Curious George books in the 1980s. Early printings: ($40.00 with dust jacket) $20.00

Weekly Reader Book Club editions, illustrated hardcovers with no dust jackets: $10.00

Curious George, 1941
Cecily G and the Nine Monkeys, 1942
Curious George Takes a Job, 1947
Curious George Rides a Bike, 1952
Curious George Gets a Medal, 1957
Curious George Flies a Kite, 1958
Curious George Goes to the Hospital, 1966
Curious George Learns the Alphabet, 1973

——————— •☞ **D** ☜• ———————

1970s white hardcovers

DANA GIRLS MYSTERY SERIES, Carolyn Keene, Grosset & Dunlap, 1970s reprints, illustrated white hardcovers, titles from *Stone Tiger* through *Haunted Lagoon.* $10.00

DANCING PEEL SERIES, Lorna Hill, 1954 – 1962, Thomas Nelson, hardcover, 6 titles. See also MAJORIE, PATIENCE, SADLER'S WELLS, and VICARAGE CHILDREN. ($20.00 with dust jacket) $10.00

Dancing Peel, 1954
Dancer's Luck, 1955
Little Dancer, 1956
Dancer in the Wings, 1958
Dancer in Danger, 1960
Dancer on Holiday, 1962

DANNY DUNN SERIES, Jay Williams and Raymond Abrashki, 1956 – 1970s McGraw-Hill, Whittlesey House and Weekly Reader editions, all hardcover. $10.00
Danny Dunn and the Anti-Gravity Paint
Danny Dunn on a Desert Island
Danny Dunn and the Homework Machine
Danny Dunn and the Weather Machine
Danny Dunn on the Ocean Floor
Danny Dunn and the Fossil Cave
Danny Dunn and the Heat Ray
Danny Dunn, Time Traveler
Danny Dunn and the Voice From Space
Danny Dunn and the Smallifying Machine
Danny Dunn and the Swamp Monster
Danny Dunn, Invisible Boy
Danny Dunn, Scientific Detective
Danny Dunn and the Universal Glue

DARK IS RISING SERIES, Susan Cooper, 1966 – 1977 Atheneum, except *Over Sea, Under Stone.* (Although *Over Sea, Under Stone* was written several years before the other books, most collectors count it as the first of the series because it features the same characters.)
Over Sea, Under Stone, 1966 Harcourt, hardcover, illustrated by Margery Gil. First edition with dust jacket: $175.00. Later editions: ($25.00 with dust jacket) $15.00

Dark is Rising, 1973. First edition with dust jacket: $75.00. Later editions: ($25.00 with dust jacket) $15.00
Greenwitch, 1974. First edition with dust jacket: $75.00. Later editions: ($25.00 with dust jacket) $15.00
Grey King, 1975. First edition with dust jacket: $65.00. Later editions: ($25.00 with dust jacket) $15.00
Grey King, 1975. First edition with Newbery Medal winner seal on dust jacket, $50.00. Later editions: ($25.00 with dust jacket) $15.00
Grey King, 1975 Chatto & Windus, Newbery seal on dust jacket: $125.00.
Silver on the Tree, 1977. First edition with dust jacket: $50.00. Later editions: ($25.00 with dust jacket) $15.00

DAUNTLESS SERIES, Peter Dawlish, 1954 Oxford University Press, hardcover, illustrated by Jobson. ($25.00 with dust jacket) $10.00
Dauntless and the Mary Baines
Dauntless Takes Recruits
Dauntless Finds Her Crew
Dauntless in Danger

DESMOND THE DOG SERIES, Herbert Best, Viking, hardcover, b/w illustrations by Lilian Obligado or Ezra Jack Keats. ($25.00 with dust jacket) $10.00
*Desmond's First Case,*1961
Desmond and the Peppermint Ghost: the Dog Detective's Third Case, 1965
Desmond and Dog Friday, 1968
Desmond the Dog Detective: the Case of the Lone Stranger, 1972

DICK AND JANE BOOKS, William Gray and others; 1927 – 1970; Scott, Foresman and Company.

The first grade primers featuring Dick and Jane were updated every five years to reflect changes in clothing, automobiles, and American lifestyles. Last update occurred in 1965. Original illustrations of early books are by Eleanor Campbell. Prices given show the date of publication of that particular book, not its original date of copyright. "Ex-school copies" are the most commonly available types and have ex-library type markings, stamped with school names, room numbers, and so forth.

Because these first grade readers are almost always ex-schoolroom books, prices vary widely, depending on condition. On books identified as ex-library or ex-school, there is stamped or inked school or library information.

Dick and Jane paperbound hardcover pre-primers, 1950s and 1960s editions: $50.00 to $100.00
Dick and Jane
More Dick and Jane Stories
We Come and Go
We Look and See
We Work and Play
Sally, Dick and Jane
Fun With Our Family
Fun Wherever We Are

Dick and Jane clothbound hardcovers, 1950s and 1960s editions: $30.00 to $65.00
Fun with Dick and Jane
New Fun with Dick and Jane
Fun with Our Friends

John and Jean hardcover readers:
Fun with John and Jean, 1951, same story as *Fun with Dick and Jane,* but revised for Catholic schools and labeled "New Cathedral Basic Reader," light green hardcover, 159 pages, illustrated by Eleanor Campbell. $50.00

Dick and Jane hardcover readers:
Our New Friends, 1950s edition: $60.00
Good Times With Our Friends, Dorothy Baruch, 1948 edition: $60.00
Happy Days with Our Friends, Elizabeth Montgomery, Bauer, Gray, 1954, blue hardcover, illustrated by Ruth Steed. Ex-school copy: $75.00
More Fun with Our Friends, Helen Robison, 1962 edition, illustrated hardcover, 192 pages, color illustrations, hard-to-find unmarked copy: $80.00 Ex-school copy: $45.00
New Our New Friends, 1956, brown hardcover, color illustrations: $60.00
New Fun with Dick and Jane, William Gray, 1956 first printing, illustrated hardcover, 160 pages, color illustrations. $125.00
New More Streets and Roads, William Gray, 1956, hardcover, illustrated. $45.00
Fun with Our Friends, Robinson, Monroe, Artley,

1963, printed illustration on yellow and white hardcover, color illustrations: $50.00 Ex-school copy : $25.00
Friends New and Old, Helen Robinson, 1963, second grade reader, illustrated green and white hardcover, 238 pages. $40.00
Dick and Jane workbook:
Think and Do Book, 1956, workbook, 71 pages, 5x8 with blue cover. $50.00
Dick and Jane "Before We Read" Picture Books, oversize oblong hardcover, also softcover workbook editions, b/w and color illustrations, no words. $40.00 to $100.00 range
Before We Read
We Read Pictures
We Read More Pictures
Dick and Jane teacher's editions:
New Guess Who, 1962 teacher's edition, hardcover, guide to pre-primers. $85.00
We Read Pictures, 1963 Cathedral Basic Reader teacher's edition, oblong oversize hardcover, 48 pages, with instructions to teacher to use John, Jean, Judy names. $60.00
We Read More Pictures, 1951 teacher's edition, oblong oversize hardcover, 48 pages. $75.00
We Read More Pictures, 1962 teacher's edition, oblong oversize softcover, 78 page "teacher notes" section precedes 48 story pages. $75.00

DIG ALLEN SPACE EXPLORER ADVENTURES, Joseph Greene, ca. 1960s Golden Press, yellow spine, illustrated hardcover, illustrators include Myron Strauss, Walter Dey, Charles Beck, and Phil Marin. $15.00
Forgotten Star, 1959
Captives in Space, 1959
Journey to Jupiter, 1961
Trappers of Venus, 1961
Robots of Saturn, 1962
Lost City of Uranus, 1962

DING DONG SCHOOL BOOKS, 1953 – 1956 Rand McNally, 25 titles. Small hardcover books with pictorial covers and silver foil spines, 28 pages, color illustrations, various illustrators. Covers state "By Miss Frances" (Dr. Frances Horwich), the host of the NBC television series. $12.00
Your Friend the Policeman, 1953
Debbie and Her Nap, 1953
Suitcase with a Surprise, 1953
Big Coal Truck, 1953
I Decided, 1953
Day Downtown with Daddy, 1953
Dressing Up, 1953
Daddy's Birthday's Cakes, 1953
Baby Chipmunk, 1953

Peek In, 1954
Growing Things, 1954
My Goldfish, 1954
In My House, 1954
Dolls of Other Lands, 1954
My Big Brother, 1954
Robin Family, 1954
Grandmother Is Coming, 1954
Looking Out the Window, 1954
Our Baby, 1955
Jingle Bell Jack, 1955
Mr. Meyer's Cow, 1955
Lucky Rabbit, 1955
Magic Wagon, 1955
My Daddy is a Policeman, 1956
Here Comes the Band, 1956
We Love Grandpa, 1956

Ding Dong School Books, ca. 1959 – 1960 Golden Press, 8 titles. Reprints of the earlier Rand McNally titles done as part of the standard Little Golden Book format, 24 pages. Gold foil spines, pictorial covers state "Golden Press" or "A Little Golden Book." $10.00

DISNEY, LITTLE GOLDEN BOOKS, (see also LITTLE GOLDEN BOOKS and MICKEY MOUSE CLUB BOOKS), 1948 – 1978 Golden Press, 148 titles including Mickey Mouse Club titles. Gold foil spine except for Mickey Mouse Club, which had red foil spines. Series numbers begin with "D", revised editions printed after 1985 begin with "105-." First editions should have "A" printed on lower right corner of inside back page (position

of "A" changes or can be hidden by binding).
1950s first editions: $15.00
1960s first editions: $12.00
1970s first editions: $10.00
Other editions: $5.00.
Titles generally commanding higher than normal prices:
Davy Crockett, 1955, by Irwin Shapiro, illustrated by Mel Crawford, $18.00
Disney Mother Goose, 1952, illustrated by Al Dempster, "A" edition, $35.00
Ludwig von Drake, 1961, by Ingolia and George, illustrated by Pratt and Statt, $20.00

DONNA PARKER SERIES, Marcia Martin, 1957 – 1964 Whitman, illustrated hardcover. $15.00
Donna Parker at Cherrydale
Donna Parker, Special Agent
Donna Parker on Her Own
Donna Parker, Spring to Remember
Donna Parker in Hollywood
Donna Parker at Camp Arawak
Donna Parker Takes a Giant Step

DORRIE SERIES, Patricia Coombs, 1960s – 1970s Lothrop Lee, oversize (10 x 6¾ inches) hardcover, b/w and color illustrations by author. ($35.00 with dust jacket) $15.00
Dorrie and the Birthday Eggs
Dorrie and the Blue Witch
Dorrie and the Fortune Teller
Dorrie and the Goblin
Dorrie and the Haunted House

Dorrie and the Weather-Box
Dorrie and the Witch Doctor
Dorrie and the Wizard's Spell
Dorrie and the Amazing Magic Elixir

DRAGON BOOKS, Ruth Stiles Gannett, Random House, hardcover, b/w illustrated by Ruth Chrisman Gannett, stories about Elmer Elevator. Book club editions: ($20.00 with dust jacket) $10.00
My Father's Dragon, 1948
Elmer and the Dragon, 1950, first edition: ($35.00 with dust jacket) $20.00
Dragons of Blueland, 1951 first edition. ($80.00 with dust jacket) $25.00

⋘ **E** ⋙

Earthsea Trilogy

EARTHSEA TRILOGY, Ursula LeGuin, hardcover. Later printings: ($25.00 with dust jacket) $15.00
Wizard of Earthsea, 1968 Parnassus, illustrated by Ruth Robbins. First edition with dust jacket: $225.00
Wizard of Earthsea, 1971 Gollancz, first UK edition, $100.00 with dust jacket.
Tombs of Atuan, 1971 Atheneum, illustrated by Gail Garrity. First edition with dust jacket: $125.00
Farthest Shore, 1972 Atheneum, illustrated by Gail Garrity. First edition with dust jacket: $125.00

EDDIE SERIES, Carolyn Haywood, 1947 – 1971 Morrow, hardcover, b/w illustrations by author. First editions: ($45.00 in dust jacket) $15.00. Later editions: ($25.00 in dust jacket) $10.00
Little Eddie, 1947
Eddie and the Fire Engine, 1949

Eddie and Gardenia, 1951
Eddie's Pay Dirt, 1953
Eddie and His Big Deals, 1955
Eddie Makes Music, 1957
Eddie and Louella, 1959
Annie Pat and Eddie, 1960
Eddie's Green Thumb, 1964
Eddie the Dog Holder, 1966
Ever-Ready Eddie, 1968
Eddie's Happenings, 1971
Eddie's Valuable Property, 1975
Eddie's Menagerie, 1978
Merry Christmas from Eddie, 1986
Eddie's Friend Boodles, 1991

EDITH THE LONELY DOLL, Dare Wright, Doubleday, oversize pictorial hardcover with photo illustrations and checkered border, photo illustrations throughout. (Now being reprinted) First edition: ($250.00 with dust jacket) $100.00
Lonely Doll, 1956
Holiday for Edith and the Bears, 1958
Doll and the Kitten, 1960
Lonely Doll Learns a Lesson, 1961
Edith and Mr. Bear, 1964
Gift from Lonely Doll, 1966
Edith and Big Bad Bill, 1968
Edith and Little Bear Lend a Hand, 1972
Edith and Midnight, 1978

ELF BOOKS, see RAND MCNALLY ELF BOOKS

ELLERY QUEEN JR. MYSTERY STORIES, Ellery Queen Jr. (pseudonym for Frederick Dannay, and Manfred B. Lee), 1941 – 1954, 8 titles. Titles added in the 1950s by Little Brown listed below; complete series also reprinted in hardcover by Grosset and Dunlap. Paperback editions published later by Berkley and Scholastic Book Service.1940s titles, hardcover: ($25.00 with dust jacket) $10.00. Last three titles published in 1950s hard-to-find. ($150.00 with dust jacket) $40.00
White Elephant Mystery, 1950
Yellow Cat Mystery, 1952
Blue Herring Mystery, 1954
Ellery Queen, Jr., Mystery Stories, 1961 – 1962 Golden Press, hardcover, 2 titles, illustrations by Robert Magnusen. New series started by authors of original Ellery Queen Jr. Series for Golden Press. This series featured different characters. Reissued in 1969 as part of the "Golden Griffon Detective Stories." $15.00.
Mystery of the Merry Magician, 1961
Mystery of the Vanished Victim, 1962
Ellery Queen, Jr., Mystery Stories, 1965 Putnam, purple hardcover.
Purple Bird Mystery $15.00

ELMER ELEVATOR, see DRAGON BOOKS

ELOISE BOOKS, Kay Thompson, Simon & Schuster, oversize hardcover, illustrations by Hilary Knight. The first book was reprinted continually, but the others had limited printings. (First new editions for all titles issued in 1999 and 2000)
Eloise, 1955, first edition, ($200.00 with dust jacket) $50.00. Later editions: ($35.00 with dust jacket) $15.00
Eloise in Paris, 1957, first edition. ($300.00 with dust jacket) $50.00
Eloise at Christmastime, 1958, first edition. ($300.00 with dust jacket) $50.00
Eloise in Moscow, 1959, first edition. ($300.00 with dust jacket) $50.00

ENCYCLOPEDIA BROWN SERIES, Donald J. Sobol, 1963 – 1970s Thomas Nelson, tweed hardcover with gilt emblem in corner which reads "America's Sherlock Holmes in Sneakers," b/w illustrations by Leonard Shortall. ($35.00 with dust jacket) $15.00
Weekly Reader editions, illustrated hardcovers, other illustrators: $20.00
Encyclopedia Brown, Boy Detective
Encyclopedia Brown and the Case of the Secret Pitch
Encyclopedia Brown Finds the Clues
Encyclopedia Brown Gets His Man
Encyclopedia Brown Solves Them All
Encyclopedia Brown Keeps the Peace
Encyclopedia Brown Saves the Day
Encyclopedia Brown Tracks Them Down
Encyclopedia Brown Shows the Way
Encyclopedia Brown Takes the Case
Encyclopedia Brown Lends a Hand

Encyclopedia Brown and the Case of the Dead Eagles

EVERYDAY LIFE SERIES, ca. 1960s Batsford, London/Putnam, NY, hardcover with gilt lettering, b/w illustrations. $15.00
Everyday Life in Prehistoric Times, M. and C. H. B. Quennell
Everyday Life in Ancient Egypt, Jon Manchip White
Everyday Life in Babylonia and Assyria, H. W. F. Saggs
Everyday Life in Ancient Greece, M. and C. H. B. Quennell
Everyday Life in Ancient Rome, F. R. Cowell
Everyday Life in Roman and Anglo-Saxon Times, M. and C. H. B. Quennell
Everyday Life in Byzantium, Tamara Talbot Rice
Everyday Life in the Viking Age, Jacqueline Simpson
Everyday Life in Medieval Times, Marjorie Rowling
Everyday Life in Renaissance Times, E. R. Chamberlin

FAMOUS FIVE SERIES, Enid Blyton, (series began ca. 1942 Hodder and Stoughton), tenth book appeared in 1951, Hodder and Stoughton, hardcover, illustrated.
First edition with dust jacket: $55.00. Later hardcover printings: ($20.00 with dust jacket) $10.00
Books 10 through 21:
Five on a Hike Together, 1950
Five Have a Wonderful Time
Five Go Down to the Sea
Five Go to Mystery Moor, 1954
Five Have Plenty of Fun
Five on a Secret Trail
Five Go to Billycock Hill
Five Get into a Fix
Five on Finniston Farm
Five Go to Demon's Rocks
Five Have a Mystery to Solve
Five Are Together Again
Famous Five Big Book, 1964 Hodder & Stoughton, first edition thus, *Five on a Treasure Island, Five Go Adventuring Again, Five Run Away Together.* $15.00

FIVE DOLLS SERIES, Helen Clare, 1960s Prentice Hall, hardcover, illustrations by Aliki. ($50.00 with dust jacket) $20.00
Five Dolls in a House, 1965
Five Dolls in the Snow, 1967
Five Dolls and the Monkey, 1967
Five Dolls and Their Friends, 1968
Five Dolls and the Duke, 1968

FIRST BOOK SERIES, Watts Publishing, hardcover, b/w illustrations, numerous titles by various authors. ($20.00 with dust jacket) $10.00

First Book of Indians, 1950
First Book of Birds, 1951
First Book of Eskimos, 1952
First Book of Chess, 1953
First Book of Holidays, 1955
First Book of Canada, 1955
First Book of the Cliff Dwellers, 1968
First Book of Congress, 1965
First Book of Tropical Mammals, 1958
First Book of Hiking, 1965
First Book of Gardening, 1956
First Book of Rhythms, 1954
First Book of American History, 1957
First Book of Codes and Ciphers, 1956
First Book of Measurement, 1960
First Book of Baseball, 1950
First Book of Conservation, 1954
First Book of Boats, 1953
First Book of Eskimos, 1952
First Book of Magic, 1953
First Book of Cowboys, 1950
First Book of Antarctic, 1956
First Book of Submarines, 1957
First Book of Snakes, 1956
First Book of Airplanes, 1958

FIRST GOLDEN LEARNING LIBRARY by Jane Werner Watson (see also LITTLE GOLDEN BOOKS), 1965, 16 volumes. Illustrations by William Dugan. Different color foil spines, full color illustrations, same format as Little Golden Books. Sample titles: *Book of B* or *First Book of S.*

Set price for complete 16 volume set in boxed carrying case: $175.00. Complete set without carrying case: $100.00. Individual titles: $5.00.

FIVE FIND-OUTERS SERIES, Enid Blyton, ca. 1950 Methuen, gray hardcover, 170+ pages, b/w illustrations by Treyer Evans. ($40.00 with dust jacket) $20.00

Mystery of the Burnt Cottage
Mystery of the Disappearing Cat
Mystery of the Secret Room
Mystery of the Hidden House
Mystery of the Spiteful Letters
Mystery of the Pantomime Cat
Mystery of the Missing Necklace
Mystery of the Invisible Thief
Mystery of the Vanished Prince
Mystery of the Strange Bundle
Mystery of Holly Lane
Mystery of the Strange Messages
Mystery of Tally-Ho Cottage
Mystery of the Missing Man

FREDDY THE PIG SERIES, Walter Brooks (1886-1958), 1930s – 1950s Knopf, hardcover, illustrated by Kurt Wiese. First editions: (to $400.00 with dust jacket) $100.00

Freddy the Cowboy, 1950
Freddy Goes to the North Pole, (ca. 1930) 1951 edition
Freddy Rides Again, 1951
Freddy the Pilot, 1952
Freddy and the Space Ship, 1953
Freddy and the Men From Mars, 1954
Freddy and the Baseball Team, 1955
Freddy and Simon the Dictator, 1956
Freddy and the Flying Saucer Plans, 1957
Freddy and the Dragon, 1958
Poetry Book:
Collected Poems of Freddy the Pig, 1953

FROG SERIES, Mercer Mayer and Mariana Mayer, short picture books without words, illustrations in brown ink, reprinted in various editions, usually with illustrated paper-over-board hardcov-

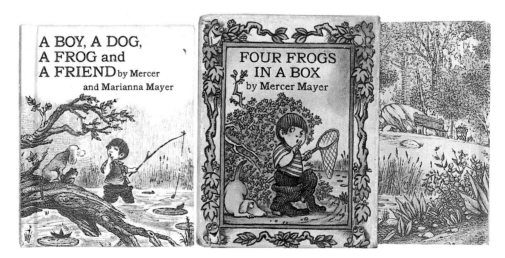

Frog Series, Four Frogs in a Box

ers. (Scholastic issued paperback editions.)

Boy, a Dog, and a Frog, 1967 Dial, hardcover. ($20.00 with dust jacket) $10.00

Frog, Where Are You?, 1969 Dial, hardcover. ($20.00 with dust jacket) $10.00

Boy, a Dog, a Frog and a Friend, 1971 Dial, hardcover. ($20.00 with dust jacket) $10.00

Frog on His Own, 1973 Dial, hardcover. ($20.00 with dust jacket) $10.00

Frog Goes to Dinner, 1974 Dial, hardcover. ($20.00 with dust jacket) $10.00

One Frog Too Many, 1975 Dial, hardcover. ($20.00 with dust jacket) $10.00

Four Frogs in a Box, undated early 1970s Dial, 3¼ inch by 4⅛ high box, covered with illustrated paper, contains four books in miniature size, illustrated paper-over-board covers plus dust jackets, first four titles. Complete set $65.00 Individual miniature books with dust jackets, $10.00, without dust jackets, $5.00

FURY SERIES, Albert Miller, ca. 1960 Grosset, pictorial hardcover. $20.00

Fury, Stallion of Broken Wheel Ranch, 1959

Fury and the Mustangs, 1960

Fury and the White Mare, 1962

Fury, other editions:

Fury, 1964 Silver Dollar Book, pictorial oversize hardcover, abridged story, illustrated by Everett Raymond Kinstler. $15.00

Fury, 1957, Little Golden Book, color illustrated hardcover. $10.00

Fury Takes the Jump, 1958, Little Golden Book, color illustrated hardcover. $10.00

Fury, Stallion of Broken Wheel Ranch, Famous Horse of Television, 1959 Winston, hardcover. ($40.00 with dust jacket) $15.00

Fury and the Mustangs, Authorized TV Edition, 1960 Holt, hardcover. ($25.00 with dust jacket) $10.00

Fury and the White Mare, 1962 Holt, hardcover, 189 pages. ($25.00 with dust jacket) $10.00

G

GEORGIE THE GHOST SERIES, Robert Bright, 1956 – 1975 Doubleday, oversize oblong hardcover, illustrations by author. (Series continued beyond these titles into the 1980s.) ($35.00 with dust jacket) $15.00

Georgie to the Rescue, 1956

Georgie and the Robbers, 1963

Georgie and the Magician, 1966

Georgie and the Noisy Ghost, 1971

Georgie's Halloween, 1958

Georgie's Christmas Carol, 1975

GINNIE SERIES, Catherine Woolley, Morrow, hardcover, illustrated by Ursula Koering. ($25.00 with dust jacket) $15.00

Ginnie and Geneva, 1948

Ginnie Joins In, 1951

Ginnie and the New Girl, 1954

Ginnie and the Mystery House, 1957

Ginnie and the Mystery Doll, 1960

Ginnie and her Juniors, 1963

Ginnie and the Cooking Contest, 1966

Ginnie and the Wedding Bells, 1967

Ginnie and the Mystery Cat, 1969

GINNY GORDON, Julie Campbell, 1950s edition Whitman, color illustrated hardcover. $15.00

Ginny Gordon and the Mystery of the Old Barn, 1951

Ginny Gordon and the Broadcast Mystery, 1956

Ginny Gordon and the Disappearing Candlesticks, 1954

Ginny Gordon and the Lending Library, 1954

GOLDEN STALLION SERIES, Rutherford Montgomery, Little Brown, reissued by Grosset & Dunlap as part of the Famous Horse Stories. British editions issued by Hodder or White Lion. Little Brown first edition: ($35.00 with dust jacket) $10.00

Little Brown later editions: ($25.00 with dust jacket) $10.00

Grosset & Dunlap hardcovers: ($15.00 with dust jacket) $10.00

Capture of the Golden Stallion, 1951

Golden Stallion's Revenge, 1953

Golden Stallion to the Rescue, 1954

Golden Stallion's Victory, 1956

Golden Stallion and the Wolf Dog, 1958

Golden Stallion's Adventure at Redstone, 1959

Golden Stallion and the Mysterious Feud, 1967

Golden Stallion, Related titles:

Golden Stallion, 1962 Grosset, Montgomery (abridgement), illustrated by Al Brule. $12.00

GOOD HOUSEKEEPING'S BEST BOOK SERIES, Pauline Evans, 1957 Good Housekeeping Publications, hardcover, b/w illustrations. ($15.00 with dust jacket) $10.00

Good Housekeeping's Best Book of Adventure Stories

Good Housekeeping's Best Book of Animal Stories

Good Housekeeping's Best Book of Fun and Nonsense

Good Housekeeping's Best Book of Nature Stories

GREAT BRAIN SERIES, John D. Fitzgerald, 1970s Dial, hardcover, b/w illustrations by Mercer Mayer. First editions: ($35.00 with dust jacket) $15.00

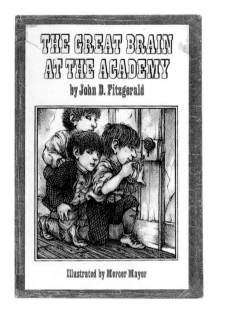

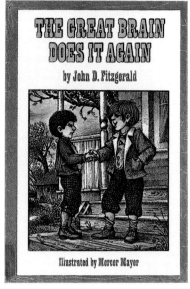

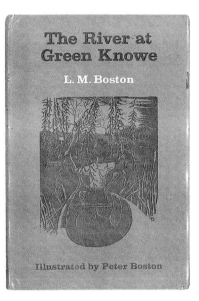

Later printings: ($20.00 with dust jacket) $10.00
Great Brain
More Adventures of the Great Brain, 1969
Me and My Little Brain
Great Brain at the Academy, 1972
Great Brain Reforms, 1973
Return of the Great Brain, 1974
Great Brain Does It Again, 1975

GREEN KNOWE SERIES, L. M. Boston, Harcourt or Atheneum, American editions, and Faber, UK editions, hardcover, illustrated by Peter Boston. This series was based on the author's own house.
Early UK editions: ($50.00 with dust jacket) $15.00
Early American editions: ($30.00 with dust jacket) $15.00
Children of Green Knowe, 1955
Treasure of Green Knowe, 1958 (British title: *Chimneys of Green Knowe*)
River at Green Knowe, 1959
Stranger at Green Knowe, 1961
Enemy at Green Knowe, 1964
Stones of Green Knowe, 1976

HALF MAGIC SERIES, Edward Eager, Harcourt Brace, illustrated by N.M. Bodecker. Loosely connected plots and characters deal with the children who first appeared in HALF MAGIC or with their children.
First edition: ($60.00 with dust jacket) $20.00
Later Harcourt editions: ($25.00 with dust jacket) $15.00
Weekly Reader editions: ($20.00 with dust jacket) $10.00
Half Magic, 1954
Knight's Castle, 1956
Magic by the Lake, 1957

Time Garden, 1958
Seven Day Magic, 1962

HAPPY HOLLISTERS SERIES, pseudonym Jerry West, (most titles credited to Andrew Sevenson, a partner in the Stratemeyer Syndicate), 1953 – 1970 Garden City or Doubleday, 33 books. Published in three formats: trade edition hardcover with dust jacket (price listed on dust jacket), trade hardcover with picture cover, and book club edition with dust jacket (dust jacket has no price, this format used for all 33 titles), two-color illustrations throughout by Helen Hamilton.
Hardcover: ($15.00 with dust jacket) $10.00
Pictorial cover: $10.00.
Note individual price for last titles in series.
Happy Hollisters on a River Trip, 1953
Happy Hollisters at Sea Gull Beach, 1953
Happy Hollisters and the Indian Treasure, 1953
Happy Hollisters at Mystery Mountain, 1954
Happy Hollisters at Snowflake Camp, 1954
Happy Hollisters and the Trading Post Mystery, 1954
Happy Hollisters at Circus Island, 1955
Happy Hollisters and the Secret Fort, 1955
Happy Hollisters and the Merry-Go Round Mystery, 1955
Happy Hollisters at Pony Hill Farm, 1956
Happy Hollisters and the Old Clipper Ship, 1956
Happy Hollisters at Lizard Cove, 1957
Happy Hollisters and the Scarecrow Mystery, 1959
Happy Hollisters and the Mystery of the Totem Faces, 1959
Happy Hollisters and the Ice Carnival Mystery, 1959
Happy Hollisters and the Mystery in Skyscraper City, 1959
Happy Hollisters and the Mystery of the Little Mermaid, 1961
Happy Hollisters and the Mystery at Missile Town, 1961

Happy Hollisters and the Cowboy Mystery, 1961
Happy Hollisters the Haunted House Mystery, 1962
Happy Hollisters the Secret of the Lucky Coins, 1962
Happy Hollisters the Castle Rock Mystery, 1963
Happy Hollisters the Cuckoo Clock Mystery, 1963
Happy Hollisters the Swiss Icho Mystery, 1963
Happy Hollisters the Sea Turtle Mystery, 1964
Happy Hollisters the Punch and Judy Mystery, 1964
Happy Hollisters the Whistle-Pig Mystery, 1964
Happy Hollisters the Ghost Horse Mystery, 1965
Happy Hollisters the Mystery of the Golden Witch, 1966
Happy Hollisters the Mystery of the Mexican Idol, 1967
Happy Hollisters and the Monster Mystery, 1969 ($25.00 with dust jacket)
Happy Hollisters and the Mystery of the Midnight Trolls, 1970 ($75.00 with dust jacket)

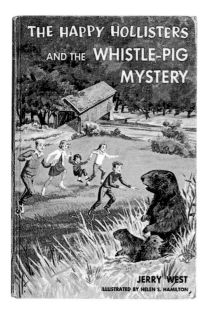

HAPPY LION SERIES, Louise Fatio, McGraw Hill, color illustrations by Roger Duvoisin. ($30.00 with dust jacket) $15.00
Happy Lion, 1954
Happy Lion, pictorial hardcover edition with 45 rpm record. $30.00
Happy Lion in Africa, 1955
Happy Lion Roars, 1957
Happy Lion and the Bear, 1964, first edition: $45.00 with dust jacket

HARDY BOYS SERIES, Franklin W. Dixon (pseudonym for Stratemeyer Syndicate authors), Grosset & Dunlap, 124 volumes published between 1927 – 1994. Starting in 1959, the Stratemeyer Syndicate began revising all books published earlier, shortening length and changing plot lines. In 1979, Simon & Schuster bought out the Stratemeyer Syndicate and published new Hardy Boys titles under the "Wanderer Books" imprint in hardcover and paperback. G&D retained publication rights to older titles. Like other G&D series, first editions are not identified, and dating is unclear. Most collectors identify "firsts" as books that do not list past their own title on the title list.

Hardy Boys, new titles 1950 – 1962 (not previously issued in any format, see also revised titles below), 1950 – 1962, hardcover. ($25.00 with dust jacket) $10.00
Later editions with pictorial cover: $10.00
Secret of Lost Tunnel, 1950
Wailing Siren Mystery, 1951
Secret of Wildcat Swamp, 1952
Crisscross Shadow, 1953
Yellow Fear Mystery, 1954
Hooded Hawk Mystery, 1954
Clue in the Embers, 1955
Secret of Pirates' Hill, 1956
Ghost of Skeleton Rock, 1957
Mystery at Devil's Paw, 1959
Mystery of the Chinese Junk, 1960
Mystery of the Desert Giant, 1961
Hardy Boys, new titles, 1962 – 1975 Grosset & Dunlap, issued only in pictorial hardcover editions. $10.00
Probable first editions: $15.00
Clue of the Screeching Owl, 1962
Viking Symbol Mystery, 1963
Mystery of the Aztec Warrior, 1964
Haunted Fort, 1965
Mystery of the Spiral Bridge, 1966
Secret Agent on Flight 101, 1967
Mystery of the Whale Tattoo, 1968
Arctic Patrol Mystery, 1969
Bombay Boomerang, 1970
Danger on the Vampire Trail, 1971
Masked Monkey, 1972
Shattered Helmet, 1973
Clue of the Hissing Serpent, 1974
Mysterious Caravan, 1975
Hardy Boys, revised titles, 1959 – 1975. These are books originally published before 1959, with stories revised or completely rewritten. Copyright shows date of original story and date of revision. Text is shortened to 20 chapters, pictorial cover format used only for books published after 1962. Hardcover with dust jacket: $15.00
Plain hardcover or pictorial hardcover: $10.00
Hardy Boys, related books:
Hardy Boys Detective Handbook, 1959 Grosset & Dunlap, hardcover, written "...in consultation with Captain D. A. Spina." ($25.00 with dust jacket) $15.00
Hardy Boys Detective Handbook, 1972 Grosset &

Dunlap, a revised edition states "in consultation with William F. Flynn." $15.00

Hardy Boys and Nancy Drew Meet Dracula, 1978 Grosset & Dunlap, softcover only, tie-in to late 1970s television series. $8.00

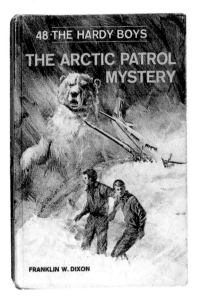

HARRY THE DOG SERIES, Gene Zion, Harper, illustrated hardcover, color illustrations by Margaret Bloy Graham. ($40.00 with dust jacket) $20.00
Weekly Reader edition: $15.00
Harry the Dirty Dog, 1956
Harry the Dirty Dog, the First Talking Storybook, 1956, with 33⅓ RPM record. $50.00
No Roses for Harry, 1958
Harry and the Lady Next Door, 1960
Harry by the Sea, 1965

HENRY HUGGINS SERIES, also see RAMONA

SERIES, Beverly Cleary, Morrow, hardcover, b/w illustrations by Louis Darling.
First edition with dust jacket: $55.00
Later printings: ($20.00 with dust jacket) $10.00
Henry Huggins, 1950
Henry and Ribsy, 1954
Henry and the Paper Route, 1957
Henry and the Clubhouse, 1962
Henry and Beezus, 1952, first edition with dust jacket: $75.00

HENRY REED SERIES, Keith Robertson, Viking, hardcover, color illustrations by Robert McClosky.
First editions: ($35.00 with dust jacket) $15.00
Later editions: ($15.00 with dust jacket) $10.00
Henry Reed, Inc., 1958
Henry Reed's Journey, 1963
Henry Reed's Babysitting Service, 1966
Henry Reed's Big Show, 1970

HOWDY DOODY, various authors, ca. 1950s, Little Golden Books, small illustrated hardcovers, 28 pages. Several of these titles were dropped or replaced in the LITTLE GOLDEN BOOKS series in the 1960s. $12.00
Howdy Doody's Circus, 1950, Don Gormley, illustrated by Liz Dauber
Howdy Doody and Clarabell, 1951, Edward Kean, illustrated by Art Seiden
Howdy Doody and the Princess, 1952, Edward Kean, illustrated by Art Seiden
Howdy Doody's Lucky Trip, 1953, Edward Kean, illustrated by Harry McNaught
Howdy Doody and His Magic Hat, 1954, Edward Kean, illustrated by Art Seiden
Howdy Doody and Mr. Bluster, 1954, Edward Kean, illustrated by Elias Marge
It's Howdy Doody Time, 1955, Edward Kean, illustrated by Art Seiden
Howdy Doody and Santa Claus, 1955, Edward Kean, illustrated by Art Seiden
Howdy Doody's Animal Friends, 1956, Kathleen Daly, illustrated by Art Seiden

——— ◁═ **I** ═▷ ———

ISLAND STALLION SERIES, see BLACK STALLION SERIES

——— ◁═ **J** ═▷ ———

JEFF WHITE SERIES, Lew Dietz, Little Brown, hardcover, illustrated by Kuhn and Moyers. ($25.00 with dust jacket) $10.00
Jeff White, Young Guide, 1951

Jeff White, Young Lumberjack, 1952
Jeff White, Forest Fire Fighter, 1954

JENNINGS SERIES, Anthony Malcolm Buckeridge, 1950 – 1977 Collins, hardcover, 22 titles. This English school series began as radio plays in 1948. In the 1990s, Collins issued two final titles: *Jennings Again!* and *That's Jennings.* Like the *Billy Bunter* or *William Brown* books, prices in England tend to be higher than in the USA ($25.00 with dust jacket) $10.00
Jennings Goes to School, 1950
Jennings Follows a Clue, 1951
Jennings' Little Hut, 1951
Jennings and Darbishire, 1952
Jennings' Diary, 1953
According to Jennings, 1954
Our Friend Jennings, 1955
Thanks to Jennings, 1957
Take Jennings, For Instance, 1958
Jennings, as Usual, 1959
Trouble with Jennings, 1960
Just Like Jennings, 1961
Leave It to Jennings, 1963
Jennings, Of Course!, 1964, first edition with dust jacket: $40.00
Especially Jennings!, 1965
Bookfull of Jennings, 1966
Jennings Abounding, 1967
Jennings in Particular, 1968
Trust Jennings! 1969
Jennings Report, 1970
Typically Jennings!, 1971
Speaking of Jennings!, 1973
Jennings at Large, 1977

JOEY BOOKS, Robert Martin, ca. 1950s Thomas Nelson, London, red hardcover, b/w illustrations by T. R. Freeman. ($15.00 with dust jacket) $10.00
Joey and the Helicopter
Joey and the Magic Pony
Joey and the River Pirates

JUNGLE DOCTOR SERIES, Paul White, ca. 1950s – 1960s, Paternoster Press, London, a church school series, small hardcover, b/w illustrations by Graham Wade. ($15.00 with dust jacket) $8.00
Jungle Doctor
Jungle Doctor on Safari
Jungle Doctor Operates
Jungle Doctor Attacks Witchcraft
Jungle Doctor's Enemies
Jungle Doctor Meets a Lion
Jungle Doctor to the Rescue
Jungle Doctor's Case-Book

Jungle Doctor and the Whirlwind
Eyes on Jungle Doctor
Jungle Doctor Looks for Trouble
Jungle Doctor Goes West
Jungle Doctor Stings a Scorpion
Jungle Doctor Hunts Big Game
Jungle Doctor on the Hop
Jungle Doctor's Crooked Dealings
Jungle Doctor's Fables
Jungle Doctor's Monkey Tales
Jungle Doctor's Tug-of-War
Doctor of Tanganyika, photo illustrations
Jungle Doctor Panorama, photo illustrations

JUNIOR DELUXE EDITIONS, various authors, 1950s – 1970s Nelson Doubleday or Country Life Press. Following is a sampling of titles only, as dozens of classic and modern children's novels appeared in these editions. ($20.00 with dust jacket) $10.00
All the Mowgli Stories, Rudyard Kipling
At the Back of the North Wind, George Macdonald
Big Wave and Other Stories, Pearl Buck
Captains Courageous, Rudyard Kipling
Christmas Stories, Charles Dickens:
Eight Cousins, Louisa May Alcott
Hans Brinker or The Silver Skates, Mary Mapes Dodge
Hans Christian Andersen's Fairy Tales
Kidnapped, Robert Louis Stevenson
Little Men, Louisa May Alcott
My Friend Flicka, Mary O'Hara
Myths Every Child Should Know
National Velvet, Enid Bagnold
New Wizard of Oz, L. Frank Baum
Oliver Twist, Charles Dickens
Penrod and Sam, Booth Tarkington
Profiles in Courage, J.F. Kennedy
Robin Hood, Howard Pyle
Stories from the Arabian Night, Laurence Housman

JUST-SO STORIES, Rudyard Kipling, 1955 – 1956 Rand McNally Elf Books. Each small book contained one story from the Just So collection. Small full-color hardcovers, see also ELF BOOKS. $8.00
Elephant's Child, illustrated by Katherine Evans
How the Camel Got His Hump, illustrated by Erika Weihs
How the Rhinoceros Got His Skin, illustrated by Erika Weihs

K

KATHY MARTIN STORIES, ca. 1960s Golden Press, yellow spine, illustrated hardcover. $15.00
Cap for Kathy
Junior Nurse

Senior Nurse
Patient in 202
Assignment in Alaska
Private Duty Nurse

KEN HOLT MYSTERY STORIES, Bruce Campbell (pseudonym of Samuel and Beryl Epstein), 1949 – 1963 Grosset & Dunlap, hardcover, 18 titles. Each came with a white dust jacket with different color illustration for each book. Spine shows head of Ken Holt in a shield-shaped panel. Uncredited illustrations. Illustrated endpapers signed James M. Will or Wills. Pre-1960 titles: ($20.00 with dust jacket) $10.00
  Later titles: see individual titles for prices
Secret of Skeleton Island, 1949
Riddle of the Stone Elephant, 1949
Black Thumb Mystery, 1950
Clue of the Marked Claw, 1950
Clue of the Coiled Cobra, 1951
Secret of Hangman's Inn, 1951
Mystery of the Iron Box, 1952
Clue of the Phantom Car, 1953
Mystery of the Galloping Horse, 1954
Mystery of the Green Flame, 1955
Mystery of the Grinning Tiger, 1956
Mystery of the Vanishing Magician, 1956
Mystery of the Shattered Glass, 1958
Mystery of the Invisible Enemy, 1959
Mystery of Gallows Cliff, 1960
Clue of the Silver Scorpion, 1961 (probable first with dust jacket, $35.00) $15.00
Mystery of the Plumed Serpent, 1962 (probable first with dust jacket, $45.00) $15.00
Mystery of the Sultan's Scimitar, 1963 (probable first with dust jacket, $60.00) $25.00

KENT BARSTOW ADVENTURE SERIES, Rutherford Montgomery, 1958 – 1964 Duell, Sloan and Pearce, 7 books, cloth hardcover. Cold war adventures featuring Barstow, a young U.S. Air Force officer. ($15.00 with dust jackets) $10.00
Kent Barstow, Special Agent, 1958
Missile Away!, 1959
Mission Intruder, 1960
Kent Barstow, Space Man, 1961
Kent Barstow and the Commando Flight, 1963
Kent Barstow Aboard the Dyna Soar, 1964
Kent Barstow on a B-70 Mission, 1964

KIM ALDRICH MYSTERY SERIES, Jinny McDonnell, ca. 1970 Whitman, pictorial hardcover.
Miscalculated Risk
Silent Partner
Long Shot

KOKO SERIES, Basil William Miller, 1947 – 1956 Zondervan, hardcover, 7 titles. Books tell the story of Kris Cory and his sled dog Koko. ($15.00 with dust jacket) $10.00
Koko, King of the Arctic Trail, 1947
Koko of the Airways, 1948
Koko and the Eskimo Doctor, 1949
Koko and the Timber Thieves, 1951
Koko and the Fur Thieves, 1953
Koko on the Yukon, 1954
Koko and the Mounties, 1956

—————— L ——————

LANDMARK BOOKS SERIES, circa 1950s – 1960s Random House, hardcover, b/w or b/w/color illustrations, a series of non-fiction books written about various historical events, biographies, and special interest topics. Books by well-known authors or unusual topics may command slightly higher prices. ($20.00 with dust jacket) $8.00
Barbary Pirates, C. S. Forester, 1953
Betsy Ross and the Flag, Jane Mayer, 1952
Chief of the Cossacks, Harold Lamb, 1959
Daniel Boone: The Opening of the Wilderness, John Mason Brown, 1952, illustrated by Lee J. Ames
Early Days of Automobiles, Elizabeth Janeway 1956, illustrated by Bertha Depper
Ethan Allen and the Green Mountain Boys, Slater Brown, 1956, illustrated by William C. Moyers
Erie Canal, Samuel Hopkins Adams, 1953, illustrated by Leonard Vosburgh
F.B.I., Quentin Reynolds, 1954, illustrated with photographs
Guadalcanal Diary, Richard Tregaskis, 1955, illustrated with photographs
Genghis Khan and the Mongol Horde, Harold Lamb, 1954
Hawaii Gem of the Pacific, Oscar Lewis, 1954
Lawrence of America, Alistair MacLean, 1962
Mr. Bell Invents the Telephone, Katherine B. Shippen 1952, illustrated by Richard Floethe
Our Independence and the Constitution, Dorothy Canfield Fisher, 1950, illustrated by Robert Doremus
Paul Revere and the Minute Men, Dorothy Canfield Fisher, 1950, illustrated by Norman Price
Peter Stusyvesant of Old New York, Crouse, 1954
Pony Express, Samuel Adams, 1950
Rise and Fall of Adolf Hitler, William L. Shirer, 1961, illustrated with photographs
Royal Canadian Mounted Police, Richard L. Neuberger, 1953, illustrated by Lee J. Ames.
Santa Fe Trail, Samuel Adams, 1951

Slave Who Freed Haiti: The Story of Toussaint Louverture, Scherman, 1954
Swamp Fox of the Revolution, Stewart Holbrook, 1959, illustrated by Ernest Richardson
Story of Albert Schweitzer, Anita Daniel, 1957
Story of the U.S. Marines, George P Hunt, 1951, illustrated by Charles J. Mazoujian
Story of the U.S. Air Force, Loomis, 1959
Trappers and Traders of the Far West, James Daugherty, 1952, illustrated by author
Wild Bill Hickok, Stewart H. Holbrook, 1952, illustrated by Ernest Richardson
Winter at Valley Forge, F. Van Wyck Mason, 1953
Wright Brothers: Pioneers of American Aviation, Quentin Reynolds, 1950, illustrated by Jacob Landau

LASSIE SERIES, Whitman, illustrated hardcover, TV tie-in. $10.00
Lassie, Forbidden Valley, Schroeder, 1959
Lassie, Treasure Hunter, Harry Timmins, 1960
Lassie and the Mystery at Blackberry Bog, Snow
Lassie and the Secret of the Summer, Snow, 1958
Lassie: The Wild Mountain Trail, Edmonds, 1966
Lassie, the Mystery of the Bristlecone Pine, Frazee, 1967
Lassie, Adventure In Alaska, Elrick, 1967
Lassie and the Firefighters, Michelson, 1968
Lassie, Secret of the Smelters' Cave, Frazee, 1968
Lassie Lost in the Snow, Steve Frazee, 1969
Lassie, Tell-a-Tale Books, Whitman, small pictorial hardcover. $10.00
Lassie and the Kittens, Grant, 1956
Lassie Finds a Friend, 1960
Hooray for Lassie, Borden, 1964
Lassie and the Cub Scout, Michelson, 1966
Lassie and the Busy Morning, Lewis, 1973
Lassie, Big Little Books, Whitman. $10.00
Lassie and the Shabby Sheik, Elrick, 1968

LEAVE IT TO BEAVER SERIES, Beverly Cleary, Berkeley, 3 books based on the popular TV series. Published in paperbacks only, $10.00
Leave it to Beaver, 1960
Beaver and Wally, 1961
Here's Beaver!, 1961
Leave it to Beaver, Little Golden Book:
Leave it to Beaver, Lawrence Alson, 1959, small color illustrated hardcover, foil spine. 24 pages, color illustrations by Mel Crawford. $15.00

LEONARD SERIES, see TIME MACHINE SERIES

LINDA CRAIG SERIES, Ann Sheldon, 1960s Doubleday, pictorial hardcover, decorated endpapers. $15.00

Linda Craig and the Clue on the Desert Trail
Linda Craig and the Palomino Mystery
Linda Craig and the Secret of Rancho Del Sol
Linda Craig and the Mystery in Mexico
Linda Craig and the Ghost Town Treasure

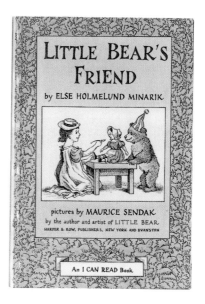

LITTLE BEAR SERIES, Else Holmelund Minarik, Harper Row, I Can Read books, small, pictorial hardcover, two-color illustrations by Maurice Sendak.
Harper first editions with dust jacket are priced to $150.00
Kingswood, Surrey, World's Work first editions with dust jacket are priced to $85.00
Early editions: ($35.00 with dust jacket) $15.00
Later editions: ($25.00 with dust jacket) $10.00
Weekly Reader illustrated hardcover editions: $15.00
Little Bear, 1957
Little Bear's Visit, 1961
Little Bear's Friend, 1960
Father Bear Comes Home, 1961
Kiss for Little Bear, 1968

LITTLE BEAR SERIES, Janice (Brustlein), Lothrop Lee and Shepard, hardcover, 32 pages, color illustrations by Mariana.
First edition with dust jacket: $50.00
Later printings: ($30.00 with dust jacket) $15.00
Little Bear's Pancake Party, 1960
Little Bear's Christmas, 1964
Little Bear's Thanksgiving, 1967
Little Bear Marches in the St. Patrick's Day Parade, 1967
Little Bear Learns to Read the Cookbook, 1969
Little Bear's Sunday Breakfast

LITTLE BLACK, Walter Farley, see BLACK STALLION SERIES

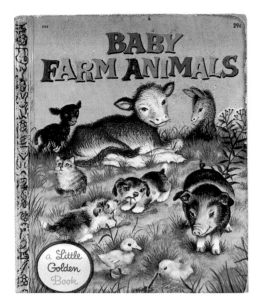

LITTLE GOLDEN BOOKS SERIES, various authors/illustrators, 1942 on, Western Publishing, (publisher listed as Western, Simon & Schuster, or Golden Press), 600+ titles through 1973. Western had sold more than a billion copies of Little Golden Books by the 1950s. Collectors seek first editions, editions with unusual gimmicks (see LITTLE GOLDEN, Band Aids) or books illustrated by name illustrators. First editions were marked with an "A" often printed on the lower right corner of the last page, slightly hidden under binding. Price printed on book, or the color of the spine, or the design on the back cover, can also help identify books. Original prices were: 25 cents (1942 – 1962), 29 cents (1962 – 1968), 39 cents (1968 – 1974), 40 cents (1974 – 1977). Early 1940s titles were 42 pages long. By the 1950s, the length was cut to 28 pages and then to 24 pages. The numbering system does not indicate the chronological order of a book in a series, as many earlier titles were replaced with new titles using the same number in the 1960s and 1970s. For example, #315 was used for *Legend of Wyatt Earp* (1958) and *Sesame Street: The Together Book*, (1971). The authors of this price guide highly recommend *Collecting Little Golden Books* by Steve Santi for complete bibliographical information. Prices given below are average prices for single titles. For books related to specific characters or series, see also DING DONG SCHOOL, DISNEY, HOWDY DOODY, LONE RANGER, MARY POPPINS, MICKEY MOUSE CLUB, OZ, ROY ROGERS, TARZAN.

Little Golden Books, general titles, 1950 – 1969, "antique gold" foil spine hardcover with leaves and flower pattern.

1950s first editions, $15.00
1960s first editions, $12.00
 Later editions: nonfiction titles such as *Airplanes*, #373: $5.00; popular comic strip characters, such as *Bugs Bunny*, #72, $8.00.
Popular illustrators Garth Williams and Eloise Wilkin, first editions, $20.00, later editions $10.00.
Titles that command higher than normal prices generally feature popular TV shows, themes, or artwork.
Little Golden Books, general titles, 1969 – 1975, "gold" foil spine hardcover with animal pattern. First editions, $8.00, later printings, $4.00. Higher prices for popular comic characters or illustrators.
Little Golden Books, general titles, 1948, cloth covers. A number of other cover materials were used for Little Golden Books besides the standard slick paper-over-board hardcover. Some titles were released in "special bound in cloth editions" (ca. 1948), "Duro-Tuff" two color covers (ca. 1950), and Goldencraft library or school editions (1950s – 1960s). Goldencraft also manufactured a stiff cardboard cover with a fabric spine. Ex-library or ex-school editions are usually priced at under $5.00
Little Golden Books, other books with novelty toys, paper dolls, or commercial products, (see also GOLDEN BOOKS, Activity Books, Band-Aids and Jig-Saw Books), **1950s – 1960s.** Several Little Golden titles were issued with toys such as paper dolls or novelty products attached. Prices shown are for books with products still attached. (If the product is missing, the price is usually in the under $5.00 range.)
Little Benny Wanted a Pony, 1950, illustrated by Richard Scarry, with a real mask intact, $25.00
Happy Birthday, 1952, illustrated by Retta Worcester, 42 pages with party favors, original cover price 35 cents, $20.00
Fun With Decals, 1952, illustrated by Corinne Malvern, #139 with decals, $30.00
Tex and His Toys, 1952, illustrated by Corinne Malvern, #129 with Texel Cellophane Tape, $50.00
Christmas Manger, 1953, 28 pages, #176 with cutout Nativity scene, $25.00
Little Golden Paper Dolls, 1951, 28 pages, #113 with paper dolls, $35.00
Little Golden Paper Dolls, later printing, 24 pages, series #280, with paper dolls, $25.00
Little Lulu and Her Magic Tricks, 1954, #203 with Kleenex package, $75.00 ($30.00 without Kleenex)
Paper Doll Wedding, 1954, #193 (also issued as an activity book) with paper dolls, $35.00
How to Tell Time, 1957, cover has Gruen "watch" with movable hands, $25.00
How to Tell Time, later printings, cover "watch" missing Gruen name, with movable hands, $20.00

Betsy McCall, 1965, #559, with Betsy paper doll, $30.00

Little Golden Books, Activity Books, 1955 – 1963, 50 titles, hardcovers. The activities books used series numbers A1 through A52 (not to be confused with the "A" indicating edition). Books featured paper dolls, stamps, wheels, or paints in cover. General prices: stamp books with stamps, $15.00; wheel books with wheel, $10.00; paper doll books with paper dolls, $35.00. Books with activities missing, $5.00.

Unusual titles, hard-to-find:

Animal Paintbook (with three paints in cover), 1955, by Hans Helweg, illustrated by author, $45.00

Cinderella (with paper dolls), 1960, illustrated by Gordon Laite, $45.00

Clown Coloring Book, 1955, illustrations by Art Seiden, with crayon box, $45.00

Gordon's Jet Flight (with paper model jet), by Naomi Glasson, illustrated by Mel Crawford, $50.00

Hansel and Gretel (with paper dolls), 1961, illustrated by Judy and Barry Martin, $40.00

Little Red Riding Hood (with paper dolls), 1959, by Sharon Kostner, $40.00

Mickey Mouse Club Stamp Book (with stamps), by Kathleen Daly, illustrated by Julius Svendsen, $50.00

My Little Golden Calendar (double-page calendar), 1961, by Richard Scarry, $30.00

Story of Baby Jesus Stamps (with stamps), 1957, by J.W. Watson, illustrated by Eloise Wilkin, $45.00

Trim the Christmas Tree (#A15 with tree punch-out), 1957, by Elsa Nast, illustrated by Doris Henderson, $35.00

Trucks (with two paper model trucks), 1955, by Kathryn Jackson, illustrated by Ray Quigley, $50.00

Little Golden Books, Band-Aid Books, 1950 – 1979, by Helen Gaspard *(Dr. Dan)* or Kathryn Jackson *(Nurse Nancy),* illustrated by Corrine Malvern. Hardcovers were issued with Johnson and Johnson Band-Aids inserted. Pre-1960 books with Band-Aids: RARE.

Pre-1960, without Band-Aids: $20.00

Later printings, without Band-Aids: $10.00

Doctor Dan the Bandage Man, 1950, series #111, 42 pages, with six Band-Aids.

Doctor Dan the Bandage Man, 1957, series #295, 24 pages, with six "stars 'n strips" Band-Aids.

Doctor Dan the Bandage Man, later reprint, series #312-07 (1970s reprint), with "two real" Band-Aids.

Doctor Dan at the Circus, 1960, by Pauline Wilkins, illustrated by Katherine Sampson, series #399, 24 pages with circus patterned Band-Aids.

Nurse Nancy, 1952, series #154 with six Band-Aids "in three shapes."

Nurse Nancy, 1959, series #346 with Band-Aids.

Nurse Nancy, 1962, series #473 with "stars 'n strips" Band-Aids.

Little Golden Books, Eager Reader Series, 1974 – 1975, boxed set of 8 volumes. Solid gold spine, large type, cover copy reads "a book you can read by yourself." Boxed set, $35.00. Individual titles, $2.00

Little Golden Books, Record Sets, ca. 1948 – 1970s. A variety of records with book formats were issued for Little Golden Books. "Little Golden Records" (1948/1950) were issued as single records pressed in yellow plastic. Prices are higher for popular characters or known narrators such as actor Danny Kaye. $35.00

Record Sets, 1956, black record accompanied by regular Little Golden Book book, series number begins with C. $30.00

Golden Story Book and Record Album, ca. 1960s, 33⅓ long playing record with 24 page soft cover book, series numbers begin with GST. $20.00

Read and Hear, ca. 1960s, 45 rpm record inserted into front cover of book. Series numbers 151 through 176. $20.00

Disneyland Record, ca. 1970s, 33⅓ rpm record inserted into back cover. Series numbers 201 through 255. $20.00

Little Golden Books, Giants, 1957 – 1959, various authors and illustrators, series numbers 5001 – 5027, 56 pages, original cover price 50 cents. Cover states "A Giant Little Golden Book." Books were often a collection of stories or reprints of earlier titles.

Individual titles: $10.00

Walt Disney titles: $20.00.

Some exceptions:

My Christmas Treasury, 1957, illustrated by Lowell Hess, 72 pages, $20.00

Adventures of Lassie, 1958, three complete stories, $15.00

Hans Christian Andersen's Fairy Tales, 1958, 72 pages, $20.00

Captain Kangaroo, 1959, "three books in one!", $15.00

Cub Scouts, 1959, by Bruce Brian, illustrated by Me Crawford, $20.00

Mother Goose Rhymes, 1959, illustrated by Feodor Rojankovsky, $30.00

My Pets, 1959, by Patsy Scarry, illustrated by Eloise Wilkin, $30.00

Nursery Tales, 1959, illustrated by Richard Scarry, 72 pages, $20.00

This World of Ours, 1959, by J.W. Watson, illustrated by Eloise Wilkin, $30.00

Little Golden Books, Jig-Saw Puzzles, ca. 1949 – 1950, various authors and illustrators. On top of cover, tag line may state "A LITTLE GOLDEN BOOK plus a real JIG-SAW PUZZLE."

Book with intact puzzle in back cover, $45.00

Book without puzzle, $10.00

Jolly Barnyard, 1950, illustrated by Tibor Gergely, 42 pages, #67

Katie the Kitten, 1949, illustrated by Alice and Martin Provenson, 28 pages #75

Baby's House, 1950, illustrated by Mary Blair, 28 pages #80

Duck and His Friends, 1950, illustrated by Richard Scarry, 28 pages, #81

Pets for Peter, 1950, illustrated by Battaglia, 28 pages, #82

Brave Cowboy Bill, 1950, illustrated by Richard Scarry, 42 pages, #93

Jerry At School, 1950, illustrated by Corinne Malvern, 42 pages, #94

When I Grow Up, 1950, illustrated by Corrine Malvern, 42 pages, #96

Little Golden ABC, 1951, illustrated Cornelius De Witt, 28 pages, #101

Ukelele and Her New Doll, 1951, illustrated by Campbell Grant, 28 pages, #102

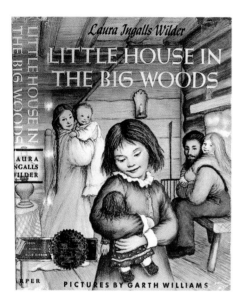

LITTLE HOUSE SERIES, Laura Ingalls Wilder, 1953 editions Harper, hardcover, (original books were illustrated by Helen Sewell) b/w illustrations by Garth Williams.
   First edition thus: ($50.00 with dust jacket) $15.00
   Later printings: ($20.00 with dust jacket) $10.00

Little House in the Big Woods
Little House on the Prairie
Farmer Boy
On The Banks of Plum Creek
By The Shores of Silver Lake
Long Winter
Little Town on the Prairie
These Happy Golden Years
The First Four Years
On the Way Home

West From Home

LITTLE LEAGUE SERIES, Curtis Kent Bishop, 1953 – 1968 Steck Co. or Lippincott, hardcover, 13 titles. Steck Co. (Austin, TX) published titles 1-5, Lippincott published titles 6-13. ($20.00 with dust jacket) $10.00

Larry of the Little League, 1953
Larry Leads Off, 1954
Larry Comes Home, 1955
Little League, 1956
Little League Way, 1957
Lank of the Little League, 1958
Little League Heroes, 1960
Little League Double Play, 1962
Little League Amigo, 1964
Little League Stepson, 1965
Little League Visitor, 1966
Little League Victory, 1967
Little League Brother, 1968

LONE HUNTER SERIES, Donald Emmet Worcester, 1956 – 1959 Oxford/Walck, hardcover. ($15.00 with dust jacket) $10.00

Lone Hunter's Gray Pony, 1956
Lone Hunter and the Cheyennes, 1957
Lone Hunter's First Buffalo Hunt, 1958
Lone Hunter and the Wild Horses, 1959

LONE RANGER BOOKS, Fran Striker, Grosset & Dunlap, ca. 1950s. Other publishers, including Whitman, have issued a variety of hardcover or paperback reprints of Lone Ranger stories.
   Early editions with dust jacket: $50.00
   Later editions: ($25.00 with dust jacket) $10.00

Lone Ranger in Wild Horse Canyon, 1950
Lone Ranger and the War Horse, 1951
Lone Ranger West of Maverick Pass, 1951
Lone Ranger on Gunsight Mesa, 1952
Lone Ranger and the Bitter Spring Feud, 1953
Lone Ranger and the Code of the West, 1954
Lone Ranger: Trouble on the Santa Fe, 1955
Lone Ranger on Red Butte Trail, 1956
Lone Ranger and the Outlaw Stronghold, 1959 Sampson, UK

Lone Ranger, Little Golden Books, small illustrated hardcovers, 24 pages, $12.00

Lone Ranger, 1956, by Steffi Fletcher, illustrated by Joseph Dreany

Lone Ranger and Tonto, 1957, by Charles Verral, illustrated by Edwin Schmidt

Lone Ranger and the Talking Pony, 1958, by Emily Brown, illustrated by Frank Bolle

Lone Ranger, other books:

Lone Ranger Annual, 1952 World, London, hardcover, cartoon strips, 93 pages. $15.00

Lone Ranger Adventure Stories, adapted by Arthur Groom for the Warner film, 1957 Western, oversize pictorial hardcover, 77 pages, photo illustrations. $30.00

Lone Ranger and the Desert Storm, Revena, 1957 Whitman Tell-a-Tale book. $10.00

Lone Ranger and the Ghost Horse, Alice Sankey, 1957 Whitman, small hardcover, illustrated by Bob Totten. $15.00

LONELY DOLL, see EDITH

LORD OF THE RINGS, J.R.R. Tolkien, 1953 – 1955 George Allen & Unwin: London, 1967, revised second edition, including a revision of *The Hobbit,* issued by Houghton Mifflin: Boston and George Allen & Unwin, UK. Revised editions (also called second editions) are clearly marked by the publishers and contain a new foreword by Tolkien as well as additional appendices.

Hobbit, 1966 Houghton, revised second edition, first printing stated on copyright page: ($100 with dust jacket) $50.00. Later printings: ($35.00 with dust jacket) $15.00

Hobbit, 1977 Harry Abrams, color illustrations taken from the Rankin/Bass animated film. (With painted acetate dust jacket, $50.00) $30.00

Fellowship of the Ring (Volume 1), 1953 George Allen & Unwin, first edition, red cloth, RARE

Fellowship of the Ring, 1967 Houghton (UK editions Allen & Unwin), revised second edition, black cloth hardcover, first printing stated on copyright page, pull-out map intact: ($100 with dust jacket) $50.00. Later printings: ($30.00 with dust jacket) $15.00

Two Towers (Volume 2), 1954 George Allen & Unwin, first edition, red cloth, RARE

Two Towers, 1967 Houghton (UK editions Allen & Unwin), revised second edition, first printing stated on copyright page: ($100 with dust jacket) $50.00. Later printings: ($30.00 with dust jacket) $15.00

Return of the King, 1955 George Allen & Unwin, first edition, red cloth, RARE

Return of the King, 1967 Houghton (UK editions Allen & Unwin), revised second edition, first printing stated on copyright page: ($100 with dust jacket) $50.00. Later printings: ($30.00 with dust jacket) $15.00

Lord of the Rings (complete set, Volume 1 through 3), 1953 – 1955 George Allen & Unwin, red cloth, gilt lettering on covers, folding maps, first printing, RARE. One such set listed in 1999 dealer's catalog as $6,000 for books in good condition with "minor soiling."

Lord of the Rings (complete set, Volume 1 through 3) 1967 Houghton (UK editions Allen & Unwin), revised second edition, first printing clearly stated on copyright page, ($350.00 with dust jackets) $150.00

Lord of the Rings (complete set, Volume 1 through 3) 1967 Houghton, book club editions, three volumes in slipcase, $50.00

LUCKY STARR SERIES, Paul French (pseudonym of Isaac Asimov), 1952 – 1958 Doubleday, hardcover, adventures of space ranger David "Lucky" Starr by a famous American science fiction author. Reissued in hardcover by Twayne in 1970s. Later issued in paperback format by Signet, Fawcett, Ballantine, and Bantam Books (double volumes).
Doubleday hardcovers: ($150.00 with dust jackets) $20.00
Twayne hardcovers: ($35.00 with dust jackets) $10.00

David Starr, Space Ranger, 1952

Lucky Starr and the Pirates of the Asteroids, 1953

Lucky Starr and the Oceans of Venus, 1954

Lucky Starr and the Big Sun of Mercury, 1956

Lucky Starr and the Moons of Jupiter, 1957

Lucky Starr and the Rings of Saturn, 1958

LYLE THE CROCODILE SERIES, Bernard Waber, Houghton Mifflin, hardcover, color illustrations by Waber. ($25.00 with dust jacket) $15.00
Weekly Reader Book Club editions: $10.00

House on East 88th Street, 1962

Lyle, Lyle, Crocodile, 1965

Lyle and the Birthday Party, 1966

Lovable Lyle, 1969

Lyle Finds his Mother, 1974

MADELINE SERIES, Ludwig Bemelmans, oversize picture books with color illustrated hardcovers and endpapers, and color illustrations throughout by author. The first book was published in 1939, and first editions are hard-to-find. The series is constantly reprinted, usually in full-size reproductions of the originals, including same-as-cover dust jackets, and price varies with publisher and date. Later editions: ($20.00 with dust jacket) $10.00
Madeline, 1939
Madeline's Rescue, 1953 Viking, first edition with dust jacket: $400.00
Madeline and the Bad Hat, 1957
Madeline and the Gypsies, 1959 Andre Deutsch, first edition with dust jacket: $60.00
Madeline in London, (1961) 1962 Andre Deutsch, first edition with dust jacket: $90.00
Related books:
Madeline, 1954 Little Golden Book $15.00

MAGGIE MUGGINS BOOKS, Mary Grannan, ca. 1960s, hardcover.
Maggie Muggins and her Animal Friends, 1959 Pennington, first edition, hardcover, illustrated by Bernard Zalusky. ($15.00 with dust jacket) $10.00
Maggie Muggins Bedtime Stories, 1959 Pennington Press, first edition, hardcover, b/w/orange illustrations. ($15.00 with dust jacket) $10.00
More Maggie Muggins, 1959 Pennington Press, hardcover, illustrations by Bernard Zalusky. ($15.00 with dust jacket) $10.00
Maggie Muggins and the Cottontail, 1960 Thomas Allen, Toronto, first edition, hardcover, illustrated by Pat Patience. ($30.00 with dust jacket)

Maggie Muggins and Mr. McGarrity, 1960 Thomas Allen, first edition, hardcover, illustrated by Pat Patience. ($30.00 with dust jacket)

MAGNUS SERIES, Hans Peterson, 1960s, translated by Marianne Turner for Pantheon, or Madeleine Hamilton for Viking, first American edition, hardcover, illustrated by Ilon Wikland. First edition with dust jacket: $50.00. Later editions: ($25.00 with dust jacket) $15.00
Magnus and the Squirrel
Magnus and the Wagon Horse
Magnus in the Harbor
Magnus in Danger
Magnus and the Ship's Mascot

MARCO SERIES, John T. Foster, Dodd Mead, b/w illustrations by Lorence Bjoklund. Boys' mystery series set in New Orleans.
Hardcovers, $10.00 (with dust jackets, $15.00)
Weekly Reader editions, $8.00.
Marco and the Tiger, 1967
Marco and the Sleuth Hound, 1969
Marco and That Curious Cat, 1970

MARCY RHODES, Rosamund du Jardin (1902 – 1963), 1950s Lippincott, hardcover. See also TOBY HEYDON and PAM AND PENNY. ($35.00 with dust jacket) $15.00
Wait for Marcy, 1950
Marcy Catches Up, 1952
Man for Marcy, 1954
Senior Prom, 1957

MARJORIE SERIES, Lorna Hill, 1948 – 1962, hardcover, first editions had various publishers (dates and publishers noted below). Titles later were reissued by Thomas Nelson. See also DANCING PEELS, PATIENCE, SADLER WELLS, and VICARAGE CHILDREN. ($20.00 with dust jackets) $10.00
Marjorie and Co., 1948 Art & Educational
Stolen Holiday, 1948 Art & Educational
Border Peel, 1950 Art & Educational
Castle in Northumbria, 1953 Burke
No Medals For Guy, 1962 Thomas Nelson

MARLOWS SERIES, Antonia Forest, 1948 – 1976, Faber and Faber, 8 titles. Although the author never meant to write a series, new accounts of the eight Marlow children appeared regularly, with an additional book published in 1982. Her two historical novels (see FOREST in authors section) also had slight ties to the series. Hardcovers in good condition are hard to find for most of the series. Prices in England tend to be double that of American bookstores.

First editions with dust jackets: $80.00

Later editions: ($35.00 with dust jackets) $20.00

Autumn Term, 1948
Marlows and the Traitor, 1953
Falconer's Lure: Story of a Summer Holiday, 1957
End of Term, 1959
Peter's Room, 1961
Thuggery Affair, 1965
Ready-Made Family, 1967
Cricket Term, 1974
Attic Term, 1976

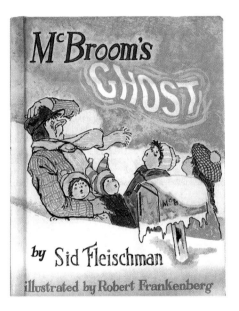

McBROOM SERIES, Sid Fleischman, 1966 – 1978 Norton, oversize hardcover, illustrated endpapers, color illustrations throughout. ($25.00 with dust jacket) $15.00

Grosset and Weekly Reader editions, hardcover. $15.00

McBroom Tells the Truth
McBroom and the Big Wind
McBroom's Ear
McBroom's Ghost
McBroom's Zoo
McBroom and the Rainmaker
McBroom Tells a Lie
McBroom and the Beanstalk

MCGURK MYSTERIES, E. Hildick, 1973 – 1990 Macmillan or Grosset & Dunlap, hardcover, 20 titles in series. ($15.00 with dust jackets) $10.00

Weekly Reader editions, $6.00

McGurk titles published in 1970s:

Nose Knows, 1973
Deadline for McGurk, 1975
Case of the Condemned Cat, 1975
Case of the Nervous Newsboy, 1976

Great Rabbit Rip-off, 1977
Case of the Invisible Dog, 1977
Case of the Secret Scribbler, 1978
Case of the Phantom Frog, 1979

MEG SERIES, Holly Beth Walker, Whitman, pictorial hardcover, illustrated endpapers, illustrated by Cliff Schule. $15.00

Meg and the Disappearing Diamonds, 1967
Meg: Secret of the Witch's Stairway
Meg: The Treasure Nobody Saw, 1970
Meg: Mystery in Williamsburg, 1972

MELLOPS BOOKS, Tomi Ungerer, Harper, oversize hardcovers, color illustrations by author. ($35.00 with dust jacket) $20.00

Mellops Go Diving for Treasure, 1957
Mellops Go Flying, 1957
Mellops Strike Oil, 1958
Christmas Eve at the Mellops', 1960
Mellops Go Spelunking, 1963

MEL MARTIN BASEBALL STORIES, John Cooper, 1947 – 1953 Cupples & Leon, hardcover, 6 titles. Baseball-related mystery stories. Reprints by Garden City or Books Inc.

Cupples & Leon editions: $30.00 with dust jackets

Later reprints: ($15.00 with dust jacket) $10.00

Mystery at the Ball Park, 1947
Southpaw's Secret, 1947
Phantom Homer, 1952
First Base Jinx, 1952
Fighting Shortstop, 1953
College League Mystery, 1953

MICKEY MOUSE CLUB, Little Golden Books, (see also DISNEY and LITTLE GOLDEN BOOKS),

1954 – 1957, illustrated hardcover, red foil spine with Disney cartoon characters, club emblem printed on cover. Numbered as part of Little Golden Disney series. First editions: $12.00
Later printings: $6.00
Popular characters, movies or TV shows may command higher prices. For example:
Davy Crockett's Keelboat Race, by Irwin Shapiro, illustrated by Mel Crawford, $18.00
Jiminy Cricket Fire Fighter, by Annie Bedford, illustrated by Samuel Armstrong, $20.00

MIKE MARS SERIES, Donald Wolheim, Doubleday, hardcover, illustrations by Albert Orbaan. Astronaut adventures. Later paperbacks published by Paperback Library update Cape Canaveral to Cape Kennedy. Hardcovers: ($25.00 with dust jacket) $15.00
Mike Mars, Astronaut, 1961
Mike Mars Flies the X-15, 1961
Mike Mars at Cape Canaveral, 1961
Mike Mars in Orbit, 1961
Mike Mars Flies the Dyna-soar, 1962
Mike Mars, South Pole Spaceman, 1962
Mike Mars and the Mystery Satellite, 1963
Mike Mars Around the Moon, 1964

MILL CREEK IRREGULARS SERIES, August Derleth, 1958 – 1970 Duell Sloan and Pearce, hardcover, 10 titles. Some titles also published by Meredith Press or Candlelight Press. ($35.00 with dust jackets) $12.00
Moon Tenders, 1958
Mill Creek Irregulars, Special Detectives, 1959
Pinkertons Ride Again, 1960
Ghost of Black Hawk Island, 1961
Tent Show Summer, 1963
Irregulars Strike Again, 1964

House by the River, 1965
Watcher on the Heights, 1966
Prince Goes West, 1968
Three Straw Men, 1968

MISHMASH SERIES, Molly Cone, 1962 – 1980s Houghton, hardcover, b/w illustrations by Leonard Shortall, dust jackets have wrap-around illustrations.
($25.00 with dust jacket) $10.00
Mishmash
Mishmash and the Substitute Teacher
Mishmash and the Sauerkraut Mystery
Mishmash and the Venus Flytrap
Mishmash and Uncle Looey
Mishmash and the Robot
Mishmash and the Big Fat Problem

MISS BIANCA SERIES, see RESCUERS SERIES

MISS PICKERELL SERIES, Ellen MacGregor, Whittlesey House and McGraw-Hill, hardcover with b/w illustrations. ($35.00 with dust jacket) $15.00
1960s Scholastic paperbacks: $5.00
Miss Pickerell Goes to Mars, 1951
Miss Pickerell and the Geiger Counter, 1953, illustrated by Paul Galdone
Miss Pickerell Goes Undersea
Miss Pickerell Goes to the Arctic
Miss Pickerell on the Moon, 1965, illustrated by Charles Geer
Miss Pickerell Goes on a Dig, 1966, illustrated by Charles Geer
Miss Pickerell Harvests the Sea, 1968, illustrated by Charles Geer
Miss Pickerell and the Weather Satellite, 1971, illustrated by Charles Geer

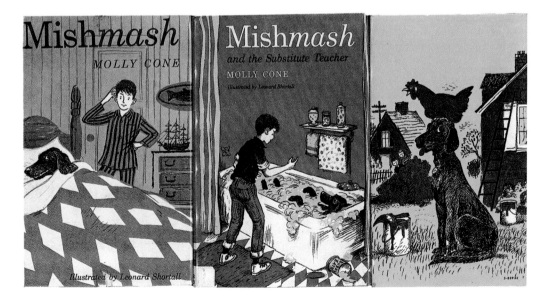

Miss Pickerell Meets Mr. H.U.M., 1974, illustrated by Charles Geer

Miss Pickerell Takes the Bull by the Horns, 1976, illustrated by Charles Geer

Miss Pickerell to the Earthquake Rescue, 1977, illustrated by Charles Geer

MOOMIN SERIES, Tove Jansson, Finland, English translations, 1960s Walck, hardcover, b/w illustrations by author. Early editions: ($50.00 with dust jacket) $20.00

Early editions by Benn, London: ($60.00 with dust jacket) $20.00

Late 1960s editions: ($20.00 with dust jacket) $10.00

Finn Family Moomintroll
Moominsummer Madness
Moominland in Midwinter
Tales from Moominvalley
Exploits of Moominpappa
Moominpappa at Sea
Comet in Moominland
Moominvalley in November

Related book:

Book about Moomin, Mymble and Little My, 1953 Benn, London, ovesize hardcover, first English edition, cut-outs and color illustrations throughout, text in script. $300.00

MRS. PEPPERPOT SERIES, Alf Proysen, translated from Norwegian by Marianne Helwig, hardcover, b/w illustrations by Bjorn Berg, Sweden. ($35.00 with dust jacket) $15.00

Little Old Mrs. Pepperpot, 1960 Astor
Mrs. Pepperpot Again, 1961 Astor
Mrs. Pepperpot to the Rescue, 1964 Pantheon
Mrs. Pepperpot in the Magic Wood, 1968 Pantheon
Mrs. Pepperpot's Outing, 1971 Pantheon

MRS. PIGGLE-WIGGLE BOOKS, continuation of series, Betty MacDonald, Lippincott, small, hardcover, about 220 pages, b/w illustrations.

Mrs. Piggle-Wiggle, (1947)1957 edition b/w illustrations by Hilary Knight. ($40.00 with dust jacket) $15.00

Mrs. Piggle-Wiggle's Farm, 1954, b/w illustrations by Maurice Sendak. First edition in dust jacket: $300.00 Later printings: ($40.00 with dust jacket) $15.00

Hello, Mrs. Piggle-Wiggle, 1957 edition b/w illustrations by Hilary Knight. ($40.00 with dust jacket) $15.00

MUSHROOM PLANET SERIES, Eleanor Cameron, ca. 1960 Little Brown, hardcover, b/w illustrations by Leonard Shortall, Robert Henneberger, or Fred Miese. First edition with dust jacket: $60.00 Later printings: ($30.00 with dust jacket) $15.00

Wonderful Flight to the Mushroom Planet
Stowaway to the Mushroom Planet
Mr. Bass's Planetoid
Mystery for Mr. Bass
Time and Mr. Bass

MYSTERY SERIES, Christine Govan and Emmy West, 1957 Sterling Publishing, hardcover, book jacket illustration by Frederick Chapman. ($20.00 with dust jacket) $10.00

Mystery at Moccasin Bend
Mystery at the Shuttered Hotel
Mystery at the Mountain Face
Mystery at Shingle Rock
Mystery at the Indian Hide-Out

MYTHS AND LEGENDS SET, 1955 Oxford University Press, 8-volume set, first edition, hardcover.

Individual books: ($20.00 with dust jacket) $10.00. Complete set of 8 volumes: $200.00 with dust jackets, $80.00 without dust jackets.

——— ➣ **N** ➣ ———

Nancy Drew Double Editions

NANCY DREW, Carolyn Keene (pseudonym for various Stratemeyer Syndicate authors), 1930 – 1979 Grosset & Dunlap, 56 titles, illustrators: Russell Tandy, Bill Gillies, Rudy Nappi, and others. Books issued from 1950 – 1953 had only a frontispiece illustration, books printed after 1954 had 6 black-and-white illustrations. In 1962, Grosset dropped the hardcover format with dust jacket and began issuing all titles in the yellow spine picture-cover hardcovers. In 1979, Simon & Schuster began publishing new Drew titles under their Minstrel or Wanderer imprints. As with Hardy Boys, collectors identify "firsts" as books that do not list beyond that title in the advertisements for series.
Nancy Drew, **new titles** published by Grosset & Dunlap after 1950, unrevised versions (see also revised, yellow picture cover).
Pre-1962 hardcover: ($35.00 with dust jacket) $20.00
Yellow spine pictorial hardcovers: $6.00 (probable first editions: $15.00)
Secret of the Wooden Lady, 1950
Clue of the Black Keys, 1951
(In 1952 Grosset switched to blue "tweed" covers for series)
Mystery at the Ski Jump, 1952
Clue of the Velvet Mask, 1953
Ringmaster's Secret, 1953

(1954 Grosset changed illustration format to 6 pictures)
Scarlet Slipper Mystery, 1954
Witch Tree Symbol, 1955
Hidden Mystery, 1956
Haunted Showboat, 1957
Secret of the Golden Pavilion, 1959
Clue in the Old Stagecoach, 1960
Mystery of the Fire Dragon, 1961
Clue of the Dancing Puppet, 1962 (first original yellow picture cover)
Moonstone Castle Mystery, 1963
Clue of the Whistling Bagpipes, 1964
Phantom of Pine Hill, 1965
Mystery of the 99 Steps, 1966
Clue in the Crossword Cipher, 1967
Spider Sapphire Mystery, 1968
Invisible Intruder, 1969
Mysterious Mannequin, 1970
Crooked Banister, 1971
Secret of Mirror Bay, 1972
Double Jinx Mystery, 1973
Mystery of the Glowing Eye, 1974
Secret of the Forgotten City, 1975
Sky Phantom, 1976
Strange Message in the Parchment, 1977
Mystery of Crocodile Island, 1978
Thirteenth Pearl, 1979
Nancy Drew, revised titles, 1959 – 1961, tweed hardcover, text shortened to 20 chapters. ($20.00 with dust jacket) $10.00
Secret of the Old Clock, 1959 (1930)
Hidden Staircase, 1959 (1930)
Bungalow Mystery, 1960 (1930)
Mystery at Lilac Inn, 1961 (1930)
Secret of Red Gate Farm, 1961 (1931)
Nancy Drew, unrevised titles, 1962 – 1977, yellow pictorial hardcovers. Text length generally 24 to 25 chapters, copyright date shown is original publication date (i.e., text written before 1960s). $15.00
Nancy Drew, revised titles, 1962 – 1977, yellow pictorial hardcovers. (See also Nancy Drew, new titles, in this section). Cover art usually by Rudy Nappi. Text shortened to 20 chapters. List below shows original publication date in parentheses. $6.00
Secret of the Old Clock, 1959 (1930)
Hidden Staircase, 1959 (1930)
Bungalow Mystery, 1960 (1930)
Mystery at Lilac Inn, 1961 (1930)
Secret of Red Gate Farm, 1961 (1931)
Clue in the Diary, 1962 (1932)
Secret of Shadow Ranch, 1965 (1930)
Clue of the Broken Locket, 1965 (1934)
Password to Larkspur Lane, 1966 (1932)
Ghost of Blackwood Hall, 1967 (1948)
Clue of the Leaning Chimney, 1967 (1949)
Secret of the Wooden Lady, 1967 (1950)

Nancy's Mysterious Letter, 1968 (1932)
Sign of the Twisted Candles, 1968 (1932)
Clue of the Black Keys, 1968 (1951)
Mystery at the Ski Jump, 1968 (1952)
Clue of the Tapping Heels, 1969 (1939)
Quest of the Missing Map, 1969 (1942)
Clue of the Velvet Mask, 1969 (1953)
Whispering Statue, 1970 (1937)
Secret in the Old Attic, 1970 (1944)
Mystery of the Moss-Covered Mansion, 1971 (1941)
Message in the Hollow Oak, 1972 (1935)
Haunted Bridge, 1972 (1937)
Clue in the Jewel Box, 1972 (1943)
Clue in the Crumbling Wall, 1973 (1945)
Mystery of the Tolling Bell, 1973 (1946)
Mystery of the Ivory Charm, 1974 (1936)
Ringmaster's Secret, 1974 (1953)
Scarlet Slipper Mystery, 1974 (1954)
Witch Tree Symbol, 1975 (1955)
Hidden Window Mystery, 1975 (1956)
Mystery of the Brass-Bound Trunk, 1976 (1940)
Clue in the Old Album, 1977 (1947)

Nancy Drew, related titles:

Nancy Drew, British editions, ca. 1960s Sampson Loew, hardcovers. ($25.00 with dust jackets) $10.00

Nancy Drew Cookbook: Clues to Good Cooking, 1973 Grosset & Dunlap, yellow illustrated hardcover. First printing (1973 on copyright page, no other dates) $20.00, other printings $15.00.

Nancy Drew Cameo Editions, 1959 – 60 Grosset & Dunlap, book club hardcovers with "cameo locket" picture of Nancy on endpapers, color dust jackets by Polly Bolian, 9 illustrations per volume. ($30.00 with dust jacket) $10.00

Nancy Drew Double Editions, ca. 1970s Grosset & Dunlap, lavender spine hardcover, each volume contains two revised (post-1959) versions of Nancy Drew novels. $10.00.

Nancy Drew Triple Editions, ca. late 1960s or early 1970s Grosset & Dunlap, hardcover, each volume contains three revised (post-1959) versions of Nancy Drew novels. $10.00.

Picture Book Nancy Drew, 1977 Grosset & Dunlap, 2 titles, oversized hardcovers, 62 pages, illustrated. $15.00

Mystery of the Lost Dogs
Secret of the Twin Puppets

NANCY KIMBALL, Carli Laklan, Doubleday, hardcover. ($15.00 with dust jacket) $10.00

At City Hospital
Nurse's Aide, 1962
Second Year Nurse, 1967

NARNIA SERIES, see CHRONICLES OF NARNIA SERIES

NATURE MYSTERIES, Mary Adrian, 1956 – 1971 Hastings House, 10 titles, various illustrators. ($20.00 with dust jacket) $10.00

Uranium Mystery, 1956
Fox Hollow Mystery, 1959
Rare Stamp Mystery, 1960
Mystery of the Night Explorers, 1962
Skin Diving Mystery, 1964
Mystery of the Dinosaur Bones, 1965
Indian Horse Mystery, 1966
Kite Mystery, 1968
Lightship Mystery, 1969
Ghost Town Mystery, 1971

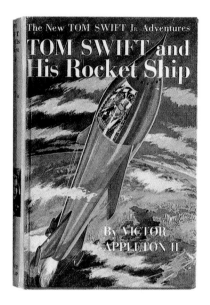

NEW TOM SWIFT JR. ADVENTURES SERIES, (based on the TOM SWIFT series), Victor Appleton II (Stratemeyer pseudonym), Grosset and Dunlap, b/w illustrations by Graham Kaye.

Tweed hardcover: ($20.00 with dust jacket) $10.00
Yellow spine, color illustrated hardcover: $15.00

Tom Swift and his Flying Lab, 1954
Tom Swift and his Jetmarine, 1954
Tom Swift and his Rocket Ship, 1954
Tom Swift and his Giant Robot, 1954
Tom Swift and his Atomic Earth Blaster, 1954
Tom Swift and his Outpost in Space, 1955
Tom Swift and his Diving Seacopter
Tom Swift in the Caves of Nuclear Fire
Tom Swift on the Phantom Satellite, 1956
Tom Swift and his Ultrasonic Cycloplane, 1956
Tom Swift and his Deep-Sea Hydrodome, 1958
Tom Swift in the Race to the Moon
Tom Swift and his Solartron
Tom Swift and his Electronic Retroscope
Tom Swift and his Spectromarine Selector, 1960
Tom Swift and the Cosmic Astronauts, 1960
Tom Swift and the Visitor from Planet X, 1961

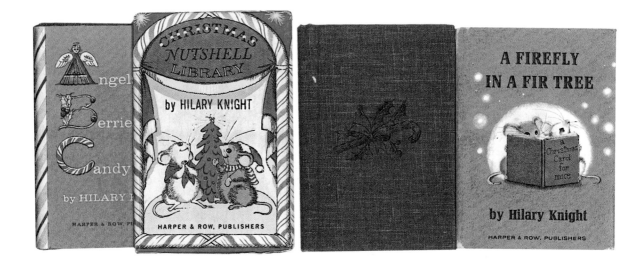

Tom Swift and the Electronic Hydrolung, 1961
Tom Swift and his Triphibian Atomicar, 1962
Tom Swift and his Polar-Ray Dynasphere, 1965
Tom Swift and his Subocean Geotron, 1966

NODDY SERIES, Enid Blyton, Sampson Low Marston, London, hardcover, color illustrated by Beek. Early editions: ($60.00 with dust jacket) $30.00
Later reprints, $15.00
Noddy Goes to Toyland
Noddy at the Seaside, 1953
Noddy and the Magic Rubber, 1954
You Funny Little Noddy, 1955
Be Brave, Little Noddy, 1956
You're a Good Friend, Noddy, 1958
Noddy and the Bunkey, 1959
Noddy Goes to the Fair, 1960
Cheer Up, Little Noddy, 1960
Plod and Little Noddy, 1961
Noddy and the Tessie Bear, 1961
Noddy and the Tootles, 1962

NOEL AND HENRY SERIES, Josephine Pullein-Thompson, 1946 – 1957 Collins, hardcover, 5 titles, English "pony" series. ($15.00 with dust jacket) $10.00
Six Ponies, 1946
Pony Club Team, 1950
Radney Riding Club, 1951
One Day Event, 1954
Pony Club Camp, 1957

NURSES THREE SERIES, Jean Kirby, Whitman, color illustrated hardcover. $10.00
Nurses Three, First Assignment, 1963
Nurses Three, A Career for Kelly, 1963
Nurses Three, Tracy's Little People, 1965

NUTSHELL LIBRARY, Harper Row, four cloth hardcover books, each with illustrated paper dust jacket, 2½ inches wide by 4 inches high, with color illustrations throughout, packaged in a paper covered bookholder box, so that the books slide in with spines out.
Bunny's Nutshell Library, Robert Kraus, 1965, includes, Silver Dandelion, First Robin, Juniper, and Springfellow's Parade. Complete first edition set with dust jackets and box: $150.00
Christmas Nutshell Library, Hilary Knight, 1963, includes Angels and Berries and Candy Canes, Firefly in a Fir Tree, Christmas Stocking Story, and Night Before Christmas, all illustrated by Knight. Complete first edition set: $150.00. Later sets: $50.00
Complete Nutshell Library, Maurice Sendak, 1962, includes Alligators All Around, Chicken Soup, One Was Johnny, and Pierre. Individual books with dust jackets, $25.00. Complete first edition set: $300.00. Later complete sets: $45.00
See FROG series, Four Frogs in a Box, for similar set by Dial.

O

OZ BOOKS, continuing books and new editions based on the series originated by L. Frank Baum.
Oz, new titles from Reilly & Lee:
Hidden Valley of Oz, Rachel Cosgrove, 1951 Reilly & Lee, first edition, blue hardcover with paste-on-pictorial, 313 pages, illustrated endpapers, b/w illustrations by Dirk Gringhuis. ($325.00 with dust jacket) $150.00
Hidden Valley of Oz, later printings, hardcover without paste-on-pictorial. $50.00

Merry Go Round in Oz, Eloise Jarvis McGraw and Lauren McGraw Wagner, 1963 Reilly & Lee, first edition, white hardcover with printed illustration, b/w illustrations by Dick Martin. $150.00 with dust jacket

Visitors from Oz, Jean Kellogg, re-telling of a selection of Baum short stories, 1960 Reilly & Lee, green background color illustration printed on white oversize hardcover, 60 pages, b/w and color illustrations by Dick Martin. ($250.00 with dust jacket) $100.00

Who's Who in Oz, Jack Snow, 1954 Reilly & Lee, tan hardcover with gilt lettering, 277 pages, Oz map endpaper, illustrated with artwork from the earlier books, a bibliography of Oz characters. ($150.00 with dust jacket) $50.00

Oz, Roycraft cover editions, ca. 1959 Reilly & Lee, hardcover, issued with new dust jackets signed "Roycraft." ($75.00 with dust jacket) $35.00

Wizard of Oz
Land of Oz
Ozma of Oz
Dorothy and the Wizard in Oz
Road to Oz
Scarecrow of Oz
Lost Princess of Oz
Tin Woodman of Oz
Hungry Tiger of Oz
Pirates in Oz
Speedy in Oz

Oz, Dick Martin cover editions, ca. 1960 Reilly & Lee, hardcover, issued with new dust jackets by Dick Martin, same book format at the "Roycraft" editions. ($75.00 with dust jacket) $35.00

Wizard of Oz
Patchwork Girl of Oz
Rinkitink in Oz
Magic of Oz
Glinda of Oz
Kabumpo in Oz
Cowardly Lion of Oz
Purple Prince of Oz
Captain Salt in Oz
Shaggy Man of Oz

Oz, Kellogg and Martin editions, 1961 Reilly & Lee, oversize, color illustrated laminated hardcover, 60 pages, rewritten by Jean Kellogg, color and b/w illustrations by Dick Martin. ($75.00 with dust jacket) $35.00

Wizard of Oz
Land of Oz
Ozma of Oz
Dorothy and the Wizard of Oz

Oz "White Cover" editions, Reilly & Lee, white cloth-over-board hardcovers with printed illustration on front, back and spine, a re-issue of the original Baum texts, original illustrations by Denslow and Neill adapted by Dick Martin. The cover designs were also adapted by Martin from Denslow and Neill illustrations. No dust jackets. $35.00

Wizard of Oz, 1964 edition, full-color wrap-around design printed on hardcover. (Although this is the first of the "white cover" editions, its cover is blue/green.)

Emerald City of Oz
Patchwork Girl of Oz
Tik-Tok of Oz
Scarecrow of Oz
Lost Princess of Oz

Oz, 1965 white cover editons: $30.00

Wizard of Oz, 1965 edition, design printed on white background on hardcover, to match the rest of the white covers.

Land of Oz
Ozma of Oz
Dorothy and the Wizard in Oz
Road to Oz
Rinkitink in Oz
Tin Woodman of Oz
Magic of Oz
Glinda of Oz

Oz, Little Golden Books, Baum, small, color illustrated hardcovers, gold spines, 28 pages, color illustrations throughout by Harry McNaught, generally use one or two rewritten adventures from the Oz original titles. $10.00

Road to Oz, 1951
Emerald City of Oz, 1952
Tin Woodman of Oz, 1952

Oz, Rand McNally papercover editions, 1971 – 1973, oversize, cover illustrations by Dick Martin, 12 of the Baum titles. $20.00

Oz, Wonder Books, Grosset & Dunlap, small hardcover books published as part of the WONDER BOOKS series. $12.00

Wizard of Oz, 1951, illustrated by Tom Sinnickson
Cowardly Lion, 1956, illustrated by Ruth Wood

Oz, Other publishers:

Marvelous Land of Oz, 1961 edition Dover, blue spine and white illustrated board, 287 pages, b/w illustrations. $20.00

New Wizard of Oz, 1955 edition Doubleday, Junior Deluxe hardcover, illustrated by Leonard Weisgard. $15.00

Wizard of Oz, 1956 edition Grosset & Dunlap, pictorial hardcover, 206 pages, b/w illustrations and color plates. $15.00

Wizard of Oz, adapted by Mary Cushing & Dorothea Williams, 1962 edition Grosset & Dunlap, oversize hardcover, illustrated by Claudine Nankivel. $45.00

Wonderful Wizard of Oz, 1961 edition Crown,

hardcover, 268 pages, full-color and two-color illustrations from the original Denslow illustrations. $20.00

The Oz titles continue to be reprinted, both in hardcover and paperback, and to be adapted into other formats, including pop-up books, color books, sticker books, and so forth, by a variety of publishers.

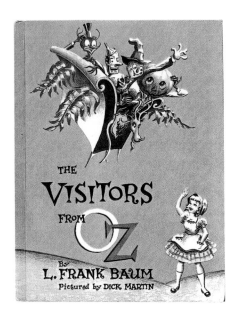

—— ≈ **P** ≈ ——

PADDINGTON SERIES, Michael Bond, Collins, London, pictorial boards, and Houghton Mifflin, Boston, cloth-over-board hardcover, b/w illustrations by Peggy Fortnum. A few Paddington books had other illustrators, as noted.
   1960s first edition with dust jacket: $65.00
   1970s first edition with dust jacket: $45.00
   Later printings: ($20.00 with dust jacket) $10.00
Bear Called Paddington, 1960
More About Paddington, (1959) ca. 1960 Houghton, first American edition
Paddington Helps Out, 1960 Collins
Paddington at Large, Collins
Paddington Marches On, 1964 Collins
Paddington at Work, 1966 Collins
Paddington Goes to Town, 1968 edition Houghton
Paddington Takes the Air, 1971 Houghton
Paddington Abroad, 1972 Houghton
Paddington Takes to TV, 1974, first American edition, illustrated by Ivor Wood.
Paddington Picture Books, 1970s, Random House, Ilustrations by Fred Banbery
Paddington Goes Shopping, 1973 Collins
Paddington's Garden, 1973
Five Paddingtons at the Circus, 1973 Collins
Paddington's Lucky Day, 1974
Paddington on Stage, 1974 Collins
Paddington on Top, 1974 Collins
 Paddington on Top, 1975 Houghton
Paddington at the Sea-Side, 1975 Collins

PAM AND PENNY SERIES, Rosamund du Jardin (1902 – 1963), 1950s Lippincott, hardcover. See also MARCY RHODES and TOBY HEYDON. ($25.00 with dust jacket) $10.00
Double Date, 1952
Double Feature, 1953
Showboat Summer, 1955
Double Wedding, 1958

PATIENCE SERIES, Lorna Hill, 1951 – 1955 Burke, hardcover. See also DANCING PEELS, MAJORIE, SADLER WELLS, and VICARAGE CHILDREN. ($15.00 with dust jacket) $10.00
They Called Her Patience, 1951
It Was All Through Patience, 1952
So Guy Came Too, 1954
Five Shilling Holiday, 1955

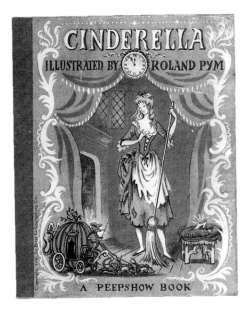

Peepshow Books

PEEPSHOW BOOKS, ca.1950 Houghton Mifflin,

224

small, carousel books produced by Folding Books Ltd., color illustrated paper-over-board cover, book opens to form a circle with six double-page cut-out 3-layered scenes, with 6 or 7 lines of print on bottom of pages. Ribbon ties to hold book closed. Price drops dramatically for any missing pieces. $150.00 each
Cinderella, illustrated by Roland Pym
Ali Baba and the Forty Thieves, illustrated by Ionicus
Puss-in Boots, illustrated by Kathleen Hale
Sleeping Beauty, illustrated by Roland Pym

PEGGY LANE THEATER SERIES, Virginia Hughes, ca. 1960s Grosset and Dunlap, color illustrated hardcover, b/w illustrations by Sergio Leone. $10.00
Peggy Finds the Theater
Peggy Plays Off-Broadway
Peggy Goes Straw Hat
Peggy on the Road
Peggy Goes Hollywood
Peggy's London Debut
Peggy Plays Paris
Peggy's Roman Holiday

PETUNIA SERIES, Roger Duvoisin, Knopf, oversize picture books, pictorial hardcovers, illustrated endpapers, color illustrations throughout.
First edition in dust jacket: $75.00
Later printings: ($35.00 in dust jacket) $20.00
Weekly Reader Book Club edition, illustrated hardcover: $20.00
Petunia, 1950
Petunia and the Song, 1951
Petunia's Christmas, 1952
Petunia Takes a Trip, 1953

Petunia, Beware!, 1958
Petunia, I Love You, 1965 Bodley Head, UK edition, with dust jacket: $40.00
Petunia, I Love You, undated flip book by Dandelion. $15.00
Petunia's Treasure, 1975

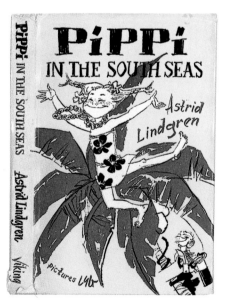

PIPPI LONGSTOCKING SERIES, Astrid Lindgren, translated by Florence Lamborn, U. S. editions ca. 1960s Viking, hardcover, b/w illustrations by Louis Glanzman. First edition with dust jacket: $40.00
Later editons: ($25.00 with dust jacket) $15.00
Glossy pictorial hardcover editions: $15.00
American titles:
Pippi Longstocking, 1950
Pippi Goes on Board, 1957

Pippi in the South Seas, 1959
Pippi on the Run, 1976

PLEASANT FIELDMOUSE SERIES, Jan Wahl, various publishers and illustrators.
Pleasant Fieldmouse, 1964 Harper, illustrations by Maurice Sendak. First edition with dust jacket, $150.00. Later editions: ($25.00 with dust jacket) $15.00
Six Voyages of Pleasant Fieldmouse, 1971 Delacorte, small hardcover, b/w drawings by Peter Parnall. ($25.00 with dust jacket) $15.00
Pleasant Fieldmouse Storybook, 1975 Prentice-Hall, small hardcover, illustrated by Erik Blegvard. ($25.00 with dust jacket) $15.00

POLLY FRENCH SERIES, Francine Lewis (Helen Wells), ca. 1954 Whitman, color illustrated pictorial boards, small, illustrated endpapers, illustrations throughout by Nina Albright. $15.00
Polly French at Whitford High
Polly French Takes Charge
Polly and the Surprising Stranger

POP-UP BOOK SERIES, see RANDOM HOUSE POP-UP

POWER BOYS SERIES, Mel Lyle, Whitman, glossy pictorial hardcover, illustrated by Raymond Burns. $10.00
Mystery of the Flying Skeleton, 1964
Mystery of the Haunted Skyscraper, 1964
Mystery of the Double Kidnapping, 1965

Mystery of the Million Dollar Penny, 1965
Mystery of the Burning Ocean, 1965
Mystery of the Vanishing Lady, 1967

PRINCE VALIANT BOOKS, Hal Foster, 1951 – 1957 Hastings House, hardcover with dust jacket and pictorial endpapers, different for each book. Stories adapted from the original Foster newspaper comic strip by Max Trell, black and white illustrations adapted from Fosters' artwork. Reprinted by Nostalgia Press, starting in 1974.
Hastings hardcovers, first editions: ($50.00 with dust jacket) $20.00
Nostalgia hardcovers: ($25.00 with dust jacket) $10.00
Prince Valiant in the Days of King Arthur, 1951
Prince Valiant Fights Attila the Hun, 1952
Prince Valiant on the Inland Sea, 1953
Prince Valiant's Perilous Voyage, 1954
Prince Valiant and the Golden Princess, 1955
Prince Valiant in the New World, 1956
Prince Valiant and the Three Challenges, 1957

PRYDAIN CHRONICLES SERIES, Lloyd Alexander, Holt Rinehart Winston, hardcover, jacket illustrations and maps by Evaline Ness. First edition with dust jacket: $125.00. Later editions: ($25.00 with dust jacket) $10.00
Book of Three, 1964
Black Cauldron, 1965
Castle of Llyr, 1966
Taran Wanderer, 1967
High King (1969 Newbery winner)

Prydain Chronicles, 1969 edition

Prydain Picture Books:

Coll and His White Pig, Lloyd Alexander, 1965 Holt, hardcover, illustrated by Evaline Ness, short story related to character in Pyrdain Chronicles, color illustrations throughout. ($35.00 with dust jacket) $20.00

Truthful Harp, Lloyd Alexander, 1967 Holt, hardcover, illustrated by Evaline Ness, short story related to character in Pyrdain Chronicles, color illustrations throughout. ($45.00 with dust jacket) $20.00

Foundling, Lloyd Alexander, 1973 Holt, 73 pages, b/w illustrations by Margot Zemach. ($35.00 with dust jacket) $20.00

RAILWAY SERIES, see THOMAS THE TANK ENGINE SERIES

─── ⇒ **R** ⇐ ───

RAMONA SERIES, also see HENRY HUGGINS SERIES, Beverly Cleary, Morrow, hardcover. First editions with dust jackets: $60.00. Later editions: ($20.00 with dust jacket) $15.00

Beezus and Ramona, 1955, b/w illustrations by Louis Darling

Ramona the Pest, 1968, b/w illustrations by Louis Darling

Ramona the Brave, 1975, b/w illustrations by Louis Darling

Ramona and her Father, 1975, b/w illustrations by Alan Tiegreen

Ramona and her Mother, 1979, b/w illustrations by Alan Tiegreen

RAND McNALLY ELF BOOKS, 1947 – 1970s Rand McNally, 450+ titles. Like the rival Little Golden Book lines, Elf Books are small, color picture books, some based on original stories, many based on classic fairy tales. Collectors pay higher prices for books with media tie-ins, cartoon characters, or popular themes. The name "Elf Books" was sold to Checkerboard Press in the 1980s. First editions prior to 1963 are identified by a letter/number code on back page: CS(Month)-(Year). For example, CS6-50 indicates printing date of June 1950. See also JUST-SO STORIES. Individual books: 1940s first editions, $15.00, 1950s first editions, $12.00, 1960 – 1962 first editions, $12.00. All later and other editions are usually less than $10.00

Four Little Puppies
Little Miss Muffet
Peppy
Fraidy Cat
Little Boy Blue
Farm for Andy
Busy Bulldozer
Little Skater
Tortoise and the Hare
Silly Joe
Mother Goose
Teddy the Terrible
Goody, a Mother Cat Story
Timothy Tiger
Forest Babies
Farm Animals
Snuggles

Rand McNally Start-Right Elf Books

Mr. Bear's House
Johnny and the Birds
Little Bobo and His Blue Jacket

RAND McNALLY JUNIOR ELF BOOKS, ca. 1960s, about 5 x 6½ inches, color illustrated hardcovers, b/w and color illustrations, many titles including the following, some are simple or shortened versions of classic stories, some are original stories. Most sell for $5.00 or less.
Five Beds for Bitsy
Cowboy Dan
Surprise in the Barnyard
Timothy the Little Brown Bear
Tim and his Train
Puppy that Found a Home
My Toys
Little Red Wagon
Myrtle Turtle
Child's Garden of Verses

RAND McNALLY START-RIGHT ELF BOOKS, ca. 1960s, about 6½ x 4¾ inches, color illustrated hardcovers, color illustrations, beginning reader books. $5.00
Animals Talk to Me
Davy Deer's New Red Scarf
Elves and the Shoemaker
Three Billy Goats Gruff
Walk with Grandpa
All Around the City
How Chicks are Born
What's in the Bakery Truck?
Count the Puppies
Beth's Happy Day
Little Red Boot
Time for a Rhyme
Backyard Circus
Treasure Trunk
My Cowboy Book
Raggedy Goat
Farm Animals
Henny Penny
Jack Sprat
Look! A Parade
Mother Goose
Giant's Shoe
Moth is Born
Tommy's Tooth

RAND McNALLY TIP-TOP ELF BOOKS, ca. 1950s – 1960s, about 6½ x 8¼ inches, color illustrated hardcovers, color illustrations, many titles including the following, some are simple or shortened versions of classic stories, some are original stories. Most sell for $5.00 or less, but

original stories on popular themes are priced higher. For example, *Little Majorette* is usually listed at $15.00.
Zippy
Forst Babies
Rumpelstiltskin
Muggins Mouse
Five Busy Bears
Present for the Princess
Jeepers, the Little Frog
Johnny and the Birds
Little Mailman of Bayberry Lane
Seven Wonderful Cats
Little Majorette

Rand McNally Tip-Top Elf Books

RANDOM HOUSE POP-UP BOOKS, undated ca. 1960s Random House, about 9½ x 6½ shiny hardcover, color illustrations, pop-ups and animations throughout, many were written by Albert Miller, designed by Paul Taylor, and illustrators include Tor Lokvig, Marvin Brehm, Dave Chambers, Gwen Gordon. All pop-ups in good working condition: $40.00
Adventures of Dr. Doolittle
Animal Alphabet Book
Bennett Cerf's Pop-Up Limericks
Bennett Cerf's Silliest Riddles
Book of Left and Right
Color Book
Hide and Seek
Mother Goose
Night Before Christmas
Riddles
Sound-Alikes

Tournament Magic
Wishing Ring

Random House Pop-Up Book

REAL BOOK SERIES, 1950s – 1960s Garden City, hardcover, illustrated. ($15.00 with dust jacket) $10.00
Numberous titles, including:
Real Book about Pets, Bates
Real Book about Treasure Hunting, Burton
Real Book about Amazing Animals, Dickinson
Real Book of Great American Journeys
Real Book about Trains, Cole
Real Book about Farms, Howard
Real Book about Horses, Sherman
Real Book about Airplanes, Whitehorse
Real Book about the Texas Rangers, Allen
Real Book About Spies, Epstein
Real Book about Stars, Goodwin
Real Book about Space Travel, Goodwin
Real Book about Sports, Bonner
Real Book about Baseball, Hopkins
Real Book about Pirates, Epstein
Real Book About Buffalo Bill, Regli

REGIONAL STORIES SERIES, see AMERICAN REGIONAL STORIES SERIES

RESCUERS SERIES, Margery Sharp, 1959 through 1978, Little Brown, American editions; Collins, London, and Heinemann, UK editions. Two Disney animated films were based on the adventures of Miss Bianca and her loyal beau, Bernard. Unless identified as UK editions, the following prices are for American editions. Later editions: ($20.00 with dust jacket) $10.00

Rescuers, 1959 Collins, London, first edition, illustrated by Judith Brook. ($50.00 with dust jacket) $20.00
Rescuers, 1959, Little Brown, first edition, illustrated by Garth Williams. ($100.00 with dust jacket) $35.00
Miss Bianca, 1962 Little Brown, first edition, illustrated by Garth Williams. ($65.00 with dust jacket) $25.00
Miss Bianca, 1962 Collins, London, first edition, illustrated by Garth Williams. ($55.00 with dust jacket) $25.00
Turret, 1963, Collins, London, first edition, illustrated by Garth Williams. ($50.00 with dust jacket) $20.00
Turret, 1963, Little Brown, first edition, illustrated by Garth Williams. ($60.00 with dust jacket) $20.00
Miss Bianca in the Salt Mines, 1966 Little Brown, first edition, illustrated by Garth Williams. ($50.00 with dust jacket) $20.00
Miss Bianca in the Orient, 1970 Heinemann, UK, first edition, illustrations by Eric Blegvad. ($40.00 with dust jacket) $20.00
Miss Bianca in the Antarctic, 1971 Little Brown, first edition, illustrated by Eric Blegvad. ($30.00 with dust jacket) $20.00
Miss Bianca and the Bridesmaid, 1972 Little Brown, first edition, illustrated by Eric Blegvad. ($30.00 with dust jacket) $20.00
Bernard the Brave, 1977, Little Brown, first edition, illustrated by Leslie Morrill. ($45.00 with dust jacket) $15.00
Bernard into Battle, 1978 Little Brown, first edition, illustrated by Leslie Morrill. ($25.00 with dust jacket) $15.00

RICK BRANT SCIENCE-ADVENTURE STORIES (or RICK BRANT ELECTRONIC ADVENTURE SERIES), John L. Blaine (pseudonym for Harold

Goodwin or Peter Harkins), 1947 – 1968 Grosset & Dunlap, 23 titles. "Rick Brant Electronic Adventure Series" and "Rick Brant Science-Adventure Stories" both used by Grosset & Dunlap as series title. "Electronic Adventure" name was the earlier, but many books use both series titles in different places in the jacket or hardcover text. "Electronic Adventure" was dropped soon after the picture cover format was introduced. First editions were not identified by publisher, who kept the same copyright date for all. Most collectors label books as probable first editions if the title listings do not exceed books published that year (often referred to by collectors as "list to self").

Rick Brant, 1947 – 1960 tweed hardcovers, illustrated endpapers, b/w frontispiece. $10.00
With dust jacket that "lists to self," $30.00
With later dust jacket, $15.00
Pictorial hardcover, $8.00
Rocket's Shadow, 1947 (probable first jacket lists to *Lost City*)
Lost City, 1947
Sea Gold, 1947
100 Fathoms Under, 1947
Whispering Box Mystery, 1948
Phantom Shark, 1949
Smuggler's Reef, 1950
Caves of Fear, 1951
Stairway to Danger, 1952
Golden Skull, 1954
Wailing Octopus, 1956
Electronic Mind Reader, 1957
Scarlet Lake Mystery, 1958
Pirates of Shan, 1958
Rick Brant, 1960 – 1962, hardcover, series titles "list to self" probable firsts: $50.00. Later printings $20.00
Blue Ghost Mystery, 1960
Egyptian Cat Mystery, 1961
Flaming Mountain, 1962
Rick Brant, 1963 – 1968, pictorial hardcover, no dust jackets issued, firsts "list to self" (for some titles, only one or two printings were done). Probable firsts: $55.00. Later printings $35.00
Flying Stingaree, 1963
Ruby Ray Mystery, 1964
Veiled Raiders, 1965
Rocket Jumper, 1966, hard-to-find, $125.00
Deadly Dutchman, 1967, hard-to-find, $125.00
Danger Below, 1968
Rick Brant, related title:
Rick Brant's Science Projects, 1960 Grosset & Dunlap, non-fiction, hard-to-find. One dealer's 1998 catalog had this listed at $975.00

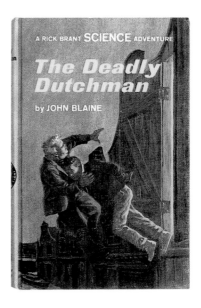

ROBIN KANE SERIES, Eileen Hill, 1960s Whitman, wrap-around pictorial hardcover, b/w illustrations. $10.00
Mystery of the Blue Pelican, 1966
Mystery of the Phantom, 1966
Mystery of Glengary Castle, 1966
Mystery in the Clouds, 1971

ROGER TEARLE SERIES, Scott Corbett, Little Brown, 5 titles, hardcover, illustrations by Paul Frame. ($30.00 with dust jacket) $15.00
Case of the Gone Goose, 1966
Case of the Fugitive Firebug, 1969
Case of the Ticklish Tooth, 1971
Case of the Silver Skull, 1974
Case of the Burgled Blessing Box, 1975

ROMPER ROOM, Little Golden Books, ca. 1950s and 1960s. Published as part of LITTLE GOLDEN BOOKS series, color illustrated hardcover with foil spine, color illustrations throughout. $8.00
Romper Room Do Bees: A Book of Manners, 1956, by Nancy Claster, illustrated by Eleanor Dart
Romper Room Exercise Book, 1964, by Nancy Claster, illustrated by Sergio Leone
Romper Room, Wonder Books, ca. 1950s and 1960s. Published as part of WONDER BOOK series, small illustrated hardcovers. $8.00.
Romper Room Book of Finger Plays and Action Rhymes, 1955, by June Pierce, illustrated by Ruth Wood
What Time Is It? A Romper Room Book, 1954, by John Peter, illustrated by Joseph Zabinski, with "a practice clock on back cover"
Can You Guess? A Romper Room Book, 1953, by Leonore Klein, illustrated by Ruth Wood
Romper Room Do Bee Book of Manners, 1960, by

Nancy Claster, illustrated by Art Seiden
Romper Room Safety Book, 1965, by Nancy Claster, illustrated by Art Seiden

ROY ROGERS BOOKS, various authors, ca. 1950s Little Golden Books, small illustrated hardcover, foil spine, color illustrations. $20.00
Roy Rogers, 1953, by Annie Bedford, illustrated by Mel Crawford
Roy Rogers and Cowboy Toby, 1954, by Elizabeth Beecher, illustrated by Mel Crawford
Dale Evans and the Lost Goldmine, 1954, by Monica Hill, illustrated by Mel Crawford
Roy Rogers and the Mountain Lion, 1955, by Ann McGovern, illustrated by Mel Crawford
Dale Evans and the Coyote, 1956, by Gladys Wyatt, illustrated by Joseph Dreany
Roy Rogers and the Indian Sign, 1956, by Gladys Wyatt, illustrated by Mel Crawford
Roy Rogers, other books:
Roy Rogers and the Ghost of Mystery Rancho, Walker Tompkins, 1950 Whitman, hardcover. $15.00
Roy Rogers and Dale Evans in River of Peril, Cole Fannin, 1957 Whitman, hardcover. ($15.00 with dust jacket) $10.00

— S —

SADLER'S WELLS SERIES, Lorna Hill, 1950 – 1964 Evans (American editions published by Holt), 14 titles. Ballet series based on the school experiences of the author's daughter at Sadler's Wells, later called the Royal Ballet School, in London. See also MAJORIE, DANCING PEELS, PATIENCE, and VICARAGE CHILDREN.
First editions: ($25.00 with dust jacket)
Later editions: ($15.00 with dust jacket) $10.00
Dream of Sadler's Wells, 1950
Veronica at the Wells, 1951
Masquerade at the Wells, 1952
No Castanets at the Wells, 1953
Jane Leaves the Wells, 1953
Ella at the Wells, 1954
Return to the Wells, 1955
Rosanna Joins the Wells, 1956
Principal Role, 1957
Swan Feather, 1958
Dress-Rehearsal, 1959
Back-Stage, 1960
Vicki in Venice, 1962
Secret, 1964

SAILOR JACK SERIES, S. and J. Wasserman, ca. 1960 Benific Press, hardcover. $10.00
Sailor Jack and Bluebell's Dive
Sailor Jack Goes North

Sailor Jack and the Jet Plane
Sailor Jack and the Target Ship
Sailor Jack's New Friend
Sailor Jack and Homer Pots

SANDY STEELE ADVENTURES, Roger Barlow, Simon & Schuster, 6 titles, hardcover. ($20.00 with dust jacket) $10.00
Black Treasure, 1959
Danger at Mormon Crossing, 1959
Stormy Voyage, 1959
Fire at Red Lake, 1959
Secret Mission to Alaska, 1959
Troubled Water, 1959

BABY'S SANTA MOUSE

By Michael Brown

SANTA MOUSE BOOKS, Michael Brown, Grosset picture books.
Santa Mouse, 1966 oversize pictorial hardcover, color illustrations by Elfrieda De Witt. $25.00
Santa Mouse, Where Are You?, 1968, pictorial hardcover, color illustrations by Elfrieda De Witt. $25.00
Santa Mouse Meets Marmaduke, ca. 1969, pictorial hardcover, illustrated by George De Santis. $20.00
Baby's Santa Mouse, 1969, stiff cardboard pages, color photos of puppets by Izawa and Hijikata. $20.00

SASEK SERIES, Miroslav Sasek, 1959 – 1974 Macmillan, oversize hardcover picture books, glossy illustrated cover, color illustrations throughout by author. The dust jackets have the same illustrations as the covers. A few of the titles had smaller printings and are harder to find. Their prices are noted after the titles. The rest: ($40.00 with same-as-cover dust jacket) $25.00
This is Paris

This is London
Questra E Londra (This is London translated into Italian)
This is Rome
This is New York
This is Edinburgh
This is Munich
This is Venice
This is San Francisco
This is Israel
This is Cape Canaveral, published in 1963, hard-to-find first edition, later editions of this title are re-named *This is Cape Kennedy.* ($75.00 with dust jacket) $45.00
This is Cape Kennedy, 1964. ($55.00 with dust jacket) $35.00
This is Ireland
This is Hong Kong
This is Greece
This is Texas
This is the United Nations
This is Australia
This is Historic Britain

Sasek Series

SECRET CIRCLE MYSTERIES, Arthur Hammond, editor, Little, Brown, hardcover, 6 titles, various authors, b/w illustrations. ($15.00 with dust jackets) $10.00
Mystery of Monster Lake, David Gammon, 1962
Riddle of the Haunted River, Lawrence Earl, 1962
Legend of the Devil's Lode, Robert Collins, 1962
Secret Tunnel Treasure, Arthur Hammond, 1962
Mystery of the Muffled Man, Max Braithwaite, 1962
Clue of the Dead Duck, Scott Young, 1962

SECRET SEVEN SERIES, Enid Blyton, ca. 1960s Brockhampton Press, hardcover. ($25.00 with dust jacket) $10.00
Secret Seven and the Mystery of the Empty House
Secret Seven and the Circus Adventure
Secret Seven and theTree House Adventure
Secret Seven and the Railroad Mystery
Secret Seven Get Their Man
Secret Seven and the Case of the Stolen Car
Secret Seven and the Hidden Cave Adventure
Secret Seven and the Grim Secret
Secret Seven and the Missing Girl Mystery
Secret Seven and the Case of the Music Lover
Secret Seven and the Bonfire Adventure
Secret Seven and the Old Fort Adventure
Secret Seven and the Case of the Dog Lover
Secret Seven and the Case of the Old Horse

SIGNATURE SERIES, 1950s Grosset & Dunlap, hardcover. ($15.00 with dust jacket) $10.00
Numerous titles including:
Story of Daniel Boone, Steele
Story of Marco Polo, Price
Story of Geronimo, Kjelgaard
Story of Crazy Horse, Meadowcroft
Story of Kit Carson, Collier NY
Story of Lafayette, Wilson
Story of Edith Cavell, Vinton
Story of Good Queen Bess, Malkus

SIMON BLACK SERIES, Ivan Southall, 1950 – 1961, Angus & Robertson, 8 titles. Australian boys' series, compared by collectors to Tom Swift Jr. or Rick Brant. At least first three books originally issued on a lower grade post-WWII paper, and then reissued with better paper and dust jackets in the late 1950s and early 1960s. Abridged editions issued in laminated hardcover. Various illustrators including I. Maher, Wal Stackpool, or Frank Norton.
Hardcover with dust jacket, $15.00
Laminated hardcover: $10.00
Meet Simon Black, 1950
Simon Black in Peril, 1951
Simon Black in Coastal Command, 1953
Simon Black in China, 1954
Simon Black and the Spacemen, 1955
Simon Black in the Antarctic, 1956
Simon Black Takes Over, 1959
Simon Black at Sea, 1961

SNUG AND SERENA SERIES, Alison Uttley (1884-1976), (appeared in 1950s in Great Britain), British Book Center and/or Bobbs-Merrill, first American edition, hardcover, 64 pages, illustrated by Katherine Wigglesworth. ($45.00 with dust jacket) $20.00

Snug and Serena Park Cowslips, 1950
Snug and the Chimney-Sweep, 1953
Snug and Serena Count Twelve, 1962
Snug and Serena Go to Town, 1963
Snug and Serena Meet a Queen, 1963

SPACE CAT SERIES, Ruthven Todd, Scribner, illustrated hardcover, illustrations by Paul Galdone. $45.00
Space Cat, 1952
Space Cat Visits Venus, 1955
Space Cat Meets Mars, 1957
Space Cat and the Kittens, 1959

SPRINGBOARD SPORTS SERIES, Alex B. Allen, Whitman, 4 titles, pictorial hardcovers, various artists. $10.00.
No Place for Baseball, 1973
Fifth Down, 1974
Danger on Broken Arrow Trail, 1974
Tennis Menace, 1975

STEP-UP BOOKS, DeKay, White, and other authors, ca. 1960s Random House, hardcover, illustrations, map or illustrated endpapers. ($15.00 with dust jacket) $10.00
Meet John F. Kennedy, 1965
Meet Andrew Jackson, 1967
Meet Theodore Roosevelt, 1967
Meet Christopher Columbus, 1968

STEVE CANYON ADVENTURE STORIES, Milton Caniff, Grosset & Dunlap, hardcover, uncredited illustrations copy Caniff's newspaper strip style. ($35.00 with dust jacket) $10.00
Steve Canyon: Operation Convoy, 1959
Steve Canyon: Operation Snowflower, 1959
Steve Canyon: Operation Foo Ling, 1959
Steve Canyon: Operation Eel Island, 1959
Steve Canyon, related books:
Milton Caniff's Steve Canyon, 1959 Golden Books, part of "Little Golden Books" series, $10.00

SWORD OF SPIRITS TRILOGY, John Christopher (b. 1922), Macmillan. (This English science fiction author's most popular series was the TRIPOD trilogy.) ($35.00 with dust jacket) $15.00
Prince in Waiting, 1970
Beyond the Burning Lands, 1971
Sword of Spirits, 1972

——— ⋙ **T** ⋘ ———

TED WILFORD MYSTERIES, Norvin Pallas, 1951 –

1967, Ives Washburn, 15 titles, hardcover. ($15.00 with dust jacket) $10.00
Secret of Thunder Mountain, 1951
Locked Safe Mystery, 1954
Star Reporter Mystery, 1955
Singing Tree Mystery, 1956
Empty House Mystery, 1957
Counterfeit Mystery, 1958
Stolen Plans Mystery, 1959
Scarecrow Mystery, 1960
Big Cat Mystery, 1961
Missing Witness Mystery, 1962
Baseball Mystery, 1963
Mystery of Rainbow Gulch, 1964
Abandoned Mine Mystery, 1965
S. S. Shamrock Mystery, 1966
Greenhouse Mystery, 1967

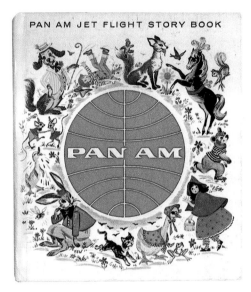

Tell-a-Tale Pan Am Jet Flight Story Book

TELL-A-TALE BOOKS, Whitman Publishing, were published in several sizes.
Tell-a-Tale Books, about 5⅝ x 6⅜ inches, color illustrated paper-over-board covers, color illustrations throughout, numerous titles including the following examples of 1950 – 1960 titles. $5.00
Circus Alphabet
Two Stories about Chap and Chippy
Especially from Thomas
Two Stories about Wendy
Frisker
Johnny Go Round
Where Timothy Lives
Princess and the Pea
Rubbles and Bamm-Bamm
Uncle Scrooge
Woody Woodpecker

Peter Potamus
Tom and Jerry and the Toy Circus
Buffy and the New Girl
Nancy and Sluggo, the Big Surprise
Buster Bulldozer
Tell-a-Tale Pan Am Jet Flight Story Books, with airline insignia cover, no price, contained a color illustrated story.
1960s book: $35.00
1980s book: $10.00
Big Tell-a-Tale Books, ca. 1960s Whitman Publishing, 6 x 8½ inches, color illustrated paper-over-board covers, color illustrations throughout. $10.00
Original stories:
Little Boy from Shickshinny
Pet at the Zoo
Funny Alphabet
My Father Can Fix Anything
Five-Star General
Solomon Shag
1 Boy Lives in My House
Casey, the Clumsy Colt
  Old Favorite Stories:
Child's Garden of Verses
Three Bears
Mother Goose
Rumpelstiltskin
Three Little Pigs
Little Red Riding Hood
Gingerbread Man
  Stories About Your TV and Movie Friends:
Visit to Disneyland
Uncle Scrooge
Flintstones
Yogi Bear
Boo Boo
Giant Tell-a-Tale Books, ca. 1960s Whitman Publishing, 10 x 12½ inches, color illustrated paper-over-board covers, color illustrations throughout. $20.00
My Dog, My Friend, in Pictures and Rhyme, 1966
Ride a Fine Horse, Robert Lee, 1967

THOMAS THE TANK ENGINE (RAILWAY SERIES), Rev. Wilbert Awdry (1911 – 1998) Kay and Ward, London, small hardcover, color illustrations, first editon with dust jacket: $40.00
  Later editions: ($20.00 with dust jacket) $10.00
Gordon the Big Engine, 1960
Three Railway Engines, 1963
Stepney the Bluebell Engine, 1963
Mountain Engines, 1964
Troublesome Engines, 1964
Very Old Engines, 1965
James the Red Engine, 1965

Percy the Small Engine, 1965
Duck and the Diesel Engine, 1965
Thomas the Tank Engine, 1966
Tank Engine Thomas Again, 1966
Little Old Engine, 1966
Main Line Engine, 1966
Gallant Old Engine, 1966
Toby the Tram Engine, 1966
Oliver the Western Engine, 1969

THREE BOYS SERIES, Nan Hayden Agle and/or Ellen Janet Wilson (Cameron), 1951 – 1968 Scribners, hardcover, illustrated endpapers, illustrations by Marian Honigman. Heroes are the triplets Abercrombie, Benjamin, and Christopher. ($15.00 with dust jacket) $10.00
Three Boys and a Lighthouse, 1951
Three Boys and the Remarkable Cow, 1952
Three Boys and a Tugboat, 1953
Three Boys and a Mine, 1954
Three Boys and a Train, 1956
Three Boys and a Helicopter, 1958
Three Boys and Space, 1962
Three Boys and H2O, 1968

THREE INVESTIGATORS, see ALFRED HITCHCOCK AND THE THREE INVESTIGATORS.

THREE JAYS, Pat Smythe, 1958 – 1961 Cassell, 6 titles, hardcover. ($15.00 with dust jacket) $10.00
Jacqueline Rides for a Fall, 1957
Three Jays Against the Clock, 1958
Three Jays on Holiday, 1958
Three Jays Go to Town, 1959
Three Jays Over the Border, 1960
Three Jays Go to Rome, 1960
Three Jays Lend a Hand, 1961

TIMBER TRAIL RIDERS, Michael Murray, 1960s Whitman, glossy pictorial $10.00
Mysterious Dude
Luck of Black Diamond
Texas Tenderfoot, A Dave Talbot Story
Long Trail North

TIME MACHINE SERIES, Gene Darby, 1960s Field Educational Publications, oversize hardcover, two-color illustrations by Barbara Robinson. $15.00
Leonard Visits Space
Leonard Visits the Ocean Floor
Leonard Discovers America
Leonard Visits Dinosaur Land
Leonard Visits Sitting Bull
Leonard Goes to the Olympics
Leonard Equals Einstein
Leonard Discovers Africa

TINKER AND TANKER SERIES, Richard Scarry, author-illustrator, early 1960s Doubleday, oversize easy-read picture books, color illustrated paper-over-board cover, color and b/w illustrations throughout by Scarry. $25.00
Tinker and Tanker
Tinker and Tanker and their Space Ship
Tinker and Tanker Out West
Tinker and Tanker and the Pirates

TOBY HEYDON SERIES, Rosamund du Jardin, Lippincott, hardcover.
($15.00 with dust jacket) $10.00
Practically Seventeen, 1949
Class Ring, 1951
Boy Trouble, 1953
Real Thing, 1956
Wedding in the Family, 1958
One of the Crowd, 1961

TOM CORBETT SPACE CADET SERIES, based on radio and TV series, Carey Rockwell, 1950s Grosset & Dunlap, hardcover, illustrated by Frank Vaughn. ($35.00 with dust jacket) $10.00
Glossy pictorial hardcover, Wonder Books: $15.00
Stand by for Mars, 1952
Danger in Deep Space, 1953
On the Trail of the Space Pirates, 1953
Space Pioneers, 1953
Revolt on Venus, 1954
Treachery in Outer Space, 1954
Sabotage in Space, 1955
Robot Rocket, 1956

TOM QUEST SERIES, Fran Striker, Grosset & Dunlap, tweed hardcover: ($20.00 with dust jacket) $10.00
Clover Books, McLoughlin Bros. glossy illustrated hardcover: $15.00
Sign of the Spiral, 1947
Telltale Scar, 1947
Clue of the Cypress Stump, 1948
Secret of the Lost Mesa, 1949
Hidden Stone Mystery, 1950
Secret Of Thunder Mountain, 1952
Inca Luck Piece, 1955
Mystery of the Timber Giant, 1955

TOM SWIFT SERIES, see NEW TOM SWIFT JR. ADVENTURES SERIES

TOP TOP TALES SERIES, ca. 1960s Whitman, small illustrated hardcover, illustrated endpapers, color illustrations throughout, generally reprints or new versions of old favorites. $10.00
Where is the Keeper?
Little Caboose

Playmate for Peter
Petunia
Dr. Goat
Hullabaloo
Big Red Pajama Wagon
Truck that Stopped at Village Small
Jolly Jingles
Wiggletail
Columbus, the Exploring Burro
Three Little Pigs
Mother Goose
Gingerbread Man
Three Bears
Huckleberry Hound
Crusader Rabbit
Little Lulu
Quick Draw McGraw
Donald Duck

Top Top Tales Series

TRIPODS TRILOGY, John Christopher, Hamish Hamilton, UK, and Macmillan, US, hardcover. English science fiction writer Christopher wrote about a trio of teenage boys who resisted an alien invasion. See also SWORD OF SPIRITS.
Hamish Hamilton first edition with dust jacket: $35.00
Macmillan first edition with dust jacket: $40.00
Later editions: ($20.00 with dust jacket) $15.00
White Mountains, 1967
City of Gold and Lead, 1967
Pool of Fire, 1968

TRIXIE BELDEN SERIES, originated by Julie Campbell, 1948 – on Whitman Publishers, 39 books, written by Campbell and other authors.

Ca. 1948 – 1951, books were published with dust jackets, interior illustrations and dust jackets by Mary Stevens.

1950s hardcovers: ($45.00 with dust jacket) $15.00

Ca. 1954 – 1961, laminated pictorial hardcovers, interior illustrations and cover by Mary Stevens. $15.00

Ca.1959, hardcovers with dust jacket and a diamond pattern on spine, illustrations by Mary Stevens. Dust jacket illustrations by Herbert Tauss. ($20.00 with dust jacket) $10.00

Ca. 1962 – 1964, "cameo" picture of Trixie appears in white or ivory-colored oval. Cover picture printed directly on cloth hardcover. Illustrations by Mary Stevens or Paul Frame. $15.00

Ca. 1965, oversized "deluxe" books, color illustration printed directly on cloth hardcover. Interior illustrations by Paul Frame or Haris Petie. Also published by Golden Press. $20.00

1970s reprints, Dean & Son Ltd, London, cameo and illustration on yellow glossy hardcover. $10.00

Secret of the Mansion, 1
Red Trailer Mystery, 2
Gatehouse Mystery, 3
Mysterious Visitor, 4
Mystery Off Glen Road, 5
Mystery in Arizona, 6

Trixie Belden Series, continued, Kathryn Kenny (pseudonym used by several authors), 1961 – 1970 Whitman, illustrated hardcover. $10.00

Ca. 1970, thinner format where books are less than one inch thick, cover picture printed directly on cloth hardcover. Illustrations by Larry Frederick. $10.00

Mysterious Code, 7
Black Jacket Mystery, 8
Happy Valley Mystery, 9
Marshland Mystery, 10
Mystery at Bob-White Cave, 11
Mystery of the Blinking Eye,12
Mystery on Cobbetts Island, 13
Mystery of the Emeralds, 14
Mystery on the Mississippi, 15
Mystery of the Missing Heiress, 16

TUCKER FAMILY SERIES, Jo Mendel, ca. 1965 Whitman, pictorial hardcover, 280+ pages, illustrated endpapers, green illustrations by Jackie Tomes. $15.00

Adventures of Plum Tucker, 1961
Special Secret, 1961
Trouble on Valley View, 1961
Turnabout Summer, 1963

Big Tell-a-Tale Tucker Family books, ca. 1965, small, color illustrated hardcover, illustrated end-papers, color illustrations by Betty Fraser. $15.00

Tuckers: One Big Happy Family
Toby Tucker
Here Come the Tuckers
Tom Tucker and Dickie-Bird

U

UNITED STATES BOOKS SERIES, Bernadine Bailey, Whitman, hardcover, Kurt Wiese illustrations. ($30.00 with dust jacket) $15.00

Florida, 1949
Missouri, 1951
Oklahoma, 1952
Georgia, 1953
Louisiana, 1954
Oregon, 1954
Vermont, 1961
Washington, 1962

V

VERONICA SERIES, Roger Duvoisin, Knopf, oversize hardcover, illustrated endpapers, color illustrations by author.

Veronica, first edition. ($40.00 with dust jacket) $20.00

Veronica, 1962 Weekly Reader Childrens Book Club edition. $15.00

Our Veronica Goes to Petunia's Farm, 1962, first edition. ($35.00 with dust jacket) $20.00

Lonely Veronica, 1963, first edition. ($35.00 with dust jacket) $20.00

Veronica's Smile, 1964, first edition. ($40.00 with dust jacket) $20.00

Veronica and the Birthday Present, 1971, first edition. ($35.00 with dust jacket) $20.00

VICARAGE CHILDREN SERIES, Lorna Hill, 1961 – 1966 Evans, hardcover, 3 titles. See also MAJORIE, DANCING PEELS, PATIENCE, and SADLER WELLS. ($25.00 with dust jacket) $10.00
Vicarage Children, 1961
More About Mandy, 1963
Vicarage Children in Skye, 1966

──────── ◁══ **W** ══▷ ────────

WE WERE THERE SERIES, Grosset and Dunlop, Sears Book Club, hardcover. ($20.00 with dust jacket) $10.00
We Were There with the Pony Express, William Steele, 1956
We Were There at the Klondike Gold Rush, Benjamin Appel, 1956
We Were There at the Battle for Battan, Benjamin Appel, 1957
We Were There at the Oklahoma Land Run, Jim Kjelgaard, 1957

WHITMAN TELEVISION FAVORITES, ca. 1960, pictorial hardcover, b/w illustrations, some times more than one book and title for a TV series. $15.00
Rebel
Real McCoys
Sea Hunt
Rifleman
Janet Lennon, Adventure at Two Rivers
Janet Lennon, Camp Calamity
Walt Disney's Annette

Leave It to Beaver
Ripcord

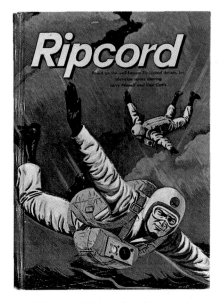

Whitman Television Favorites

WILDERNESS MYSTERY SERIES, Troy Nesbit (pseudonym of Franklin Brewster Folsom), Harvey House, hardcover, illustrated by John Joseph Floherty. Some titles appear to have been published in earlier editions by Whitman with different illustrators. $15.00
Mystery at Rustler's Fort, 1960
Sand Dune Pony Mystery, 1960
Indian Mummy Mystery, 1962
Mystery at Payrock Canyon, 1962
Diamond Cave Mystery, 1962
Forest Fire Mystery, 1963
Hidden Ruin, 1966

WILLIAM BROWN SERIES, (also called JUST WILLIAM), Richmal Crompton, 1922 – 1969 George Newnes, 38 titles. Female author worked as a school teacher until forced to retire by the onset of polio. School series based on her experiences and the character of her brother, Jack, also an author. Illustrations by Thomas Henry.
William Brown, reprints of titles published between 1922 and 1950, hardcovers: ($20.00 with dust jacket) $10.00
William Brown, new titles issued between 1950 and 1969, hardcovers: ($20.00 with dust jacket) $10.00
William the Bold, 1950
William and the Tramp, 1952
William and the Moon Rocket, 1954
William and the Space Animal, 1956

William's Television Show, 1958
William the Explorer, 1960
William's Treasure Trove, 1962
William and the Witch, 1964
William and the Pop Singers, 1965
William and the Masked Ranger, 1966
William the Superman, 1968
William the Lawless, 1970

Wolves Chronicles

WOLVES CHRONICLES, Joan Aiken, 1960s, Doubleday, various illustrators. Aiken's spoof of the Victorian melodrama takes place in the time of James III, a Stuart king who never was, ruling a definitely Dickensian England. The most popular character in the series, Dido Twite, and her family continued to inspire new novels into the 1990s. The original series deals, mostly, with the wicked plots of the Hanoverians bent on overthrowing the Stuart monarchy.

Early editions: ($35.00 with dust jacket) $15.00
Wolves of Willoughby Chase, 1962, b/w illustrations by Pat Marriot
Black Hearts In Battersea, 1964, b/w illustrations by Robin Jacques
Nightbirds in Nantucket, 1966, map endpapers, b/w illustrations by Robin Jacques
Cuckoo Tree, 1971, b/w illustrations by Susan Obrant

WONDER BOOKS, Grosset and Dunlap, 1947 – 1976, 440+ titles, 28 to 42 pages. Small hardcover books advertised as "Wonder Books with the Washable Covers." Like most Grosset and Dunlap series, first editions are generally identified through advertisements in books. If a book's advertisement does not show titles published after original copyright date, it may be a first edition. Like LITTLE GOLDEN BOOKS or RAND MCNALLY ELF BOOKS, titles devoted to popular children's characters or media tie-ins command higher than usual prices. Stephen King collectors seek *Mr. Bear Squash-You-All-Flat,* due to the title being mentioned in one of the horror-meister's stories. See also RAGGEDY ANN, ROMPER ROOM, and OZ. 1940s individual titles: $8.00, post 1950 titles: $5.00. Some exceptions:
Mr. Bear Squash-You-All-Flat, 1950, by Morrell Gipson, illustrated by Angela, lists up to $300.00
Felix the Cat, 1953, by Pat Sullivan, illustrated by author, $10.00
Blondie's Family, 1954, by Chic Young, illustrated by Chic Young, $12.00

YOUNG FOLKS SHELF OF BOOKS, Margaret E. Martignoni, Sr. Editor, 1962 Crowell-Collier, 10-volume set, various colors, hardcover. Price for complete set: $55.00

The value of a particular edition of a child's book often depends on the collectibility of the illustrator. We began our search for information about these talented artists in *Children's Books, 1850 – 1950*. Here are more names and information to help collectors identify favorite illustrators.

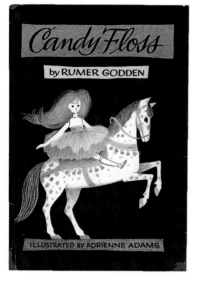

Adrienne Adams

Adams, Adrienne (b. 1906 Arkansas)
Adams' work made her twice a runner-up for the Caldecott (1959, 1961) as well as a recipient for the 1973 Rutgers University Award for contributions to children's literature. She started her career in 1942, illustrating her husband's book *Bag of Smoke*. By the 1960s, she was turning out a variety of work, with a particular emphasis on the quality control of the color printing; she did her own color separations rather than them being prepared by others. A lovely example of her use of color is the dust jacket for Rumer Godden's *Candy Floss.* Adams also added design elements to books, such as the pawprint endpapers for Aileen Fisher's *Going Barefoot* (1960). In the 1970s, she began to write and illustrate her own books including *A Woggle of Witches* (1971).

Anderson, C.W. (1891 – 1971, b. Nebraska)
Horses were Anderson's major love, probably due to his Nebraska childhood, and most of this author/illustrator's work revolves around the beauty of having an equine pal. Anderson attended the Chicago Institute of Art, later working in New York and then Boston as a freelance artist. His series, *Billy and Blaze*, concentrated on a boy and his pony, but he also wrote novels for older readers such as *Afraid to Ride* (1957). He was a stickler for accuracy in his drawings and wanted his readers to understand proper horsemanship as well as horses from his illustrations. His last published work was *Blind Connemara,* drawn in his Boston studio.

Anno, Mitsumasa (b. 1926 Japan)
A graduate of Yamaguchi Teacher Training College in Japan, Anno began his career as a primary grade teacher. He plays games with his art to engage very young readers; creating *tromp-l'oeil* (literally "fool the eye") designs or hiding pictures within pictures. His wordless books such as *Topsy-Turvies* (1970) don't require any translation and have built up a worldwide network of fans. His awards include the Golden Apple from the Biennale at Bratislava and the First Prize for Graphic Excellence in Books for Children from the Bologna Children's Book Fair. In the late 1970s, Anno began working with his son, Masaichiro, on a series of books to teach mathematical concepts.

Aruego, Jose (b. 1932 Manila)
After earning a law degree from the University of Philippines, Aruego left his native Manila to attend the Parsons School of Design in New York. By 1969, he was working in children's book illustrations. A number of collaborations with his former wife Ariane Dewey (also listed as Ariane Aruego) used Areugo's drawings while Dewey provided the color wash.
See Author section, Robert KRAUS

Babbitt, Natalie (b. 1932 Ohio)
According to Babbitt's own recollections, she set out to be an illustrator like John Tenniel. She studied art at the Laurel School in Cleveland and at Smith College and then illustrated her husband's book, *The Forty-Ninth Magician* (1966) as well as some works of poetry. Finally, she turned to writing her own stories to have something to illustrate. This led to a long list of work where Babbitt's words received more attention than her pen-and-ink drawings, including such popular titles as *Tuck Everlasting* (1975) and *The Devil's Storybook* (1974).

Baker, Jeannie (b. 1950 Australia)
Baker relies on detailed collage constructions using leaves, grass, and other common materials to ilustrate her own books. She began her career by preparing material for animated children's programs on Thames Television in London, after attending the Croydon College of Art and the Brighton College of Art. Her first published work was *Polar* by Elaine Moss (1975).

Barton, Byron (b. 1930 Rhode Island)
California artist Barton attended the Chouinard Art Institute and worked in television animation as well as illustration. In 1979, he embarked on a series of nonfiction books for preschoolers with such titles as *Wheels*. His 1975 picture book, *Hester*, is a good example of his use of bright color and strong shapes.

Baskin, Leonard (b. 1922 New Jersey)
American artist Baskin's work can be found in museum collections, on the campus of Smith College, in the works of his literary press Gehenna Press, and in his contributions to children's books. Trained at the Yale School of Art as well as in Paris and Florence, he became professor of graphics and artist-in-residence at Smith College in 1953. His watercolor illustrations for *Hosie's Alphabet* (1972) earned him a Caldecott Honor, and he later illustrated Ted Hughes' poetry for young adult readers including *Season Songs* (1975).

Berson, Harold (b. 1926 Los Angeles)
Berson studied art in Paris, then graduated from the University of California, L.A. Berson's travels through Europe and the Middle East gave him the opportunity to develop his style. His illustrations for children's books display his clever use of color and humor.
See Author section, Hilaire BELLOC

Blake, Quentin (b. 1932 Kent, England)
Blake lists his major influences as the French illustrator and cartoonist, Honore Daumier, and the English humor magazine, *Punch*. He received his training at the Chelsea School of Art and later became an instructor at the Royal College of Art in London. In collaboration with Russell Hoban, Blake received the Whitbread Literary Award for the picture book, *How Tom Beat Captain Najork and His Hired Sportsmen* (1974). In the late 1970s, he started illustrating the works of Roald Dahl.

Blegvad, Erik (b. 1923 Denmark)
During World War II, Blegvad attended art school in Denmark. In post-war 1947, illustrating jobs were hard to find in Copenhagen, so Blegvad moved to Paris. There he met and married his American wife, Lenore, who would eventually collaborate with him on children's books. In 1951, they moved to New York and Blegvad became a prolific illustrator for both novels and picture books. In 1979, he wrote and illustrated *Self-Portrait: Erik Blegvad* about his career in art.
See Author section, Richard JACKSON and Marjorie WINSLOW

Bodecker, N. M., (Nils Mogens) (b. 1922 Copenhagen, Denmark)
Bodecker studied archictecture and economics in Copenhagen, and art at the School of Applied Arts, Copenhagen. He began his career as a writer, on staff at a magazine and free-lancing to newspapers, which led to cartooning and then to illustrating. His illustrations appear in children's books and in magazines. In 1972 he was named as one of the ten best illustrators by *The New York Times* for his own book *Miss Jaster's Garden*.
See Author section, JENNINGS; see Series section, HALF MAGIC.

Raymond Briggs

Briggs, Raymond (b. 1934 London)
Briggs often combines pictures and text in a comic book format to tell his stories. From the "bloomin" *Father Christmas* (1973) to later wordless work such as the *Snowman* (1978), Briggs seems likely to replace Dickens as England's best Christmas export. He earned his first Kate Greenaway Medal for the *Mother Goose Treasury* (1966) which featured a typical Briggs' working class look imposed on the classical figures of nursery rhyme. The next Greenaway was for *Father Christmas* (1973), which tells its story through panels and word balloons as Father Christmas grumps his way through his job of delivering packages. Briggs studied at Wimbledon School of Fine Art, the Slade School of Fine Art, and the University of London.

Brown, Marcia (b. 1918 Rochester, NY)
During her long career, Brown has won three Caldecott Medals and six Caldecott Honors. After graduating from the New York College for Teachers in 1940, she taught English and later worked as an assistant librarian for the New York Public Library.

Brown studied art at the Woodstock School of Painting and at the Art Students League in New York, working with such artists as Stuart Davis and Yasuo Kuniyoshi. Her first Caldecott Medal book, *Stone Soup* (1948), was one of Brown's many popular recreations of a classic fairy tale. Brown worked in a variety of mediums ranging from pen-and-ink to woodcuts for *Once A Mouse* (1962 Caldecott) to match the art to the mood. In 1992, she received the Laura Ingalls Wilder Award for her contributions to children's literature.

Bryan, Ashley (b. 1923 New York)
Bryan's varied background includes majoring in philosophy at Columbia University, studying drawing at the Cooper Union Art School (as well as Columbia), working with the Head Start program to introduce children to art, and teaching at New York colleges such as Queens College, Lafayette College, and others. In the 1970s, he joined Dartmouth College's faculty, eventually serving as chairman of the Art Department. His work reflects his interest in his African-American heritage, often using African motifs to illustrate folk tales like *Ox of the Wonderful Horns and Other African Tales* (1971).

Burchard, Peter (b. 1921 Washington, D.C.)
Burchard began his art career illustrating Army manuals during World War II. After leaving the Army, he studied at the Philadelphia Museum of Art's School of Industrial Art. During his career as an artist in New York, he designed book jackets and illustrated more than 100 books. His love of sports, including sailing, can be seen in his brightly colored illustrations of action scenes painted for dust jackets of young adult novels. In the 1970s, he began writing historical novels and nonfiction works such as *One Gallant Rush: Robert Gould Shaw and His Brave Black Regiment*, which served as the basis for the 1989 movie, *Glory*.

See Author section, Clyde BULLA

Burkert, Nancy (b. 1933 Colorado)
Burkert earned her MA degree at the University of Wisconsin. Her delicate use of color and fine ink linework distinguish her illustrations for Roald Dahl's *James and the Giant Peach,* (1961), her first book assignment, as well as Randall Jarrell's *Snow White and the Seven Dwarfs,* (1972), a Caldecott Honor book. Among other recognitions of her work, she received the 1966 Gold Medal of the Society of Illustrators.

Burningham, John (b. 1936 Surrey, England)
Burningham attended the Central School of Art and Craft in London, where he met his wife, illustrator Helen Oxenbury. Following stints as a poster designer for London Transport and an art school instructor, Burningham moved into a regular career as an author/illustrator, winning England's Kate Greenaway Medal for *Borka* (1963) and *Mr. Gumpy's Outing* (1973). He also won a number of international awards including the New York Times Best Illustrated Children's Books of the Year Award and the Boston Globe-Horn Book Award for Illustration.

Burton, Virginia Lee (1909 – 1968)
Burton intended to be a dancer, but she studied drawing with George Demetrios in Boston and ended up marrying him and pursuing a career in art. When creating picture books, she often looked to her own sons for subjects they would enjoy. The author/illustrator of *Choo Choo* (1937) and *Mike Mulligan and His Steam Shovel* (1939) became a well-established figure in American picture books in the 1940s. A true perfectionist, she often reworked drawings or stories leading to a revised edition of *Calico the Wonder Horse or the Saga of Stewy Stinker* (1950 edition; the 1941 edition calls him Stewy Slinker, not Burton's first choice). Toward the end of her career, she abandoned book illustration in favor of textile design.

Carle, Eric (b. 1929 Syracuse, NY)
According to Carle, ninety-nine percent of his illustrations are made with tissue paper, with just a little added crayon or ink. His parents returned to Germany in 1935, where Carle studied art. Around 1950 Carle moved back to New York, where he worked for a time as a graphic designer for the *New York Times*, and also as a freelance commerical artist. In the 1960s Carle began to make his own picture books. For almost 20 years, his editor Ann Beneduce encouraged him to create educational picture books that didn't sacrifice entertainment to learning. His vivid colors and humorous cut-out shapes accomplish that goal.

Carrick, Donald (1929 – 1989, b. Michigan)
Carrick, a landscape and portrait painter, started illustrating children's nonfiction. When an editor asked Carrick if he wanted to do his own picture book, he turned to his wife, Carol, for help. She wrote and he drew *The Old Barn* (1966) which led to several other collaborative ventures. Carrick also wrote and illustrated his own books such as *The Tree,* as well as providing illustrations for others. Carrick attended Colorado Springs Fine Art Center, Art Students League, and Vienna Academy of Fine Art.

Barbara Cooney

Cooney, Barbara (b. 1917 Brooklyn)
Cooney attended Briarcliff and Smith College, then studied lithography and etching at the New York Art Students League. Much of her life was spent in New England, and that influence is apparent in many of her drawings. In 1959, her illustrations for *Chanticleer and the Fox* won the Caldecott Award. Early works used scratchboard, but after *Chanticleer,* she experimented with collage, watercolor, acrylics, and other techniques.

Cuffari, Richard (1925 – 1978, b. Brooklyn)
Cuffari studied at the Pratt Institute following service in World War II. For years a freelance com-

merical artist, he turned to illustrating children's books in the 1960s and later became an instructor of book illustration for the Parsons School of Design. Much of his work centers on historical recreations, such as *Perilous Gard* (1974, Pope), or natural history. With more than 200 books to his credit, Cuffari received a number of design awards including two Citations of Merit from the Society of Illustrators.

de Paola, Tomie (b. 1934 Connecticut)
Like many American illustrators of the 1970s, DePaola received his early education at the Pratt Institute in Brooklyn, New York, and also at the Skowhagen School of Painting. During his graduate years at the California College of Arts and Crafts, he worked as a stage set designer and a muralist. His work often draws upon his own Irish-Italian heritage, including his most famous picture book, *Strega Nona* (Caldecott Honor Award, 1976). His highly recognizable style relies on a strong brown line with color supplied by acrylic, although he occasionally uses color pencils. The strong use of shapes, rather than photographic renderings, grew out of De Paola's interest in folk art.
See Author section, FARBER

Dillon, Leo (b. 1933 Brooklyn)
Dillon, Diane (b. 1933 California)
New Yorker Leo and Californian Diane grew up on opposite coasts, then met when they both attended Parsons School of Design. Although they pursued separate freelance careers after marriage, they eventually pooled their talents to create a "third

Tomie de Paola

style." From science fiction paperbacks to picture books, the prolific Dillons turned out hundreds of distinct, colorful illustrations, often incorporating American-Indian or African motifs. In the 1990s, their son, Lee, joined the family collaboration by creating the borders for the picture book, *Aida*. Due to the beauty of their work as well as its themes, the Dillons' picture books, especially out-of-print works, draw serious interest from collectors.

Domanska, Janina (1912 – 1995)

Polish Domanska was imprisoned in a concentration camp during World War II, but her artwork earned her an early release. After the war, she studied art in Rome and eventually emigrated to the United States. In America, she worked as a textile designer while studying English. As soon as she felt comfortable speaking the language, she sought work as a book illustrator. Many of her picture books retell popular folk tales and the art reflects the traditions of the country. *Marilka* (1970) is a lovely example of Domanska's use of Slavic designs.

Carp with a harp

Fritz Eichenberg

Eichenberg, Fritz (1901 – 1990, b. Germany)

As a successful German political cartoonist in the 1930s, Eichenberg annoyed a rising politician named Adolf Hitler. Leaving Germany where he had studied at the Academy of Graphic Arts in Leipzig, Eichenberg worked in Central America before emigrating to the United States. Much of his work concentrated on illustrating new editions of classics, such as Bronte's *Wuthering Heights*, but the birth of a son inspired a couple of picture books: *Ape in a Cape* (1952) and *Dancing in the Moon* (1955).

Emberley, Edward (b. 1931 Massachusetts)

Emberley studied art at the Rhode Island School of Design and the Massachusetts College of Art. His first art assignment was painting signs for the Army. Following his military service, he worked as a commercial artist and cartoonist before becoming interested in children's books. Starting in the 1950s, he produced a number of picture books, often collaborating with his wife Barbara. *Drummer Hoff* received the 1968 Caldecott Award while *One Wide River to Cross* was a Caldecott Honor Book for 1967. In the 1970s, Emberley produced a series of books on drawing, including *Ed Emberley's Drawing Book of Animals* (1970) and *Ed Emberley's Great Thumbprint Drawing Book* (1977).

Ets, Marie Hall (b. 1895 Wisconsin)

Ets began her art career as an interior decorator then worked as a social worker in Chicago. She studied art at the New York School of Fine and Applied Art and at the Chicago Art Institute, and after a series of personal challenges, began her career as an illustrator of children's books in the 1930s. Much of her work was black-and-white illustration, but her 1960 Caldecott Medal was awarded for the full-color illustrated *Nine Days to Christmas.*

Feelings, Tom (b. 1933 Brooklyn)

African-American Feelings grew up in Brooklyn and studied cartooning, which led to a strip entitled "Tommy Traveler in the World of Negro History" carried by the *New York Age*. Discouraged by the problems of racism, he moved to Ghana, where he illustrated books for the Ghana government. Upon his return to the United States in the late 1960s, he sought to work with African-American writers as well as producing picture books based on his own African experiences such as *Jambo Means Hello* (1971). Throughout his career, Feelings provided positive images of black children to counteract the lack of such books in his own childhood.

Fitzhugh, Louise (1928 – 1974 Tennessee)

Fitzhugh came from a wealthy but unhappy Southern background. The only child of divorced parents, she never completed her college education, dropping out to move to New York and train as a painter. She studied at the Art Students League and at Cooper Union. Her first picture book was co-written with Sandra Scoppettone in 1961. Then she produced the book that became an almost instant classic, *Harriet the Spy* (1964). Several of Fitzhugh's works, including more picture books, were published posthumously in the late 1970s and early 1980s.

Antonio Frasconi

Frasconi, Antonio (b. 1919)
Frasconi was born in Argentina to Italian parents, grew up in Uruguay, and moved to the United States to study at the Art Students League in the 1940s. He soon became recognized as an exceptional woodcut artist. When children's editor Margaret McElderry asked him to create a picture book, he wrote and illustrated *See and Say* (1955) in four different languages: English, Spanish, Italian, and French. His multilingual picture books, including the Caldecott Medal book *The House That Jack Built* (1959), broke new ground for diversity in American children's publishing. He provided woodcut illustrations for other authors through the 1990s as well as teaching at a number of prestigious schools. In 1989, Frasconi was honored by the Library of Congress for his contributions to children's literature.

Freeman, Don (1908 – 1978, b. San Diego)
Freeman moved to New York to become a professional musician, but he also studied at the Art Students League during the 1920s and 1930s. The loss of his trumpet on the subway led to a career as a freelance artist, covering the New York shows for the newspapers. His most famous picture book, *Corduroy* (1968), weaves an appealing story and pictures into a seamless whole.

Goble, Paul (b. 1933 Oxford, England)
Paul Goble graduated from London's School of Arts and Crafts, where he met his wife and co-author, Dorothy Goble. He lectured at Ravensbourne College of Art and Design, primarily in the area of furniture design. His interest in graphic art creates strong images in his children's books. Goble's fascination with American Indians

prompted his move to the Black Hills of South Dakota, and he proudly claims adoption by the Sioux and Yakima tribes, as well as close friendships with other tribes. His first book retold the story of Custer and Little Big Horn from an Indian boy's point of view. Many of his picture books draw their stories from the myths of the Plains Indians.

Paul Goble

Goffstein, M.B. (Marilyn Brooke) (b. 1940 Minnesota)
After graduation from Bennington College in Vermont, Minnesotan Goffstein moved to New York to find work as a children's book illustrator. In the 1960s, she began writing her own books, illustrated with her humorous drawings, such as *Two Piano Tuners*. She taught book illustration at the Parsons School of Design.

Goodall, John S. (b. 1908 Norfolk, England)
Goodall studied at the Royal Academy School of Art In 1968, he created a series of wordless picture books to entertain very young children. *The Adventures of Paddy Pork* won the Boston Globe-Horn Book Award and he later received the New York Times Best Illustrated Children's Book of the Year for *The Surprise Picnic* (1977). A member of the Royal Institute of Water Colour Painters, Goodall continued to produce exhibitions of seascapes and landscapes as well as annual picture books through the 1990s.

Gorey, Edward (b. 1925 Chicago)
The Gothic tone of Gorey's pen-and-ink drawings is instantly recognizable from his now famous opening credits for the Mystery series on PBS. After attending Harvard, Gorey studied

at the Art Institute of Chicago. He worked as a freelance artist and later as a staff artist for Doubleday starting in 1953. Besides his own macabre picture books, Gorey provided dust jackets and illustrations for dozens of children's books during the 1960s and 1970s. With a huge legion of fans, Gorey's own picture books, especially first editions and out-of-print works, draw increasingly high prices in the collector's market and his illustrations usually enhance the resale value of other works.

See Author section, Frank JACOBS

Haley, Gail (b. 1939)
Haley grew up in North Carolina and attended the University of Virginia. Her retelling of the Ananse legends grew out of a year spent living in the Carribbean islands. *A Story, a Story* (1970) won the Caldecott. Haley has used a variety of techniques to illustrate her tales including woodcuts, block prints, and paintings. In the 1980s, she established the Gail Haley Collection of the Culture of Childhood at the Appalachian State University in North Carolina.

Hogrogrian, Nonny (b. 1932 New York)
Hogrogrian graduated from Hunter College. She studied woodcut art with Antonio Frasconi and entered the publishing business as a designer and art buyer. Because of her interest in design, she chooses the layout, cover, end papers, and typography for her works. She also changes her medium to suit her story, including pen-and-ink for *Always Room for One More* by Sorche Leodhas (1965), and oils for her own *One Fine Day* (1971), both awarded Caldecott Medals.

Houston, James (b. 1921 Canada)
Houston's education included Ontario College of Art as well as study at art schools in Paris and Tokyo. Houston's meticulous recreations of Innuit life come from his long fascination with Canada's northern territories. He first went to Hudson Bay in 1948, worked as a civil administrator of West Baffin, and regularly returned to the Queen Charlotte Islands, even after he established a career in New York designing Steuben glass. In the 1960s, he began writing and illustrating books about the Innuit.

Hutchins, Pat (b. 1942 Yorkshire, England)
Hutchins entered art school at the age of sixteen, studying at Darlington School of Art, and then at Leeds College of Art. She worked for a time in advertising art. Her children's book, *The Wind Blew* (1974), was a Kate Greenaway Medal winner. She also writes books for older children, many of which are illustrated by her husband, film director Laurence Hutchins.

Hyman, Trina Schart (b. 1939 Philadelphia)
Hyman attended the Philadelphia Museum College of Art and the Museum School of Fine Arts in Boston, then continued her art education at the Swedish State Art School for Applied Arts in Stockholm. She started working in book illustration during the 1960s. In 1972, she began a seven-year stint as the art director for *Cricket* magazine, producing a number of magazine covers and illustrations for them. Although best known for her picture books of classic fairy tales such as Howard Pyle's *King Stork* (1973), she has also done dust jackets and interior illustrations for more than 100

Trina Schart Hyman

245

books. Today, her earlier work is beginning to climb in value in the collector's market, although much is still in print.

See Author section, CAMERON, NICHOLS, VANCE

Keats, Ezra Jack, (1916 – 1983, b. Brooklyn, NY)
Keats' art work includes portraits and landscape paintings as well as magazine and book illustrations. His popular paintings for children's books are easily recognizable by the bold use of shape and clear colors. His best known book, *Snowy Day* (1962), began as a deliberate attempt to introduce a black child having an ordinary adventure into a mainstream picture book. Like so many illustrators, he attended the Art Students League, and also studied with Jean Charlot.

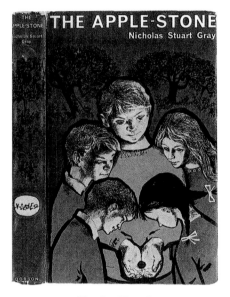

Charles Keeping

Keeping, Charles (1924 – 1988, England)
After serving in the British navy, Keeping attended the Polytechnic School of Art in London. He began illustrating books for adults and children in the 1960s. For children, his work ranged from picture books like *Through the Window* (1970) to the historical novels of Rosemary Sutcliff or Leon Garfield. He received numerous international awards for his work including the Kate Greenaway Medal.

See Author section, Nicholas GRAY

Knight, Hilary (b. 1926 Long Island, NY)
Knight grew up in an artistic household. His mother, Katherine Sturges, provided the pictures in *Little Pictures of Japan* (1925). His father, Clayton Knight, worked in a Manhattan studio, painting magazine covers, advertising art, and book illustrations. Following service in the Navy during

WWII, Hilary Knight studied with Reginald Marsh at the Art Students League in New York. During the 1940s, he entered the commercial art world doing greeting cards and magazine illustrations. A friend introduced him to Kay Thompson, suggesting his style complemented Thompson's breezy texts. They collaborated closely on the *Eloise* picture books. Knight also provided the Plaza Hotel, which was the setting of the stories, with two oil paintings of Eloise (the first was stolen, the second is still displayed in the lobby).

Kurelek, William (1927 – 1977, Canada)
A fine artist whose work can be seen in such collections as New York's Museum of Modern Art, Kurelek attended the University of Manitoba, then went to England to study painting. While many of his adult works concentrated on religious themes, his picture books portray life in the Canadian prairies during the 1930s. *A Prairie Boy's Winter* (1973) and its sequel, *A Prairie Boy's Summer* (1975), reflect his own childhood years in a farming community.

Lent, Blair (b. 1930 Boston)
After studying graphics and design at the Boston Museum School, Lent traveled through Europe on an art scholarship. He worked for several years in advertising and produced his first picture book in 1964. Lent used a variety of mediums including cardboard cuts (like woodcuts but made from the more flexible cardboard) as well as pen-and-ink. He won the Caldecott for *Funny Little Woman* (1972) by Arlene Mosel, but is probably best remembered for another Mosel picture book, *Tikki Tikki Tembo* (1968).

Lewin, Ted (b. 1935 Buffalo, NY)
Lewin is probably one of the few children's illustrators to have had a career in professional wrestling. He studied design at the Pratt Institute and supplemented his income after graduation with wrestling jobs. In the late 1970s, Lewin began to emphasize his interests in conservation and ornithology by illustrating a number of science and nonfiction books.

Lionni, Leo (b. 1910 Amsterdam)
Dutch-American illustrator Lionni earned a Ph.D. in economics before turning to graphic design. He headed the graphic arts department at the Parsons School of Design as well as working as an art director in the corporate world. Lionni started creating picture books in 1959 to entertain his grandchildren. Works like *Alexander and the Wind-Up Mouse* (1969) feature colorful paper collages. Four of his books, including *Alexander*, were named as Caldecott Honor books.

Leo Lionni

Lobel, Anita Kempler (b. 1934)
Lobel, Arnold (1933 – 1987)
Polish-born Anita Kempler survived the German concentration camps of World War II, eventually being reunited with her parents in Sweden. While attending the Pratt Institute, she met her husband, Arnold Lobel. During the early days of their careers, Anita Lobel worked more in textile design while Arnold concentrated on children's books. Encouraged by Arnold's editor, Anita eventually went into illustration, starting with *Sven's Bride* (1965). Arnold Lobel was one of several artist/authors who created the popular I-Can-Read books. His *Frog and Toad* series are probably his best known creation. In the 1980s, Lobel won the Caldecott Medal as well as several citations for his contribution to children's literature. Besides his own books, he illustrated more than 20 books for other authors.

See Author section, Cheli RYAN

Macaulay, David (b. 1946 England)
Born in England, Macaulay moved to the U.S. when he was eleven. Anyone who has seen Macauley's highly detailed drawings of cathedrals and pyramids won't be surprised to learn that he earned a bachelor's degree in architecture from the Rhode Island School of Design. Starting with his first book, *Cathedral* (1973), Macaulay created a series of nonfiction books that intrigued both children and adults. His exacting pen-and-ink drawings make the process of building easy to understand as well as beautiful to look at. In the 1980s, he began a series of books on the way that things work, bringing the same meticulous and fascinating sense of detail to illustrating the world of machines.

Mayer, Mercer (b. 1943 Arkansas)
Mayer studied at the Honolulu Academy of Arts and at the Art Students League. His earliest works were a series of wordless picture books for the preschool set as well as simple books about childhood fears, such as *There's a Nightmare in My Closet*, (1968). He also provided illustrations for other authors' works, including Fitzgerald's series, *Great Brain*. Occasionally, Mayer used the pseudonym of "Professor Wormbog." In the 1980s, he started on a series of classic fairy tale books illustrated in a lavish, full-color style.

See Series section, FROG and GREAT BRAIN

THERE'S A NIGHTMARE IN MY CLOSET

written and illustrated by MERCER MAYER

Mercer Mayer

247

McCully, Emily Arnold (b. 1939 Illinois)
After McCully attended Brown and Columbia universities, she started her career in advertising and magazine illustration. Her real success in commercial art came in the 1960s when she began illustrating children's books, including DeJong's *Journey from Peppermint Street* (1968). Her career continued into the 1990s. She received the Caldecott Medal in 1993 for *Mirette on the High Wire*.
  See Author section, Mildred KANTROWITZ

Montresor, Beni (b. 1926 Italy)
Montresor studied at the Verona Art School and the Academy of Fine Arts in Venice. Following graduation, he designed sets and costumes for the films of Fellini, De Sica, and Rossellini. Montresor came to the United States in the 1960s to work for the Metropolitan Opera. He was awarded the Caldecott in 1965 for his colorful, lush illustrations for *May I Bring A Friend?*, by Beatrice DeRegniers.

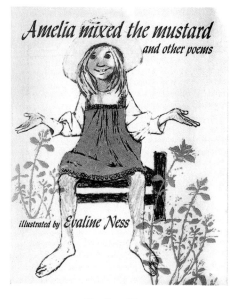

Evaline Ness

Ness, Evaline (1911 – 1986, b. Chicago)
After studying fine art at the Art Institute of Chicago and the Corcoran Gallery of Art, Ness continued her art education at the Art Students League and in Italy. She pursued a career in commercial art, including work for *Seventeen* magazine. In the 1960s, she began illustrating children's books, often writing her own charming stories such as *Sam, Bangs & Moonshine* (1967 Caldecott Medal). Ness used a variety of artistic techniques from ink and color wash to woodcuts, depending upon the mood of her tale.
  See Series section, PRYDAIN

Oxenbury, Helen (b. 1938 Suffolk, England)
Oxenbury attended the Ipswich School of Art and the Central School of Arts and Crafts, London. At art school, she met her husband, British illustrator John Burningham. Oxenbury pursued a career in theater design while Burningham concentrated on book illustration. After the birth of her first child, Oxenbury also began to design picture books so that she could work at home. She received two Kate Greenaway awards for her illustrations. In the 1980s, Oxenbury wrote and illustrated a series of board books for the preschoolers.

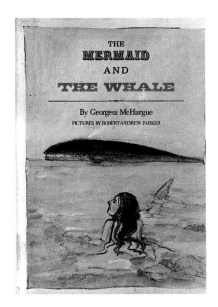

Robert Andrew Parker

Parker, Robert Andrew (b. 1927)
Parker studied at the Chicago Art Institute and the Atelier 17 in New York. His commerical art projects ranged from creating the paintings for the 1956 movie, *Lust for Life*, to album covers for Thelonious Monk. Parker's book illustrations have received many awards including a Caldecott Honor in 1970 for *Pop Corn and Ma Goodness* by Edna Mitchell Preston.

Peet, Bill (b. 1915 Indiana)
Peet began his career studying at the John Herron Art Institute in Indianapolis. This was followed by 27 years with the Walt Disney Company, one of the few companies actively recruiting artists during the Depression years. While with Disney, Peet first worked on continuity drawings, telling the story of the movie through a series of pictures. This led to writing screenplays and, eventually, to illustrating his own books, including the charming animal legend, *Ant and the Elephant,* 1972. *Bill Peet: An Autobiography* (1989) supplies the reader

with fascinating tales of Peet's artistic adventures, each one well illustrated by Peet.

Pinkney, Jerry (b. 1939 Philadelphia)
Illustrator Pinkney won a scholarship to the Philadelphia Museum College of Art, where he studied advertising and design. After his marriage, a move to Boston led to meetings with publishers. The demand for more African-American writers for children in the late 1960s also led to increased demand for African-American illustrators like Pinkney. Pinkney has worked on a variety of projects, illustrating his own stories as well as the works of others. In later years, Pinkney's career included commemorative stamps for the U.S. Postal Service's Black Heritage Series (1983) and working on the NASA artist team for the space shuttle Columbia.

Pinkwater, Daniel Manus (b. 1941 Tennessee)
Although admired as much for his writing as his illustrations, Pinkwater's college career emphasized fine art as he studied sculpture at Bard College. Early works such as *Blue Moose* (1975) match highly absurd tales with even more absurd drawings. Much of Pinkwater's work is still in print, but early editions or first editions continue to rise in value. Young collectors remember Pinkwater's books as their "absolute favorites" in grade school or junior high.

Politi, Leo (b. 1908 – 1996)
Born in California, Politi moved to Italy with his parents when he was seven and studied art there at the National Art Institute of Monza. In 1931, he returned to the United States. Much of his work reflects his home city of Los Angeles and the lives of the immigrants who settled in Southern California.

Provensen, Alice (b. 1918 Chicago)
Provensen, Martin (1916 – 1987, b. Chicago)
Unlike many other artist duos listed in this book, the Provensens liked to explain that they did not meet in art school. Both attended the Chicago Art Institute and the University of California, but they didn't meet until they both took jobs in Hollywood in the 1940s. Alice worked for the Walter Lantz Studios as an animator, while Martin made naval training films at Universal. In 1946, they left California to move east and start their joint career as illustrators for Golden Press (Simon and Schuster), their exclusive publisher for more than 20 years.

Raskin, Ellen (1928 – 1984, b. Wisconsin)
Raskin studied fine arts at the University of Wisconsin and then left the Midwest for New York

and a career as a freelance commerical artist. She designed or illustrated more than one thousand book jackets and advertisements, receiving many awards for her work. She started illustrating books with Dylan Thomas' *A Child's Christmas in Wales* (1959). Her first venture into illustrating her own words, *Nothing Ever Happens On My Block* (1966), was named Best Picture Book of the Year by the *New York Herald Tribune*. Books for older children, such as *The Mysterious Disappearance of Leon (I Mean Noel),* (1971), used type to create both illustrations and puzzles for her readers.

Rockwell, Anne (b. 1934 Tennessee)
Rockwell, Harlow (1910 – 1988)
Illustrator/author Anne Rockwell studied at the Sculpture Center in New York City as well as the Pratt Institute in Brooklyn. Many of her 70 titles were aimed at the preschool set. With her husband, Harlow, she wrote a number of nonfiction works such as *The Toolbox* (1971) or *My Dentist* (1975). Together, the Rockwells created more than 20 books for children. Harlow received his art education at the Albright Knox Art Gallery in Buffalo, NY, and at the Pratt Institute.

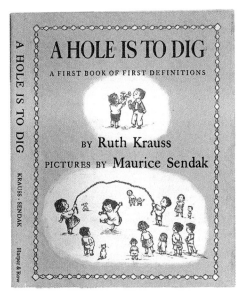

Maurice Sendak

Sendak, Maurice (b. 1928 Brooklyn)
Since the publication of *Where the Wild Things Are* (1963, 1964 Caldecott Award), Sendak has been the acknowledged artist king of American picture books. His distinctive style and innovative use of art and words make his picture books instantly recognizable. Before the publication of *Wild Things*, Sendak had illustrated a number of books for other

authors including his first assignment, *A Hole Is to Dig,* by Ruth Krauss (1952), and the delightful Little Bear series by Else Holmelund Minarik. Sendak's education included time at Art Students League, NY. *The Art of Maurice Sendak* by Thelma G. Lanes documents the enormous scope of his work. Today first editions and out-of-print works continue to escalate in value as Sendak's many fans search out his unique brand of art.

See Author section, JARRELL and KRAUSS; See Series section, LITTLE BEAR

Seuss, Dr. (1904 – 1991, b. Maine)
Theodor Geisel took his pen name from his middle name of Seuss. Seuss studied at Dartmouth, Oxford, and the Sorbonne and was a well-established illustrator by the 1930s (see *Collector's Guide to Children's Books, Vol. 1).* Seuss' greatest invention of the 1950s and 1960s was the beginning reader series for Random House. From *The Cat in the Hat* (1957) to *Green Eggs and Ham* (1960), Seuss demonstrated that you didn't need a lot of words to tell a story that a child will love. Much of his work remains in print. The sheer volume of copies printed during his lifetime (*Cat* sold more than a million books in its first year) has kept the prices relatively low for an artist of his popularity. Seuss used a number of pseudonyms for books that he wrote but did not illustrate, including the name LeSieg.

Shulevitz, Uri (b. 1935 Poland)
Displaced from Warsaw by World War II, Shulevitz's family eventually emigrated to Israel where he attended the Tel-Aviv Art Institute. As a young man, he left Israel for New York to study at the Brooklyn Museum Art School. His first picture book appeared in 1963, *Moon in My Room,* and was followed by a number of other works, including illustrations for Arthur Ransome's *Fool of the World and the Flying Ship* (1968 Caldecott Medal). Shulevitz taught illustration at several art schools and also wrote *Writing With Pictures: How to Write and Illustrate Children's Books* (1985).

Silverstein, Shel (1932 – 1999, b. Chicago)
Silverstein was considered a Renaissance man by his friends, with talents ranging from art to music to writing, and he even did some acting in films. As a cartoonist, Silverstein's art appeared in *Pacific Stars and Stripes* as well as *Playboy* magazine. As a songwriter, his lyrics include such hits as "A Boy Named Sue." As an artist for children, Silverstein's simple drawings perfectly match his stories in such books as *The Giving Tree* (1964), or the poems of *Where the Sidewalk Ends* (1974).

Simont, Marc (b. 1915 Paris)
Simont's father worked as a draftsman for the French magazine, *L'Illustration.* Simont trained in France at the Academie Julien as well as attending the National Academy of Design in New York. He began illustrating children's books in 1939 and even shared an apartment with Robert McCloskey and a bunch of ducklings. Simont received a Caldecott Honor in 1950 for *Happy Day,* by Ruth Krauss, and won the Caldecott Medal in 1955 for *A Tree Is Nice* by Janice May Udry. Also in the 1950s, he provided stylized color illustrations for James Thurber's two classic tales, *The Thirteen Clocks* (1951) and *The Wonderful O* (1957). Simont continued to illustrate through the 1980s including new illustrations for an earlier Thurber tale, *Many Moons* (1990 edition, originally illustrated by Slobodkin in 1943).

See Author section, Richard KENNEDY and James THURBER

Spier, Peter (b. 1927 Netherlands)
Spier moved to the United States from his native Netherlands in 1953. Prior to that, he studied art at the Royal Academy in Amsterdam, served in the Dutch Navy, and worked in publishing. Over the decades, he has won numerous awards and citations for his detailed and often wordless (or nearly wordless) picture books. Several of his books turned song lyrics into stories including *Fox Went Out on A Chilly Night* (1961) and *London Bridge is Falling Down* (1967).

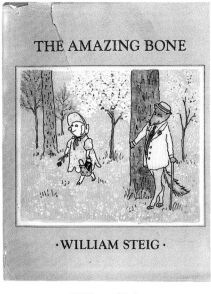

William Steig

Steig, William (b. 1907 New York)
Steig attended City College in New York, then continued his art education at the National Academy

of Design. He built his art career around his clever sketching techniques and a wry sense of humor, obvious in both his cartoons and his books. This author-illustrator has been awarded both the Caldecott for art and the Newbery for writing in the children's book field.

Stevenson, James (b. 1929 New York)
Stevenson studied at Yale and worked as a reporter for *Life* magazine before joining the staff of the *New Yorker* in the 1950s as a cartoonist and writer. He began illustrating books for children in the 1960s, starting with a collaboration written by his eight-year-old son called *If I Owned a Candy Factory* (1968).

Tomes, Margot (1917 – 1991, b. New York)
Tomes trained at the Pratt Institute. A cousin of the Pene DuBois family of artists including illustrator William Pene DuBois, she found her own niche in illustrating the works of others. Among her dozens of credits, early works such as Jean Fritz's *And Then What Happened, Paul Revere?* earned her critical praise. By the late 1970s, she'd been recognized by the *New York Times* list of best illustrated books for children and earned the Society of Illustrators' certificate of merit.

Faith Towle

Towle, Faith
Librarian Faith Towle graduated from Simmons Library School, worked as a librarian in Los Angeles, and then expanded her career to an American Embassy school library in India. Combining her love of children's illustrated books and folklore with her admiration of Indian art, she found a teacher in India to instruct her in authentic batik methods of tie-dying cloth. The process included

drying the pieces on the rooftop of her home in India. The stunning results became illustrations for her lovely picture book, *Magic Cooking Pot,* (1975).

Ungerer, Tomi (b. 1931 France)
A rare adult work by Ungerer, *Tomi: A Childhood Under the Nazis* , (1998), chronicles his early years in Strasbourg, France. His childhood experiences triggered much of Ungerer's interest in art. Drawing became a way to both comment about and escape from the chaos that surrounded him. Following a brief time at the Ecole des Arts Decoratifs in Strasbourg, France, Ungerer spent many years wandering Europe and working in odd jobs as an illustrator. In 1956, he emigrated to the United States and worked for a time in magazine illustration. His first book, *The Mellops Go Flying* (1957), led to a prolific career in writing and illustrating picture books for children, including a series of titles about the Mellops.

Watson, Wendy (b. 1942 New Jersey)
Collaborating with her sister, Clyde Watson, Wendy Watson's *Father Fox's Pennyrhymes* (1971) earned a National Book Award nomination. Other collaborations by the sisters included *Tom Fox and the Apple Pie* (1972). Watson attended Bryn Mawr College, studied painting at the National Academy of Design in New York, and spent several summers at Cape Cod studying with portrait painter Jerry Farnsworth. As an author-illustrator, she has created more than a dozen children's books and has illustrated more than 60 titles for other authors.

Weil, Lisl (b. 1910 Vienna)
Weil immigrated to the United States in 1939. Starting in the 1940s, she illustrated more than 100 books, often writing the text as well as supplying the pictures. In her hometown, New York City, she became well-known for her performances with the Little Orchestra Society of New York. As the orchestra played the music for a story, such as Stravinsky's "Firebird," Weil would draw the characters on panels stretched across the stage.

Wildsmith, Brian (b. 1930 England)
Wildsmith grew up in a coal mining family in Yorkshire. After earning a scholarship to the Slade School of Fine Art, University of London, he took up painting as a profession. While early work was primarily book jackets, his first picture book for children, *Brian Wildsmith's ABC* (1962), won the Kate Greenaway Award. Wildsmith proceeded to illustrate a number of fables based on the works of La Fontaine as well as his own books such as

Brian Wildsmith's Birds (1967), with his boldly stylistic forms and bright colors.

Young, Ed (b. 1931 China)
After spending his early childhood in Shanghai, China, and attending high school in Hong Kong, Ed Young started his college career by studying architecture in Los Angeles but soon switched to art classes. While he was working in advertising in New York, a friend suggested that he try illustrating children's books. His first assignment, Janice May Urdy's *Mean Mouse and Other Mean Stories* (1962), earned an American Institute of Graphic Arts award. Other illustration work drew on his Chinese background, including the papercuts and calligraphy. *Emperor and the Kite* (1967), edited by Jane Yolen, became a Caldecott Honor Book.

Zemach, Margot (1931 – 1989, b. California)
Margot Zemach used a Fulbright scholarship to study art at the Vienna Academy of Fine Arts. There she met fellow Fulbright scholar, Harvey Fischstrom. During her early career, she often worked with her husband and their collaborations were published under the name Harve Zemach. Twice nominated for the Hans Christian Andersen Award, which honors an artist for an entire body of work rather than an individual book, Zemach also received the 1974 Caldecott Medal for *Duffy and the Devil,* as well as many other citations for her work. Following her husband's death in 1974, Zemach concentrated on illustrating folk tales.

Margot Zemach

When the postwar baby boom hit the school room in the 1950s, it created its own tidal wave of demand for books that teach children to read.

From Dick and Jane to Dr. Seuss, the books geared to first grade readers, which focus on simple vocabulary and repeating words, became a huge part of the children's publishing industry from 1950 through the early 1970s.

For many collectors, these early books inspired their love of reading. They want copies to share with their children or grandchildren. School readers from the 1950s, featuring the angelic Dick and Jane, suddenly became a hot collector's item in the late 1990s, even inspiring their own book. *Growing Up With Dick and Jane*, which included Dick and Jane paper dolls as well as a sample reader, created many new collectors when it was published in 1996.

Dick and Jane Formula

Dick and Jane are much older than they look. Although most collectors are seeking the readers they first encountered in the 1950s, Dick and his sister Jane actually date back to 1927. Reading consultant Zerna Sharp pitched the idea of school readers that reflected the lives of the children reading them.

William Gray (the credited author on many Dick and Jane readers) was already developing books for publisher Scott, Foresman and Company that used big, colorful illustrations to convey the meaning of the story. Unlike the drab, black-and-white phonetic readers, such as McGuffey's, these books would teach "silent" reading where children could work out the meanings of words through a combination of pictures and repeating words.

Sharp's idea of using "real children" matched perfectly with this format. Dick and Jane were born, and their family would eventually grow to include a dog, a cat, a little sister, and parents. The simple, repeating vocabulary was based on words that children actually used in their conversations. The story situations, such as splashing in puddles, imitated real children's play.

Illustrator Eleanor Campbell added to the appeal by providing bright, full-color illustrations. Her lively children point, exclaim, and fall down with all the abandon of real children.

Philadelphia illustrator Campbell worked from snapshots of children and pets in her neighborhood. The kids acted out the story lines developed by the books' editorial team, and then Campbell refined her pictures from the photographs, giving the books their lively, true-life look.

1950s Readers

The boom years for the Scott Foresman readers occured in the 1950s. By that time, approximately 80% of all first-graders in the United States read Dick and Jane stories.

These readers formed part of what the publisher called the New Basic Reading Program. To make the teacher's job easier, Scott Foresman published pre-primers, primers, workbooks, word cards and charts, all featuring Dick and Jane, along with little sister Sally, the dog Spot, the kitten Puff, and, of course, Mother and Father.

Besides teaching reading, certain books were designed to promote personal safety (how to cross the street) or good health (drink your milk). These titles, *Good Times With Our Friends* and *Happy Times With Our Friends*, first appeared in 1948. Like the primers, these came with teacher's editions that discussed how to promote the ideas to the classroom.

Scott Foresman revised their books every five years, adding new words or updating illustrations to reflect changes in the American lifestyle. Illustrators used popular catalogs, such as Sears Roebuck, to create new dresses for Jane. Gauze bandages became Band-aids. The family also changed, slightly, to reflect the new looks. Grandma and Grandpa stopped wearing spectacles and started wearing denim jackets on the farm.

For collectors, these constant revisions mean that they may want to match their first grade year to the books collected, just to get the look they remember, or collect a set of the same primer reflecting the changes over the years.

While the basic school books, usually ex-classroom copies, show up frequently in the market, the supporting material such as the teacher's workbooks are much scarcer. These supplementary materials command higher prices from collectors because of their rarity.

John and Jean: The Catholic Readers

Parochial schools wanted to use the Scott Foresman readers but needed religious editions. So in 1930, Scot Foresman began to produce Dick and Jane stories with a religious theme for that market.

By the 1950s, Dick, Jane, and Sally had been rechristened John, Jean, and Judy for the Catholic readers. Spot and Puff kept their names. Primers like *We Come and Go* included revised stories about going to church or teaching the Nativity.

Scott Foresman also produced books for the Seventh Day Adventist market.

For Dick and Jane collectors, the parochial books may be harder to find, due to the smaller printings, but they may also have slightly lower prices. They're simply not as well known or as sought after as the regular primers.

Copycat Readers

Scott Foresman controlled the first grade textbook market by the 1950s, and their success did not go unnoticed.

A number of textbook publishers copied the look of Dick and Jane readers. These primers included such series as Alice and Jerry (Row, Peterson and Company); Susan and Tom (Ginn and Company); and Ned and Nancy (D.C. Heath and Company). Again, because of the smaller exposure, these readers generally don't command as high prices as the Dick and Jane readers in the secondary market, despite their rarity.

The most sucessful challenge to Scott Foresman's lock on first grade minds came not from a textbook publisher, but from a doctor named Seuss.

1957: The Cat in the Hat

By the end of the 1950s, Dick and Jane may have taken over the schools, but they'd gotten their knocks in the popular press. A number of newspaper and magazine critics attacked the first grade primer formula as bland, too literal, and showing uniformly dull little children. Such books, they claimed, lacked appeal for young readers.

William Spaulding, director of the educational division of Houghton Mifflin, asked popular picture book artist Ted Geisel, better known as Dr. Seuss, to come up with a picture book for the school trade. Spaulding wanted Geisel to use no more than 225 basic words in the text, like any first grade primer, but he also wanted that Seuss touch of nonsense. Spaulding asked for a book that first-graders couldn't put down.

Geisel took the list of words home, looked at it, and told his wife that it was impossible. But he kept coming back to the idea. He tossed the manuscript across the room more than once, but slowly the repeating rhymes of *The Cat in the Hat* came together. Houghton Mifflin brought out the school edition in 1957. Random House, Geisel's regular publisher, printed a trade edition at the same time.

Random House found themselves with a runaway hit on their hands. By 1960, they had sold nearly a million *Cats* in the $1.95 trade edition.

1958: Beginner Books

Editor Phyllis Cerf immediately recognized the potential of *The Cat in the Hat.* She asked her husband, publisher Bennet Cerf of Random House, to lend her his star author to start a new publishing venture. The new company would publish supplementary readers like *The Cat in the Hat* for the booming first grade market. Bennet Cerf agreed, on the condition that Random House retain the rights to distribution of the books.

Geisel agreed to take over as head of the new company as long as he and his wife Helen would be stockholders and equal partners in the enterprise. Phyllis Cerf agreed, Random House loaned them the start-up money, and Beginner Books was born.

Phyllis Cerf sat down and read every possible first grade primer in 1957 (including, one assumes, a lot of Dick and Jane). From this homework, she developed a list of 379 words that authors could use in the Beginner Books. No story was to exceed 200 words out of the 379, but authors could go outside the basic words for 20 "emergency words" to complete their story.

Cerf also found many of the contract authors and illustrators to write and design books. Manuscripts were then submitted to the Geisels for editorial work, with Helen Geisel often playing mediator between the strong-willed Phyllis Cerf and equally strong-willed Ted Geisel. Sometimes, the process was reversed, with the Geisels commissioning a work and Cerf giving the final editorial approval.

Both Helen and Ted Geisel would also write beginner books. Sometimes they worked under their own names or under various pseudonyms. Ted used LeSieg for books that he wrote but did not illustrate.

Cerf came up with the vocabulary list, but Ted Geisel developed the look of these new readers. Under Ted Geisel's direction, the formula of Beginner Books was simple: no more than one illustration on any page; the text should not describe anything not pictured; children should be able to work out the story from the illustrations as much as the text; and each pair of facing pages should act as an artistic unit.

Beginner Books launched four titles in 1958, with first printings of 60,000 copies each. It was a smash success, not only with parents but with the library and school trade.

By 1960, Beginner Books exceeded one million dollars a year in sales and already produced 18 titles. Random House bought back its runaway success by giving the principal shareholders stock in Random House. Phyllis Cerf and the Geisels continued to have editorial control over the books, until Cerf finally left Beginner Books in 1963 to move into another division of Random House.

Although most authors fussed about Cerf's vocabulary list and the restrictions of only using 200 words in their stories, Geisel designed a Beginner Book using only 50 vocabulary words. Done in response to a bet, *Green Eggs and Ham* (1961) had nothing to do with the safe world of Dick and Jane, but it certainly takes the idea of repeating simple words to its illogical limits.

A number of other authors and illustrators worked for Beginner Books over the years. One husband-and-wife team, Stan and Jan Berenstain, launched their famous Berenstain Bears as Beginner Books.

1965: Mike, Pam, and Penny

By the 1960s, Scott Foresman faced some serious competition in the beginning reader market. Schools and libraries were beginning to pick up the Beginner Books, such as *The Cat in the Hat*, which had much greater appeal to children than the somewhat staid Dick and Jane.

Educators, even those that deplored the frivolity of Seuss, were arguing for more multicultural, diverse textbooks to teach reading.

In 1965, Scott Foresman introduced the first black family into Dick and Jane's neighborhood. Big brother Mike had twin sisters, Pam and Penny, who appear to be about Sally's age. Mother and Father, like Dick and Jane's Mother and Father, have no first or last name.

The authors of *Growing Up With Dick and Jane* also noted that the Scott Foresman plots got slightly more mischievous. The children now used words like "Don't. Can't. No." Dick even dumped his ice cream cone on Tom's head, something that the children of the 1950s readers would never have done.

The 1965 editions of the Dick and Jane readers, even with their more diverse cast and slightly more complicated plots, came at the end of the primers' popularity. The pressure mounted, as reading scores dropped, to change how reading was taught in American schools.

A new television program, "Sesame Street," debuted in 1969, with a very different look and take on teaching reading. Muppets and their multicultural, inner-city world bear a greater resemblance to that Seuss approach to reading than the Dick and Jane format. In fact, Christopher Cerf, Phyllis's son, left Random House to work on the early Sesame Street, where he was joined by another Seuss editor, Mike Frith.

In 1970, instead of doing a five-year revision of their long-going primers, Scott Foresman retired the Dick and Jane books.

Beginner Books continued going strong, with new Dr. Seuss titles added to the series on a regular basis through the 1980s. At the time of Seuss' death in 1991, columnist Anna Quindlen eulogized his contribution to first graders, stating that Geisel would be best remembered "for the murder of Dick and Jane."

For collectors, however, both types of beginning readers remain enormously popular. Dick and Jane still command strong loyalty among their fans, as do the works of Random House's Beginner Books. As the children of the 1970s start their own collections, the same nostalgia adds an extra glow to the books of Big Bird and Oscar the Grouch.

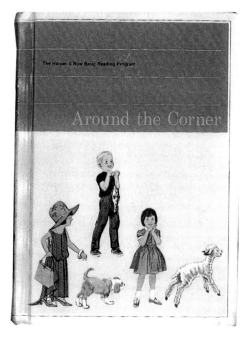

So when exactly is a first edition a first edition and how can you tell if your book is a first? Publishers and collectors do not necessarily mean the same thing when they discuss first editions — something that has led to considerable confusion for new collectors over the past few years.

For publishers, the term "first edition" indicates the first time that their company published an original work. The "edition" would not change until such time as the publisher substantially changed the work. An example of this would be *The Hobbit* by J.R.R. Tolkien, which was revised by the author in the mid-1960s to better fit into the larger Lord of the Rings sequence. This 1960s revision became known as the "second edition," so that all copies of the *Hobbit* printed from 1938 until those 1960s text changes could be classified as part of the first "edition," from the publisher's point-of-view.

For collectors, the designation of "first edition" has come to mean a book that was printed during the first run of the press or the "first printing." So only a *Hobbit* printed in 1938 would be seen as a "true" first edition and later printings would be later "editions" from the collector's point-of-view. Until the middle of the century, this information was not necessarily indicated by publishers in their books. Children's books, in particular, were often unmarked or poorly marked, even by publishers who were very careful in marking their adult novels.

In the 1970s, most publishers adopted a numeric or alphabetic system such as 1 2 3 4 5 6 7 8 9 or A B C D E. In most cases, the 1 or the A indicated a first printing (some exceptions are noted in the list below). The "1" was removed, as in 2 3 4 5 6 7 8 9, to indicate a second printing and so on. Sometimes publishers used numbers in an reverse pattern such as 10 9 8 7 6 5 4 3 2 1 or in an alternating pattern of odds and evens. In most cases, the appearance of the "1" or "A" still indicated a first printing, and a line starting or ending with the "2" or "B" a second printing and so on (see RANDOM HOUSE for one variation on this system).

Booksellers seem to fall somewhere between collectors and publishers in their definition of first editions. Today, most sellers catalog books as "first editions" if that information is clearly stated on the copyright page. They may also add such information as "first edition, first printing" if that information is available. For books with no clearly stated information on the copyright page, they will generally look to other factors to identify first editions, but may or may not be able to identify the first printing. In this case, they may still label the book a "first edition" following the publisher's definition of that term but give no indication of printing, or use phrases such as "first edition, early printing."

Collectors who only want "first printings" as opposed to "first editions" should state that desire clearly to the seller. In the case of famous books, many of the indications of a first printing, even if not stated by the publisher, have been cataloged by magazines such as *Firsts* or collector's clubs such as the International Wizard of Oz Club. Doing the research can make a difference of hundreds of dollars for very famous books (and no difference at all for obscure titles!).

In the case of this price guide, we use "first edition" to indicate the first time that the book was published in the country of the publisher. So first editions are either the American first edition or the British first edition even if not specifically stated as such. We do not distinguish which was actually published first if they came out in the same year.

We took "first edition thus" to be the first time published in a particular format by a publisher where significant changes from the original work had occurred (usually a change of illustrations).

Some people use "first edition thus" to indicate a change of publisher. This can be confusing to collectors. Most collectors and booksellers call such books "reprints" if no significant change has taken place i.e., a Grosset book in a series such as Famous Horse Stories is most often classified as a reprint, not a "first edition thus." Some publishers, like Holt and Greenwillow, will indicate the original publisher on their copyright page for reprints. Some just give the year of the original copyright.

A paperback, if containing the same information as the original hardcover, is seen as a reprint and not as a "first edition thus." Only those books issued originally in softcover would be classified as "first editions" in the paperback form.

Throughout this guide, "first editions" and "first editions thus" were used for books that were either marked first printings or had no subsequent printings indicated on the copyright page. For example, if the copyright page stated "first published 1951" and "reprinted 1954" then we would see that as a later edition.

The following information shows some of the ways that collectors and booksellers generally identify first editions and first printings for various publishers. These points apply only to books published after 1950. Publishers changed systems often (see Volume 1 of our *Collector's Guide* for first edition markings for earlier periods). Always there are exceptions to the rule, and the books listed in our bibliography explore these points in far greater depth than we can provide in the space allotted.

Caldecott and Newbery books: Collectors should also remember that changes in dust jackets may indicate later printings. The most obvious clue is the appearance of the Caldecott or Newbery medal on the dust jacket. These awards are always given after the book has been published and do not appear on the dust jackets until several months to a year after the first printing.

ISBN numbers did not start appearing on book jackets or copyright pages until the late 1960s (see Glossary) and bar codes appeared even later.

Experienced booksellers and collectors also date books by examining the type of paper used in the text and the dust jacket and the type of cover material. Although this can seem a little daunting to a new collector, we suggest regular browsing through bookstores and other people's collections to get the "feel" of the books from a particular era. The more examples that you see from a particular era, the easier it becomes to spot books from the same time period.

Following is general information to help the collector identify marking systems for first editions used by specific publishers:

ABELARD-SCHUMAN
Copyright page may state "First Published" followed by the year. First editions may also be indicated by having no additional information about printing on the copyright page.

ALADDIN BOOKS
"First Edition" is usually stated.

APPLETON-CENTURY-CROFTS
The same date on the title page and copyright page at the front of the book usually indicated a first edition after the 1950s. In some cases, a first edition may have had no additional information about printings on the copyright page.

ATHENEUM
This publisher stated on the copyright page "First Edition" or "First American Edition." They did not adopt a numeric system for printings until the mid-1980s.

ATLANTIC MONTHLY PRESS
First editions are stated on the copyright page.

BLACKIE & SON
An English publisher, Blackie reprinted a number of classic tales as well as new works, and printings/editions were rarely indicated. The words "First published" followed by the year and no other information may indicate a first edition, according to McBride (see Bibliography).

BROCKHAMPTON
First editions should state "first published" followed by year and no other information on the copyright page.

BOBBS-MERRILL
Besides doing originals, Bobbs-Merrill often acted as a reprint publisher for classic children's books or for books originally published in England (see SLEIGH, Barbara). First editions may not be clearly marked, and the copyright dates often refer to the original copyright rather than the year printed by Bobbs-Merrill.

BODLEY-HEAD
The copyright information usually indicated "First Published" or "First Edition Published" followed by the date and no other information.

BOOK CLUB/BOOK OF THE MONTH CLUB
Book club editions sometimes have a depression or imprint on the bottom of the right-hand corner of the back cover (this is more common in adult than juvenile fiction) — it should be noted that many publishers like Knopf use such a mark on their trade editions. The BOMC notation or the words "book club edition" often appear on the lower corner of the inside flap of the dust jacket. Book club editions generally fall into the same price range as reprints for collectors and booksellers. See also WEEKLY READER.

BUCCANEER
A reprint house, Buccaneer started re-issuing a number of hard-to-find children's books in the 1990s. Their books are clearly marked, lack dust jackets, and should be priced as modern reprints in the secondary market.

JONATHAN CAPE (CAPE)
The UK division used "first published" followed by the year and no other information on the copyright page for most first editions.

CASSELL & CO. (CASSELL)
Through the mid-1950s, the copyright pages of first editions should have no information other than the year of copyright. Later first editions may

state "first published" followed by the year.

CENTURY CO.
The copyright page usually shows the date of the first printing as well as any successive printing. First printings should show one date only.

CHILTON
Books usually stated "first edition" or "first published" with no additional printings indicated.

COWARD McCANN & GEOGHEGAN
The words "first edition," or "first edition" followed by the year were used, but some first editions simply show no other printings on the copyright page.

THOMAS Y. CROWELL COMPANY (CROWELL)
First editions probably show only the copyright notice on the copyright page. "Second Printing," etc. on the copyright page would indicate subsequent printings. When a numeric system was used, the "1" indicated a first printing.

DIAL PRESS
The date on the title page and the copyright page usually match for first editions printed prior to 1966. After that time, the words "First Published" followed by a date appeared on the copyright page.

DODD, MEAD AND COMPANY
This publisher noted second and later printings on the copyright page. If no such information appears, the book is probably a first edition. The numeric system was adopted in 1976.

DOUBLEDAY
First editions are usually marked on the copyright page. A numeric system may appear also.

DUELL, SLOAN AND PEARCE
First editions may state "First Edition" on the copyright page. If the copyright page has a numeric sequence, the Roman numeral "I" marks a first edition.

E.P. DUTTON & COMPANY, INC (DUTTON)
Copyright page may state "First Edition," but some firsts simply show no further information on this page except the date of copyright. Subsequent printings are usually noted on the copyright page.

FABER & FABER
A variety of systems was used to indicate first editions including "first published" followed by the year; "first published" followed by month and year; or just the words "first published."

FARRAR, STRAUS or FARRAR, STRAUS & GIROUX
Their books generally state "First Published" or "First Edition" on copyright page. Some books that were originally published elsewhere, such as Tanith Lee's *Dragon Hoard*, state "First American Edition."

FREDERICK WARNE & CO., LTD
Later reprints of their classic titles, such as the Beatrix Potter books, usually stated the date of printing on the copyright page. This publisher has been very inconsistent in marking first editions. Unless the printing is clearly stated on copyright page, it is extremely difficult to distinguish first printings from later printings.

FUNK & WAGNALLS
A Roman numeral "I" appearing on copyright page indicated a first edition, as did the words "first published" followed by the month and year (and no other information). In the 1970s, the company switched to a numeric system.

GARDEN CITY PUBLISHING COMPANY
This American publisher largely reprinted classic children's works, although they occasionally commissioned new illustrations for a work (a "first edition thus"). Copyright dates may be the date of the original copyright or the date that Garden City copyrighted their edition but are rarely an accurate reflection of the year printed.

GARRARD PUBLISHING
No additional publishing dates would be listed on the copyright page for a first edition.

GOLDEN PRESS, LITTLE GOLDEN BOOKS
This publisher uses an alphabetic sequence with an "A" indicated a first printing. The "A" may appear on the title page, the copyright page or the last page of the book. For the Little Golden series, the "A" often is hidden by the binding.

GREENWILLOW
This publisher of young adult fantasy did both original works and many reprints. Their reverse numeric system indicates printing with the "1" indicating a first printing for both originals and reprints. Read the copyright page carefully, as it often starts with the original copyright date, then the date when published by the original publisher, and then lists in small print below that the date of the Greenwillow copyright for reprints.

GROLIER

Generally printing information was not included on copyright page. Only a change of text would create a "second edition" designation.

GROSSET & DUNLAP (GROSSET)

Book printed by this publisher may be originals or reprints of works purchased from other publishers. Copyright information almost always refers to the original copyright date of the work and cannot be used as a reliable guide for the year of printing. For series books, such as HARDY BOYS or NANCY DREW, collectors generally identify first editions as books that only show the titles published in the same year as the copyright date.

HARCOURT, BRACE

The words "First Edition" may appear on the copyright page and subsequent printings are usually noted.

HARPER & BROTHERS

First edition indicated on the copyright page. The publisher used an alphabetical code to indicate the actual month and year of printing.

HARPER & ROW

In 1962, Harper merged with the textbook publisher, Row, Peterson & Company and began using the imprint Harper & Row. For this imprint, "first edition" was printed on the back of the title page for firsts published in the early 1960s. The company started using a numeric code for printings in the late 1960s which would appear on the last page of the text.

HARPER & ROW, PETERSON

"First edition" or a numeric code was used.

HASTINGS HOUSE

Printing information often appeared on the dust jacket.

HAWTHORN BOOKS

The first edition information followed by month and year was stated on the copyright page. Some books may use a numeric code.

WILLIAM HEINEMANN (HEINEMANN)

This British publisher used "First published" followed by the year on their copyright page. No other information usually appeared on first editions, and later printings clearly stated "reprinted" followed by the year. Like many English and some Australian publishers, the price was printed on the lower (not upper) corner of the inside dust jacket flap, so a clipped dust jacket does not necessarily indicate a book club edition.

HODDER & STOUGHTON (HODDER)

The copyright page of a first edition usually stated "first published" followed by the year or "first printed" followed by the year and no other information.

HOLIDAY HOUSE

This publisher did a number of classic works with new illustrations ("first editions thus") as well as other books. Many of their books have stayed in print for decades. The date on the copyright page usually refers to the original copyright by Holiday rather than the date of printing.

HENRY HOLT AND COMPANY (HOLT)

The copyright notice usually stated "First Printing" or "First Edition." Copyright information clearly indicated reprints of earlier works when appropriate.

HOLT, RINEHART AND WINSTON

The copyright page stated when the book was first published and any subsequent printings. For example, books in the PRYDAIN series have later printings clearly labeled as "fourth printing, March 1969" and so on.

HOUGHTON MIFFLIN COMPANY

The term "First Printing" was commonly used from the late 1950s to the early 1970s. Later books used a number sequence with "1" indicating a first edition.

ALFRED A. KNOPF (KNOPF)

The term "First Edition" was used. A numeric sequence may be used on the back page. The same date on the title page and the copyright page might be used to indicate a first edition. We've also seen date codes on the back flap of Knopf dust jackets from the mid-1970s.

J.B. LIPPINCOTT COMPANY (LIPPINCOTT)

The words "Second Printing," "Third Printing," and so on indicated later printings. First editions may be marked "first edition" or "printed" followed by the original month and year (matches copyright date) or by a numeric system.

LITTLE, BROWN

For the time period covered in this guide, the most common wording on the copyright page was "First Printing" or "First Edition."

LITTLE GOLDEN BOOKS

See GOLDEN PRESS

MACMILLAN COMPANY (US)
From the 1950s through the 1970s, the copyright page stated the month and year of publication or the words "first published" were used with this information. Later printings and revisions are usually noted below this date. A numeric code was adopted in the early 1970s. The British and Canadian companies did not always use the "first printed" or "published" designation. First editions for these companies may simply have no additional printing information on the copyright page.

McGRAW-HILL BOOK COMPANY, INC.
"First Edition" may be indicated on the title page for books printed after 1957. Otherwise a single date of printing on the copyright page probably indicated a first. The company started using a numeric system in the 1970s.

DAVID McKAY COMPANY (McKAY)
In the 1950s, the publisher would usually indicate subsequent printings on the copyright page. A numbering system was adopted in the 1970s.

MEREDITH PRESS
The copyright page usually stated first edition or "first published" followed by the year.

WILLIAM MORROW AND COMPANY (MORROW)
Through the 1950s and 1960s, subsequent printings or editions were clearly marked "Second Printing" or "Second Edition" and so on. First printings usually had no additional information on the copyright page. In 1973, the publisher started using a numeric sequence where the "1" indicated a first edition.

W.W. NORTON (Norton)
This publisher usually indicated "first edition" or used a numeric code.

PANTHEON BOOKS
Until the mid-1960s, no additional information would appear on the copyright page of first editions. After 1965, "first printing" or "first American edition" or "first edition" would be used.

PARENTS' MAGAZINE PRESS
Many books were reprints (see also WEEKLY READER CLUB) although they did originals, as well as the first hardcover editions of works originally published in softcover. Later printings should be indicated on copyright page. A numeric system was not adopted until after 1975.

PRENTICE-HALL
This publisher used several systems. Later printings were often noted on the copyright page. A first edition could have no information past the copyright date or it could say "first printed" or it could show "1" in the number line.

G.P. PUTNAM'S SONS (PUTNAM)
The copyright page may state "First Edition" but this publisher also used other systems. If the date on the title page and the date on the copyright page match, it is probably a first edition. Later printings may be indicated by such terms as "second impression" and so on appearing on the copyright page.

RAND MCNALLY
Original works usually state "first published" followed by the year, or use an alphabetical code with "A" indicating the first printing. This publisher also purchased the Oz series from Reilly & Lee and issued a number of reprints of those books.

RANDOM HOUSE
This publisher used a variety of systems for its children's books. Series such as the Black Stallion novels clearly state "first printing" or subsequent printings on the copyright page. However picture books such as the Dr. Seuss books often have no printing information and the date/printing must be guessed from the title lists, dust jacket prices, and other such clues. After 1968, the words "First Printed" or "First Edition" appear in the copyright page of many Random House books (and disappear from subsequent printings). The number sequence adopted in the 1970s, unlike that of most publishers, uses the words "First Edition" and "2" in the number line to indicate first editions ("1" never appears).

REILLY & LEE COMPANY
Reprints of the company's classic series, such as the Oz books, do not indicate the actual year of printing or any other information beyond the original copyright date. Books printed in the 1960s may still show the original copyright dates of 1912 and so on. Collectors date these books by the cover designs, dust jacket prices, and other information (see Oz in series section).

ST. MARTIN'S PRESS
First editions should have no other indication of an additional printing on the copyright page. Like many publishers, St. Martin's adopted a numeric system in the late 1970s.

SCRIBNER'S
The company used the letter "A" on the copyright

page to indicate many first editions. The "A" may be followed by the publisher's code for the location and date of printing. The company went to a numeric system in the mid-1970s.

SIMON & SCHUSTER

"First Edition" or "First Printing" appeared on copyright pages from 1952 to the early 1970s. Later printings and date would usually be shown. A numeric system was adopted in the 1970s that used "1" to indicate a first printing.

HENRY Z. WALCK (WALCK)

This British publisher often showed their original date on the title page; it should match the original copyright date on the back of the title page for a first edition. Reprints or later printings were noted on the copyright page. Books such as the Moomin series list the original date of the Finnish copyright, the date of original English publication, and reprint information on the copyright page.

VIKING PRESS, INC.

The copyright page usually states "First Published in ..." followed by the year and no other information. Viking book club editions also have this information on the copyright page and are only identified on the dust jacket (front flap).

WEEKLY READER CHILDREN'S BOOK CLUB

These book club editions show the original publisher on the spine, such as Doubleday or Scribners, but are clearly marked in several places: back cover, title page, and copyright page. They are considered book club editions (reprints) by collectors and not true first editions, even when this is the first time that the book appeared in hardcover.

WHITMAN

This publisher issued many reprints of children's classics as well as original series. Copyright information almost always refers to the original copyright date of the title and cannot be used as a reliable guide for the year of printing.

Annuals: Books issued once a year that collected the works published in a magazine. Most commonly for this time period, these refer to the collections of newspaper comic strips or magazine stories published in Great Britain.

Board: The paste-boards were covered with another material to form the hardcover of a book, leading to the terms such as "cloth bound" or "paper over board."

Board books: The books were originally designed for very small children. Each page is made of a stiff "board" material that babies and toddlers can handle without tearing. Board books became very popular at the end of the 1970s and continue to be a major part of publishing for small children today. It's not unusual to find board books with teething marks.

Cloth binding, cloth hardcover, clothbound: Cloth wrapped around a "board" (usually paste-board or another stiff base) and glued on the edges to form a cover. See also "pictorial cover" and "laminated cover."

Color plate: Color plates are colored pictures printed on a glossy paper that is different from the paper used for the text. This technique was extremely popular for children's books at the beginning of the century but was used less during the period covered in this guide.

Collage: Collage pictures are usually created by tearing pieces of paper and arranging them into shapes (see Eric Carle in Illustrators section).

Copyright date: The copyright date indicates when the publisher or author registered the copyright for a work, but not necessarily the date that the book was printed. For example, most Grosset & Dunlap series books show the original date that the book was copyrighted and not necessarily the date that it was issued. See also first edition.

Copyright page: Generally, the copyright page is located on the back of the title page. However, this term is used for any page that shows the copyright information. Some publishers, such as Garden City, put this information on the title page. Picture books may have this information on the title page, the endpapers, or hidden somewhere in the back depending on the design of the book.

Dust jacket, dust wrapper, dust cover: The loose paper cover used to both protect and advertise the book's contents. See also "pictorial cover" and "laminated cover."

Edition: see "first edition."

Endpapers: The double leaves (pages) added at the front and back during the binding process. The outer leaf is pasted to the inner surface of the cover, while the inner leaf forms the first or last page of the book. Endpapers can be plain or form a double-page illustration related to the text. Sometimes they are called endleaves. See also "flyleaf."

Errata: Errors made in the printing or binding of the book. Sometimes, the errata can be used to identify first editions as such mistakes are usually corrected by the publisher as soon as possible.

Ex-library: This term applies to a book that has been removed from the collection of a public library. Ex-library editions are usually priced far less than originals because they have been altered or marked by the library. They might be rebound by the library, have cards pasted over the endpapers, or be stamped with the library's name throughout the text. See also "library binding."

First edition: A first edition is generally defined to be the first time that a book appeared in print. See Identifying First Editions section for more information.

Flyleaf: The blank loose page found in the front or back of the book is often described as the flyleaf. See also "endpaper."

Folio: The largest size paper sheet used by printers to make a book. The term is also used by book dealers to designate books that are over 13 inches in height. See also "size."

Frontispiece: The illustration that faces the title-page of the book.

Gilt edges, gilt lettering: When the letters are printed with gold-colored, metallic ink, the book has "gilt lettering." Gilt lettering usually appears on the cover. Gilt edges refer to pages with gold decoration on the edge of the paper.

Hardcover, hardback: A book with stiff cover created from "boards." Almost all the prices in this guide refer to hardcover editions of a title.

ISBN: The International Standard Book Number (ISBN) system was adopted between 1967 and 1969 by publishers in Great Britain and North America. Each book is assigned a unique series of digits, such as 0-89145-717-8 (the ISBN for our first book). This information was usually printed on the copyright page and also the dust jacket. The number is changed when the publisher changes the binding (a paperback is assigned a different number from the hardback edition). The number will also be changed when the book is reprinted by another publisher (the Macmillan edition would have a different number from the Grosset & Dunlap edition of the same title). A new ISBN will be assigned if the book goes through a rewrite or other changes that make the book a new "edition" from the publishers' point-of-view. The ISBN does not usually change between printings. RR Bowker assigns and tracks the ISBN for American publishers. The Standard Book Numbering Agency Ltd. in the United Kingdom tracks the British ISBN. See also "Library of Congress" and "SBN."

Laminated covers: These are hardcovers issued with pictorial covers that have been laminated with a shiny clear gloss coating over the cover. Many of the Whitman books were issued with laminated covers. See also "pictorial cover."

Library binding: As books are worn by library patrons, they may be rebound. These library bindings replaced the original binding, and often required the page edges to be trimmed slightly from the original size. Library bindings are usually easy to spot because they are of a thicker, more durable material than regular book covers (bright orange seems a popular color). The library bindings do not have the usual publisher marks on the spine and cover. They also considerably reduce the price of the book (see also "ex-library"). Sometimes, library binding may also refer to the reinforced binding used by the publishers; this type of binding does not reduce the value of the book as it generally looks just like the regular trade edition.

Library of Congress catalog card number, LOC number: The card number assigned by the Library of Congress started appearing regularly in books around 1960. Eventually this information was replaced by the Library of Congress Cataloging-in-Publication Data (a paragraph that looks like a library card) in the late 1970s. This information appears on the copyright page and is just one of the many clues that can be used to date a book when the date of printing is unclear. Publishers of childrens' books were very inconsistent during the early days of this system (and the SBN), so these dates should be used as a general guideline only.

Limited edition: This type of book was issued in a limited number of copies.

No date: In this guide and most dealer catalogs, "no date" means a book that has no date of publication printed on the copyright or title page.

Paper boards, paper covered: The paper boards are the stiff material that forms the outer cover of a book. Generally, these are made from paste boards (layers of paper). When used by a dealer to describe the cover of a book, this generally means that the boards are plain and not covered by cloth. This is different from a paperback (see "softcover").

Paperback: A small book issued with a soft cover is usually called a paperback. The standard size is approximately 4.25 inches by 6.5 inches, but children's books, such as the Scholastic paperbacks, may be slightly larger. Unless specifically noted, we did not price paperbacks in this guide. See also "softcover."

Picture book: In this text, a picture book is a book that relies mostly on pictures to convey the story to very young readers.

Pop-ups: These three-dimensional pictures have been cut and glued so they "pop up" when the book is opened. The term is also used as a name for books illustrated by this type of picture.

Pictorial Cover: A hardcover, usually issued without a dust jacket, decorated with a printed picture on the front cover. The 1960s Nancy Drew books were issued as pictorial covers. Many picture books were printed as pictorial covers but issued with a dust jacket. If the dust jacket and cover have the same illustration, the hardcover is often referred to as "same as" pictorial cover. See also "laminated covers" and "dust jackets."

Price clipped: In many cases, dust jackets had the price clipped off them before being given as gifts. Some collectors are looking for completely intact dust jackets, some don't care if the price is clipped as long as it doesn't affect the look of the dust jacket. Generally this is considered a minor fault on dust jackets, but something that should be noted if you are selling a book.

Provenance: The pedigree of a book's ownership presented by a dealer. We did not look at the provenance of books when creating this guide and this type of information should be treated like an author's signature, something that takes the book outside the normal realm of pricing.

Re-backed: When the spine or backstrip of a book has been replaced, the book is called "re-backed."

SBN: Standard Book Number (SBN) was the forerunner of the ISBN and appeared on copyright pages mostly in the mid-1960s. See also "ISBN."

Series: A set of books with an on-going theme, a continuation of stories about specific characters, or a label put on a set of books by a publisher, can be defined as a series.

Set: Several books meant to be sold together, typically in sets of six or twelve volumes.

Size: In this guide, we've tried to stay with general terms like "oversize" or "small." Some dealers use "folio" or "quarto" to refer to size. These terms originally referred to the size of the paper sheet on which the book was printed and the number of times that sheet was folded to form the book. There is much debate over the proper use of these terms, so we have avoided them whenever possible. See also abbreviations below.

Softcover: A "softcover" book is one that is issued with a soft outer cover but is larger than the standard paperback (this book is a softcover). Today, booksellers and publishers may use the term "trade paperback" to refer to softcovers of a medium size (approximately six inches by nine inches). Unless specifically noted, we did not price softcovers in this guide.

Spine: The spine is the part of the book which is visible when the book is closed and placed on the shelf.

Volume: As used in this guide, a volume generally means one book in a set, such as a volume in a set of encyclopedias.

Wood-block, wood-cut: A wood-block illustration is originally created by carving the picture on a wooden block and then printing the page (for late 20th century, these pictures are then photographed and reproduced in the mass market printing). Generally, this type of picture has a very strong, bold line and is fairly easy to spot when

looking at picture books. Frasconi (see Illustrators) used the wood block technique to create many of his picture books.

ABBREVIATIONS

Many dealers use abbreviations to describe books and their conditions in their catalogs and Internet listings. The abbreviations listed below seem to be the most commonly used, but be aware that dealers often invent their own abbreviations or use a standard abbreviation for another meaning. When in doubt, query first, especially if this information makes a difference in the desirability of the book for you.

4to – Quarto, usually meaning quarto sized (approximately 12" tall)

8to – Octavo, usually meaning octavo sized (approximately 9" tall)

12mo – Twelvemo or duodecimo, usually meaning approximately 7" tall

16mo - Sixteenmo, usually meaning 5½" tall.

(**Special note on sizes:** librarians, bibliographical references, and many antiquarian booksellers use 4to, etc., to refer to the original size of the paper and the number of folds taken by the printer, rather than the height of the book. It is wise to check how a particular dealer is using the term.)

Anon., anony. – Anonymous author.

BCE – Book club edition.

Bndg. – Binding.

BW, b/w – Black-and-white, as in black-and-white illustrations.

C. – Copyright date (c. 1967) or circa, meaning about that time (c. 1970s). One of those abbreviations that you want to doublecheck. Some dealers also use "ca" for circa.

Ca. – Circa (approximate date or era).

CP – Copyright page.

Cond. – Condition.

DJ, dw, dc – Dust jacket, dust wrapper, or dust cover.

Ed. – Editor or edited by as in "short stories ed. Andre Norton."

Ex. lib., exlib, ex-lib – Ex-library.

F. – Fine, describing condition.

FAE – First American edition.

FE – First edition rather than fine edition (but doublecheck if unsure).

Fly, fr. fly, r. fly – Flyleaf, front flyleaf, rear flyleaf.

Fr. – Front or frontispiece.

G, gd – Good, describing condition.

Ill., illus. – Illustrated or illustrations: "illus. by M. Sendak"

Lg., lge. – Large

Lt. – Light: "lt. marks on dust jacket."

Ltd. – Limited, referring to edition.

Med. – Medium size.

NAP – No additional printing, i.e., no additional printings shown on copyright page.

ND, nd – No date, usually means no date of printing available

Obl. – Oblong, as in a book that is wider than it is tall.

O.P., OOP – Out of print.

PC, p.c. – Price clipped as in "dust jacket pc"

Phots., photos – Photographs, referring to illustrations.

Pg., pgs. – Page, pages

Pub., pu. – Published, as in "pu. 1967" or publisher as in "pub. Random House."

Prtg. – Printing such as "first prtg."

Qto. – Quarto, often used for quarto-sized (approx. 12" tall)

Rev. – Revised, referring to edition.

Rpt. – Reprint or reprinted as in "rept. by G&D" (reprint by Grosset & Dunlap).

Sigd., sgd., /s/ – Signed as in "sigd. by author." May also use sig. for signature.

Sm. – Small

Sp. – Spine as in "dust jacket sp torn"

SS, ss – short stories as in "ss by various authors."

TP – Title page.

Trans. – Translator or translated by.

V., v. – Very.

VG, vg – Very good.

VG/VG, G/VG, etc. – Refers to condition of book and dust jacket. The first is used for a very good edition, very good dust jacket. A reference like VG/0 usually means that there is no dust jacket available, but this is one of those abbreviations that it is wise to doublecheck.

Vol. – Volume, referring to a single book in a set.

W/ or w/o – With or without.

Internet, Newsletters, and Other Resources

For collectors, there is a variety of resources to help find used bookstores, chat with other collectors, research titles, and swap want lists. Below you'll find Internet resources, newsletters, and some other research tools that we've enjoyed or that have been recommended to us by other collectors.

If you are connected to a commercial on-line service such as America Online, check the members' bulletin boards for areas of interest to book collectors.

If you have found another resource for children's book collectors, we would like to hear from you. You can reach us at lostlvs@aol.com or write to: Rosemary Jones, P.O. Box 9432, Seattle, WA 98109.

Internet Newsgroups
Book Collecting
rec.books.collecting

This very busy Internet newsgroup spends most of its time discussing issues of interest to collectors. Everything from getting musty smells out of old books to identifying first editions can turn up during the day. The group strongly protests any type of "for sale" or "for auction" notice being posted. The FAQs (frequently asked questions) are posted on a regular basis and contain many useful tips for book collectors.

Children's Books
rec.arts.books.childrens

This Internet newsgroup discusses everything from new titles to collecting various series books. Members are extremely helpful in identifying books, and this is one of our favorite places to describe that book that we read in childhood but can't remember the title or author. Like most Internet newsgroups, advertising is not welcome, and you should read a few messages before posting, or check the group's FAQ file. "For Sale" (FS) notices have been actively discouraged by many participants.

Marketplace
rec.arts.books.marketplace

This is the one newsgroup where any individual can post For Sale (FS) and Want To Buy (WTB) notices without any fear of flaming. Regard this newsgroup as an unregulated electronic flea market and take the usual precautions before sending money or credit card numbers.

Nancy Drew
alt.books.nancy-drew

Besides discussing everybody's favorite girl sleuth, members of this newsgroup are very knowledgeable about series books, Hardy Boys, and other topics of interest to fans of the Stratmeyer Syndicate.

Internet Sites For Research:
Bowker's Out-of-Print Database
http://www.reedref.com/bowker/index.html

The official (U.S.) Books-Out-Of-Print database allows users to search by author, title, subject, series or ISBN. Bowker also publishes a number of books of interest to the children's book collector; the index should contain links to their catalog of printed material. The out-of-print database is most useful for fairly recent children's books. You will be given a user ID and password the first time that you sign on. No charge for this service at this time, but like all Web resources, this may be subject to change. Many public libraries also have this information available through their computer systems.

International Book Collectors Association
http://www.rarebooks.com

This large web site contains many topics of interest to collectors including lists of award winners, identification of first editions, and links to many more sites.

Library of Congress
http://www.loc.gov/

The Library of Congress offers an on-line version of their catalog. This is a useful tool for searching for more information about books if you don't have the full name of the author or only the title. Many collectors use it for finding other titles written by a favorite author.

Internet Sites For Buying And Selling Books:

Many collectors now use the Internet as a major source for books. Below, we've listed web sites that we use or have had recommended to us by other collectors.

Some web sites listed are professional services where dealers pay to list their catalogs. The customer makes arrangements directly with the bookseller, usually a store, for payment and shipping. Others, like Bookfinder, help you search through all the services and compare prices. Still others, like e-Bay, give collectors a chance to buy and sell directly with fellow enthusiasts.

Addall
http://www.addall.com/

Like Bookfinder, Addall allows you to search multiple sites and compare prices. The sites searched in 1999 included ABE, Alibris, Antiq-Book, Bibliocity, Bibliofind, Gutenberg Holdings, and Powell's.

Advanced Book Exchange
http://www.abebooks.com/

At ABE, you can search for out-of-print books by author, title, or other factors such as illustrators or category, through the on-line catalogs of thousands of book dealers. Searches are free, and you can leave free want lists on the database. You will receive direct e-mail notification if a "match" occurs any time that a dealer posts a book that you wanted. When ordering books, you deal directly with the bookstore rather than the web service so there is no middleman mark-up.

Alibris
http://www.alibris.com/

Unlike ABE or Bibliofind, when you order a book for Alibris, you pay the web service directly, they order the book from the dealer for you, ship it into their warehouse to check condition, and then ship it out to you. The service may cost you a little more but if you're nervous about buying through the Internet, this site offers all sorts of security features and guarantees.

Amazon Auctions
http://auctions.amazon.com/

Like e-Bay's auctions, Amazon provides a forum for individual sellers to offer items for auction. The terms of payment, shipping, and so on are arranged directly between the seller and buyer.

Antiquarian Booksellers Association
http://www.abaa-booknet.com/booknetl.html

The homepage of the Antiquarian Booksellers Association of America serves as a great launching place to search for antiquarian book dealers or bookfairs in your area. The ABAA site has links to their member booksellers with catalogs on the Web, information about book fairs throughout the country, a directory of member booksellers by region or specialty, and links to international organizations of booksellers.

Bibliocity
http://www.bibliocity.com/

Like ABE or Bibliofind, Bibliocity allows you to search through the databases of their member bookstores. The site also contains a page with links to current book auctions at the major auction houses such as Bloomsbury Book Auctions; Butterfield & Butterfield; Pacific Book Auctions; Sotheby's, and many more.

Bibliofind
http://www.bibliofind.com/

Like ABE, Bibliofind lets you search for free through the on-line catalogs of their members and leave free want lists. Once you find a book, you deal directly with the member bookstore.

Bookfinder.com
http://www.bookfinder.com

Bookfinder searches through a variety of Internet databases such as ABE and Bibliofind. This is a good way to do some quick comparison shopping (you still have to go to the other sites to order the books).

Booksales
http://www.book-sales-in-america.com/

This site helps you locate library and other non-profit groups' book sales in the US. Just click on your region and see what's going on.

e-Bay
http://www.e-bay.com/

This popular auction site has literally hundreds of children's books for sale every day. If you win an auction by having the highest bid, you are responsible for making arrangements with the seller for payment. Anybody can offer books for sale through this service.

Pacific Book Auction Galleries
http://www.pacificbook.com/

This San Francisco auction house specializes in books. Auctions may be one famous collection from a single source or several small collections grouped around a theme such as the Oz series. In 1999, PBA started offering on-line bidding. When purchasing books, you deal directly with the auction house. The terms of sales and guarantees on book descriptions are fully explained on their site. The site also contains information on their regular auctions and how to sell large collections through their services.

Library Research

If you're doing research in a public or university library, ask if they subscribe to the CD-ROM called Children's Reference Plus. This CD is updated annually and contains information from several Bowker reference works including *Fiction,*

Folklore, Fantasy and Poetry for Children 1876 – 1985; Children's Books in Print; and *Books Out of Print* (children's section).

See also our bibliography for a listing of favorite reference books available through most public libraries.

Newsletters

Firsts: The Book Collector's Magazine
www.firsts.com
This magazine covers all aspects of book collecting with a special emphasis on the identification of first editions. Issues will often focus on a single author or subject area. Subscription information is available by writing *Firsts* Magazine, Dept. I, P.O. Box 65166 , Tucson, AZ 85728 or at their web site: www.firsts.com

Martha's KidLit Newsletter
http:// www.kidlitonline.com
This monthly printed newsletter covers a wide variety of topics concerning children's books including auction news, exhibitions, biographies of authors and illustrators, and tips for collectors. The web site contains sample articles as well as links to other sites. For current subscription rates, check the web site or write to: Martha's KidLit Newsletter, Box 1488, Ames, IA 50014.

Updates

Lost Loves Collector Guide's Link Page
http://members.aol.com/lostlvs/links.htm
This is the web site where the authors of this guide maintain links to various web sites mentioned here. Check here for updates and new resources.

Billman, Carol, *Secret of the Stratemeyer Syndicate,* 1986 Ungar Publishing.

Doyle, Brian, *Who's Who of Children's Literature,* 1968 Schocken Books.

Feaver, William, *When We Were Young: Two Centuries of Children's Book Illustration*, 1977 Holt, Rinehart and Winston.

Hanrahan, Joyce, *Works of Maurice Sendak, 1947 – 1994.*

Haviland, Virginia, editor, *Children's Literature,* 1966 Library of Congress.

Horne, Alan, *Dictionary of 20th Century British Book Illustrators*, 1994 Antique Collector's Club, Woodbridge Suffolk, UK.

Houfe, Simon, *Dictionary of British Book Illustrators and Caricaturists 1800 – 1914*, 1981 (revised edition) Antique Collector's Club, Woodbridge Suffolk UK.

Kismaric, Carole and Marvin Heiferman, *Growing Up With Dick and Jane,* 1996 Collins.

Lanes, Selma G., *Art of Maurice Sendak,* 1980 Harry N. Abrams, Inc.

Lynn, Ruth Nadelman, *Fantasy Literature for Children and Young Adults: An Annotated Bibliography,* 4th edition. 1995, R.R. Bowker.

Mahoney, Bertha, and Elinor Whitney, *Realms of Gold in Children's Books,* 1930 Doubleday.

Marcus, Leonard, *75 Years of Children's Book Week Posters*, 1994 Alfred A. Knopf, New York.

McBride, Bill, *Pocket Guide to the Identification of First Editions*, 1995 McBride/Publisher, West Hartford.

McBride, Bill, *Points of Issue*, 1996 McBride/Publisher.

Meyer, Susan E., *America's Great Illustrators*, 1978 H. N. Abrams, NY.

Miller, Betha E. Mahoney, editor, *Illustrators of Children's Books, 1744 – 1945*, 1947 Horn Book.

Morgan, Judith and Neil, *Dr. Seuss & Mr. Geisel: A Biography*, 1995 Random House.

Pitz, Henry Clarence, *Treasury of American Book Illustration*, 1947 American Studio Books and Watson-Guptill Publications, Inc., New York, London.

Santi, Steve, *Collecting Little Golden Books*, 1998 Krause Publications

Silvey, Anita, editor, *Children's Books and Their Creators*, 1995 Houghton Mifflin.

Weinberg, Robert, *A Biographical Dictionary of Science Fiction and Fantasy Artists,* 1988 Greenwood Press, Westport, CT.

Whalley, Joyce Irene and Chester, Tessa Rose, *History of Children's Book Illustration,* 1988 John Murray Ltd., London.

COLLECTOR BOOKS

Informing Today's Collector

For over two decades we have been keeping collectors informed on trends and values in all fields of antiques and collectibles.

DOLLS, FIGURES & TEDDY BEARS

4707	A Decade of **Barbie** Dolls & Collectibles, 1981–1991, Summers	$19.95
4631	**Barbie** Doll Boom, 1986–1995, Augustyniak	$18.95
2079	**Barbie** Doll Fashion, Volume I, Eames	$24.95
4846	**Barbie** Doll Fashion, Volume II, Eames	$24.95
3957	**Barbie** Exclusives, Rana	$18.95
4632	**Barbie** Exclusives, Book II, Rana	$18.95
4557	**Barbie**, The First 30 Years, Deutsch	$24.95
5252	The **Barbie** Doll Years, 3rd Ed., Olds	$18.95
3810	**Chatty Cathy Dolls**, Lewis	$15.95
1529	Collector's Encyclopedia of **Barbie** Dolls, DeWein	$19.95
4882	Collector's Encyclopedia of **Barbie** Doll Exclusives and More, Augustyniak	$19.95
2211	Collector's Encyclopedia of **Madame Alexander Dolls**, Smith	$24.95
4863	Collector's Encyclopedia of **Vogue Dolls**, Izen/Stover	$29.95
3967	Collector's Guide to **Trolls**, Peterson	$19.95
5253	Story of **Barbie**, 2nd Ed., Westenhouser	$24.95
1513	**Teddy Bears & Steiff** Animals, Mandel	$9.95
1817	**Teddy Bears & Steiff** Animals, 2nd Series, Mandel	$19.95
2084	**Teddy Bears, Annalee's & Steiff** Animals, 3rd Series, Mandel	$19.95
1808	Wonder of **Barbie**, Manos	$9.95
1430	World of **Barbie** Dolls, Manos	$9.95
4880	World of **Raggedy Ann** Collectibles, Avery	$24.95

TOYS, MARBLES & CHRISTMAS COLLECTIBLES

3427	**Advertising Character** Collectibles, Dotz	$17.95
2333	Antique & Collector's **Marbles**, 3rd Ed., Grist	$9.95
4934	**Breyer Animal** Collector's Guide, Identification and Values, Browell	$19.95
4976	**Christmas** Ornaments, Lights & Decorations, Johnson	$24.95
4737	**Christmas** Ornaments, Lights & Decorations, Vol. II, Johnson	$24.95
4739	**Christmas** Ornaments, Lights & Decorations, Vol. III, Johnson	$24.95
4649	Classic Plastic **Model Kits**, Polizzi	$24.95
4559	Collectible **Action Figures**, 2nd Ed., Manos	$17.95
3874	Collectible Coca-Cola Toy **Trucks**, deCourtivron	$24.95
2338	Collector's Encyclopedia of **Disneyana**, Longest, Stern	$24.95
4958	Collector's Guide to **Battery Toys**, Hultzman	$19.95
5038	Collector's Guide to **Diecast Toys & Scale Models**, 2nd Ed., Johnson	$19.95
4651	Collector's Guide to **Tinker Toys**, Strange	$18.95
4566	Collector's Guide to **Tootsietoys**, 2nd Ed., Richter	$19.95
5169	Collector's Guide to **TV Toys** & Memorabilia, 2nd Ed., Davis/Morgan	$24.95
4720	The Golden Age of **Automotive Toys**, 1925–1941, Hutchison/Johnson	$24.95
3436	**Grist's** Big Book of **Marbles**	$19.95
3970	Grist's Machine-Made & Contemporary **Marbles**, 2nd Ed.	$9.95
5267	**Matchbox** Toys, 1947 to 1998, 3rd Ed., Johnson	$19.95
4871	**McDonald's Collectibles**, Henriques/DuVall	$19.95
1540	**Modern Toys** 1930–1980, Baker	$19.95
3888	**Motorcycle** Toys, Antique & Contemporary, Gentry/Downs	$18.95
5168	Schroeder's Collectible **Toys**, Antique to Modern Price Guide, 5th Ed.	$17.95
1886	Stern's Guide to **Disney** Collectibles	$14.95
2139	Stern's Guide to **Disney** Collectibles, 2nd Series	$14.95
3975	Stern's Guide to **Disney** Collectibles, 3rd Series	$18.95
2028	**Toys**, Antique & Collectible, Longest	$14.95

FURNITURE

1457	American **Oak** Furniture, McNerney	$9.95
3716	American **Oak** Furniture, Book II, McNerney	$12.95
1118	Antique **Oak** Furniture, Hill	$7.95
2271	Collector's Encyclopedia of **American** Furniture, Vol. II, Swedberg	$24.95
3720	Collector's Encyclopedia of **American** Furniture, Vol. III, Swedberg	$24.95
1755	Furniture of the **Depression Era**, Swedberg	$19.95
3906	**Heywood-Wakefield** Modern Furniture, Rouland	$18.95
1885	**Victorian** Furniture, Our American Heritage, McNerney	$9.95
3829	**Victorian** Furniture, Our American Heritage, Book II, McNerney	$9.95

JEWELRY, HATPINS, WATCHES & PURSES

1712	Antique & Collector's **Thimbles** & Accessories, Mathis	$19.95
1748	Antique **Purses**, Revised Second Ed., Holiner	$19.95
1278	Art Nouveau & Art Deco **Jewelry**, Baker	$9.95
4850	Collectible **Costume Jewelry**, Simonds	$24.95
3875	Collecting Antique **Stickpins**, Kerins	$16.95
3722	Collector's Ency. of **Compacts, Carryalls & Face Powder Boxes**, Mueller	$24.95
4854	Collector's Ency. of **Compacts, Carryalls & Face Powder Boxes**, Vol. II	$24.95
4940	**Costume Jewelry**, A Practical Handbook & Value Guide, Rezazadeh	$24.95
1716	Fifty Years of Collectible **Fashion Jewelry**, 1925–1975, Baker	$19.95
1424	**Hatpins** & Hatpin Holders, Baker	$9.95
1181	100 Years of Collectible **Jewelry**, 1850–1950, Baker	$9.95
4729	**Sewing Tools** & Trinkets, Thompson	$24.95
4878	Vintage & Contemporary **Purse Accessories**, Gerson	$24.95
3830	Vintage **Vanity Bags & Purses**, Gerson	$24.95

INDIANS, GUNS, KNIVES, TOOLS, PRIMITIVES

1868	Antique **Tools**, Our American Heritage, McNerney	$9.95
1426	**Arrowheads** & Projectile Points, Hothem	$7.95
4943	Field Guide to **Flint Arrowheads & Knives** of the North American Indian	$9.95
2279	**Indian Artifacts** of the Midwest, Hothem	$14.95
3885	**Indian Artifacts** of the Midwest, Book II, Hothem	$16.95
4870	**Indian Artifacts** of the Midwest, Book III, Hothem	$18.95
5162	Modern **Guns**, Identification & Values, 12th Ed., Quertermous	$12.95
2164	**Primitives**, Our American Heritage, McNerney	$9.95
1759	**Primitives**, Our American Heritage, 2nd Series, McNerney	$14.95
4730	Standard **Knife** Collector's Guide, 3rd Ed., Ritchie & Stewart	$12.95

PAPER COLLECTIBLES & BOOKS

4633	**Big Little Books**, Jacobs	$18.95
4710	Collector's Guide to **Children's Books**, 1850 to 1950, Jones	$18.95
1441	Collector's Guide to **Post Cards**, Wood	$9.95
2081	Guide to Collecting **Cookbooks**, Allen	$14.95
5271	Huxford's **Old Book** Value Guide, 11th Ed.	$19.95
2080	Price Guide to **Cookbooks & Recipe Leaflets**, Dickinson	$9.95
3973	**Sheet Music** Reference & Price Guide, 2nd Ed., Pafik & Guiheen	$19.95
4654	**Victorian Trade Cards**, Historical Reference & Value Guide, Cheadle	$19.95
4733	**Whitman Juvenile Books**, Brown	$17.95

GLASSWARE

4561	Collectible **Drinking Glasses**, Chase & Kelly	$17.95
4642	Collectible **Glass Shoes**, Wheatley	$19.95
4937	Coll. **Glassware** from the 40s, 50s & 60s, 4th Ed., Florence	$19.95
1810	Collector's Encyclopedia of **American Art Glass**, Shuman	$29.95
4938	Collector's Encyclopedia of **Depression Glass**, 13th Ed., Florence	$19.95
1961	Collector's Encyclopedia of **Fry Glassware**, Fry Glass Society	$24.95
1664	Collector's Encyclopedia of **Heisey Glass**, 1925–1938, Bredehoft	$24.95
3905	Collector's Encyclopedia of **Milk Glass**, Newbound	$24.95
4936	Collector's Guide to **Candy Containers**, Dezso/Poirier	$19.95
4564	**Crackle Glass**, Weitman	$19.95
4941	**Crackle Glass**, Book II, Weitman	$19.95
4714	**Czechoslovakian Glass** and Collectibles, Book II, Barta/Rose	$16.95
5158	**Elegant Glassware** of the Depression Era, 8th Ed., Florence	$19.95
1380	Encyclopedia of **Pattern Glass**, McCain	$12.95
3981	Evers' Standard **Cut Glass** Value Guide	$12.95
4659	**Fenton** Art Glass, 1907–1939, Whitmyer	$24.95
3725	**Fostoria**, Pressed, Blown & Hand Molded Shapes, Kerr	$24.95
4719	**Fostoria**, Etched, Carved & Cut Designs, Vol. II, Kerr	$24.95
3883	**Fostoria Stemware**, The Crystal for America, Long & Seate	$24.95
4644	**Imperial Carnival Glass**, Burns	$18.95
3886	**Kitchen Glassware** of the Depression Years, 5th Ed., Florence	$19.95
5156	Pocket Guide to **Depression Glass**, 11th Ed., Florence	$9.95

5035	Standard Encyclopedia of **Carnival Glass**, 6th Ed., Edwards/Carwile	$24.95
5036	Standard **Carnival Glass** Price Guide, 11th Ed., Edwards/Carwile	$9.95
5272	Standard Encyclopedia of **Opalescent Glass**, 3rd ed., Edwards	$24.95
4731	**Stemware Identification**, Featuring Cordials with Values, Florence	$24.95
3326	**Very Rare Glassware** of the Depression Years, 3rd Series, Florence	$24.95
4732	**Very Rare Glassware** of the Depression Years, 5th Series, Florence	$24.95
4656	**Westmoreland Glass**, Wilson	$24.95

POTTERY

4927	**ABC Plates & Mugs**, Lindsay	$24.95
4929	**American Art Pottery**, Sigafoose	$24.95
4630	**American Limoges**, Limoges	$24.95
1312	**Blue & White Stoneware**, McNerney	$9.95
1958	So. Potteries **Blue Ridge Dinnerware**, 3rd Ed., Newbound	$14.95
1959	**Blue Willow**, 2nd Ed., Gaston	$14.95
4848	Ceramic **Coin Banks**, Stoddard	$19.95
4851	Collectible **Cups & Saucers**, Harran	$18.95
4709	Collectible **Kay Finch**, Biography, Identification & Values, Martinez/Frick	$18.95
1373	Collector's Encyclopedia of **American Dinnerware**, Cunningham	$24.95
4931	Collector's Encyclopedia of **Bauer Pottery**, Chipman	$24.95
4932	Collector's Encyclopedia of **Blue Ridge Dinnerware**, Vol. II, Newbound	$24.95
4658	Collector's Encyclopedia of **Brush-McCoy Pottery**, Huxford	$24.95
5034	Collector's Encyclopedia of **California Pottery**, 2nd Ed., Chipman	$24.95
2133	Collector's Encyclopedia of **Cookie Jars**, Roerig	$24.95
3723	Collector's Encyclopedia of **Cookie Jars**, Book II, Roerig	$24.95
4939	Collector's Encyclopedia of **Cookie Jars**, Book III, Roerig	$24.95
4638	Collector's Encyclopedia of **Dakota Potteries**, Dommel	$24.95
5040	Collector's Encyclopedia of **Fiesta**, 8th Ed., Huxford	$19.95
4718	Collector's Encyclopedia of **Figural Planters & Vases**, Newbound	$19.95
3961	Collector's Encyclopedia of **Early Noritake**, Alden	$24.95
1439	Collector's Encyclopedia of **Flow Blue China**, Gaston	$19.95
3812	Collector's Encyclopedia of **Flow Blue China**, 2nd Ed., Gaston	$24.95
3813	Collector's Encyclopedia of **Hall China**, 2nd Ed., Whitmyer	$24.95
3431	Collector's Encyclopedia of **Homer Laughlin China**, Jasper	$24.95
1276	Collector's Encyclopedia of **Hull Pottery**, Roberts	$19.95
3962	Collector's Encyclopedia of **Lefton China**, DeLozier	$19.95
4855	Collector's Encyclopedia of **Lefton China**, Book II, DeLozier	$19.95
2210	Collector's Encyclopedia of **Limoges Porcelain**, 2nd Ed., Gaston	$24.95
2334	Collector's Encyclopedia of **Majolica Pottery**, Katz-Marks	$19.95
1358	Collector's Encyclopedia of **McCoy Pottery**, Huxford	$19.95
3963	Collector's Encyclopedia of **Metlox Potteries**, Gibbs Jr.	$24.95
3837	Collector's Encyclopedia of **Nippon Porcelain**, Van Patten	$24.95
2089	Collector's Ency. of **Nippon Porcelain**, 2nd Series, Van Patten	$24.95
1665	Collector's Ency. of **Nippon Porcelain**, 3rd Series, Van Patten	$24.95
4712	Collector's Ency. of **Nippon Porcelain**, 4th Series, Van Patten	$24.95
1447	Collector's Encyclopedia of **Noritake**, Van Patten	$19.95
1037	Collector's Encyclopedia of **Occupied Japan**, 1st Series, Florence	$14.95
1038	Collector's Encyclopedia of **Occupied Japan**, 2nd Series, Florence	$14.95
2088	Collector's Encyclopedia of **Occupied Japan**, 3rd Series, Florence	$14.95
2019	Collector's Encyclopedia of **Occupied Japan**, 4th Series, Florence	$14.95
2335	Collector's Encyclopedia of **Occupied Japan**, 5th Series, Florence	$14.95
4951	Collector's Encyclopedia of **Old Ivory China**, Hillman	$24.95
3964	Collector's Encyclopedia of **Pickard China**, Reed	$24.95
3877	Collector's Encyclopedia of **R.S. Prussia**, 4th Series, Gaston	$24.95
1034	Collector's Encyclopedia of **Roseville Pottery**, Huxford	$19.95
1035	Collector's Encyclopedia of **Roseville Pottery**, 2nd Ed., Huxford	$19.95
4856	Collector's Encyclopedia of **Russel Wright**, 2nd Ed., Kerr	$24.95
4713	Collector's Encyclopedia of **Salt Glaze Stoneware**, Taylor/Lowrance	$24.95
3314	Collector's Encyclopedia of **Van Briggle** Art Pottery, Sasicki	$24.95
4563	Collector's Encyclopedia of **Wall Pockets**, Newbound	$19.95
2111	Collector's Encyclopedia of **Weller Pottery**, Huxford	$29.95
3876	Collector's Guide to **Lu-Ray Pastels**, Meehan	$18.95
3814	Collector's Guide to **Made in Japan** Ceramics, White	$18.95
4646	Collector's Guide to **Made in Japan** Ceramics, Book II, White	$18.95
2339	Collector's Guide to **Shawnee Pottery**, Vanderbilt	$19.95

1425	**Cookie Jars**, Westfall	$9.95
3440	**Cookie Jars**, Book II, Westfall	$19.95
4924	**Figural & Novelty Salt & Pepper Shakers**, 2nd Series, Davern	$24.95
2379	Lehner's Ency. of **U.S. Marks** on Pottery, Porcelain & China	$24.95
4722	**McCoy Pottery**, Collector's Reference & Value Guide, Hanson/Nissen	$19.95
4726	**Red Wing Art Pottery**, 1920s–1960s, Dollen	$19.95
1670	**Red Wing Collectibles**, DePasquale	$9.95
1440	**Red Wing Stoneware**, DePasquale	$9.95
1632	**Salt & Pepper Shakers**, Guarnaccia	$9.95
5091	**Salt & Pepper Shakers** II, Guarnaccia	$18.95
2220	**Salt & Pepper Shakers** III, Guarnaccia	$14.95
3443	**Salt & Pepper Shakers** IV, Guarnaccia	$18.95
3738	**Shawnee Pottery**, Mangus	$24.95
4629	Turn of the Century **American Dinnerware**, 1880s–1920s, Jasper	$24.95
3327	**Watt Pottery** – Identification & Value Guide, Morris	$19.95

OTHER COLLECTIBLES

4704	Antique & Collectible **Buttons**, Wisniewski	$19.95
2269	Antique **Brass & Copper** Collectibles, Gaston	$16.95
1880	Antique **Iron**, McNerney	$9.95
3872	Antique **Tins**, Dodge	$24.95
4845	Antique **Typewriters & Office Collectibles**, Rehr	$19.95
1714	**Black** Collectibles, Gibbs	$19.95
1128	**Bottle** Pricing Guide, 3rd Ed., Cleveland	$7.95
4636	**Celluloid Collectibles**, Dunn	$14.95
3718	Collectible **Aluminum**, Grist	$16.95
4560	Collectible **Cats**, An Identification & Value Guide, Book II, Fyke	$19.95
4852	Collectible **Compact Disc** Price Guide 2, Cooper	$17.95
2018	Collector's Encyclopedia of **Granite Ware**, Greguire	$24.95
3430	Collector's Encyclopedia of **Granite Ware**, Book 2, Greguire	$24.95
4705	Collector's Guide to **Antique Radios**, 4th Ed., Bunis	$18.95
3880	Collector's Guide to **Cigarette Lighters**, Flanagan	$17.95
4637	Collector's Guide to **Cigarette Lighters**, Book II, Flanagan	$17.95
4942	Collector's Guide to **Don Winton Designs**, Ellis	$19.95
3966	Collector's Guide to **Inkwells**, Identification & Values, Badders	$18.95
4947	Collector's Guide to **Inkwells**, Book II, Badders	$19.95
4948	Collector's Guide to **Letter Openers**, Grist	$19.95
4862	Collector's Guide to **Toasters** & Accessories, Greguire	$19.95
4652	Collector's Guide to **Transistor Radios**, 2nd Ed., Bunis	$16.95
4864	Collector's Guide to **Wallace Nutting Pictures**, Ivankovich	$18.95
1629	**Doorstops**, Identification & Values, Bertoia	$9.95
4567	Figural **Napkin Rings**, Gottschalk & Whitson	$18.95
4717	Figural **Nodders**, Includes Bobbin' Heads and Swayers, Irtz	$19.95
3968	**Fishing Lure** Collectibles, Murphy/Edmisten	$24.95
5259	**Flea Market Trader**, 12th Ed., Huxford	$9.95
4944	**Flue Covers**, Collector's Value Guide, Meckley	$12.95
4945	**G-Men and FBI Toys** and Collectibles, Whitworth	$18.95
5263	**Garage Sale & Flea Market Annual**, 7th Ed.	$19.95
3819	**General Store Collectibles**, Wilson	$24.95
5159	Huxford's Collectible **Advertising**, 4th Ed.	$24.95
2216	**Kitchen Antiques**, 1790–1940, McNerney	$14.95
4950	The **Lone Ranger**, Collector's Reference & Value Guide, Felbinger	$18.95
2026	**Railroad** Collectibles, 4th Ed., Baker	$14.95
5167	**Schroeder's Antiques** Price Guide, 17th Ed., Huxford	$12.95
5007	**Silverplated Flatware**, Revised 4th Edition, Hagan	$18.95
1922	Standard **Old Bottle** Price Guide, Sellari	$14.95
5154	**Summers' Guide to Coca-Cola**, 2nd Ed.	$19.95
4952	Summers' Pocket Guide to **Coca-Cola** Identifications	$9.95
3892	**Toy & Miniature Sewing Machines**, Thomas	$18.95
4876	**Toy & Miniature Sewing Machines**, Book II, Thomas	$24.95
5144	Value Guide to **Advertising Memorabilia**, 2nd Ed., Summers	$19.95
3977	Value Guide to **Gas Station** Memorabilia, Summers & Priddy	$24.95
4877	Vintage **Bar Ware**, Visakay	$24.95
4935	The W.F. Cody **Buffalo Bill** Collector's Guide with Values	$24.95
5281	**Wanted to Buy**, 7th Edition	$9.95

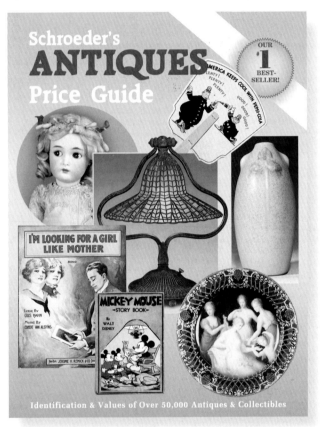